Societies and Cultures
IN WORLD HISTORY

Societies and Cultures
IN WORLD HISTORY
VOLUME B   1300 TO 1800

MARK KISHLANSKY
Harvard University

PATRICK GEARY
University of California, Los Angeles

PATRICIA O'BRIEN
University of California, Irvine

R. BIN WONG
University of California, Irvine

With

ROY MOTTAHEDEH
Harvard University

LEROY VAIL
Harvard University

ANN WALTNER
University of Minnesota

MARK WASSERMAN
Rutgers University

JAMES GELVIN
Massachusetts Institute
of Technology

HarperCollinsCollegePublishers

Executive Editor: Bruce Borland
Development Editor: Barbara Muller
Project Coordination: Ruttle, Shaw & Wetherill, Inc.
Cover Design: Mary McDonnell
Text Design: Anne O'Donnell
Photo Research: Sandy Schneider
Cartographer: Maps produced by Mapping Specialists, Inc.
Manufacturing Manager: Willie Lane
Compositor: Publication Services, Inc.
Printer and Binder: R.R. Donnelley & Sons Company
Cover Printer: The Lehigh Press, Inc.

For permission to use copyrighted material, grateful acknowledgment is made to the copyright holders on pp. C-1–C-10, which are hereby made part of this copyright page.

Cover and Frontispiece: Anonymous Japanese Screen: The Tale of the Genji (detail). Isabella Stewart Gardner Museum, Boston, USA/Art Resource, NY.

Societies and Cultures in World History, Volume B 1300 To 1800

Library of Congress Cataloging-in-Publication Data
    Societies and cultures in world history / Mark Kishlansky ... [et al.] ;
       p.   cm.
    Includes indexes.
    Contents: v. A. To 1500 — v. B. 1300 to 1800 — v. C. 1789 to the present.
    ISBN 0-06-500348-9 (v. A).—ISBN 0-06-500349-7 (v. B)—ISBN 0-06-500350-0 (v. C)
    1. Civilization—History. I. Kishlansky, Mark A.
CB69.S633   1995
909—dc20
                          93-49369
                            CIP

94 95 96 97   9 8 7 6 5 4 3 2 1

BRIEF CONTENTS

DETAILED CONTENTS

DOCUMENTS

MAPS

CHARTS, TABLES, AND FIGURES

COLOR ESSAYS

PREFACE

There is no more difficult subject for an introductory textbook than world history. While textbook writers are always faced with the dilemma of what to include and what to leave out, for the authors of a world history text this choice usually involves entire civilizations across centuries. And now more than ever—with the explosion in scholarship on world societies over the past decade—there are no easy answers. Decisions once made on the basis of too little knowledge to reconstruct a story must now be made on other grounds. It is an extraordinarily daunting task.

In writing *Societies and Cultures in World History*, we first considered how the book would be used among the variety of courses currently taught under the title World Civilizations. We designed the book for courses that combine the teaching of Western and world civilizations. It devotes more space to the history of the West, broadly construed, than to that of any other civilization. This design will give students a base of knowledge from which to compare and contrast the experiences of other civilizations as well as to help them understand the impact (for good or ill) that the West has had on the rest of the world. In coverage of world civilizations, we have allocated most space to Asian civilizations and have attempted to treat equally Africa, the Middle East, and Latin America. Although this presentation conforms to the broad outlines of most world civilization courses, we recognize there are nearly as many configurations of the course as there are places where it is taught. We hope the strengths of our presentation will outweigh its shortcomings.

We believe our book offers two outstanding distinctions: an intellectual respect for the integrity of all civilizations and a concern for the demands placed on student users. In planning our world civilization text, we decided not to follow the well-beaten path of adding one or two specialists to the author team and requiring them to write about civilizations (or epochs) in which they had neither scholarly training nor teaching experience. Instead we have contributions from a diverse team of experts—specialists in African, Latin American, and Middle Eastern history, as well as in early and modern Asia. This means that *Societies and Cultures in World History* has the benefit of the most up-to-date knowledge of world societies presented by experts on those societies.

Ann Waltner of the University of Minnesota has written on early Asia for part or all of Chapters 1, 4, 8, and 11. Leroy Vail of Harvard University has written on Africa for part or all of Chapters 1, 7, 14, 18, 19, 27, and 33. Mark Wasserman of Rutgers University has written on Latin America for part or all of Chapters 1, 14, 28, and 33. Roy Mottahedeh of Harvard University has written on early Islamic civilization for part or all of Chapters 15, 19, and 33; and James Gelvin of the Massachusetts Institute of Technology has written on modern Islamic civilization for part or all of Chapters 19 and 33.

Secondly, we are acutely aware that studying world history can be as daunting as reconstructing it, and throughout the process we have been concerned that the book meet the diverse needs and abilities of the students who will study it. We have tried to write a book that students will want to read. A number of decisions contributed to our goal. First, we would not write an encyclopedia of world civilization. Information would never be included in a chapter unless it fit within the themes of that chapter. There would be no information for information's sake and we would need to defend the inclusion of names, dates, and events whenever we met to critique our chapters. To our surprise, we found that by adhering to the principle that information appear only to illustrate a particular point or a dominating theme, we included as much, if not more, than books that habitually listed names, places, and dates with no other context. In addition, we were committed to integrating the history of women and of ordinary people into the narrative. In this endeavor, we had the assistance of two reviewers who were assigned no other responsibilities than to evaluate our chapters for the inclusion and integration of these materials within our chapters.

To construct a book that students would want to read, we needed to develop fresh ideas about how to involve the readers with the material, how to transform them from passive recipients to active participants. From computer science we borrowed the concept of "user friendly." Seeking ways to stimulate the imagination of the student, we realized the most dynamic way to do this was visually. Thus we initiated the technique of the pictorial chapter opener. At the beginning of each chapter, we explore a picture, guiding students across a canvas or an artifact or a photograph, helping them see things that are not immediately apparent, unfolding both an image and a theme. In some chapters we highlight details in the manner of an art history course, pulling out a section of the original picture to take a closer look. In others we attempt to shock readers into recognition of horror or beauty. Some openers are designed to make students ask, "What was it like to be there?" All are chosen to illustrate a dominant theme within the chapter, and the lingering impression they make helps reinforce that theme. We believe the combination of words and images will actively involve our readers—grabbing their attention and drawing them into the narrative.

To reinforce our emphasis on involving readers through visual learning, we included eight color inserts, built around the single theme, "Gender and Culture." The images and essays were prepared by Debra Mancoff, Professor and Chair of the Art History Department at Beloit College. Professor Mancoff has contributed her scholarly expertise in writing and teaching about representations of women to a compelling set of images that students will be able to compare and contrast over time and across cultures. These pictorial essays are substantive—not merely decorative—text, and we hope instructors will build on students' experience in reading the chapter pictorial features to analyze these photographs.

Similarly, we have taken an image-based approach to our presentation of geography. When teachers of world civilization courses are surveyed, no single area of need is highlighted more often than geography. Students simply have no mental image of the world beyond its shape, no familiarity with the geophysical features that are a fundamental part of the realities of world history. No world civilization textbook is without maps and ancillary map programs, yet no survey of teachers shows satisfaction with the effectiveness of these presentations. In *Societies and Cultures in World History*, we have tried to ensure that each place identified in the text is also identified in a map located within the chapter. The second device we developed to engage students with historical subjects is the in-depth chapter feature. These two-page, illustrated essays focus on a single event or personality chosen to demonstrate or enhance the students' sense that history is as real and exciting as

life itself. They are written with more drama or sympathy or wonder than would be appropriate in the body of the text, and we believe they will captivate the imagination of their readers.

Finally, so that students can grasp the past firsthand, we have provided a wide variety of excerpts from primary source documents. Two criteria guided the selection of these excerpts: accessibility and immediacy. We believe students will be able to engage with these primary sources with no further introduction than that provided by the contextual headnotes that introduce each selection. In choosing these excerpts, we have tapped the widest variety of genres—literature, popular culture, philosophy, religion, and all manner of political accounts. For those instructors who wish to make primary materials more central to their course, *Societies and Cultures in World History* also comes with a two-volume supplementary source book, *Sources of World History*.

Although our text includes much that is new and out of the ordinary, we do not mean to suggest that we have attempted to appeal to students only by adding "whistles and bells." *Societies and Cultures in World History* is a mainstream text in which most of the authors' energies have been placed in developing a solid, readable narrative of world civilizations that integrates women and the masses into the traditional sequence of periods and major events. We have highlighted personalities while identifying trends. We have spotlighted social history while maintaining a firm grip on political developments. We hope there are many qualities in this book that every teacher of world civilization will find valuable. But we also hope that there are things here you will disagree with, themes you can develop better, arguments and ideas that will provoke you. A textbook is only one part of a course, and it is always less important than a teacher. We have attempted to produce a book that your students will read so that you will not need to read it to them. We hope that by doing our job successfully we have made your job easier and your students' job more enjoyable.

Mark Kishlansky
Patrick Geary
Patricia O'Brien
R. Bin Wong

ACKNOWLEDGMENTS

We wish to thank the many conscientious historians who reviewed our manuscript and gave generously of their time and knowledge. Their valuable critiques and suggestions have contributed greatly to the final product. We are grateful to the following:

Mark Bartusis
Northern State University

Doris L. Bergen
University of Vermont

Martin Berger
Youngstown State University

Timothy Brook
University of Toronto

Charles J. Bussey
Western Kentucky University

Lee Cassanelli
University of Pennsylvania

Weston F. Cook, Jr.
Kutztown University

Todd A. Diacon
University of Tennessee at Knoxville

Ross E. Dunn
San Diego State University

Ainslie T. Embree
Columbia University

Charles T. Evans
Northern Virginia Community College-Loudoun

William Edward Ezzell
DeKalb College-Central Campus

Jonathan Goldstein
West Georgia College

Joseph Gowaskie
Rider College

John Mason Hart
University of Houston

Kandice Hauf
Babson College

Gerald Herman
Northeastern University

Mark C. Herman
Edison Community College

Ira M. Lapidus
University of California, Berkeley

Alan LeBaron
Kennesaw State College

Geri H. Malandra
University of Minnesota

Jon E. Mandaville
Portland State University

Patrick Manning
Northeastern University

Thomas Metcalf
University of California, Berkeley

James A. Miller
Clemson University

Joseph C. Miller
University of Virginia

Barbara A. Moss
University of Georgia

On-cho Ng
Penn State University

Donathon C. Olliff
Auburn University

James B. Palais
Jackson School of International Studies at the University of Washington

Peter C. Perdue
Massachusetts Institute of Technology

Paul J. Smith
Haverford College

Alexander Sydorenko
Arkansas State University

Steven C. Topik
University of California, Irvine

Karen Turner
College of the Holy Cross

Anne Walthall
University of California, Irvine

Eric L. Wake
Cumberland College

Allen Wells
Bowdoin College

David L. White
Appalachian State University

Alexander Woodside
University of British Columbia

Madeline C. Zilfi
University of Maryland

Supplements

The following supplements are available for use in conjunction with this book:

For the Instructor

Instructor's Resource Guide, by George F. Jewsbury, Oklahoma State University. This unique Instructor's Resource Guide provides new materials not found in the text through the use of lecture modules, lecture launchers, critical thinking exercises relating to the text's primary documents, detailed chapter summaries, test questions, and listings of additional resources for videos and films. As a **special feature**, there are six essays by Dr. Robert Edgar, Professor of African History at Howard University which incorporate the African history portions of the text into the lectures and discuss many of the most important and controversial issues in the teaching of world history.

Discovering World History Through Maps and Views, by Gerald Danzer of the University of Illinois at Chicago, winner of the AHA's 1990 James Harvey Robinson Prize for his work in the development of map transparencies. This set of 100 four-color transparencies from selected sources is bound in a three-ring binder and available free to adopters. It also contains an introduction on teaching history with maps and detailed commentary on each transparency. The collection includes cartographic and pictorial maps, views and photos, urban plans, building diagrams, classic maps, and works of art.

Test Bank, by John Paul Bischoff, Oklahoma State University. A total of 2000 questions, including 50 multiple-choice questions and five essay questions per text chapter. Each test item is referenced by topic, type, and text page number. Available in print and computerized format.

TestMaster Computerized Testing System. This flexible, easy-to-master computer test bank includes all the test items in the printed test bank. The TestMaster software allows you to edit existing questions and add your own items. Available for IBM and Macintosh computers.

QuizMaster. The new program enables you to design TestMaster generated tests that your students can take on a computer rather than in printed form. QuizMaster is available separate from TestMaster and can be obtained free through your sales representative.

Grades. A grade-keeping and classroom management software program that maintains data for up to 200 students.

Map Transparencies. A set of 40 transparencies of maps taken from the text.

The HarperCollins World Civilization Media Program. A wide variety of media enhancements for use in teaching world civilization courses. Offered to qualified adopters of HarperCollins world history texts.

For the Student

Study Guide, in two volumes. Volume I (Chapters 1 through 16) and Volume II (Chapters 14 through 35), prepared by John Paul Bischoff, Oklahoma State University. Includes chapter outlines; timeline; map exercises; lists of important terms, people and events; and sections on "Making Connections" and "Putting Larger Concepts Together."

World History Map Workbook: Geographic and Critical Thinking Exercises, in two volumes. Prepared by Glee Wilson of Kent State University, each volume of this workbook contains 40 maps accompanied by over 120 pages of exercises. Each of the two volumes is designed to teach the students the location of various countries and their relationship to one another and events. Also included are numerous exercises aimed at enhancing students' critical thinking abilities.

Sources of World History, by Mark Kishlansky, a collection of primary source documents available in two volumes. These volumes provide a balance among constitutional documents, political theory, philosophy, imaginative literature, and social description. Represented are examples of the works of each of the major civilization complexes, Asia, Africa, Latin America, and the Islamic world as well as the central works of Western Civilization. Each volume includes the introductory essay, "How to Read a Document," which leads students step by step through the experience of using historical documents.

SuperShell II Computerized Tutorial, prepared by John Paul Bischoff, Oklahoma State University. This interactive program for IBM computers helps students learn the major facts and concepts through drill and practice exercises and diagnostic feedback. SuperShell II provides immediate correct answers; the text page number on which the material is discussed, and a running score of the student's performance is maintained on the screen throughout the session. This free supplement is available to instructors through their sales representative.

TimeLink Computer Atlas of World History, by William Hamblin, Brigham Young University. This Hyper-Card Macintosh program presents three views of the world—Europe/Africa, Asia, and the Americas—on a simulated globe. Students can spin the globe, select a time period, and see a map of the world at that time, including the names of major political units. Special topics such as the conquests of Alexander the Great are shown through animated sequences that depict the dynamic changes in geopolitical history. A comprehensive index and quizzes are also included.

Mapping World History: Student Activities, a free student map workbook by Gerald Danzer of the University of Illinois at Chicago. It features numerous map skill exercises written to enhance students' basic geographical literacy. The exercises provide ample opportunities for interpreting maps and analyzing cartographic materials as historical documents. The instructor is entitled to one free copy of *Mapping World History* for each copy of the text purchased from HarperCollins.

About the Authors

Mark Kishlansky

Recently appointed Professor of History at Harvard University, Mark Kishlansky is among today's leading young scholars. Professor Kishlansky received his Ph.D. from Brown University and is a member of the Harvard University faculty. A Fellow of the Royal Historical Society, his primary area of expertise is seventeenth-century English political history. Among his main publications are *Parliamentary Selection: Social and Political Choice in Early Modern England* and *The Rise of the New Model Army*. He is the editor of the *Journal of British Studies* and the recipient of the 1989 Most Distinguished Alumnus Award from SUNY Stony Brook.

Patrick Geary

Holding a Ph.D. in Medieval Studies from Yale University, Patrick Geary is both a noted scholar and teacher. Professor Geary was named outstanding undergraduate history teacher for the 1986–87 year at the University of Florida. He currently teaches at the University of California, Los Angeles, where he is Director for the Center for Medieval and Renaissance Studies. He has also held academic positions at the École des Hautes Études en Sciences Sociales, Paris; the Universitat Wien; and Princeton University. His many publications include *Readings in Medieval History; Before France and Germany: The Creation and Transformation of the Merovingian World; Aristocracy in Provence: the Rhone Basin at the Dawn of the Carolingian Age;* and *Furta Sacra: Thefts of Relics in the Central Middle Ages.*

Patricia O'Brien

Professor O'Brien teaches at the University of California, Irvine, and is Associate Vice Chancellor in the Office of Research and Graduate Studies. Professor O'Brien holds a Ph.D. from Columbia University in modern European history. Among her many publications are *The Promise of Punishment: Prisons in 19th Century France; "l'Embastillement de Paris: The Fortification of Paris During the July Monarchy";* and *"Crime and Punishment as Historical Problems."*

R. Bin Wong

R. Bin Wong holds a Ph.D. from Harvard University where he studied both Chinese and European history. In addition to research publications in the United States, which include *Nourish the People: The State Civilian Granary System in China, 1650–1850* (with Pierre-Etienne Will), he has published articles in mainland China, Taiwan, Japan, France, and Holland. He has held a number of research and teaching positions, including ones in the Society of Fellows, the University of Michigan; the Institute of Economics, Chinese Academy of Social Sciences; Institute of Oriental Culture, University of Tokyo; and the École des Hautes Études en Sciences Sociales in Paris. Currently, Professor Wong teaches history and directs a research program in Asian Studies at the University of California, Irvine.

James L. Gelvin

Holding a Ph.D. in History and Middle Eastern Studies from Harvard University, James L. Gelvin's particular field of interest is Syrian history during the late nineteenth and twentieth centuries. An award-winning teacher, Professor Gelvin has taught history and politics at Harvard University, Boston College, and Massachusetts Institute of Technology.

Roy P. Mottahedeh

Professor of History at Harvard University, Roy Mottahedeh has served as Director of the Center for Middle Eastern Studies and is currently Chair of the Committee on Islamic Studies at that University. He received his B.A. and Ph.D. at Harvard University and taught for many years at Princeton University. His publications include *Loyalty and Leadership in an Early Islamic Society* and *The Mantle of the Prophet: Religion and Politics in Iran.*

LEROY VAIL

Professor of African History at Harvard University, Leroy Vail is a leading scholar of Africa. Having received his Ph.D. from the University of Wisconsin (Madison), he spent a dozen years in Africa, teaching at the Universities of Malawi and Zambia and carrying out research on the languages and history of southeast Africa. He is the author of numerous articles on the region's history and linguistics. In collaboration with Landeg White, he has written *Capitalism and Colonialism in Mozambique* and *Power and the Praise Poem: Southern African Voices in History.* He has also edited the important *The Creation of Tribalism in Southern Africa* and is currently editing a dictionary of Lakeside Tonga, a language of Malawi.

ANN WALTNER

An Associate Professor of History at the University of Minnesota and Director of Graduate Studies there, Professor Waltner holds a Ph.D. in Chinese history from the University of California at Berkeley. Her research interests center on the social and intellectual history of China in the sixteenth and seventeenth century, and include topics such as gender, kinship, and religion. She is presently completing a book on Tanyangzi, a young woman mystic who lived in south China in the sixteenth century. Her publications include numerous articles, as well as *Getting an Heir: Adoption and the Construction of Kinship in Late Imperial China.*

MARK WASSERMAN

With his Ph.D. from the University of Chicago, Mark Wasserman is professor of history at Rutgers, The State University of New Jersey. He has won prestigious post-doctoral fellowships from the Social Science Research Council, the Tinker Foundation, the American Philosophical Society, and the U.S. Department of Education. Among his main publications are *Capitalists, Caciques and Revolution: The Native Elite and Foreign Enterprise in Chihuahua, Mexico, 1854-1911, Persistent Oligarchs: Elites and Politics in Chihuahua, Mexico, 1910-1940, A History of Latin America,* and *Provinces of the Revolution: Essays on Regional Mexican History, 1910-1929.* He won the Arthur P. Whitaker Prize in 1984 from the Middle Atlantic Council of Latin American Studies for *Capitalists, Caciques, and Revolution.*

Societies and Cultures
IN WORLD HISTORY

CHAPTER 11

East Asia, 1100–1600

Sentimentalizing Peasant Life

They are idyllic images, men leaning against a shaded railing as they operate a waterwheel, watching one of their fellows as he fills a bucket with irrigation water from the stream below, and women sitting in the shade of a spreading tree as they do their mending and spinning. Both paintings, Song dynasty images, are literati representations of peasant life. The seals and calligraphic inscriptions on the illustration of the irrigators were placed there by successive owners of the piece, and attest to its value as a collector's item. The style of the inscription to the far right mimics the writing found on antique bronzes, a style which would have been utterly incomprehensible to the men in the painting, or most men and women, for that matter.

Let us look more closely at the way these images represent Chinese agrarian life. Much agriculture in south China was flooded-field rice cultivation, which demanded ingenious technology and constant vigilance on the part of villagers. The government did not intervene in matters such as the irrigation project we see under way here: villagers themselves, perhaps under the direction of local gentry, took the responsibility for maintaining the irrigation works.

Women's work in traditional China was conventionally defined as textile work, although in fact women engaged in a wide variety of labor. Here we see four women, open to our view but concealed from the public gaze by a thatched fence. The fence solves a thorny problem: How is a respectable woman to take advantage of summer breezes without exposing herself to public view? And how is an artist to represent her doing so?

This painting, which is part of a scroll illustrating an instructional text for women, entitled the *Lady's Classic of Filial Piety*, is labeled as depicting "common people." Perhaps they are common, but they are not inelegant. And, in keeping with the tenor of the instructional text in which they appear, they are concerned with modesty and propriety. And "common" seems to be a relative term: The woman second from the left seems to be a servant, presenting cloth to the seated woman for her attention. In the eyes of this painter, even ordinary people have servants.

These paintings are the product of an elite culture and were designed for an elite audience. They portray contented, aesthetically pleasing, productive peasants. (The men in the picture at the left may appear to be idling, but the rice is flourishing. Someone has been hard at work.)

The images of modest and industrious peasant women were perhaps also intended to serve as models for elite women, to urge them to greater frugality, diligence, and chastity. The images valorize hard work, but they have sentimentalized peasant life. These images are far removed from any social problems peasants may have faced. They are pretty peasants, at peace with themselves and their world.

The literati who painted these images imagined a world that was whole and harmonious, and in which women and peasants were content with their roles. It is true that in both China and Japan during this period cultures became more inclusive. Literacy expanded, and commerce linked regions and social classes to a greater degree than ever before.

But do not be deluded by the literati visions of a unified society. Peasants did not always conceptualize their interest in a way which meshed with literati notions. During this period, peasants on occasion rebelled. The most serious of these rebellions brought down the Yuan dynasty (1279–1368) in China and put a peasant on the throne.

317

Tang China and Heian Japan, for all their differences, were both aristocratic societies. In the years 1000 to 1300, the aristocratic society in both countries collapsed. In Song dynasty China (960–1276) the old aristocracy was replaced by a literati elite, and in Kamakura Japan (1185–1333) the warrior elite became the most politically powerful class. Changes in access to political power characterized this period in Asian history.

These changes were accompanied by other changes. In both China and Japan during this period towns grew, and in Japan merchants began to play a more active role in the development of culture. In both China and Japan, the social and political roles of women became more circumscribed. Men attained their elite status by passing civil service exams in China or by demonstrating their prowess on the battlefield in Japan. The battlefield and the examination hall were both gendered arenas, restricted to men.

In this chapter we discuss the diffusion of culture among various elements within China and within Japan. It would be misleading to suggest that by 1600 the culture of either China or Japan was homogeneous. But expanding literacy, the growth of vernacular literature, and the proliferation of forms of entertainment like the theater, which could be enjoyed by people from a wide variety of backgrounds, led to a more cohesive culture in both China and Japan than had existed in the past. At the same time, regional differences remained profound.

The Glories of Civilian Society Under the Song

Several seemingly paradoxical themes stand out in the history of the Song dynasty. First, the international situation was characterized by constant difficulties between the Song and the peoples on China's northern frontier, problems that culminated in the northern peoples' invading Chinese territory. The Jin took north China in 1126 and the Mongols conquered all of China in 1276. But in spite of these problems, the Song in many ways flourished. Not only was the Song dynasty a great age of commercial expansion and urban prosperity, but the Song state was remarkably effective at capturing commercial revenues to finance its activities. The Song state was an activist, effective state. Many Song institutional arrangements, such as the civil service examinations, proved durable. But in other ways, later dynasties were not able to equal the performance of the Song.

The foreign insecurity and the domestic prosperity contributed to intellectual changes that led to the development of a revised Confucianism, commonly known as neo-Confucianism, which was to have an important impact on Chinese life.

The Border Issue

From early in the dynasty, northern neighbors were a problem for the Song. In 1004, anxious to establish peaceful relations with the Liao, the Song concluded a treaty in which they agreed to pay tribute to the Liao. That the Chinese paid tribute to a neighboring state had more than an economic significance. In the traditional Chinese world order, states on China's periphery would send tribute to China as an acknowledgment of China's cultural superiority. In the early eleventh century, the Liao were able to turn the tables on the Song. In 1042, because the Liao had allied with the Chinese against the Tangut state of Western Xia, they were able to extract even more tribute from the Chinese. Both the

Gender and Culture

THE FALL OF MAN

Figure 1

In the late medieval era, the European world view shifted. For more than a millennium, earthly experience had been overshadowed by the promise of heavenly salvation. However, by the thirteenth century, with the rise of the cities, the new, cosmopolitan attitudes gained through trade and travel, and the emergence of powerful monarchs balancing the power of clergy, this focus began to change. The visual arts reflected this shift, adding images of individuals and scenes from daily life to the reigning repertoire of biblical heroes and narratives. Every aspect of men and women's lives offered subjects for the visual record, and marriage, previously a neglected subject in the arts, drew unprecedented attention.

In Judeo-Christian societies, Adam and Eve forged the prototype for all marriages. Tradition held that Eve was created to heal Adam of his loneliness. After their defiance of divine order and their expulsion from the garden, they lived a life together. The punishments imposed upon them for disobedience—that Eve would bear children in pain and that Adam would live by the sweat of his brow—cast a gendered matrix for matrimonial roles. Images of Adam and Eve after the expulsion are rare in western art. More typical is the depiction of their moment of temptation, as seen on the preceding page in Hugo Van Der Goes's *The Fall of Man* (ca. 1486–70, Flanders; Figure 1). As was common in this period, this panel was originally paired with a scene of the lamentation over Christ. The message to the faithful was clear: Follow the pattern ordained before the fall and redeem the sin with sacrifice.

The union of man and woman served the secular society as well as the sacred. The importance of marriage to the civic structure is illustrated in an unusual sculpture ensemble in the Romanesque cathedral in Naumburg. Six pairs of figures, natural in scale and detail, stand in tabernacles of the choir. These portray six married couples—the original benefactors of the church—each a descendant from the reigning houses of Billung and Wettin. *Ekkehard and Uta* (ca. 1250–60, Germany; Figure 2) are a striking pair. Their portraits seem real, a record of actual appearance. But this couple, like the others, died long before the

EKKEHARD AND UTA

Figure 2

GIOVANNI ARNOLFINI AND HIS BRIDE   *Figure 3*

VENUS AND MARS   *Figure 4*

sculptures were carved. Their individuality reflects the ancient theory of the four humors, a discourse on personality based on the proportions of bodily fluids. Ekkehard, with his firm stance and self confident gaze, represents the sanguine type, dominated by blood. Uta is phlegmatic. Her timid nature and the constant chill caused by the excess of cold phlegm in her system prompts her to retreat from view in the folds of her voluminous cloak. These idealized portraits may be based on an outdated biology, but they suggest a modern cliche. In male and female relationships we still believe that opposites attract.

Jan Van Eyck's painting of *Giovanni Arnolfini and His Bride* (1434, Flanders; Figure 3), seen on the preceding page, is more than a matrimonial portrait. The symbols in the painting read as a wedding certificate. Arnolfini, an agent for the Medici, takes the hand of his Florentine bride and pledges his faith. Both have removed their shoes, suggesting that the bed chamber is transformed into sacred ground through the sacrament of marriage. There are signs of divine presence—the eye-like mirror, the single candle burning in the chandelier—and references to the fruits of matrimony—the whiskbroom for domesticity, the bride calling attention to the fullness of her skirt, indicating pregnancy. Even the little dog plays a role; it embodies fidelity. The officiating priest is seen in the mirror, as is the artist, whose signature, "Jan Van Eyck Was Here" bears witness to the ceremony.

Botticelli's *Venus and Mars* (ca. 1480, Italian; Figure 4) also celebrates a wedding, but its message is a metaphor. Commissioned for the marriage of Guiliano de'Medici to Simonetta Vespucci, the presentation of a slumbering Mars and an alert Venus corresponds with a Neo-Platonic discourse written by Marsilio Ficino. The chaste Venus of Neo-Platonism tames Mars, balancing his excessive and violent temperament. Ficino writes that Venus may master Mars, but Mars will never master Venus. In Botticelli's painting, Venus has vanquished her languid lover. The painting was seen by some contemporaries as an insult to the bridegroom. This may have been Botticelli's intention, for he based his vision of Venus on the bride Simonetta, and he positioned the Vespucci symbol of the wasp prominently in the background.

Western Xia and the Liao used these Chinese goods to trade with other Central Asian countries.

The Song policy of buying peace met with only temporary success. In the twelfth century the Song met with adversaries who were more interested in conquest than in commodities. In 1114, a people known as the Jurched had proclaimed the Jin dynasty, and rose to power with meteoric speed. In 1120 they allied with the Chinese against the Liao, but shortly thereafter they attacked China. In 1126, they took the Song capital Kaifeng and all of north China. After the fall of Kaifeng, the Song government fled south and in 1135 established a new capital at Lin'an, the city now called Hangzhou.

The year 1126 marks an important division in the history of the Song dynasty. The period prior to 1126 is known as the Northern Song, the period after, as the Southern Song. The Southern Song controlled a much smaller territory than did the Northern Song, and faced an ever present threat of further incursions from northern neighbors. The threat became reality in 1276 when the Mongols, invaders from the north, finally destroyed the dynasty.

The Triumph of Domestic Politics

The loss of the north not only divided the political history of the Song dynasty but also created a poignant sense of loss that pervaded all aspects of Southern Song culture. But it would be a mistake to read the history of the Song as the history of loss. The Song dynasty made permanent and far-reaching contributions to Chinese political culture. One of the most important contributions was the large-scale implementation of civil service examinations as the primary means of recruiting the bureaucracy. The civil service examination system had been used earlier, but not until the Song did it become the dominant means of recruiting the bureaucracy. Although the details of the curriculum varied to some extent, the core was unwavering: Students were tested on their knowledge of the Confucian classics. In general, practical knowledge, such as knowledge of the legal codes, was not subject to examination. Confucian political theory rested on the premise that the best training for a political career was a thorough grounding in the classics. The details of political administration—law, tax collection, agricultural management—could be learned on the job or entrusted to specialist assistants.

A job in the bureaucracy was not merely a job. It conferred political power and social prestige not only on the man who held it but on his family. His wife, his parents, and his grandparents were granted official titles. A man from a well-to-do family of scholars would clearly stand a better chance of doing well on the examinations than would a man from a more modest family background, but a young man from a prominent family still had to pass the examinations. Although failure would not doom him to poverty, or even necessarily to obscurity, it would preclude a career in government. There were several levels of examination a young man had to pass: first at the provincial level, then at the national level, and finally a palace examination. The entire cycle of examinations was repeated every three

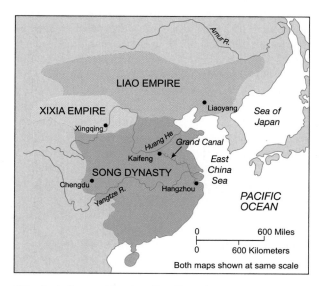

China in the Song and Southern Song Dynasties

Statue of an early Northern Song civil official holding a hu, *a tablet that symbolizes high office.*

kind of demon who have come to distract the young man from the serious business of study.

The examination system shaped Chinese political culture in several ways. Because most Chinese men were eligible to take the examinations, the system fostered a great deal of social mobility among the upper strata of society. An ambitious man need not oppose the political elite; by dint of hard work he could hope to enter it. In this way, the myth of social mobility may have served as a safety valve for social tensions. The examination system also promoted cultural cohesion in traditional China. Because young men of the upper classes in all parts of China aspired to take the same tests, they studied the same curriculum. As a result, there was a broad consensus about social values, about human nature, and about what government could and could not do. The civil service examination system was not abolished until 1905. It is true that during the course of this long history, the examinations occasionally had a stultifying effect on political life. But they also enriched that political life and provided it with rare cohesion.

The close connection between education and politics made the education of daughters problematic. On the one hand, a daughter would never take the civil service exam, so the elaborate classical education required for sons of the elite class was wasted on a daughter. On the other hand, mothers were by and large in charge of early childhood education. When an elite family was selecting a wife for a son, they looked for a woman who was well enough educated to teach the rudiments of reading to their grandsons. And when that same family was making decisions about whether or not to invest in educating a daughter, they would be attentive to the demands of the marriage market. Although during this time there was a well-developed system of academies and private schools, many elite families preferred to call in tutors to teach their sons. There is no way of knowing how many daughters picked up scraps of classical knowledge from a brother's tutor. Indeed, such exposure to the classics might well have been involuntary. One of the most important ways in which a boy would learn texts was by reciting them aloud. One can imagine that everyone in the household would learn the texts along with him, whether they wanted to or not.

The examination system is perhaps the most distinctive aspect of Chinese political culture in the Song and later periods. But, while it was crucial in shaping the national political elite, that elite was only a small portion of the total population. Elite status on the local level was conferred by other means: One became a

years. Failure was the rule rather than the exception, but a candidate who failed the examinations might take them again. In the Song, one out of every five candidates would pass the palace exams, and the successful candidate was often in his mid-thirties.

This test upon which so much rested was fraught with anxiety. Chinese literature is full of stories of vulnerable young men on their way to take civil service examinations who are seduced by beautiful young women. These beauties, it often turns out, were often not human beings at all, but fox-fairies or some other

member of the elite through education, through wealth, and through landholding. During the Song, a local elite that was more or less independent of the national government developed. This local elite proved crucial in providing stability and continuity during the period of Mongol rule during the Yuan dynasty (1279–1368), and would remain a powerful force throughout the Ming dynasty (1368–1644).

Commercial and Agricultural Productivity

Commerce flourished during the Song dynasty. The growing prosperity of the landed class provided a market for luxury goods, which stimulated economic growth. Long-distance trade, both domestic and international, prospered. Because water transport was the most efficient way of moving goods, an elaborate system of rivers and canals was developed for water traffic. The Song also participated in maritime trade. By the tenth or eleventh century, boats capable of high-seas navigation had been perfected, and the compass had been in use since the late eleventh century.

The prominence of long-distance trade led to technical innovations such as paper money. The first Chinese paper money was printed in 1024 in Sichuan province, supplementing the copper and silver coins that had been in circulation for more than a millennium. The amount of paper money in circulation under the Song was substantial: At its height it amounted to the equivalent of 400 million strings of copper cash (a string was a thousand coins). Paper money was a success during the Song. In later dynasties, however, governments under financial duress succumbed to the temptation to print more money, and inflation became a serious problem.

During the Song dynasty agricultural productivity increased modestly. Part of this increase was due to an increase in the amount of land under cultivation. Some of the new land was hills that were terraced. But much of it was wetlands around lakes, which were drained for agriculture. New strains of rice were also introduced. Sometime after 1012 Champa rice from Southeast Asia was introduced to China. This new strain had several advantages. It was quick-ripening and disease resistant. Champa rice enabled more Chinese farmers to grow two crops of rice a year on the same field. The Song government took an active role in agricultural development. Government officials systematically distributed the new seeds, along with information about other agricultural techniques, such as improved irrigation and

Painting of a knickknack peddler by Southern Song artist Li Sung. A woman and her children look over the hundreds of items on display.

soil preparation. Agricultural handbooks detailing the latest in farming techniques began to be widespread during the Song. Because most peasants were illiterate, landlords or county magistrates read these books and conveyed the techniques to peasants under their supervision.

Rural markets held on a periodic basis linked communities commercially and to some extent socially. Traveling peddlers would go from town to town, on a fixed route, carrying gossip and other news with their wares as they went from market to market. Parents sent matchmakers to a nearby market town to find spouses for their children. Marriage networks thus formed another way of linking these communities.

Mining played an important role in the Song economy, as did the production of cast iron. Porcelain was perfected in the twelfth century, and both government and private merchants sponsored its manufacture.

The cities that emerged during the Song represented a new kind of urban growth. The Tang dynasty capital of Chang'an, for all its splendor, had been principally an administrative center. The Song capital of Kaifeng, however, was dominated by commercial life and amusements. The wards within the cities were no longer walled, and some entertainment shops were open all night. The state no longer controlled markets as it had during the Tang. Various informal organizations, such as mutual aid societies and guilds, arose.

These informal organizations were important in promoting regional integration.

Even more remarkable than the degree of commercial development under the Song was the degree to which the Song government was able to exploit commercial wealth as a source of revenue. In the eleventh century, revenues from commercial taxes and monopolies equaled those produced by the land tax. By the thirteenth century they had exceeded it. The Song was, to an extent remarkable in a premodern state, based on commercial rather than agrarian wealth.

New Ways of Looking at the World

During the Song dynasty, social and economic change was accompanied by intellectual change. During the Period of Disunion (206–589) and the Tang dynasty, Confucianism had been eclipsed to some degree by Buddhism and Taoism. Buddhism had been introduced into China from India in the third century C.E., and it became an important religion remarkably rapidly. During the same period, Taoism also became prominent. Buddhism and Taoism had raised questions that were not central to classical Confucianism, questions dealing with how the universe was created, the generation of human life, and so forth. In the Song, a transformed Confucianism reasserted itself on the intellectual and social scene. In the classical era, Confucianism had been concerned primarily with questions of order in human society. Neo-Confucianism, as the revived Song Confucianism is called in the West, was much more involved in metaphysical speculation than classical Confucianism had been. In addition to being a political philosophy, it became a religion of personal salvation.

Neo-Confucianism described the universe as being made up of two components, *li* and *chi*. The root meaning of *li* is "pattern," and what the neo-Confucians meant by it was an ordering principle. *Chi* is the material of the universe, which li orders. The li that structures a bamboo leaf is the same as the li that structures

ZHU XI ON MIND, NATURE, AND FEELINGS

■ *In this excerpt, the neo-Confucian master is explaining the thorny relationship among feelings, nature, and the mind. Zhu Xi does not condemn feelings, as that would be Buddhist, and he is ever careful to distinguish himself from Buddhism. He offers a qualified endorsement of emotions here. Even anger, when appropriate, has a place in a balanced life.*

Nature is the state before activity begins, feelings are the state when activity has started, and the mind includes both of these states. As the saying goes: "the mind unites and commands one's nature and feelings." Desire emanates from feelings. The mind is like the flow of water, and the desire is like its waves. Just as there are good and bad waves, so there are good desires, such as "I desire to be humane," and bad desires which rush out like violent waves. When bad desires are substantial, they destroy the principle of Heaven, as water bursts a dam. When Mencius said that "feelings enable people to do good," he meant that the feelings flowing from our nature are originally all good.

Question: Is it correct to suppose that sages never show anger?

Answer: How can they never show anger? When they ought to be angry, they will show it . . . When one becomes angry at the right time, he will be acting to the proper degree. When the matter is over, anger disappears, and none of it will be retained.

Question: How can desires be checked?

Answer: Simply by thought. In learning there is nothing more important than thought. Only thought can check desires.

Someone said: If thought is not correct, it will not be adequate to check desires. Instead, it will create trouble. How about the saying: "Have no depraved thoughts"?

Answer: Thoughts that are not correct are merely desires. If we think through the right and wrong of a thing in accordance with its principle, then our thought will surely be correct.

the cosmos. Thus studying and understanding a bamboo leaf will lead to an understanding of the cosmos, and an understanding of the cosmos implies an understanding of one's place in it.

There are two primary ways in which knowledge can be acquired in the neo-Confucian program. The first is through the study of books, especially the classics and history. The second is through quiet-sitting, which is derived from Chan Buddhist meditational techniques. The public, political aspects of Confucianism that were so important in the classical era remain, but added to them is an element of personal enlightenment. The mastery of the self, known as self-cultivation, was central to the neo-Confucian program. In the document cited on page 322, Zhu Xi (1130–1200), one of the most important of the Song neo-Confucian thinkers, describes the proper role emotions should play in a well-balanced life.

Women's Place in the New World

Associated with the many changes occurring in the Song dynasty was a decline in the status of women. Chinese women had gained fame as poets in preceding centuries, and they were not necessarily confined to domestic roles. But the growing prosperity of the Song economy, coupled with the moral seriousness of the neo-Confucians, combined to restrict the role of women in China.

Palace Ladies Bathing Children, *a Song dynasty painting.*

Most symptomatic of the change in the status of women is foot binding. Tang women did not bind their feet. The origins of the custom are unclear—legend suggests that a dancer at the Tang court had extraordinarily tiny feet and that other women bound their feet to imitate her. A wife with bound feet became a symbol of conspicuous consumption. A man announced to the world that he was well off by marrying someone whose capacity for productive labor was literally hobbled. Furthermore, bound feet restricted a woman's physical ability to move about at the same time moralists were suggesting that her mobility ought to be restricted. Whatever the origins of the custom, its durability lies in the dark recesses of the erotic imagination. Chinese women bound their daughters' feet because tiny lotus-like feet made them more attractive on the marriage market.

The extent to which foot binding was prevalent among all the classes of Chinese society is unclear. It was widespread among the upper classes, though more so after the Song than during it. Parents who were planning for their daughters' futures might well have hoped that the girl would grow up and marry (or be a concubine) in a social stratum where bound feet were expected. As a result of such parental pretensions, countless peasant women labored in the fields with bound feet.

The most important unit in Chinese local society was the family. It was an economic unit, as well as a biological and moral one. Moreover, it was the fundamental unit of production and consumption among peasants. Marriage was almost universal for women, but was less so for men. Because upper-class men might marry several women as concubines, there were simply not enough women to go around. Women married relatively young, in their late teens or early twenties. In the most common form of marriage, known as virilocal marriage, the young woman lived with her new husband's family, which was frequently in another village. She was subject to the authority of her in-laws, particularly her mother-in-law. Her visits to her home village were restricted to ceremonial occasions.

Concubinage, always legal, became more widespread in the Song. A man might have only one legal wife, but he might have as many concubines as he could afford. A wife had certain protections against divorce, but a concubine had none.

The ideal household size was large, but its actual size was quite modest. Although the size varied with time, with class, and with region, it seems to have averaged five or six people. It was unusual for married brothers to continue living together in an undivided household.

Although marriage was arranged, an ideal marriage was not devoid of romance. One of the most celebrated poets of the Song dynasty, a woman named Li Qingzhao (1084–1141), wrote erotic poems to her husband. The following may serve as an example:

How many evenings in the arbor by the river,
when flushed with wine we'd lose our way back.
The mood passed away, returning late by boat
we'd stray off into a spot thick with lotus
    and thrashing through
       and thrashing through
startle a shoreful of herons by the lake.

Servants played an important role in the households of the elite. Children were often nursed by wet nurses, who usually lived with the families of their young charges. Such nurses might remain for life with the children they had nursed, and retain significant influence in their lives. The fact that women of the lower classes had such a profound role in raising children of the upper classes probably fostered cultural integration among various levels of society. The stories servant women told their young masters became transformed into part of the culture of the elite.

Song Religion and Popular Culture

Chinese religion during the Song and later periods differs in many ways from Western religion. Chinese religion tended to be characterized by pragmatism rather than doctrinaire approaches. Although there were a number of different religions—Buddhism, Taoism, and Confucianism—which did not always approach problems in the same way, these different religions coexisted quite harmoniously. Not only did individual people subscribe to more than one, temples often housed images from all three traditions. Furthermore, there was no strong separation between secular and sacred. Neither Buddhism nor Taoism had weekly services that the faithful were expected to attend. Services were held to celebrate particular rituals; otherwise, believers entered temples to worship as it seemed appropriate to them to do so.

Temples, whether they were Buddhist, Taoist, or shrines to local gods, were always community centers. With the possible exception of the capital, Chinese cities and towns in general did not have public civic space the way European towns did. Temples served as public spaces. Markets and theatrical performances often took place at temples.

In addition to being entertainment centers, Buddhist temples were important sources of social welfare.

They functioned as orphanages, hospitals, soup kitchens, and schools. This function was even more important after the Song, when the state spent fewer resources on welfare.

Festivals were important components of local religion. Some festivals were calendrical, that is, they marked off seasonal changes. Calendrical festivals celebrated the passing of the seasons, such as the coming of spring. They sought to ensure the fertility of the land and of the people. At the root of this is a belief in correspondences between the world (and the actions) of humans and the cosmos. The lunar New Year, which falls on a date in the Western calendar sometime between mid-January and mid-February, marks the beginning of spring. It is the biggest festival of the year, and marks a new beginning. Celebrations last for much of the first lunar month. On the fifteenth of the first lunar month, there is a lantern festival, which is described in this poem by Xin Chiji (1140–1207):

One night's east wind made a thousand trees burst into flowers
    And breathe down still more
    Showers of fallen stars.
Splendid horses, carved carriages, fragrance filled the road
    Music resounded from paired flutes,
    Light swirled on the water-clock towers.
All night long, the fabled fish-dragons danced.
Gold-threaded jacket, moth or willow-shaped hair ornaments
Melted into the throng, giggling, a trail of scents.
In the crowd I looked for her a thousand and one times;
    And all at once, as I turned my head,
    I was startled to find her
Among the lanterns where candles were growing dim.

Festivals such as the lantern festival were one of the rare occasions when women of the upper classes went out and mingled with crowds. The poet is strolling amid the festive splendor, looking for a particular woman, whom he in fact finds. This poem indicates the erotic overtones to festival life.

Another sort of festival is life-cycle rituals. Funerals are the only one of these rituals that required the assistance of a priest. Weddings were not religious ceremonies. They were solemn, they were much written about in ritual texts, but they did not require the intervention of a priest. The transition between life and death is dangerous, and a ritual expert was needed both to guide the dead person on his or her journey and to console the living.

Two major festivals to propitiate the dead were held in late traditional China. The first is called *Qingming*, which means "clear and bright." Qingming did not belong to Buddhism or Taoism or Confucianism, but rather was part of a culture common to all three religions. It was held in mid-spring, on a day calculated by the solar calendar, falling in the Western month of April. On this day, families would gather and sweep the graves of the dead. The festival, perhaps analogous to our Memorial Day, was a celebration of the lives of those no longer living. The dead were not threatening on Qingming.

But the dead were threatening at the ghost festival, which was celebrated on the fifteenth of the seventh lunar month. This festival had as its core a Taoist ghost festival, and was marked by danger. On that day the boundaries between the dead and the living were fluid; normally the gates of heaven and hell are guarded by tigers and leopards, and the boundaries between the living and the dead are fixed. Added to the Taoist festival was a Buddhist festival called Ulambana.

The story behind Ulambana illustrates several important points about Chinese Buddhism. A young monk named Mulian left some money with his mother so that she could give alms to wandering monks. She spent the money on herself. The money that should have gone to feed monks went for food, wine and musicians. When she dies she goes to hell. When Mulian discovers that she is suffering dreadful punishments in hell, he undertakes a horrendous journey to find her and save her. She can neither eat nor drink. The Buddha tells Mulian that he can save his mother by offering food and drink to monks and to "hungry ghosts" on the fifteenth of the seventh lunar month. Hungry ghosts are people whose descendants do not sacrifice to them, or people who died untimely or violent deaths.

In many senses the story of Mulian is a myth that reconciles Buddhism and filial piety. Its hero quite literally goes to hell to save a parent. It is worth noting that the filial tie honored here is not the father-son tie, but rather the mother-son tie.

The Chinese spirit world, especially the world of Taoism, resembled the world of the mundane bureaucracy. For example, when a person had a request to make of a Taoist divinity—for health, long life, prosperity—he or she would write a petition using the same form that would be used to petition the emperor. The believer would then burn the petition. If the deity did not grant the petition, the believer might then appeal to a higher deity.

In the Song, Yuan, and Ming dynasties, Taoism was articulated into a complex textual religion, with numerous rituals, meditation techniques, and other

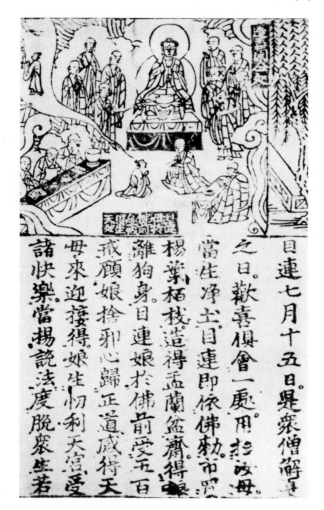

Japanese scroll dated 1346, showing Mulian administering the precepts to his mother. They kneel in the presence of the Buddha and an assembly of monks.

practices. It had a large following among the elite, and was particularly attractive to several of the late Ming emperors.

Buddhism in China survived the late Tang persecutions. But the forms that survived with the most vitality were Chan, which could be studied with a teacher, and Pure Land, in which the simple recitation of the name of the Amida Buddha would ensure salvation. The three religions in China usually had an easy coexistence. Individuals might believe that their own religious orientation was superior to that of their neighbor, but they had enough respect for the reality of the spirit world not to scorn their neighbor. Chinese religion was pragmatic rather than doctrinaire. If prayers to a Buddhist deity failed, then the sensible thing to do would be to pray to a Taoist or Confucian one.

A number of local deities who are neither Buddhist nor Taoist played an important role in Chinese religious life. One of these is the city god, who might well be a deity of local significance, or might be one with broader appeal. What often happened with these local deities was that the state incorporated them into the official orthodox pantheon. They became the representatives of the state cult at the local level, just like the magistrate is the representative of the emperor at the local level.

During the Song dynasty, cities prospered and trade flourished. The civil service examination system became the primary means of recruitment into the bureaucratic elite. Neo-Confucianism suggested new ways of looking at the interaction between human beings and the cosmos, and a wide variety of rituals and festivals were practiced among various social groupings.

Mongols and the Yuan Dynasty

The world of the Mongols was very different from the world of the Chinese, and the story of how they conquered and ruled China is a remarkable one. Equally remarkable is the way in which Chinese local society emerged from a century of Mongol domination essentially unscathed. While it might be an exaggeration to assert, as generations of Chinese historians have done, that Mongol domination exerted no influence on Chinese life, it is true that Chinese religion, family structures, and even political philosophy remained remarkably durable through the years of conquest.

Conquering from Horseback

The Mongols' homeland was on the steppe lands of northern Asia, land that was arid and inhospitable to sedentary agriculture. Their economy was based on raising sheep and horses, and they engaged in a minimal trade with the settled agricultural people of northern China in order to obtain commodities like grain, tea, textiles, and metals. They engaged in seasonal migrations—in the summer they pastured their animals on open plains, but in the winter they moved to more sheltered pastures. As befitted a nomadic people, they made their homes in felt tents called yurts.

Not only did the Mongol economy differ from the Chinese, their society was constructed along fundamentally different lines. The most important social unit of the Mongols was the clan, which was headed by a chieftain. Although the chief might be the eldest man in the clan, he was chosen primarily on the basis of his abilities rather than on seniority. Women held relatively high positions in Mongol society. A daughter might inherit her father's property if there were no sons, and a woman had the right to divorce her husband.

In the late eleventh and twelfth centuries, the Mongol clans began to consolidate and turn their attention to their neighbors to the south. The man who united the Mongol clans was Temujin (1167–1227), better known by his title of Genghis Khan. By invoking ties of personal loyalty, he forged a formidable military and political empire. In 1206 he was named Genghis Khan, a title meaning "universal ruler," of the Mongol tribes. In 1215 the Mongols captured the Jin capital, and by 1233 they had defeated the remnants of the Jin state. From the conquest of the Jin, the Mongols continued their southern expansion and by 1276, all of China was in their hands. Kublai Khan (1216–94) became the emperor of all China. He ruled the vast multicultural Mongol empire not from the traditional capital of Karakorum in Mongolia, but rather from Khanbaliq, near modern Beijing.

The success of the Mongols can be explained partly in terms of their military superiority. The military might of the Mongols was legendary, as was their battle prowess. But despite their military advantages, the Mongols were severely outnumbered by the Chinese. There were perhaps 1.5 million Mongols at the time of the conquest of China, and only one hundred thousand or so of them were in China. The total population of China at that time was about 60 million. Superior horsemanship might account for the conquest, but it does not explain nearly a century of Mongol rule of China. Chinese advisers were fond of quoting an old proverb to the Mongols: "One can conquer the world on horseback, but one cannot govern it on horseback." The story goes that Ogodai (1229–41), Genghis's successor, had imagined turning north China into pastureland, but was persuaded that it would be more profitable to leave the splendid cities and lush farmlands intact and extract wealth from them. Consequently, when the Mongols proclaimed the Yuan dynasty, they left more or less intact the bureaucratic structure of China.

Nor did they try to convert the Chinese to a Mongol way of life. The Mongol language, Mongol religion—a

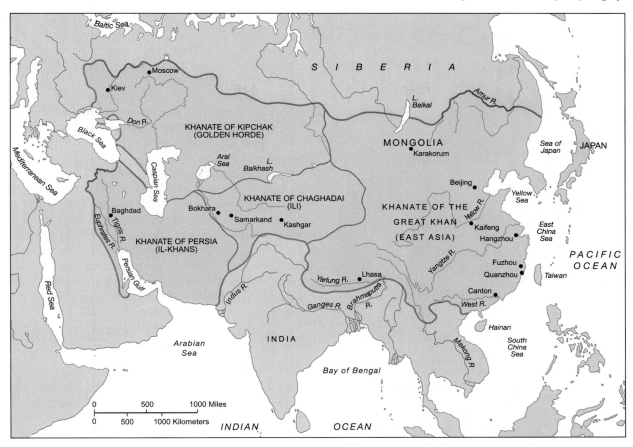

The Mongol Empire

Yuan Achievements

form of Tibetan Buddhism known as lamaism—and even the Mongol law code remained restricted to Mongols.

After the conquest of China was complete, the Yuan allowed the large estates in the south to remain more or less intact. The rich agricultural lands of south China continued to prosper. During the Yuan dynasty, cotton became a significant Chinese crop for the first time. The policy of leaving south China alone contrasted with Mongol policies elsewhere in the world, and won for the Yuan the neutrality, if not the support, of the large landowners there.

The Mongols were astute traders, and under their rule trade prospered. The sheer size of the Mongol empire facilitated contact between east and west, which enhanced trade. They improved the commercial infrastructure in China. Their most famous innovation was a postal system with couriers who could travel 250 miles in a day, set up in 1236. The Yuan dynasty continued using paper currency, but the Chinese did not necessarily benefit from Yuan dynasty trade. Much of the trade under the Yuan was in the hands of non-Chinese middlemen, and hence much of the profit also went into non-Chinese hands.

China may have been a glittering prize the Mongols desperately desired, but Mongol ambitions extended well beyond China's boundaries. The Mongol empire stretched over much of the Eurasian continent. Much of the Mongol success in governing in fact lay with their strategy of leaving local societies and institutions more or less intact.

But that does not mean that the Mongol conquest was not brutal. The Koreans resisted the Mongol attacks, which began in 1231, with every resource at their disposal. They attempted to elicit divine aid as well by carving woodblocks to print the entire body of Buddhist scripture (known as the Tripitika). The project,

Pottery figurine of a dancing actor, Yuan dynasty, found in 1963 in Hunan province.

completed in 1236, required 81,000 woodblocks, which are still extant. But it was to no avail; the Mongols devastated Korea. A Korean dynastic history records the devastation of those years:

> Those who died of starvation were multitudinous, the corpses of the old and weak clogged ravines, and in the end some even left babies tied in trees.

The Mongols used Korea as a staging ground for their attempts to invade Japan in the late thirteenth century (see discussion below). The Mongols, believing that Vietnam had been a part of China, attempted to gain control of it in the 1280s, but failed.

Despite the fact that the preconquest Mongols lacked a written language, they were interested in cultural matters. Kublai Khan sent envoys to south India to bring back doctors and craftworkers. He established an

imperial library in Beijing in 1238. The Mongols even followed the Chinese practice of commissioning the dynastic history of their predecessors. Dynastic histories of the Song, Liao, and Jin were compiled under Yuan auspices in 1344–45.

During the Yuan dynasty, the traditional arts of painting and poetry both thrived in China, and a major new art form, the drama, evolved. While the older art forms were appreciated primarily by the connoisseurs who were members of the educated elite, drama found a wider audience.

Yuan drama was highly stylized and combined singing and the spoken word. The language of the drama was a mixture of Yuan dynasty colloquial and classical forms. It featured familiar stories, historical heroes, and romantic heroines. Earthy humor and poignant romance were both prominent. The plays may be categorized as comedies: the genre demanded a happy ending. Drama formed an important cultural link between literate and nonliterate segments of the population.

Downfall of the Yuan

The Yuan dynasty was brought down by rebellions precipitated by a combination of administrative inefficiency and natural disasters. The late Yuan dynasty was plagued by natural catastrophes, which in the Chinese political context were apt to be interpreted as signaling the loss of the Mandate of Heaven. In the 1330s, famine hit north China hard. Making matters worse, the Yellow River flooded repeatedly. The Yellow River is heavily laden with silt, hence its name. Because it has been dredged and diked for countless centuries, in many places the riverbed is higher than the surrounding land. Dikes must be maintained with absolute vigilance or the river will burst from its dikes and flood the surrounding land. In 1344, dikes downriver from Kaifeng broke, and they were not repaired for five years. Many catastrophes, like floods, which we are in the habit of calling natural, are often precipitated by human negligence. The fourteenth-century flooding of the Yellow River is an example of nature and humanity working in tandem to create calamity.

In the waning years of the dynasty, the Yuan court was plagued by factional disputes. In the years between 1320 and 1329 four different emperors occupied the throne. In 1328, a virtual civil war broke out among the princes. These problems both weakened the technical capacity of the government to govern and lessened its credibility among the populace.

A regime threatened by natural catastrophe and factional dissent might still survive if it has the support of the political elite. But the Yuan had never completely won over the Chinese literati. When the political situation began to decay in the fourteenth century, the elite were quick to throw their support behind rebels with whom they may in fact have had very little in common.

This combination of factors left the Yuan vulnerable to rebellion. Among the rebel groups that arose in the late Yuan was a group known as the White Lotus, a heterodox offshoot of Buddhism. The White Lotus sect was founded in 1133 by a man named Mao Ziyuan in Suzhou. It attracted a following among salt workers and boatmen in the lower Yangzi River area. White Lotus religion was millenarian, messianic, and salvational. It held that the coming of the Buddha of the Future, Maitreya, was imminent. In the coming age, Maitreya would save those who believed in him. Although many White Lotus groups were communities of law-abiding peasants, others rose in rebellion to destroy the existing society and prepare for the new order. Orthodox Buddhism regarded sectarian cults like the White Lotus with a great deal of skepticism. Moreover, the government was hostile to these sects and proscribed them whether or not they were rebellious. For example, laws that prohibited the mingling of men and women together after dark to eat vegetables were clearly aimed at vegetarian egalitarian sects. The state sought to proscribe these cults because they represented a challenge to its authority. White Lotus religion appealed to an authority structure outside the realm of the state, indeed even outside this world. In addition to invoking the Maitreya Buddha, some of these groups claimed descent from the Song ruling house, hence hearkening back to a pre-Mongol era of Chinese political legitimacy.

Mongol rule over China did not last a full century. The Chinese model of government was powerful enough that even conquerors adopted it. The Yuan dynasty was a time of political complexity and cultural innovation, especially in the arenas of painting and drama.

The Restoration of Chinese Power Under the Ming

After a century of Mongol rule, the Chinese Ming dynasty reasserted indigenous rule. The man who succeeded in establishing the Ming dynasty, Ming Taizu (1368–98) was the son of an itinerant agricultural worker and the grandson of a master sorcerer. He rose to power through the ranks of a White Lotus sect. Taizu was the second peasant rebel to found a Chinese dynasty—Liu Bang, the Han founder, had been the first. When he became emperor, he made sectarian religion illegal, not because he underestimated it but because he knew how powerful it could be. Ming emperors were much more autocratic than previous rulers had been. Early rulers, were energetic men who had a clear vision of what Chinese society ought to be. But later emperors were often ineffective.

Chinese society under the Ming dynasty continued to function, even thrive. The local elites that began forming in the Song continued to prosper in the Ming. Indeed, they provided a center of gravity that provided for continuity. The growth of printing, which underwent a veritable explosion in the sixteenth century, meant that all kinds of texts could be printed and circulated like never before. Popular art forms like the drama served to link all classes of society.

Ming Continuity and Change

Ming Taizu was a man with a vision who had the political authority and will to enforce that vision. At the center of his vision was the establishment of a stable agrarian society, a society radically different from the vibrant commercial economy of the Song and early Yuan dynasties. But he was not a simple reactionary: The agrarian economy of north China had been ravaged during the Yuan by natural catastrophes and civil wars. Revitalizing the agrarian economy of the north was a pressing need. One aspect of the revitalization was a reforestation project, in which one hundred million trees were planted.

The administrative structure of the Ming dynasty resembled that of the Song, but the political reality was very different. Most Song emperors consulted on a regular basis with their ministers. It is perhaps an exaggeration to say that the Song emperor had a collegial relationship with his ministers of state—he was, after all, the Son of Heaven—but the emperor was not the sole and central focus of authority. The Ming emperor, however, was a supreme autocrat.

Comparisons between Song and Ming politics do not redound to the advantage of the Ming. Ming government was simultaneously more despotic and less efficient than Song government had been. The concentration of political power in the person of the emperor led to these seemingly conflicting trends. In a system where power is concentrated in the emperor, should the emperor choose not to exercise power—and some late Ming emperors were more interested in carpentry than they were in affairs of state—or should he exercise power badly, then the system is in trouble.

The autocratic tendencies of the early Ming were reinforced by some institutional changes. A crisis was precipitated in 1380 when Hu Weiyong, the prime minister, was charged with treason. He was executed along with thousands of his family members, friends, and supporters. Moreover, the position of prime minister was abolished. Hence, there was no one bureaucrat in the early Ming who had an institutional position that might have enabled him to provide a counterbalance to despotic or incompetent imperial power.

The third Ming emperor, commonly referred to by his reign name as Yongle (1403-24), was a powerful and energetic ruler. Under his reign, Ming rule was further consolidated and expanded. The Ming attempted to reincorporate Vietnam into the Chinese empire, but failed after twenty years of occupation. Ironically, after their expulsion in 1427, Chinese cultural influence in Vietnam, especially neo-Confucianism, experienced a resurgence.

The early Ming was a great maritime power, as had been the Song. But under the Ming, maritime expansion reached a new scale. Zheng He (1371-1433), a Moslem eunuch from Yunnan province, led seven expeditions. The voyages were massive: There were more than twenty thousand men on each trip. The overt purpose of the voyages was neither trade nor colonization. Rather, they aimed at securing recognition of the power and prestige of the Ming empire, and they were by and large successful. The tribute missions sent to the Ming court by Mamluk Egypt, for example, were probably prompted by the voyages. Another measure of the success of these voyages is the fact that in places in Southeast Asia, Zheng He was later deified as a popular god.

Zheng He returned from his last voyage in 1433, bringing the era of Chinese exploration to a close. After the death of the Yongle emperor, no one else at court seems to have been particularly interested in continuing the voyages. The voyages of Zheng He seem to have satisfied the curiosity of his imperial patrons about the outside world. This attitude is in marked contrast to that of Europeans later in the same century, who would embark upon an era of exploration and colonization. The Chinese in the early fifteenth century had technical navigational skills that were superior to those of the Europeans, but they chose not to continue to use them.

The retreat from expansionism can also be seen in policies toward the steppe peoples. Ming problems in dealing with the frontier can be seen in the Tumu incident in 1449, when Mongols captured the Ming emperor. The capture of the emperor created a profound political crisis, but it did not bring down the dynasty. The emperor was succeeded by his brother, who reigned until 1457, when the captive emperor was released.

Another aspect of Ming politics worthy of note is the growing power of eunuchs. Eunuchs had access to the Forbidden City, the residence of the emperor and his consorts. Men who were sexually intact were denied entrance into the emperor's private quarters because of an obsessive concern with the sexual purity of the emperor's consorts. But the imperial household was immense, and the system used to run it amounted to a shadow bureaucracy. In the Song, many of the positions were staffed by women. But under the Ming, most of those positions were held by eunuchs.

Eunuchs also controlled access to the emperor, since civil service bureaucrats were forbidden entry into the Forbidden City. It was easy for unscrupulous eunuchs to abuse power, especially if the emperor was indolent, as so many of the later Ming emperors were. Taizu had recognized the potential danger posed by the eunuchs, and had forbidden them to learn to read. But in the Chinese bureaucracy, knowledge was power and literacy was one of the most precious tools of the powerful. Recognizing this fact, eunuchs learned to read. After they gained control of the secret police, they became a truly formidable force.

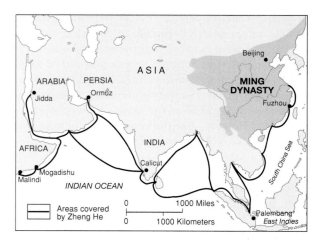

Ming China and the Zheng He Expeditions

Ming Commerce, Culture, and Corruption

The Ming vision of an ideal society was a stable agrarian order, and early Ming society reflected that vision. By the thirteenth century, cotton was grown widely in China. Hemp, another textile fiber, and mulberry, used to feed silkworms, were also widely grown. Chinese silk continued to be a luxury commodity prized on the international market. Cotton and mulberry had important implications for the gendered division of labor in the areas where they were important crops, such as the lower Yangzi valley. Textile production was lucrative, and it was women's work. By the sixteenth century in this area a woman spinning could produce as much income as a man working in the fields. The prominence of cash crops, which of course varied from place to place and even from time to time within the same place, implied a commercialized economy: a peasant family who grew cotton, for example, had cash to buy their grain.

Beginning in the sixteenth century, crops from the New World began to be introduced into China—corn, peanuts, potatoes, and sweet potatoes. The new crops gradually and profoundly transformed the Chinese agricultural economy. They had high nutritional value and could be grown on land that was marginal for rice. They fueled a population growth that would loom large in eighteenth-century China.

During the Yuan and early Ming dynasties, cities and commerce had been less important and less highly developed than they had been in the Song. But by the sixteenth century, Chinese cities were flourishing once again. Along with urban growth at this time, a distinctive urban culture developed. Printing increased dramatically, and—for the first time—fiction began to appear in the vernacular language. Some collections of fiction were printed with illustrations running across the top of each page, as if the pictures were for the benefit of the marginally literate. Novels printed in this way were found in the grave of a fifteenth-century official's wife, indicating not only that she read but that novels were treasured.

Several important popular novels were first published in the sixteenth century. *Journey to the West* is a comic novel about salvation. In it, a monkey, a monk, a pig, and a sand demon leave China for India on a quest for Buddhist scriptures. The novel, one hundred chapters long, is filled with their misadventures and their gradual awakening to the reality that all is illusion. *Jin ping mei* is a domestic tragedy, chronicling the life of Ximen Qing, a wealthy merchant, and his six wives. It is a bitter tale of jealousy, greed, and sexual excess, told by a master storyteller. The world in the novel is a far cry from that of the Confucian moralist.

For all the strength of the new urban cultural forms, they did not replace older literati forms. Indeed they never gained the cultural prestige held by the great literati artistic triad of painting, poetry, and calligraphy. Because the brush was used both to paint and to write, there was a close connection between painting and calligraphy in traditional China. Poems might be inscribed on a painting, either by the painter or by a later collector. If the inscription was done by the painter, the positioning of the words on the page would be an integral part of the spatial composition of the painting. If the inscription, or colophon, was written by a later collector, it would alter the spatial relationships in the painting. This was not regarded by painter or collector as an act defacing the painting. A work of art existed in dynamic interaction with later generations of viewers. It was only fitting that a collector who felt moved to inscribe a poem on the painting do so, provided of course that he had an elegant hand and a strong sense of space.

A splendid example of this is a poem and painting, both done by the fifteenth-century painter Shen Zhou:

> White clouds like a scarf enfold the mountain's waist,
> stone steps hang in space—a long, narrow path.
> Alone, leaning on my cane, I gaze intently at the scene,
> and feel like answering the murmuring brook with the music of my flute.

The poem inscribed on this painting is an integral part of the work of art. Besides describing the scene, the poem serves to locate the painter in it. The poem makes explicit the resonances between the world of the human and the natural world that are implied in the painting and makes the work function on a scale both human and grandiose. The placing of the poem on the painting is not accidental: the small human figure seems to be speaking the words.

In other matters, however, values were less humane. During the Song, attitudes about widow remarriage had begun to harden. Zheng Yi, the neo-Confucian philosopher, said that it was a small thing to starve to death but a large thing to lose one's chastity. In the early fourteenth century the government first established memorial arches for widows who had been widowed before they were thirty and had remained chaste until their fiftieth birthday. Such virtue had practical consequences; for example, the families of such women were granted tax exemptions. Political loyalty was analogous

Poet on a Mountain Top. *Leaf from an album with a poem and an ink drawing on paper by Shen Zhou (1427–1509).*

to sexual loyalty: by promoting the latter, the government doubtless hoped to promote the former. During the Ming and Qing (1644–1912) dynasties, the cult of widow chastity became widespread. At the same time, there were practical reasons for a woman to remarry, and she might be under pressure to do so. There was a sad and shocking proliferation of women who, under pressure from family members to remarry, committed suicide rather than do so.

Philosophy also flourished in sixteenth-century Ming culture. The most important philosopher of the Ming dynasty was Wang Yangming (1472–1529), who believed everyone had the innate capacity to know good, and that the point of moral cultivation was to extend that capacity. He asserted that external sources of authority, both texts and teachers, had only secondary significance. As he put it, "If words are examined in the mind and found to be wrong, even though they come from the mouth of Confucius, I dare not accept them as correct." Wang Yangming also articulated another position implicit in earlier Confucian thought when he asserted the unity of knowledge and action. For example, a person who does not treat his or her parents with filial piety cannot be said to understand filial piety. Real understanding of the concept would mandate action.

Although Wang Yangming asserted that everyone had the potential for sagehood, he by no means implied that the attaining of sagehood would be easy. But some of his followers did. The most radical of these thinkers, called the Taizhou school after the place where the school originated, took the precept that every person was a sage literally. The most important of these thinkers was Wang Gen (1483–1541). When Wang Gen preached, so

the story goes, thousands of people would flock to hear him—so many that shouters would stand in the audience and convey his words, as a kind of low-technology sound system. Influenced by these philosophical developments, as well as by the growth in urban commercial wealth and the growing importance of literacy, was a literary genre called Ledgers of Merit and Demerit. These texts provided a kind of popularized moral handbook for society.

Paradoxically, this period of great flourishing of Ming society in the sixteenth century also had serious social problems. One of the consequences of the Ming vision of an ideal society as a stable agrarian order was that when commerce began to flourish in the sixteenth century, the state was not able to capture revenues from the new prosperity. Ming taxes were consistently lower than taxes had been in the Song, and as a result the number of services the state could provide was much lower. Functions such as poor relief, which the Song state had shown some interest in financing, were funded entirely by local elites or religious organizations during the Ming dynasty. Moreover, this was a period of stunning imperial incompetence and corruption. Zhang Zhuzheng (1525–82), who held the extremely important and powerful position of Senior Grand Secretary, implemented a number of financial reforms. But what is most remembered about him is not the reforms but the fact that at his death his estate was lavish beyond even the Ming imagination. He has become emblematic of late Ming corruption. The reasons for the fall of the Ming are complex, but the problems of cumbersome and incompetent government play a significant role.

Japan: Aristocrats into Warriors

In Japan during the period from the twelfth to the seventeenth centuries, central power disintegrated and was reconstituted along new lines. The aristocratic culture of early Japan was replaced by a culture dominated by warriors, monks, and merchants. The Kamakura (1185–1338) and Ashikaga (1338–1573) periods are characterized by a growing trend toward political decentralization. The Ashikaga is marked by frequent warfare, and by its end, central power was completely meaningless. Yet, ironically, this period was also a time of economic growth and cultural flourishing. Much of what

MERITORIOUS DEEDS AT NO COST

■ *This work is typical of the genre of morality books, which flourished in the sixteenth and seventeenth centuries. These texts reflect a popularized notion of the possibilities for enlightenment.*

The moral precepts in this particular text are categorized by social status. Here are excerpts from what is expected of the local gentry, the peasantry, and finally of people in general. Note the ways in which one can infer social tensions by which kinds of behavior are prohibited.

LOCAL GENTRY

Take the lead in charitable donations. Rectify your own conduct and transform the common people. Do not make remarks about women's sexiness. Do not be arrogant, because of your own power and wealth, toward relatives who are poor or of low status. Do not ignore your own relatives and treat others as if they are of your kin. Persuade others to settle lawsuits through conciliation. Do not keep too many concubines.

PEASANTS

Do not miss proper times for farm work. Do not steal and sell your master's grain in connivance with his servants. In plowing, do not infringe on graves or make them hard to find.

PEOPLE IN GENERAL

Do not divulge your parents' faults to others. Respect women's chastity. Do not put curses on those from whom you have become estranged. When you meet fishermen, hunters, or butchers, try to have them change their occupations. Disseminate morality books which teach retribution and reward. Take good care of paper on which characters are written. Make peace between husbands and wives who are about to separate. Do not speak ill of Buddhist or Taoist monks. Do not listen to your wife or concubines if they should encourage you to neglect or abandon your parents. When helping to put out a fire, do not take advantage of it to steal others' belongings. Even if you see bad men prosper, do not lose faith in ultimate recompense.

From Tadao Sakai, "Confucianism and Popular Educational Works."

we think of as representing traditional Japanese culture—the tea ceremony, warrior ethics, Noh drama—had its beginnings during the Kamakura or Ashikaga period.

One of the clearest contrasts between China and Japan is in the nature of the imperial institution. In China, imperial legitimacy was conferred by the Confucian concept of the Mandate of Heaven, a mandate that did not rest permanently with any one ruling family. The mechanism for legitimating dynastic change is described as a change in mandate. By contrast, Japanese political theory does not allow for a changeable mandate. The legitimacy of the Japanese imperial house rested upon the mythology of its descent from the sun goddess. This made the emperor of Japan quasi-divine. Because of the charisma of the authority surrounding him, the emperor was not overthrown. But this did not

mean that the authority of the emperor could not be usurped. In the Kamakura period, a family named Minamoto established themselves as shoguns. Although the shogun was originally a military official, in fact shoguns held civil as well as military power. For example, they had the authority to appoint provincial officials. The emperor appointed the shogun, and granted him legitimacy. The shogun ruled in the name of the emperor, using his charisma rather than usurping it.

Kamakura: Warrior Rule

The first shogun was Minamoto Yoritomo (1147–99), who established his power base in the fishing village of Kamakura, which then gave its name to an era. During the Kamakura period, the emperor remained on the

Wooden sculpture of Minamoto Yoritomo, the first shogun of Japan, from the thirteenth century.

throne in Kyoto and the shogun ruled from Ka-makura—a situation that created an uneasy balance of authority between the two centers of power.

Many of the early Kamakura policies were designed to give the shogun better control of the land and the revenues it produced. By the tenth century most of the land in Japan was divided into estates called *shoen*. A shoen was a privately held estate that was often tax-exempt. Yoritomo placed a steward on each shoen, who collected rent and dues from it. In return the stewards were granted military and judicial powers and a portion of the income from the estate. The shogun also appointed an official called the *shugo*, in each province, who oversaw the stewards. Yoritomo also offered protection and rights to land to his followers in return for their promise of military allegiance to him. In several important respects this resembles the feudalism of the European Middle Ages: Military and civil functions were fused into a single authority, and the vertical bond between lord (*daimyo* in the Japanese case) and vassal was the primary bond that tied society together. This system, whether or not we choose to call it feudalism, enabled the Kamakura to govern localities and provide for defense with minimal central government expenditures. But there were also negative consequences: Kamakura central control was very fragile.

After Yoritomo's death, his widow Hojo Masako (1157—1225) retained a position of power. Moreover, she manipulated her own family into positions of authority, and the Hojo became hereditary regents for the Minamoto shoguns, dominating the politics of the Ka-makura shogunate until its demise in 1333. Thus another layer was added to the complicated picture of central authority in Kamakura Japan.

One consequence of the decentralization of Japan under the Kamakura was the fragmentation of legal authority. Neither the imperial government nor the shogunal government had the authority to promulgate a legal code that had force throughout the land. The important daimyo would have house codes, which would govern the behavior not only of members of the family but also of the peasants who resided on their estates. In order to bring about some uniformity in the legal structure for samurai (the warrior aristocracy), the Hojo regents to the shogun promulgated a legal code, the Joei code, in 1232. The Joei code was the first codification of feudal customary law in Japan. The main author, a man named Hojo Yasutoki (1183–1242), wrote that "the ancient codes and regulations are like complicated Chinese characters, understood only by a very few people. They are rendered useless to those who understand only the Japanese syllabary. This code is presented in such a way that the great majority of people can take comfort in it, just as there are many people who can understand the Japanese syllabary, so must this code be uniformly known." The code is at pains to assure vassals that they will be treated equally. It also demonstrates a clear concern with public order—it exhorts samurai to obey shoen law. It enshrined warrior values, such as loyalty, honor, and frugality, and celebrated aspects of warrior culture, such as horsemanship, archery, and swordsmanship. Despite the pretensions of the code to universality, its provisions pertained only to samurai. Justice for peasants remained a local matter, to be decided under local codes promulgated at the shoen level.

Important families, such as the Hojo regents, produced family instructions to regulate the behavior of family members. The Hojo instructions, written in 1247, reflect the ethical aura of the period. Some of the instructions advocate a person fear the gods and the Buddhas, and that he obey his lord. A person is cautioned to be aware of the Buddhist law of *karma* and the effect his or her actions will have on future generations. Bravery is a virtue that is celebrated—not surprising in a warrior society. The instructions also contain detailed rules of etiquette that reveal a highly elaborated social structure. Other exhortations resemble those that one might find in instruction books in any society. For example, the Hojo instructions tell the reader that one should obey one's parents and be generous and diligent.

This painting depicts Kublai Khan's massive seaborne invasion of Japan in 1274. The Mongol fleet has landed in northern Kyushu, and the ships are attacked by samurai armed with long swords.

Perhaps the most serious threat to face the Kamakura regime came from the Mongols, who had already conquered China and much of the rest of the world. In November of 1274 a force of 30,000 Mongols, Chinese, and Koreans sailed from Korean ports to Japan. They took the islands of Tsushima and Iki and landed at Hakata Bay. On the night of November 19, a violent storm came up, and the bulk of the Mongol army retreated. Later Japanese referred to this propitious storm as a *kamikaze,* or "divine wind." To prevent further attacks, the shogun ordered the building of a long defensive wall around all of Hakata Bay. But the Mongols were dissuaded neither by the weather nor by the wall. In 1281 Kublai Khan dispatched another force from China and Korea, this one of 140,000 men. After about two months of brutal fighting, once again the kamikaze intervened and forced the Mongol forces to retreat to Korea. The attempted Mongol invasions of Japan were the largest maritime expeditions in history prior to modern times. The expenses of defense sapped the resources of the central government, and the anxiety produced by the threat of Mongol conquest had a profound effect on Kamakura culture, especially religious culture.

Kamakura Culture: The Peasant, the Monk, the Warrior, and the Merchant

Although the economy of Kamakura Japan remained predominantly agrarian, towns and cities grew and prospered. In the late Kamakura period, peasants increased the productivity of their land by using more night soil (a

Tokugawa Japan

euphemism for human excrement) and animal manure. Farms were worked more intensively than they had been in earlier periods. Ordinary peasants in the Kamakura increasingly used metal plows and hoes and owned their own draft animals. All of these changes worked together to promote an increase in agricultural output. As villages became more prosperous, rural commerce became more highly developed. Markets held in villages became more frequent, meeting between three and six times a month. Goods produced in villages were also sold at regional markets, as well as in the growing cities.

Kamakura culture was dominated by Buddhism. In the Kamakura, we begin to see warrior values replace the aristocratic values of earlier Japanese history. And merchants begin to play a role as cultural patrons.

Three forms of Buddhism were important in Kamakura Japan—Zen, Pure Land, and Nichiren. Zen and Pure Land were imported from China, but the particular cast of Kamakura society influenced their development. Nichiren Buddhism, named after its founder, Nichiren (1222–82), on the other hand, was an indigenous development in Japanese Buddhism. Changes in the social order, such as the growth of a class of mer-

chants and warriors, coupled with the anxieties of the age, had a transformative impact on Buddhism. In earlier periods, Japanese Buddhism had been elite in its appeal and abstract in its theology. During the Kamakura, it became a popular religion.

Zen Buddhism was extremely important in Kamakura Japan. Its influence extended beyond religion into the realm of aesthetics and politics. The Zen monk Dogen (1200–53) reminded his audience that the Buddha was not born enlightened, but rather attained enlightenment through meditation. For Dogen, this implied that even ordinary humans could attain enlightenment the same way. Zen Buddhists stressed that meditation had a value separate from and superior to intellectual thinking. Dogen advised:

> Do not study the words and letters of the sutras intellectually but rather reflect upon your self-nature inwardly. Thus, your body and mind will be cast off naturally and your original nature will be revealed. If you wish to do this, be diligent in meditation.

A Zen practitioner might meditate on a *koan*, a spiritual riddle, a question with no answer, as an aid to enlightenment. A famous koan asks what is the sound of one

"DEDICATION TO THE LOTUS" BY NICHIREN

■ *This excerpt, reflecting the beautiful cadences of Kamakura Buddhist preaching, reveals the profound reverence Nichiren holds for the* Lotus Sutra.

If you desire to attain Buddhahood immediately, lay down the banner of pride, cast away the club of resentment, and trust yourselves to the unique Truth. Fame and profit are nothing more than vanity of this life; pride and obstinacy are simply fetters to the coming life . . . When you fall into an abyss and some one has lowered a rope to pull you out, should you hesitate to grasp the rope because you doubt the power of the helper? Has not Buddha declared, "I alone am the protector and savior"? There is the power! Is it not taught that faith is the only entrance [to salvation]? There is the rope! One who hesitates to seize it, and will not utter the Sacred Truth, will never be able to climb the precipice of Bodhi (Enlightenment) . . . Our hearts ache and our sleeves are wet [with tears], until we see face to face the tender figure of the One, who says to us, "I am thy Father." At this thought our hearts beat, even as when we behold the brilliant clouds in the evening sky or the pale moonlight of the fast-falling night . . . Should any season be passed without thinking of the compassionate promise, "Constantly I am thinking of you"? Should any month or day be spent without revering the teaching that there is none who cannot attain Buddhahood? . . . Devote yourself wholeheartedly to the "Adoration to the Lotus of the Perfect Truth," and utter it yourself as well as admonish others to do the same. Such is your task in this human life.

hand clapping. Because ultimate spiritual reality differs from ordinary physical and social reality (which is but an illusion), techniques like koan were needed to startle the practitioner out of the frame of reference of ordinary reality. Dogen also preached on the capacity of women for salvation:

> When we speak of the wicked, there are certainly some men among them. When we talk of the noble, these surely include women. Learning the Law of the Buddha and achieving release from illusion have nothing to do with whether one happens to be a man or a woman.

Zen also valued manual labor and taught a rigid discipline. Its spare aesthetics had a profound influence on Kamakura and later Japanese art. As secular society became more and more the preserve of the warrior, Zen monasteries became more and more sanctuaries of learning. It was not uncommon for a warrior to retire to a Zen monastery after his career in battle was over. But it would be a mistake to regard Zen as an alternative to the life of the warrior. It was the religion of choice of the warrior aristocracy. Many shoguns were important patrons of Zen.

If Zen was characterized by monastic retreat, other forms of Kamakura Buddhism were taught by street preachers, who used parables and anecdotes featuring vivid portrayals of heaven and hell to entice and convert their listeners. A Heian monk named Genshin (942–1017) wrote a very popular text called the *Essentials of Salvation*, which characterized hell as the realm of the hungry spirits who were constantly thwarted in their attempts to obtain even the most basic essentials:

> When they happen to come to an orchard the various fruits suddenly disappear, and when they approach a pure stream of water this quickly dries up.

The hungry spirits were constantly tormented by mirages of satiation and salvation. According to Genshin, faith in the Amida Buddha could save hungry spirits, and by extension all of humankind. This faith would be made manifest by chanting his name, a practice called *nembutsu*. Faith in Amida was sufficient to cause a believer to be reborn in the Pure Land.

Honen (1133–1212) and Shinran (1173–1262) were both deeply influenced by the *Essentials of Salvation*, and further developed Pure Land Buddhism. Honen took Genshin's position one step further and argued that human beings cannot attain salvation on their own merits, no matter how hard they labor. In order to obtain salvation, it was necessary to invoke the power and grace of the Amida Buddha. Honen further asserted the equality of all in the eyes of the Buddha. Shinran, who was married to the nun Eshin (1182–1270), made Pure Land Buddhism more appealing by arguing that there was no need for clerical celibacy.

But it was Nichiren (1222–82) who developed what was to be the most characteristically Japanese of all the varieties of Kamakura Buddhism. Nichiren based his teachings on the *Lotus Sutra*, an Indian Buddhist scripture that had enormous influence in both China and Japan. The *Lotus Sutra* portrays the Buddha as eternal, ever present, and existing in many forms. According to the *Lotus Sutra*, the historical Buddha had not been a human being, but was rather a manifestation of all-pervading Buddha nature. The *Lotus Sutra* stressed that everyone has the potential for salvation.

Nichiren lived during dangerous times, and his vision of human life and history was apocalyptic. The mid-thirteenth century saw widespread famine, and the Mongol invasions began in 1274. But Nichiren's vision of the apocalypse was not conditioned merely by secular catastrophe. Buddhist cosmologists calculated that in a year corresponding to 1052 in the Western calendar, an era called *mappo*, the end of Buddhist law, had begun. Mappo meant a precipitous decline in all aspects of life and society. Buddhists interpreted the social chaos of the Kamakura era as indicative of the degeneracy of the law (mappo). The opening of one of Nichiren's tracts gives the flavor of his apocalyptic vision:

> During recent years cosmic cataclysms, natural disasters, famines and epidemics have filled the world. Oxen and horses collapse at the crossroads; skeletons fill the lanes. Already more than one-half of the population has died; no one is unafflicted.

At the end of the degenerate age, Nichiren predicted, the period of the true law would come, and it would be ushered in by an ideal ruler, a Buddhist-Confucian sage-king.

The religion Nichiren founded was a national religion, and he declared the *Lotus Sutra* to be a nation-protecting sutra. When a believer invoked the text, he or she was performing an act that had implications for both personal and national salvation. But Nichiren was also universalistic: He advocated missionary work to spread the truth of the *Lotus Sutra* abroad. Japanese Buddhists, like their Chinese counterparts, were generally fairly tolerant of dissent. Here, too, Nichiren was exceptional. He was intolerant of Pure Land practitioners, and they reciprocated. He advocated suppressing them, and they burned his house to the ground.

Buddhism played an important role in Kamakura arts. Among the great achievements of the early

THE CONFESSIONS OF LADY NIJO

■ *This passage opens with the lament of the lady Nijo that the retired emperor is no longer an attentive lover. This exposes the cost of a relaxed marriage system.*
   The text then moves to a description of the empress giving birth. Note how the shamanistic rituals are central to the procedure. The lady Nijo is operating in a realm where medicine and shamanism are not separate.

I was in no position to complain about the Retired Emperor's failure to visit me at night, but it was very disappointing to wait in vain time after time. Nor could I very well grumble like my companions about the women who visited him from outside the palace, but I rebelled inwardly against the conventions whenever I had to escort one of them. Was the time likely to come when I would recall this period in my life with nostalgia? The days went by and autumn arrived.

   The approach of Higashinijoin's confinement, which was to take place in the Corner Palace, was causing concern because of the Imperial Lady's relatively advanced age and history of difficult births. I believe the time was around the Eighth Month. Every conceivable large ritual and secret ritual had been commissioned—prayers to the Seven Healing Buddhas and the Five Mystic Kings, prayers to Fugen for the prolongation of life, prayers to Kongo Doji and the Mystic King Aizen, and so on. At Father's special request, he assumed responsibility for the prayers to Kongo Doji this time, in addition to the ones to Kundali, which had always been supported by Owari Province in the past. The exorcist was the Jojuin bishop.

Kamakura period are lifelike wooden sculptured images of monks, such as those made by Unkei (ca. 1163–1233). The influence of Buddhism can be seen in the written word as well. The *Tales of Uji* are simple and powerful tales of Buddhist morality. The *Confessions of Lady Nijo*, written in the late fourteenth century by a court lady, portray life at the imperial court. But in the final two chapters, the lady Nijo abandons the court and becomes a wandering Buddhist nun.

   Another important genre of Kamakura literature is the military romance. Perhaps the most famous of these is the *Tale of the Heike*, in which the Buddhist values of the warrior culture are made clear. The famous opening of the tale can be taken as emblematic of the period:

> The sound of the bell of the Gion temple echoes the impermanence of all things. The pale hue of the flowers of the teak-tree show the truth that they who prosper must fall. The proud do not last long, but vanish like a spring-night's dream. And the mighty ones will perish in the end, like dust before the wind.

Thus we see reflected in Kamakura culture the combination of a concern with Buddhist impermanence and the beginnings of a new society infused with warrior

values and merchant wealth. These are trends that will develop more fully in the centuries to follow.

Ashikaga: Politics with No Center

If politics in Kamakura Japan was decentralized, in the Ashikaga (also known as Muromachi) period, the center ceased to hold entirely. From the Onin War (1467–77) until the Tokugawa reunification at the beginning of the seventeenth century, there was no effective central government in Japan. And yet, as we saw in the Kamakura period, these periods of political chaos do not preclude an era of cultural and economic flourishing.

   In 1333, in what is known as the Kemmu restoration, an alliance between the forces of the Ashikaga family and the emperor Go-Daigo (1318–39) overthrew the Hojo regents to the Kamakura shoguns. But the alliance soon broke down, and the emperor Go-Daigo fled south and established his court at Yoshino. Although Go-Daigo insisted that he remained the only legitimate emperor, Ashikaga Takauji (1305–58) established on the throne his puppet, a man from a collateral line of the imperial house. Takauji declared himself shogun

THE DEATH OF ATSUMORI

■ *The* Tale of the Heike *is a chronicle that recounts the rise of the Ashikaga shoguns. The portion excerpted here is a famous exposition of the warrior ethos. Naozane is overcome by grief and remorse at the fact that duty compels him to kill the handsome young Atsumori, who is, we are told in a portion of the text not reproduced here, the age of Naozane's son. But Naozane is a warrior and Atsumori must die. The poignant discovery of the flute on the body of the dead youth leads Naozane to contemplate renouncing war and assuming the religious life of a monk.*

At the beginning of the passage excerpted here, Naozane is speaking to Atsumori.

"I would like to spare you," he said, restraining his tears, "but there are warriors everywhere. You cannot possibly escape. It will be better if I kill you than if someone else does it, because I will offer prayers on your behalf."

"Just take my head and be quick about it."

Overwhelmed by compassion, Naozane could not find a place to strike. His senses reeled, his wits forsook him, and he was scarcely conscious of his surroundings. But matters could not go on like that forever: in tears, he took the head.

"Alas! No lot is as hard as a warrior's. I would never have suffered such a dreadful experience if I had not been born into a military house. How cruel I was to kill him!" He pressed his sleeve to his face and shed a flood of tears.

He removed the youth's armor so that he might wrap it around the head. A brocade bag containing a flute was tucked in at the waist. "Ah, how pitiful! He must be one of the people I heard making music just before dawn. There are tens of thousands of riders in our eastern armies, but none of them has brought a flute to the battlefield. Those court nobles are refined men!"

When Naozane's trophies were presented for Yoshitsune's inspection, they drew tears from the eyes of all the beholders. It was learned later that the slain youth was Atsumori.

After that, Naozane thought increasingly of becoming a monk. It is deeply moving that music, a profane entertainment, should have led a warrior to the religious life.

in 1338, and moved the seat of the shogun's power from Kamakura to Kyoto. Thus began the period we call Ashikaga.

Until 1392, two emperors remained on the throne, one located at the southern court at Yoshino and the other at the northern court at Kyoto. The split was the occasion for sporadic but debilitating civil war. Contemporaries debated the competing claims of the two courts. One of the strongest proponents of the southern court was the historian Kitabatake Chikafusa (1293–1354), who said that the emperor's direct lineal descent from the sun goddess precluded any changes in the imperial line. The idea of direct lineal descent from the sun goddess first appeared in eighth-century texts, and Kitabatake Chikafusa's invoking it here shows how politics could summon both history and legend to its aid.

Early Ashikaga shogunal attempts to reassert central power met with some temporary success, but the decline in central power proved irreversible. Several of the early fifteenth-century shoguns, such as Yoshimitsu (1353–1408) and Yoshinori (1428–41), were strong leaders. Some of the institutional arrangements made by these leaders to consolidate central control backfired. For example, Yoshimitsu attempted to restrict the power of the *shugo*, military leaders whose lands often included more than one province. He required each shugo to maintain a residence in Kyoto in addition to his provincial residence. This eroded their local power base, as well as making it easier for the shogun to supervise them. The shugo were forbidden to return to their provincial base without official permission, and returning without prior permission constituted treason.

However, these policies did not, in the end, strengthen the central government. The absence of the shugo from the land precipitated the rise of a new group of locally powerful warrior families, called *kokujin*.

During the early years of the fifteenth century the shugo lost control of the provinces to the kokujin and political power became even more decentralized.

During the course of the Ashikaga period, there was a change in Japanese inheritance practices. In earlier Japanese history, property was shared among sons and daughters. Women could hold property, and indeed, during the Heian period, houses were in general held by women. But during the Ashikaga, a system known as primogeniture—where one son, usually the eldest, inherits all property—became the norm. As a consequence, women lost rights to hold property. In general in the warrior society of Kamakura and Ashikaga Japan, women played a much more restricted role than they had in earlier Japanese history.

The effective end of Ashikaga control was marked by the Onin War (1467–77), though Ashikaga power continued in name only for another century. The war was caused by a succession dispute in the Ashikaga ruling house, a struggle that was entwined with a power struggle among shugo. By the end of the war, the splendid city of Kyoto lay in ruins, the power of the shugo was exhausted, and the Ashikaga was a government in name only.

But, ironically enough, the political chaos was not socially debilitating. Agricultural productivity continued the rise begun in the Kamakura period. Early-ripening Champa rice from Southeast Asia facilitated double cropping. Furthermore, other new crops such as soybeans and tea were introduced during the Ashikaga. The use of the water wheel and increased use of draft animals also stimulated agricultural productivity. Technical progress in mining, paper production, and sake brewing also stimulated economic growth.

Local villages became even more autonomous during the Ashikaga than they had been during the Kamakura. These villages were governed by assemblies of male residents. According to a fifteenth-century set of rules, male peasants who did not attend village assemblies would be fined. But village autonomy does not translate into peasant contentment. During the course of the fifteenth century, peasants rebelled with increasing frequency. Often peasants demanded that their debts be canceled, and on several occasions they met with success. Because the pawnbrokers to whom the peasants were in debt were often city dwellers, these uprisings on occasion took on the cast of a conflict between city and countryside.

Urban areas, like their rural counterparts, had a striking degree of autonomy during the Ashikaga period. During this period the tendency toward the develop-

A Japanese painting celebrates communal agriculture. To the tune of special "music of the fields," men in rush skirts carry rice plants to kimono-clad women, who set them out in the rice paddies.

ment of town culture we saw during the Kamakura increased. Not only did cities grow, but residents were increasingly identifying themselves as townsfolk of the city in which they lived. Confucian disdain for merchants, which often surfaced in both China and Japan, seemed absent during this period: Merchants were referred to as "men of virtue." By the beginning of the Ashikaga period, warriors and merchants were playing a significant role in the creation of an urban culture, which featured drama and other forms of popular entertainment. (See Special Feature, "The Flowering of Noh Drama," pp. 342–343.)

Ashikaga towns were subdivided into units called *machi*, which began to take on responsibility for important functions such as protection against fire and the maintenance of law and order. As the central power of the shogunal government declined, these local organizations became more and more important.

Another social organization that was gaining in importance was the guild. Guilds were formed by merchants and artisans to protect their rights over the production of particular goods or services. They often sought the protection of great families or great monasteries. For example, the pawnbrokers of Kyoto were protected by the famous Tendai monastery on Mt. Hiei, located just outside the city. The protection they sought was not just spiritual; on more than one occasion armed monks from Mt. Hiei fought on behalf of their clients.

From the middle of the fifteenth century, tension between urban and rural areas became more clearly expressed. Armed peasants attacked the city of Kyoto several times. Their specific targets varied: They targeted wealth, specific proprietors, or moneylenders and pawnbrokers. But when they attacked, the whole machi was subject to risk, and the machi fought back as a unit. Thus the crucial fault line in these uprisings seems not to lie on occupational or class lines, but rather between rural and urban society.

Under the Ashikaga, two new commercial groups rose to prominence—moneylenders and sake brewers. In fact, the groups overlapped to a considerable degree because sake brewing required a significant amount of capital. During the Ashikaga, the use of money had become more widespread, and bills of exchange were introduced. The moneylenders' power stemmed from the fact that everyone, including the shogun, owed them money. The shogunal government periodically issued edicts that wiped out all debts, but this proved only a temporary solution.

International trade played a significant role in the Ashikaga economy. The threat of Mongol invasions in the late Kamakura had stimulated Japanese shipbuilding. Prior to the Mongol invasions, most trade between Japan and the mainland had been carried by Chinese or Korean ships. But this began to change in the fourteenth century with the rise of Japanese shipbuilding, and with the fifteenth-century decline of China as a sea power.

During the early Ashikaga period, international trade in East Asia was not regularized, and it was often hard to tell the difference between piracy and trade. About 1350, Korea began to complain about Japanese pirates raiding the Korean coast, and in 1373 two monks traveling as envoys of the emperor of China asked that the raids against the Chinese coast be stopped. Between 1376 and 1384, Japanese pirates staged an average of forty raids a year. These raids could be substantial, the largest of them consisting of 400 ships with 3,000 men. The main objectives of the raids seem to have been the acquisition of grain and slaves. The impact of the raids

was serious. The disorder they produced contributed to the fall of the Korean Koryo dynasty in 1392. So-called Japanese pirates remained a problem for the rest of early modern East Asian history, though as time went on, more and more of the pirates were actually Chinese or Korean.

A regulated and restricted trade between China and Japan, known as the tally trade, was set up in 1404. When a merchant was granted permission to carry on the trade, he would receive a tally signifying his authority, hence the name of the trade. This trade was initially carried out under the rubric of tribute trade. In 1401, the shogun Yoshimitsu, using the title "king of Japan" sent tribute to the Chinese, and promised that the pirate raids would stop. The tally trade was profitable, but limited in scope. Only seventy or eighty of these trips were made before the system broke down in 1551. The Japanese exported copper, sulfur, folding fans, painted screens, and steel swords. Much to the consternation of the Ming government, tens of thousands of high-quality swords found their way to China from Japan. The Chinese exported silk, porcelain, paintings, medicine, books, and coins. During the fifteenth century, objects from China enjoyed resurgent prestige in Japan, especially among Buddhist monks.

In the early Ashikaga, trade with China was a monopoly of the shoguns. Later, the trade was carried out as joint ventures between the shogun, temples, and important daimyo. By the early sixteenth century, important warrior families, notably the Ouchi and the Hosokawa, monopolized the China trade, and the shogun was not even a participant. This is indicative of his declining general significance. Japanese merchants also conducted important trade with Korea, which was regulated by the So family from Tsushima. Textiles, especially cotton, were the chief commodity involved.

The period following the Onin War is known as the Warring States period, and it lasted until the Tokugawa reunification in 1600. In the late fifteenth century, a new group of locally powerful military leaders, called warring states daimyo, emerged. With few exceptions, they are new families, often descended from the kokujin. Of 142 major daimyo families existing in 1563, only 32 were descended from shugo families. Indeed, the old shugo had been destroyed as a class, and no longer played a role in the political arena. The great social upheavals of this era were often described by contemporaries with the phase "the lowly are overturning the mighty."

The warring states daimyo were even more independent of central authority than the shugo had been. In

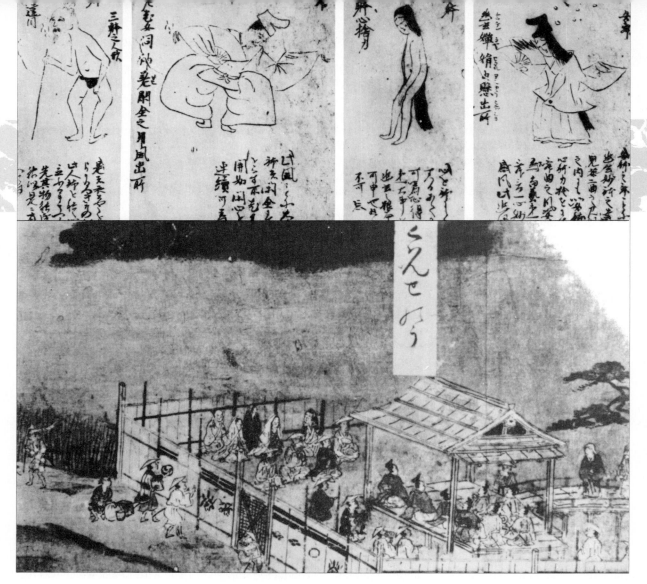

The figure at the top presents details of illustrations for Nikyoku Santai no Ezu *("Dance and Music"), a work of criticism by Zeami, the Japanese drama theorist. The human figures show how the body should be held in the performance of Noh drama. The bottom figure shows "Scenes Within and Without the Capital Screen," a painting from the early seventeenth century, which depicts the forms of popular entertainment available in Tokyo, including this Noh drama.*

The Flowering of Noh Drama

The story goes that in 1374 the shogun, the great Yoshimitsu, was out on the town and happened upon a performance of a play called "The Old Man." The performers were Kan'ami (1333–84) and his captivating twelve-year-old son Zeami (1363–1443). Yoshimitsu was taken by the performance, and perhaps smitten by the boy as well. He took the father and son back to the palace and became their patrons. The result of this happy meeting of artist and patron was the flowering of Noh drama.

Noh drama had its roots in peasant performances. One of its precursors was *dengaku*, field music, which had originated as songs that Japanese farmers sang when they did their fieldwork. These songs attracted the attention of the elite, already in the Heian period, dengaku was popular with members of the court. The *Taiheike*, a fourteenth-century text, tells us of the dance:

Around that time in the capital, men made much of the dance called field music, and high or low there was none that did not seek after it eagerly. Hearing of this a lay monk called down the New Troupe and the Original Troupe to Kamakura, where he amused himself with them day and night and morning and evening, with no other thought in his mind. When those dancers danced at a feast, the monk and all his kinsmen and captains took off their robes and trousers and tossed them out, none willing to be outdone.

Now drinking on a certain night, the monk grew merry with wine, so that he rose up and danced. (His dancing was only the vain dancing of a drunken old monk of more than forty years.) Suddenly from nowhere there came more than ten field music dancers of the New and Original Troupes, who lined up in the room dancing and singing with surpassing skill.

There was a lady-in-waiting who looked through a crack in the sliding door, irresistibly diverted by the sound of those voices. And she saw that of those who had seemed to be dancers, not one was a human being, but all were specters of divers kinds and shapes who had changed themselves into humans.

Sorely affrighted, the lady sent a man running to a castle lay monk, who made haste to go toward the room, sword in hand. But when his footsteps advanced violently through the middle gate, the phantoms vanished. And all the while the other monk slept drunkenly, knowing nothing of it.

The plays of Noh drama are divided into five categories by subject matter: plays about gods, warriors, women, demons, and miscellaneous subject matter. The stage was simple, open on three sides, with no curtain and no background scenery. The actors were often masked, and mime was one of the most important dramatic techniques employed.

After Noh became a palace art, it became less realistic and more abstracted and refined. These abstractions appealed to the taste of sophisticated connoisseurs. History is full of examples of elite culture being used on the popular level. But Noh drama is a clear example of the reverse: peasant work songs transformed into austere art forms for the court and the aristocracy.

1482, the shogun Yoshimasa (1435–90) lamented that "The daimyo do as they please and do not follow orders. This means there can be no government." Indeed, after the Onin War the shogun was a puppet of the most powerful daimyo. These powerful daimyo governed their lands more or less as independent principalities, and sixteenth-century European visitors often called them kings.

During the Warring States period, daimyo built splendid castles. Towns to serve the needs of these lords arose in the shadow of the castles. To be sure, the primary purpose of these castles was as defensive strongholds, but they were also strong expressions of cultural identity. Most of the Warring States castles have been destroyed, but the castles of Himeji in Hyogo Prefecture and Matsumoto in Nagano Prefecture are still extant. Castle towns were extremely important in promoting urban growth in Japan.

The warfare of the Warring States period does not seem to have had a negative impact on economic development. Warfare was bloody and protracted, and doubtless had locally negative economic consequences. But it stimulated demand, especially in the burgeoning castle towns.

Around 1550, the old order had completely disintegrated, and ambitious men imagined the reunification of Japan into a more strongly centralized state. The reunification of Japan was accomplished by three men: Oda Nobunaga (1534–82), Toyotomi Hideyoshi (1536–98) and Tokugawa Ieyasu (1542–1616). In 1573 Oda Nobunaga sent the last Ashikaga shogun into permanent exile. Through a combination of diplomacy and military skill, cooperation and treachery, these three men forged a unified country. The new state was called the Tokugawa, and will be discussed in chapter 23.

Ashikaga Culture: Temple and Ceremony

Despite the political chaos of this era, culture flourished. Merchants and warriors were crucial players in Ashikaga culture, but so were monks and nuns. In this era, Buddhism became an important part of lay life, and the monastic life was an attractive option for both men and women. Especially as civil society became war-torn during the Warring States period, the monastery became a repository of learning, Confucian as well as Buddhist. As an anonymous seventeenth-century author said, describing the situation during the civil wars in the fifteenth and sixteenth centuries,

> If you wanted a cure for an illness, a horoscope read, a picture painted or a document written, it was to a temple that you went. All the arts became the monopoly of priests.

In this respect they fulfilled a role not unlike that played by monasteries in Europe during the Middle Ages.

The Kamakura cults that were discussed earlier all persisted, and Zen became even more important than it had been. As warrior values permeated society, Zen monasteries were used by the Ashikaga as the literate branch of government. In Kyoto a temple named Shokokuji, which had been established by the shogun Yoshimitsu, served as a center of foreign relations. Monks there drafted communications in Chinese for the Ming court.

Ashikaga merchants and monks showed a keen interest in Chinese objects. They eagerly studied Chinese religion, arts, and technology. For example, Song dynasty monochrome paintings became fashionable, and exerted an influence on Japanese art. These paintings, rendered in ink on silk with a minimum of color, were described as "transcending color."

The tea ceremony was an Ashikaga cultural form that occupied a ground somewhere between religious ritual and performance art. Often sponsored by, and even performed by, merchants, it flourished in the fifteenth and sixteenth centuries. The tea ceremony consisted of the preparation and serving of tea in a carefully arranged setting. The most highly regarded tea ceremonies were carried out in austere settings; the ascetic surroundings of the ceremony were symbolic of Buddhist renunciation. The aesthetics of the tea ceremony influenced secular architecture. The straw *tatami* mats covering the entire surface of the floor and the sliding paper *shoji* screens that we think of as characteristic of traditional Japanese architecture became popular as a result of their association with the tea ceremony.

The most famous tea master in all of Japan was not a warrior or a monk but a merchant from Sakai named Sen no Rikyu (1522–91). He founded a school of tea ceremony which stressed the utmost simplicity. Despite this, he became the tea master to both Oda Nobunaga and Hideyoshi, two of the men who played a prominent role in the unification of Japan. The fact that these sturdy warriors had a tea master indicates both the pervasiveness of the aesthetic sensibility reflected in the tea ceremony, and the ways in which the ceremony could be used for cultural legitimation. For reasons that remain obscure, Sen no Rikyu incurred Hideyoshi's displeasure and in 1591 was forced to commit suicide by disemboweling himself.

"The Four Seasons" by the Japanese painter Sesshu (1420–1506). He adapted Chinese models to Japanese artistic ideas.

The aesthetics of the tea ceremony propounded by Sen no Rikyu profoundly influenced the potter Chojiro (1576–92), the originator of a style of pottery known as Raku ware. While earlier ceramics were delicate and refined, Raku brings out the quality of the clay, and looks very modern to our eyes.

Literary forms remained important in this period, and one of the most important was a verse forms known as *renga,* or linked verse. These poems were often composed at social occasions. "Three Poets as Minase," composed in 1488 by Sogi and his disciples Shohaku and Socho, is one of the most famous. It opens with the following verses.

Sogi: Snow clinging to slope,
On mist-enshrouded mountains
At eveningtime
Shohaku: In the distance water flows
Through plum-scented villages.
Socho: Willows cluster
In the river breeze
As spring appears.
Sogi: The sound of a boat being poled
In the clearness of dawn.

Shohaku: Still the moon lingers
As fog o'er spreads
The night.
Socho: A frost covered meadow;
Autumn has drawn to a close.
Sogi: Against the wishes
Of droning insects
The grasses wither.

The various voices of this poem link the landscape and the passage of time. The poem is not dominated by a single authorial voice, rather, there are three voices drawing on a common tradition and writing by common rules. Renga melds multiple voices into a single poem without denying their multivocality.

Linked verse had a great comic capacity as well. Comic renga might be posed as answers to a riddle, as in the following sixteenth-century example:

It is dangerous
But also makes us joyful.
The log bridge
We cross in the evening
To welcome the groom.

The first two lines are anonymous, the final three are by Arakida Moritake (1473–1549). The danger represented by the log bridge might well be literally that. But the poem also invokes the dangerous moment at which a new member joins the family. Note that the wedding here is effected when the groom joins the bride's house, probably in a uxorilocal marriage.

China and Japan both underwent dramatic changes during the period covered by this chapter. The two societies were, if anything, even more different one from another by the end of the period. The most pronounced difference is of course in the way the elite was constituted; in China it was a literati elite recruited through civil service examinations, while in Japan it was a warrior elite recruited through battle.

Should we need any proof that history is not the story of progress, the fate of women in China and Japan during this period should suffice. Women, who in China had once played polo, now had their feet bound. Women, who in Japan had been the primary producers of what still ranks as one of the world's great literatures, lost the right to inherit property.

Both China and Japan saw the growth of splendid cities during this period. In Japan during the Ashikaga, a distinctive urban culture began to evolve. Townsfolk, people who were neither warriors nor aristocrats, began to identify themselves with their cities and began producing a culture that was distinctively urban. This was

much more pronounced in Japan than it was in China. A Chinese merchant could always aspire for his son to take the civil service exam. The possibility of joining the literati was a potent lure, and was significant in inhibiting the formation of an independent merchant culture.

SUGGESTIONS FOR FURTHER READING

THE GLORIES OF CHINA UNDER THE SONG

*Jacques Gernet, *Daily Life in China on the Eve of the Mongol Invasion* (New York: MacMillan, 1962). A lively and readable account of daily life in the Song capita.

Valerie Hansen, *Changing Gods in Medieval China. 1127–1276* (Princeton, NJ: Princeton University Press, 1990). A splendid study of the transmission and transformation of popular religion in Song dynasty China.

Patricia Ebrey, *Chu Hsi's Family Rituals: A Twelfth Century Manual for the Performance of Cappings, Weddings, Funerals and Ancestral Rites* (Princeton, NJ: Princeton University Press, 1991). A translation of a crucial ritual text.

Robert Hymes, *Statesmen and Gentlemen: The Elite of Fu-chou, Chiang-hsi, in Northern and Southern Sung* (Cambridge, MA: Cambridge University Press, 1986). An analysis in changes in elite status and society from the Northern to the Southern Song.

John Chaffee, *The Thorny Gates of Learning in Sung China: A Social History of Examinations* (Cambridge, MA: Cambridge University Press, 1985). An account of the examination system and its implications.

MONGOLS AND THE YUAN DYNASTY

Morris Rossabi, *Khubilai Khan: His Life and Times* (Berkeley and Los Angeles: University of California Press, 1988). A highly readable account of the man who ruled most of Eurasia in the thirteenth century.

Thomas Allsen, *Mongol Imperialism: The Politics of the Grand Qan Mongke in China, Russia and the Islamic Lands 1251–1259* (Berkeley and Los Angeles: University of California Press, 1987). The Mongol empire in world perspective.

Elizabeth Endicott-West, *Mongolian Rule in China: Local Administration in the Yuan Dynasty* (Cambridge, MA: Harvard University Press, 1989). A careful study of Yuan local administration.

*John Langlois, ed., *China under Mongol Rule* (Princeton, NJ: Princeton University Press, 1981). A collection of essays treating various aspects of Yuan history.

THE RESTORATION OF CHINESE POWERS UNDER THE MING

*Ray Huang, *1587, A Year of No Significance: The Ming Dynasty in Decline* (New Haven, CT: Yale University Press, 1981). A collection of biographies of key players in late Ming politics and society.

*John Dardess, *Confucianism and Autocracy: Professional Elites and the Founding of the Ming Dynasty* (Berkeley and Los Angeles:

University of California Press, 1983). An analysis of the role of the Confucian literati in the formation of the Ming state.

Craig Clunas, *Superfluous Things: Material Culture and Social Status in Early Modern China* (Urbana, IL: University of Illinois Press, 1991). A study of elite consumption with suggestive comparisons to early modern Europe.

Cynthia J. Brokaw, *The Ledgers of Merit and Demerit: Social Change and Moral Order in Late Imperial China* (Princeton, NJ: Princeton University Press, 1991). A study of popular morality books and the ways in which they are rooted in changing social contexts.

JAPAN: ARISTOCRATS INTO WARRIORS

Hitomi Tonomura, *Community and Commerce in Late Medieval Japan: The Corporate Villages of Tokuchin-ho* (Stanford, CA: Stanford University Press, 1992). A local study of the peasant economy in the sixteenth century.

Thomas Keirstead, *The Geography of Power in Medieval Japan* (Princeton, NJ: Princeton University Press, 1992). An examination of the shoen as a cultural system, with particular attention to how power is negotiated within that system.

Thomas Rimer and Masaku Yamazaki, *On the Art of the No Drama: The Major Treatises of Zeami* (Princeton, NJ: Princeton University Press, 1984). An informative and readable introduction followed by translations of nine treatises on the No drama.

Peter Arneson, *The Medieval Japanese Daimyo: The Ouchi Family's Rule in Suo and Nagato* (New Haven, CT: Yale University Press, 1979). A good, detailed discussion of the rise of the Ashikaga. It assumes an intelligent reader with some background knowledge of the subject.

Martin Collcutt, *Five Mountains: The Rinzai Zen Monastic Institution in Medieval Japan* (Cambridge, MA: Harvard University Press, 1981). An institutional study of Zen monasticism in Japan.

Kenneth A. Grossberg, *Japan's Renaissance: The Politics of the Muromachi Bakufu* (Cambridge, MA: Harvard University Press, 1981). A readable political history of the Muromachi era.

Janet Goff, *Noh Drama and the Tale of Genji: The Art of Allusion in Fifteen Classical Plays* (Princeton, NJ: Princeton University Press, 1991). A cogent analysis of Noh plays based on the novel *Tale of Genji*, coupled with a translation of selected texts.

Helen Craig McCullough, compiler and editor, *Classical Japanese Prose: An Anthology* (Stanford, CA: Stanford University Press, 1990). An easily readable accessible anthology of prose.

Jacob Raz, *Audience and Actors: A Study of their Interaction in the Japanese Theater* (Leiden, Netherlands: E.J. Brill, 1983). A survey beginning with the earliest theaters and continuing to modern times.

Mary Elizabeth Berry, *Hideyoshi* (Cambridge, MA: Harvard University Press, 1982). A look at political culture in the late sixteenth century through a biography of one of the unifiers.

Michael Cooper, *They Came to Japan: An Anthology of European Reports on Japan, 1543–1640* (Berkeley and Los Angeles: University of California Press, 1965). A collection of missionary and other travel accounts, arranged topically.

*Indicates paperback edition available.

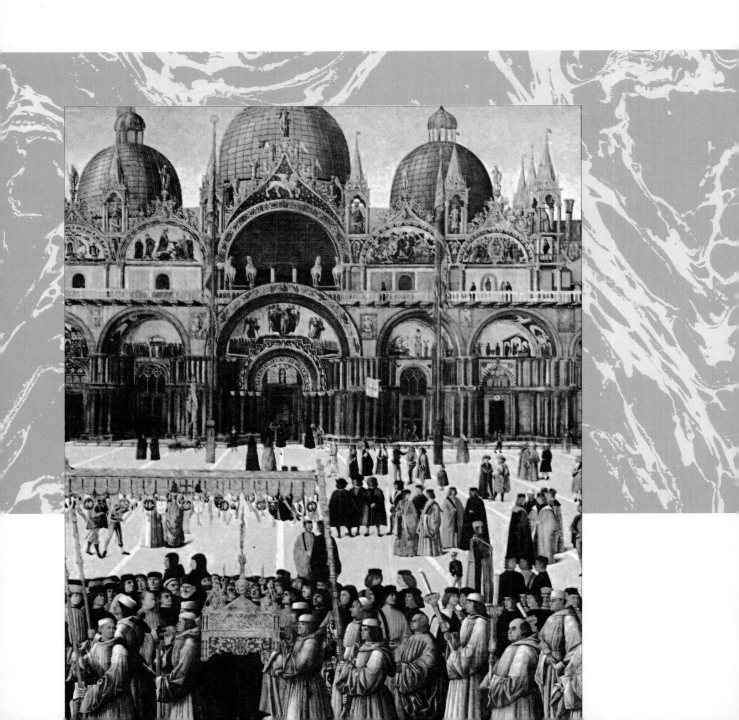

A CIVIC PROCESSION

It is 25 April 1444. On this day each year the city of Venice celebrates its patron, Saint Mark, with a procession around the square that bears his name. Processions are a common form of civic ritual through which a community defines itself. The special features that identify Venice for its citizens are all on display. Flags and emblems of the city are mounted on poles, and clothes bear the insignia of various orders and groups. The procession re-creates all forms of communal life. Here are the religious orders (the white-clad brothers of the Confraternity of Saint John are passing before us now), and the civic leaders can be seen just behind them. Musicians entertain both marchers and onlookers. An entire band files by on the right. The procession is orderly, but it is by no means contrived. It is not staged, as would be a modern ceremony, and this difference is evident in the relaxed attitude of the ordinary citizens who stand in groups in the middle of the square. There is no apparent drama to observe, and they walk and talk quite naturally. So, too, do the participants. In the lower left-hand corner, some friars are reading music; at the lower right, members of the confraternity carry their candles negligently.

Yet the painting, *The Procession of the Relic of the Holy Cross* (1496) by Gentile Bellini (ca. 1429–1507), was commissioned to commemorate a miracle rather than a civic procession. On the evening before Saint Mark's day, a visiting merchant and his son were touring the square when the boy accidentally fell and cracked his skull. The doctors who were called to treat him regarded the case as hopeless and advised the father to prepare for his son's death. The next morning, the Brothers of the Confraternity of Saint John carried the relic of a piece of the true cross beneath an embroidered canopy. The merchant approached the golden altarpiece that contained the relic, dropped to his knees, and prayed that Saint Mark would miraculously cure his son. He is the figure kneeling just to the right of center where the line of brothers breaks. The next day, the boy revived and his injury healed.

The Brothers of Saint John commissioned Bellini to commemorate this event. Bellini came from the most distinguished family of painters in Venice. His father Jacopo had studied in Florence and had brought both of his sons into his workshop when they were young boys. Until the age of thirty Gentile and his younger and more famous brother, Giovanni, worked on their father's commissions, learning the difficult craft of painting. Art was very much a family business in fifteenth-century Italy. The large workshops with their master and hordes of apprentices turned out vast canvases with almost assembly-line precision. The master created the composition and sketched it out; his skilled assistants, like the Bellini brothers, worked on the more complex parts; and young apprentices painted backgrounds and indistinct faces. The master was first and foremost a businessman, gaining commissions to sustain his family and his workers. The Bellinis were well connected to the Confraternity of Saint John, and it was only natural that Gentile would receive this lucrative contract.

Though *The Procession of the Relic of the Holy Cross* was designed to re-create a central moment in the history of the confraternity, it is not the confraternity that dominates the picture. Miracles were part of civic life, and each town took pride in the special manifestations of heavenly care that had taken place within it.

And it is very much Venice that is the center-piece of Bellini's canvas. Dominating the painting is the Basilica of San Marco, with its four great horses over the center portico and the winged lion, the city's symbol, on the canopy above the horses. The procession emanates from the duke's palace to the right of the church, and the great flags of the city are seen everywhere. By the end of the fifteenth century, Venice was one of the greatest powers on earth, the center for international trade and finance. Home to the largest concentration of wealthy families anywhere in Europe, it could well afford the pomp and splendor of its processions. The achievements of God and the achievements of humans blend together in this painting as they blended together in that era of remarkable accomplishments that historians call the Renaissance.

Renaissance Society

Perhaps the most surprising result of the Black Death was the way in which European society revived itself in the succeeding centuries. Even at the height of the plague a spirit of revitalization was evident in the works of artists and writers. Petrarch (1304–74), the great humanist poet and scholar, was among the first to differentiate the new age in which he was living from two earlier ones: the classical world of Greece and Rome, which he admired, and the subsequent Dark Ages, which he detested. This spirit of self-awareness is one of the defining characteristics of the Renaissance. "It is but in our own day that men dare boast that they see the dawn of better things," wrote Matteo Palmieri (1406–75). The Renaissance was a new age by self-assertion. In that self-assertion wave after wave of artistic celebration of the human spirit found its wellspring and created a legacy that is still vibrant five hundred years later.

What was the Renaissance? A French word for an Italian phenomenon, *Renaissance* literally means "rebirth." The word captures both the emphasis on humanity that characterized Renaissance thinking and the renewed fascination with the classical world. But the Renaissance was an age rather than an event. There is no moment at which the Middle Ages ended. Late medieval society was artistically creative, socially well developed, and economically diverse. Yet eventually the pace of change accelerated, and it is best to think of the Renaissance as an era of rapid transitions. Encompassing the two centuries between 1350 and 1550, it passed through three distinct phases. The first, from 1350 to 1400, was characterized by a declining population, the uncovering of classical texts, and experimentation in a variety of art forms. The second phase, from 1400 to 1500, was distinguished by the creation of a set of cultural values and by artistic and literary achievements that defined Renaissance style. The large Italian city-states developed stable and coherent forms of government and the warfare between them gradually ended. In the final period, from 1500 to 1550, invasions from France and Spain transformed Italian political life, and the ideas and techniques of Italian writers and artists radiated to all points of the Continent. Though Renaissance ideas and achievements did spread throughout western Europe, they are best studied where they first developed, on the Italian peninsula.

Cities and Countryside

The Italian peninsula differed sharply from other areas of Europe in the extent to which it was urban. By the late Middle Ages nearly one in four Italians lived in a town, in contrast to one in ten elsewhere. There were more Italian cities and more people in them. By 1500 seven of the ten largest cities in Europe were in Italy.

The streets of Florence were narrow and dark, with an incredible jumble of buildings in all sizes, shapes, and states of repair. All public inns were on a single street, and their management was strictly regulated.

Naples, Venice, and Milan, each with a population of more than one hundred thousand, led the rest. But it was the numerous smaller towns, with populations nearer to one thousand, that gave the Italian peninsula its urban character. Cities were still the wonder of the world, dominating their regions economically, politically, and culturally. The diversified economic activities in which the inhabitants engaged created vast concentrations of wealth. Cities also served as convenient centers of judicial and ecclesiastical power, and Italy was the banking capital of the world.

Cities acted as central places around which a cluster of large and small villages was organized. Urban areas, especially the small towns, provided markets for the agricultural produce of the countryside and for the manufactured goods of the urban craftsmen. This allowed for the specialization in agricultural and industrial life that increased both productivity and wages. Cities also

caught the runoff of rural population, especially the shower of younger sons and daughters who could not be accommodated on the farms. Thus the areas surrounding a city were critical to its prosperity and survival. Florence, the dominant city in the region of Tuscany, exemplifies this relationship. Though it possessed two-thirds of its region's wealth, Florence contained only 14 percent of the regional population. The surrounding countryside was agriculturally rich, for marketing costs were low and demand for foodstuffs high. Smaller cities like Prato and Pistoia to the north and Pisa to the west channeled their local produce and trade to Florence.

Though cities may have dominated Renaissance Italy, by present standards they were small in both area and population. A person could walk across fifteenth-century Florence in less than half an hour. In 1427 its population was thirty-seven thousand, only half its preplague size. Most Italian cities contained large fields for agricultural production, and within the outer walls of Florence were gardens and grain fields. Inside the inner city walls the people crowded together into tightly packed quarters. The intensity of the stench from raw sewage, rotting foodstuffs, and slaughtered animals was equaled only by the din made by hoofs and wooden cartwheels on paving stones.

Urban populations were organized far differently from rural ones. On the farms the central distinctions involved ownership of land. Some farmers owned their estates outright and left them intact to their heirs. Others were involved in a sharecropping system by which absentee owners of land supplied working capital in return for half of the farm's produce. A great gulf in wealth separated owners from sharecroppers. But within the groups the gaps were not as great. There were gradations, but these were ordinarily temporary conditions that bad harvests, generous dowries, or divided inheritances balanced out over time.

In the city, however, distinctions were based first on occupation, which largely corresponded to social position and wealth. Cities began as markets and it was the privilege to participate in the market that defined citizens. City governments provided protection for consumers and producers by creating monopolies through which standards for craftsmanship were maintained and profits for craftsmen were guaranteed. These monopolies were called guilds or companies. Each large city had its own hierarchy of guilds. At the top were the important manufacturing groups—clothiers, metalworkers, and the like. Just below them were bankers, merchants, and the administrators of civic and Church holdings. At the bottom were grocers, masons, and other skilled workers. Roughly speaking, all of those within the guild structure, from bottom to top, lived comfortably. Yet the majority of urban inhabitants were not members of guilds. Many managed to eke out a living as wage laborers; many more were simply destitute. As a group these poor constituted as much as half of the entire population. Most were dependent upon civic and private charity for their very survival.

The disparities between rich and poor were overwhelming. The concentration of wealth in the hands of an ever narrowing group of families and favored guilds characterized every large city. One reason for this was the extreme instability of economic life. Prices and wages fluctuated wildly in response to local circumstance. After an epidemic of plague, wages climbed and the prices of consumer goods tumbled. A bad harvest sent food prices skyrocketing. Only those able to even

out these extreme swings by stockpiling goods in times of plenty and consuming them in times of want were safe. Capital, however initially accumulated, was the key to continued wealth. Monopolies ensured the profitability of trade and manufacturing, but only those with sufficient capital could engage in either. In Florence, for example, 10 percent of the families controlled 90 percent of the wealth, with an even more extreme concentration at the top.

Production and Consumption

This concentration of wealth and the way in which it was used defined Renaissance economy. Economic life is bound up in the relationship between resources and desires, or, as economists would have it, supply and demand. The late medieval economy, despite the development of international banking and long-distance trade, was still an economy of primary producers: between 70 and 90 percent of Europe's population was involved in subsistence agriculture, only producing enough each year for survival. Even in Italy, which contained the greatest concentration of urban areas in the world, agriculture predominated. The manufacture of clothing was the only other significant economic activity, and it was dwarfed in comparison to farming. Moreover, most of what was produced was for local consumption rather than for the marketplace. The relationship between supply and demand was precisely measured by the full or empty stomach. Even in good times more than 80 percent of the population lived at subsistence level with food, clothing, and shelter their only expenses. Thus when we discuss the market economy of the Renaissance, we are discussing the circumstances of the few rather than the many.

The defining characteristic of the early Renaissance economy was change in population. Recurring waves of plague kept population levels low for more than a century. In the century between 1350 and 1450 one in every six years was characterized by an unusually high mortality rate. At the end of this period Florence's population was only a quarter of what it had been at the beginning. This dramatic reduction in population depressed economic growth. The general economy did not revive until the sustained population increase toward the end of the fifteenth century. Until then, in both agriculture and manufacturing supply outstripped demand. On the farms overabundance resulted from two related developments, the concentration of surviving farmers on the

Cloth making was a major contributor to European economic growth during the Middle Ages. In this 1470 portrait of Cloth Merchants' Street, Bologna, a tailor (center) measures a prospective client.

luxury became more alluring than ever. It was not merely the perceived shortage in profitable investments that brought on the increase in conspicuous consumption during the fifteenth century. In the psychological atmosphere created by unpredictable, swift, and deadly epidemics, people became more concerned with the present than the future. Secondly, in order to pay for wars, both offensive and defensive, rates of taxation increased. Since both houses and personal property were normally exempt from the calculations of wealth upon which taxation was based, the richest members of the community could escape this additional burden by purchasing luxury goods.

For whatever reasons, the production and consumption of luxuries soared. By the middle of the fourteenth century Florence was known for its silks and jewelry as much as for its cloth. Venice became a European center for the glass industry, especially for the finely ground glass that was used in eyeglasses. Production of specialty crops like sugar, saffron, fruits, and high-quality wine expanded. International trade increasingly centered on acquiring Eastern specialties, resulting in the serious outflow of gold and silver that enriched first the Byzantine and then the Ottoman emperors. Both public and private building projects increased, spurring the demand for architects, sculptors, and painters. The rise in the consumption of luxuries was everywhere apparent, taken by some as a sign of the vitality of the age, by others as an indication of its decay.

The Experience of Life

Luxury helped improve a life that for rich and poor alike was short and uncertain. Nature was still people's most potent enemy. Renaissance children who survived infancy found their lives governed by parentage and by sex. In parentage the great divide was between those who lived with surplus and those who lived at subsistence. The first category encompassed the wealthiest bankers and merchants down to those who owned their own farms or engaged in small urban crafts. The vast majority of urban and rural dwellers comprised the second category. About the children of the poor we know very little other than that their survival was unlikely. If they did not die at birth or shortly afterward, they might be abandoned—especially if female—to the growing number of orphanages in the cities, waste away from lack of nutrition, or fall prey to ordinary childhood diseases. Eldest sons were favored, younger daughters were disadvantaged. But in poor families this favoritism meant

best land and the enlargement of their holdings. In the shops finished products outnumbered the consumers who survived the epidemics. Overproduction meant lower prices for basic commodities, and the decline in population meant higher wages for labor. At the lowest levels of society survivors found it easier to earn their living and even to create a surplus than had their parents. For a time the lot of the masses improved.

But for investors, such economic conditions meant that neither agriculture nor cloth making were particularly lucrative. Expensive investments in land or equipment for sharecropping were paid off in inexpensive grain; high wages for the few surviving skilled workers brought a return in cheap cloth. In such circumstances, consumption was more attractive than investment and

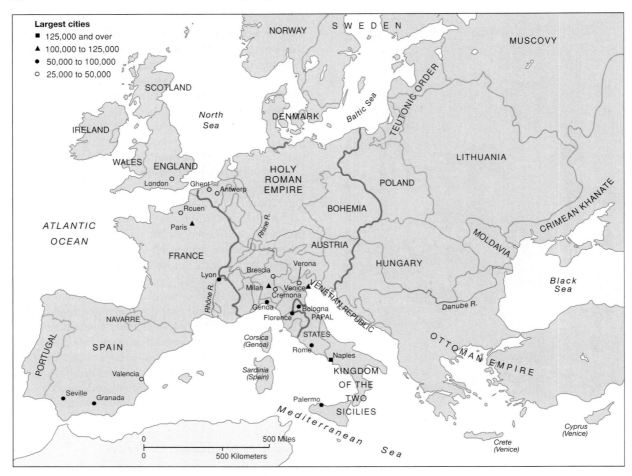

Europe, ca. 1500

little more than early apprenticeship to day labor in the city or farm labor in the countryside. Girls were frequently sent out as domestic servants far from the family home.

Children of the wealthy had better chances for survival than did children of the poor. For the better off, childhood might begin with "milk parents," life in the home of the family of a wet nurse who breast-fed the baby through infancy. Only the very wealthy could afford a live-in wet nurse, which increased the child's chances of survival. Again, daughters were more likely to be sent far from home and least likely to have their nursing supervised. The use of wet nurses not only emancipated parents from the daily care of infants, it also allowed them to resume sexual relations. Nursing

women refrained from sex in the belief that it affected their milk.

During the period between weaning and apprenticeship Renaissance children lived with their families. There was no typical Renaissance family. Nuclear families—that is, parents and their children under one roof—were probably more common than extended families, which might include grandparents and other relatives. But the composition of the family changed over the course of the life cycle and included times in which married children or grandparents were present and others when a single parent and small children were the only members. Moreover, even nuclear families commonly contained stepparents and stepchildren as well as domestic servants or apprentices.

Thus a child returning to the parental household was as likely to form emotional bonds with older siblings as with parents.

The family was an economic unit as well as a grouping of relatives. Decisions to abandon children, to send them away from the household when very young, or to take in domestic servants were based on economic calculations. In the competition for scarce resources, the way in which children were managed might determine the survival of the family unit. Sons could expect to be apprenticed to a trade probably between the ages of ten and thirteen. Most, of course, learned the crafts of their fathers, but not necessarily in their father's shop. Sons inherited the family business and its most important possessions, tools of the trade or beasts of labor for the farm. Inheritance customs varied. In some places only the eldest son received the equipment of the family occupation; in others, like Tuscany, all the sons shared it. Still, in the first fifteen years of life, these most

Ginevra de'Benci *by Leonardo da Vinci, painted around 1481. With its serenity and mystery, this portrait brings to mind the artist's more famous* Mona Lisa.

Old Man With a Child *by the Florentine painter Domenico del Ghirlandaio (1449–94).*

favored children spent between one-third and one-half of their time outside the household in which they had been born.

Expectations for daughters centered on their chances of marriage. For a girl, dowry was everything. If a girl's father could provide a handsome one, her future was secure; if not, the alternatives were a convent, which would take a small bequest, or a match lower down the social scale, where the quality of life deteriorated rapidly. Daughters of poor families entered domestic service in order to have a dowry provided by their masters. The dowry was taken to the household of their husband. There the couple resided until they established their own separate family. If the husband died, it was to his parental household that the widow returned.

Women married in late adolescence, usually around the age of twenty. Among the wealthy, marriages were perceived as familial alliances and business transactions rather than love matches. The dowry was an investment on which fathers expected a return, and while the bride might have some choice, it was severely limited. Compatibility was not a priority in matchmaking. Husbands

ALBERTI, *ON THE FAMILY*

■ *Leon Battista Alberti wrote a number of important tracts that set out the general principles of a subject, including* On Architecture, *which was considered the basic text for three hundred years. His writings on the family bring insight into the nature of a male-dominated, patriarchal institution.*

They say that in choosing a wife one looks for beauty, parentage, and riches . . . Among the most essential criteria of beauty in a woman is an honorable manner. Even a wild, prodigal, greasy, drunken woman may be beautiful of feature, but no one would call her a beautiful wife. A woman worthy of praise must show first of all in her conduct, modesty, and purity. Marius, the illustrious Roman, said in that first speech of his to the Roman people: "Of women we require purity, of men labor." And I certainly agree. There is nothing more disgusting than a coarse and dirty woman. Who is stupid enough not to see clearly that a woman who does not care for neatness and cleanliness in her appearance, not only in her dress and body but in all her behavior and language, is by no means well mannered? How can it be anything but obvious that a bad mannered woman is also rarely virtuous? We shall consider elsewhere the harm that comes to a family from women who lack virtue, but I myself do not know which is the worse fate for a family, total celibacy or a single dishonored woman. In a bride, therefore, a man must first seek beauty of mind, that is, good conduct and virtue.

In her body he must seek not only loveliness, grace, and charm but must also choose a woman who is well made for bearing children, with the kind of constitution that promises to make them strong and big. There's an old proverb, "When you pick your wife, you choose your children." All her virtues will in fact shine brighter still in beautiful children. It is a well-known saying among poets: "Beautiful character dwells in a beautiful body." The natural philosophers require that a woman be neither thin nor very fat. Those laden with fat are subject to coldness and constipation and slow to conceive. They say that a woman should have a joyful nature, fresh and lively in her blood and her whole being. They have no objections to a dark girl. They do reject girls with a frowning black visage, however. They have no liking for either the undersized or the overlarge and lean. They find that a woman is most suited to bear children if she is fairly big and has limbs of ample length. They always have a preference for youth, based on a number of arguments which I need not expound here, but particularly on the point that a young girl has a more adaptable mind. Young girls are pure by virtue of their age and have not developed any spitefulness. They are by nature modest and free of vice. They quickly learn to accept affectionately and unresistingly the habits and wishes of their husbands.

were, on average, ten years older than their wives and likely to leave them widows. In the early fifteenth century about one-fourth of all adult women in Florence were widows.

Married women lived in a state of nearly constant pregnancy. Alessandra Strozzi, whose father was one of the wealthiest citizens of Florence, married at the age of sixteen, gave birth to eight children in ten years, and was widowed at the age of twenty-five. Not all pregnan-

cies produced children. The rates of miscarriages and stillbirths were very high, and abortions and infanticide were not unknown. Only among the families who hovered between surplus and subsistence is there any evidence of attempts to control pregnancies. These efforts, which relied upon techniques like the rhythm method and withdrawal, were not particularly effective. The rhythm method was especially futile because of the misunderstanding of the role of women in conception. It was not yet known that the woman contained an egg that was fertilized during conception. Without this knowledge it was impossible to understand the cycle of ovulation. Practically speaking, family size was limited on the one end by late marriages and on the other by early deaths.

Life experiences differed for males. Men married later, near the age of twenty-five on the farms, nearer thirty in the cities because of the cost of setting up in trade or on the land. Late marriage meant long supervision under the watchful eye of father or master, an extended period between adolescence and adulthood. The reputation that Renaissance cities gained for homosexuality and licentiousness must be viewed in light of the advanced age at which males married. The level of sexual frustration was high and its outlet in ritual violence and rape was also high.

The establishment of one's own household through marriage was a late rite of passage considering the expectations of early death. Many men, even with families, never succeeded in setting up separately from their fathers or elder brothers. Men came of age at thirty but were thought to be old by fifty. Thus for men marriage and parenthood took place in middle age rather than in youth. Valued all their lives more highly than their sisters, male heads of households were the source of all power in their domicile, in their shops, and in the state. They were responsible for overseeing every aspect of the upbringing of their children. But their wives were essential partners who governed domestic life. Women labored not only at the hearth, but in the fields and shops as well. Their economic contribution to the well-being of the family was critical, both in the dowry they brought at marriage and in the labor they contributed to the household. If their wives died, men with young children remarried quickly. While there were many bachelors in Renaissance society, there were few widowers.

In most cases death came suddenly. Epidemic diseases, of which plague was the most virulent, struck with fearful regularity. Even in the absence of a serious outbreak, there were always deaths in town and country attributable to the plague. Epidemics struck harder at the young—children and adolescents who were the majority of the population—and hardest in the summer months when other viruses and bacteria weakened the population. Medical treatment was more likely to hasten death than to prolong life. Lorenzo de Medici's physician prescribed powdered pearls for the Florentine ruler's gout. After that Lorenzo complained more of stomach pains than of gout. Such remedies revealed a belief in the harmony of nature and the healing power of rare substances. They were not silly or superstitious, but they were not effective either. Starvation was rare, less because of food shortage than because the seriously undernourished were more likely to succumb to disease than to famine. In urban areas, the government would intervene to provide grain from public storehouses at times of extreme shortage; in the countryside large landholders commonly exercised the same function.

The Quality of Life

Though life may have been difficult during the Renaissance, it was not unfulfilling. Despite constant toil and frequent hardship, people of the Renaissance had reason to believe that their lives were better than those of their ancestors and that their children's lives would be better still. On the most basic level, health improved and, for those who survived plague, life expectancy increased. Better health was related to better diet. Improvement came from two sources, the relative surplus of grain throughout the fifteenth century and the wider variety of foods consumed. At the upper levels of society, sweet wine and citrus fruits helped offset the lack of vegetables. This diversification of diet resulted from improvements in transportation and communication, which brought more goods and services to a growing number of towns in the chain that linked the regional centers to the rural countryside.

But the towns and cities contributed more than consumer goods to Renaissance society. They also introduced a new sense of social and political cohesiveness. The city was something to which people belonged. In urban areas they could join social groups of their own choosing and develop networks of support not possible in rural environments. Blood relations remained the primary social group. Kin were the most likely source of aid in times of need, and charity began at home. Kin groups extended well beyond the immediate family, with both cousins and in-laws laying claim to the privileges of blood. The urban family could also depend upon the connections of neighborhood. In some Italian cities wealth or occupation determined housing patterns. In others, like Florence, rich and poor lived side by side and identified themselves with their small administrative unit and with their local church. Thus they could participate in relationships with others both above and below them in the social scale. From their superiors they gained connections that helped their families; from their inferiors they gained devoted clients.

As in the Middle Ages, the Church remained the spatial, spiritual, and social center of people's lives. Though the Renaissance is singled out as a time when people became more worldly in their outlook, this worldliness took place within the context of an absorbing devotional life. There was not yet any separation between faith and reason. The Church provided explanations for both the mysterious and the mundane. In it were performed the rituals of baptism, marriage, and burial that measured the passage of life. The Church was also the source of the key symbols of urban society. The flags of militia troops, the emblems of guilds, the regalia of the city itself were all adorned by recognizably religious symbols. The Church preserved holy relics that were venerated for their power to protect the city or to endow it with particular skills and resources. Through its holy days, as much as through its rituals, the Church helped channel leisure activities into community celebrations.

A growing sense of civic pride and individual accomplishment were underlying characteristics of the Italian Renaissance, enhanced by the development of social cohesion and community solidarity that both Church and city-state fostered. It is commonly held that the Renaissance was both elitist and male dominated, that it was an experience separate from that of the society at large. There can be no question that it was the rich who commissioned works of art or that it was the highly skilled male craftsmen who executed them. But neither lived in a social vacuum. The Renaissance was not an event whose causes were the result of the efforts of the few or whose consequences were limited to the privileged. In fact, the Renaissance was not an event at all. Family values that permitted early apprenticeships in surrogate households and that emphasized the continuity of crafts from one generation to the next made possible the skilled artists of the Renaissance cities. The stress on the production of luxury goods placed higher value upon individual skills and therefore upon excellence in workmanship. Church and state sought to express social values through representational art. One of the chief purposes of wall murals was to instruct the unlettered in religion, to help them visualize the central episodes in Christian history. The grandiose architecture and statuary that adorned central places were designed to enhance civic pride, nurture loyalty, and communicate the protective power of public institutions.

For ordinary people the world of the Renaissance was not much different from the world of the Middle Ages.

Though urban areas grew, providing a wider variety of occupations and a varied material life, most people continued to scratch a meager living from the soil. The crucial difference from generation to generation was the degree of infectious diseases or the rate of rising or falling population. For the lucky ones there was surplus; for the unfortunate there was dearth. Within these confines men were privileged over women, having greater security and status and monopolizing power. But the tightly knit organization of family life protected the weak and the poor while the Church provided faith, hope, and charity.

Renaissance Art

In every age, artistic achievement represents a combination of individual talent and predominant social ideals. Artists may be at the leading edge of the society in which they live, but it is the spirit of that society that they capture in word or song or image. Artistic disciplines also have their own technical development. Individually, Renaissance artists were attempting to solve problems about perspective and three-dimensionality that had defeated their predecessors. But the particular techniques or experiments that interested them owed as much to the social context as they did to the artistic one. For example, the urban character of Italian government led to the need for civic architecture, public buildings on a grand scale. The celebration of individual achievement led to the explosive growth of portraiture. Not surprisingly, major technological breakthroughs were achieved in both areas.

This relationship between artist and social context was all the more important in the Renaissance, when artists were closely tied to the crafts and trades of urban society and to the demands of clients who commissioned their work. Although it was the elite who patronized art, it was skilled tradesmen who produced it. Artists normally followed the pattern of any craftsman, an apprenticeship begun as a teenager and a long period of training and work in a master's shop. This form of education gave the aspiring artist a practical rather than a theoretical bent and a keen appreciation for the business side of art. Studios were identified with particular styles and competed for commissions from clients, especially the Church. Wealthy individuals commissioned art as investments, as marks of personal distinction, and as displays of public piety. Isabella d'Este (1474-1539), one of the great patrons of Renaissance artists, wrote hundreds of letters specifying the details of the works she commissioned. She once sent an artist a thread of the exact dimensions of the pictures she had ordered. Demand for art was high. The vast public-works projects needed buildings, the new piazzas (public squares) and palazzos (private houses) needed statuary, and the long walls of churches needed murals.

The survival of so many Renaissance masterpieces allows us to reconstruct the stages by which the remarkable artistic achievements of this era took place. Although advances were made in a variety of fields during the Renaissance, the three outstanding areas were architecture, sculpture, and painting. While modern artists would consider each a separate discipline, Renaissance artists crossed their boundaries without hesitation. Not only could these artists work with a variety of materials, their intensive and varied apprenticeships taught them to apply the technical solutions of one field to the problems of another. Few Renaissance artists confined themselves to one area of artistic expression, and many created works of enduring beauty in more than one medium. Was the greatest achievement of Michelangelo his sculpture of David, his paintings on the ceiling of the Sistine Chapel, or his design for the dome of Saint Peter's? Only a century of interdisciplinary cross-fertilization could have prepared the artistic world for such a feat.

An Architect, a Sculptor, and a Painter

The century that culminated in Michelangelo's extraordinary achievements began with the work of three Florentine masters who deeply influenced one another's development—Brunelleschi (1377-1446), Donatello (1386-1466), and Masaccio (1401-28). In the Renaissance the dominant artistic discipline was architecture. Buildings were the most expensive investment patrons could make and the technical knowledge necessary for their successful construction was immense. The architect not only designed a building, he served as its general contractor, its construction supervisor, and its inspector. Moreover, the architect's design determined the amount and the scale of the statuary and decorative paintings to be incorporated. By 1400 the Gothic style of building had dominated western Europe for over two centuries. Its characteristic pointed arches, vaulted ceilings, and slender spires had simplified building by

removing the heavy walls formerly thought necessary to support great structures. Gothic construction permitted greater height, a characteristic especially desirable in cathedrals, which stretched toward the heavens. But though the buildings themselves were simplified, the techniques for erecting them became more complex. By the fifteenth century architects had turned their techniques into an intricate style. They became obsessed by angular arches, elaborate vaultings and buttresses, and long, pointed spires.

It was Brunelleschi who decisively challenged the principles of Gothic architecture by recombining its basic elements with those of classical structures. Basing his designs on geometric principles, Brunelleschi reintroduced planes and spheres as dominant motifs. His greatest work was the dome on the cathedral in Florence, begun in 1420. His design for the dome was simple but bold. The circular windows are set inside a square of panels, which in turn are set inside a rectangle. Brunelleschi is generally credited with

Florence Cathedral was begun by Arnolfo di Cambio in 1296. The nave was finished about 1350, and the dome, designed by Brunelleschi, was added in the 1420s. This view shows the dome and the apse end of the cathedral.

having been the first Renaissance artist to have understood and made use of perspective, though it was immediately put to more dramatic effect in sculpture and painting.

The sculptor's study was the human form in all of its three-dimensional complexity. The survival of Roman and Hellenistic pieces, mostly bold and muscular torsos, meant that the influence of classical art was most direct in sculpture. Donatello translated these classical styles into more naturalistic forms. His technique is evident in the long flowing robes in most of his works, sculpted in the natural fashion in which cloth hung. Donatello revived the free-standing statue, which demanded greater attention to human anatomy because it was viewed from many angles. He also led the revival of the equestrian statue, sculpting the Venetian captain-general *Gattamelata* (1445–50) for a public square in Padua. This enormous bronze horse and rider relied upon the standpoint of the viewer to achieve its overpowering effect. This use of linear perspective is also seen in Donatello's breathtaking altar scenes of the mir-acles of Saint Anthony in Padua, which resemble nothing so much as a canvas cast in bronze.

These altar scenes clearly evince the unmistakable influence of the paintings of Masaccio. His frescoes in the Brancacci Chapel in Florence were studied and sketched by all of the great artists of the next generation, who unreservedly praised his naturalism. What most claims the attention of the modern viewer is Masaccio's shading of light and shadow and his brilliant use of linear perspective to create the illusion that a flat surface has three dimensions. Masaccio's work was on standard Christian themes, but he brought an entirely novel approach to them all. In an adoration scene he portrayed a middle-aged Madonna and a dwarfish baby Jesus; in a painting of Saint Peter paying tribute money, he used his own likeness as the face of one of the Apostles. His two best-known works are the *Holy Trinity* (1425) and the *Expulsion of Adam and Eve* (ca. 1427). In the *Holy Trinity* Masaccio provides the classic example of the use of linear perspective. In the painting, the ceiling of a Brunelleschi-designed temple recedes to a vanishing point beyond the head of God, creating the simultaneous illusion of height and depth.

Renaissance Style

By the middle of the fifteenth century a recognizable Renaissance style had triumphed. The outstanding architect of this period was Leon Battista Alberti (1404–72), whose treatise *On Building* (1452) remained the most influential work on the subject until the eighteenth century. Alberti consecrated the geometric principles laid down by Brunelleschi and infused them with a humanist spirit. He revived the classical dictum that a building, like a body, should have an even number of supports and, like a head, an odd number of openings. This furthered precise geometric calculations in scale and design.

No sculptor challenged the preeminence of Donatello for another fifty years, but in painting there were many contenders for the garlands worn by Masaccio. The first was Piero della Francesca (ca. 1420–92) who, though trained in the tradition of Masaccio, broke new ground in his concern for the visual unity of his paintings. From portraits to processions to his stunning fresco *The Resurrection* (ca. 1463) Piero concentrated upon the most technical aspects of composition. Another challenger was Sandro Botticelli (1445–1510), whose classical themes, sensitive portraits, and bright colors set him

Gattamelata, *Donatello's equestrian statue of the Venetian captain-general Erasmo da Narni stands in a square in Padua.*

apart from the line of Florentine painters with whom he studied. His mythologies of the *Birth of Venus* and *Spring* (ca. 1478) depart markedly from the naturalism inspired by Masaccio.

This concern with beauty and personality is also seen in the paintings of Leonardo da Vinci (1452–1519), whose creative genius embodied the Renaissance ideal of the "universal man." Leonardo's achievements in scientific, technical, and artistic endeavors read like a list of all of the subjects known during the Renaissance. His detailed anatomical drawings and the method he devised for rendering them, his botanical observations, and his engineering inventions (including models for a tank and an airplane) testify to his unrestrained curiosity. His paintings reveal a continuation of the scientific application of mathematics to matters of proportion and perspective. Leonardo's psychological portrait *La Gioconda* (1503–06), popularly called the Mona Lisa, is quite possibly the best-known picture in the world.

From Brunelleschi to Alberti, from Masaccio to Leonardo da Vinci, Renaissance artists placed a unique stamp upon visual culture. By reviving classical themes, geometric principles, and a spirit of human vitality, they broke decisively from the dominant medieval traditions. Art became a source of individual and collective pride, produced by masters but consumed by all. Cities and wealthy patrons commissioned great works of art for public display. New buildings rose everywhere, adorned with the statues and murals that still stand as a testimony to generations of artists.

Michelangelo

The artistic achievements of the Renaissance culminated in the creative outpourings of Michelangelo Buonarroti (1475–1564). Poet, sculptor, painter, and architect, Michelangelo imparted his genius to everything he touched. Uncharacteristically, Michelangelo came from a family of standing in Florentine society. At the age of fourteen, over the opposition of his father, he was apprenticed to a leading painter and spent his spare time in Florentine churches copying the works of Masaccio among others.

In 1490 Michelangelo gained a place in the household of Lorenzo de' Medici. During this two-year period he claimed to have taught himself sculpturing, a remarkable feat considering the skills required. In fact, what was unusual about Michelangelo's early development was that he avoided the long years of apprenticeship

In The Expulsion of Adam and Eve, *Masaccio's mastery of perspective helps create the illusion of movement. Eve's anguish is shown in her deep eyes and hollow mouth, which are accentuated by casting the source of light downward and shading what otherwise would be lit.*

THE LIFE OF LEONARDO

■ *Giorgio Vasari celebrated the creativity of the artists who made Italy the center of cultural activity in the late Middle Ages. His commemoration of their achievements through the medium of biography helped to create the aura that still surrounds Renaissance art.*

The most heavenly gifts seem to be showered on certain human beings. Sometimes supernaturally, marvelously, they all congregate in one individual. Beauty, grace, and talent are combined in such bounty that in whatever that man undertakes, he outdistances all other men and proves himself to be specially endowed by the hand of God. He owes his pre-eminence not to human teaching or human power. This was seen and acknowledged by all men in the case of Leonardo da Vinci, who had, besides the beauty of his person (which was such that it has never been sufficiently extolled), and indescribable grace in every effortless act and deed. His talent was so rare that he mastered any subject to which he turned his attention. Extraordinary strength and remarkable facility were here combined. He had a mind of regal boldness and magnanimous daring. His gifts were such that his celebrity was worldwide, not only in his own day, but even more after his death, and so will continue until the end of time.

Leonardo was frequently occupied in the preparation of plans to remove mountains or to pierce them with tunnels from plain to plain. By means of levers, cranes, and screws, he showed how to lift or move great weights. Designing dredging machines and inventing the means of drawing water from the greatest depths were among the speculations from which he never rested. Many drawings of these projects exist which are cherished by those who practice our arts.

Leonardo, with his profound comprehension of art, began many things that he never completed, because it seemed to him that perfection must elude him. He frequently formed in his imagination enterprises so difficult and so subtle that they could not be entirely realized and worthily executed by human hands. His conceptions were varied to infinity. In natural philosophy, among other things, he examined plants and observed the stars—the movements of the planets, the variations of the moon, and the course of the sun.

From Giorgio Vasari, *The Life of Leonardo Da Vinci*.

during which someone else's style was implanted upon the young artist. In the Medici household he came into contact with leading Neoplatonists, who taught that man was on an ascending journey of perfectibility toward God. These ideas can be seen as one source of the heroic concept of humanity that Michelangelo brought to his work.

In 1496 Michelangelo moved to Rome. There his abilities as a sculptor quickly brought him to the attention of Jacopo Galli, a Roman banker who was interested in art and learning. Galli commissioned a classical work for himself and procured another for a French cardinal, which became the *Pietà*. Although this was Michelangelo's first attempt at sculpting a work of religious art, it was a masterpiece in beauty and composition. The *Pietà* created a sensation in Rome and by the time that

Michelangelo returned to Florence in 1501, at the age of twenty-six, he was already acknowledged as one of the great sculptors of his day. He was immediately commissioned to work on an enormous block of marble that had been quarried nearly a half-century before and had defeated the talents of a series of carvers. He worked continuously for three years on his *David* (1501–04), a piece that completed the union between classical and Renaissance styles.

Though Michelangelo always believed himself to be primarily a sculptor, his next outstanding work was in the field of painting. In 1508 Pope Julius II summoned Michelangelo to Rome and commissioned him to decorate the ceiling of the small ceremonial chapel that had been built next to the new papal residence. Michelangelo's plan was to portray, in an extended narrative, man's

Botticelli's Primavera (Spring), *also called* Garden of Venus. *Venus, in the center, is attended by the three Graces and by Cupid, Flora, Chloris, and Zephyr. Botticelli's figures have a dreamlike quality, an unreality highlighted by the beautiful faces and lithe figures of his characters.*

creation and those Old Testament events that foreshadowed the birth of the Savior. First Michelangelo framed his scenes within the architecture of a massive classical temple. In this way he was able to give the impression of having flattened the rounded surface on which he worked. Within the center panels came his fresco scenes of the events of the creation and of human history from the Fall to the Flood. His representations were simple and compelling: the fingers of God and Adam nearly touching; Eve with one leg still emerging from Adam's side; the half-human snake in the temptation are all majestically evocative.

The *Pietà*, the *David*, and the paintings of the Sistine Chapel were the work of youth. Michelangelo's crowning achievement, the building of Saint Peter's basilica in Rome, was the work of age. The intervening years saw the production of masterpiece after masterpiece, enough completed and unfinished work to have established his genius. The basework of St. Peter's had already been laid and drawings for its completion had been made thirty years earlier by Bramante. Michelangelo altered these plans in an effort to bring more light within the church and provide a more majestic facade outside. His main contribution, however, was the design of the great dome, which centered the interior of the church on Saint Peter's grave. More than the height, it is the harmony of Michelangelo's design that creates the sense of the building thrusting upward like a Gothic cathedral of old. Michelangelo did not live to see the dome of Saint Peter's completed.

Renaissance art served Renaissance society. It reflected both its concrete achievements and its visionary ideals. It was a synthesis of old and new, building upon classical models, particularly in sculpture and architecture, but adding newly discovered techniques and skills. When Giorgio Vasari (1511–74) came to write his *Lives of the Great Painters, Sculptors, and Architects* (1550) he found over two hundred artists worthy of distinction. But Renaissance artists did more than construct and adorn buildings or celebrate and beautify spiritual life. Inevitably their work expressed the ideals and aspirations of the society in which they lived, the new

The creation of Adam and Eve. Detail from Michelangelo's frescoes on the ceiling of the Sistine Chapel. The Sistine frescoes had become obscured by dirt and layers of varnish and glue applied at various times over the years. In the 1980s they were cleaned to reveal their original colors.

emphasis upon learning and knowledge; upon the here and now rather than the hereafter; and most importantly upon humanity and its capacity for growth and perfection.

Renaissance Ideals

Renaissance thought went hand in glove with Renaissance art. Scholars and philosophers searched the works of the ancients to find the principles on which to build a better life. They scoured monastic libraries for forgotten manuscripts, discovering among other things, Greek poetry, history, the works of Homer and Plato, and Aristotle's *Poetics*. Their rigorous application of scholarly procedures for the collection and collation of these texts was one of the most important contributions of those Renaissance intellectuals who came to be known as humanists. Humanism developed in reaction to an intellectual world that was centered on the Church and dominated by otherworldly concerns. Humanism was by no means antireligious, but it was thoroughly secular in outlook.

Humanists celebrated worldly achievements. Pico della Mirandola's *Oration on the Dignity of Man* (1486) is the best known of a multitude of Renaissance writings influenced by the discovery of the works of Plato. Pico believed that people could perfect their existence on earth because humans were divinely endowed with the capacity to determine their own fate. This emphasis on human potential found expression in the celebration of human achievement.

Thus humanists studied and taught the humanities, the skills of disciplines like philology, the art of language, and rhetoric, the art of expression. Though they were mostly laymen, humanists applied their learning to both religious and secular studies. Humanists were not antireligious. Although most reacted strongly against Scholasticism (see chapter 13), they were heavily indebted to the work of medieval churchmen and most were devoutly religious. Nor were they hostile to the Church. Petrarch, Bruni, and Alberti were all employed by the papal court at some time in their careers, as was Lorenzo Valla, the most influential of the humanists. Their interest in human achievement and human potential must be set beside their religious beliefs. As Petrarch stated quite succinctly: "Christ is my God; Cicero is the prince of the language I use."

Humanists and the Liberal Arts

The most important achievements of humanist scholars centered upon ancient texts. It was the humanists' goal to discover as much as had survived from the ancient world and to provide texts of classical authors that were as full and accurate as possible. Though much was already known of the Latin classics, few of the central works of ancient Greece had been recovered. Humanists preserved this heritage by reviving the study of the Greek language and by translating Greek authors into Latin, the language of the Church. After the fall of Constantinople in 1453, Italy became the center for Greek studies as Byzantine scholars fled the Ottoman conquerors. Humanists also introduced historical methods in studying and evaluating texts, establishing principles for determining which of many manuscript copies of an ancient text was the oldest, the most accurate, and the least corrupted by their copyists. This was of immense importance in studying the writings of the ancient Fathers of the Church, many of whose manuscripts had not been examined for centuries. Their emphasis upon the humanistic disciplines fostered new educational ideals. Along with the study of theology, logic, and natural philosophy, which had dominated the medieval university, humanist scholars stressed the importance of grammar, rhetoric, moral philosophy, and history. They believed that the study of these "liberal arts" should be undertaken for its own sake. This emphasis gave a powerful boost to the ideal of the perfectibility of the individual that appeared in so many other aspects of Renaissance culture.

A miniature portrait of Petrarch is seen within the illuminated initial a in a manuscript of the poet's treatise De remediis utriusque fortunae *("Remedies Against Fortune").*

Humanists furthered the secularization of Renaissance society through their emphasis on the study of the classical world. Philology became one of the most celebrated humanist skills and the study of ancient manuscripts one of the most common humanist activities. The rediscovery of Latin texts during the late Middle Ages spurred interest in all things ancient. Petrarch, who is rightly called the father of humanism, revered the great Roman rhetorician Cicero above all others. Leonardo Bruni (1370–1444) was reputed to be the greatest Greek scholar of his day. He translated Plato and Aristotle and did much to advance mastery of classical Greek and foster the ideas of Plato in the late fifteenth century.

The study of the origins of words, their meaning, and their proper grammatical usage may seem an unusual foundation for one of the most vital of all European intellectual movements. But philology was the human-

ists' chief concern. This can best be illustrated by the work of Lorenzo Valla (1407–57). Valla was brought up in Rome, where he was largely self-educated, though according to the prescriptions of the Florentine humanists. Valla entered the service of Alfonso I, king of Naples, and applied his humanistic training to affairs of state. The kingdom of Naples bordered on the Papal States, and its kings were in continual conflict with the papacy. The pope asserted the right to withhold recognition of the king, a right that was based upon the jurisdictional authority supposedly ceded to the papacy by the Emperor Constantine in the fourth century—the so-called Donation of Constantine. Valla settled the matter definitively. Applying historical and philological critiques to the text of the Donation, Valla proved that it could not have been written earlier than the eighth century, four hundred years after Constantine's death. He mercilessly exposed words and terms that had not existed in Roman times, like *fief* and *satrap*, and thus proved beyond doubt that the Donation was a forgery and papal claims based upon it were without merit.

Valla's career demonstrates the impact of humanist values on practical affairs. Although humanists were scholars, they made no distinction between an active and a contemplative life. A life of scholarship was a life of public service. This civic humanism is best expressed in the writings of Leon Battista Alberti (1404–72), whose treatise *On the Family* (1443) is a classic study of the new urban values, especially prudence and thrift. Alberti extolled the virtues of "the fatherland, the public good, and the benefit of all citizens." An architect, a mathematician, a poet, a playwright, a musician, and an inventor, Alberti was one of the great virtuosi of the Renaissance.

Alberti's own life might have served as a model for the most influential of all Renaissance tracts, Castiglione's *The Courtier* (1528). Baldesar Castiglione (1478–1529) directed his lessons to the public life of the aspiring elite. It was his purpose to prescribe those characteristics that would make the ideal courtier, who was as much born as made. He prescribed every detail of the education necessary for the ideal state servant from table manners to artistic attainments. Castiglione's perfect courtier was an amalgam of all that the elite of Renaissance society held dear. He was to be educated as a scholar, he was to be occupied as a soldier, and he was to serve his state as an advisor.

Machiavelli and Politics

At the same time that Castiglione was drafting a blueprint for the idealized courtier, Niccolò Machiavelli (1469–1527) was laying the foundation for the realistic sixteenth-century ruler. No Renaissance work has been more important or more controversial than Machiavelli's *The Prince* (1513). Its vivid prose, its epigrammatic advice—"men must either be pampered or crushed"— and its clinical dissection of power politics have attracted generation after generation of readers. With Machiavelli, for better or worse, begins the science of politics in Europe.

Machiavelli came from an established Florentine family. He entered state service as an assistant to one of his teachers and unexpectedly rode those coattails into the relatively important office of secretary to the Council of Ten, the organ of Florentine government that had responsibility for war and diplomacy. Here Machiavelli received his education in practical affairs. He was an emissary to Cesare Borgia during his consolidation of the Papal States at the turn of the century and carefully studied Borgia's methods. Machiavelli was a tireless correspondent and he began to collect materials for various tracts on military matters.

But as suddenly as he rose to his position of power and influence, he fell from it. The militia that he had advocated and in part organized was soundly defeated by the Spaniards, and the Florentine republic fell. Machiavelli was summarily dismissed from office in 1512 and was imprisoned and tortured the following year. Released and banished from the city, he retired to a small country estate. Immediately he began writing what became his two greatest works, *The Prince* (1513) and *The Discourses on Livy* (1519).

Machiavelli has left a haunting portrait of his life in exile, and it is important to understand how intertwined his studies of ancient and modern politics were.

> On the coming of evening, I return to my house and enter my study; and at the door I take off the day's clothing covered with mud and dust, and put on garments regal and courtly; and reclothed appropriately, I enter the ancient courts of ancient men, where, received by them with affection, I feed on that food which only is mine and which I was born for.

The Prince is a handbook for a ruler who would establish a lasting government. It attempts to set down principles culled from historical examples and contemporary events to aid the prince in attaining and maintaining power. By the study of these precepts and by their swift and forceful application, Machiavelli believed that the prince might even control fortune itself. What made *The Prince* so remarkable in its day, and what continues to enliven debate over it, is that Machiavelli was able to separate all ethical considerations from his analysis. Whether this resulted from cynicism or from his own expressed desire for realism, Machiavelli uncompromisingly instructed the would-be ruler to be half man and half beast—to conquer neighbors, to murder enemies, and to deceive friends. Steeped in the humanist ideals of fame and virtù—a combination of virtue and virtuosity, of valor, character, and ability—he sought to reestablish Italian rule and place government upon a stable, scientific basis that would end the perpetual conflict among the Italian city-states.

The careers of Lorenzo Valla and Niccolò Machiavelli both illustrate how humanists were able to bring the study of the liberal arts into the service of the state. Valla's philological studies had a vital impact on

Terra-cotta bust of Niccolò Machiavelli by an unknown artist. Because of the ideas set forth in The Prince, *Machiavellianism has passed into the language as a label for the ruthless, amoral pursuit of power.*

diplomacy, and Machiavelli's historical studies were directly applicable to warfare. Humanists created a demand for learning that helps account for the growth of universities, the spread of literacy, and the rise of printing. They also created a hunger for knowledge that characterized intellectual life for nearly two centuries.

The Politics of the Italian City-States

Like studs on a leather boot, city-states dotted the Italian peninsula. They differed in size, shape, and form. Some were large seaports, others small inland villages; some cut wide swaths across the plains, others were tiny islands. The absence of a unifying central authority in Italy, resulting from the collapse of the Holy Roman Empire and the papal schism, allowed ancient guilds and confraternities to transform themselves into self-

governing societies. By the beginning of the fifteenth century the Italian city-states were the center of power, wealth, and culture in the Christian world.

This dominion rested on several conditions. First, their geographical position favored the exchange of resources and goods between east and west. Until the fifteenth century, and despite the crusading efforts of medieval popes, east and west fortified each other. A great circular trade had developed, encompassing the Byzantine Empire, the North African coastal states, and the Mediterranean nations of western Europe. The Italian peninsula dominated the circumference of that circle. Its port cities, Genoa and Venice especially, became great maritime powers through their trade in spices and minerals. Second, just beyond the peninsula to the north lay the vast and populous territories of the Holy Roman Empire. There the continuous need for manufactured goods, especially cloth and metals, was filled by long caravans that traveled from Italy through the Alps. Milan specialized in metal crafts. Florence was a financial capital as well as a center for the manufacture of fine luxury goods. Finally, the city-states and their surrounding areas were agriculturally self-sufficient.

Because of their accomplishments we tend to think of these Italian city-states as small nations. Even the term *city-state* implies national identity. Each city-state governed itself according to its own rules and customs, and each defined itself in isolation from the larger regional or tribal associations that once prevailed. Italy was neither a nation nor a people.

The Five Powers

Although there were dozens of Italian city-states, by the early fifteenth century five had emerged to dominate the politics of the peninsula: Naples, the Papal States, Florence, Milan, and Venice. Among them developed the principle of the balance of power that governed Italian politics. In the south was the kingdom of Naples, the only city-state governed by a hereditary monarchy. Its politics were mired by conflicts over its succession. During the fourteenth century Naples was successively ruled by French and Hungarian princes. The fifteenth century began with civil warfare between rival claimants of both nations and it was not until the Spaniard Alfonso I of Aragon (1442–58) secured the throne in 1443 that peace was restored and Naples and Sicily were reunited. Bordering Naples were the Papal States, whose capital was Rome but whose territories

FROM *THE PRINCE*

■ *Niccolò Machiavelli wrote* The Prince *in 1513 while he was under house arrest. It is one of the classics of Western political theory, in which the author separates the political from the moral.*

Every one understands how praiseworthy it is in a prince to keep faith, and to live uprightly and not craftily. Nevertheless we see, from what has taken place in our own days, that princes who have set little store by their word, but have known how to overreach men by their cunning, have accomplished great things, and in the end got the better of those who trusted to honest dealing.

Be it known, then, that there are two ways of contending,—one in accordance with the laws, the other by force; the first of which is proper to men, the second to beasts. But since the first method is often ineffectual, it becomes necessary to resort to the second. A prince should, therefore, understand how to use well both the man and the beast . . . But inasmuch as a prince should know how to use the beast's nature wisely, he ought of beasts to choose both the lion and the fox; for the lion cannot guard himself from the toils, nor the fox from wolves. He must therefore be a fox to discern toils, and a lion to drive off wolves.

To rely wholly on the lion is unwise; and for this reason a prudent prince neither can nor ought to keep his word when to keep it is hurtful to him and the causes which led him to pledge it are removed. If all men were good, this would not be good advice, but since they are dishonest and do not keep faith with you, you in return need not keep faith with them.

From Niccolò Machiavelli, *The Prince*.

stretched far to the north and lay on both sides of the spiny Apennine mountain chain that extends down the center of the peninsula. Throughout the fourteenth and early fifteenth centuries, the territories under the nominal control of the Church were largely independent and included such thriving city-states as Bologna, Ferrara, and Urbino. Even in Rome the weakened papacy had to contend with noble families for control of the city.

The three remaining dominant city-states were bunched together in the north. Florence, center of Renaissance culture, was one of the wealthiest cities of Europe before the devastations of the plague and the sustained economic downturn of the late fourteenth century. The city itself was inland and its main waterway, the Arno, ran to the sea through Pisa, whose subjugation in 1406 was a turning point in Florentine history. Nominally Florence was a republic, but during the fifteenth century it was ruled in effect by its principal banking family, the Medici.

To the north of Florence was the duchy of Milan, the major city in Lombardy. It too was landlocked, cut off from the sea by Genoa. But Milan's economic life was oriented northward to the Swiss and German towns beyond the Alps, and its major concern was preventing foreign invasions. The most warlike of the Italian cities, Milan was a despotism, ruled for nearly two centuries by the Visconti family.

The last of the five powers was the republic of Venice. Ideally situated at the head of the Adriatic Sea, Venice became the leading maritime power of the age. Until the fifteenth century, Venice was less interested in securing a landed empire than in dominating a seaborne one. The republic was ruled by a hereditary elite, headed by an elected doge, who was the chief magistrate of Venice, and a variety of small elected councils.

The political history of the peninsula during the late fourteenth and early fifteenth centuries is one of unrelieved turmoil. Wherever we look, the governments of the city-states were threatened by foreign invaders, internal conspiracies, or popular revolts. In the 1370s the Genoese and Venetians fought their fourth war in little more than a century, this one so bitter that the Genoese risked much of their fleet in an unsuccessful effort to conquer Venice itself. At the turn of the century, the Hungarian occupant of the throne of Naples invaded both Rome and Florence. Florence and Milan were constantly at war with each other. Nor were foreign threats the only dangers. In Milan three Visconti brothers inherited power. Two murdered the third, and then the son of one murdered the other to reunite the inheritance. The Venetians executed one of their military leaders who was plotting treachery. One or another Florentine family usually faced exile when governments there changed hands. Popular revolts channeled social and economic discontent against the ruling elites in Rome, Milan, and Florence. The revolt of the "Ciompi" (the wooden shoes) in Florence in 1378 was an attempt by poorly paid wool workers to reform the city's exclusive guild system and give guild protection to the wage laborers lower down the social scale. In Milan an abortive republic was established in reaction against strong-arm Visconti rule.

By the middle of the fifteenth century, however, two trends were apparent amid this political chaos. The first was the consolidation of strong centralized governments within the large city-states. These took different forms but yielded a similar result—internal political stability. The return of the popes to Rome after the Great Schism restored the pope to the head of his temporal estates and began a long period of papal dominance over Rome and its satellite territories. In Milan, one of the great military leaders of the day, Francesco Sforza (1401–66), seized the reins of power after the failure of the Visconti line. The succession of King Alfonso I in Naples ended a half-century of civil war. In both Florence and Venice the grip that the political elite held over high offices was tightened by placing greater power in small advisory councils and, in Florence, by the ascent to power of the Medici family. In sum, this process is known as the rise of signorial rule. The rise of the signories—whether individual families or small councils—made possible the second development of this period, the establishment of a balance of power within the peninsula.

It was the leaders of the Italian city-states who first perfected the art of diplomacy. Constant warfare necessitated continual alliances, and by the end of the fourteenth century the large city-states had begun the practice of keeping resident ambassadors at the major seats of power. This provided leaders with accurate information about the conditions of potential allies and enemies. Diplomacy was both an offensive and defensive weapon. This was especially so because the city-states hired their soldiers as contract labor. These mercenary armies, whose leaders were known as *condottieri* from the name of their contract, were both expensive and dangerous to maintain. If they did not bankrupt their employers, they might desert them or, even worse, turn on them. Thus Francesco Sforza, the greatest *condottiere* of the fifteenth century, gained power in Milan. Sforza's consolidation of power in Milan initially led to warfare, but ultimately it formed the basis of the Peace of Lodi (1454). This established two balanced alliances, one between Florence and Milan, the other between Venice and Naples. These states, along with the papacy, pledged mutual nonaggression, a policy that lasted for nearly forty years.

The Peace of Lodi did not bring peace. It only halted the long period in which the major city-states struggled against one another. Under cover of the peace, the large states continued the process of swallowing up their smaller neighbors and creating quasi-empires. This was a policy of imperialism as aggressive as that of any in the modern era. Civilian populations were overrun, local leaders exiled or exterminated, tribute money taken, and taxes levied. Each of the five states either increased its mainland territories or strengthened its hold upon them. Venice and Florence especially prospered.

Venice: A Seaborne Empire

Water was the source of the prosperity of Venice. Located at the head of the Adriatic Sea, the city is formed by a web of lagoons. Through its center snakes the Grand Canal, whose banks were lined with large and small buildings that celebrated its civic and mercantile power. At the Piazza San Marco stood the vast palace of the doge, elected leader of the republic, and the Basilica of Saint Mark, a domed church built in the Byzantine style. At the Rialto were the stalls of the bankers and moneylenders, less grand perhaps but no less important. Here, too, were the auction blocks for the profitable trade in European slaves, east European serfs, and battlefield captives who were sold into service to Egypt or Byzantium.

Its prosperity based on trade rather than conquest, Venice enjoyed many natural advantages. Its position at the head of the Adriatic permitted access to the raw

Woodcut illustration of Venice, from Breydenbach's Peregrinations *(1486).*

materials of both east and west. The rich Alpine timberland behind the city provided the hardwoods necessary for shipbuilding. The hinterland population were steady consumers of grain, cloth, and the new manufactured goods—glass, silk, jewelry, and cottons—that came pouring onto the market in the late Middle Ages.

But the success of Venice was owed more to its own achievements than to these rich inheritances. The triumph of the Venetian state was the triumph of dedicated efficiency. The heart of its success lay in the way in which it organized its trade and its government. The key to Venetian trade was its privileged position with the Byzantine Empire. Venice had exchanged with the Byzantines military support for tax concessions that gave Venetian traders a competitive edge in the spice trade with the East. The spice trade was so lucrative that special ships were built to accommodate it. These galleys were constructed at public expense and doubled as the Venetian navy in times of war. By controlling these ships, the government strictly regulated the spice trade. Rather than allow the wealthiest merchants to dominate it, as

they did in other cities, Venice specified the number of annual voyages and sold shares in them at auction based on a fixed price. This practice allowed big and small merchants to gain from the trade and encouraged all merchants to find other trading outlets.

Like its trade, Venetian government was also designed to disperse power. Although it was known as the Most Serene Republic, Venice was not a republic in the sense that we use the word; it was rather an oligarchy—a government by a restricted group. Political power was vested in a Great Council whose membership had been fixed at the end of the thirteenth century. All males whose fathers enjoyed the privilege of membership in the Great Council were registered at birth in the Book of Gold and became members of the Great Council when adults. From the body of the Great Council, which numbered about twenty-five hundred at the end of the fifteenth century, was chosen the Senate, a council about one-tenth the size, whose members served a one-year term. It was from the Senate that the true officers of government were selected: the doge, who was chosen for life, and members of a number of small councils, who administered affairs and advised the doge. Members of these councils were chosen by secret ballot in an elaborate process by which nominators were selected at random. Terms of office on the councils were extremely short in order to limit factionalism and to prevent any individual from gaining too much power. Though small groups exercised more power in practice than they should have in theory, the Venetian oligarchy was never troubled by either civil war or popular rebellion.

With its mercantile families firmly in control of government and trade, Venice created a vast overseas empire in the east during the thirteenth and fourteenth centuries. Naval supremacy allowed the Venetians to offer protection to strategic outposts in return for either privileges or tribute. But in the fifteenth century Venice turned west. In a dramatic reversal of its centuries-old policy, it began a process of conquest in Italy itself. There were several reasons for this new policy. First, the Venetian navy was no longer the unsurpassed power that it once had been. The Genoese wars had drained resources, and the revival of the Ottoman Turks in the east posed a growing threat that ultimately resulted in the fall of Constantinople (1453) and the end of Venetian trading privileges. Outposts in Dalmatia and the Aegean came under assault from both the Turks and the king of Hungary, cutting heavily into the complicated system by which goods were circulated by Venetian merchants. It was not long before Portuguese competition affected the most lucrative of all the commodities traded by the Venetians—pepper. Perhaps most importantly, mainland expansion offered new opportunities for Venice. Not all Venetians were traders, and the new industries that were being developed in the city could readily benefit from control of mainland markets. Most decisively of all, opportunity was knocking. In Milan Visconti rule was weakening and the Milanese territories were ripe for picking.

Venice reaped a rich harvest. From the beginning of the fifteenth century to the Peace of Lodi, the Most Serene Republic engaged in unremitting warfare. Its successes were remarkable. It pushed out to the north to occupy all the lands between the city and the Habsburg territories; it pushed to the east until it straddled the entire head of the Adriatic; and it pushed to the west almost as far as Milan itself. The western conquests in particular brought large populations under Venetian control which, along with their potential as a market, provided a ready source of taxation. By the end of the fifteenth century the mainland dominions of Venice were contributing nearly 40 percent of the city's revenue at a cost far smaller than that of the naval empire a century earlier.

Florence: Spinning Cloth into Gold

Florentine prosperity was built on two foundations: money and wool. Beginning in the thirteenth century, Florentine bankers were among the wealthiest and most powerful in the world. Initially their position was established through support of the papacy in its long struggle with the Holy Roman Empire. Florentine financiers established banks in all the capitals of Europe and the east. In the Middle Ages, bankers served more functions than simply handling and exchanging money. Most were also tied to mercantile adventures and underwrote industrial activity. So it was in Florence where international bankers purchased high-quality wool to be manufactured into the world's finest woven cloth.

The activities of both commerce and cloth manufacture depended on external conditions, and thus the wealth of Florence was potentially unstable. In the mid-fourteenth century instability came with the plague that devastated the city. Nearly 40 percent of the entire population was lost in the single year 1348, and recurring outbreaks continued to ravage the already weakened survivors. Loss of workers and loss of markets seriously disrupted manufacturing. By 1380 cloth production had fallen to less than a quarter of preplague levels. On the heels of plague came wars. The property of Florentine bankers and merchants abroad was an easy target, and in this respect the wars with Naples at the end of the fourteenth century were particularly disastrous. Thirty years of warfare with Milan, interrupted by only a single decade of peace (1413–23), resulted in total bankruptcy for many of the city's leading commercial families. More significantly, the costs of warfare, offensive and defensive, created a massive public debt. Every Florentine of means owned shares in this debt, and the republic was continually devising new methods for borrowing and staving off crises of repayment. Small wonder that the republic turned for aid to the wealthiest banking family in Europe, the Medici.

As befitted a city whose prosperity was based on manufacturing, Florence had a strong guild tradition. The most important guilds were associated with banking and cloth manufacture but they included the crafts and food-processing trades as well. Only guild members could participate in government, electing the nine *Signoria* who administered laws, set tax rates, and directed foreign and domestic policy. Like that of Venice, Florentine government was a republican oligarchy and like Venice, it depended upon rotated short periods in office and selections by lot to avoid factionalism. But Florence had a history of factionalism longer than its history of republican government. Its formal structures were occasionally altered so that powerful families could gain control of the real centers of political power, the small councils and emergency assemblies through which the Signoria governed. Conservative leadership drawn from the upper ranks of Florentine society guided the city through the wars of the early fourteenth century. But soon afterward the leaders of its greatest families, the Albizzi, the Pazzi, and the Medici, again divided Florentine politics into factions.

The ability of the Medici to secure a century-long dynasty in a government that did not have a head of state is just one of the mysteries surrounding the history of this remarkable family. Cosimo de' Medici (1389–1464) was one of the richest men in Christendom when he returned to the city in 1434 after a brief exile. His leading position in government rested upon supporters who were able to gain a controlling influence on the *Signoria*. Cosimo built his party carefully, banishing his Albizzi enemies, recruiting followers among the craftsmen whom he employed, and even paying delinquent taxes to maintain the eligibility of his voters. Most importantly, emergency powers were invoked to reduce the number of citizens qualified to vote for the Signoria until the majority were Medici backers.

Cosimo was a great patron of artists and intellectuals. He collected books and paintings, endowed libraries, and spent lavishly on his own palace, the Palazzo Medici. Cosimo's position as an international banker brought him into contact with the heads of other Italian city-states, and it was his personal relationship with Francesco Sforza that finally ended the Milanese wars and brought about the Peace of Lodi.

It was Cosimo's grandson, Lorenzo (1449–92), who linked the family's name to that of the age. He held strong humanist values instilled in him by his mother, Lucrezia Tornabuoni, who organized his education. He brought Michelangelo and other leading artists to his garden; he brought Pico della Mirandola and other leading humanists to his table. Lorenzo's power was based on his personality and reputation. His diplomatic abilities were the key to his survival. Almost immediately after Lorenzo came to power, Naples and the papacy began a war with Florence, a war that was costly to the Florentines in both taxation and lost territory. In 1479 Lorenzo traveled to Naples and personally convinced the Neapolitan king to sign a separate treaty. This restored the Italian balance of power and ensured continued Medici rule in Florence.

There is some doubt whether Lorenzo should be remembered by the title "the Magnificent" that was bestowed upon him. His absorption in politics came at the expense of the family's commercial enterprises, which were nearly ruined during his lifetime. Branch after branch of the Medici bank closed as conditions for international finance deteriorated, and the family fortune was dwindling. Moreover, the emergency powers that Lorenzo invoked to restrict participation in government changed forever the character of Florentine republicanism, irredeemably corrupting it. There is no reason to accept the judgment of his enemies that Lorenzo was a tyrant, but the negative consequences of his rule cannot be ignored. In 1494, two years after Lorenzo's death, the peninsula was plunged into those wars that turned it from the center of European civilization into one of its lesser satellites.

Lorenzo de' Medici. His patronage of artists and philosophers made Florence the leading Renaissance city.

HOLY ROMAN EMPIRE

SWISS CONFEDERATION

SAVOY

FRANCE

Milan •

MILAN

VENETIAN

Venice •

HUNGARY

Genoa •

GENOA

MODENA

Florence •

FLORENCE

OTTOMAN EMPIRE

Adriatic Sea

Ragusa •

SIENA

PAPAL STATES

Corsica (Genoa)

Rome •

BENEVENTO

KINGDOM OF SARDINIA

Tyrrhenian Sea

Naples •

KINGDOM OF THE TWO SICILIES

Sicily

Boundary of the Holy Roman Empire

0   100   200 Miles

0   100   200 Kilometers

Mediterranean Sea

Italy, 1494

The End of Italian Hegemony, 1450–1527

In the course of the Renaissance western Europe was Italianized. For a century the city-states dominated the trade routes that connected East and West. Italian manufactures, such as Milanese artillery, Florentine silk, and Venetian glass, were prized above all others. The ducat and the florin, two Italian coins, were universally accepted in an age when every petty prince minted his own. The peninsula exported culture in the same way that it exported goods. Humanism quickly spread across the Alps, aided by the recent invention of printing (which the Venetians soon dominated), while Renaissance standards of artistic achievement were known worldwide and everywhere imitated. The city-states shared their technology as well. The compass and the navigational chart, projection maps, double-entry bookkeeping, eyeglasses, the telescope—all profoundly influenced what could be achieved and what could be hoped for. In this spirit Christopher Columbus, a Genoese seaman, successfully crossed the Atlantic under the Spanish flag, and Amerigo Vespucci, a Flo-

rentine merchant, gave his name to the newly discovered continents.

But it was not in Italy that the rewards of innovation or the satisfactions of achievement were enjoyed. There the seeds of political turmoil and military imperialism, combined with the rise of the Ottoman Turks, were to reap a not-unexpected harvest. Under the cover of the Peace of Lodi, the major city-states had scrambled to enlarge their mainland empires. By the end of the fifteenth century they eyed one another greedily and warily. Each expected the others to begin a peninsula-wide war for hegemony and took the steps that ultimately ensured the contest. Perhaps the most unusual aspect of the imperialism of the city-states was that it had been restricted to the peninsula itself. Each of the major powers shared the dream of recapturing the glory that was Rome. Long years of siege and occupation had militarized the Italian city-states. Venice and Florence balanced their budgets on the backs of their captured territories. Milan had been engaged in constant war for decades and even the papacy was militarily aggressive.

And the Italians were no longer alone. The most remarkable military leader of the age was not a Renaissance *condottiere* but an Ottoman prince, Mehmed II (1451–81), who conquered Constantinople and Athens and threatened Rome itself (see chapter 15). The rise of the Ottomans, whose name is derived from Osman, their original tribal leader, is one of the most compelling stories in world history. Little more than a warrior tribe at the beginning of the fourteenth century, a hundred and fifty years later the Ottomans had replaced stagnant Byzantine rule with a virile and potent empire. First they gobbled up the towns and cities in a wide arc around Constantinople. Then they fed upon the Balkans and the eastern kingdoms of Hungary and Poland. By 1400 they were a presence in all the territory that stretched from the Black Sea to the Aegean. By 1450 they were its master. (See Special Feature, "The Fall of Constantinople," pp. 374–375.)

Venice was most directly affected by the Ottoman advance. Not only was its favored position in eastern trade threatened, but during a prolonged war at the end of the fifteenth century the Venetians lost many of their most important commercial outposts. Ottoman might closed off the markets of eastern Europe, and by 1480 Venetian naval supremacy was a thing of the past.

The Italian city-states might have met this challenge from the east had they been able to unite in opposing

Manuscript illustration of the siege of Constantinople. The tents of Turkish invaders are seen in the foreground, while their ships surround the city.

*T*he Fall of Constantinople

The prayers of the devout were more fervent than ever on Easter Sunday, 1453. The Christians of Constantinople knew that it was only a matter of time before the last remaining stronghold of the Byzantine Empire came under siege. For decades the ring of Ottoman conquests had narrowed around this holy city until it alone stood out against the Turkish sultan. Constantinople, the bridge between Europe and Asia, was tottering. The once teeming center of Eastern Christianity had never recovered from the epidemics of the fourteenth century. Dwindling revenues matched the dwindling population. Concessions to Venetian and Genoese traders reduced customs while Ottoman conquests eliminated tribute money.

Perhaps it was this impoverishment that had kept the Turks at bay. Constantinople was still the best-fortified city in the world. Two of its three sides faced the sea, and the third was protected by two stout rings of walls and a trench lined with stones. No cannon forged in Europe could dent these battlements and no navy could hope to force its way through the narrow mouth of the Golden Horn.

A siege of Constantinople hardly seemed worthwhile as long as there were conquests to be made in eastern Europe and Asia Minor. Thus an uneasy peace existed between sultan and emperor. It was shattered in 1451 when a new sultan, the nineteen-year-old Mehmed II, came to the throne. Mehmed's imagination was fired by the ancient prophecies that a Muslim would rule in all of the territories of the east. Only Constantinople was a fitting capital for such an empire, and Mehmed immediately began preparations for its conquest.

In 1452 Mehmed had constructed a fortress at the narrow mouth of the Bosporus and demanded tribute from all ships that entered the Golden Horn. The Byzantine emperor sent ambassadors to Mehmed to protest this aggression. Mehmed returned their severed heads. The Turks now controlled access to the city for trade and supplies. An attack the following spring seemed certain. The emperor appealed far and wide for aid for his beleaguered city. But the Europeans were in no hurry to pledge their support, as it was inconceivable that the Ottomans could assemble the army necessary to besiege Constantinople before summer.

But they reckoned without Mehmed. While the Italians bickered over their share of the expedition and Christians everywhere made ready to celebrate Holy Week, the Ottomans assembled a vast army of fighters and laborers and a huge train of weapons and supplies. Mehmed's forces, which eventually numbered more than 150,000, of which 60,000 were soldiers, assembled around the walls of Constantinople on April 5. During the next week a great flotilla sailed up the Bosporus and anchored just out of reach of the Byzantine warships in the Golden Horn. A census taken inside the city revealed that there were only 7,000 able-bodied defenders, about 5,000 Greek residents and 2,000 foreigners, mostly Genoese and Venetians. The Italians were the only true soldiers among them.

Though the defenders were vastly outnumbered, they still held the military advantage. As long as their ships controlled the entrance to the Golden Horn, they could limit the Ottoman attack to only one side, where all of the best defenders could be massed. The Byzantines cast a boom—an iron chain supported by wooden floats—across the mouth of the bay to forestall a naval attack. By the middle of April the Turks had begun their land assault. Each day great guns pounded the walls of the city and each night residents worked frantically to repair the damage. The Turks suffered heavily for each attempt to follow a cannon shot with a massed charge. But the attack took its toll among the defenders as well. No one was safe from the flaming arrows and catapulted stones flung over the city's walls. Nevertheless, in the first month of siege the defenders held their own.

The vigorous defense of the city infuriated Mehmed. As long as there was only one point of attack, the defenders could resist indefinitely. The line of assault had to be extended, and this could only be done by sea. With the boom effectively impregnable and with Italian seamen superior to the Turks, the prospects seemed dim. But what could not be achieved by force might be achieved by intelligence. A plan was devised to carry a number of smaller ships across land and then to float them behind the Christian fleet. Protected by land forces, the ships could be used as a staging point for another line of attack. Thousands of workmen were set the task of building huge wooden rollers, which were greased with animal fat. Under cover of darkness and the smoke of cannon fire, seventy-two ships were pulled up the steep hills and pushed down into the sea. Once they were safely anchored, a pontoon bridge was built and cannon were trained on the seaward walls of the city.

Moving ships across dry land was not the only engineering feat that sapped the defenders. One night a tower higher than the city's battlements was assembled in front of the landward walls. From there archers pelted the city and sorties of attackers sallied forth. The attacks and bombardments were now relentless. The city had withstood siege for nearly six weeks without any significant reinforcement. At the end of the month there was a sudden lull. A messenger from the sultan arrived to demand surrender. The choice was clear. If the city was taken by force the customary three days of

unrestricted pillage would be allowed, but if it yielded, the sultan pledged to protect the property of all who desired to remain under his rule. The emperor replied feebly that no one who had ever laid siege to Constantinople had enjoyed a long life. He was ready to die in defense of the city.

On May 30 the final assault began. Mehmed knew that his advantage lay in numbers. First he sent in waves of irregular troops, mostly captured slaves and Christians, who suffered great losses and were finally driven back by the weakened defenders. Next, better-trained warriors attacked and widened the breaches made by the irregulars. Finally came the crack Janissaries, the sultan's elite warriors, disciplined from birth to fight. It was the Janissaries who found a small door left open at the base of the wall. In they rushed, quickly overwhelming the first line of defenders and battering their way through the weaker second walls. By dawn the Ottoman flag was raised over the battlements and the sack of Constantinople had begun.

There was no need for the customary three days of pillage. By the end of the first day there was nothing left worth taking. The churches and monasteries had been looted and defaced, the priests and nuns murdered or defiled, and thousands of civilians had been captured to be sold into slavery. Large areas of the city smoldered from countless fires. The desolation was so complete that not even Mehmed could take joy in the ceremonial procession into the new capital of his empire. The bastion of Eastern Christendom was no more.

it. Successive popes pleaded for holy wars to halt the advance of the Turks. The fall of Constantinople in 1453 was an event of epochal proportions for Europeans, many believing that it foreshadowed the end of the world. Yet it was Italians rather than Ottomans who plunged the peninsula into those wars from which it never recovered.

The Wars of Italy (1494–1529) began when Naples, Florence, and the Papal States united against Milan. At first this alliance seemed little more than another shift in the balance of power. But rather than call upon Venice to redress the situation, the Milanese leader, Ludovico Sforza, sought help from the French. An army of French cavalry and Swiss mercenaries, led by Charles VIII of France (1483–98) invaded the peninsula in 1494. With Milanese support the French swept all before them. Florence was forced to surrender Pisa, a humiliation that led to the overthrow of the Medici and the establishment of French sovereignty. The Papal States were next to be occupied, and within a year Charles had conquered Naples without engaging the Italians in a single significant battle. Unfortunately, the Milanese were not the only ones who could play at the game of foreign alliances. Next it was the turn of the Venetians and the pope to unite and call upon the services of King Ferdinand of Aragon and the Holy Roman Emperor. Italy was now a battleground in what became a total European war for dynastic supremacy. The city-states used their foreign allies to settle old scores and to extend their own mainland empires. At the turn of the century Naples was dismembered. In 1509 the pope conspired to organize the most powerful combination of forces yet known against Venice. All of the mainland possessions of the Most Serene Republic were lost, but by a combination of good fortune and skilled diplomacy Venice itself survived. Florence was less fortunate, becoming a pawn first of the French and then of the Spanish. The final blow to Italian hegemony was the sack of Rome in 1527.

The sense of living in a new age, the spirit of human achievement, and the curiosity and wonderment of writers and artists all characterized the Renaissance. The desire to re-create the glories of Rome was not Machiavelli's alone. It could be seen in the palaces of the Italian aristocracy; in the papal rebuilding of the Holy City; and in the military ambitions of princes. But the legacy of empire, of "ancient and heroic pride," had passed out of Italian hands.

SUGGESTIONS FOR FURTHER READING

GENERAL READING

Ernst Breisach, *Renaissance Europe 1300–1517* (New York: Macmillan, 1973). A solid survey of the political history of the age.

* Denys Hay, *The Italian Renaissance* (Cambridge: Cambridge University Press, 1977). An elegant interpretive essay. The best first book to read.

J. R. Hale, ed., *A Concise Encyclopedia of the Italian Renaissance* (Oxford: Oxford University Press, 1981). A treasure trove of facts about the major figures and events of the era.

* P. Burke, *Culture and Society in Renaissance Italy* (Princeton, NJ: Princeton University Press, 1987). A good introduction to social and intellectual developments.

RENAISSANCE SOCIETY

* M. Aston, *The Fifteenth Century: The Prospect of Europe* (London: Thames and Hudson, 1968). A concise survey of Continental history; well written and illustrated.

* J. R. Hale, *Renaissance Europe: The Individual and Society* (Berkeley, CA: University of California Press, 1978). A lively study that places the great figures of the Renaissance in their social context.

* Carlo Cipolla, *Before the Industrial Revolution: European Society and Economy, 1000–1700* (New York: Norton, 1976). A sweeping survey of social and economic developments across the centuries.

* Harry Miskimin, *The Economy of Early Renaissance Europe 1300–1460* (Englewood Cliffs, NJ: Prentice Hall, 1969). A detailed scholarly study of economic development.

D. Herlihy and C. Klapische-Zuber, *The Tuscans and Their Families* (New Haven, CT: Yale University Press, 1985). Difficult but rewarding study of the social and demographic history of Florence and its environs.

* Christiane Klapische-Zuber, *Women, Family, and Ritual in Renaissance Italy* (Chicago: University of Chicago Press, 1985). A sparkling collection of essays on diverse topics in social history from wet-nursing to family life.

RENAISSANCE ART

* Michael Baxandall, *Painting and Experience in Fifteenth Century Italy* (Oxford: Oxford University Press, 1972). A study of the relationship between painters and their patrons, of how and why art was produced.

Frederick Hartt, *History of Italian Renaissance Art* (Englewood Cliffs, NJ: Prentice Hall, 1974). The most comprehensive survey, with hundreds of plates.

* Michael Levey, *Early Renaissance* (London: Penguin Books, 1967). A concise survey of art; clearly written and authoritative.

* Rudolph Wittkower, *Architectural Principles in the Age of Humanism* (New York: Norton, 1971). A difficult but rewarding study of Renaissance architecture.

Roberta Olson, *Italian Renaissance Sculpture* (New York: Thames and Hudson, 1992). A brief, up-to-date guide with good illustrations.

* Linda Murray, *High Renaissance and Mannerism* (London: Thames and Hudson, 1985). The best introduction to late Renaissance art.

* Howard Hibbard, *Michelangelo* (New York: Harper & Row, 1974). A compelling biography of an obsessed genius.

RENAISSANCE IDEALS

* Hans Baron, *The Crisis of the Early Italian Renaissance* (Princeton, NJ: Princeton University Press, 1966). One of the most influential intellectual histories of the period.

* Ernst Cassirer, ed., *The Renaissance Philosophy of Man* (Chicago: University of Chicago Press, 1948). Translations of the works of Petrarch, Valla, and Pico della Mirandola, among others, with excellent introductions.

George Holmes, *The Florentine Enlightenment* (New York: Pegasus, 1969). The best work on the successive generations of Florentine humanists.

Albert Rabil, ed., *Renaissance Humanism* (Philadelphia: University of Pennsylvania Press, 1988). A multi-authored multi-volume collection of essays on humanism, with all of the latest scholarship.

* Quentin Skinner, *Machiavelli* (Oxford: Oxford University Press, 1981). A brief but brilliant life.

THE POLITICS OF THE ITALIAN CITY-STATES

* Lauro Martines, *Power and Imagination: City-States in Renaissance Italy* (New York: Alfred A. Knopf, 1979). An important interpretation of the politics of the Italian powers.

* Frederic C. Lane, *Venice: A Maritime Republic* (Baltimore: Johns Hopkins University Press, 1973). A complete history of Venice, which stresses its naval and mercantile developments.

* Gene Brucker, *Renaissance Florence, 2d ed.* (Berkeley, CA: University of California Press, 1983). The best single-volume introduction to Florentine history.

* J. R. Hale, *Florence and the Medici* (London: Thames and Hudson, 1977). A compelling account of the relationship between a city and its most powerful citizens.

* Eugene E. Rice, Jr., *The Foundations of Early Modern Europe 1460-1559* (New York: Norton, 1970). The best short, synthetic work.

*Indicates paperback edition available.

CHAPTER 13

The Religious Reformation in Europe, 1500–1555

SOLA SCRIPTURA

"In the beginning was the Word, and the Word was with God, and the Word was God." In no other period of European history was this text of the apostle John so appropriate. Men and women shared a consuming desire to hear and to read the Word of God as set down in the Bible. In the early sixteenth century, Europeans developed an insatiable appetite for the Bible. Scriptures rolled off printing presses in every shape and form, from the great vellum tomes of Gutenberg, pictured here, to pocket Bibles that soldiers carried into battle. They came in every imaginable language. Before 1500 there were fourteen complete Bibles printed in German, four each in Italian, French, and Spanish, one in Czech, and even one in Flemish. There were hundreds more editions in Latin, the official Vulgate Bible first translated by Saint Jerome in the fourth century. Whole translations and editions of the Bible were only part of the story. Separate sections, especially the Psalms and the first books of the Old Testament, were printed by the thousands. There were twenty-four French editions of the Old Testament before an entirely new translation appeared in 1530. When Martin Luther began his own German translation of the Bible in 1522, it immediately became an international best-seller. In twenty-five years it went into 430 editions. It is estimated that one million German Bibles were printed in the first half of the sixteenth century—at a time when Europe had a German-speaking population of about 15 million people, 90 percent of whom were illiterate.

Bible owning was no fad. It was but one element in a new devotional outlook that was sweeping the Continent and that would have far-reaching consequences for European society during the next 150 years. A renewed spirituality was everywhere to be seen. It was expressed in a desire to change the traditional practices and structures of the Roman church. It was expressed in a desire to have learned and responsible ministers to tend to the needs of their parishioners. It was expressed in a desire to establish godly families and godly cities and godly kingdoms. Sometimes it took the form of sarcasm and bitter denunciations; sometimes it took the form of quiet devotion and pious living. The need for reform was everywhere felt; the demand for reform was everywhere heard. It came from within the Roman church as much as from without.

The inspiration for reform was based on the Word of God. Scholars, following humanist principles, worked on biblical translations in an attempt to bring a purer text to light. Biblical commentary dominated the writings of churchmen as never before. Woodcut pictures, depicting scenes from the life of Jesus or from the Old Testament, were printed in untold quantities for the edification of the unlettered. For the first time common people could, in their own dwellings, contemplate representations of the lives of the saints. Many of the Bibles that were printed in vernacular—that is, in the languages spoken in the various European states rather than in Latin—were interleaved with illustrations of the central events of Christian history. Preachers spoke to newly aware audiences and relied on biblical texts to draw out their message. Study groups, especially in urban areas, proliferated so that the literate could read and learn together. Bible reading became a part of family life, which mothers and fathers could share with their children and their servants. *Sola Scriptura*—by the Word alone—became the battle cry of religious reform.

The Intellectual Reformation

Nothing is as powerful as an idea whose time has come. But the coming of ideas has a history as complex as the ideas themselves. In the early sixteenth century reformers throughout western Europe preached new ideas about religious doctrine and religious practice. At first these ideas took the form of a sustained critique of the Roman Catholic church, but soon they developed a momentum of their own. Some reformers remained within traditional Catholicism; others moved outside and founded new Protestant churches. Wherever this movement for religious reform appeared, whether Catholic or Protestant, it was fed by new ideas. This was made possible by the development of printing, which appeared in Germany in the late fifteenth century and rapidly spread across Europe in the succeeding decades. Yet printing was as much a result as it was a cause of the spread of ideas. The humanist call for a return to the study of the classics and for the creation of accurate texts, first heard in Italy, aroused scholars and leaders in all of the European states. Their appetite for manuscripts exhausted the abilities of the scribes and booksellers who reproduced texts. Printing responded to that demand.

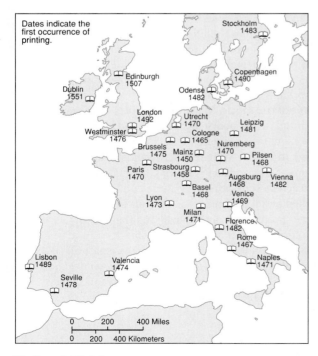

The Spread of Printing

The Print Revolution

The development of printing did not cause religious reform, but it is difficult to see how reform would have progressed in its absence. The campaign to change the doctrine and practice of Catholicism was waged through the press, with millions of flyers and pamphlets distributed across Europe to spread the new ideas. But the ways in which printing came to be used by religious reformers could hardly have been foreseen by the artisans, bankers, and booksellers who together created one of the true technological revolutions in Western history.

Printing was not invented. It developed as a result of progress made in a number of allied industries, of which papermaking and goldsmithing were the most important. Scholars and university students needed copies of manuscripts. Their need led to the development of a trade in bookselling that flourished in almost every university town. The process of reproduction was slowed by difficulties in obtaining the sheep and calf skins on which the manuscripts were written. In the early fifteenth century, copyists began to substitute paper made from linen rags for the expensive vellum skins. A number of German craftsmen experimented with using movable metal type to make exact reproductions of manuscripts on paper. In the 1450s in Mainz, Johannes Gutenberg (ca. 1400–1468) and his partners succeeded and published their famous Bibles.

The association of early printing with goldsmithing resulted from the high level of technical skill that was necessary to create the hard metal stamps from which the softer metal type was produced. Printing was an expensive business. Only the press itself was cheap. Any corn or wine press could be used to bring the long flat sheets of paper down upon a wooden frame filled with ink-coated metal type. Booksellers initially put up the capital needed to cast the stamps, mold the type, and buy the paper. They bound the printed pages and found the markets to distribute them. At first sales were slow. Printed books were considered inferior to handwritten manuscripts. Nor at first were printed books less expensive. Bibles, like those printed by Gutenberg, were major investments, equivalent to purchasing a house today.

Still, once it was begun, printing spread like wildfire. By 1480 over 110 towns had established presses, most in Italy and Germany. After that the pace quickened. By the beginning of the sixteenth century Venice and Paris were the centers of the industry, with the Paris presses producing over three hundred new titles annually. Most of the early printed works were either religious or classical. Bibles, church service books, and the commentaries of the Church Fathers were most common. Cicero topped the list of classical authors.

What is most amazing about the printing revolution is how rapidly printing came to be a basic part of life. In the first forty years after the presses began, perhaps as many as twenty million books were produced and distributed. Printing changed the habits of teachers and students and therefore the possibilities of education. It altered the methods by which the state conducted its business. It affected both legal training and legal proceedings. Compilations of laws could now be widely distributed and more uniformly enforced. Printing had a similar effect on the development of scientific study. The printing press popularized the discoveries of the New World and contributed to the reproduction of more accurate charts and maps, which in turn facilitated further discovery. Printing also helped standardize language, both Latin and vernacular, by frequent repetition of preferred usage and spelling. Perhaps most importantly, printing created an international intellectual community whose ideas could be dispersed the length and breadth of the continent. The printing press enhanced the value of ideas and of thinking. Nothing could be more central to the reform of religion.

Christian Humanism

Many of the ideas that spread across Europe as the result of the printing revolution originated in fifteenth-century Italian humanism (see chapter 12). The revival of classical literature, with its concern for purity in language and eloquence in style, was one of the most admired achievements of the Renaissance. Students from all over Europe who descended upon Italian universities to study medicine and law came away with a strong dose of philology, rhetoric, moral philosophy, and the other liberal arts. By the beginning of the sixteenth century, the force of humanism was felt strongly in northern and western Europe. The combination was a powerful intellectual movement known as Christian humanism.

Though the humanism of the north differed from that of the Italian city-states, this is not to say that northern humanists were Christians and Italian humanists were not. But Italian intellectual interests were in secular subjects, especially in mastering classical languages and in translating classical texts. Italian humanists had established techniques for the recovery of accurate texts and had developed principles for compiling the scholarly editions that now poured forth from the printing presses. Christian humanists applied these techniques to the study of the authorities and texts of the Church. Most of the new humanists had been trained in Italy, where they devoted themselves to the mastery of Greek and Latin. They had imbibed the idea that scholars, using their own critical faculties, could establish the authority of texts and the meaning of words. Building upon the patient work of their predecessors and the advantages offered by printing, this new generation of humanists brought learning to educated men and women throughout Europe.

Christian humanism was a program of reform rather than a philosophy. It aimed to make better Christians through better education. Humanists were especially interested in the education of women. Thomas More (1478–1535) raised his daughters to be among the educated elite of England. Renowned women scholars even held places at Italian universities. Humanist educational principles posed an implicit challenge to Roman Catholicism. Schools had once been the monopoly of the Church, which used them to train clergymen. Literacy itself had been preserved over the centuries so that the gospel could be propagated.

By the sixteenth century these purposes had been transformed. Schools now trained many who were not destined for careers in the Church, and literacy served the needs of the state, the aristocracy, and the merchant classes. More importantly, as the humanists perfected their techniques of scholarship, the Church continued to rely on traditional methods of training and on traditional texts. The dominant manner of teaching at the schools and universities was known as Scholasticism. Passages of biblical texts were studied through the commentaries of generations of Church Fathers. Rote memorization of the opinions of others was more highly valued than critical thinking. Argument took place by formal disputation of questions on which the Fathers of the Church disagreed. The Vulgate Bible was used throughout Western Christendom. It was now a thousand years old.

The Humanist Reform Movement and Erasmus

Many humanist criticisms of Church teaching focused on its failure to inspire individuals to live a Christian life. Humanist writers were especially scathing about popular practices that bordered on superstition, like pilgrimages to holy places or the worship of relics from the early history of the Church. Such beliefs became the butt of popular humor: "If the fragments [of the Lord's Cross] were joined together they would seem a full load for a freighter. And yet the Lord carried his whole cross."

This map by Ambrosius Holbein was published in Thomas More's Utopia, *1518. The mythical island's capital, Amaurote, is shown in the center.*

Utopia

"It is a general rule that the more different anything is from what people are used to, the harder it is to accept." So warned the imaginary traveler Raphael Hythloday as he described Utopia, a fabulous society he had visited in the New World. Utopian society was different indeed. In Utopia, all property was held in common—there were no social classes; families were extended to include grandparents, in-laws, and flocks of children; and all work and most social activities were regulated by the state. Utopians were rarely tempted to sin. Everyone wore the same practical clothes to abolish vanity. "No matter how delicate the thread, they say a sheep wore it once and still was nothing but a sheep." Everyone ate the same food in large common halls to abolish jealousy. "A man would be stupid to take the trouble to prepare a worse meal at home when he had a sumptuous one near at hand in the hall." To abolish greed, Utopians scorned gold and silver. "Criminals who are to bear through life the mark of some disgraceful act are forced to wear golden rings on their ears, golden bands on their fingers, golden chains around their necks, and even golden crowns on their heads." Utopians lived harmoniously in planned cities, honored their elders, cared for their sick, and brought up their children to love learning and respect hard work. They "lead a life as free of anxiety and as full of joy as possible." There were many ways in which Christian humanists attempted to instruct their contemporaries to lead a joyful life. None has proved more enduring than the imaginary community Sir Thomas More created in *Utopia,* a social satire so convincing that a Catholic priest sought to become its bishop and sea travelers tried to learn its location. More's creation has proven so compelling that it has given its name to the entire genre of dreamworlds that followed in its wake, although in Greek *Utopia* means "nowhere." His vision of a carefully planned and permanently contented society has passed into our language, but in a way that would not have pleased the author. Now, *utopian* has a wistful ring. It is a label for impractical ideals that will never come to pass, a name for well-meaning but misguided daydreams. For More, as for his generation of humanists, the goal of teaching Christians to lead a Christian life was neither wistful nor impractical.

Sir Thomas More was a London lawyer by vocation but a humanist scholar by avocation. His father practiced law, and planned a similar career for his son. But Thomas's stay at Oxford University coincided with the first flush of humanist enthusiasm there, especially in the study of Greek. More proved so exceptionally able that his father removed him to London in fear that reading Greek would turn him away from Catholicism. More proved as able at law school as he had at the university, and he was soon singled out as one of the best lawyers of his day. But in his spare time he continued to study the classics and became part of the growing humanist circle in London. There he met Erasmus, who became his lifelong friend.

More wrote *Utopia* in 1516, before he embarked upon the public career that would result in his becoming Chancellor of England, Speaker of the House of Commons, Privy Councilor and companion to Henry VIII, and finally a victim of the king's divorce and assumption of the title Supreme Head of the Church of England. More ended his life on the chopping block, and his death was mourned by humanists throughout Europe.

Utopia is written in the form of a dialogue in which the author pretends to be one of the charac-

ters. On a visit to Antwerp, the character More is introduced to an imaginary traveler named Raphael Hythloday. During a long evening, Hythloday relates a tale of a remarkable society that he encountered on his voyages. Utopia was a self-sufficient island, protected from invasion by the sea and thus able to develop its social customs without interference.

Hythloday contrasted the practices of the Utopians with those of contemporary Europeans and confounded the character More's objections that such arrangements were impractical. For example, where European peasants or craftsmen worked for fourteen hours a day, Utopians worked for only six. But all Utopians worked. There were no idle aristocrats with their marauding retainers, no priests and monks and nuns, no beggars unable to find jobs. Moreover, there was no surplus of workers in one field and shortage in another. For two years, each Utopian worked on the farm. After that, Utopians worked at a craft according to the needs of the city. Both males and females were educated to be of service to their community. Women were trained in less strenuous but no less essential trades like weaving or

spinning. The population of cities was strictly controlled so that there was neither poverty nor homelessness. In their spare time Utopians engaged in uplifting activities like music, gardening, or artistic pursuits. Severe punishment awaited transgressors, but in contrast to the European practice of executing thieves, Utopian criminals were enslaved so that they could work for the restitution of the wrongs that they committed. Though they had not the benefit of Christian religion, the Utopians believed in a single divinity as well as an afterlife and their worship was simple and natural.

By ironic contrast with the unfulfilling life led by Europeans, grasping for riches, dominated by vanity, motivated by pride, the peaceful and simple life of the Utopians held great attraction. By contrasting the success of heathen Utopians with the failure of Christian Europeans, More called upon his contemporaries to reform their own lives. The purpose of *Utopia* was not to advocate the abolition of wealth and property or the intervention of the state in the affairs of the individual but to demonstrate that a society founded upon good principles would become a good society.

This ironic strain in humanist writing is most closely associated with the great Dutch humanist, Desiderius Erasmus, but it is also visible in the humanist social criticism of Sir Thomas More's *Utopia* (See Special Feature, "Utopia," pp. 382-383). Christian humanists wanted to inspire Christians.

Christian humanism was an international movement. The humanists formed the elite of the intellectual world of the sixteenth century, and their services were sought by princes and peers as well as by the most distinguished universities. In fact, monarchs supported the humanists and protected them from their critics. Marguerite of Navarre, sister of King Francis I of France (1515-47), was an accomplished writer who frequently interceded on behalf of the leading French humanists. Ferdinand of Aragon, Henry VIII of England (1509-47), and the Holy Roman Emperors Maximilian I (1486-1519) and Charles V (1519-56) all brought humanists to their courts and aided their projects. Maria of Hungary and Henry VIII's daughters, Mary and Elizabeth Tudor, were trained in humanist principles and participated in humanist literary achievements. This support was especially important for educational reforms. Under the influence of the French humanist Jacques Lefèvre d'Etaples (ca. 1455-1536), Francis I established the Collège de France; under the direction of Cardinal Jiménez de Cisneros, the University of Alcalà was founded in Spain. Throughout northern Europe professorships in Greek and Latin were endowed at universities to help further the study of classical languages.

The centerpiece of humanist reforms was the translation of Christian texts. Armed with skills in Greek and Latin, informed by scholars of Hebrew and Aramaic, humanist writers prepared new editions of the books of the Bible and of the writings of the early Church Fathers. The Polyglot Bible—literally "many languages"—that was produced in 1522 at the University of Alcalà took a team of scholars fifteen years to complete. They rigorously compared texts of all known biblical manuscripts and established the principle that inconsistencies among Latin manuscripts were to be resolved by reference to Greek texts and difficulties in Greek texts by reference to Hebrew texts. The result was six volumes that allowed scholars to compare the texts. The Old Testament was printed in three parallel columns of Hebrew, Latin Vulgate, and Greek. The New Testament was printed in double columns of Greek and Vulgate. The Greek edition of the Bible and its establishment as a text superior to the Vulgate caused an immediate sensation throughout humanist and Church circles.

Engraving of Erasmus by the German master Albrecht Dürer. The title, date, and signature appear behind the philosopher. The Greek inscription reads "His writings depict him even better."

Though the Polyglot Bible contained the first completed Greek edition of the New Testament, it was not the first published one. That distinction belongs to the man whose name is most closely associated with the idea of Christian humanism, Desiderius Erasmus of Rotterdam (ca. 1466-1536). Orphaned at an early age, Erasmus was educated by the Brothers of the Common Life, a lay brotherhood that specialized in schooling children and preparing them for a monastic life. Singled out early for his extraordinary intellectual gifts, Erasmus entered a monastery and was then allowed to travel to pursue his studies, first in France and then in England.

In England Erasmus learned of new techniques for instructing children both in classical knowledge and in Christian morals, and he became particularly interested in the education of women. While in England, Erasmus decided to compose a short satire on the lines of his conversations with Thomas More, extolling what was silly and condemning what was wise. The result was *In Praise of Folly* (1509), a work that became one of the first best-sellers.

Before his visit to England, Erasmus had worked solely on Latin translations, but he came to realize the

FROM *IN PRAISE OF FOLLY*

■ In Praise of Folly *was a witty satire on the abuses to be found in the Catholic church. Desiderius Erasmus wrote it on a lark to be presented to his friend Sir Thomas More, on whose name its Latin title puns. It was probably the first best-seller of the age of printing.*

These various forms of foolishness so pervade the whole life of Christians that even the priests themselves find no objection to admitting, not to say fostering, them, since they do not fail to perceive how many tidy little sums accrue to them from such sources. But what if some odious philosopher should chime in and say, as is quite true: "You will not die badly if you live well. You are redeeming your sins when you add to the sum that you contribute a hearty detestation of evil doers: then you may spare yourself tears, vigils, invocations, fasts, and all that kind of life. You may rely upon any saint to aid you when once you begin to imitate his life."

As for the theologians, perhaps the less said the better on this gloomy and dangerous theme, since they are a style of man who show themselves exceeding supercilious and irritable unless they can heap up six hundred conclusions about you and force you to recant; and if you refuse, they promptly brand you as a heretic,—for it is their custom to terrify by their thunderings those whom they dislike. It must be confessed that no other group of fools are so reluctant to acknowledge Folly's benefits toward them, although I have many titles to their gratitude, for I make them so in love with themselves that they seem to be happily exalted to the third heaven, whence they look down with something like pity upon all other mortals, wandering about on the earth like mere cattle.

---

importance of recovering the Greek texts of the early Church Fathers. At the age of thirty he began the arduous task of learning ancient Greek and devoted his energies to a study of the writings of Saint Jerome, the principal compiler of the Vulgate, and to preparing an edition of the Greek text of the Bible. Erasmus's New Testament and his edition of the writings of Saint Jerome both appeared in 1516.

Erasmus devoted his life to restoring the direct connection between the individual Christian and the textual basis of Christian doctrine. Although he is called the father of biblical criticism, Erasmus was not a theologian. He was more interested in the practical impact of ideas than in the ideas themselves. His scathing attacks upon the Scholastics, popular superstition, and the pretensions of the traditionalists in the Church and the universities all aimed at the same goal: to restore the experiences of Christ to the center of Christianity. Though his patrons were the rich and his language was Latin, Erasmus also hoped to reach men and women lower down the social order, those whom he believed the Church had failed to educate. "The doctrine of Christ casts aside no age, no sex, no fortune or position in life. It keeps no one at a distance."

In his life Erasmus encapsulated the intellectual reformation of the early sixteenth century. Taking advantage of the new technology of printing, Erasmus became a best-selling author able to influence thousands beyond his northern European home. He learned Greek, translated scripture, and wrote in the vernacular. Erasmus championed educational reforms, as did his friend Sir Thomas More, and a new spirit of critical thinking. The greatest of the Christian humanists, Erasmus imparted a vision that extended from the reorganization of the principles of scholarship to the reorientation of life in the Church, a vision that made possible religious reform.

The Lutheran Reformation

On the surface the Roman Catholic church at the end of the fifteenth century appeared as strong as ever. The growth of universities and the spread of the new learning had helped create a better-educated clergy. The printing press proved an even greater boon to the Church than it had to the humanists by making widely available both instructional manuals for priests and up-to-date service books for congregations. In Rome successive late medieval popes had managed to protect Church interests in the wake of the disintegration of the autonomous power of the Italian city-states. Popes had become first diplomats and then warriors in order to repel French and Spanish invaders. Rome was invaded, but never conquered. And it was more beautiful than ever as the great artists and craftsmen of the Renaissance built and adorned its churches. On the surface all was calm.

Yet everywhere in Europe the cry was for reform. Reform the venal papacy and its money-sucking bishops. Reform the ignorant clergy and the sacrilegious priests. Raise up the fallen nuns and the wayward friars. Wherever one turned one saw abuses. Parish livings were sold to the highest bidder to raise money. This was simony. Rich appointments were given to the kinsmen of powerful Church leaders rather than to those most qualified. This was nepotism. Individual clergymen accumulated numerous positions whose responsibilities they could not fulfill. This was pluralism. Some priests who took the vow of chastity lived openly with their concubines. Some mendicants who took the vow of poverty dressed in silk and ate from golden plates.

The cry for reform at the beginning of the sixteenth century came at a moment when people from all walks of life demanded greater spiritual fulfillment and held to higher standards those whose vocation it was to provide such fulfillment. Expectation rather than experience powered the demands for reform.

The Spark of Reform

Europe was becoming more religious. Cities hired preachers to expound the gospel. Pilgrims to the shrines of saints clogged the roadways every spring and summer. Rome remained the greatest attraction, but pilgrims covered the continent. The shrine of the apostle Saint James at Compostela in Spain was believed to cure the ill. Endowments of masses for the dead increased. Henry VII of England provided money for ten thousand masses to be said for his soul. In the chantries, where such services were performed, there were neither enough priests nor enough altars to supply the demand.

People wanted more from the Church than the Church could possibly give them. Humanists condemned visits to the shrines as superstitious; pilgrims demanded that the relics be made more accessible. Reformers complained of pluralism; the clergy complained that they could not live on the salary of a single office.

Civic authorities demanded that the established Church take greater responsibility for good works; the pope demanded that civic authorities help pay for them.

Contradiction and paradox dominated the movements for reform. Though the most vocal critics of the Church complained that its discipline was too lax, for many ordinary people its demands were too rigorous. The obligations of penance and confession weighed heavily upon them. Church doctrine held that sins had to be washed away before the souls of the dead could enter heaven. Until then they suffered in purgatory. Sins were cleansed through penance, the performance of acts of contrition assigned after confession. But the ordeal of confession kept many people away. "Have you skipped mass? Have you dressed proudly? Have you thought of committing adultery?" These were just a few of the uncomfortable questions that priests were instructed to pose in confession. In towns merchants were asked about their trading practices, shopkeepers about the quality of their goods.

Thus it is hardly surprising that the sale of indulgences became a popular substitute for penance and confession. An indulgence was a portion of the treasury of good works performed by righteous Christians throughout the ages. They could be granted to those who desired to atone for their sins. Strictly speaking, an indulgence supplemented penance rather than substituted for it. It was effective only for the contrite—for sinners who repented of their sins. But as the practice of granting indulgences spread, this subtle distinction largely disappeared. The living bought indulgences to cleanse the sins of the dead, and some even bought indulgences in anticipation of sins they had not yet committed.

By the sixteenth century, to limit abuses by local Church authorities, only the pope, through his agents, could grant indulgences. Popes used special occasions to offer an indulgence for pilgrimages to Rome or for contributions to special papal projects. Other indulgences were licensed locally, usually at the shrines of saints or at churches that contained relics.

The indulgence controversy was a symptom rather than a cause of the explosion of feelings that erupted in the small German town of Wittenberg in the year 1517. In that year the pope was offering an indulgence to help finance the rebuilding of Saint Peter's Basilica in Rome. The pope chose Prince Albert of Brandenburg (1490-1545) to distribute the indulgence in Germany, and Albert hired the Dominican friar Johann Tetzel (ca. 1465-1519) to preach its benefits. Tetzel offered little warning about the theological niceties of indulgences

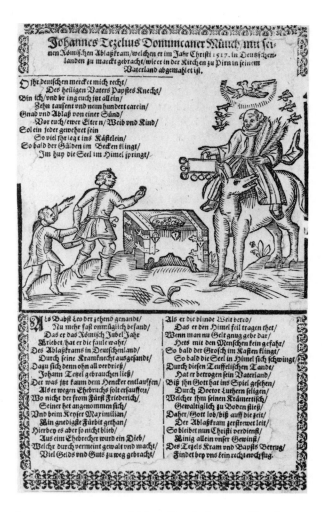

An anonymous caricature of Johann Tetzel, whose preaching of an indulgence inspired Martin Luther's Ninety-five Theses. Tetzel answered with 122 theses of his own, but was rebuked and disowned by the Catholics.

to those who paid to mitigate their own sins or alleviate the suffering of their ancestors in purgatory.

Enthusiasm for the indulgence spread to the neighboring state of Saxony, where the ruler, Frederick III, the Wise (1463–1525), banned its sale. Frederick's great collection of relics carried their own indulgences and Tetzel offered unwelcome competition. But Saxons flocked into Brandenburg to make their purchases, and by the end of October, Tetzel was not very far from Wittenberg Castle, where Frederick's relics were housed. On All Saints' Day the relics would be opened to view and, with the harvest done, one of the largest crowds of the year would gather to see them. On the night before, Martin Luther (1483–1546), a professor of

theology at Wittenberg University, posted on the door of the castle church ninety-five theses attacking indulgences and their sale.

Other than the timing of Luther's action, there was nothing unusual about the posting of theses. In the Scholastic tradition of disputation, scholars presented propositions, or theses, for debate and challenged all comers to argue with them in a public forum. Luther's theses were controversial, but as that was the whole point of offering them for discussion, they were meant to be. Only circumstance moved Luther's theses from the academic to the public sphere. Already there was growing concern among clergy and theologians about Tetzel's blatant sale of indulgences. Hordes of purchasers believed that they were buying unconditional remission of sin. Individual priests and monks began to sound the alarm: an indulgence without contrition was worthless.

Luther's theses focused this concern and finally communicated it beyond the walls of the church and university. The theses were immediately translated into German and spread throughout the Holy Roman Empire by humanists who had long criticized as superstitious such practices as the sale of indulgences. Prospective buyers became wary; past purchasers became angry. They had been duped again by the Church and by the Italian pope who cared nothing for honest hard-working Germans.

The Faith of Martin Luther

Martin Luther was not a man to challenge lightly. Although he was only an obscure German professor, he had already marked himself out to all who knew him. In his youth Luther was an exceptionally able student whose father sent him to the best schools in preparation for a career in law. But against the wishes of his father he entered an Augustinian monastery, wholeheartedly followed the strict program of his order, and was ordained a priest in 1507. He received his doctorate at the university in Wittenberg and was appointed to the theology faculty in 1512.

Luther attracted powerful patrons in the university and gained a reputation as an outstanding teacher. He began to be picked for administrative posts and became overseer of eleven Augustinian monasteries. His skills in disputation were widely recognized and he was sent to Rome to argue a case on behalf of his order. He fulfilled each task beyond expectation. In all outward appearances Luther was successful and contented.

But beneath this tranquil exterior lay a soul in torment. As he rose in others' estimation, he sank in his own. Through beating and fasting he mortified his flesh.

Through vigil and prayer he nourished his soul. Through study and contemplation he honed his intellect. Still he could find no peace. Despite his devotion, he could not erase his sense of sin; he could not convince himself that he could achieve the righteousness God demanded of him.

Knowledge of his salvation came to Luther through study. His internal agonies led him to ponder over and over again the biblical passages that described the righteousness of God. In the intellectual tradition in which he had been trained, that righteousness was equated with law. The righteous person either followed God's law or was punished by God's wrath. It was this understanding that tormented him. "I thought that I had to perform good works till at last through them Jesus would become a friend and gracious to me." But no amount of good works could overcome Luther's feelings of guilt for his sins. Almost from the moment he began lecturing in 1512 he searched for the key to the freedom of his own soul.

Even before he wrote his Ninety-five Theses, Luther had made the first breakthrough by a unique reading of the writings of Saint Paul. "I pondered night and day until I understood the connection between the righteousness of God and the sentence 'The just shall live by faith.' Then I grasped that the justice of God is the righteousness by which through grace and pure mercy, God justifies us through faith. Immediately I felt that I had been reborn and that I had passed through wide open doors into paradise!" Finally he realized that the righteousness of God was a gift freely given to the faithful. It was this belief that fortified Luther during his years of struggle with both civil and Church powers.

Over the next several years, Luther refined his spiritual philosophy and drew out the implications of his newfound beliefs. His religion was shaped by three interconnected tenets. First came justification by faith alone—*sola fide*. An individual's everlasting salvation came from faith in God's goodness rather than from the performance of good works. Sin could not be washed away by penance, and it could not be forgiven by indulgence. Second, faith in God's mercy came only through the knowledge and contemplation of the Word of God— *sola scriptura*. All that was needed to understand the

LUTHER ON THE RELATIONSHIP OF HUSBAND AND WIFE

■ *Martin Luther wrote thousands of pages of theological and devotional literature in establishing a new religious movement. His simple style and everyday examples made his message accessible to hundreds of thousands of ordinary people. In this selection from his tract* On Good Works *(1520) he compares the relationship of the husband and wife to that of the Christian and Christ.*

We can understand this whole matter [of good works] by an obvious human example. When husband and wife are fond of one another and live together in love and in confidence in one another, and each believes truly in the other, who shall teach them how they should act, what they should do or leave undone, say or not say, think or not think? Their own insight tells them all that need be, and more too. There is no distinction in their "works" for one another. They do the long, hard, and heavy tasks as willingly as the slight and easy things, and moreover they act with glad, peaceful, and secure hearts and are altogether free and unconstrained. But when doubt comes they begin to ask what is best, and begin to distinguish between their acts in order to gain the other's favor, and go about with troubled and heavy hearts, perhaps well-nigh in despair or driven to downright desperation.

So the Christian who lives in confidence toward God knows what things he should do, and does all gladly and freely, not with a view to accumulating merit and good works, but because it is his great joy to please God and to serve him without thought of reward, contented if he but do God's will. On the contrary, he who is not at one with God, or is in doubt, will begin to be anxious how he may satisfy God and justify himself by his works. He runs off on a pilgrimmage to St. James of Compostella, to Rome, to Jerusalem,—here, there, anywhere; prays to St. Bridget, or some other saint, fasts this day and that, confesses here and confesses there, asks this man and that, but finds no peace.

From Martin Luther, *On Good Works.*

justice and mercy of God was contained in the Bible. Reading the Word, hearing the Word, expounding upon and studying the Word, this was the path to faith and through faith to salvation. Finally, all who believed in God's righteousness and had achieved their faith through the study of the Bible were equal in God's eyes. The priesthood was of all believers. Each followed his or her own calling and found his or her own faith through Scripture. Ministers and preachers could help others learn God's Word, but they could not confer faith.

Luther's spiritual rebirth and the theology that developed from it posed a fundamental challenge to the Roman Catholic church. Though for centuries the Church had met doctrinal challenges and had absorbed many seemingly unorthodox ideas, Luther's theology could not be among them. It struck too deeply at the roots of belief, practice, and structure. Yet for all of the transforming power of these apparently simple ideas, it was not Luther alone who initiated the reform of religion. Justification by faith alone provided an alternative to the combination of works and faith that many Roman Catholics found too difficult to fulfill. Luther's insistence that faith comes only through the study of the Word of God was facilitated by the new learning and the invention of printing. The printing press prepared the ground for the dissemination of his thought as much as it disseminated it. This was a contribution of the Renaissance. Luther's hope for the creation of a spiritual elite, confirmed in their faith and confident of their salvation, readily appealed to the citizens of hundreds of German towns who had already made of themselves a social and economic elite. This was a contribution of the growth of towns. The idea of the equality of all believers meant that all were equally responsible for fulfilling God's commandments. This set secular rulers on an equal footing with the pope at a moment in Western history when they were already challenging papal power in matters of both church and state. For all his painful soul-searching, Luther embodied the culmination of changes of which he was only dimly aware.

From Luther to Lutheranism

The first to feel the seriousness of Luther's challenge to the established order was the reformer himself. The head of his order, a papal legate, and finally the Emperor Charles V all called for Luther to recant his views on indulgences. Excommunicated by Pope Leo X in 1521, Luther was ordered by Charles V to appear before the diet, or assembly, in Worms, Germany, in April of that year. The emperor demanded that Luther retract his teachings. To all he gave the same infuriating reply: if he could be shown the places in the Bible that contradicted his views he would gladly change them. Charles V declared Luther an enemy of the empire. In both church and state he was now an outlaw.

In fact, during the three years between the posting of his theses and his appearance before the Diet of Worms, Luther came to conclusions much more radical than his initial attack on indulgences. He came to believe that the papacy was a human rather than a divine invention. Therefore he denounced both the papacy and the general councils of the Church. In his *Address to the Christian Nobility of the German Nation* (1520) he called upon the princes to take the reform of religion into their own hands.

Martin Luther (far left), Zwingli, Melancthon, and other dissenters surround their protector, Elector John Frederick the Magnanimous.

But Luther had attracted powerful supporters as well as powerful enemies. Prince Frederick III of Saxony consistently intervened on his behalf, and the delicate international situation forced Luther's chief antagonists to move more slowly than they might have wished. The pope hoped first to keep Charles V off the imperial throne and then to maintain a united front with the German princes against him. Charles V, already locked in his lifelong struggle with the French, needed German military support and peace in his German territories. These factors consistently played into Luther's hands.

While pope and emperor were otherwise occupied, Luther refined his ideas and thus was able to hold his own in the theological debates in which he won important converts. More importantly, as time passed Luther's reputation grew, not only in Germany, but all over Europe. Between 1517 and 1520 he published thirty works, all of which achieved massive sales. Yet Luther alone could not sustain what came to be called Lutheranism. The Roman Catholic church had met heresy before and knew how to deal with it. What turned Luther's theology into a movement, which after 1529 came to be known as Protestantism, was the support he received among German princes and within German cities.

There were many reasons that individual princes turned to Luther's theology. First and foremost was sincere religious conviction. Matters of the hereafter were a pressing concern in a world in which the average life span was thirty years and nearly all natural phenomena were inexplicable. And they were more pressing still among the educated elites infected by the new learning and self-confident of their power to reason critically. Yet there were secular reasons as well. The formation of large states had provided a model for civil government. On a smaller scale, German princes worked to centralize their administration, protect themselves from predatory neighbors, and increase their revenues. Taxes and gifts flowed south to a papacy dominated by Italians. Luther's call for civil rulers to lead their own churches meant that civil rulers could keep their own revenues.

The Reformation spread particularly well in German cities, especially those that the emperor had granted the status of freedom from the rule of any prince. Once Protestant ideas were established entire towns adopted them. Many cities had long struggled with the tension of the separate jurisdictions of state and church. Much urban property was owned by the Church, and thus exempt from taxation and law enforcement, and the clergy constituted a significant proportion of urban populations. Reformed religion stressed the equality of clergy and laity and thus the indisputable power of civil

authorities. Paradoxically, it was because the cities contained large numbers of priests that Luther's ideas reached them quickly. Many of his earliest students served urban congregations and began to develop doctrines and practices that, though based on Luther's ideas, were adapted to the circumstances of city life. The reform clergy became integrated into the life of the city in a way that the Catholic clergy had not. They married the daughters of citizens, became citizens themselves, and trained their children in the guilds. Moreover, the imperial free cities were also the center of the printing trade and home to many of the most noted humanists, who were initially important in spreading Luther's ideas.

Luther's message held great appeal for the middle orders in the towns. While it was necessary for the leader of a state to support reform if it was to survive, in the cities it was the petty burghers, lesser merchants, tradesmen, and artisans who led the movements that ultimately gained the approval of city governments. These groups resented the privileges given to priests and members of religious orders, who paid no taxes and were exempt from the obligations of citizenship. The level of anticlericalism, always high in Germany, was especially acute in cities that were suffering economic difficulties. The evangelism of reforming ministers created converts and an atmosphere of reform. Support from members of the ruling oligarchy both mobilized these pressures and capitalized upon them. Town governments secured their own autonomy over the church, tightening their grip upon the institutions of social control and enhancing the social and economic authority of their members. Once Protestant, city governments took over many of the functions of the religious houses, often converting them into schools or hostels for the poor. Former monks were allowed to enter trades. Former nuns were encouraged to marry. Luther himself married an ex-nun after the dissolution of her convent.

Religious reform appealed to women as well as men, but it affected them differently. Noblewomen were among the most important defenders of Protestant reformers, especially in states in which the prince opposed it. Marguerite of Navarre (1492–1549), sister of Francis I, frequently intervened with her brother on behalf of individual Lutherans who fell afoul of Church authorities. She created her own court in the south of France and stocked it with both humanists and Protestants. Her devotional poem, *Mirror of the Sinful Soul* (1533), inspired women reformers and was translated into English by Elizabeth I. Mary of Hungary (1505–58) served a similar role in the Holy Roman Empire. Sister

Portrait of Marguerite de Valois, queen of Navarre, the cultured and talented sister of King Francis I.

of both Charles V and Ferdinand I, queen of Hungary and later regent of the Netherlands, Mary acted as patron to Hungarian reformers. Though she was more humanist than Protestant, Luther dedicated an edition of Psalms to her, and she read a number of his works. Her independent religious views infuriated both of her brothers. Bona, wife of Sigismund I of Poland, was especially important in eastern reform. An Italian by birth, Bona (1493–1558) was a central figure in spreading both Renaissance art and humanist learning into Poland. She became one of the largest independent landowners in the state and initiated widespread agricultural and economic reforms. Her private confessor was one of Poland's leading Protestants.

Luther's reforms also offered much to women who were not so highly placed in society. The doctrine of the equality of all believers put men and women on an equal spiritual footing even if it did nothing to break the male monopoly of the ministry. But the most important difference that Protestantism made to ordinary women was in the private rather than the public sphere. Family life became the center of faith when salvation was removed from the control of the Church. Luther's marriage led him to a deeper appreciation of the importance of the wife and mother in the family's spirituality.

By following humanist teaching on the importance of educating women of the upper orders and by encouraging literacy, the reformers did much that was uplifting. Girls' schools were founded in a number of German cities and townswomen could use their newly acquired skills in their roles as shopkeepers, family accountants, and teachers of their children. But there were losses as well as gains. The attack upon the worship of saints and especially of the Virgin Mary removed female images from religion. Protestantism was male-dominated in a way that Catholicism was not. Moreover, the emphasis upon reading the Bible tended to reinforce the image of women as weak and inherently sinful. The dissolution of the convents took away the one institution that valued their gender and allowed them to pursue a spiritual life outside marriage.

The Spread of Lutheranism

By the end of the 1520s the empire was divided between cities and states that accepted reformed religion and those that adhered to Roman Catholicism. Printing presses, traveling merchants, and hordes of students who claimed—not always truthfully—to have attended Luther's lectures or sermons spread the message. Large German communities across northern Europe, mostly founded as trading outposts, became focal points for the penetration of reformist ideas. In Livonia the Teutonic Knights established a Lutheran form of worship that soon took hold all along the shores of the Baltic. Lutheran-inspired reformers seized control of the Polish port city of Gdansk, which they held for a short time, while neighboring Prussia officially established a Lutheran church. Polish translations of Luther's writings were disseminated into Poland-Lithuania, and Protestant communities were established as far south as Kraków.

Merchants and students carried Luther's ideas into Scandinavia, but there the importance of political leaders was crucial. Christian III (1534–59) of Denmark had been present at the Diet of Worms when Luther made his famous reply to Charles V. Christian was deeply impressed by the reformer and after a ruinous civil war, confiscated Catholic church property in Denmark and created a reformed religion under Luther's direct supervision.

Paradoxically, Lutheranism came to Sweden as part of an effort to throw off the yoke of Danish dominance.

Cartoon showing Martin Luther carting a host of former priests away from their vows of chastity, followed by his wife, the former nun Katharina von Bora.

Here, too, direct connection with Luther provided the first impulses. Olaus Petri (1493–1552) had studied at Wittenberg and returned to preach Lutheran doctrine among the large German merchant community in Stockholm. He was a trained humanist who used both Erasmus's Greek New Testament and Luther's German one to prepare his Swedish translation (1526). When Gustav I Vasa (1523–60) led a successful uprising against the Danes and became king of Sweden, he encouraged the spread of Protestant ideas and allowed Petri to continue his translations of the mass and the Lutheran service. Luther's impact extended into central Europe.

Bohemia had had a reforming tradition of its own that antedated Luther. Though the teachings of Jan Hus (1373–1415) had been condemned by the Catholic church, Hussitism was in fact the all but established religion in most parts of Bohemia. Ferdinand I, king of Bohemia, was bound by law to allow its moderate practice. Hussites had already initiated many reforms, for Luther had been influenced by Hus. The mass was said in Czech, and the Bible had been translated into the vernacular. Hussites believed that communion in both forms was mandated by the Bible. This was the real issue that separated them from Roman Catholics, for the Hussites refused to accept the traditional view that the authority of either the pope or the general council of the Church could alter God's command. On all these issues, Hussites and Lutherans shared a common program. But the Hussites were conservative in almost everything else. While the German communities in Bohemia accepted the core of Lutheran doctrine, most Czechs rejected justification by faith alone and maintained their own practices.

As important as Protestant ideas were in northern and central Europe, it was in the Swiss towns of the empire that they proved most fertile. Here was planted the second generation of reformers, theologians who drew from Luther's insights radical new conclusions. In the east, Huldrych Zwingli (1484–1531) brought reformed religion to the town of Zurich. Educated at the University of Basel and deeply influenced by humanist thought early in his career, Zwingli was a preacher among the Swiss mercenary troops that fought for the empire. In 1516 he met Erasmus in Basel and under his influence began a study of the Greek writings of the Church Fathers and of the New Testament. Zwingli was also influenced by reports of Luther's defiance of the pope, for his own antipapal views were already developing. Perhaps most decisively for his early development, in 1519 Zwingli was stricken by plague. In his life-and-death struggle he came to a profoundly personal realization of the power of God's mercy.

These experiences became the basis for the reform theology Zwingli preached in Zurich. He believed that the Church had to recover its earlier purity and reject the innovations in practices brought in by successive popes and general councils. He stressed the equality of believers, justification by faith alone, and the sufficiency of the gospel as authority for church practice. He attacked indulgences, penance, clerical celibacy, prayers to the Virgin, statues and images in churches, and a long list of other abuses. He also stressed that the mass was to be viewed as a commemorative event rather than one that involved the real presence of Christ. He preferred to call the service the Lord's Supper. His arguments were so effective that the town council adopted them as the basis for a reform of religion.

The principles Zwingli preached quickly spread to neighboring Swiss states. He participated in formal religious disputations in both Bern and Basel. In both places his plea for a simple, unadorned religious practice met widespread approval. Practical as well as theological, Zwingli's reforms were carried out by the civil government, with which he allied himself. This was not the same as the protection that princes had given to Lutherans. Rather, in the places that came under Zwingli's influence, there was an important integration of church and state. He stressed the divine origins of civil government and the importance of the magistrate as an agent of Christian reform. "A church without the magistrate is mutilated and incomplete." This theocratic idea—that the leaders of the state and the leaders of the church

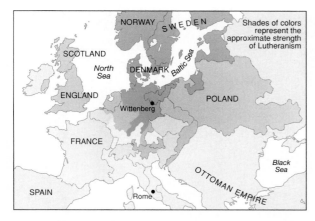

The Spread of Lutheranism

were linked—became the basis for further social and political reform.

The reformation that had begun with the personal struggles of an individual German priest had now spread across Europe. Luther's quest for salvation transformed religious life for millions of people. His insistence on reading the Scriptures, preaching the word, and living through faith struck a responding chord everywhere. Though he was excommunicated and banished from the Holy Roman Empire, Luther was protected by princes who were soon labeled Protestant. The conversion of princes and the spread of Lutheranism in towns ensured that the new religion would become a powerful political force even beyond the boundaries of the empire. In Scandinavia, Bohemia, and the Swiss cantons the message received a ready reception. In barely more than a decade a new religion had been established.

The Protestant Reformation

By the middle of the 1530s Protestant reform had entered a new stage. Luther did not intend to form a new religion; his struggle had been with Rome. Before he could build he had to tear down—his religion was one of protest. Most of his energy was expended in attack and counterattack. The second generation of reformers faced a different task. The new reformers were the church builders who had to systematize doctrine for a generation that had already accepted religious reform. Their challenge was to draw out the logic of reformed ideas and to create enduring structures for reformed churches. The problems they faced were as much institutional as doctrinal. How was the new church to be governed in the

absence of the traditional hierarchy? How could discipline be enforced when members of the reformed community went astray? What was the proper relationship between the community of believers and civil authority? Whatever the failings of the Roman Catholic church, it had ready answers to these critical questions.

Geneva and Calvin

The Reformation came late to Geneva. In the sixteenth century Geneva was under the dual government of the Duchy of Savoy and the Catholic bishop of the town, who was frequently a Savoy client. The Genevans also had their own town council, which traditionally struggled for power against the bishop. By the 1530s the council had gained the upper hand. The council confiscated Church lands and institutions, secularized the Church's legal powers, and forced the bishop and most of his administrators to flee the city. War with Savoy inevitably followed and Geneva would certainly have been crushed into submission except for its alliance with neighboring Bern, a potent military power among the Swiss towns. Geneva was saved and was free to follow its own course in religious matters. In 1536 the adult male citizens of the city voted to become Protestant. But as yet there was no reformer in Geneva to establish a Protestant program and no clear definition of what that program might be.

Martin Luther had started out to become a lawyer and ended up a priest. John Calvin started out to become a priest and ended up a lawyer. The difference tells much about each man. Calvin (1509–64) was born in France, the son of a bishop's secretary. His education was based on humanist principles, and he learned Greek and Hebrew, studied theology, and received a legal degree from the University of Orléans. Around the age of twenty he converted to Lutheranism. Francis I had determined to root Protestants out of France, and Calvin fled Paris after one of his close friends was burned for heresy. These events left an indelible impression upon him. In 1535 he left France for Basel, where he wrote and published the first edition of his *Institutes of the Christian Religion* (1536), a defense of French Protestants against persecution. Calvin returned briefly to France to wind up his personal affairs, and then decided to settle in Strasbourg, where he could retire from public affairs and live out his days as a scholar.

To Calvin, providence guided all human action. He could have no better evidence for this belief than what happened next. War between France and the empire clogged the major highways to Strasbourg. Thus Calvin

This painting shows a Calvinist service in Lyon, France, in 1564. The sexes are segregated and the worshipers are seated according to rank. An hourglass times the preacher's sermon.

and his companions detoured through Geneva, where Guillaume Farel (1489–1565), one of Geneva's leading Protestant reformers, implored Calvin to remain in Geneva and lead its reformation. Calvin was not interested. Farel tried every means of persuasion he knew until, in exasperation, Farel declared "that God would curse my retirement if I should withdraw and refuse to help when the necessity was so urgent." For a quarter of a century, Calvin labored to bring order to the Genevan church.

Calvin's greatest contributions to religious reform came in church structure and discipline. He had studied the writings of the first generation of reformers and accepted without question justification by faith alone and the biblical foundation of religious authority. Like Luther and Zwingli he believed that salvation came from God's grace. But more strongly than his predecessors he believed that the gift of faith was granted only to some and that each individual's salvation or damnation was predestined before birth. The doctrine of predestination was a traditional one, but Calvin emphasized it differently and brought it to the center of the problem of faith. "Many are called but few are chosen," Calvin quoted from the Bible. Those who were predestined to salvation, the "elect," were obliged to govern; those who were predestined to damnation were obliged to be governed.

Calvin structured the institution of the Genevan church in four parts. First were the pastors who preached the Word to their congregations. While the pastors preached, the doctors, the second element in Calvin's church, studied and wrote. Deacons, the third element in Calvin's four-part structure, were laymen chosen by the congregation to oversee the institutions of social welfare, such as hospitals and schools, run by the church. The last element were the elders of the church, who were its governors in all moral matters. They were the most controversial part of Calvin's establishment and the most fundamental. They had the power to discipline. Chosen from among the elite of the city, the twelve elders enforced the strict Calvinist moral code that extended into all aspects of private life. Sexual offenses were the most common. Adultery and fornication were vigorously suppressed and prostitutes, who had nearly become a recognized guild in the early sixteenth century, were expelled from Geneva.

The structure that Calvin gave to the Genevan church soon became the basis for reforms throughout the Continent. The Calvinist church was self-governing, independent of the state, and therefore capable of surviving and even flourishing in a hostile environment. Expanded in several subsequent editions, *Institutes of the Christian Religion* became the most influential work of Protestant theology. It had begun as an effort to extend Protestantism to Calvin's homeland, and waves of Calvinist-educated pastors returned to France in the mid-sixteenth century and established churches along Calvinist lines. Calvinism spread north

CALVIN ON PREDESTINATION

■ *John Calvin was born in France but led the reformation in the Swiss town of Geneva. He was one of the leaders of the second generation of reformers, whose task was to refine church doctrinal structure. Calvinism was propounded in* Institutes of the Christian Religion *(1534), from which this section on the doctrine of predestination is taken.*

We must be content with this,—that such gifts as it pleased the Lord to have bestowed upon the nature of man he vested in Adam; and therefore when Adam lost them after he had received them, he lost them not only from himself but also from us all . . . Therefore from a rotten root rose up rotten branches, which sent their rottenness into the twigs that sprang out of them; for so were the children corrupted in their father that they in turn infected their children . . .

And the apostle Paul himself expressly witnesseth that therefore death came upon all men, because all men have sinned and are wrapped in original sin and defiled with the spots thereof. And therefore the very infants themselves, since they bring with them their own damnation from their mothers' womb, are bound not by another's but by their own fault. For although they have not as yet brought forth the fruits of their own iniquity, yet they have the seeds thereof inclosed within them; yea, their whole nature is a certain seed of sin, therefore it cannot be hateful and abominable to God . . .

Predestination we call the eternal decree of God, whereby he has determined with himself what he wills to become of every man. For all are not created to like estate; but to some eternal life and to some eternal damnation is foreordained. Therefore as every man is created to the one or the other end, so we say that he is predestinate either to life or to death.

From John Calvin, *Institutes of the Christian Religion.*

to Scotland and the Low Countries, where it became the basis for Dutch Protestantism, and east, where it flourished in Lithuania and Hungary. It reached places untouched by Luther and revitalized reform where Lutheranism had been suppressed. Perhaps its greatest impact was in Britain, where the Reformation took place not once but twice.

The English Reformation

The king of England wanted a divorce. Henry VIII had been married to Catherine of Aragon (1485–1536) as long as he had been king, and she had borne him no male heir to carry on his line. She had given birth to six children and endured several miscarriages, yet only one daughter, Mary, survived. Nothing so important as the lack of a male heir could happen by accident, and Henry came to believe that it was God's punishment for his marriage. Catherine had been married first to Henry's older brother, who had died as a teenager, and there was at least one scriptural prohibition against marrying a

brother's wife. A papal dispensation had been provided for the marriage, and now Henry wanted a papal dispensation for an annulment. For three years his case ground its way through the papal courts. Catherine of Aragon was the aunt of the Emperor Charles V, and the emperor had taken her side in the controversy. With imperial power in Italy at its height, the pope was content to hear all of the complex legal and biblical precedents argued at leisure.

By 1533 Henry could wait no longer. He had already impregnated Anne Boleyn (ca. 1507–36), one of the ladies-in-waiting at his court, and if the child—which Henry was certain would be a boy—was to be legitimate a marriage would have to take place at once. Legislation was prepared in Parliament to prevent papal interference in the decisions of England's courts, and Thomas Cranmer (1489–1556), archbishop of Canterbury, England's highest ecclesiastical officer, agreed to annul Henry's first marriage and celebrate his second. This was the first step in a complete break with Rome. Under the guidance of Thomas Cromwell (ca. 1485–1540), the

English Parliament passed statute after statute that made Henry supreme head of the church in England and owner of its vast wealth. Monasteries were dissolved, and a Lutheran service was introduced. On 7 September 1533, Anne Boleyn gave birth not to the expected son, but to a daughter, the future Queen Elizabeth I.

Henry's reformation was an act of state, but the English Reformation was not. There was an English tradition of dissent from the Roman church that stretched back to the fourteenth century. Anticlericalism was especially virulent in the towns, where citizens refused to pay fees to priests for performing services like burial. And humanist ideas flourished in England, where Thomas More, John Colet, and a host of others supported both the new learning and its efforts to reform spiritual life. Luther's attack on ritual and the mass and his emphasis on Scripture and faith echoed the lost Lollard program and found many recruits in London and the northern port towns.

Protestantism grew slowly in England because it was vigorously repressed. Like Francis I and Charles V, Henry VIII viewed actual attacks on the established church as potential attacks on the established state. The first published English translation of the New Testament, made by William Tyndale in 1525, had to be smuggled into England. As sensitivity to the abuses of the Church grew and Lutheran ideas spread, official persecution sharpened.

Henry's divorce unleashed a groundswell of support for religious change. The king's own religious beliefs remained a secret, but Anne Boleyn and Thomas Cromwell sponsored Lutheran reforms and Thomas Cranmer put them into practice. Religion was legislated through Parliament, and the valuable estates of the Church were sold to the gentry. These practices found favor with both the legal profession and the landed elites and made Protestantism more palatable among these conservative groups. It was in the reign of Edward VI (1547–53), Henry's son by his third wife, that the central doctrinal and devotional changes were made. Church service was now conducted in English and the first two English Prayer Books were created. The mass was reinterpreted along Zwinglian lines and became the Lord's Supper, the altar became the communion table, and the priest became the minister. Preaching became the center of the church service and concern over the education of learned ministers resulted in commissions to examine and reform the clergy.

Beginning in the 1530s, state repression turned against Catholics. Those who would not swear the new oaths of allegiance or recognize the legality of Henry VIII's marriage suffered for their beliefs. Thomas More and over forty others paid with their lives for their opposition. An uprising in the north in 1536, known as the Pilgrimage of Grace, posed the most serious threat to the English Crown since the Wars of the Roses. Henry's ability to suppress the Pilgrimage of Grace owed more

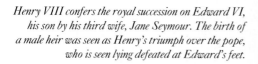

Henry VIII confers the royal succession on Edward VI, his son by his third wife, Jane Seymour. The birth of a male heir was seen as Henry's triumph over the pope, who is seen lying defeated at Edward's feet.

to his political power than to the conversion of his governing classes to Protestantism. Catholicism continued to flourish in England, surviving underground during the reigns of Henry and Edward, and reemerging under Mary I (1553–58).

Mary Tudor was her mother's child. The first woman to rule England, she held to the Catholic beliefs in which Catherine of Aragon had raised her, and she vowed to bring the nation back to her mother's church. She reestablished papal sovereignty, abolished Protestant worship, and introduced a crash program of education in the universities to train a new generation of priests. The one thing that Mary could not achieve was restoration of monastic properties and Church lands. They had been scattered irretrievably and any attempt at confiscation from the landed elite would surely have been met with insurrection. Catholic retribution for the blood of their martyrs was not long in coming. Cranmer and three other bishops were burned for heresy.

Nearly 800 Protestants fled the country rather than suffer a similar fate. These Marian exiles, as they came to be called, settled in a number of reformed communities. There they imbibed the second generation of Protestant ideas, especially Calvinism, and from there they began a propaganda campaign to keep reformed religion alive in England. It was the Marian exiles who were chiefly responsible for the second English reformation, which began in 1558 when Mary died and her half-sister, Elizabeth I (1558–1603), came to the throne.

Under Elizabeth, England returned to Protestantism, but what was reestablished was not what had come before. Even the most advanced reforms during Edward's reign now seemed too moderate for the returning exiles. Against Elizabeth's wishes, the English church adopted the Calvinist doctrine of predestination and the simplification (but not wholesale reorganization) of the structure of the church. But it did not become a model of thoroughgoing reformation. The Thirty-nine Articles (1563) continued the English tradition of compromising points of disputed doctrine and of maintaining traditional practices wherever possible.

The Reformation of the Radicals

Schism breeds schism. That was the stick with which the Catholic church and civil authorities beat Luther from the beginning. By attacking the authority of the established church and flouting the authority of the established state he was fomenting social upheaval. But he insisted that his own ideas buttressed rather than subverted authority, especially civil authority under

whose protection he had placed the Church. As early as 1525 peasants in Swabia appealed to Luther for support in their social rebellion. They based some of their most controversial demands, such as the abolition of tithes and labor service, on biblical authority. Luther instructed the rebels to lay down their arms and await their just rewards in heaven. But Luther's ideas had a life of their own. He clashed with Erasmus over free will and with Zwingli over the mass. Toward the end of his life he felt he was holding back the floodgates against the second generation of Protestant thinkers. Time and again serious reformers wanted to take one or another of his doctrines further than he was willing to go himself. The water was seeping in everywhere.

The most dangerous threat to the establishment of an orthodox Protestantism came from groups who were described, not very precisely, as Anabaptists. Though it identified people who practiced adult baptism—literally "baptism again"—the label was mainly used to tar religious opponents with the brush of extremism. Anabaptists appeared in a number of German and Swiss towns in the 1520s. Taking seriously the doctrine of justification by faith, Anabaptists argued that only believers could be members of the true church of God. Those who were not of God could not be members of his church. As baptism was the sacrament through which entry into the church took place, Anabaptists reasoned that it was a sacrament for adults rather than infants. But infant baptism was a core doctrine for both Catholics and Protestants. It symbolized the acceptance of Christ and without it eternal salvation was impossible. Unbaptized infants who died could not be accepted in heaven, and infant mortality was appallingly common.

Thus the doctrine of Anabaptism posed a psychological as well as a doctrinal threat to the reformers. But the practice of adult baptism paled in significance to many of the other conclusions that religious radicals derived from the principle of *sola scriptura*—by the Word alone. Some groups argued the case that since true Christians were only those who had faith, all others must be cast out of the church. These true Christians formed small separate sects. Many believed that their lives were guided by the Holy Spirit who directed them from within. Some went further and denied the power of civil authority over true believers. Some argued for the community of goods among believers and rejected private property. Others literally followed passages in the Old Testament that suggested polygamy and promiscuity.

Wherever they settled, these small bands of believers were persecuted to the brutal extent of the laws of heresy. Catholics burned them, Protestants drowned them, and they were stoned and clubbed out of their communities. There was enough substance in their ideas and enough sincerity in their patient sufferings that they continued to recruit followers as they were driven from town to town, from Germany into the Swiss cities, from Switzerland into Bohemia and Hungary.

There on the eastern edges of the empire the largest groups of Anabaptists finally settled. Though all practiced adult baptism, only some held goods in common or remained pacifist. Charismatic leaders such as Balthasar Hubmaier (1485–1528) and Jacob Hutter (d. 1536) spread Anabaptism to Moravia in southern Bohemia, where they converted a number of the nobility to their views. They procured land for their communities, which came to be known as the Moravian Brethren. Independent groups existed in England and throughout northwest Europe, where Menno Simons (1496–1561), a Dutch Anabaptist, spent his life organizing bands of followers who came to be known as Mennonites.

The reformation begun by Luther was spread by different hands. The second-generation reformers, led by John Calvin, deepened theological and social changes. Calvin's emphasis upon predestination generated a vanguard of Protestant saints who believed it was their duty to govern on earth. They reordered church government and redefined moral discipline. Calvinism spread in Switzerland and France, but most importantly in England, where it was adopted as the foundation of the Elizabethan church. Though Calvinism was the most influential of the new forms of Protestantism, it was not the only one. Anabaptists could be found in a number of Swiss and German towns, and they were especially influential in Bohemia and Hungary. Together with the Lutherans, these groups and their churches constituted a potent new religious force in Europe.

The Catholic Reformation

Like a rolling wave Protestant reform slapped up across the face of Europe, but the rock of the Roman Catholic church endured. Though pieces of the universal church crumbled away, in northern Germany, Switzerland, Bohemia, Scandinavia, England, and Scotland, the dense mass remained in southern Germany, Italy, Poland-Lithuania, Spain, France, and Ireland. Catholics felt the same impulses toward a more fulfilling religious life as did Protestants and complained of the same abuses of clerical, state, and papal powers. But the Catholic re-

sponse was to reform the Church from within. A new personal piety was stressed, which led to the founding of additional spiritual orders. The ecclesiastical hierarchy became more concerned with pastoral care and initiated reforms of the clergy at the parish level. The challenge of converting other races, Asians and Native Americans especially, led to the formation of missionary orders and to a new emphasis on preaching and education. Protestantism itself revitalized Catholicism.

The Spiritual Revival

The quest for individual spiritual fulfillment dominated later medieval Roman Catholicism. Erasmus, Luther, and Zwingli were all influenced by a Catholic spiritual movement known as the New Piety. It was propagated in Germany by the Brethren of the Common Life, a lay organization that stressed the importance of personal meditation upon the life of Christ. *The Imitation of Christ* (1427), the central text of the New Piety, commonly attributed to Thomas à Kempis (1379–1471), was among the most influential works of the later Middle Ages. The Brethren taught that a Christian life should be lived according to Christ's dictates as expressed in the Sermon on the Mount. They instructed their pupils to lead a simple ascetic life with personal devotion at its core. These were the lessons that the young Erasmus found so liberating and the young Luther so stifling.

The New Piety, with its emphasis on a simple personal form of religious practice, was a central influence upon Christian humanism. It is important to realize that humanism developed within the context of Catholic education and that many churchmen embraced the new learning and supported educational reform or patronized works of humanist scholarship. The Polyglot Bible was organized by Cardinal Jiménez de Cisneros (1436–1517), Archbishop of Toledo and Primate of Spain. Without any of his famed irony, Erasmus dedicated his Greek Bible to the pope.

This combination of piety and humanism imbued the ecclesiastical reforms initiated by Church leaders. Archbishop Jiménez de Cisneros, who also served as Inquisitor-General of the Spanish Inquisition, undertook a wide-ranging reorganization of Spanish religious life in the late fifteenth century. Though not every project was successful, Jiménez de Cisneros's program took much of the sting out of Protestant attacks on clerical abuse, and there was never a serious Protestant movement in Spain.

The most influential reforming bishop was Gian Matteo Giberti (1495–1543) of Verona. Using his own frugal life as an example, Giberti rigorously enforced vows, residency, and the pastoral duties of the clergy. He founded almshouses to aid the poor and orphanages to house the homeless. In Verona Giberti established a printing press, which turned out editions of the central works of Roman Catholicism, especially the writings of Augustine.

The most important indication of the reforming spirit within the Roman church was the foundation of new religious orders in the early sixteenth century. Devotion to a spiritual life of sacrifice was the chief characteristic of the lay and clerical orders that had flourished throughout the Middle Ages. In one French diocese, the number of clergy quadrupled in the last half of the fifteenth century, and while entrants to the traditional orders of Franciscans and Dominicans did not rise as quickly, the growth of lay communities like the Brethren of the Common Life attested to the continuing appeal of Catholic devotionalism.

Devotionalism was particularly strong in Italy where a number of new orders received papal charters. The Capuchins were founded by the Italian peasant Matteo de Bascio (ca. 1495–1552). He sought to follow the strictest rule of the life of Saint Francis of Assisi, a path that even the so-called Observant Franciscans had found too arduous. In contrast, the Theatines were established by a group of well-to-do Italian priests who also wished to lead a more austere devotional existence than was to be found in the traditional orders. Like the Capuchins they accepted a life of extreme poverty, in which even begging was only a last resort.

This spiritual revival spread all over Catholic Europe and was not limited to male orders. In Spain, Saint Teresa of Avila (1515–82) led the reform of the Carmelites. She believed that women had to withdraw totally from the world around them in order to achieve true devotion. Against the wishes of the male superiors

FROM *THE LIFE OF SAINT TERESA*

■ *Teresa of Avila was a Carmelite nun whose life became a model of spirituality for Spanish Catholics in the seventeenth century. She founded a number of monasteries and convents and wrote popular devotional literature. Her autobiography was published after her death.*

My love of, and trust in, our Lord, after I had seen Him in a vision, began to grow, for my converse with Him was so continual. I saw that, though He was God, He was man also; that He is not surprised at the frailties of men; that He understands our miserable nature, liable to fall continually, because of the first sin, for the reparation of which He had come. I could speak to Him as a friend, though He is my Lord, because I do not consider Him as one of our earthly lords, who affect a power they do not possess, who give audience at fixed hours, and to whom only certain persons may speak. If a poor man have any business with these, it will cost him many goings and comings, and currying favour with others, together with much pain and labour before he can speak to them. Ah, if such a one has business with a king! Poor people, not of gentle blood, cannot approach him, for they must apply to those who are his friends; and certainly these are not persons who tread the world under their feet; for they who do this speak the truth, fear nothing, and ought to fear nothing; they are not courtiers, because it is not the custom of a court, where they must be silent about those things they dislike, must not even dare to think about them, lest they should fall into disgrace.

O my Lord! O my King! who can describe Thy Majesty? It is impossible not to see that Thou art Thyself the great Ruler of all, that the beholding of Thy Majesty fills men with awe. But I am filled with greater awe, O my Lord, when I consider Thy humility, and the love Thou hast for such as I am. We can converse and speak with Thee about everything whenever we will; and when we lose our first fear and awe at the vision of Thy Majesty, we have a greater dread of offending Thee—not arising out of the fear of punishment, O my Lord, for that is as nothing in comparison with the loss of Thee!

of her order she founded a convent to put her beliefs into practice and began writing devotional tracts like *The Way of Perfection* (1583). In 1535 Angela Merici (ca. 1474–1540) established another female order. The Ursulines were one of the most original of the new foundations, composed of young unmarried girls who remained with their families but lived chaste lives devoted to the instruction of other women.

Loyola's Pilgrimage

At first sight Saint Ignatius of Loyola (1491–1556) appears an unlikely candidate to lead one of the most vital movements for religious reform in the sixteenth century. The thirteenth child of a Spanish noble family, Loyola trained for a military life in the service of Castile. In 1521 he was one of the garrison defenders when the French besieged Pamplona. A cannonball shattered his leg, and he was carried home for a long enforced convalescence. There he slowly and carefully read the only books in the castle, a life of Christ and a history of the saints. His reading inspired him.

Loyola was not a man to do things halfway. He resolved to model his life on the sufferings of the saints about whom he had read. He renounced his worldly goods and endured a year-long regimen of physical abstinence and spiritual nourishment in the town of Manresa. He deprived himself of food and sleep for long periods and underwent a regimen of seven hours of daily prayer, supplemented by nearly continuous religious contemplation. "But when he went to bed great enlightenment, great spiritual consolations often came to him, so that he lost much of the time he had intended for sleeping." During this period of intense concentration he first began to have visions, which later culminated in a mystical experience in which Christ called him directly to his service.

Like Luther, Loyola was tormented by his inability to achieve grace through penance, but unlike Luther he redoubled his efforts. At Manresa Loyola encountered the *Imitation of Christ*, which profoundly influenced his conversion. He recorded the techniques he used during this vigil in *The Spiritual Exercises*, which became a handbook for Catholic devotion. In 1523, crippled and barefoot, he made a pilgrimage to Jerusalem. He returned to Spain intent upon becoming a priest.

By this time Loyola had taken on a distinctive appearance that attracted a following but also suspicion. Twice the Spanish ecclesiastical authorities summoned him to be examined for heresy. In 1528 he decided to complete his studies in France. Education in France

St. Teresa of Avila, the Carmelite reformer. The personal example and devotional works of this mystic and visionary inspired a rebirth of Catholicism in Spain.

brought with it a broadening of horizons that was so important in the movement that Loyola was to found. He entered the same college that Calvin had just left, but given his own devotional experiences, Protestantism held little attraction. While in France, Loyola and a small group of his friends decided to form a brotherhood after they became priests. They devoted themselves to the cure of souls and took personal vows of poverty, chastity, and obedience to the pope. On a pilgrimage to Rome, Loyola and his followers again attracted the attention of ecclesiastical authorities. Loyola explained his mission to them and in 1540 won the approval of Pope Paul III to establish a new holy order, the Society of Jesus.

Loyola's Society was founded at a time when the spiritual needs of the church were being extended beyond the confines of Europe. Loyola volunteered his followers, who came to be known as Jesuits, to serve in the remotest parts of the world. One disciple, Francis Xavier (1506–52), made converts to Catholicism in the Portuguese port cities in the East and then in India and Japan. Other Jesuits became missionaries to the New World, where they offered Christian consolation to the Native American communities. By 1556 the Society of Jesus had grown from ten to a thousand and Loyola had become a full-time administrator in Rome.

Loyola never abandoned the military images that had dominated his youth. He enlisted his followers in military terms. The Jesuits were "soldiers of God" who served "beneath the banner of the Cross." Loyola's most fundamental innovation in these years was the founding of schools to train recruits for his order. Jesuit training was rigorous. Since they were being prepared for an active rather than a contemplative life, Jesuits were not cloistered during their training. Jesuit schools were opened to the laity and lay education became one of the Jesuits' most important functions. Loyola lived to see the establishment of nearly a hundred colleges and seminaries and the spread of his order throughout the world. He died while at prayer.

The Counter-Reformation

The Jesuits were both the culmination of one wave of Catholic reform and the advance guard of another. They combined the piety and devotion that stretched from medieval mysticism through humanism, diocesan reforms, and the foundations of new spiritual orders. But they also represented an aggressive Catholic response that was determined to meet Protestantism head on and repel it. This was the Church militant. Old instruments like the Inquisition were revived, and new weapons like the Index of prohibited books were created. But the problems of fighting Protestantism were not only those of combating Protestant ideas. Like oil and water, politics and religion failed to combine. The Holy Roman Emperor Charles V and the hierarchy of the German church, where Protestantism was strong, demanded thoroughgoing reform of the Catholic church; the pope and the hierarchy of the Italian church, where Protestantism was weak, resisted the call. As head of the Catholic church, the pope was distressed by the spread of heresy in the lands of the empire. As head of a large Italian city-state the pope was consoled by the weakening of the power of his Spanish rival. Brothers in Christ, pope and emperor were mortal enemies in everything else. Throughout the Catholic states of Germany came the urgent cry for a reforming council of the Church. But the voices were muffled as they crossed the Alps and made their way down the Italian peninsula.

At the instigation of Charles V, the first serious preparations for a general council of the Church were made in the 1530s. The papacy warded it off. The complexities of international diplomacy were one factor—the French king was even less anxious to bring peace to the Holy Roman Empire than was the pope—and the complexities of papal politics were another. The powers of a general council in relation to the powers of the papacy had never been clarified. In fact, Catholic reformers were as bitter in their denunciations of papal abuses as were Protestants. The second attempt to arrange a general council of the Church occurred in the early 1540s. Again the papacy warded it off.

These factors ensured that when a general council of the Church did finally meet, its task would not be an easy one. The northern churches, French and German alike, wanted reforms of the papacy; the papacy wanted a restatement of orthodox doctrine. Many princes whose states were divided among Catholics and Protestants wanted compromises that might accommodate both. Ferdinand I, king of Bohemia, saw the council as an opportunity to bring the Hussites back into the fold. Charles V and the German bishops wanted the leading Protestant church authorities to offer their own compromises on doctrine that might form a basis for reuniting the empire. The papacy wanted traditional Church doctrine reasserted.

The general council of the Church that finally met in Trent from 1545 to 1563 thus had nearly unlimited potential for disaster. It began in compromise—Trent was an Italian town under the government of the emperor—

Spanish wood carving showing St. Ignatius Loyola, the founder of the Society of Jesus.

but ended in total victory for the views of the papacy. For all of the papacy's seeming weaknesses—the defections of England and the rich north German territories cut into papal revenues, and Italy was under Spanish occupation—an Italian pope always held the upper hand at the council. Fewer than one-third of the delegates came from outside Italy. The French looked upon the council suspiciously and played only a minor role, and the emperor forbade his bishops to attend after the council moved to Bologna.

Yet for all of these difficulties, the councillors at Trent made some real progress. They corrected a number of abuses, of which the sale of indulgences was the most substantive. They formulated rules for the better regulation of parish priests and stressed the obligation of priests and bishops to preach to their congregations. They ordered seminaries to be founded in all dioceses where there was not already a university so that priests could receive sufficient education to perform their duties. They prepared a new modern and uniform Catholic service and centralized and updated the Index of prohibited books to include Protestant writings from all over the Continent.

The Council of Trent made no concessions to Protestants, moderate or radical. The councillors upheld justification by faith and works over justification by faith alone. They confirmed the truth of Scripture and the traditions of the Church against Scripture alone. They declared the Vulgate the only acceptable text of the Bible and encouraged vast bonfires of Greek and Hebrew Scriptures in an effort to undo the great scholarly achievements of the humanists. They reaffirmed traditional Catholic doctrines. They upheld clerical celibacy. The redefinition of traditional Roman Catholicism drew the doctrinal lines clearly and ended decades of confusion. But it also meant that the differences between Catholics and Protestants could now be settled only by the sword.

The resolutions of the Council of Trent demonstrated the vitality and self-confidence of Roman Catholicism. The pietistic movements that had founded new spiritual orders for men and women, the zealotry that had inspired Ignatius of Loyola and his Jesuits—these could be seen in every Catholic nation. Protestantism had issued a challenge, and Catholicism had responded. Catholics, too, felt the need for spiritual regeneration, but they found its source not in breaking away from the universal church of Rome but by reforming from within. There could be no doubt that by the middle of the sixteenth century the Catholic church had a stronger hold on the hearts of its practitioners than it had had fifty years earlier.

The Council of Trent, painted by Titian in 1586. Despite interruptions and delays, the Council arrived at a definitive restatement of Catholic doctrine, even though it failed at the original goal of reconciliation with the Protestants.

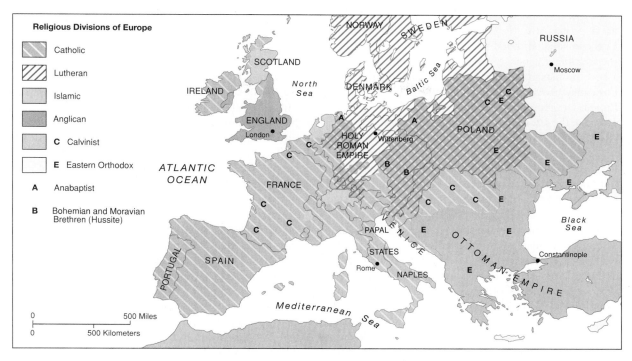

Religious Divisions of Europe

- Catholic
- Lutheran
- Islamic
- Anglican
- C Calvinist
- E Eastern Orthodox
- A Anabaptist
- B Bohemian and Moravian Brethren (Hussite)

Religious Divisions of Europe, 1555

The Reformation and the Counter-Reformation

1517	Luther writes his Ninety-five Theses
1521	Luther is excommunicated and declared an enemy of the empire
1523	Zwingli expounds his faith in formal disputation
1533	Henry VIII divorces Catherine of Aragon, marries Anne Boleyn, and breaks with the church of Rome
1536	Calvin publishes *Institutes of the Christian Religion*
1540	Loyola receives papal approval for Society of Jesus
1545–63	Council of Trent
1553	Mary I restores Catholicism in England
1563	Elizabeth I enacts the Thirty-nine Articles, which restores Protestantism to England

The Empire Strikes Back

Warfare dominated the reform of religion almost from its beginning. The burnings, drownings, and executions by which both Catholics and Protestants attempted to maintain religious purity were but raindrops compared to the sea of blood that was shed in sieges and on battlefields beginning in the 1530s. The Catholic divisions were clear. The Holy Roman Emperor continued to be engaged in the west with his archenemy France, and in the south with the ever expanding Ottoman Empire. Charles V needed not only peace within his own German realms, but positive support for his offensive and defensive campaigns. He could never devote his full resources to suppressing Protestant dissent.

Yet there was never a united Protestant front to suppress. The north German towns and principalities that accepted Lutheranism in the 1520s had had a long history of warfare among themselves. Princes stored up grievances from past wars and contested inheritances, cities stored up jealousies from commercial rivalries and special privileges. Added to this was the division between Luther and Zwingli over doctrinal issues that effectively separated the German and Swiss components of the reformation from each other.

Though both the Protestant and the Catholic sides were internally weak, it was the greater responsibilities of Charles V that allowed for the uneasy periods of peace. Each pause gave the Protestant reformers new life. Lutheranism continued to spread in the northern part of the empire, Zwinglian reform in the south. Charles V asked the papacy to convoke a general council and the Protestants to stop evangelizing in new territories. But Protestant leaders were no more capable of halting the spread of the reformation than were Catholics. Thus each violation of each uneasy truce seemed to prove treachery. In 1546, just after Luther's death, both sides raised armies in preparation for renewed fighting. In the first stage of war Charles V scored a decisive victory, capturing the two leading Protestant princes and conquering Saxony and Thuringia, the homeland of Lutheran reform.

Charles V's greatest victories were always preludes to his gravest defeats. The remaining Protestant princes were driven into the arms of the French, who placed dynastic interests above religious concerns. Again Europe was plunged into general conflict, with the French invading the German states from the west, the Turks from the south, and the Protestant princes from the north. Charles V, now an old and broken man, was forced to flee through the Alps in the dead of winter and was brought to the bargaining table soon after. By the Peace of Augsburg in 1555 the emperor agreed to allow the princes of Germany to establish the religion of their people. The Peace of Augsburg ended forty years of religious struggle in Germany, but it settled nothing.

In 1547 the then-victorious Charles V stood at the grave of Martin Luther. He had been buried in the shadow of the church in which he had been baptized, and now other shadows darkened his plot. Imperial troops were masters of all Saxony and were preparing to turn back the religious clock in Luther's homeland. The emperor was advised to have the body exhumed and burned, to carry out twenty-five years too late the Edict of Worms that had made Luther an outlaw from church and state. But Charles V was no longer the self-confident young emperor who had been faced down by the Saxon monk on that long-ago day. Popes had come and gone, and his warrior rivals Francis I and Henry VIII were both dead. He alone survived. He had little stomach for the petty revenge that he might now exact upon the man who more than any other had ruined whatever hope there might have been for a united empire dominant over all of Europe. "I do not make war on dead men," Charles declared as he turned away from the reformer's grave. But the ghosts of Luther and Zwingli, of Calvin and Ignatius of Loyola were not so easily laid. For another century they would haunt a Europe that could do nothing else but make war on dead men.

Fishing for Souls, *by Adriaen Van De Velde, 1614. This allegorical painting shows Protestants (on the left) and Catholics (on the right) vying for the souls of Christians. In the water, parties from both banks try to drag naked men and women into their boats. Overhead, uniting them all, shines the unheeded rainbow of God.*

SUGGESTIONS FOR FURTHER READING

GENERAL READING

* G. R. Elton, ed., *The New Cambridge Modern History, Vol. II, The Reformation 1520–1559* (Cambridge: Cambridge University Press, 1958). A multi-authored study of the Protestant movement with sections on social and political life.

* Owen Chadwick, *The Reformation* (London: Penguin Books, 1972). An elegant and disarmingly simple history of religious change.

* Steven Ozment, *The Age of Reform 1250–1550* (New Haven, CT: Yale University Press, 1980). An important interpretation of an epoch of religious change.

* Evan Cameron, *The European Reformation* (Oxford: Oxford University Press, 1991). The most up-to-date survey of the Reformation period. Difficult but rewarding.

THE INTELLECTUAL REFORMATION

Lucien Febvre and Henri Martin, *The Coming of the Book* (Atlantic Highlands, NJ: Humanities Press, 1976). A study of the early history of bookmaking.

* E. Eisenstein, *The Printing Revolution in Early Modern Europe* (Cambridge: Cambridge University Press, 1983). An abridged edition of a larger work that examines the impact of printing upon European society.

R. W. Scribner, *For the Sake of Simple Folk* (Cambridge: Cambridge University Press, 1981). A study of the impact of the Reformation on common people. Especially good on the iconography of reform.

* Richard Marius, *Thomas More* (New York: Knopf, 1984). A recent reinterpretation of the complex personality of England's greatest humanist.

* Roland Bainton, *Erasmus of Christendom* (New York: Charles Scribner's Sons, 1969). Still the best starting point and the most compelling biography.

Richard L. DeMolen, *Erasmus* (New York: St. Martin's Press, 1974). Selections from Erasmus's writings.

THE LUTHERAN REFORMATION

* Francis Oakley, *The Western Church in the Later Middle Ages* (Ithaca, NY: Cornell University Press, 1979). A study of the spiritual and intellectual state of the Roman Catholic church on the eve of the Reformation.

* Hajo Holborn, *A History of Modern Germany, Vol. I, The Reformation* (New York: Knopf, 1964). A widely respected account in a multivolume history of Germany. Especially strong on politics.

* Roland Bainton, *Here I Stand* (New York: New American Library, 1968). The single most absorbing biography of Luther.

* John Dillenberger, *Martin Luther: Selections From His Writings* (New York: Doubleday, 1961). A comprehensive selection from Luther's vast writings.

* Eric Erikson, *Young Man Luther* (New York: Norton, 1958). A classic psychoanalytic study of Luther's personality.

* Heiko Oberman, *Luther, Man Between God and the Devil* (New York: Doubleday, 1992). English translation of one of the best German biographies of Luther. Sets Luther within the context of late medieval spirituality.

* Bernd Moeller, *Imperial Cities and the Reformation* (Durham, NC: The Labyrinth Press, 1982). A central work that defines the connection between Protestantism and urban reform.

R. Po-chia Hsia, ed., *The German People and the Reformation* (Ithaca, NY: Cornell University Press, 1988). A collection of essays exploring the social origins of the Reformation.

G. R. Potter, *Huldrych Zwingli* (New York: St. Martin's Press, 1977). A difficult but important study of the great Swiss reformer.

THE PROTESTANT REFORMATION

E. William Monter, *Calvin's Geneva* (London: John Wiley & Sons, 1967). A social and political history of the birthplace of Calvinism.

T. H. L. Parker, *John Calvin: A Biography* (Philadelphia: Westminster Press, 1975). The classic study.

William Bouwsma, *John Calvin* (Oxford: Oxford University Press, 1987). A study that places Calvin within the context of the social and intellectual movements of the sixteenth century.

* John Dillenberger, *John Calvin: Selections From His Writings* (New York: Doubleday, 1971). A comprehensive collection.

* J. J. Scarisbrick, *Henry VIII* (Berkeley: University of California Press, 1968). The classic biography of the larger-than-life monarch.

* A. G. Dickens, *The English Reformation* (New York: Schocken Books, 1964). An important interpretation of the underlying causes of the English Reformation.

* Rosemary O'Day, *The Debate on the English Reformation* (London: Methuen, 1986). A survey of conflicting views by eminent scholars.

George H. Williams, *The Radical Reformation* (Philadelphia: Westminster Press, 1962). A comprehensive synthesis of the first generation of radical Protestants.

Claus-Peter Clasen, *Anabaptism, A Social History 1525–1618* (Ithaca, NY: Cornell University Press, 1972). A study of the Anabaptist movement.

Steven Ozment, *Protestants: The Birth of a Revolution* (New York: Doubleday, 1992). An accessible study of the origins of Protestant beliefs and the impact of Protestant ideas among ordinary people.

THE CATHOLIC REFORMATION

Jean Delumeau, *Catholicism Between Luther and Voltaire* (Philadelphia: Westminster Press, 1977). A reinterpretation of the Counter-Reformation.

* John C. Olin, *The Autobiography of St. Ignatius Loyola* (New York: Harper & Row, 1974). The best introduction to the founder of the Jesuits.

* A. D. Wright, *The Counter-Reformation* (New York: St. Martin's Press, 1984). A comprehensive survey.

* A. G. Dickens, *The Counter Reformation* (London: Thames and Hudson, 1968). An excellent introduction, handsomely illustrated.

*Indicates paperback edition available

CHAPTER 14

World Encounters, 1350–1700

THE VIRGIN OF GUADALUPE

The Virgin of Guadalupe is perhaps the best known and the most important symbol of the Mexican nation. Her image reflects the complexity of the encounter between European and Indian cultures. Every year hundreds of thousands of people visit her shrine in Tepeyac just north of Mexico City. The most common version of the shrine's origin is that in 1531, barely a decade after the Spaniards had destroyed the Aztec capital of Tenochtitlán, the Virgin Mary appeared at Tepeyac to Juan Diego, a humble Indian, and spoke to him in his native language, Nahuatl. The Virgin ordered Juan Diego to tell the archbishop of Mexico that she desired a church to be built in her honor at Tepeyac. Of course, the Indian could not gain an audience with the great churchman. The Virgin then sent Juan Diego to gather roses in a place where only cactus grew, to put the roses in his cloak, and to present them to the archbishop. When the Indian unfolded his cloak, the image of the Virgin was stamped upon it. Acknowledging the miracle, the archbishop ordered the shrine built where Mary had appeared.

Over the following centuries the Virgin of Guadalupe was the subject of controversy, adoration, and manipulation. She came to illustrate much of the process and impact of colonial rule following the European encounters of the sixteenth century: the syncretization of folk religion and Catholicism; the flexibility of Spanish government; the conflicts within the Church over the plight of the Indian; the mestization, or mixture, of the native and European populations; and both the fierce and passive resistance of the Indians to the whites. The Virgin represented the "forging of the cosmic race," the Mexican people. It signified too the emergence of a sense of nationality among whites born in the New World. The Virgin became an important symbol of the new Mexican nation, and under her banner Father Miguel Hidalgo rallied the masses during the revolt for independence in 1810.

The site at Tepeyac exemplified the syncretic relation between native and Catholic religions, for it had previously been sacred to Tonantzin, the goddess of fertility. In the early years of the Christian shrine, the Indians may well have come to worship Tonantzin, and called out to her rather than to the Virgin Mary in their prayers. With the fusion of Indian and Spanish culture, the Virgin gradually integrated into the popular culture. The Virgin of Guadalupe may have served to restore the hope of salvation to the Indians, who had suffered in the conquest the death of all their old beliefs. The return of Tonantzin, through the Virgin of Guadalupe, rescued their gods.

The picture of the Virgin shown here from the seventeenth century is typical. She is usually represented standing on a crescent moon, surrounded by a crown of sunrays, which in turn is encompassed by clouds. She is clothed in a rich robe, ornamented with stars. Often a little cherub bears her on his head. The Virgin is dark-skinned.

Even before their encounters with the New World, the Virgin Mary, or Our Lady of the Immaculate Conception, was an important figure among Spaniards. One widely known version of her in Spain was the Virgin of Estremadura, which was coincidentally the birthplace of many of the *conquistadores*, or conquerors. Hernán Cortés's campaign banner carried a picture of Mary, who was a "symbol of Spanish power."

At first some clerics opposed the Virgin of Guadalupe cult. Their opposition ended, however, when during the first decades of the seventeenth century, the Virgin's intervention protected New Spain from desperate crises. Most notably, in 1629 displaying her image at the head of a procession protected Mexico City from inundation by floods. During the eighteenth century the Virgin became *patrona*, or patron saint, of New Spain.

The Guadalupe myth was important because it showed that Indians were capable of salvation; in other words, they could be Christians. This factor was crucial in the sixteenth-century debate over the humanity of the Indians. Some churchmen thought the Indian incapable of conversion and therefore rightfully exploited. Others maintained the Indians' humanity and resisted their oppression. For the Indian the most important aspect of the legend was that the Virgin appeared dark-skinned like an Indian. To rural Mexicans, the Virgin of Guadalupe was a "protectress" and an intermediary. In her were absorbed the ancient rites of agriculture. In the harshness of Christianity as it was imposed on the Indians by crusading clerics, the Virgin Mary, depicted as "the approachable little woman," mediated, praying for them to the Father and the Son. She was a "modest house-wife," who as such eased the way to the acceptance of colonial authority. The Guadalupe myth also provided a place for the *mestizo* in the new order that emerged during the seventeenth century.

In one image, then, Indian, *mestizo*, and white were brought together. In their enthusiasm for her, they shunted aside class and racial differences. At a time when the Indians' world seemed destroyed by conquest and disease, when they were helpless and terrified, they gained comfort and hope in the Indian Virgin of Guadalupe. Later, when it was time to throw off the burden of Spanish colonial rule, Mexicans again called on the Virgin to unite and protect them.

Europe and the Encounters

In the history of the world, the fifteenth and sixteenth centuries were an age of encounters. Europeans, led by the Portuguese and the Spanish, set out to explore the world known to them in Africa and Asia and wound up discovering a world totally unknown to them—America. There were many reasons why this was the moment that Europeans would look beyond their own shores. Technological changes made long sea voyages possible, and the demands of commerce provided incentives. This was especially true in the trade for eastern spices, long dominated by Italian merchants but now gradually opening to traders along the Atlantic seaboard. Spices were rare and expensive, but they were not merely luxuries. Some acted as preservatives, others as flavorings to make palatable the rotting foodstuffs that were the fare of even the wealthiest Europeans. Some spices were used as perfumes to battle the noxious gases that rose from urban streets and invaded homes and workplaces. The drugs of the East, the nature of which we can only guess at, helped soothe chronic ill health. The demand for all of these "spices" continued to rise at a rate greater than their supply.

It was the Portuguese who made the first dramatic breakthroughs in exploration and colonization. In the early fifteenth century, they gained a foothold in northern Africa and used it to stage voyages along the continent's unexplored western coast. Like those of all explorers, the motives of the Portuguese were an unselfconscious mixture of faith and greed. Establishing bases there would enable them to surround their Muslim enemies while also giving them access to the

African bullion trade. The Portuguese navigator Bartolomeu Dias (ca. 1450–1500) summarized these goals succinctly: "To give light to those who are in darkness and to grow rich."

But those who were "in darkness" turned out to have rich cultures of their own. The cultures of the African peoples encountered by Dias and succeeding generations of Portuguese, Dutch, English, and French explorers and traders challenged many of the assumptions that Europeans made about non-Christians and initiated an encounter that transformed both European and African civilization. The Portuguese came to Africa seeking a passage to India and the gold that Africans were rumored to possess. Though they ultimately found both, they also found something that would prove more valuable still: slaves. At first, Europeans participated in the indigenous slave trade among the Africans, but soon they transformed it into an organized commercial activity that uprooted hundreds of thousands of black Africans to work plantations in the New World and on Atlantic and Indian Ocean islands.

While the Portuguese were the first Europeans to encounter African civilization, the Spaniards were the first to encounter the native populations of America. Queen Isabella of Castile was persuaded to take an interest in an expedition to the Indies led by a Genoese adventurer, Christopher Columbus (ca. 1446–1506). Like all well-informed people of his day, Columbus believed the world was round. By carefully calculating routes and distances, he concluded that a western track would be shorter and less expensive than the path the Portuguese were breaking around Africa. Because Columbus's conclusions were based on erroneous calculations, the land he reached on 12 October 1492 was not Japan, as he believed, but a hemisphere entirely unknown to Europeans.

Successive voyages by Columbus and others established that vast tracts of rich lands lay to the west of Europe. Indeed, in 1519 Ferdinand Magellan (ca. 1480–1521), a Portuguese mariner in the service of Spain, began a voyage that resulted in the circumnavigation of the globe. By then the globe had been divided between the Spanish and the Portuguese by the Treaty of Tordesillas (1494). The Portuguese were given the right to the eastern route to the Indies as well as to any undiscovered lands east of an imaginary Line of Demarcation fixed about 1,250 miles west of the Cape Verde Islands. This entitled Portugal to Brazil. The Spaniards received whatever lands lay west of the line.

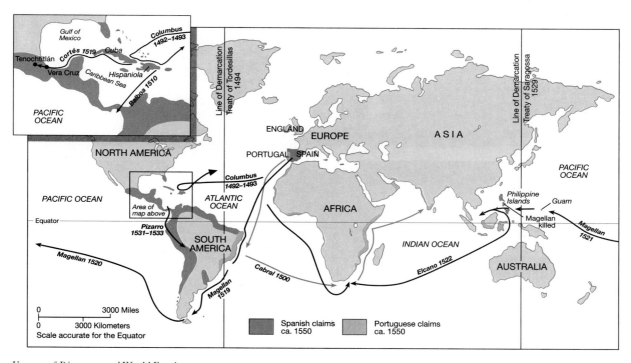

Voyages of Discovery and World Empires

CHRISTOPHER COLUMBUS, LETTER FROM THE FIRST VOYAGE, 1493

■ *Christopher Columbus seemingly needs no introduction. His name has forever been associated with the European discovery of the New World, although the meaning of that discovery has been continually contested. In the summer of 1492 Columbus sailed west from the Canary Islands, believing that he would reach the coast of China. Instead he landed on an island in the Carribbean. This passage from a letter addressed to the royal treasurer of Spain contains his first impressions of the people he encountered.*

A Letter addressed to the noble Lord Raphael Sanchez, Treasurer to their most invincible Majesties, Ferdinand and Isabella, King and Queen of Spain, by Christopher Columbus, to whom our age is greatly indebted, treating of the islands of India recently discovered beyond the Ganges, to explore which he had been sent eight months before under the auspices and at the expense of their said Majesties.

The inhabitants of both sexes in this island, and in all the others which I have seen, or of which I have received information, go always naked as they were born, with the exception of some of the women, who use the covering of a leaf, or small bough, or an apron of cotton which they prepare for that purpose. None of them are possessed of any iron, neither have they weapons, being unacquainted with, and indeed incompetent to use them, not from any deformity of body (for they are well-formed), but because they are timid and full of fear.

They carry however in lieu of arms, canes dried in the sun, on the ends of which they fix heads of dried wood sharpened to a point, and even these they dare not use habitually; for it has often occurred when I have sent two or three of my men to any of the villages to speak with the natives, that they have come out in a disorderly troop, and have fled in such haste at the approach of our men, that the fathers forsook their children and the children their fathers. This timidity did not arise from any loss or injury that they had received from us; for, on the contrary, I gave to all I approached whatever articles I had about me, such as cloth and many other things, taking nothing of theirs in return: but they are naturally timid and fearful. As soon however as they see that they are safe, and have laid aside all fear, they are very simple and honest, and exceedingly liberal with all they have; none of them refusing any thing he may possess when he is asked for it, but on the contrary inviting us to ask them. They exhibit great love towards all others in preference to themselves: they also give objects of great value for trifles, and content themselves with very little or nothing in return.

Such are the events which I have briefly described. Farewell.

Lisbon, the 14th of March. Christopher Columbus, *Admiral of the Fleet of the Ocean.*

West of the line lay the ancient cultures of the Americas. The Spanish encounters with the Native Americans—the peoples they dubbed "Indians"—were no less momentous than were those of the Portuguese in Africa. Among the Aztecs and the Incas the Spanish beheld unimaginable marvels, at once appealing and repulsive. But the Spaniards came as conquerors and brought with them deadly microbes that took the lives of millions of native peoples. European diseases proved far more potent than European weapons in destroying the mighty American empires.

Africa and the Encounters

At the beginning of the fifteenth century two of sub-Saharan Africa's three "coasts" had long been frontiers of change. For centuries, Muslim traders and preachers had crossed to the Sahel, the southern shore of the Sahara, using camels as their "ships of the desert." Their influence, both economic and religious, had penetrated southward from the Sahel into the West African forest zone. Similarly, trade and Islam, borne on the

This woodcut of Christopher Columbus landing on the island of Hispaniola accompanied the first illustrated edition of a letter that Columbus wrote about his first voyage. The ship is inaccurately depicted as a Mediterranean galley.

The Portuguese Pursuit of African Pepper and Gold

Changes in the economy of northern Europe that occurred at the end of the fourteenth century prompted Portugal's early leadership in European explorations along Africa's Atlantic coast. Through its exports of fish and sugar Portugal had had commercial connections with northern Europe for some time. But northern Europe's economic recovery from the Black Death after 1380 stimulated demands for other commodities that Portugal's rulers felt Portugal might also fill. Northern Europeans, for example, were raising more animals for meat. Lacking fodder to feed all of them through the winter, however, they had to slaughter many more animals in the autumn than they could consume immediately. To prevent the meat from spoiling, they needed tremendous quantities of preservatives. One commonly used preservative was malagueta pepper, known at the time as "Grains of Paradise" and obtained from West Africa through the trans-Saharan trade. Europe's reviving economy also demanded more and more gold, another commodity long supplied through the trans-Saharan trade.

Portugal's rulers therefore decided to attempt to sail along the Atlantic coast of Africa to reach the actual sources of the pepper and gold south of the Sahara. Perhaps, they thought, they might even establish direct links with the fabled trading center of Timubuktu by striking overland from the west coast of Africa, eastward along the Sahel zone. If they succeeded in establishing such a direct trade link, they would both eliminate the North African middlemen from the profitable trade and, as Christians, also strike a blow against Islam by undermining the prosperity of Muslim states. They knew that Portugal was well placed to attempt such a strategy. Most obviously, its location at the edge of Europe, facing outward toward the Atlantic, had given Portuguese fishermen ample experience with its currents and winds, making them among Europe's best mariners. At the start of the fifteenth century Portugal also had a centralized government at a time when most other parts of Europe were politically fragmented, and hence the state could be directly involved in explorations. Moreover, it was a small country with a serious lack of land to provide estates for a group of fairly well-educated younger sons of the nobility, who were thus forced to search for new ways to make their fortunes. Finally, through earlier investments in Portugal, Genoese bankers had established links with it that ensured that capital would be available for profitable overseas ventures.

Indian Ocean's predictable monsoon winds, had affected the East Coast of Africa and helped create its Swahili culture. But the Atlantic coast had remained almost wholly unaffected by outsiders and almost purely African. This situation was soon to change.

After centuries of political disunity, by 1400 a new Europe was stirring. As a consequence, led by the Portuguese, but with Spanish, English, Dutch, and French merchants close behind, Europeans began to visit Africa's Atlantic coast. These visits began a process of change that affected large areas of Africa. They also created new kinds of relationships with Africans living along the west coast that gradually came to be overshadowed by a single factor: the growing need of New World plantation owners for African slaves.

Portuguese Explorations

As a small country in Europe, Portugal's future seemed to require overseas expansion. In 1415 this expansion began with the seizure of Ceuta, a wealthy Moroccan city on the Mediterranean coast, as the Portuguese sought access to Moroccan grain, cloth, and Berber slaves.

But very real technical problems had to be solved if Portuguese mariners were to overcome the barriers that had prevented them from sailing south of Cape Bojador, on the coast of the western Sahara, into the "Ocean Sea," as the Atlantic was then called. Northeast trade winds that blow in the same direction throughout the year dominate the ocean to the south of Cape Bojador. The Canary Current is strong and constant, and it flows in roughly the same direction as the winds. This meant that, while a vessel found it easy to sail south as it was pushed along by both currents and winds, it was almost impossible to sail back to Europe against these forces. Theoretically, mariners could sail into an adverse wind by tacking back and forth, but doing this was exceedingly difficult when they were opposed by a strong current as well.

Prince Henry, known as "the Navigator" (1394–1460), brother of the king of Portugal, was the person who sought to discover the solution to this technical problem and thereby open the way for serious Portuguese expansion. Henry's interests were many. He was

administrator of the Order of Christ, a religious order dedicated to anti-Muslim crusades, and he continued to make war on Morocco. He possessed plantations and other lands. He was closely linked to Portuguese trading interests and invested much of his and his order's money in overseas trading ventures. And every year after 1419 Prince Henry sponsored one or two expeditions to explore how to sail beyond Cape Bojador and return safely. The crucially important knowledge of tides, currents, and wind patterns he accumulated encouraged Henry to establish a formal center for his work on the south coast of Portugal in 1433. In 1434, Gil Eanes, a Portuguese sailor, ventured south past Cape Bojador and then, using the new understanding of the Atlantic's wind patterns, sailed westward into the Atlantic to return home, discovering the islands of Madeira on the way.

Eanes's discoveries encouraged the Portuguese to combine elements of navigational technology from around the world into a new synthesis. From the Arabs they learned about the compass and the lateen sail, a type of sail shaped so as to create a vacuum on its leeward side, effectively causing the vessel to be pulled along even when sailing very close to the wind. From northern Europe they took the single-piece keel and other elements of hull construction, changes that allowed the building of smaller shallow-draft boats known as caravels that were well suited to move into dangerous uncharted waters. These adaptations created almost limitless possibilities for exploration. And so, after 1433, the Portuguese, followed closely by Castilians from Spain, sailed farther and farther down the west coast of Africa, making steady progress toward their ultimate goal of gaining direct access to gold and pepper and other exotic products such as ivory. In the process they gathered additional valuable information about the lands and peoples they encountered.

Prince Henry died in 1460. But the decade after his death witnessed continuing Portuguese explorations along Africa's Guinea coasts, with the most promising discoveries coming at decade's end. In 1469, Portuguese navigators passed the bulge of West Africa and coasted southeastward to what later came to be known as the Ivory, Gold, and Slave Coasts. In 1471, the Portuguese discovered in the Gulf of Guinea two islands with rich volcanic soils, São Tomé and Principe. The warm and wet regions of the Guinea coasts had many more people living in them than did the desert coasts the Portuguese had encountered north of the Senegal River. The area's people produced pepper and hunted for ivory. But best of all, the people of the Gold Coast, known today as

Ghana, produced gold. At last, the Portuguese had reached a major source of the ancient trans-Saharan gold trade. In 1482 they built the fortress of São Jorge da Mina—Elmina—as a base for their trade there.

Sugar and the Rise of Plantation Slavery

In 1443, in the process of their trading explorations, the Portuguese had added a new commodity to their shopping list. Sailing one of the new lateen-rigged caravels, Nuno Tristão landed on Arguin, an island off the north coast of Mauritania, and, extending Portuguese practices in Morocco, he purchased some African slaves in the course of his trading. He sold them in Portugal. In 1444 six vessels set sail from Portugal specifically seeking slaves to be taken home as well as other items. So great were the profits of the new trade for human cargo that in 1445 no fewer that twenty-six ships participated in it as part of their larger trading enterprise. To dispel any doubts about its propriety, in 1452 Pope Nicholas V promulgated a bull, *Dum Diversas*, sanctioning the enslavement of pagans and infidels. While the slaves traded in the years before 1500 were of distinctly secondary importance in the context of the overall trade, numbering only about 1,800 to 2,000 annually, and while gold remained the primary interest for the Portuguese, the establishment of the new trade in slaves nonetheless inaugurated an activity that was to characterize for centuries European activities on Africa's Atlantic coast.

That there were slaves available for the Portuguese to purchase was hardly surprising. Virtually every pre-capitalist society in human history has used slaves to

The Portuguese fortress of São Jorge da Mina was built with labor and materials imported from Portugal.

perform arduous work for little cost. Those in Africa were no different. Significantly, a slave was defined as a person without relatives to protect him or her and, after being acquired, a slave was usually viewed as being in the process of being incorporated into the acquiring family as a subordinate relative. There were three basic categories of people who could find themselves "without relatives" and hence slaves. First, there were those given by one family to another as a way of redressing an injury. For example, if a man killed another man in a hunting accident, the dead man's family could be placated by the killer's family ceding a woman or young girl to the family of the dead man to compensate for his loss. Rather quickly, this slave would become a member of the new family, probably with a new name to signal her new social identity.

Second, families could sever ties of protection for criminals and other social misfits and then sell them into slavery. Disinheritance and the resulting status of slavery were mechanisms to punish serious criminal offenses or blatantly antisocial behavior in societies generally lacking prisons. Finally, and of special importance in the large states that were in time to become the main sources for the full-blown Atlantic slave trade, slaves were produced by warfare when enemies were captured. Such war captives might be treated badly and forced to do only menial work at first, but, if sold to a family, even they might be absorbed gradually into it. In short, considering the shortage of labor power in precapitalist Africa, it was quite natural that slavery was a social institution and that there were many ways of becoming a slave.

When the Portuguese appeared on the West African coast, therefore, they found Africans who were already slaves and who were available for purchase. But the destiny of those unfortunates was different from that which most slaves had experienced within Africa. In Africa there was a tendency to absorb slaves into the families that acquired them, but no such destiny awaited slaves purchased by the Portuguese and other European traders. For the most part, they became chattel slaves, who remained without kin and who were destined to labor long and hard on the plantations that were being developed in the Atlantic basin. The increase in the slave trade from West Africa and the development of the plantation as a system of production were linked inextricably. And it was sugar production that underlay both.

Sugar had had a long history. It was in India, around 500 C.E., that the discovery of a process for turning sugarcane juice into granulated sugar had made sugar

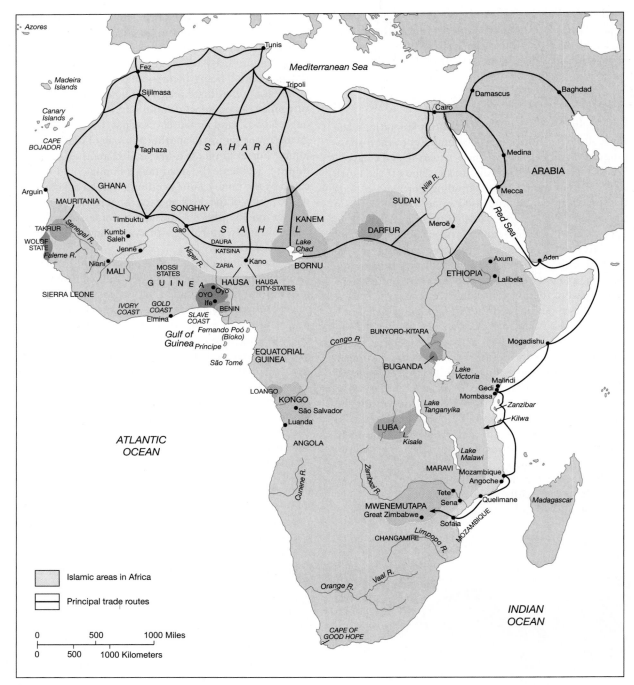

Africa, ca. 1400–1600

commercially important, for it could be stored indefinitely and traded over long distances. A luxury item valued widely for its many uses—medicinal, preservative, decorative, and as a sweetener—sugar was also highly profitable. Because all stages of its cultivation, harvesting, and processing required large numbers of highly disciplined workers, it was a crop ideal for production by slaves.

When the Crusaders from western Europe occupied Palestine in the eleventh century, they operated

Gender and Culture

VESPUCCI "DISCOVERING" AMERICA

Figure 1

The European encounter with the cultures of the western hemisphere posed a problem for visual artists. Prior to the voyages of discovery, the peoples of the world were represented according to Ovid's scheme of the *triplex mundus* or triple world, including Asia, Europe, and Africa. However, by the sixteenth century, the concept of a four or even five part world emerged, requiring a new and expanded symbolic mode. The allegory of the four continents first appeared in Abraham Ortelius's *Theatrum Orbis Terrarum*, published in Antwerp in 1570. Using the classical form of personification, a female figure bearing appropriate attributes signified a geographic location, and a new symbolic entity—America—was forged. The iconography confirmed fears about the strange new world, and long after Europe gained familiarity with the cultures of the indigenous peoples of America and elsewhere, the language of the arts retained the fantastic forms invented to describe the earliest encounters.

In the first depictions of new world allegories, "civilized" Europe contrasted with "savage" America. Theodor Galle's engraving *Vespucci "Discovering" America* (late sixteenth century, after a painting by Jan van der Street; Figure 1), seen on the preceding page, portrays the cartographer as a man of breeding, position, and science. He is stylishly dressed, and he holds the banner of the Southern Cross and an astrolabe. America, a massive woman, dressed in a scant feathered skirt and crowned with a feathered cap, springs from her hammock to greet him. Her domain is exotic and frightening. Odd animals, only the tapir and sloth can be identified, lurk in the lush foliage of her jungle home. In the distance, native people prepare a human leg on a spit. Cannibalism remained a persistent theme in the allegory; well into the seventeenth and eighteenth centuries, figures of America presided over grisly feasts, holding a severed head as an attribute.

The elegant interpretation of *America* by Giovanni Battista Tiepolo (1753, Italy; Figure 2) seems far removed from Galle's naive engraving. Painted in the stairwell of the Wurzburg Residenz of Prince-Bishop Carl Phillip von Greiffenklau, Tiepolo's handsome personification commands a procession of exotic people and extraordinary goods. She is presented with similar images of Africa and Asia, all bringing the wealth of their lands to Europe. Her trappings are magnificent. Decked in gold and multicolored feathers, she rides on the back of an alligator. Her tributes include powerful stags, bundles of brazil wood, and a cornucopia of ripe fruit. However, her savage heritage is not forgotten. Inconspicuously placed on

Figure 2

THE INDIAN WIDOW

Figure 3

the ground to the right of her retinue is a pile of severed heads, gruesomely pierced with arrows.

In the course of the eighteenth century, knowledge of the culture of the Americas increased. But, other inventions colored new world imagery. Rousseau's vision of the "Noble Savage," coupled with rising ethnographic interest about the beliefs and habits of the native Americans, informed a new ideal: the heroic Indian. Stories that proved the valor and nobility of the indigenous people provided the subjects for romantic painting. These works were a curious hybrid. Although often inspired by authentic lore, the artistic interpretation presented European values as Native American instinct. *The Indian Widow* by Joseph Wright of Derby (1783–85, England; Figure 3) praises the stoicism of indigenous women. According to tradition, on the first full moon after a chief is slain, his wife displays his war trophies and commemorates the day in silent reflection. Wright of Derby places the hero's widow in a potentially dangerous setting. Ominous clouds darken the sky, lightening crackles near the shore, and in the distance, smoke pours from an erupting volcano. Her quiet

BEAUTY ON A PALACE TERRACE

Figure 4

vigil becomes an act of bravery; she will fulfill her duties to her slain husband even at the risk of her own life.

Europe was not alone in projecting their ideas on other cultures. Asians and Americans similarly recorded the strange appearance and bizarre habits of the new people they encountered. A Moghul painting, *Beauty on a Palace Terrace* (late seventeenth century, Indian; Figure 4), depicts three European visitors, two women and a man, attended by an Indian serving girl. Their origins are distinguished by position and clothing rather than by facial features. But the daring necklines of the women's dresses, otherwise cut in a European fashion, are pure fantasy. Such decolletage would never be acceptable in Europe.

hundreds of sugar plantations using both free wage and slave labor. After the fall of their small Crusader kingdoms in the late twelfth century, Europeans moved sugar production onto Mediterranean islands such as Cyprus, again using a mixture of free and slave labor. It then moved steadily westward from island to island, often financed by Genoese bankers, until it finally reached Spain and Portugal. Sugar was, however, a crop that demanded special types of soils, which it quickly exhausted, as well as ample water. It was also a commodity that seemed to have an unlimited market in Europe. Therefore, while they continued their search for African gold, the Portuguese and their Castilian competitors also eagerly established new sugar plantations on the Atlantic islands of Madeira, which Portugal had claimed, and the Canaries, claimed by Castile. It was for these new sugar plantations that many African slaves were purchased, firming the link between plantation slavery and sugar production.

Clearly, the best sites for the Portuguese to obtain slaves were also best for them to trade for the other things they sought, places where African leaders had established states that could mobilize the labor needed for producing not only gold and ivory but also numbers of war captives. One should remember that the Portuguese were primarily traders in sub-Saharan Africa, not colonial settlers, and that they did not initially seek to obtain large pieces of territory. But they did need African partners to deliver the goods they wanted and to provide them with security while they were in the area. Quite naturally, therefore, they found it easiest to trade with powerful figures in large states. As a French visitor to the Lower Guinea coast reported, all aspects of the local slave trade were "the businesses of kings, rich men, and prime merchants exclusive of the lower sorts of blacks." Where powerful African states did not exist, trade could still be carried out, but only with greater difficulty and risk.

As they moved down the West African coast, the Portuguese found that the leaders of the peoples of the Lower Guinea coast were especially eager to deal with them. Not only did the Portuguese bring items from Europe that the rulers valued, such as hardware, alcohol, and cloth, but with their superior maritime skills, the Portuguese could also provide a useful service to the African elite by carrying a complex regional coastal trade on their caravels. Thus, for example, kola nuts were purchased for cloth and alcohol at Sierra Leone and then exchanged for slaves at the mouth of the Gambia River. Or, as the leaders of the Gold Coast sought labor to mine their gold, they became the annual purchasers of about

500 slaves whom the Portuguese obtained from the rulers of the states of Oyo and Benin, farther east, and whom they then exchanged for gold at the Portuguese trading post at Elmina.

In the process of their explorations and trading, the Portuguese also transplanted plantation agriculture to São Tomé. This occurred at the start of sixteenth century. Using African slaves obtained from nearby coastal areas of Africa, São Tomé became the world's largest single producer of sugar by the 1510s and 1520s. The combination of rich volcanic soils, disciplined slave labor, and the technological superiority of Portuguese transportation meant that sugar produced at this isolated outpost of empire could be delivered profitably to Lisbon and Genoa despite the long distance it had to be shipped.

Portuguese Success and Failure in the Indian Ocean Basin

Portugal's commercial successes along Africa's Guinea coasts inspired King John II (1455–95), the spiritual descendant of Henry the Navigator, to press on along the West African coast in search of yet greater successes. After a war between Portugal and Castile (1475–79) over the succession to the throne of Castile, the peace treaty recognized the Canary Islands as Castilian in exchange for the recognition of all African continental territory south of Cape Bojador as being within Portugal's commercial sphere. In the 1480s the Portuguese pressed onward to take advantage of this agreement. But by the 1480s it was really Asia, not Africa, that lay at the core of royal dreams. West Africa had been rewarding, but its trade was limited to a few commodities, and the amount of gold the Portuguese could obtain annually was stalled between 13,000 and 14,000 ounces. With the European economy improving steadily, Europeans more and more wanted to reach the fabulous riches of Asia directly, by sea, thereby eliminating middlemen located in eastern Europe and western Asia. In the context of the debate at the time over how best to reach Asia, John firmly believed the best route to Asia lay southward along the coast of Africa and was determined that his own fleets would pioneer it.

As part of this quest, in 1482, the explorer Diogo Cão arrived at the mouth of the Congo River and, somewhat surprisingly, was warmly welcomed by the leaders of the Kongo state, many of whom converted to Catholicism and asked for a Portuguese presence in their country.

THE NATURE OF THE PORTUGUESE PRESENCE IN WEST AFRICA: ELMINA, 1523

■ *King John III of Portugal well understood that Portugal was on the Guinea Coast to trade. The factory at Elmina, to which much West African gold gravitated, was crucially important for Portugal's success. By 1523 it had become a little city-state, with many local Africans having abandoned their earlier ties of loyalty and now living as Christian clients of the Portuguese governor. The governor had, however, expelled some people as punishment for alleged crimes. The king knew that successful trading required a contented population and peaceful conditions. In this letter he writes to the governor of Elmina admonishing him that his policy of harsh punishments is undermining the Portuguese's very purpose in being there to trade for gold.*

We have been informed that you are treating the knights of our village of Mina there harshly, in such a manner that the village is depopulated and men are going away to other parts; and we regard it as a matter very prejudicial to our interest and primarily to the welfare of that city and its trade. Since they are Christians and have received the water of baptism, they must be defended, protected and instructed, and not banished; and this also, since they are our vassals, and live there in obedience to us, serving in our name everything ordered them for our service, and with their people and their canoes conveying to the chiefs the wood for all our ships, and, furthermore, since many of them buy on a large scale in that factory, and all generally make purchases of old linen, which is bought by them and sold in their markets. Moreover, we are told that there are rich men among them, and that slaves may be had from them, and all of them are at our command, or may be, should they be treated well and protected with that moderation in punishment and also in instruction, which is meet and proper for our service and their security; then men tell us that for all their services, they neither have, nor expect, from us any other reward than we should protect them and command them to be maintained in justice. For this reason, it seems to us that you should not take it for granted that our interest would be promoted by your expelling them abroad. We command you, therefore, to treat them better and to dispense with banishments, otherwise, besides losing them and the service which we receive from them, the merchants will not come with similar new things [to trade].

From King John III to Affonso de Albuquerque, Governor of São Jorge da Mina, 13 October 1523.

(See Special Feature, "The Ambiguity of First Encounters: The Portuguese and the Kongo," pp. 418–419.) The Portuguese pressed onward, and in 1488 Bartholomeu Dias set sail from Portugal under orders to sail to the end of Africa to see if he could reach the Indian Ocean. Dias's ship was overtaken by a storm and blown far to the southwest. When the storm abated, Dias sailed eastward, expecting to strike the African coast. Without realizing it, he sailed past Africa into the Indian Ocean. At this point, however, his men mutinied and forced him to return to Portugal. As he sailed for home, he glimpsed the tip of South Africa and called it the Cape of Storms. When King John heard his story, the king aptly decided to rename it the Cape of Good Hope, for he saw it as a hopeful sign of future Portuguese successes in the Indian Ocean.

In 1492 Christopher Columbus, seeking Asia, discovered the New World of the Americas instead. In 1497, John's successor, King Manuel I (1495–1521), sent out the explorer Vasco da Gama (ca. 1460–1524) with four ships to enter the Indian Ocean and trade there. Engaging a Swahili pilot to guide him, da Gama succeeded in his venture, opening the Indian Ocean to Europeans for the first time. The Indian Ocean presented a far different situation from that which the Portuguese had been encountering for decades on the uncharted Atlantic coast of Africa. Romans, Persians, Arabs, Chinese, and others had sailed it for centuries and its sea-lanes were well mapped. Silks and spices, gold and jewels, ivory and slaves—all were available, and their presence seemed to testify to the wisdom of the Portuguese state's persisting with their explorations along the West

African coast. When Da Gama's ships returned home in 1499, the king was delighted, and he determined to use Portugal's naval power to try to dominate the Indian Ocean by force.

In the 1480s, after Spain had recognized Portugal's trading monopoly on the West Coast, Portugal became far more aggressive as they explored and traded. The king, for example, decreed that any non-Portuguese traders encountered along the coast were to be thrown into the ocean. When Vasco da Gama sailed into the Indian Ocean, he brought with him this new royal vision of a total Portuguese monopoly over important aspects of trade. In pursuit of this goal, he traumatically disrupted the region's flourishing trade, which was highly vulnerable to the superior Portuguese naval armaments. Portugal moved quickly to dominate the region's commercial life, trying to turn the trade in some items, such as pepper, ginger, cinnamon, and silk, into royal monopolies and charging merchants dealing in other commodities protection money. In 1505 the Portuguese captured the valuable flow of gold out of Zimbabwe from Swahili traders by seizing both the port of Sofala and the pivot of the gold trade, the city of Kilwa. In 1507, they constructed a fortress on Mozambique Island as their trading post in the area. In the following years the Portuguese continued their conquests and after defeating Muslim naval forces at the battle of Diu, off the coast of India, in 1509, the Portuguese ruled the seas, gradually adding to their list of fortified trading posts such places as Goa, in India (1510); Malacca, in Malaysia (1511); Hormuz, at the mouth of the Persian Gulf (1517); Macao, in China (1557); and Mombasa, in East Africa (1594).

But despite its striking naval successes, rather surprisingly the Portuguese state's share in the trade soon stagnated. This stagnation occurred for several reasons. First, its monopolies over the most lucrative trade items discouraged investments from private enterprises in Portugal because they could not legally trade in the commodities most likely to enrich them. Many individual Portuguese evaded the state's control by participating in a complex web of private deals that did the state little good. A second reason was fiscal. The Portuguese had few desirable manufactured goods to offer the sophisticated peoples of Asia in exchange for the commodities they sought. Forced, therefore, to purchase Asian products with gold and silver, Portugal soon found itself drained by a troubling balance of payments deficit to Asia. Finally, the Portuguese were never wholly unchallenged in their attempts to dominate the Indian Ocean. Their navies

had failed to take Aden, in southern Arabia, and this failure gave their Muslim rivals a base from which to attack Portuguese shipping in the Indian Ocean. The Portuguese usually responded effectively to such attacks, but their responses were costly and badly taxed their resources.

In short, while impressive for their rapid establishment, the series of trading posts that the Portuguese state established in the Indian Ocean was equally striking for their failure to transform or create much of anything new or enduring in the region. As a consequence of the growing problems in the middle of the sixteenth century, Portuguese leaders began to think of fresh and perhaps more satisfactory venues for their energies. Their thoughts turned to the New World.

Growing Links Between Africa and the New World

In 1494, soon after Columbus's first voyage, Spain and Portugal negotiated the Treaty of Tordesillas, formally dividing the world between themselves in order to forestall conflict. On one of Portugal's voyages of exploration, in 1500, Pedro Alvares Cabral (ca. 1468–1520) sailed out into the Atlantic far to the west and landed in Brazil. When he consulted his instruments, he discovered that this surprising piece of the New World was east of the line of division and hence belonged to Portugal. Aside from gathering some dyewoods there, however, the Portuguese largely ignored their new possession. Only in 1549 did the crown finally take direct control over some of Brazil's coastal areas and begin to send thousands of Portuguese settlers, government officials, and missionaries to occupy them.

The discovery that sugar grew extremely well in Brazil and that it could be the base of a prosperous economy motivated this change of policy. Gradually, a sugar industry was built up with Native Americans used as slave labor. But its major expansion occurred in the 1570s when an increase in Dutch investment and a decline in slave prices in Africa allowed large numbers of African slaves to be imported from across the Atlantic on the dreaded "Middle Passage." The new Brazilian sugar industry soon undercut the already established Spanish sugar industry on the island of Hispaniola as well as the older Portuguese industries on Madeira and São Tomé.

The success of Brazilian sugar affected West Africa greatly by demonstrating once again how profitable a plantation system based on highly disciplined slave labor could be. The specific parts of Africa to which the

An engraving of São Salvador (1686), illustrates an idealization of the capital of the Kingdom of Kongo.

The Ambiguity of First Encounters: The Portuguese and the Kongo

It is commonly believed that Europeans, with their superior military technology, have always been able to dominate Africans. Yet, in fact, before the late nineteenth century African leaders were generally able to act independently, in what they saw as their own best interests, when dealing with Europeans. It is in the revealing ambiguities embedded in such African dealings with Europeans that one can discover the contradictory self-interest and flawed humanity of all participants. None is more interesting than the Kongo welcome of the Portuguese between 1483 and 1543.

When the explorer Diogo Cão arrived at the mouth of the Congo River in 1482, he expected a cool reception similar to those his countrymen had earlier received from West African leaders farther north. But this was not the case. Instead, the Kongo king welcomed the Portuguese with startling enthusiasm. Over the next several decades, Kongo leaders converted to Roman Catholicism, took Christian names, made Catholi-cism a state religion, renamed their capital São Salvador, enthusiastically embraced reading and writing, gave rich gifts to the Portuguese, and clamored for westernization. One Kongo prince became a Catholic bishop.

Why? Some have suggested that the Kongo were overawed by the Portuguese and the magic of their technology. This answer is unconvincing for it ignores African motivation. Other African leaders encountered Europeans without acting as the Kongo did. Why were the Kongo different? The explanation lies in the nature of Kongo politics when Cão appeared on the scene.

The people of Kongo were typical of other African peoples. Although sharing a common culture, they had long been fragmented geographically and politically, with the local extended family being the main social unit. But, as among other peoples, a family's head, if powerful enough, was known as a "big man" because of his links of clientage with people not actually of his family. One such big man, who was situated at the crossroads of two important trade routes, had been able to levy tolls on the trade in cloth, salt, and copper, build up his power, and extend his authority over neighboring areas and fellow big men. Finally, he had assumed the title of *maniKongo* and become the "king" of all the Kongo.

Yet his position was not a dictator's, for he ruled within a complex system of checks and balances. His own family appointed influential counselors to advise him. The state's bureaucracy often acted independently. Religious leaders were prepared to oppose him. Groups on the fringe of the state sought opportunities to resist him or even secede from his control. In short, when Diogo Cão dropped anchor, the *maniKongo* was searching for allies, which would grant him greater independence, legitimacy, and freedom of action. When the Portuguese said that they wanted to be his friends, the *maniKongo* accepted them as allies who could supply him with European weapons. When Catholic missionaries arrived, the *maniKongo* also made them his allies, believing that they would give him a source of independent religious legitimacy he currently lacked.

The *maniKongo's* initial dependence on Portuguese support continued. When the *maniKongo* died in 1506, one of his sons, Afonso, was ambitious to succeed him. According to Kongo custom, however, the kingship should have gone to a nephew. Convinced that European primogeniture was appropriate, the Portuguese supported Afonos, an old friend and ardent Catholic, and he was able to usurp the throne after a "miracle" enabled his army to defeat his rival's force and execute the rightful heir. Afonso rewarded the Portuguese by giving them access to the copper, ivory, cloth, and slaves that they sought.

Did the *maniKongo's* policies work? To the extent that the Portuguese strengthened his position, they clearly did. When Afonso died in 1543, the central government was still going strong and the economy was thriving.

Yet once established in Kongo territory, the Portuguese proved difficult to control. This was because they split into various factions, each with its own aims and strategies. Many of these Portuguese sought to expand slave trading for their own private benefit. Seeking slaves for sugar production on São Tomé, however the Portuguese crown tried to win Afonso's favor by sending him presents in 1508 and 1512. In response, he yielded to the crown a monopoly in buying war captives as slaves. The other Portuguese were outraged, for they wanted to participate in the lucrative trade, and they successfully pressured the crown to abandon its monopoly. All Portuguese in Kongo were then granted the right to trade for slaves. But there were not enough war captives to supply the demand, and the Portuguese sought slaves wherever they could, trading arms to anyone who could provide them, legally or not, and ignoring Afonso and his interests. This situation endangered the *maniKongo's* position in two ways. First, ambitious local big men acquired arms from the Portuguese and, once they had established their own private armies, they pursued their own political goals. Second, the illegal enslavement of Kongo citizens led to popular discontent with Afonso's government for its inability to guarantee public safety. Ironically, then, only with the support he obtained from the Portuguese did he survive the problems precipitated by the Portuguese. In time, during the 1530s, the focus of the slave trade moved inland beyond the state's borders. This eased the pressures on the Kongo state and even permitted Afonso to increase his income by levying tolls on the new slave trade to the coast.

Clearly, the nature of the Kongo reception of the Portuguese can be explained only in terms of Kongo politics. But, as with most political initiatives, it was filled with ambiguities. The Portuguese shored up the *maniKongo* by supplying guns and bringing Catholicism. But they also brought the growing international slave trade, and, with its corrosive impact on society, it could not but lead to profound troubles in the long run not only for the Kongo leadership, but for the Kongo people as a whole.

View of a sugar mill in Pernambuco, Brazil. Sugar and tobacco were the two labor-intensive crops that fostered the growth of plantation agriculture and of slave labor in the New World.

Portuguese turned most for slaves for their Brazilian enterprises were Kongo and Angola, an area to the southwest of Kongo. The story of the new phase in the extraction of slaves from these areas is filled with contradictions.

After the 1540s, the *maniKongo* had ended relations with the Portuguese because of their interference in local affairs. During the 1560s and into the 1570s internal political problems had plagued the *maniKongo* Alvaro I, however, and it was only through accepting renewed Portuguese military support that he had survived the challenges from ambitious rival leaders within the state. The price tag for this military support was that the Portuguese be allowed to increase the level of slave trading from the Kongo region to supply labor to São Tomé and to Brazil's expanding plantations.

In later decades, the Brazilian demand grew more insistent as the plantation economy increased and as the slave population in Brazil did not reproduce itself. This was so for several reasons. The high mortality rate of slaves, plantation owners' discouragement of marriage and family life, psychological stress, the use of abortifacients, and being simply worked too hard all hindered tropical slave societies from reproducing themselves, and Brazil was no different. Furthermore, the trade was mostly in young men, with the number of women always far, far below that of men. As long as slaves could be obtained relatively cheaply in Africa, it made good economic sense for plantation owners to obtain young males, work them to death, and then replace them. If a slave lived for a minimum of four years, he had paid for the cost of his acquisition, transport, and food.

As elsewhere in Africa, despite the appalling sufferings of those enslaved, the burgeoning slave trade through Kongo and Angola greatly increased the power of the participating elites and, in the process, transformed the very nature of the Kongo state as it also changed the nature of slavery within the state. More and more societies of the interior, to the east beyond the Kongo state, became involved in catching people to supply the Portuguese demand. As a consequence, the *maniKongo* was able to increase his tolls on the trade from the interior to the coast. As the trade grew, the *maniKongo* invested much of the state's growing income from the tolls in acquiring slaves for his own state.

The state's leadership used these slaves in two wholly new ways. First, they provided the labor for large plantations established to grow food to be supplied to the Portuguese port of Luanda, founded in 1575 on the coast of Angola, and to the ships involved in the transatlantic slave trade. The introduction of maize and cassava (manioc), new crops from the New World, made this novel use of slave labor especially attractive. These crops yielded far more calories per unit of land than older native crops and hence produced far more income to plantation owners who grew them.

Second, the state also employed slaves as civil servants and, especially, as soldiers. In this way, the government of the *maniKongo* was able to reduce its former dependence upon subsidiary leaders for military support. With his own loyal army of an estimated 20,000 troops, the *maniKongo* effectively curtailed the independence of local big men and expanded the boundaries of his state. As a result of these changes, while in 1550, before the expansion of the slave trade to Brazil, there had been very few slaves in Kongo, by 1650 there were more slaves than free people.

But it was not only in the realms of economic prosperity and military power that the increased Portuguese presence aided the *maniKongo*. For example, literacy was used to strengthen bureaucratic efficiency in Kongo as written Arabic had done in the Sudanic region, with written records allowing for greater exactitude in levying taxes. The use of written letters also permitted the *maniKongo* to communicate directly with people both in his country and in Europe. And making Catholicism a state religion guaranteed that Catholic missionaries would become involved in the day-to-day administration of the state and helped to legitimize the power of the central government.

As a consequence of all this, between 1578, when Alvaro I received renewed support from the Portuguese after the long period of estrangement, and 1614, when Alvaro II died, the Kongo state reached new heights of centralization and prosperity. The *maniKongo* skillfully used the Portuguese to overcome and blunt tendencies within the Kongo political structure to fragment and shatter. Yet support from the Portuguese had become an addiction for the *maniKongo*, and it, like all addictions, was dangerously unpredictable. This was so particularly as the Portuguese developed interests that conflicted with those of the *maniKongo*.

Such conflicting interests arose as a result of Portuguese activities in Angola, to the southwest of the Kongo state. In 1568 a Portuguese adventurer, Paulo Dias de Novais (d. 1589), had landed on Angola's coast. Sebastian (1557–78), the new Portuguese king, a romantic youth of fourteen, had ordered him to conquer the area, a radical departure from past Portuguese policy, which had relied upon cooperation with West African leaders and the maintenance of only small fortified posts such as Elmina. Novais's instructions were different because Portugal wanted direct access to two commodities thought to exist in the interior: silver and slaves. At the time of Novais's landing, there were a number of refugees also entering the area, fleeing the political instability in the Kongo state to the north. These refugees allied themselves with Novais and used Portuguese-supplied arms to raid for slaves for markets in Brazil, São Tomé, and elsewhere.

There was an element of perpetual motion in the slave raiding that came to typify the area, with new groups of people acquiring arms and carrying a slave-raiding frontier deeper and deeper into the interior. And with it came the Portuguese—some government officials and other adventurers working on their own—establishing their fortresses in the interior in the decades after 1600. By 1640 the interior of Angola had become an area of very real and expansive Portuguese military and economic activity, a situation up to then unknown on the West Coast of Africa.

This new situation to the south undermined the Kongo state in two ways. First, much of the earlier trade in slaves that had enriched the *maniKongo's* government for so long was drawn southward through Matamba, an area claimed by the Kongo, toward the Portuguese port of Luanda, on the Angolan coast. Using the income drawn from this new trade, the leaders of this area were able to break free from the overlordship of the Kongo and declare their independence under a remarkable queen, Nzinga. She then outfitted a strong army with Portuguese arms, and by the 1640s, virtually all 13,000 slaves annually exported to Brazil from Luanda were coming through Matamba, cutting off one of the *mani-Kongo's* main sources of income and enriching Nzinga's coffers.

A type of shell known as *nzimbu* was used in the region as a currency. Harvesting them from Luanda Bay, the Portuguese introduced immense quantities of these shells into the Kongo economy. The result was as if unlimited counterfeit money had been placed in circulation. A huge surge of inflation occurred at the very moment that the Kongo leadership was losing its control over the profitable slave trade from the interior. The inflation and the loss of control over its lucrative trade was a combination that the Kongo leadership could not long endure. When the Kongo state was challenged by Nsoyo, a rival coastal state to its west whose leaders had begun to strengthen themselves through trade with British and Dutch merchants challenging Portuguese commercial dominance in the region, the Kongo state entered upon a period of prolonged decline, defeat, and dismemberment. At last, in 1649, after a military defeat, the *maniKongo* surrendered his southern territories to the Portuguese, yielded them a trade monopoly, agreed to stop taxing the slave trade, and sent hostages to Lisbon as guarantors of his good behavior. The state of Kongo, long famous in Europe for its wealth and its adoption of many European customs, quickly collapsed. São Salvador, the Kongo capital, which had had tens of thousands of people living in it at the start of the century, was finally abandoned in 1678, with its people returning to the countryside.

A Portuguese delegation meets the formidable Queen Nzinga of Matamba. When the Portuguese governor refused her a chair, she sat down on one of her attendants.

Portuguese and Africans in Mozambique

During the sixteenth century the Portuguese also expanded their presence on the East Coast, in Mozambique, where gold was their main motivation. At the start of the century, they thought they could remain in their coastal settlements at Sofala and on Mozambique Island and that the gold trade would flow naturally down to them as it had long done in West Africa, at Elmina. These expectations were not fulfilled, however, and gradually the Portuguese felt that they had no choice but to intervene in the interior. One reason for such involvement was that they encountered stiff competition. Portuguese naval forces were too weak to prevent Swahili merchants from developing new inland trade routes for Zimbabwe's gold, bypassing the Portuguese settlements, and arriving at the coast at Angoche, a new Swahili port at which they offered better deals than the Portuguese did. The Portuguese quickly realized that if they were to prosper, they would have to compete by sending their own agents inland to seek direct access to the gold and cut out the Swahili competition.

Competition also came from individual Portuguese beyond official control. In establishing their empire, Portugal's rulers had largely relied upon a group of people whom they felt Portugal itself could well do without. Many of the foot soldiers of empire were criminals, not people from whom much loyalty to the Portuguese state could be expected. Once beyond Lisbon's direct control, these people often struck out on their own, seeking their fortunes by venturing beyond governmental control into the interior. As they pushed up into the hot and humid Zambezi valley in search of gold, they formed a second group of competitors to the official traders in coastal settlements. As time passed, more and more of these Portuguese adventurers traveled into the interior, married local African women, and settled down as Africanized *sertanejos*, or "backwoodsmen." As had happened earlier along the Guinea coast and was to happen later in Angola, an Africanized group of people of mixed race and culture developed in Mozambique after 1580.

That the Swahili merchants and Portuguese sertanejos were welcome in the interior was largely because of a situation there remarkably similar to that in Angola during the same period. Successors of the Great Zimbabwe state occupied the area, but none was as unified or powerful as its predecessor. Instead, several states competed with each other over access to gold and other resources. One of these was "Monomotapa," named after its ruler, the *Mwene Mutapa*. Other substantial states in the area included Changamire and a set of Maravi kingdoms north of the Zambezi River. Changamire posed an especially severe threat to the Mwene Mutapa, and so he welcomed outsiders to come into his area to trade and be his allies.

It was in this political context that Portuguese officials reluctantly moved up the Zambezi valley to compete more effectively for gold and other products. In the 1530s they established trading stations at Sena and Tete, both on the south bank of the Zambezi River. In 1544 they founded the coastal town of Quelimane as a commercial alternative to the Swahili port of Angoche. By 1560 the official Portuguese settlements were flourishing, but by then, too, their English, French, and Dutch rivals were beginning seriously to challenge the Portuguese naval dominance of the Indian Ocean basin.

A portrait of a Mwene Mutapa. *The Portuguese artist depicts the king with a European-style scepter and crown.*

The Portuguese began to think that it would be wise for them to consolidate their still tenuous position in Mozambique by taking direct control over the mines of the interior. Perhaps Mozambique was destined to become "the Brazil of Africa" and, if so, it should remain Portugal's.

During this period of reevaluation, in 1568, Sebastian, the new Portuguese king, became convinced that God had chosen him to lead a crusade against the Muslims. He decided that the Muslim Swahili traders competing with the Portuguese in Mozambique were ideal targets for his wrath. He dispatched an army to conquer the Mwene Mutapa and his Swahili allies and to seize Monomotapa's mines for Portugal. Things went well initially, and in 1569 the Portuguese handily defeated an African army and massacred Muslims they encountered. But soon malaria began to kill the Portuguese, sleeping sickness killed their horses, and the army gradually evaporated.

In the midst of this action, the Mwene Mutapa, both concerned with the Portuguese military advance into the interior and eager to gain their aid against his African enemies, especially the state of Changamire, executed several Muslim merchants at his capital to show his good intentions. In 1575 he concluded a treaty of friendship with the Portuguese. The treaty gave them the right to trade freely in his lands, to build churches, to mine gold, and to expel any Muslims that they might encounter. In subsequent years, as the Mwene Mutapa sought additional Portuguese arms, he made more concessions and further undermined the integrity of his state. As in the case of the Kongo, a situation was fast developing from which the African elite had no real escape. On the one hand, the Mwene Mutapa felt that Portuguese support was necessary for his campaigns against his local enemies. On the other hand, however, with the expulsion of the Muslims, he now had no one to balance against the Portuguese and their demands for concessions.

The dependency of the Mwene Mutapa on the Portuguese grew. In 1607 he signed a treaty that turned over to them the area's gold, copper, and iron mines and yielded five of his children as hostages, so that they might be trained as Catholics and educated as Portuguese. While these concessions kept the Portuguese state at bay, more and more unruly Portuguese sertanejos were coming to live in the interior beyond the reach of Portuguese officials and as laws unto themselves, frequently ignoring the Mwene Mutapa and his laws. At the death of the old Mwene Mutapa in 1624, a succession dispute occurred, which was marked by efforts by

Portugal and Africa, 1415–1650

1415	Seizure of the Moroccan city of Ceuta
1434	Discovery of the Madeira Islands in Atlantic Ocean
1444	First slaves traded from Argiun, on Mauritanian coast
1482	Fortified trading station built at Elmina, Guinea coast; Diogo Cão welcomed by the king of Kongo
1494	Treaty of Tordesillas divides the world between Spain and Portugal
1498	Vasco da Gama enters Indian Ocean
1509	Battle of Diu, near India, establishes Portugal as dominant naval power in Indian Ocean basin
1531	Portugal establishes trading station of Sena, in Mozambique's Zambezi valley
1549	Portugal decides to build sugar industry in Brazil
1568	Sebastian, an intense anti-Muslim, becomes king of Portugal
1569	Portugal's first serious invasion of inland Mozambique
1575	Establishment of colony at Luanda to facilitate slave trade from Angola
1629	*Mwene Mutapa* becomes "vassal" of Portuguese king and cedes concessions in Mozambique to Portugal
1649	*ManiKongo* cedes concessions of Portugal and Kongo state begins final collapse

a pretender, Kaparidze, to bring the Portuguese under control. He first seized some Portuguese trading stations and demanded tribute from the Portuguese government. In response, the Portuguese supported another pretender, whom they placed on the throne in 1629. He then signed an agreement with the Portuguese that formally made him a vassal of the Portuguese king and opened his country without any restriction to Portuguese traders and prospectors.

Monomotapa's people were unhappy to see their independence disappear in this way, and in 1631, Kaparidze organized a campaign of resistance to the Portuguese takeover. Missionaries, traders, prospectors, and Africans identified as collaborators with the Portuguese were killed, with the final death count reportedly running into the thousands. The Portuguese government sent an army to reestablish order, and through the army's successes in 1632 the Portuguese government secured a powerful position in the whole Zambezi valley. Once established there, the Portuguese went to work in succeeding decades to dismantle further the Mwene Mutapa's state as well as those of other Africans. Perhaps the greatest threat, however, came not from the Portuguese state itself but from the Portuguese sertanejos, who used slaves to create private mercenary armies that allowed them to rule over large tracts of the Zambezi valley utterly heedless of Lisbon and its laws and largely beyond the control of local Africans as well. In this way, large areas of Mozambique's interior experienced the same sort of changes then occurring in Angola's interior, with local Africans being drawn into an economic system largely dominated by Portuguese adventurers and with the Portuguese state laying the foundations of a colony destined to remain Portugal's until 1974.

The impact of Portuguese trade and intervention in the internal affairs of regions in the African hinterland was highly contradictory. Initially, for rulers who were able to supply what the Portuguese wanted, there were real benefits, and their governments were able to strengthen themselves. But one of Portugal's demands—for slaves to work sugar plantations—had especially negative consequences. It not only brought misery to the unfortunates who were enslaved and forced to experience the harrowing "Middle Passage" to the New World, but Portugal's demand for slaves also created extreme difficulties for African rulers, especially in places such as Kongo where the needs of the newly established Brazilian plantations prompted the Portuguese to intervene actively in the procurement of slaves. By the start of the seventeenth century, however, other European nations had decided to challenge Portugal's hegemony along all the coasts of Africa, beginning an era of far greater African contact with other European powers, far greater challenges for Africans, and far greater changes within Africa itself.

America and the Encounters

The regions of Mesoamerica and the central Andes underwent enormous changes during the half millennium between the mid-thirteenth and eighteenth centuries. Two powerful peoples, the Aztecs of the Valley of Mexico and the Incas of the Andean highlands, moved into the void left by the collapse of classic civilizations and constructed vast empires. At the zenith of their achievements they in turn fell before the Spanish *conquistadores* (conquerors).

The reaction of the peoples of Mesoamerica and the Andes to the Europeans framed the history of the succeeding two centuries. They resisted the imposition of European rule and the intrusion of European culture, particularly religion—fiercely and violently on occasion, passively and relentlessly most of the time. The conjunction of the two groups, combined with a third, the African peoples brought forcefully to work in the New World, forged a hybrid culture and produced new peoples of mixed blood (*mestizos*, the offspring of European and Indian; mulattos, or *pardos*, the progeny of European and African; *zambos*, the offspring of Indian and African).

The Spanish and Portuguese succeeded in controlling the vast territory from the Californias south to the Strait of Magellan at the tip of South America. Their success was due to a combination of their own administrative flexibility and the effects of the catastrophic decline in native population that resulted from the introduction of European diseases.

The Rise of the Aztec and Inca Empires

Mesoamerica and the Andes produced artistic, intellectual, and political accomplishments that rivaled and sometimes surpassed those of the Old World. (See Chapter 1.) The Olmec, Chavín, and Maya civilizations produced magnificent achievements. But these societies crumbled under circumstances that we only partially understand, leaving both the central Andes and Mesoamerica fragmented. After 200 to 300 years, in the fourteenth and fifteenth centuries, powerful new empires arose, the Aztec in Mesoamerica and the Inca in South America, unifying vast expanses of territory and millions of people. Both Aztecs and Incas rose meteorically; the Incas built their domain in the short span of thirty years. Neither had been in power long enough to consolidate and stabilize their conquered lands. Each faced the Europeans with a divided empire. Their vul-

nerabilities became all too apparent when they were confronted with the challenge of the Spaniards.

The Aztecs were one of the barbarian peoples called Chichimecas who migrated from the north to the Valley of Mexico. The Mexicas, as they were also known, arrived in the region and settled at Chapultepec on Lake Texcoco around 1250 C.E. Because of their extreme brutality, they were unwelcome neighbors, and in 1319 an alliance of city-states expelled them. The Mexica worked as mercenaries, eventually finding safe haven on an island in the middle of the lake, where in 1345 they founded what was to be Tenochtitlán. Borrowing the technology of the valley dwellers, they built an ingenious hydraulic farming system based on floating gardens, called *chinampas*, which enabled the city to grow to a population that exceeded 200,000 at its height.

The road to empire began between 1429 and 1433 when the Triple Alliance of Tenochtitlán and two neighboring city-states, Texcoco and Tlacopán, defeated the dominant power in the Valley of Mexico, Atzcapotzalco. The alliance conquered the Valley of Mexico and its neighboring regions, then set about to unify the high plateau under its rule and extend the empire south and east into what is now the state of Veracruz and then west to the Pacific Coast. To ensure the food supply, devastated in a four-year-long famine at mid-century, the alliance constructed an extensive system of irrigation and flood control for the lakes in the valley. The unprecedented series of military victories ended when the Aztecs attempted unsuccessfully to defeat the Tarascans in what is now Michoacán. Further defeats followed. In 1502 Moctezuma II (1466–1520) took power. He presided over the destruction of the empire by the Spanish.

Historians vary widely in their interpretations of the Aztec empire. The differing views focus on the nature of the relationship between the Aztecs and their subject peoples and on the extent of and the reasons for the practice of human sacrifice. There is substantial agreement that the Aztecs erected no significant bureaucracy, that they used marriage to link the city-states of the valley, and that they kept lesser local rulers in power as long as they paid the required tribute. The Aztecs maintained military control not by occupation but through threats and reconquest. No such consensus exists about the nature of the relations between the Aztecs and neighboring states. The nature of the "flowery wars" fought between the Triple Alliance and five city-states just over the mountains in the Puebla Valley, southeast of Tenochtitlán, is at the heart of the debate. Why did the Aztecs allow these states, most

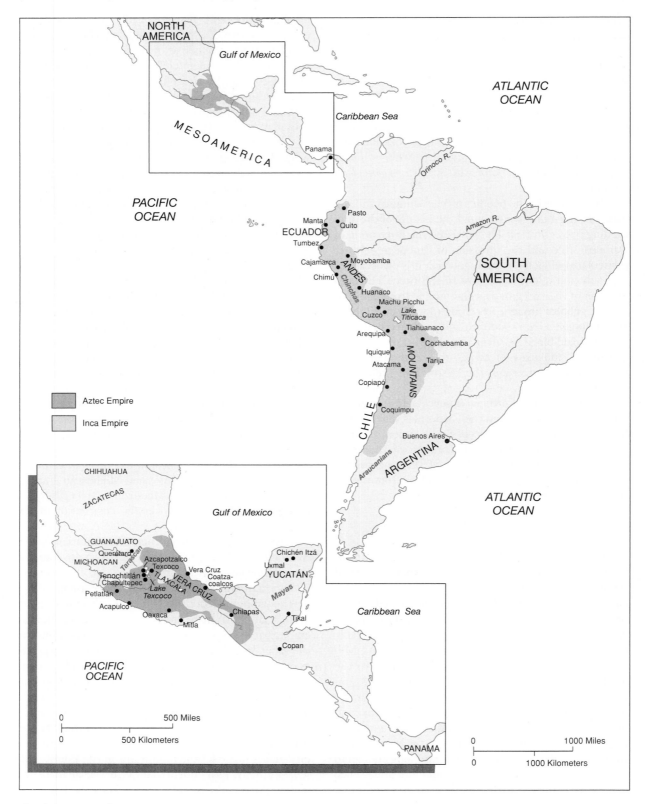

America, ca. 1300–1600

notably Tlaxcala, to maintain their autonomy, when Aztec military might should have brought easy victory over them? One possible answer is that these were phony wars used to provide a guaranteed supply of captives for human sacrifice. Another possible reason is that the Aztecs used these conflicts to furnish much-needed high-level military training for their young soldiers. The overall question of just how much control the Aztecs exerted over their empire is still only partially answered.

The extent of and motivation for human sacrifice by the Aztecs is perhaps the most controversial topic. Undoubtedly, human sacrifice was an integral part of Aztec religion. According to Aztec tradition, the world had gone through four previous stages or Suns, each destroyed by catastrophe. In order to maintain the Fifth Sun in place and ward off the predicted next disaster, the Aztecs sought to keep their deities satisfied. This required human blood obtained from bloodletting and sacrifice. Some observers see human sacrifice as an invention of imperial rule, aimed at terrorizing military foes into quick surrender and subject peoples into submission. The extent of the practice is also much debated. The Spanish chroniclers, who recorded the conquerors' exploits and who tried to compile a version of the Aztecs' history after their defeat, told of extensive sacrifice. At the dedication of a new temple in Tenochtitlán in the late fifteenth century, Aztec priests supposedly sacrificed tens of thousands of lives. Others believe the practice existed on a far more modest scale and that the chroniclers exaggerated the numbers to enhance the glory of the Aztec empire and, thus, the glory of its conquerors.

The Aztec capital, Tenochtitlán, rivaled the great cities of Europe. The city was laid out like Venice, and its canals furnished the major means of transportation. Although the chinampas were extremely productive, most supplies had to be brought in from the mainland on three causeways. Consequently, Tenochtitlán was a bustling commercial center. An extensive system of aqueducts transported drinking water. Large temples and palaces rose from the lake, forming a magnificent skyline.

The basic social unit of Aztec society was the *calpulli*, a kin-based community with landholding, religious, and military functions. At the top was the *tlatoani* or chief speaker (emperor). Originally elected by the calpulli, by the time of Moctezuma II the chief speaker reached the status of deity. As Aztec conquests expanded, society stratified; what began as bureaucratic and citizen military meritocracies became a hereditary nobility and a

The founding of Tenochtitlán, from Codex Mendoza. *The drawings at the bottom depict the early Aztec conquests of Colhuacan and Tenayucan.*

professional military. In the middle of the social scale were merchants and artisans. Merchants occupied perhaps the most precarious position in society, not only because they risked death as military spies for the Aztec armies, but because, if too successful and ostentatious in their display of wealth, they were subject to drastic punishment by their rulers. Artisans were assured an important status, for they crafted the gold and feather ornaments for the chief speaker and nobility, providing them with the necessary conspicuous consumption their exalted positions required. The common people, called *macehualtin*, were members of the calpulli and owned land. Beneath them were the *mayeques*, or bondsmen, who comprised perhaps as many as one-third of the population. We know very little about them other than that they were probably landless people attached to the lands of the nobility. The *tlacotin*, or slaves, made up roughly five percent of the population. One could become a slave by committing a crime, through debts, or by selling oneself. As society grew more hierarchical and social classes more stratified, women experienced less independence. Nonetheless, they could own their own property, conduct business such as trade (through traders), and practice quite autonomous professions like midwife, healer, or priestess. Women who died in childbirth were revered equally with those males who died in battle, the greatest glories an Aztec could attain.

There is little historical evidence about the rise of the other great American empire, the Incas. They had no writing, and archaeological discoveries in the Andes, especially in the environs of Cuzco, the Inca capital, are limited. Most likely, the Incas arrived in the region of Cuzco around 1250 C.E. For nearly two hundred years, they lived as one of numerous tribes in the region. They began their meteoric rise to mighty empire in 1438, when Inca Yupanqui, a disinherited son of the reigning Inca Viracocha, saved them from defeat by a local rival. Legend has it that, unable to gather enough recruits to battle, he turned stones into soldiers. The new ruler, now known as Pachacuti, began an unprecedented series of conquests. During the next thirty years, he and his successors carried the empire south to the region of Lake Titicaca and into what is now Argentina and Chile and north as far as Ecuador. They controlled the central Andean highlands and the Pacific Coast. Only the Amazonian jungles proved an impenetrable barrier.

In an extraordinarily short period, the Incas built an empire that rivaled in territory and population the great conquests of the Greeks and Romans. The expansion depended more on persuasion than on military prowess. Inca policies were meant to give subject peoples a stake in the empire and to foster loyalty to it. Whereas Aztec armies were composed of professional soldiers from the Triple Alliance, Inca armies consisted primarily of peasants from the most recently conquered states mobilized as part of their tribute obligations to the empire. Including subject peoples in the new military campaigns served two practical purposes. Since there were far too few Incas to carry out large-scale conquest, it furnished needed soldiers. In addition, it gave conquered people a stake in the empire. Local elites retained their power. The Incas also realized the need for at least the threat of coercion behind their persuasion. Consequently, they established a clear record of atrocities to back up their material incentives.

The Incas controlled their empire by means of a vast bureaucracy and tax system, more remarkable because they lacked a written language and because the Andes presented enormous difficulties in transportation and communication. They built their rule on existing polit-

An Inca "accountant." The Inca lacked writing, but they used the quipu, *knotted strings of different lengths and colors, to keep accurate and detailed records.*

ical structures. They were very flexible, treating small-scale chiefdoms differently from complex city-states. The Incas rewarded subject peoples with participation in the glory and spoils of new conquests, shrewdly taking advantage of regional rivalries, pitting a newly conquered people against an old, neighboring enemy. Moreover, the Incas provided other benefits, such as irrigation works, terraces, and roads.

The Incas closely administered conquered peoples. They resettled much of their subject population. The sons of the rulers of conquered states were sent to school in Cuzco, partly as hostages to assure cooperation, but also to indoctrinate them into Inca language and ideology. The Incas sought to spread their language, Quechua, and their religion. But they also absorbed other deities and beliefs into their pantheon. As always their inclusiveness and openness had a purpose. They often brought the idols of subject peoples to Cuzco to hold as hostages. The Incas' primary form of retribution against rebels was deportation, not death.

When they began their conquests, the Incas relied on peasant soldiers. As the empire grew, however, there evolved a professional military centered in specialized ethnic groups. Inca-led armies did not plunder or forage, but rather used provisions stored in warehouses along their famous road system.

By the early sixteenth century the Inca military campaigns slowed or ended. There was no method to maintain the satisfaction of peripheral subject peoples, and they frequently rebelled. When two rivals for leadership clashed in 1525, an underutilized military proved restless and dangerous and moved easily to civil war.

Inca social organization revolved around the family unit, called the *ayllu*. The ayllu distributed land among its members every two years. Its members cared for the old and infirm by working common lands. As in the case of the Aztecs, the social structure became more stratified as the empire grew. At the top of society was the Sapay-Inca, or emperor. By the time of the Spaniards' arrival, his position had evolved from tribal leader to god-king. Originally a council of ayllu elected the Sapay-Inca, but after the conquests, the ruler chose his successor. Below the Sapay-Inca was the hereditary nobility, the ruling Inca clan. Underneath them were the ayllus of Cuzco and the chieftains of conquered peoples. There was also a class of bondsmen called *yanacona*.

The Inca capital, Cuzco, was not nearly as elaborate as Tenochtitlán, but it had more than 100,000 residents. Each inhabitant had to wear the costume of his or her home tribe or city-state. Cuzco was an administrative and religious center, but unlike Tenochtitlán it was not a hub of commerce. The Inca state controlled trade in the Andes, and the medium of trade was barter.

Despite better administration and more benevolent rule, the Inca empire, like the Aztec, was in crisis in the years before the Spaniards arrived in Peru. The Inca Huayna Capac, who reigned from 1493 to 1525, had taken a number of measures that led to civil war. He moved his capital from Cuzco to Ecuador in the far northern reaches of the empire, which led to a geographic split between north and south. In addition, the emperor fostered rivalry between his legitimate heir and successor, Huáscar, and his son by a concubine, Atahuallpa. When Huayna Capac died, Atahuallpa refused to recognize his half-brother as Sapay-Inca and civil war ensued. With northern support, the rebel won. But the bloody civil war left wounds that never healed.

The Fall of the Aztec and Inca Empires

By the first decade of the sixteenth century the great empires were weakened and divided, having apparently reached their limits. The Aztecs had encountered the fierce resistance of western Tarascans and northern Chichimecs; bitter old enemies like Tlaxcala festered in their hate. There is evidence too that when slowed conquest diminished the supply of luxury items and sacrifice victims, internal dissension arose. Moreover, the population of the Valley of Mexico may have reached its ecological limits. In the mid-fifteenth century, when a massive famine struck, the Aztecs had trouble feeding a smaller version of the empire. Based on tribute, which often was in the form of sacrifice victims, the Aztec empire elicited no loyalty. Tlaxcalans, after a nasty defeat at the hands of the Spaniards, and imbued with old grudges against Tenochtitlán, allied with the newcomers. If the Aztec empire was held together by the terror of human sacrifice, it was not a lasting bond. The empire of the Incas tore itself apart by civil war between north and south. Hence, on the eve of the encounters, both empires were vulnerable.

The stories of the conquests of Mexico and Peru are epic tales told by the victors. Glorified by the chronicles of their companions, the *conquistadores*, or conquerors, especially Hernán Cortés (1485–1547), emerged as heroes larger than life. In 1517 the Spaniards sent a scouting expedition to the region of Veracruz. Cortés landed in the same region in 1519. He scuttled his ships and set off westward. After soundly thrashing a Tlaxcalan army and inducing the losers to join them against the Aztecs, the Spaniards marched to Tenochtitlán. They quickly captured and publicly humiliated Moctezuma, forcing him to rule as their puppet. Cortés had to return to the coast to head off an expedition led by Pánfilo de Narváez (ca. 1480–1528), sent to arrest him for insubordination to the governor of Cuba, under whose auspices the expedition had sailed. Cortés defeated Narváez, incorporating Narváez's remaining soldiers in his army, now numbering 1,300. While Cortés was away from Tenochtitlán, his second-in-command, Pedro de Alvarado (ca. 1485–1541), provoked a bloody confrontation with the Aztecs, leading to the overthrow of Moctezuma, who fell victim to a lethal stone thrown by one of his subjects. When Cortés returned, he realized he must retreat from the city. This he did on the night of 30 June 1520, known as *La Noche Triste*, the Night of Sorrows. The retreat cost the conquistador two-thirds of his men and most of his horses. The Aztecs, however, did not pursue the Spaniards, who fled to Tlaxcala. The Aztecs

THE MASSACRE AT THE CANAL OF THE TOLTECS

■ *The Aztecs and Incas did not relinquish their rule without persistent, fierce resistance to the Spaniards. As this passage from* The Broken Spears *indicates, the natives defeated the conquerors rather badly. If not for the ravages of disease on the population of Tenochtitlán, especially on the Aztec leadership, and the alliance of other cities once subordinated or allied with the Aztecs, the Spaniards might have perished.*

When the Spaniards reached the Canal of the Toltecs . . . they hurled themselves headlong into the water, as if they were leaping from a cliff . . .

The canal was soon choked with the bodies of men and horses; they filled the gap in the causeway with their own drowned bodies. Those who followed crossed to the other side by walking on the corpses . . .

The dawn was breaking as they entered the village. Their hearts were cheered by the brightening light of this new day: they thought the horrors of the retreat were all behind them. But suddenly they heard war cries and the Aztecs swarmed through the streets and surrounded them. They had come to capture the Tlaxcaltecas for their sacrifices. They also wanted to complete their revenge against the Spaniards.

remained in Tenochtitlán and reconstituted their forces. The Spaniards returned to besiege Tenochtitlán, now ruled by the emperor Cuauhtémoc. The Aztecs held out miraculously for nearly three months, during which time the city was almost completely destroyed by bombardment from ships on the lake and house-to-house fighting. The end of the siege came on 13 August 1521 with the capture of Cuauhtémoc. The resistance of native peoples did not end then, however.

Francisco Pizarro (ca. 1475–1541) arrived in Cajamarca, Peru, in November 1532. Like Cortés, he sought to capture the emperor, cutting off the head of the empire. This he did on 16 November, when the haughty Atahuallpa fatally miscalculated his military power. The Spaniards executed Atahuallpa and conducted an appalling slaughter of the Inca army. Pizarro needed a puppet to act as titular head of the Inca empire. Manco Capac, son of Huayna Capac, began as a collaborator. From 1533 to 1536 he acted as the Spaniards' stooge, humiliated and imprisoned. Finally, after the Europeans raped his wives in front of him, he escaped, gathered an army, and began the Inca resistance. Despite a numerically superior army—over 40,000 against 200 Spaniards—Manco was unable to successfully besiege Cuzco. When his army dissipated, Manco established a mountain retreat, from which he harassed the conquerors until betrayed by Spaniards to whom he had offered refuge. His son Sayri Tupac, only ten years old, succeeded him, only to sur-

render in 1555 to the enticements of a royal life under Spanish rule. When he died in 1560, another son of Manco, Titu Cusi, rekindled the resistance and ten years of guerrilla war ensued, ending with his death. The Spanish viceroy, Francisco de Toledo, penetrated the Inca redoubt, capturing the last Inca, Tupac Amarú, in 1572.

After the initial shocks of losing their leaders and their capitals, the Aztecs, Incas, and other native peoples fiercely resisted the Spaniards. They quickly learned how to fight against the guns and horses. Throughout the three hundred years of colonial rule, they resisted, if not by shedding blood then passively, day by day, to maintain their language and customs. Some fought into the twentieth century. Latin American culture today remains a testimony to their persistence.

The native population of Brazil was composed of nonsedentary and semisedentary peoples, who also fiercely resisted the incursions of the Europeans. Because of their mobility and the vastness and harshness of the land into which they could escape, they proved difficult to defeat permanently, though their numbers were decimated by disease.

The Portuguese in many ways obtained Brazil much as the British were later said to have acquired their empire—"in a fit of absence of mind." In 1500 Pedro Alvares Cabral, en route to Asia via the coast of Africa, was blown far off course across the Atlantic and landed

CAPITVLODELOSPASAGEROS
ESPAÑOLESDELTA
bo y criollos mestizos ymula
tos ycriollas mestizas yespa
ñoles cristianos
decastilla

The Spanish attitude toward the Indians is demonstrated in this sixteenth-century drawing of a Spaniard kicking an Indian. Spanish colonial society was divided into classes on the basis of birthplace and race.

How then did barely four hundred Spaniards under Hernán Cortés and perhaps one hundred with Francisco Pizarro destroy them?

The Spaniards recognized weakness and division and exploited both. Native soldiers comprised the preponderance of the army that Cortés led against Tenochtitlán. Pizarro allied with the losing side in the Inca civil war, the followers of Huáscar. Cortés and Pizarro provided brilliant leadership compared to the Aztecs and Incas. Early in the struggles the Spaniards captured both Moctezuma II and Atahuallpa, leaving a vacuum in these highly centralized empires.

The Spaniards had a number of advantages in the war against the Aztec and Inca empires. At first glance they appear to have enjoyed superior weaponry; they had guns, cannon, and metal armor. They also had horses, which added speed and mobility and frightened their opponents. Ultimately, though, their technology may not have been advantageous. The Spaniards quickly discarded their heavy armor, which in tropical climates or high altitudes was burdensome, and adopted the natives' woven cotton. Archers could reload faster than gunners. Although the noise of the cannon terrorized the native troops at first, they quickly got used to it. The initial advantage of the horses was soon lost, as they were a distinct hazard in closed spaces like Tenochtitlán.

The Spaniards' greatest advantage, perhaps, lay in their persistence and ruthlessness and in the profound cultural misunderstanding between them and their opponents, especially the Aztecs. The Spaniards, deeply motivated by greed and ambition, employed vicious tactics. Cortés's scuttling his ships in order to prevent any turning back clearly indicates the extent of the Spaniards' desperate motivation. The Spaniards also benefited from their view of warfare. To the Aztecs, war was a sacred undertaking, in which the goal was to capture the bravest, most capable opponents for sacrifice. At its utmost, war was one man against another, face to face. Aztec warriors did not retreat, did not hide behind walls or horses, did not kill civilians indiscriminately. The Spaniards did all of these, for their concept of war was quite different. To them, as to all Europeans, the goal of war was victory at any cost. This helps explain why the Spanish suffered so few casualties.

Another example of the radically different and mutually misunderstood worldviews of Aztecs and Spaniards was their respective perceptions of the gifts Aztec emperor Moctezuma II sent to Cortés after the latter landed in the region of Veracruz in 1519. These opulent presents were meant by the Aztecs as a haughty display

on the coast of what is now Brazil. He discovered, evidently to his surprise, that under the terms of the Treaty of Tordesillas, which was signed in 1494 by Spain and Portugal and divided the world between them, the territory he landed on belonged to Portugal. At the time, however, the Portuguese were preoccupied by trade with Asia. Aside from gathering brazilwood—from which the colony derived its name—for use in dyes, they largely ignored their new possession. Since no precious metals were readily available, there was no pressing need for attention.

Controversy as well as curiosity abounds about the reasons for the Spanish conquest, which was decisive and relatively swift. Vulnerable or not, the great Aztec and Inca empires were formidable foes and vastly outnumbered the Europeans. They had the advantage of knowing the land. They were brave, brilliant warriors.

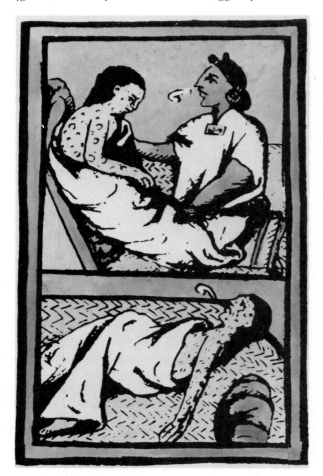

Aztec Indians suffering from smallpox during the conquest. The disease took a terrible toll among the inhabitants of Mexico, who had no immunity to the plagues of the Old World.

of their power; they were insults to the Spaniards. The Spaniards interpreted the gifts as a sign of Aztec weakness, attempted bribes to keep them from Tenochtitlán.

Perhaps the crucial factor in the defeat of the Aztec and Inca empires, however, was neither the military prowess of the Spaniards nor the internal weaknesses of the American empires, but rather the rapid spread of diseases like smallpox, measles, and plague, which devastated the native population. There is little question that disease preceded the arrival of the Spaniards to both Mesoamerica and Peru. Early landings had spread smallpox to Tenochtitlán. Several important leaders fell to the disease, weakening Aztec war-making power. In the Andes, half the population may have perished even before Pizarro arrived. So badly weakened, the Incas were easier prey for the Spaniards.

Spanish and Portuguese Colonial America, 1550–1700

Once the initial military victories in Mesoamerica and the Andes were complete, the Europeans, thousands of miles from their homelands across the Atlantic Ocean, confronted a vast extent of territory, with a population far larger than that of the Iberian Peninsula. The problems of ruling such an enormous domain were as vast and complex as the land and the people. The natives resisted fiercely, and rebellions punctuated the sixteenth century; some less sedentary peoples continued to fight for three hundred years to avoid the colonial yoke. Moreover, the New World colonies were constantly threatened by European rivals. English pirates, Dutch merchants, and French adventurers nibbled at Iberian hegemony. In Europe the Spanish crown engaged in continual warfare, with unfortunate consequences for its colonies.

The Spanish and Portuguese ruled their New World empires with utmost flexibility, bare-bones administration, and minimal use of force. The Spaniards, especially, centered their efforts on the extraction and removal of gold and silver, which the crown used to finance its European involvements.

A complex mixture of motivations, which historians have characterized as gold, glory, and God, comprised the psyche of the conquerors and colonists. They were exceptionally greedy and ruthless in their pursuit of riches and—particularly the earliest arrivals—fervent in their desire to Christianize the natives. They believed that military conquest and religious proselytization would bring honor to them and to the crown. To Ferdinand and Isabella, the first Spanish rulers of the New World, and their successors, Charles I and Philip II, the defense and spread of Christianity were paramount considerations. They were literally the defenders of the faith, second only to the pope. But it was enormously expensive to defend Christianity and the huge Spanish empire in Europe, which expanded when King Charles I of Spain became Holy Roman Emperor Charles V in the mid-sixteenth century. Spanish kings' demands for revenues from the New World were aggressive and unending. When faced with conflict between Christian virtue and treasure, the crown most assuredly chose the latter.

The administrative and economic complex of Spanish colonial rule evolved around the extraction of precious metals, such as gold and silver. For three hundred years the crown managed to walk a tightrope between meddling in the smallest matters involving revenue and

Spanish and Portuguese Colonial America

The phrase *obedezco pero no cumplo*, which means "I obey but do not comply," aptly describes the ability of the colonists to refuse laws that they opposed.

There is considerable debate over the size of the population of the New World at the time of the arrival of the Europeans. For Mesoamerica in 1519, estimates range from 4.5 to 25.2 million, and for Peru from 3 to 32 million inhabitants. The best current estimates are probably 12 to 25 million for Mesoamerica, 9 million for Peru, and 2.4 million for Brazil. But there is no question that the population underwent a catastrophic decline. One estimate based on postconquest tribute (taxation) records posits that the population of Mesoamerica stood at 25.2 million in 1519 and then fell to 16.8 million in 1532; 6.3 million in 1548; 2.65 million in 1568; 1.9 million in 1580; 1.375 million in 1595; 1.075 million in 1605; 0.75 million in 1622. The destruction took place in successive epidemics, first of smallpox and measles, later influenza. In the mid-seventeenth century yellow fever and malaria arrived from Africa. By 1650 contact with Europeans had eliminated 90 to 95 percent of the native population. (Accepting the lower range of estimates for Mesoamerica in 1519, the percentage loss is over 80 percent for a population of 12 million.)

The demographic collapse changed landholding patterns, crop production, ecology, labor systems, and methods of administration. Formerly dense populations of native peoples disappeared, replaced by Europeans, Africans, and migrants from other regions. The decline was uneven, some areas were harder-hit than others. However, the devastating physical and psychological toll did not destroy the indigenous cultures.

Given the scarce resources and manpower and the vast distances between Spain and its empire, the first impulse of the Spanish was to merely take over the top ranks of the hierarchical indigenous societies. The native elite would remain in place, retaining most of its privileges, and ensuring that their subjects furnished tribute in the form of taxes and labor. However, the drop in population forced the Spaniards to involve themselves more extensively with the native people.

Because the revenues from Peru and New Spain, as the Spaniards named the Mesoamerican part of the empire, were so important, the crown constructed a large bureaucracy to administer them. These Spanish bureaucrats, with their propensity for paperwork, generated tons of laws, regulations, reports, and correspondence, which historians have used to study the period. Much of importance that happened was unrecorded, however.

At the top of the administrative pyramid, just below the Spanish king and based in Spain, was the Council of

pushing the colonists to rebellion. Colonial administration functioned differently in the regions central to mining than in those in the periphery. The central mining regions were highly regulated, while the far regions were left for the most part to rule themselves. The entire economic system, including commerce, landholding, and labor organization, was based on a complex of mining center, city, and *hacienda* (a large landed estate). A similar situation existed in Brazil, where the Portuguese concentrated their efforts on the production of sugar, with interludes for gold and diamonds.

Two practical considerations shaped Iberian governance in the New World. First, the precipitous and catastrophic decline of the native population forced constant readjustments of Spanish policies. Demographic recovery resulting not only from increased immunities of the native peoples to European diseases after the mid-seventeenth century but also from the growing population of mixed-bloods (*mestizos* and mulattos) and white immigrants also forced important shifts. Second, the great distances between Spain and Portugal and their colonies and the inability of either to station large number of soldiers in the New World meant that flexibility was crucial. Colonists were in a favorable position to oppose onerous laws or policies.

III.
INDI, QVA ARTE AVRVM EX
MONTIBVS ERVANT.

A silver mine at Potosi, in Peru. The mine provided enormous wealth for the Spaniards, but many of the Indian laborers lost their lives in the harsh working conditions.

the Indies. It was responsible for the legislative, judicial, and consultative functions of colonial administration, both recommending the appointment of officeholders and scrutinizing their work. Unfortunately, very few members of the Council had any experience in the colonies. The crown's ranking representatives in the Americas were the viceroys. Initially, there were two viceroys, one for New Spain and one for Peru. Each viceroy was responsible for general administration, tax revenues, public works, social order, defense, and protection of the native peoples. Although in theory they were substitute kings, in practice the viceroys were limited in power by the overlapping jurisdictions of the crown's financial officers and the Church. Because the viceroyalties proved far too large to administer, the crown divided them into smaller units known as *audiencias* (the equivalent of provinces). These in turn were divided into even smaller, local units known as *corregimientos*,

alcaldias mayores, and *gobernaciones* (the equivalent of districts). And finally, at the lowest level were the municipalities. The viceroy headed the audiencia in his capital; in the other regions they were headed by captain-generals. The *cabildo* (or city council) administered the municipalities. Each of these organizations had legislative and judicial as well as administrative functions.

The crown bureaucracy was meddlesome, corrupt, and inefficient. Because Spanish kings were always short of funds, they resorted to selling colonial offices. This practice had one positive and one negative effect. In the first instance, it enabled American-born Spaniards, known as *criollos* (creoles), to obtain offices, and thus presumably assured that colonial administration, especially at the municipal level, would be more responsive to local needs. In the second instance, however, the initial cost of acquiring office and the poor salaries offered forced officeholders to use their positions for profit-making enterprise. This situation ensured a high degree of corruption and suffering for subject people. The crown's colonial bureaucracy closely regulated all aspects of society and economy, often to the smallest detail. The rules and regulations were not always based on colonial realities and therefore were often widely ignored. The discrepancy between law and practice, then, became so large that it discredited law and government.

The introduction of sugar into Brazil made that colony a money-making enterprise and led to building permanent settlements. The native population, for the most part comprised of nonsedentary and semisedentary peoples, proved quite unwilling to subject themselves to the harsh labor conditions on sugar plantations. Resisting such work, they fled into the interior out of their tormentors' reach. Like their brethren in Spanish America, they lacked immunity to European diseases and died in great numbers. The Portuguese then turned to the importation of African slaves to work the sugar plantations and *engenhos*, or sugar mills.

The Portuguese were somewhat more relaxed in their governance than the Spanish. Their administration began as private enterprise in the form of vast grants of land by the crown, known as donatory captaincies. The recipients in turn had wide latitude to grant land to settlers and name officials, in return for which they were obligated to pay revenue to the crown. Most of the captaincies failed from the lack of capital, inability to attract enough colonists, or poor management. The danger of French intrusions in the mid-sixteenth century forced the crown to take a more formal role in the administration of Brazil. For this purpose, the Portuguese crown established the Overseas Council, which

LETTER OF VICEROY FRANCISCO DE BORJA TO HIS SUCCESSOR, 1621

■ *On the occasion of the completion of their term, the viceroys reviewed their terms in* memorias *or* memoirs *to their successors. This selection clearly indicates that Borja's priorities lay in the extraction of silver. It also reveals his deep-seated contempt for the native peoples. The Indians reported for work in the mines as part of a system of forced labor known as the* mita.

The Indians assigned for the labor [in the mines] are supposed to enter on Monday morning, and for this they assemble at a place called Guaina at the foot of the hill. Here the corregidor reviews them and delivers them to the recipients . . . and they work through the following Saturday. In fact, given their laziness and drunkeness that appears on holidays, it has always been difficult to get them rounded up before Monday afternoon, or even Tuesday morning . . . The holidays that they are supposed to observe are few . . . and the mineowners have tried to make them work on the holidays that the councils have left open, it has not seemed convenient to concede this. For they are miserable people and recently converted, and the labor of those few is hardly worth considering.

functioned like the Council of the Indies. The Portuguese equivalent of the viceroy in Spanish America was the governor-general. Both Spanish and Portuguese decentralized governance, with regions and localities operating quite independently in routine matters. Powerful family groups arose to rule over these geographic fragments.

Both crowns paid close attention to revenue-producing areas. In New Spain the central corridor extended from Parral in Chihuahua, through Zacatecas and Guanajuato into Mexico City, and then to Veracruz, the major Caribbean port. This corridor was intensely monitored because it included the most important mining camps and trading routes. The same was true for the highland mining centers in Peru. The Spanish crown demanded one-fifth of the value of all ores mined in its empire. It also maintained a monopoly over the production and supply of mercury, which was essential for silver extraction. Both Iberian colonial empires tried to limit their colonies' trade to the mother country. Spain went further, restricting New World trade to only one port in Spain, Seville, and two in the Americas, Veracruz and Panamá, and allowing goods to be transported on only one or two heavily guarded convoys sent back and forth across the Atlantic each year. (This was known as the *flota*, or fleet system.) Constructed to maximize crown revenues, the overbearing economic system added greatly to the cost of living in the colonies and resulted in widespread smuggling. The most notorious example of the adverse effects of the system was the

prohibition of direct trade between Spain and Buenos Aires (in what is now Argentina). The colonial administration required goods to be shipped from Spain to Panamá, then to Peru, then across the Andes and Pampas to Buenos Aires on the Atlantic coast. The extra cost of this wayward route was large. Obviously, these rules were made to be broken. Crown customs officials were easily bribed, and smuggling in the vast underadministered territory was easy and rampant. Corruption and inefficiency made the system less onerous.

It was crucial for the Iberians to integrate the native peoples into their economic system, for without their labor, the colonies could not have survived. The two most important institutions for this acculturation were the Catholic church and the *hacienda*, or large landed estate.

The Church came early to the Americas to convert the native peoples to Christianity. A small number of regular clergy, composed of members of the Franciscan, Dominican, Augustinian, and later Jesuit orders, often heroically led the way into new territories. Initially, they tried to destroy the vestiges of the heathen religions. Unfortunately, in doing so, they erased much of the historical and cultural record of pre-Columbian times. But the friars quickly realized that they had to learn native cultures, religions, and languages in order to teach the people the word of their god. The regular clergy also sought to protect the native peoples from the rapacious European settlers. The resulting conflicts often led to violence. In one case in northern Brazil, several regular priests were forcefully put to sea in a raft;

the raft capsized and the passengers drowned, to the great satisfaction of the Portuguese settlers.

The most famous Spanish protector of the native peoples was friar Bartolomé de las Casas (1474–1566). In the early sixteenth century he gained the ear of the Spanish crown, who at his behest prohibited Indian slavery. Later in the colonial era the regular clergy were replaced by secular clergy, who were often American-born, far more pragmatic, and less solicitous of the native population. However, the crown itself was rarely willing to sacrifice mineral production for the spiritual well-being of the natives. In a choice between religion and the need for native labor, gold and silver took precedence.

By indoctrinating the native peoples into Catholicism, the priests taught them obedience and passivity. The misery of this world would be rewarded by heaven in the next. Any deviance from the norm was expurgated by the Inquisition, the Church's investigative arm.

Most native and mixed-blood (*mestizo*) people blended their folk culture and religion with Christianity to produce a unique form of Catholicism. Especially in the countryside, Catholicism was only imperfectly absorbed. There were never very many regular clergy. As a result, they touched the people of the periphery only lightly. The nomadic peoples fiercely resisted any incursions. In the cities many more priests presided and Catholicism was more conventional.

The Church also functioned as an important financial institution. It became enormously wealthy because many rich colonists bequeathed their funds and estates, others purchased penance in the form of indulgences, and the entire population was supposed to pay the tithe, usually a ten percent assessment on their income. Collectively, the Church was the largest rural property holder and urban landlord in New Spain and operated as the most important commercial and mortgage banker.

The hacienda evolved as a consequence of population decline in the demographic disaster, which caused a severe shortage of labor and the abandonment of large tracts of land. Originally the Spaniards adopted an institution from the Iberian Peninsula, later adapted to the Caribbean, the *encomienda*, which was a grant of tribute from the native people of a specified geographic entity, usually paid in the form of labor. The encomienda, however, presented serious problems for the Spanish crown. The owners of the encomiendas showed every indication of turning themselves into a New World hereditary nobility, a development the crown vigorously resisted. Most important, the decline in population wiped out the basis of the grant—people. Next the Spaniards turned to *repartimiento*, a forced labor system, but there

were not enough natives to fill the work quotas. The hacienda proved a solution to the shortage of labor, for it attracted native workers by offering to pay their tribute and church fees (for marriage, baptism, funeral). Hacienda laborers accumulated large debts that were passed on unpaid to their children. This system of debt peonage, however, offered some advantages, for it protected laborers from oppressive taxation or other obligations and provided an opportunity for security. In areas such as northern Mexico, indebtedness was more of an advance in wages than a burden. The evolution from encomienda to hacienda occurred unevenly. In some areas encomienda lasted centuries; in others different labor systems existed side by side.

The decline in native population caused both Spanish and Portuguese to turn to Africa to supply labor needed for New World plantations and mines. Large numbers of slaves were imported into Brazil, Mexico, and Peru. By 1800 2.5 million African slaves had been brought to the Americas, three-quarters of them to Brazil. The most profound impact was in Brazil. Because of a seemingly unending potential supply from Africa, the plantation owners of Brazil determined it was cheaper to work slaves to death than to feed or treat them well.

Life in Latin America Under Colonial Rule

The influx of Iberians, the loss of native population, and the realignment of landholding brought vast changes to life in the New World. The Europeans demanded different foods, most importantly wheat, olives, and wine. They brought with them new plants and animals. Their cattle, sheep, and goats required a completely altered pattern of land ownership and land usage. In an effort to better acculturate and administer the native peoples, the Spanish colonial government often tried to congregate or resettle them. Agriculture reorganized to supply markets in the mining camps and cities.

The great empires that preceded the Iberians were socially stratified, and colonial society was no different, but the Europeans added the new dimension of race. Under Spain and Portugal, whites were at the top of the social pyramid. Being white did not by any means assure one such an exalted position, however. There were poor and middle-class Spaniards. Moreover, there were two types of Spaniards, those born in the New World, known as *criollos* (creoles), and those born in Spain, *peninsulares*, or as they were known disparagingly, *gachupines* (greenhorns). Occupationally, the colonial elite were

This painted wooden beaker from Spanish colonial Peru is decorated with a multiracial portrait of a Spanish trumpeter, an African drummer, and a Native American official.

large landowners, miners, merchants, upper-level clergy, and government officials. These categories often overlapped, for example, when successful merchants and miners purchased large estates. In the middle were artisans, retail merchants, intermediate-level bureaucrats, and priests in the cities and, though their ranks were few in number, small farmers and ranchers in the countryside. Racially the middle comprised whites and some mixed-bloods, most likely *mestizos* or less often, *pardos.* The vast majority of the population, which included mestizos, pardos, Indians, and free Africans, was poor and lived in a continual state of deprivation. Most of the lower class lived in rural areas. At the very bottom were the African slaves, commodities to be bought and sold. Economically, urban and household slaves may have at times been better off than their mestizo or Indian counterparts, for their masters generally guaranteed them a minimal subsistence. Those who depended on market forces to determine their wages had no such guarantee. The distribution of wealth was extremely unequal, for the rich had almost all the resources and the poor virtually none. There was minimal chance for upward mobility. Mestizos and pardos were known to have purchased certificates of purity of blood that attested to their whiteness. Money could sometimes buy social standing, but rarely was the opportunity available.

The primary institution for the survival of Indian culture was the village, enduring through the demographic losses, the overbearance of the hacienda, and resettlement. It was most resilient in the regions on the periphery outside Spanish centralized rule. Communal landholding persisted, but most Indians had to work outside the village to obtain merchandise unavailable there. Hacienda and village developed a complex relationship, which was symbiotic when the hacienda needed labor and the villagers needed to supplement the subsistence yield of their individually or communally owned land, and which conflicted when the two fought over scarce land and water resources. Many Indians moved to towns and cities to escape tribute exactions. They earned a bare subsistence as day laborers or in textile factories.

In a society obsessed with matters such as honor and manhood, women were repressed by a double standard of behavior. There were, however, various ways to escape these constraints. Indeed, entrance into a convent was an important means for wealthy women to obtain their independence. Widows also obtained considerable autonomy, especially if they were beyond childbearing age and thus free of pressure to remarry, because they were entitled to one-half their husbands' estates.

Rural and urban working-class women worked, for few families could survive without their income. In the countryside they planted and harvested. In the cities and towns the market vendors were often women. Other employment was available as domestic servants for the rich and as factory workers, particularly in the textile mills.

For men and women of the lower classes, life was a struggle to subsist. One of the most remarkable statistics of Latin American history is the fact that wages on the haciendas on the central plateau of Mexico stayed the same from 1650 to 1800, at a level that was not sufficient to provide the basics of food and shelter for a family. Wages rose only in areas such as the northern mining districts where labor was scarce.

The population of Latin America began to increase in the second half of the seventeenth century, when at last the Indian population, having developed immunities to European diseases, began to recover and the number of mixed-bloods and whites grew, the latter through immigration. This growth added to the general misery of the people and presented colonial rulers with a new set of difficulties. When these new pressures combined with a series of external events in Europe, they caused a crucial political realignment in the New World empires.

From 1519 to 1700 the great empires of the New World fell to the onslaught of internal dissension,

America and the Encounters

1325	Aztecs settle on Lake Texcoco
1427	Triple Alliance: Tenochtitlán, Tlacopán, Texcoco
1438–71	Reign of Sapay-Inca Pachacuti
1471–93	Reign of Sapay-Inca Topa Inca Yupanqui
1492	First voyage of Columbus
1493–1525	Reign of Sapay-Inca Huayna Capac
1500	Cabral discovers Brazilian coast
1516	Charles I ascends Spanish throne
1519	Hernán Cortés lands in Veracruz
1521	Tenochtitlán destroyed by Spanish-Tlaxcalan siege
1525	Civil war between Inca factions led by Huáscar and Atahuallpa
1527	First *Audiencia* and bishopric established in New Spain
1531	Francisco Pizarro reaches Peru
1555	Philip II succeeds to Spanish crown
1572	Execution of Tupac Amarú ends Inca resistance
1650	Low point of native population in Mexico, less than one million

Iberian arms, and European diseases. The new rulers, intolerant of the conquered, tried mightily to destroy indigenous culture and religion. They achieved only limited success. The vanquished did not succumb easily, fighting for centuries to preserve their ways. The Spanish and Portuguese never conquered all of Latin America, but rather succeeded only in occupying crucial areas. Flexible but authoritarian, meddlesome but inefficient, religious but ruthless, both Spanish and Portuguese colonial rule comprised a series of paradoxes.

The changes wrought by the encounter between Europeans and the native peoples of the Americas were extensive and profound. The very face of the land changed: where corn had once sprouted, wheat grew and cattle grazed. Where once the temples of Aztec gods had stood, Catholic churches dominated the skyline. But in many respects, life for most native people changed little with the coming of the Europeans. The Aztecs were feared and loathed throughout Mesoamerica. They were cruel conquerors, who at times demanded terrible tribute in the form of victims for human sacrifice, and who at the very least required the payment of luxury commodities while contributing little to their subjects. Though the Incas offered opportunity to share in the spoils of conquest and the benefits of tribute labor, such as roads and emergency food stores, they too exacted a high price from their subjects, who were forcibly resettled, held hostage, deprived of their gods, and forced to work for no recompense. The Spaniards who replaced the Aztecs and Incas were also takers. Those who defend the Iberians claim that religion, language, and peace were considerable contributions, but the Spaniards and Portuguese brought little to improve the lives of their subjects. They ruled for so long because the calamitous population decline of the native peoples made sustained resistance impossible for two centuries. But after the mid-seventeenth century, when the population began to recover, unrest recurred. As we will see (in Chapter 28), in the eighteenth century colonial rule became so burdensome to Latin America that it threw off its Iberian shackles.

In the centuries following the discovery of America and a passage to the East Indies by the Cape of Good Hope, a worldwide marketplace for the exchange of commodities emerged—a living symbol of the mixture these encounters had engendered. First the Dutch and then the English established monopoly companies to engage in exotic trades in Asia. First the Spanish and Portuguese, then the English and French established colonial dependencies in the Atlantic, which they carefully nurtured in hope of economic gain. Protected trade flourished beyond the wildest dreams of its promoters. Luxury commodities became staples; new commodities became luxuries. Trade enhanced the material life of all European peoples, though it came at great cost to the Asians, Africans, and Latin Americans whose labor and raw materials were converted into the new crazes of consumption. The consequences of black slavery and the destruction of native populations had as significant an impact on the modern world as the discoveries and encounters themselves.

SUGGESTIONS FOR FURTHER READING

EUROPE AND THE ENCOUNTERS

Felipe Fernández-Armesto, *Columbus* (Oxford: Oxford University Press, 1991). The best of the new studies. Reliable, stimulating, and up-to-date.

Felipe Fernández-Armesto, *Before Columbus: Exploration and Colonisation From the Mediterranean to the Atlantic 1229-1492* (London: Macmillan, 1987). A comprehensive survey. Difficult but rewarding.

C. R. Boxer, *The Portuguese Seaborne Empire 1415-1825* (London: Hutchison, 1968). A comprehensive history of the first of the explorer nations.

* Samuel Morrison, *Christopher Columbus, Mariner* (New York: New American Library, 1985). A biography by a historian who repeated the Columbian voyages.

* Dan O'Sullivan, *Age of Discovery 1400-1550* (London: Longman, 1984). Best short, synthetic work.

* J. H. Parry, *The Age of Reconnaissance* (New York: New American Library, 1963). A survey of technological and technical changes that made possible the European discovery of America.

* Eugene Rice, *The Foundations of Early Modern Europe 1460-1559* (New York: Norton, 1970). An outstanding synthesis.

AFRICA AND THE ENCOUNTERS

* Philip Curtin, *The Rise and Fall of the Plantation Complex: Essays in Atlantic History* (New York: Cambridge University Press, 1990). A highly readable survey of the context in which the African slave trade arose.

* Sidney W. Mintz, *Sweetness and Power: The Place of Sugar in Modern History* (New York: Viking Penguin, 1985). A fascinating history of sugar's impact on historical development.

* J. F. Ade Ajayi and Michael Crowder, eds., *History of West Africa*, 3d ed., Vol. I (New York: Longman, 1985). An encyclopedic treatment of all West African history.

A. F. C. Ryder, *Benin and the Europeans, 1485-1897* (New York: Humanities Press, 1969). A detailed discussion of one important West African state and its relationship with Europeans.

* David Birmingham and Phyllis Martin, eds., *History of Central Africa*, Vol. I (Harlow, UK: Longman, 1983). An edited survey of the history of a broadly defined central Africa in the precolonial era.

Anne Hilton, *The Kingdom of Kongo* (Oxford: Oxford University Press, 1985). A recent, comprehensive, but somewhat controversial analysis of the Kingdom of Kongo.

John Thornton, *The Kingdom of Kongo: Civil War and Transition, 1641-1718* (Madison, WI: University of Wisconsin Press, 1983). A standard survey of the decline of the Kongo state.

M. D. D. Newitt, *Portuguese Settlement on the Zambesi: Exploration, Land Tenure and Colonial Rule in East Africa* (London: Longman, 1973). A dense, extremely thorough analysis of Portuguese activity in Mozambique.

David Beach, *The Shona and Zimbabwe, 900-1850* (London: Heinemann, 1980). A historical analysis of the region of the Mwene Mutapa.

AMERICA AND THE ENCOUNTERS

Mark A. Burkholder and Lyman L. Johnson, *Colonial Latin America*. (New York: Oxford University Press, 1990). This comprehensive introduction to colonial history incorporates the latest research on social history.

Inga Clendinnen, *Ambivalent Conquests: Maya and Spaniard in Yucatan, 1517-1570* (New York: Cambridge University Press, 1987). Innovative look at the interaction of Spanish and Indian.

Inga Clendinnen, *Aztecs* (New York: Cambridge University Press, 1991). Broad interpretation using Aztec texts.

Hernán Cortés. *Five Letters of Cortes to the Emperor*, trans. J. Bayard Morris (New York: Norton, n.d.). Illuminating propaganda.

Alfred W. Crosby, Jr., *The Columbian Exchange: Biological and Cultural Consequences of 1492* (Westport, CT: Greenwood, 1972). Standard study of the plants, animals, and diseases exchanged by new world and old.

Charles Gibson, *Spain in America* (New York: Harper, 1966). Classic examination of the institutions of Spanish rule.

Ramon A. Gutierrez, *When Jesus Came, the Corn Mothers Went Away: Marriage, Sexuality, and Power in New Mexico, 1500-1846* (Stanford, CA: Stanford University Press, 1991). Brilliant and provocative view of the interchange of Spanish and native societies from the native perspective.

Miguel Leon-Portilla, *The Broken Spears: The Aztec Account of the Conquest of Mexico* (Boston: Beacon, 1969). Gripping story of the conquest from the Aztec side.

James Lockhart and Stuart B. Schwartz, *Early Latin America: A History of Colonial Spanish America and Brazil* (New York: Cambridge University Press, 1983). This is a sophisticated analysis of Iberian colonial rule.

Alfred Metraux, *The History of the Incas* (New York: Schocken Books, 1969). Comprehensive study.

R. C. Padden, *The Hummingbird and the Hawk* (New York: Harper, 1970). A provocative and controversial view of the Aztecs, it presents a brilliant picture of a terroristic state.

Thomas C. Patterson, *The Inca Empire* (New York: Berg, 1991). An up-to-date survey.

Caio Prado, Jr., *The Colonial Background of Modern Brazil*, trans. Suzette Macedo (Berkeley, CA: University of California Press, 1971). Standard introduction to Brazilian colonial history.

Jacques Soustelle, *Daily Life of the Aztecs*, trans. Patrick O'Brian (Stanford, CA: Stanford University Press, 1961). Thorough examination of life in the Aztec empire.

Stuart B. Schwartz, *Sugar Plantations in the Formation of Brazilian Society, 1550-1835* (New York: Cambridge University Press, 1985). Comprehensive study of the most important aspect of Brazilian economy during the colonial era.

Karen Spalding, *Huarochi: An Andean Society under Inca and Spanish Rule* (Stanford, CA: Stanford University Press, 1984). Insightful view of the interchange of conquerors and conquered.

Stanley J. and Barbara H. Stein, *The Colonial Heritage of Latin America* (New York: Oxford University Press, 1970). The classic exposition of the burden of colonial rule on the new nations of Latin America.

Steven J. Stern, *Peru's Indian Peoples and the Challenge of the Spanish Conquest* (Madison, WI: University of Wisconsin Press, 1982). Provocative examination of the ways in which the native people of Peru resisted their oppressors.

* Indicates paperback edition available.

CHAPTER 15

The Islamic World, 1400–1700

The Old *Bezestan:* Markets, Merchants, and Patron Saints

Evliya Chelebi, a Turkish traveler born in 1611 in Istanbul, the capital of the Ottoman Empire, writes of the Old *Bezestan* (shown here), the oldest part of the central marketplace in his native city: "It is a great warehouse like a fortress, where the goods of all the military men and viziers are deposited . . . [with] six hundred shops." Evliya enumerates twenty-five kinds of merchants and artisans who work in the Old *Bezestan* or in the uncovered markets that surround it, which together employ several thousand people. An example of the professions enumerated are the satin merchants, of whom he says: "They are three hundred men, with one hundred and five shops. Their patron is Mansur, from Islamic Spain, who was girded [for his saintliness] by Salman [a companion of the Prophet Muhammad] . . . They are for the most part Jews."

With its lofty vaults and well-lit avenues, the Old *Bezestan*, built by the Ottoman sultan Mehmed the Conqueror after his acquisition of the Byzantine capital in 1453, was an impressive monument for the sultan's new seat of government. Evliya's description suggests areas of dependency between the market and the government. The market was used by government officials as a secure place to store goods and to deposit money with large merchants, who were the bankers of this world. Yet the government's attempts to control these merchants and artisans had limits. In the reign of the Ottoman sultan Murad III (1574–95), when the government's attempts to fix meat prices ran counter to all real economic conditions, wholesale butchers simply disappeared from Istanbul and the government was ultimately forced to relent.

The marketplace and mosque were the two breathing spaces of the Islamic town—large public spaces in which people gathered freely, exchanged information and formed public opinion. But the central mosque served this function principally on Friday when attendance at the noonday prayer was obligatory and men and women were separated, whereas the markets were open most or all days of the week, and in them men and women, and Muslims and non-Muslims, circulated freely, although certain sections of the market—or, in large cities, small separate markets such as the "thread market"—tended to be dominated by women.

The culture of the marketplace in the early modern Islamic empires—the Ottoman, Safavid, Sharifian, and Moghul empires—shows both continuity and change. As in earlier Islamic regimes, the area of the marketplace was considered a legal entity, although its boundaries were defined by custom, since there were distinctions between sales made in and outside the market. As in earlier centuries, the wholesale merchants rented or owned space in vast caravansaries, secure buildings on which the ground or lower floors had space for pack animals, offices, and storage, and the upper floors space for travelers and artisans. And, as in previous centuries, an official market inspector, an official sanctioned by Islamic law, supervised weights and measures.

Yet the changed functions of the market inspector in the Ottoman and Safavid empires show the ambitions of central governments to regulate society in these new empires much more closely. The tax system canonized in Islamic law was fairly rigid about taxes on agriculture but specified very few taxes on trade.

But, although the law forbade tolls within the Islamic world, in practice Islamic governments had always maintained toll stations to collect such noncanonical taxes.

The new empires owed their strength in significant part to an increased volume of world trade, and they used the market inspectors to organize the professions into guilds and to tax the guilds and the merchants. In the Safavid empire the market inspector was also supposed to fix prices on basic commodities such as food; the Ottomans did the same, more effectively, through other officials.

The early modern empires were not, however, very successful in acquiring deep commit-ment from the merchant community to their regimes. While some categories of merchants might be treated as a unit for tax purposes, they viewed their collective nature as coming from some saintly figure who, like the Mansur of the satin merchants, had practiced their profession in the past. In general, societies looked to themselves and not to their ruling centers for their identity. The merchants, like the religious experts, preserved their distance from the powerful ruling establishments of these new empires, and remained a truly international community in the premodern Islamic world.

The Islamic World Before the Early Modern Empires

By the end of the thirteenth century, Muslims had more reason than ever to regard their world, the Islamic world, as the center of civilization. Muslims inhabited and ruled a vast band of territory from Spain to northern India, prominently positioned between the other major land areas of the Old World—sub-Saharan Africa, East and Southeast Asia, and Europe. Throughout this vast territory the great majority of governments relied on elite slave soldiers to control their subjects and protect their interests. The populations they ruled adapted to this institution, nearly unique in world history. They did so partly because their more vivid loyalties were not to governments but to many overlapping groups, some of them truly international. These multiple group identities wove societies together and made them flexible enough to survive violent invasions and changes of regime. Two of the most important groups, the large merchants and the religiously learned, wove together the basic fabric of the entire Islamic world. The merchants created networks of trade, credit, and agreed forms of contract. The religiously learned interpreted the laws of contract and fostered the study and exchange of written culture, thereby giving the Islamic world a surprising degree of intellectual unity. Thanks largely to these groups, cultural life in the Islamic world flourished even in periods of political turmoil.

The Emergence of New Rulers: 1100–1400

For the Islamic world of the Middle East in the premodern world, there were two great physical and moral lineages: Muhammad, the prophet to whom the revelation of Islam came in the seventh century, and Genghis Khan, the Mongolian conqueror and military genius who convinced the peoples of Central Asia in the thirteenth century that he and his descendants had a mandate from heaven to rule all the known world. Of the two, lineage from the Prophet, his clan and his tribe, proved the more durable; and even today the royal families of Jordan and Morocco claim direct descent from Muhammad. But the later claim of Genghis Khan that he had a God-given grant of rulership was able not only to legitimize many lines of royal descent but also to create a style of rulership that survived from the thirteenth to the eighteenth century.

Central Asian people first entered the Middle East as slaves. By the eleventh century many of the people of Central Asia spoke Turkish languages. (While "Turkish" can be used in its modern political sense for things related to the nation of Turkey, it is used in this chapter for the family of closely related languages that includes modern Turkish and the peoples who speak them.) Like their ancestors—peoples such as the Huns—they were superb horsemen. The 'Abbasid caliphs, the descendants of Muhammad's uncle who ruled the Islamic empire from 750, began in the ninth century to buy young Turkish slaves to raise as the elite cavalry needed to control their vast territories. On the completion of their training, in the course of which they invariably converted to Islam, these slaves, somewhat like successful Roman gladiators, were freed. But rulers and commanders had strong personal bonds to their former slaves because freed slaves were legally clients of their former owners who had often acted as foster parents to them while young. Usually, these owners became their employers when they were freed.

In the long run, however, the Turkish soldiers of the 'Abbasids proved more interested in enriching themselves from the caliph's treasuries or in ruling the caliph's provinces as independent governors than in saving the empire. But they did not dare assume formal independence because, to their Muslim subjects, legitimacy came only from the governors' recognition of an overlord, such as a caliph, whose lineage was connected with the Prophet. Therefore, most such soldier-rulers, who were in effect kings of their own lands, acknowledged the nominal overlordship of the 'Abbasid caliphs. Consequently, though the 'Abbasids lost the last fragment of real power when a Turkish commander took over their capital city of Baghdad in the 930s, they were preserved for three more centuries because, like the emperors of Japan, the caliphs gave legitimacy to the dynasties that inherited their empire. Even as a fiction, the claim that most of the Islamic world remained united under a caliph meant that Muslims had freedom of movement within that world. And, more important, the contracts Muslims formed, for marriage or for sale of goods, were recognized throughout the Islamic world, regardless of the temporary borders and changes of regime created by the caliphs' nominal governors.

One of the most important dynasties descended from Turkish military slaves was the Ghaznavids, named after their capital Ghazna, in what would later become Afghanistan, overlooking the mountain passes

to India. The Ghaznavid king Mahmud (998–1030) took advantage of his position to conquer over half of the Indian subcontinent. These conquests were rarely permanent, but they had many consequences. Mahmud, like future Muslim rulers, gained admiration and legitimacy by succeeding in his chosen role as a *ghazi*, a warrior who fought for Islam. He also opened the road for Muslim expansion into India. And the enormous amount of booty he brought back allowed him to be even more independent of his subjects than the kings before him. He even took the title *sultan*, which meant "dominion" or "authority" in Arabic; he was, literally, "Mr. Authority."

This separation between the people (often called the *ra'aya*, the "flocks") and a government headed by a military commander, was characteristic of most Middle Eastern Islamic regimes until the nineteenth century. The governments might be founded by tribes or, occasionally, even religious leaders, but they soon had to resort to slave and former slave soldiers as the mainstay of their rule. These slaves were expensive to buy, train, maintain, and equip in the most effective armor and weapons of the period. But, unlike tribes, they formed standing armies. Moreover, these military slaves were almost always from outside the Islamic world, not only because Islamic law forbade the enslaving of Muslims or protected peoples—such as the Christians and Jews—but also because rulers knew that outsiders were less likely to collude with the indigenous population.

The Arrival of The Turkish and Mongolian Tribes

Turks did not enter the Middle East only as slave soldiers. From the eleventh to the fifteenth centuries, whole tribes of Turkish nomads entered the Middle East in great waves of migration. The first wave entered in the eleventh century under the leadership of a royal clan called the Seljuqs. These Seljuq Turks, who were pious Muslims, preserved much of the social and cultural life of the area and created new forms of patronage, which in turn fostered Islamic Middle Eastern culture. They began using the developing Islamic law for pious endowments to found *madrasa*s (colleges), mosques, hospitals, and libraries.

Yet the foundations of Seljuq rule were far from stable. Despite their use of a large army of Turkish slave soldiers to rein in their unreliable army of Turkish tribes, they were defeated by these tribes in 1153. Disorder prevailed for about eighty years until a force appeared mightier than any seen in the Middle East since the Islamic conquests: the Mongols under Genghis

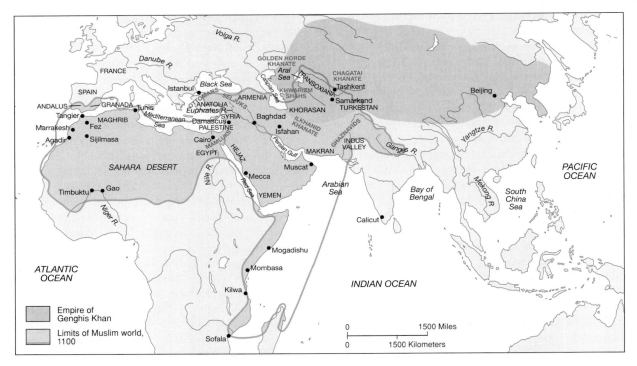

The Islamic World, 1100–1500

Khan. In 1219 Genghis launched an attack on the Islamic regime that ruled Transoxiana and Persia. His forces easily swept aside all Muslim opposition while they unleashed on many of the great cultural centers a wave of killing and destruction from which some never recovered; in Nishapur, for example, whose madrasas and men of learning were famous throughout the Islamic world, the Mongol troops carried out an order that neither a human of any age, nor "even cats and dogs should be left alive"; and the army returned several times to kill any inhabitants who might have survived in hiding.

As conquests continued under the descendants of Genghis Khan, who were, like him, not Muslims, the Mongol empire soon stretched from Hungary to Korea. But the real unity of the Mongol empire soon disappeared; and almost all of their Muslim subjects were ruled by the Mongols of Iran, the Il-Khans, or the Mongols of Russia, the Golden Horde. The Il-Khans ruled western Asia and their kingdom, whose rulers and troops eventually converted to Islam, lasted until the early fourteenth century. Toward the end of that century the Il-Khans were replaced by an empire that began with a wave of destruction rivaling the early Mongols: the em-

pire of Tamerlane. A Muslim of Mongolian descent, Tamerlane (1370–1405) reconstituted the empire of the Il-Khans, often with horrifying and very public demonstrations of his violence, such as the towers of skulls he made from the victims of his massacres. Tamerlane married a descendant of Genghis Khan and carried along a Genghisid puppet *khan* to give himself legitimacy. His far less warlike descendants ruled over dwindling kingdoms, as nomadic Turkish peoples divided the bulk of Tamerlane's lands between tribal rulers.

The influx of Turkish and Mongolian peoples had dramatic effects on the history of the Middle East. In their own historical tradition the people of the Middle East portrayed the Mongols as the villains of this great historical change, partly because most of the early Mongol rulers were hostile to Islam, now the religion of the overwhelming majority of the population. In contrast, the equally bloody conquests of the Muslim Tamerlane, who with few exceptions chose other Muslim powers as his victims, received a far better press.

The Mongols put a lasting stamp on the character of succeeding centuries of Turkish rule. Since so many of the troops the Mongols brought into or enlisted in the Middle East were Turks, the language of the Mongol ruling families of the Il-Khans and the Golden Horde soon became Turkish. And the long-term movement of the Slavic peoples south and east was halted for centuries as Turkish-speaking peoples dominated a great band of Asia from the area north of the Black Sea to the Pacific Ocean. Correspondingly, Turkish peoples regarded as nearly sacred descent from Genghis Khan and the customary law established by the Mongols. The universal mandate claimed by Genghis—"One sun in heaven, one lord on earth"—had such a dazzling effect both in creating the world's largest premodern empire and in momentarily uniting most of the Turks of Eurasia, that it was long remembered among Turkish peoples.

The Mongols had a strong tradition of unwritten law that originated in the decisions and maxims of tribal leaders. Genghis Khan's word weighed as that of no previous figure in Turco-Mongolian history had done, and gradually the story took hold that he had laid down a code called the Great Yasa. Before the Mongols, customary law and royal administrative law had existed uneasily alongside Islamic law. The Yasa was not fundamentally more acceptable to the specialists in Islamic law than any earlier form of customary law. However, it had greater authority than earlier non-Muslim law, and it was seen as a cumulative body of royal law that existed apart from the personality of the ruler, one that a ruler could change or amend but not cancel. Even Tamerlane, for all the authority he acquired as a world conqueror, reaffirmed the allegiance of his dynasty to the Yasa.

A fifteenth-century Egyptian painted leather figure in the form of a riverboat containing three archers. The figure was used in the shadow plays of the Mamluk period.

A Slave Aristocracy Rules Egypt and Syria

In Cairo in 1250, the freed slave soldiers of Saladin's much-weakened dynasty thrust aside their former masters and began to rule in their own right. They were called *Mamluks*, which literally means "those owned," and they represent a further step in the evolution of elite slave armies in the Middle East. Occasionally father-son successions appeared among these former slaves, but usually whichever Mamluk commander was most powerful would succeed his predecessor through persuasion or open warfare. This "slave" aristocracy bought its future commanders and sultans as boys from Turkish areas of Central Asia and from the Caucasus. The Mamluks recalled their Central Asian roots, even invoking the Yasa to settle disputes, although they remained free of Mongol rule.

In fact, the role of the Mamluks as champions of Islam against the Mongols was an important part of their success. In 1260 the Mamluk sultan handed the Mongols their first significant defeat in the Islamic world at a battle at Ain Jalut in Syria. Despite repeated attempts by the Mongol Il-Khans and their successors to conquer Syria, the Mamluks maintained control of Syria as well as Egypt for most of the next two and a half centuries. With non-Muslim Mongols ruling the Muslim east until 1295, Muslims came to see the Mamluk empire to their west both as a place of refuge and as a bastion of true belief. The Mamluks campaigned hard and successfully to drive the last Crusaders from the eastern Mediterranean. And, under the Mamluks, the emerging system of recognizing four schools of Islamic law as equally legitimate was established as a lasting element of orthodox Sunni Islam, the form of Islam accepted by the majority of Muslims.

People, Trade, and Culture in the Premodern Islamic World

The subjects of these Islamic regimes—perhaps half of whom had converted to Islam by the time of Mahmud of Ghazna—also found advantages in this system of military rule by outsiders, even though these military regimes often extorted heavy taxes in order to maintain themselves and sometimes acted like occupying armies. After the moral and military failure of the first two dynasties of caliphs, the Umayyads and 'Abbasids, Muslim subjects seldom felt committed to any regime; they settled for governments that at best kept violence restricted to fights within the military elite or against neighboring regimes.

Madrasa of the Shah's Mother in Isfahan, Iran.

The College with the Gilded Cage

In 1694, Shah Sultan Husayn (1694–1722) at age twenty-six emerged from the harem to rule the Safavid empire. Raised in the harem—where rulers sometimes kept their sons to prevent rebellions—Shah Sultan Husayn had little knowledge of the world. He was by nature quiet and studious, and when his mother built the college shown here he had a gilded cage prepared for himself so that he could take part in discussions among the religiously learned faculty who taught and studied at the college. Shah Sultan Husayn showed no aptitude for kingship and, while at first violently against the drinking of alcohol, soon became addicted to it. A weak man, he quickly found himself caught in a struggle between the court eunuchs and the specialists in religious learning, the ulama, who in the Safavid empire belonged to the Shi'ite branch of Islam. The empire more or less spontaneously disintegrated as subject peoples and neighbors became aware that no one was minding the throne, and in 1722 Shah Sultan Husayn gave his insignia of office to a former subject, an Afghan leader, who occupied the capital city of Isfahan.

Around the central courtyard of the *Madraseh-ye Madar-e Shah* (Madrasa of the Shah's Mother) are arcades of cells or rooms for students as well as rooms and recesses for classes. The *madrasa* contains a prayer hall and a library. Like many madrasas, it has nearby property, the income from which was dedicated by the founder to its upkeep. In this case, a building rented to merchants for offices, storage space, and even sleeping space helps maintain the college. It was not unusual for a woman to found a madrasa. Wealthy women, especially of royal families, often endowed madrasas and mosques, in part because of ties to leading religious figures.

Madrasas were colleges for training the ulama. With curricula centered on religious subjects, the madrasas are sometimes called theological colleges. But their curricula varied and might even include subjects such as astronomy, important for determining the time of prayer and its direction, since Muslims face Mecca to pray. Usually the terms of the endowment determined the curricula, although over time the number of subjects taught tended to increase and many subjects, such as philosophy were offered in private classes.

Even the public classes were not as formal as in modern schools. The students entered the madrasa with a basic literacy gained at a Qur'an school and sometimes, as in the Azhar, the major college of Cairo, memorization of the Qur'an was a prerequisite to entrance. Students in good standing could count on a bread ration to keep them alive during their years at the madrasa. Classes at the madrasa were largely based on reading and interpreting set texts until the highest levels of education, when the students engaged in open debate on subjects determined by the teacher. Students had a great deal of freedom, for there were seldom any formal degrees, only "permissions" granted by a reputable teacher for a student to teach a book or, at the highest level, to give a legal opinion.

Despite variations, in the thirteenth and fourteenth centuries a body of widely recognized classics on grammar, law, and kindred subjects began to emerge. After that time madrasa education gave a remarkable unity to the educated elite of the Islamic world. The ulama were not part of any church that could unify their opinions; but they wanted to prevent religious opinion from diverging in many directions, and the madrasas helped them. Ibn Battuta, probably the most traveled man in the world before the fifteenth century, during the years between 1325 and 1349 found employment among Muslims as a judge or religious authority in many areas he visited—from sub-Saharan Africa to India, Central Asia, and even China—because Muslims recognized that the education he had received in his native Tangier in Morocco was similar to the education of Islamic learned men everywhere. Similarly, many of the bureaucracies of Islamic governments were staffed by men who had received some madrasa training and shared a common background.

In Persian and in many languages influenced by Persian, such as Urdu, the ulama were also called *mullahs*—one of whom is seen here entering a vestibule of the madrasa. The Shi'ite mullahs lived in an uneasy symbiosis with the Safavid monarchs. They were hungry for royal patrons but, at the same time, were never quite sure of the legitimacy of Safavid claims to rule. The proximity of this madrasa to the royal palace facilitated the Shah Sultan Husayn's participation and, at the same time, emphasized the building's royal patronage. The power of the Shi'ite mullahs at the end of the Safavid period encouraged them to develop the theory that they should run the government, a theory realized in the Iranian Revolution of 1978.

The nonmilitary elites also accommodated themselves to these regimes. The upper level of bureaucrats, among whom the vizier was most important as the public face of the sultan and the head of the civil bureaucracy, played a high-risk game in which they could become rich or lose their lives overnight. In contrast, the lower bureaucracy, as long as it remained appropriately faceless, often survived great upheavals in government unharmed. Like the upper level of bureaucrats, the wealthiest merchants were subject to arbitrary confiscation when governments had urgent need for money. But, as they were the only subjects of the sultan with large sums of cash the government could borrow, a sultan who was too greedy might lose all his credit in the marketplace and even be faced with the migration of his leading merchants. By and large the rest of the merchant community was left alone.

The situation of large landlords was more precarious. Like the lower bureaucrats, they were important to the governments because they often had a role in tax collection. But, unlike the lower bureaucrats, they were more exposed to the economic changes brought by the new regimes. From the tenth century the government began to assign land-tax revenues to soldiers, especially officers. This method of payment—in which the assignment was called *iqta‘*—suited both soldiers and sultans so well that until the nineteenth century it was as characteristic of Islamic regimes as military slavery. Landlords were seldom directly harassed by the central government, but they were frequently harassed and sometimes replaced by the soldiers and their bailiffs who descended on the countryside to collect the revenues assigned to them. This system tended to discourage investment in improving the land, and most landlords chose to live in the cities to the further disadvantage of the countryside. The iqta‘ loosely resembled the European fief, but there was no hierarchy among fiefholders as in western Europe; and, while some iqta‘s did become hereditary, the government could always step in and reassign them to different holders.

Islam had no priesthood, but specialists in religious learning gradually became a semiprofessionalized elite and were collectively called *ulama*, "knowers" (See Special Feature, "The College With the Guilded Cage," pp. 446–447). But even after the foundation of special schools to train the ulama in the last half of the eleventh century, religious learning continued to be cultivated in various degrees by men who were also landlords, merchants, and bureaucrats.

In fact, almost all groupings in society overlapped: a craftsman who made silk brocade, lived in the quarter next to the citadel, subscribed to the Shafi‘i version of Islamic law and the Ash‘ari school of Islamic theology, and participated in the Qadiri order of Sufi mystics, would have a real loyalty to each of the groups to which he belonged. And each group would connect him with other groups: some makers of silk brocades might be Jews and some members of his Qadiri Sufi order might be wholesale grain merchants. Moreover, from the tenth to the nineteenth centuries in many Middle Eastern cities the population was also divided into two roughly equal factions that, although named after a profession such as the butchers or, more often, after a law school, included members of the community from other professions and law schools. The feuding between these factions became fierce at times when central government was weak, and it resembled the feuding between rival factions in some Italian city-states of the late Middle Ages. The majority of the population knew that if people did not maintain their multiple and overlapping identities they would become involved in factionalism of quarter, profession, or citywide groups to a degree that would inspire arson, murder, and other forms of destructive violence. This fear gave them yet another reason to want the rule of alien peoples such as slave-soldiers who, while commanding no vivid loyalty from their subjects, would act as arbiters generally more interested in order than in siding with any faction among the local population.

Middle Easterners were, more than ever, a "middle" people. An unwitting achievement of the Mongols was to bring to the Middle East a better knowledge of the Old World than any people had previously possessed. A vizier of the Il-Khans, Rashid ad-Din (1247–1318), wrote in Persian the most informed account of his time of all the cultures of Europe and Asia, including China. This was possible because the Pax Mongolica had for the first time created a continuous and busy overland traffic between the Mediterranean, the northeast European world, and East Asia. This overland trade continued with surprising vigor until the eighteenth century. Although western Europeans, especially Italians, continued to dominate merchant shipping in the Mediterranean, as they had since the eleventh century, Byzantine and Muslim participation in this trade was far from negligible.

The Indian Ocean was quite another matter. From the ninth century a network of Muslim traders spread all the way from East Africa to China. They came to dominate this area through daring, but they maintained their control through sound commercial practice. Islamic law had developed a sophisticated law of sale and partnership adaptable to a variety of market conditions. Thanks in significant part to a fairly uniform commercial law, Muslim traders knew what to expect of each other. The rise of Egypt under the Mamluks to preeminence among the centers of Islamic culture in the Arabic-speaking world owed a great deal to its position as an intermediary between the trade of the Indian Ocean and the Mediterranean.

In Islamic lands to the north and east of the Mamluks, an important feature of Turco-Mongolian rule was its cultural allegiance to the Persian tradition. Turkish tribes entered the Middle East through an area in which Persian was spoken. This meant that the leaders of these Turkish peoples saw Islamic Middle Eastern culture through a Persian filter. For many centuries the only major alternative to Arabic as a vehicle of written expression was Persian. Used principally in Iran, Afghanistan, and Central Asia, Persian appeared in the tenth century as a language of lyric poetry and became in the eleventh century the language of epic poems, historical chronicles, and administrative correspondence, including most of the correspondence between Turkish-speaking rulers.

From India to Anatolia, Turkish-speaking rulers carried Persian court culture. This culture included a taste for long poems, unlike Arabic literature, which excelled in the short poem of praise and lamentation. Persian poetry was the vehicle for long imaginative epics on the semilegendary Iranian past, on romantic themes, and on mystical themes. These epics became the focus of a tradition of extraordinarily beautiful book illustration that spread to India, Anatolia, and Central Asia. Not only the descendants of Genghis Khan but also Tamerlane—who tried to save people of talent from the general slaughters he ordered—and his descendants were discriminating patrons of literature, the arts, and even the scholastic sciences (such as logic and jurisprudence), which were usually written about in Arabic.

Islamic lands west of the Mamluks—Arabic-speaking like Mamluk Egypt and Syria—were called by their inhabitants the Maghrib (roughly, Morocco, Algeria, Tunisia, and Libya) and Andalus (Islamic Spain and Portugal). Nowhere in the Muslim West did cultural life develop more brilliantly than in Andalus. Here, under tolerant Muslim rulers, Christians, Jews, and Muslims exchanged ideas freely. Europeans received their first extensive knowledge of Aristotle through Latin translations from the Arabic, along with the ingenious commentaries of the Muslim scholar Ibn Rushd (in Latin, Averroës, often called by the Europeans simply The Commentator). And here, as in many other places, Muslims brought about a "green revolution" by introducing crops such as cotton, sugarcane, and oranges (all three English words were borrowed from the Arabic). But Christian zeal for the reconquest of the Iberian Peninsula, officially considered to be a "crusade," proved too strong for the Muslim kingdoms; after the Muslim defeat at Las Navas de Tolosa in 1212, it was all downhill for the Muslims. Granada, the last Muslim kingdom in Spain, hung on until 1492. Its conquest was considered so important that the inscriptions around the tombs of Ferdinand and Isabella, which have no reference to the discovery of the New World, mention as their great achievement the capture of Granada and the expulsion of the Jews from Spain.

A curious complement to the history of the Iberian Peninsula of Spain and Portugal is the history of the Anatolian Peninsula, which was to become the backbone of the Ottoman Empire. In both peninsulas—one European, the other Asian—a holy war, waged by the

Life in the City, *a Persian watercolor miniature of the sixteenth-century by Mir Sayyid 'Ali, ca. 1540. The scene, showing preparations for a betrothal feast, was painted to illustrate a story.*

FROM THE *TRAVELS OF IBN BATTUTA*

■ *Ibn Battuta, the fourteenth-century Moroccan traveler who, by virtue of twenty-five years of travel in Asia, Africa, and Europe, was probably the most widely traveled person in premodern times, wrote a detailed account of his travels that is a fundamental source for its period. Here he relates an incident that began in the Turkish-speaking part of the Middle East and ended in China.*

My purpose in traveling to these mountains was to meet a notable saint who lives there, namely Sheikh Jalal al-Din of Tabriz. At a distance of two days journey from his abode I was met by four of his disciples, who told me that the Sheikh had said to his dervishes who were with him: "The traveler from the west has come to you: go out to welcome him." He had no knowledge whatever about me but this had been revealed to him. I went with them to the Sheikh and arrived at his hermitage, situated outside the cave. There is no cultivated land there, but the inhabitants of the country, both Muslim and infidel, come to visit him, bringing gifts and presents, and the dervishes and travelers live on these offerings. The Sheikh, however, limits himself to a single cow, with whose milk he breaks his fast every ten days. It was by his labors that the people of these mountains became converted to Islam, and that was the reason for his settling among them. When I came into his presence he rose to greet me and I embraced him. He asked me about my native land and my travels, and when I had given him an account of them he said to me: "You are the traveler of the Arabs." Those of his disciples who were there said: "And the non-Arabs, too, our Master." "And of the non-Arabs too," he repeated, "so show him honor." Then they took me to the hermitage and gave me hospitality for three days.

On the day when I visited the Sheikh I saw that he was wearing a wide mantle of goatshair. It took my fancy and I said to myself: "I wish the Sheikh could have given it to me." When I visited him to bid him farewell, he . . . took off the mantle and placed it upon me . . . The dervishes told me that the Sheikh was not in the habit of wearing this mantle and had put it on only when I arrived, saying to them: "This mantle will be asked for by the Moroccan, and it will be taken from him by an infidel king, who will give it to our brother Burhan al-Din of Sagharj, whose it is, for whom it was made."

Now it came about a long time afterwards that I visited China and eventually reached the city of Khansa . . . [The king summoned me and] questioned me about the Muslim sultans and when I replied to his questions, he looked at the mantle and took a liking to it. The *wazir* said to me: "Take it off," and I could not resist his order.

This incident roused my anger, but afterwards I recalled the Sheikh's saying that an infidel king would seize it and I was deeply amazed at the fulfillment of the prediction.

The following year I entered the palace of the king of China at Khan-Beliq [Beijing] and sought out the convent of the Sheikh Burhan al-Din of Sagharj. I found him reading and wearing that identical mantle . . . "This mantle," he went on, "was specially made for me by my brother Jalal al-Din, who wrote me saying: 'This mantle will reach you by the hand of so and so.' " Then he brought out the letter and I read it and marvelled at the Sheikh's perfect knowledge.

From *Travels of Ibn Battuta in Asia and Africa, 1325–1359.*

majority religion of the continent to which they were attached, eventually triumphed: Christianity in Iberia and Islam in Anatolia. In both peninsulas a sense of historical mission carried the conquerors far beyond their original homeland, and lent legitimacy to their ruling families. Both the Habsburgs, who succeeded Ferdinand and Isabella, and the Ottomans needed the economic and military resources of subject peoples to sustain their enterprise of expansion. By the second half of the sixteenth century the Habsburgs and the Ottomans were the two mightiest powers of the European and Mediterranean world.

The Islamic World Divides Into Four Empires

In the sixteenth century most of the Islamic world belonged to four empires, generally known after their ruling families: the Sharifians, the Ottomans, the Safavids, and the Moghuls. Morocco, the most westerly part of the Maghrib, was the seat of the Sharifian empire. The rest of the Maghrib and the lands immediately to its east, namely Egypt, Palestine, Syria, many parts of Arabia and Iraq, and the great peninsula known as Anatolia, or Asia Minor, belonged to the Asian part of the Ottoman Empire. Iran was the seat of the Safavid empire, which controlled much of what is modern Afghanistan as well as areas of the Caucasus, the knot of mountains to the west of the Caspian Sea, and areas further east that are now considered parts of Central Asia. The Indian subcontinent was the seat of the Moghul empire.

The Ottomans, Moghuls, Safavids, and Sharifians, often called the early modern Islamic empires, created a degree of order that the Islamic world had not known for some centuries, and for periods succeeded in controlling their realms more effectively and at deeper social levels than had any Islamic governments prior to them. In this respect the Ottomans were the most successful and the three other empires were influenced by their example. These empires (with the exception of the Moghuls) made new use of the established practice of creating slave elites, and they all got more use out of their (often non-Muslim) vassals. They represented themselves as warriors for Islam, whether fighting for the extension of their governments into non-Muslim areas or defending Islamic governments against an increasingly aggressive Europe. Their success was in part due to the ability of their populations to produce for—and act as middlemen in—a considerably intensified world trade. At their height, the stability and wealth of their central governments enabled the material culture of these areas to reach new heights.

The Ottomans: From Border State to Mightiest Empire of Islam

The Ottomans enter world history around 1300 as leaders of a small group of Turks in charge of the area of Anatolia closest to the Byzantines. As a border state fighting the most venerable opponent of Islam, they considered themselves *ghazi*s, fighters for Islam, and consequently were joined by volunteers who also wanted the honor of being ghazis. Like other border people they shared many cultural traits with their opponents so that, when they began to have modest success in acquiring nearby territory, Byzantine nobles often joined them. And, like many border peoples, they were not subject to the scrutiny of orthodox scholars of their religion and could take advantage of the enthusiasm of various slightly heterodox groups such as the Anatolian devotees of Sufism, the mystical tradition of Islam.

From very small beginnings the Ottomans expanded rapidly. By the 1350s they had a permanent foothold in Europe. Soon after, the Ottoman ruler assumed the style of Sultan. The reaction in western Europe to Ottoman success was mild, but in eastern Europe a coalition including Serbs, Hungarians, and Bulgarians took on the Ottomans at Kosovo Polje in Serbia in 1389. In the ensuing battle—famous in Serbian history for the heroism shown by their side—so many Serbs were killed that it was a foregone conclusion that the Ottomans would, as they did, soon occupy and control Serbia and the rest of the Balkans.

At the end of the fourteenth century, western Europeans woke up to the threat the Ottomans posed. With the support of the papacy a large army of crusaders, composed not only of the nobility of areas neighboring the Ottomans but also of the knighthood of England, France, and Germany, proceeded with great pomp under the leadership of the king of Hungary and Bohemia down the Danube toward the Ottomans. Despite their bravery, the crusaders were completely overwhelmed by the Ottoman sultan Bayazid, in 1396 at Nicopolis in Greece. The Ottomans now had the best ghazi credentials of any ruler since Mahmud of Ghazna.

Anatolia, however, still consisted of a welter of dynasties, most of them Turkish; and when the Ottoman sultan Bayazid annexed their territories, these rulers appealed to Tamerlane. Bayazid, known in Turkish as "the Lightningbolt," did not hesitate to face this latest world conqueror as he entered Anatolia. In 1402 at Ankara, Tamerlane dealt Bayazid a resounding defeat and—according to one story—after taking him prisoner carried him around in a cage until the hapless Ottoman died in captivity.

Defeat at the battle of Ankara showed the weaknesses and strengths of the Ottoman system. A major Ottoman weakness was dependence on an army that included many Turkish tribes, who could be fickle and undisciplined, and many troops led by Christian vassal rulers, some of whom would throw aside their allegiance to the Ottomans in the moment of the sultan's weakness. However, the anti-Catholic sentiment of the

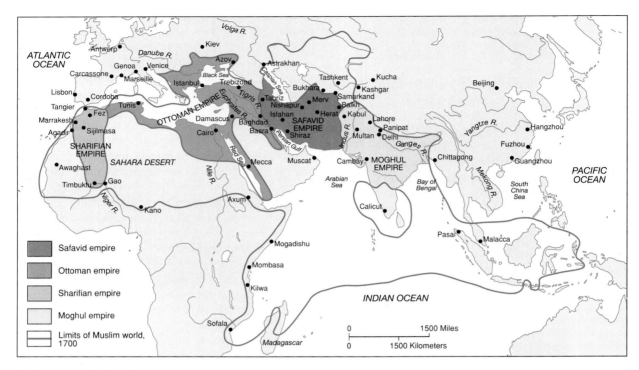

The Four Early Modern Islamic Empires, ca. 1700

Greek Orthodox church, which predominated in the Balkans, continued to help Ottoman rule and echoed the feeling of the Orthodox Patriarch, who said he would rather see in Constantinople the turban of the Turk than the mitre of the pope.

Nevertheless, the strengths of the Ottoman Empire were real enough to allow it to weather the storm. Very prominent among these strengths was the *timar* system, the Ottoman version of the Seljuk *iqta'*, upon which the Ottomans would increasingly depend after the defeat at Ankara. As they moved territory from vassalage to direct rule, they painstakingly recorded each region in registers listing the ownership of land and the number of households in the region. Then they assigned the tax revenues of the region to the sultan's loyal military supporters, including a fair number of Christians. These assignments or timars were at least large enough to support a single well-equipped mounted soldier, and sometimes large enough to support several other soldiers who fought alongside the timar-holder. Regional commanders had even larger assignments and acted both as provincial administrators and as field commanders. Timar-holders had a strong interest in keeping the Ottoman Empire a conquest state; for, as long as there was conquest, there were new territories to be divided into timars for relatives and retainers and new revenues to

keep the government from interfering with the income of timar-holders from existing timars.

By the reign of Bayazid's grandson, Murad II (1421–51), the Ottomans had developed significant new institutions that rendered them capable of creating the greatest Islamic empire in the Mediterranean since the early Caliphate of the eighth and ninth centuries. The Ottomans found that they needed, just as previous Islamic dynasties had needed, a standing army of freed slaves like the Mamluks; but in a bold innovation they domesticated the *mamluk* system. In contradiction to Islamic law, which guarantees the safety and possessions of Christians and Jews as long as they pay the taxes required of them, the Ottomans began a periodic levy of Christian boys inside their empire. They raised these boys as Muslims and trained them for service in the newly formed Janissary army corps and the Ottoman civil service. The prominence of this levy under Murad II opportunely fitted in with the new importance he gave to guns and artillery and his need to strengthen the central government against local heroes, especially renowned ghazis. The well-armed Janissary infantry protected the sultan in his palaces and surrounded him in battle; well-trained Janissary cannoneers gave his armies an advantage over Christian and Muslim opponents alike; and those in training for the Janissary corps who were spotted for administrative talent were separated and specially trained for high office in the sultan's administration. Gradually the training of the boys collected by the levy became the most elaborate and well-organized education ever created for soldiers and bureaucrats in Islamic history; and from 1453 most of the grand viziers, officials second only to the sultan, came from this background. Celibate until their "graduation" (usually in their twenties), slaves of the sultan and subject to his whim, the boys harvested by the levy were nevertheless offered a career with dazzling prospects. Bosnian Muslims were guaranteed a quota in the levies, and sometimes other Muslims tried to bribe levy officers to accept their children.

With its revived and new institutions, the Ottoman Empire saw over a century of nearly uninterrupted expansion. In 1453 Sultan Mehmed II, the son of Murad II, took Constantinople, the symbol of Christian resistance to Islamic conquest for seven centuries; and he rebuilt the city—usually called Istanbul by the Ottomans—with great splendor to give the empire a permanent capital worthy of his accomplishments. Mehmed gave to the Greek patriarch, the Grand Rabbi, and to other religious leaders theoretical and—often—real authority over the internal affairs of their people. The Ottomans not only tolerated religious diversity but also welcomed the Jews expelled from Spain.

On land the Ottomans carried all before them, and their European empire included Hungary, Croatia, Serbia, Bosnia, Albania, Greece, Bulgaria, Romania, and almost all of the districts of modern Russia and Ukraine adjacent to the Black Sea. In 1475, with the loss of Kaffa in the Crimea by the Genoese, the last route to Asia not in Muslim hands passed under Ottoman control. This loss contributed to the long-standing western European determination to reach East Asia by circumnavigating Africa (as Vasco da Gama did) or by finding a westerly

Venetian drawing of Suleiman the Magnificent leading a procession of Janissaries.

route (as Christopher Columbus attempted to do). The Ottomans acquired the largest segment of their Middle Eastern empire in one blow when they defeated the Mamluks in Syria at Marj Dabiq and then occupied Cairo in 1517. Not only did the Ottomans fall heir to the Mamluk role as guardian of the two holy places, Mecca and Medina, but they also gained responsibility as a sea power both on the Mediterranean and in the Indian Ocean, which had been newly invaded by the Portuguese. As rulers of the Arabic-speaking heartlands of the Middle East, the Ottomans inevitably came to see the Islamic tradition as much through Arab as Persian eyes.

The energies of the Spanish and Portuguese that had gone into the "reconquest" of the Iberian Peninsula were now fiercely directed toward North Africa, and a papal bull of 1494 required the faithful to help Spain in this "crusade." In 1497 the Spanish occupied the port of Malila in Morocco and subsequently took a whole string of ports including Algiers, which they occupied in 1510. Resistance to the Spaniards found its champions in an assortment of fearless North African sea captains, the most famous of whom was Khayr ad-Din Barbarossa (d. 1546). Barbarossa was by origin an Ottoman subject and a brilliant naval commander who lacked only the material support that the Ottomans could offer. With Barbarossa's help all of the North African coast except Morocco fell under Ottoman rule with its center at the recaptured port of Algiers. The interior, however, was seldom under Ottoman control and remained largely autonomous.

The acquisition of North Africa took place largely under Suleiman the Magnificent, whose reign from 1520 to 1566 has been considered the height of the empire. In Turkish Suleiman is known as Kanuni, the giver of *kanun*, or nonreligious law. Even the *shari'a*, the Islamic religious law, allowed some room for the ruler to dispense justice at his own discretion, and in practice most rulers in the Islamic world had taken a great deal of the law into their own hands and the hands of their officials rather than allowing it to remain in the hands of the *qadi*s, the judges appointed to adjudicate according to the shari'a. The Ottomans integrated the two systems of royal and religious law, and it was Suleiman who gave the combined system its fully mature form. The Ottomans even obliged the qadis to apply royal law alongside Islamic law in their courts.

This integration of royal and religious law reflects the degree to which the Ottomans penetrated and regulated society. The Ottomans were heirs to the Turco-Mongolian heritage of dynastic royal law and also to late-Roman traditions of law and bureaucracy preserved by the Byzantines. Like the Byzantines the Ottomans

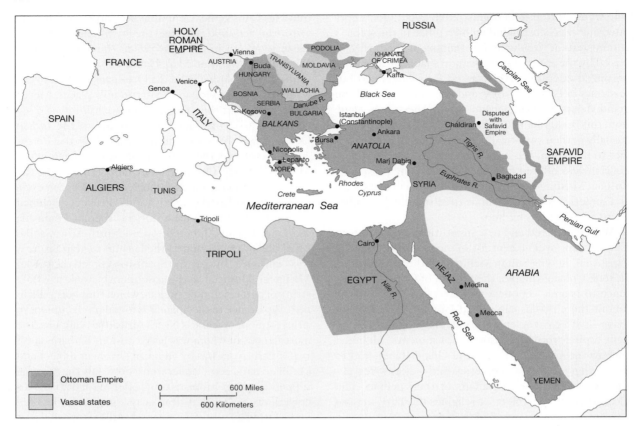

The Ottoman Empire at Its Peak in the 17th Century

organized the professions into guilds, counted households, and established supreme religious officials in their capital. While the Ottomans very often failed to control society to the extent that they wished, they came nearer to achieving such control than had any previous Islamic regime.

By the end of Suleiman's reign the empire had reached its natural limits. The Ottomans were never as successful at sea as on land. With their conquest of Egypt in 1517 they inherited the Mamluk struggle to push the Portuguese out of the Indian Ocean. For a while the Ottoman navy kept open the old route through Egypt, although they could never decisively defeat the Portuguese; and in the seventeenth century, when the larger fleets of the Dutch and English entered the Indian Ocean, these routes too were lost, and consequently the eastern Arab provinces of the Ottoman Empire became impoverished.

In the Mediterranean the Ottomans did not have the commercial fleet that the major Christian powers possessed; and they were dependent on the seafaring skills of such Ottoman subjects as Barbarossa in North Africa.

But the Ottomans had commercial interests, new provinces to protect and logistical needs to meet for further expansion in the Mediterranean, along which they controlled more than half the coast. They built a mighty navy and the Spaniards and Venetians, often enemies, allied themselves for a major confrontation. In 1571 at the battle of Lepanto off the coast of Greece in a ferocious fight with over two hundred galleys on each side, the Ottomans were defeated. Although the Ottomans rebuilt their fleet with amazing rapidity and although the Spaniards and Venetians quarreled and were unable to build upon their success, Lepanto was one of the great victories in the history of Christian Europe. The Ottomans had reached the limits of their expansion at sea. After Lepanto, seaborne Ottoman conquest in the Mediterranean was limited to the conquest of islands off their territories. And, as a further consequence, the independence of Morocco, the most distant part of North Africa and the only part of the Arab world to remain free of Ottoman rule, was assured.

Ottoman land expansion in Europe also reached its limit at this time. The Ottomans were hampered by the overland distance between Istanbul and Vienna, in miles and in time. They were also trapped by the rise of a formidable power immediately to their east in Persia, the Safavids. The Ottomans could neither move their army's barracks westward toward Vienna nor concentrate on their western front. These weaknesses grew out of a more serious weakness in Ottoman government: the central government remained too narrowly based on personal loyalty to the sultan, and any vital initiative—military or otherwise—required the personal commitment and attention of the sultan or his public face, the grand vizier.

The Safavids: From Sufi Mystics to Persian Emperors

In less than a decade the Safavid family rose from relative obscurity to world prominence, largely due to their long-established role as spiritual leaders of a Sufi religious order in Azerbaijan, the Turkish-speaking northwestern province of Iran. The mystical tradition of Islam known as Sufism holds that disciples of organized Sufi orders achieve spiritual advancement through complete obedience to their spiritual masters, who were believed to be powerful intercessors in heaven for those venerating them or their tombs. Usually Safavid rule is dated from 1501 when Isma'il (1501–24), a handsome youth, assumed the title of Shah of Iran. But the seed of Safavid rule had been planted over two centuries earlier when a Sufi leader in Azerbaijan established a Sufi mystical order that grew in respect and influence under his descendants, called Safavids. Such orders had increased after the appearance of the Mongols, partly because they offered points of social cohesion in times of political disruption and partly because Turco-Mongolian rulers respected holy men as seers and welcomed Sufis into their courts.

The Safavids soon acquired authority as spiritual leaders beyond Azerbaijan. At some point in the largely unrecorded history of the Safavid leaders before 1500, a large number of Turkish—and a few Kurdish—tribes in eastern Anatolia, northern Iraq, and eastern Iran were converted by Safavid propagandists and became fervently devoted to the Safavid leadership. The Safavids, while remaining Sufi leaders, also gained credit as ghazis by leading expeditions against the Georgian Christians in the Caucasus. With the advent of Shah Isma'il, the Safavids emerged as a genuine government with an unexpectedly effective army.

Isma'il stepped forward with virtually all the cards of legitimacy in his hand: He was a ghazi; a mystical leader who was owed total obedience; a near-divine being who fulfilled the esoteric speculations of Turkish nomads and others who awaited a Messianic leader; and a supposed descendant of the Prophet through the Prophet's son-in-law 'Ali, who was seen as the font of all wisdom. He reunited the area of the Iranian plateau and became the "Shah of Iran" and therefore heir to the royal tradition most deeply respected in western Asia. Lastly—and to the ultimate unmaking of his dynasty—he was the actual heir of the working tradition of tribally oriented Turco-Mongolian administration, which had existed continuously in Iran, while the Ottomans had only inherited certain attitudes toward statecraft from this tradition.

With his army of devoted followers Isma'il soon united most of the area that had constituted the empire called Iran before the coming of Islam. A latent identification of the linguistically varied people of this area as Iranians worked in Isma'il's favor. Isma'il proclaimed Twelver Shi'ism the only publicly acceptable form of Islam in his empire; and he and his followers set about systematically imposing this form of Shi'ism in the parts of the Safavid realm most firmly under their control. Twelver Shi'ism holds that the leadership rests with a line of descent in the Prophet Muhammad's family, the first of whom was 'Ali and the twelfth of whom had disappeared in the ninth century and would reappear as the Messiah at the end of time. Under the Safavids, being an Iranian gradually became identified with being a Twelver Shi'ite. The identification was never complete, however: significant communities in the Arab world and India were (and remain) Twelver Shi'ites, and significant minorities in Iran clung to the Sunni version of Islam espoused by the majority of non-Iranian Muslims. Meanwhile, the Turkish nomadic followers of Isma'il devotedly believed their leader to be infallible, even though Twelver Shi'ite ulama were horrified at such a claim; and Isma'il's Turkish poetry, which found an audience among Turks everywhere, implied that Isma'il saw himself as more than human.

The rise of the Safavids posed a threat to the Ottomans very different from the threat of the European powers. Many elements in the Ottoman Empire, especially the Turkish tribesmen of Anatolia and Syria, admired Isma'il and shared some of the religious beliefs of his closest followers. Turkish-speaking tribes had played a role in earlier Ottoman conquests but were no longer a significant part of the Ottoman army. They were still, however, a warlike presence in central and eastern Anatolia, and the Ottomans could not afford to have them rally to the new Shi'ite power on their eastern flank. The Ottomans marched on Azerbaijan and in

1514 the two new empires of the Middle East faced each other in battle at Chaldiran. Shah Isma'il's smaller force of mounted archers, convinced of his invincibility, charged repeatedly at the Ottomans, shouting (in Turkish) the battle cry: "My spiritual leader and master, for whom I sacrifice myself"! The handguns of the Ottoman infantry were effective against these troops but even more so was the Ottoman artillery, for which the Safavids had no counterpart. It did not matter that the individual bravery of Safavid horsemen carried some of them through the Ottoman lines to hack at the chains that held the Ottoman gun carriages together: Ottoman numbers, discipline, and technological superiority carried the day.

The battle of Chaldiran was as least as decisive as the battle of Lepanto for the future of the Middle East. As befitted a power that was far wealthier and more experienced in the new technologies of war, the Ottomans kept the upper hand in their confrontations with the Safavids and the Iranian powers that would succeed them. And Shah Isma'il lost his aura of invincibility.

LETTER FROM THE SULTAN

■ *This letter was sent by the Ottoman sultan Selim shortly before the battle of Chalidiran in 1514 to the Safavid ruler, Shah Isma'il.*

I, sovereign chief of the Ottomans, master of the heroes of the age, who unites the force and power of Feridun [a legendary king of ancient Persia], the majesty and glory of Alexander the Great, the justice and clemency of Khusraw [the famous king of Persia, in whose reign the Prophet Muhammad was born]; I, the exterminator of idolators destroyer of the enemies of the true faith, the terror of the tyrants and pharaohs of the age; I, before whom proud and unjust kings have humbled themselves, and whose hand breaks the strongest sceptres; I, the great Sultan-Khan, son of Sultan Bayezid-Khan, son of Sultan Muhammad-Khan, son of Sultan Murad-Khan, I address myself graciously to you, Amir Isma'il, chief of the troops of Persia, comparable in tyranny to Zahhak and Afrasiab [legendary tyrants mentioned in the Persian national epic], and predestined to perish like the last Darius, in order to make known to you that . . . it is He [the Almighty] who has set up Caliphs on earth . . . it is then only by practicing the true religion that man will prosper in this world and merit eternal life in the other. As to you, Amir Isma'il, such a recompense will not be your lot; because you have denied the sanctity of the divine laws; because you have deserted the path of salvation and the sacred commandments; because you have impaired the purity of the dogmas of Islam; because you have dishonored, soiled and destroyed the altars of the Lord, usurped the sceptre of the East by unlawful and tyrannical means; because coming forth from the dust, you have raised yourself by odious devices to a place shining with splendor and magnificence; because you have opened to Muslims the gates of tyranny and oppression; because you have joined iniquity, perjury and blasphemy to your sectarian impiety; because under the cloak of the hypocrite, you have sowed everywhere trouble and sedition; because you have raised the standard of irreligion and heresy . . . you have dared . . . to permit the ill-treatment of the *ulama*, the doctors and amirs descended from the Prophet, the repudiation of the Koran, the cursing of the legitimate Caliphs. Now as the first duty of a Muslim and above all of a pious prince is to obey the commandment, "O, you faithful who believe, be the executors of the decrees of God!" the ulama and our doctors have pronounced sentence of death against you, perjurer and blasphemer, and have imposed on every Muslim the sacred obligation to arm in defense of religion and destroy heresy and impiety in your person and that of all your partisans.

Animated by the spirit of this *fetwa*, conforming to the Koran the code of divine laws, and wishing on one side to strengthen Islam, on the other to liberate the lands and peoples who writhe under your yoke, we have resolved to lay aside our imperial robes in order to put on the shield and coat of mail, to raise our ever-victorious banner, to assemble our invincible armies.

But the Safavids survived, and Ottoman occupation of parts of Iran after Chaldiran did the occupiers little good because of the scorched-earth policy of the retreating Safavids and the hostility of the local population. Moreover, the Ottoman troops, which included elements secretly sympathetic to the Safavids, disliked these campaigns and grumbled that they would prefer to fight non-Muslim powers in Europe. In any case, it took the Ottoman central army as long or longer to reach the Safavids as it did to reach Vienna. Ottoman expansion had reached its physical and its ideological limits in the east as well as in the west.

For the Safavids the consequences were even more dramatic. Isma'il was not invincible, and normative Twelver Shi'ism (which had regarded him as a mere human all along) increasingly set the religious tone for the Safavid court. The most devoted followers of Shah Isma'il commonly called him "the friend and representative" of God; and it was possible for ordinary Twelver Shi'ites to accept the more conservative claim of the Safavids to be the representative of the Messiah, a claim that still allowed them ample authority.

The Safavids wanted infantry troops on the Ottoman model; and, thanks to their efforts in the sixteenth century to increase the extent of crown lands, they were able by the seventeenth century to buy slaves from the Caucasus and create their own version of the Janissaries. In the seventeenth century, under the long reign of Shah Abbas I (1587–1629), the Safavid dynasty reached its political apogee. The Turkish tribal supporters of the Safavids were assigned to specific provinces where, somewhat in the style of the Seljuk *iqta'*, they received the revenue of the provinces in exchange for providing a tribal levy for major campaigns. A small force chosen from these tribes was the original element in the standing army, to which Shah Abbas added cavalry, infantry, and artillery. Some of these troops were of slave origin, but some were recruited from very diverse elements, including—most exceptionally in the history of the premodern Islamic Middle East—the Iranian peasantry.

In Abbas's stunningly beautiful new capital of Isfahan in the center of Iran, the court language changed from Turkish to Persian, and Persian-speaking bureaucrats directly supervised taxation and expenditure in the central provinces. The luxury products of the central provinces, especially silk textiles, had an avid market and gave the crown significant income. By the early seventeenth century Safavid Iran was acknowledged by its far larger and richer neighbors, in particular the Moghuls of India, to have a certain cultural hegemony within the Islamic world.

Miniature of Shah Abbas I as a young man by an unknown Moghul painter.

The Moghuls: Tamerlane's Descendants Seize India

The Moghuls of India were the true biological heirs of Genghis Khan and of Tamerlane. Babur, the founder of the Moghul dynasty, was a great-great grandson of Tamerlane and, on his mother's side, a direct descendent of Genghis Khan. Babur wandered through Central Asia and Afghanistan, winning and losing parts of the heartland of Tamerlane's empire until, having gained control of the Afghan city of Kabul, he found himself overlooking the passes to India. In his engaging—and amazingly candid—memoirs, he wrote: "India is a wonderful country . . . [for, while it] is a land of few charms . . . the pleasant things of India are that it is a large country and has masses of gold and silver." At the battle of Panipat in 1526 Babur defeated the far more numerous forces of the Muslim kings of Delhi with an Ottoman tactic, placing a barrier of carts linked by chains behind which musketeers fired at repeated cavalry charges. Shortly afterward he defeated the leader of the Rajputs, who formed a powerful Hindu military confederacy. His grandson Akbar (1556-1605) continued his conquests, uniting the greater part of India under one rule for the first time since the Buddhist emperor Asoka in the third century B.C.E. Indians used the term "Mongols" to describe Central Asians, and they called the largely Turkish dynasty of Babur the Moghuls, a Persian form of the word *Mongols.*

India on the eve of the Moghul invasion was divided into numerous kingdoms, very few of which were truly centralized. In the fifth century Indian rulers had assigned hereditary rights to land in exchange for the services of the assignees in collecting taxes and keeping order at a local level. As many of these assignees were members of the Hindu religious elite called the Brahmans, they also controlled the extensive lands owned by Hindu temples. This hereditary group worked, generally without much commitment, for the many changing rulers of following centuries, who usually came from low-caste groups—that is, groups of low social status—or from foreign invaders. Rulers were therefore not considered to be divinely appointed; they were supposed to maintain the norms of society, which meant maintaining the local control of traditional elites. As long as they did so, they had more to fear from each other than from the people they ruled; and, in fact, they very often did not seek to replace each other but only to become the head of confederacies of kingdoms, or the "great" king from whom lesser kings derived their greatness.

This image of society and kingship was only slightly altered by the invasion from the northwest of Turkish and Afghan rulers from the Muslim world. Occasionally, a Muslim ruler took the position that Hindus were polytheistic pagans and should be given a choice of Islam or death. But the overwhelming majority of Muslim rulers agreed with an early Muslim commander that Hindus were a "people of the book" and therefore should be tolerated just as Jews and Christians were. By and large, the Muslims left local administration intact and welcomed the military support of warlike Hindu elites such as the Rajputs. The Rajputs were a social category, or caste, of northern and central India whose traditional occupation was warfare and who exalted the virtues of a courageous death on the battlefield.

Akbar at the siege of the great Rajput fortress of Ranthambhor in 1568.

The Moghuls immediately understood their situation: without the support of the Hindu Rajputs they could never maintain an extensive empire in India. Babur's grandson, Akbar, the true organizational founder of the Moghul empire, married several Rajput princesses (though only after defeating their fathers and/or brothers), and used a Rajput stronghold as the base from which his armies would establish a vast empire. By his death in 1605 the Moghul empire stretched from the heart of Afghanistan on the west to the Bay of Bengal on the east, and from The Himalaya on the north to the center of the Deccan plateau. Under Babur's successors, the Moghuls gained control of almost all remaining parts of India.

The administration created by Akbar was remarkably durable, and important aspects of it survived during the period of direct British rule of India after 1858. Akbar gave all the great officials of the empire the title of *mansabdar*, meaning "holder of a position of rank," and arranged the mansabdars into a hierarchy of thirty-three grades. The mansabdars held their position at the pleasure of the emperor and received payment through *jagirs*, assignments of revenues, the Moghul equivalent of iqta's. In the time of a vigorous emperor like Akbar, much of the actual revenue collection was performed by treasury officials, who used surveys to control revenues down to the village level and who dispensed salaries to the mansabdars. The system was open to both talent and favoritism: Muslim warriors and administrators from other Islamic regions were welcomed, and of Indian-born officials and officers a very high percentage were Hindus.

The Sharifians: The Islamic "Far West" Becomes an Empire

Morocco also emerged as a reconstituted political unit at the time of the founding of the three larger early modern Islamic empires. In the late fifteenth and early sixteenth centuries the Portuguese acquired direct or indirect control of most of the Atlantic coast of Morocco, as well as such strategic Mediterranean ports as Tangier. The Portuguese not only tried to extract as much tax as they could from their Moroccan subjects and tributaries but also raided the interior for plunder and slaves. It is often forgotten that the North African seafarers depicted as "pirates" in the literature of early modern Europe were mirror images of many of their Christian European counterparts.

The Moroccans reacted violently, and an upswell of religious sentiment shaped the destiny of Morocco to the twentieth century. Much of this sentiment found its focus in Sufism. Moroccans of all classes showed greater devotion than Muslims in other parts of the Arab world to their local Sufi leaders, who were seen as healers and miracle workers. Thanks to the contributions they received and the trade routes they dominated, many of these Sufi leaders were more independent of sultans than the ulama.

In the eighth century a *sharif*, or descendant of the Prophet Muhammad, had fled the caliphs of the Islamic Middle East and founded a minor but long-lived dynasty in Morocco. Sharifian lineage acquired particular prestige in this area, and sharifs continued to emigrate to Morocco over the centuries. In 1511 one line of sharifs agreed to lead the people of southern Morocco against the Portuguese; and the Sufi leaders, greatly empowered by the new religiosity of Moroccans, rallied to support their cause. In 1550 Muhammad (who adopted the regnal title al-Mahdi, "the Messiah"), took the greatest town of the interior, Fez.

This line of Sharifians (as the rulers of Morocco are known up to the present day) reunified Morocco and gradually expelled the Europeans. Since an important goal of European expansion along the Atlantic coast was to trade for gold (and, later, slaves) from the sub-Saharan interior, to compete with them the Sharifians moved overland far to the south, conquering Timbuktu in 1590; and, for half a century, they were the predominant power in a vast region of Africa immediately to the south of Timbuktu.

The first line of Sharifians, the Sa'dians, created a government more centralized than Morocco had experienced in some centuries and added to their tribal support a standing army of European renegades—Muslims expelled from Spain, and black troops trained by Ottoman deserters. The new state apparatus, much influenced by the Ottoman example, managed to survive in spite of continually disputed successions, competing tribal powers, and, finally, the disaffection of the Sufi leaders.

The Early Modern Islamic Empires Compared

The great Islamic empires of the early modern period shared many points of origin and of ongoing contact. In their appeal for legitimacy they all looked back to sacred history or sanctified lineages. The Moroccan rulers used the titles "caliph" and "commanders of the faithful," implying that they were rightful successors to the Prophet in temporal affairs, because they were descendants of the Prophet through 'Ali. The early Ottomans such as Bayazid, used the title caliph, as well as sultan, as did the Ottomans of the eighteenth and nineteenth centuries. The Moghuls also called themselves caliphs. The Safavid claim—quite probably false—that they were descended from the Prophet through 'Ali was generally accepted. None of the dynasties turned its back on the longing among Muslims for a universal Islamic state led by a descendant of the Prophet and/or a rightful political successor to the revered caliph or caliphs that had directly succeeded the Prophet. In a sense, the Islamic world continued to be a unit within which intellectual, mercantile, and artisanal elites moved freely.

For all these dynasties except the Moroccans, succession to the Turco-Mongolian heritage was of immense importance. Naturally, they used the title sultan, which had represented authority ever since

Mahmud of Ghazna. The grandiose title *khaqan*, originally reserved for the leader of the descendants of Genghis Khan, was used very commonly by the Ottomans, who also designated the khans of the Crimea, direct descendants of Genghis Khan, as their successors in the unlikely event that all members of the Ottoman house should expire. The Safavids, who used few titles in addition to their regnal names, nevertheless constructed a hierarchy of military officials using the Central Asian Turkish titles *khan* and *beg*, as did the Moghuls and Ottomans—for these titles carried immediate authority with their Turkish-speaking troops. Just as distinctive as the titles used by the Safavids, Ottomans, and Moghuls was their use of the Persian title shah or padishah (king) or shahanshah (king of kings). Safavid territory closely corresponded to the territory of the Sassanian shahs who ruled Iran before Islam; hence their use of the title shah. The centuries-old Iranian tradition of court culture remained the archetype to which not only the Safavid dynasty but also the more distant Ottoman and Moghul dynasties looked back.

All four early modern Islamic dynasties gained as much or more from their reaction to the contemporary world as from their association with the great physical and spiritual lineages. All four gained legitimacy by their fight against non-Muslim powers and therefore proudly bore the title of ghazi. They arose at a time when European Christian powers were assuming control of the sea, and they survived into periods of vigorous European onslaughts by land; thus, their role as ghazis carried great respect.

All four empires made use of the Sufi orders, which had emerged as huge brotherhoods with endowed lodges and teaching institutions supervised by hierarchies of leadership. The Safavid dynasty sprang directly from Sufi leadership to imperial rule. The connection of the Sharifian dynasties of Morocco to local Sufi saints often provided their most vital link to the masses. In Ottoman society, all of the rulers as well as most of the elite were interested in or affiliated with a Sufi order. The Moghuls maintained Sufi leaders as favored members of their court; and Sufi mysticism acted as a bridge to the Hindu mysticism espoused by many of their non-Muslim subjects.

Why did so much of the early modern Islamic world compose itself into fairly stable empires around 1500? For the Ottomans, Safavids, and Moghuls a reinterpretation of the Turco-Mongolian heritage played an important role. All three governments aspired to give legal authority to royal commands and to control the traditional experts of religion more than previous Islamic dynasties. All three drew upon the tradition represented by the Yasa, ascribed to Genghis Khan, which gave a special aura to royal law. The Ottomans did this most successfully; their courts applied Islamic law as well as royal law. All three tried to standardize Islamic law (which ideologically resisted standardization because it accepted an established variety of interpretations). The Ottomans and the Safavids tried to supervise the affairs of the ulama. These attempts at organizing the religiously learned—their legal functions and their assets—did not always work; but they showed an ambition to control and standardize with few precedents in Islamic history.

This drive for central control manifested itself in other areas of government. All three empires, partly in the Mongol tradition, attempted extraordinarily careful surveys of their resources. Nevertheless, all three empires turned their backs on the fairly frequent Turco-Mongolian practice of dividing an empire between royal sons. But, ironically, the Safavids, inheriting the actual personnel and practices of the Turco-Mongolian tradition of administration, at first continued the tradition of assigning provinces to tribal peoples as hereditary "fiefs." Although they later attempted to suppress this system, they were unable to do so; and their failure severely undermined their attempts to build a central army and administration on the Ottoman model.

The Ottomans, Safavids, Moghuls, and Sharifians also owed their origins and ability to endure in part to the economic vitality of their greatest rivals, the Christian Europeans. The growing population and increasing sophistication of the European market gave an advantage to large centralized empires that controlled a significant part of the trade. It was no accident that Bursa, near the Sea of Marmara, a major depot for luxury goods crossing to the Mediterranean world, was for half a century the capital of the infant Ottoman government. The Sharifian dynasties of Morocco pushed hundreds of miles southward to control Timbuktu, the collection point for the gold from the rich West African mines. The Iranians controlled overland trade between the Persian Gulf and the Caspian Sea; in addition, their strong artisanal traditions made their products widely sought and gave them significant exports. The far more numerous Indians also had strong artisanal traditions and, from Roman times on, seem to have had a highly favorable balance of trade with areas to the west. As a result India, which has few sources of precious metal, was probably the most monetized large economy in the world in the sixteenth century; and truly astonishing sums of gold and silver passed through the Indian treasury. The new empires were fiscal empires, interested in enriching royal treasuries, as they sought to wring advantage out of a world market greatly increased by improvement in travel, growth of population, and the rise of Europe.

One European export proved essential to the centralizing activities of the later Islamic empires: guns. It is hard to imagine that the Ottoman Empire would have emerged as *the* Middle Eastern state without gunpowder weapons. The Mamluks were among the world's finest cavalry forces in the fifteenth century, and the Safavid Shah Isma'il had an army completely and selflessly devoted to him; but neither could stand up against Ottoman weapons. The Safavids and Moghuls learned to imitate the Ottoman tradition of gunnery. This achievement not only enabled them to withstand external threats but made them very different kinds of regimes internally. Thanks to guns, they subdued their own realms with unprecedented thoroughness. Whereas earlier empires had to come to terms with the local leaders in remote areas, the new empires could and often did gain direct rule, in some cases replacing small local dynasties whose origins dated back many centuries.

These empires also survived because they became emblematic of the cultural area they ruled. Their territories constituted a cultural area that their subjects felt would exist less fully or even disappear if their dynasties disappeared. Although far from modern nationalism, this sense of a culturally shared identity endured in both the Sharifian and Safavid empires. By the seventeenth century, the Ottoman-Safavid struggle had produced a border that has with small modification lasted to the present.

The Ottomans and Moghuls ruled empires far more ethnically and religiously diverse, but they nevertheless produced distinctive cultural styles, which their elites aspired to imitate. In the Ottoman case, this cultural style implied the knowledge of certain revered and/or admired classics of the Persian and Arabic traditions, the ability to speak and write the ornate form of Ottoman Turkish, and the observance of elaborate norms of polite behavior as defined by court culture. Properly trained, almost any people of the Ottoman Empire, Slavs, Arabs or Turks, could become "Ottomans." In the Moghul case, a distinctively Indian cultural synthesis emerged at the Moghul court. From this synthesis came Urdu, which is a northern Indian dialect written in characters like Persian and sprinkled with words borrowed from Persian, the official language of the Moghul court. Together with its sister language Hindi, essentially the same language but with an alphabet ultimately derived from Sanskrit and with somewhat fewer Persian words, Urdu was to become the most important intercommunal language of the Indian subcontinent.

Seventeenth-century allegorical representation of Shah Abbas I and Jahangir, emperor of India (1605–27). The two rulers embrace while standing on the symbols of peace on a globe of the world.

Artistic Refinement in the Early Modern Islamic Empires

The early modern Islamic dynasties were great patrons of culture, partly by individual whim and partly by political design. Court culture of this period shone most brilliantly in the production of material objects, both of practical and of aesthetic intent. Architecture throughout the region reached an astonishing refinement from the Sa'dian tombs in Morocco to the madrasas of Central Asia. In the central Islamic lands, above all Iran, color-tiled decoration gave buildings a visual brilliance and unity almost unrivaled to this day. The richer Ottomans and Moghuls were able to build enormous stone structures of great dignity, the best known of which is the Taj Mahal in India. Court patronage of painting brought the Persian miniature, with its slightly magical atmosphere, and Moghul painting, with its dramatic realism, to their highest points of perfection. Similarly, textiles such as brocades and rugs, some manufactured in royal workshops, became luxury items widely sought for their beauty on the international market.

The intellectual world did not flourish to the same degree. Practical items were imported and practical skills learned, but mainly to enhance existing cultural forms or to defend against European onslaught. Large numbers of grandfather clocks were imported for mosques, and European seafaring techniques were adopted; yet the more abstract sciences needed to understand and develop technologies were still cultivated largely along traditional Middle Eastern lines with little awareness of European developments. Ibn Khaldun (1332–1406), a North African Muslim scholar who was a highly original social thinker, reflects the difficulty faced in the Islamic world between about 1400 (when he wrote) and about 1800 by those persons curious about European thought and intellectual achievement: "We hear now that the philosophical sciences are greatly cultivated in western Europe . . . Existing systematic expositions of them are said to be comprehensive, the people who know them numerous and the students of them many. God knows best what exists there."

The Resilience of Islamic Societies

From the thirteenth to the eighteenth centuries Islam continued to spread as a world religion. In Central Asia it became the predominant religion, even among the Mongols, whose "paganism" had once seemed such a threat to the Islamic Middle East. Under the Moghuls the numbers of Muslims increased dramatically until Muslims accounted for over one-fifth of the inhabitants of the Indian subcontinent. The East Indies (modern Indonesia) became predominantly Muslim due to the continuing influence of Muslim traders in the Indian Ocean and to the persistence of Indian influence in Southeast Asia. The success of the Mamluks and Ottomans in controlling the Nile Valley and of the Moroccans in extending their state southward contributed to the conversion of a large area in sub-Saharan Africa. The presence of the Ottomans in the Balkans facilitated the conversion to Islam of Albania, Bosnia, and other areas.

The empires cared far more about the extraction of taxes than religious affiliation, however. Conversions were overwhelmingly the result of lay activity such as trade and, above all, the spread of the Sufi brotherhoods. The great majority of Muslims had some Sufi connection, whether they belonged to a Sufi order or merely visited the tombs of Sufi "saints," which existed throughout the Islamic world. Sufi themes dominated

Islamic poetry. Sufism's success at directly reaching the masses also accounts for the use of writing in a host of hitherto largely unwritten languages, such as Pushtu in Afghanistan. And international Sufi orders, with chapter houses all the way from the Ottoman Empire to China, facilitated the movement of believers traveling throughout the Islamic world, who found like-minded Sufi "brothers" to give them shelter.

Local elites persisted, although religion often connected local life to much larger units. For example, the tomb of a Sufi saint might connect the villagers living nearby to more important saints' tombs around which yearly pilgrimages and organized Sufi life were centered. And the village Qur'an teacher might send humble boys of great talent to a distant madrasa, where they could rise to the top of the ulama hierarchy. The position of village headman, however, would most likely be hereditary in one of the richer families. As a rule, pastoralists and farmers remained interdependent. The pastoralists would use marginally cultivable land when regimes allowed them to do so, and often villages had long-standing agreements with tribal pastoralists in which food and seasonal land use was exchanged for protection of the village. In the Middle East proper a surprisingly large percentage of the population would alternate between full or part-time pastoralism and full or part-time farming according to political and ecological conditions. Pastoralists, particularly fully nomadic ones, could play an important role in the distribution of power.

In many parts of the Islamic world of this period members of the local elite were called *a'yan*, "notables." The notables usually consisted of landlords, prominent merchants, and locally distinguished religious scholars. This group tended to view themselves as hereditary; they intermarried and claimed ancient origins, but, in fact, people of new wealth became notables fairly easily. The notables had often played an important role as intermediaries between the government and the local community in earlier regimes, but when the new empires were at their strongest, the central governments often bypassed them and instead used bureaucrats assigned to local administrators. Nonetheless, the notables survived, their numbers often strengthened by the addition of former officials, civil and military, or their sons; and by the eighteenth century they had assumed the importance they once held under previous dynasties.

The life of cities was more volatile, reflecting the variety of their interest groups and the presence of government. Most cities were networks of narrow alleyways, overlooked by houses with grilled windows. Large cities were divided into quarters, often with their own

A sixteenth-century drawing of the Turkish city of Bitlis shows a typical Islamic townscape.

gates. The large and more open spaces regularly included the citadel or the governor's residence, the principal mosque (often called the Friday mosque, since Muslims of the region were all expected to gather at one specially designated mosque on Fridays) and the marketplaces. Outside many towns was an enormous area especially designated for the entire local community of Muslims to gather for such communal religious events as the yearly feast of sacrifice and the prayer for rain in times of extreme drought. Imperial cities also had parade grounds, some portion of which might be incorporated into the heart of the city as a central square and, upon occasion, as a royal polo field.

Town and city organization varied greatly, but a number of features recurred. Near the principal mosques, the ritually "cleanest" professions existed, such as the cloth trade; and since wholesale cloth sales were such an important element in big business, other professions that dealt with large sums, such as jewellers and money changers were located nearby. The madrasas and the court of the *qadi*, or judge, were also located near this more desirable part of the market quarter. Since ritual and physical cleanliness were obviously associated, the public baths were there as well. In contrast, professions involving the use of ritually unclean materials (such as animal dung for tanning leather) were placed on the outskirts of town, since these workers had to wash themselves in a specified way before they could pray.

The market inspector supervised the town market, enforcing a variety of rules considered essential to the proper function of the market, such as the use of proper weights or the wearing of proper garments. The market inspector could order summary punishments, some trivial and some intended to terrify, such as nailing a grossly dishonest shopkeeper by his ear to his shop door. In general, the operation of market forces set prices, and the saying ascribed to Muhammad, that "God sets prices" was widely quoted. In fact, a customer could return goods within three days if she or he could prove that the object sold had hidden defects or that the price was above the prevailing market price. There were also very strict injunctions against hoarding, which amounted to a demand that all goods held by merchants for sale should be offered immediately so that no merchant gain an "unjust" profit margin. The merchant communities generally respected the market inspectors, and so valued their services that in formerly Muslim parts of Spain the Christian merchants perpetuated the office. The Ottomans and Safavids gave new functions to the market inspectors, and their governments tended more and more to control retail prices (see p. 466).

The legal official of highest prestige was the qadi. The qadi not only rendered judgments in his court but also acted as the eyes and ears of the sultan in the maintenance of all the major functions of government. In the case of the Ottomans this included the levy of boys and, in later centuries, the regulation of market prices. Usually a select group of local notables worked closely with the qadi and served as witness-notaries, attesting to important legal acts such as the signature of contracts, manumission of slaves, the establishment of *waqf*s (pious endowments) and the like.

Pious endowments were an enormously important instrument for the recirculation of wealth. They maintained street fountains, hospitals, libraries, madrasas, hostels, tomb gardens, baths, free kitchens, and often all manner of public and semipublic institutions. Through such endowments rulers memorialized their names on earth and won a place in heaven. The endowments also fulfilled the contract by which God gave them sovereignty in exchange for their good and just care of their subjects. In fact, people at all levels of society established endowments out of communal feeling. These pious endowments (guarded for perpetuity by the record in the qadi's court) helped keep social peace in large cities with extremes of wealth and poverty, such as Istanbul, which, in the seventeenth century, had a population of at least seven hundred thousand, larger than its nearest competitors in Europe—London and Paris.

The economic elites, however, held on tenaciously to the basic sources of their wealth, often using the waqf to set up family trusts and keep money in the family. The ranks of the ulama, although open to talented students of humble background, tended to form a hereditary class, who passed on judgeships and teaching positions to their more talented children and the supervision of waqfs to less talented children. Large merchants still maintained networks that reached around the world because—in a world without banks—they were the principal source of risk capital and could invest as silent partners with ship captains and other small traders, who would settle for a relatively limited percentage of the profit. These and other elites held their own and flourished as the empires flourished; but in the seventeenth and eighteenth centuries, when signs of imperial decay appeared and the price revolution disoriented the economies of many parts of the world, both the governments and the elites of the Islamic empires found themselves on the defensive.

Political Decline and Transformation in the Seventeenth and Eighteenth Centuries

The seventeenth and eighteenth centuries saw an end to the expansion of these empires and to their organization as conquest states. Not surprisingly, by the eighteenth century positions tended to become hereditary: the central governments lacked the income to buy and/or train military elites, and they also needed the continuity offered by groups willing to exchange loyalty for the prestige of imperial recognition. But that loyalty was weak, and rebellions were a chronic danger in all the empires. Moreover, the loss of transit trade to Europeans and other economic setbacks shrank the empires' economies. Increasingly, they lost territory to the more able European powers. Yet, despite losses and periods of chaos, the early modern Islamic empires or their successors retained their core territories, which formed the basic elements of later nation-states. Furthermore, the social categories through which they administered society retained a greater degree of institutionalization, even under weak imperial governments, than they had achieved under earlier regimes. The decline of these empires in military power did not necessarily imply the decline of their society and cultures.

The Sharifians and the Safavids Confront Turmoil

Both the Sharifians of Morocco and the Safavids of Iran owed their rule to Sufi backing, sanctified lineage, and a regional cultural identification. Both governments tried to imitate the Ottoman example; both were undone by tribal forces. Paradoxically, the Sharifians of Morocco, who were far less successful at creating central institutions, survived; the Safavids did not.

The first family of Sharifians, the Sa'dians, for all their success in reconstituting a Moroccan political unit between the Ottomans and the Spanish, were too weak to sustain their balancing act between the rivalries of the tribes, the cities, and even the different branches of their family. It was rare when the ulama of Fez and of Marrakech agreed on the successor to any Sa'dian ruler. And if the two most important internal cities of Morocco disagreed, the people on the periphery and even the Ottomans and the Spaniards found ways of interfering in nearly every succession. The weakness of the dynasty resulted in Christians gaining control of port cities, as the Spanish did in 1610. The Sufi holy men whose support had been so vital to the rise of the Sa'dians, now became hostile to them.

Finally, from this disorder, in the mid-seventeenth century, a Sharifian family called the Alawis reconstituted the empire. Their most powerful leader, Moulay Isma'il (1672–1727) created a large new army of black slaves. He also presided over the ejection of Europeans from several port cities, including Tangier, and gained prestige as a great defender of the faith. But ultimately his resources were so slender and the consequent weight of his taxation so heavy, that without his forceful leadership this centralizing process proved impossible to continue. Continual turmoil from Moulay Isma'il's death until the late eighteenth century limited the authority of the central government over its subjects and made the Sharifian the least powerful of the early modern Islamic empires.

The Safavids, as we have seen, succeeded in building an impressive imperial bureaucracy and army under Shah Abbas I. His successors were for the most part mediocre, and it is a tribute to the structures Shah Abbas created that the empire survived at all. After a century of struggle to keep southern Iraq, the Safavids lost this province more or less permanently to the Ottomans in 1638. In the center of the empire the Shi'ite ulama grew more powerful, while in the empire's outer provinces the tribes grew more independent. When Shah Sultan Husayn (1694–1722), who succeeded to the throne in 1694, tried to impose Shi'ism on his distant Sunni Afghan subjects, the Afghans defeated his armies and marched virtually unopposed to Isfahan, the Safavid capital in the heart of Iran, in 1722. A decade of disorder ensued, in which Peter the Great of Russia, the Ottomans, descendants of the Safavids, and Afghan leaders all attempted unsuccessfully to take over the remnants of the Safavid empire.

Then, in the 1730s a Turkish leader named Nader Shah not only reconstituted the empire but soundly beat the powers surrounding Iran. The Russians withdrew from the southern Caspian shores, both Turks and Russians lost hegemony over most of the Caucasus, the Uzbeks were driven from the nearer parts of Central Asia, and—most spectacular of all—Nader Shah in 1739 defeated the Moghuls, sacked Delhi, levied an indemnity of millions of gold pieces, and carried home the world's most elaborate throne—the Peacock Throne—and the world's most famous diamond, the Koh-i-noor. All of this did little to create a durable government because Nader Shah relied on tribal armies, whose loyalty was sustained only by success, and on extortionate taxation. When he was murdered by one of his own tribesmen, Iran again reverted to anarchy until the end of the eighteenth century, only briefly relieved by the benevolent rule of Karim Khan Zand, who controlled much of Iran from his southern capital of Shiraz from 1750 to 1779.

The Slow Decline of the Ottomans

At the death of Suleiman the Magnificent in 1566 it was far from clear to the Ottomans that they had reached the limits of their expansion; if the Ottoman Empire had failed to grow significantly for over a century, it had not shrunk. The Ottomans succeeded in capturing two important islands from the Venetians: Cyprus in 1571 and Crete in 1669. An Ottoman victory against the poorly organized Poles in 1676 made the Ottomans immediate neighbors to the growing power of eastern Europe—Russia. Most of these Ottoman victories were possible because their European opponents were locked in deadly struggles or were undergoing decline within the European system. Ottoman sultans seldom led their troops in battle anymore, and sometimes took little interest in the affairs of state. Fortunately, the grand viziers to whom they confided much of their power were often men of great ability, notably the Koprulu family, who ran the empire for much of the last half of the seventeenth century.

FROM A REGISTER OF PIOUS ENDOWMENTS

■ *The following passage is an entry in the register of the pious endowments of Tangier in Morocco, consisting in the most part of copies of deeds written in the second half of the eighteenth and throughout the nineteenth century.*

When Ahmad ibn Muhammad Al-Susi was named overseer of the pious endowments of the students [attached to] the Great Mosque, he did not find any document establishing these pious endowments. In fear that they might be confused with those of the Great Mosque he decided to make a list of them. The pious endowments of the students consist of a small hostel sharing a wall with the Great Mosque, consisting of fourteen rooms with a fig tree in the middle; the large weavers' workshop opposite the hostel; a room opposite the room for funerals; a room near the shops of the witness-notaries; another room above it; the house Khadda; the oven of the mosque, above which, two apartments; the house of Hajj Abdullah al-Katib; a weavers' workshop in the Aqbal quarters; a shop in the grocers' market; two shops in the perfumers' market; a shop above that of the sons of Ibn Jallul; [another] shop in the perfumers' market; the shop of Haddu; the oven of Zaghmuri; two shops opposite that of Haddu; a shop in the cobblers section; another shop at the end of the cobblers' section; a shop in which is found a shoeing smith and a maker of packsaddles, against the wall of the city; a shop on the small square; a little apartment in ruins at the same place . . . three-quarters of a weavers' workshop, called the workshop of Isa ibn Muqaddin; a weaving loom in the possession of Abd al-Qadir Misbah; a loom in the possession of Ali Azyad; three salt caves in the salt mines of [the district] old Tangier. First of the month Jumada ath-Thaniya 1183 [1769 C.E.]. Witnessed by two witness-notaries.

From *Archives Marocaines XXIII* (1914).

FROM A MANUAL ON SAFAVID ADMINISTRATION

■ *The following passage is from a manual on Safavid administration written about 1726. The author is unknown to us but he was thoroughly acquainted with the tradition of later Safavid administration and compiled this manual to explain it to the Afghan leaders who had recently overthrown the Safavids.*

The duties of the exalted Market Inspector of the Entire Kingdom. Every month [an official] obtains from the elders of each guild an undertaking concerning the prices of the goods [in which they deal]. Having satisfied himself [as to the accuracy of the document] he seals it and hands it to the Market Inspector of the Entire Kingdom. The latter must confirm every point of it and send it to the Overseer of the Royal Workshop. The latter too considers it and, if he feels satisfied, seals it and passes it on to the Heads of the Departments, in order that, in accordance with it, the Supervisors may draw up the documents for the goods to be bought.

As regards the pricing of the goods sold by guilds to the inhabitants of the town, if any of the artisan-merchants eludes the Market Inspector's regulations, the latter makes him wear a transportable pillory, that he may serve as an example to others.

The Market Inspector of the Entire Kingdom appoints Deputies everywhere in the God-protected provinces. In every place, the traders, month by month, sell goods to people in accordance with the Deputy's certificate [of prices], so that tranquility may reign among the people [the *ra'aya* or "flocks"] and the inhabitants and residents [of towns], and that the latter may pray for the most sacred person of the King.

The Ottoman system had entered a period of internal transformation which, by the seventeenth century, was apparent to intelligent Ottoman statesmen and thinkers. Officials of the empire were no longer devotees of the Ottoman house and the Ottoman way who owed their advancement to the favor of the sultan, but men who owed as much to their family as to their ruler. The Janissary corps had swollen in numbers from about 8,000 in 1527 to about 38,000 in 1609, in part because a larger infantry was needed to use increasingly heavy firearms. They had become unruly, extravagantly expensive, and—in part because of relaxation of the celibacy requirement—a partly hereditary and far less effective military force. A quick turn in Ottoman fortunes revealed their basic military weakness within a decade. In 1683, when the Ottomans marched on Vienna to stop the alliance of the Austrian Habsburgs, the Russians, and the Poles, they were repulsed and repeatedly defeated as they retreated to Istanbul. In 1687 the defeat of the Ottomans at Mohacs ended a century and a half of direct Ottoman rule of Hungary. Further defeats followed, and only the outbreak of war between France and Austria saved the Ottomans. In the landmark Treaty of Karlowitz in 1699, the Ottomans conceded a large part of the Balkans, almost all of Hungary, and even a part of Greece to their enemies. The initiative had passed into the hands of the Europeans, who were checked only by their own rivalries, the rivalries between the European Christian subjects of the Ottomans, and by a modest recovery of Ottoman abilities in the first half of the eighteenth century.

The second half of the eighteenth century was even less favorable to the Ottomans. Russia as the leading Eastern Orthodox power posed as the champion of the Christian population of the Ottomans and stirred up trouble inside the Ottoman Empire while attacking from outside. Ottoman control of local administration had grown so weak that even in Anatolia holders of timars had become semi-independent and these "lords of the valleys" had to be coerced to send the soldiers and taxes they owed the central government. An important point in the Ottoman-Russian duel was the Treaty of Kuchuk Kainarji in 1774, which established the Russians firmly on the Black Sea with rights to navigate past Istanbul to the Mediterranean. Just as important for the future was recognition in the treaty that the Russians had some kind of protectorate over certain Eastern Orthodox institutions in the Ottoman Empire in exchange

More than a century before the 1687 battle of Mohacs, an army of Janissaries led by Suleiman the Magnificent routed the Hungarians under their young king Louis II at the "first battle of Mohacs" in 1526. In this miniature of the battle, Suleiman directs the army from behind a row of cannon.

for a recognition of the Ottoman sultan as the "caliph" of the Muslims with some kind of protectorate over the Muslims of the Crimea. The new extraterritorial character of the Russian-Ottoman confrontation as well as the revival of a hitherto little-regarded Ottoman claim to the caliphate was to have dramatic consequences in the next century and a half.

The Costly Expansion of the Moghuls

After the death in 1605 of Akbar, the administrative founder of the empire, the Moghuls, unlike the Ottomans, had a series of able and energetic leaders. Of these the most militarily successful was Akbar's great-grandson, Aurangzeb. Early Moghul emperors had sparred with the Safavids over control of Qandahar, in what is now southwestern Afghanistan, or led campaigns toward Central Asia, with which—as descendants of Ta-

merlane and Genghis Khan—they felt a natural link. In his long reign from 1658 to 1707 Aurangzeb turned his attention southward and was able to conquer or reduce to vassalage virtually all of the Indian subcontinent, as well as the surrounding northern mountainous regions of the Hindu Kush and The Himalaya. Only Kerala at the southern tip of India and the strongholds of Marathas, warlike tribal people of central India who threw off Moghul rule, successfully resisted Aurangzeb's attacks.

The situation of the Moghuls was fundamentally different from that of the other Islamic empires in that they alone had a population that was overwhelmingly not Muslim. Of all the Moghul emperors, Akbar, a stocky, burly man with a hearty laugh but a regal presence, went the furthest toward making a synthesis of Islamic ideas and non-Islamic Indian culture and religion (much of which we loosely associate under the name of Hinduism). From early in his reign Akbar tried to remove all stigma from being non-Muslim. His only problem was that while a policy of tolerance made sense, and was followed by his son and grandson, it convinced almost none of the Hindu, Muslim, Zoroastrian, Jewish, Jain, and Jesuit holy men he brought to his court, who disliked each other as bitterly after Akbar as before.

Although both emperors were men of great military ability, Aurangzeb was markedly different from his celebrated great-grandfather. Whereas Akbar had a poor education (though an open and extremely keen mind) and was barely literate, Aurangzeb was well-educated and wrote a handsome Persian style, as befitted a Moghul monarch. Aurangzeb was thin and ascetic and had, as one Italian observer wrote, "a craze for being held a saint." He partly reversed Akbar's policy of toleration. He made some Hindus serving in his army pay the poll tax prescribed in Islamic law for non-Muslims in exchange for military exemption. He even showed intolerance for Muslims, such as Shi'ites, who did not fit his vision of religious orthodoxy. He was wise enough, however, to limit most of these acts of intolerance on the grounds of expediency. Through his gift of leadership and strategy, through his lavish bestowal of jagirs to buy the loyalty of his many hesitant vassals, and through sheer doggedness—he was carried in his litter to battles whenever possible right up to his death in his eighty-eighth year—he created an empire that under its surface unity had already begun to unravel.

Aurangzeb had given some of his most intractable enemies, the Maratha leaders, large *mansab*s, or assignments of revenues in order to buy their loyalty. As the empire stopped growing, however, and Aurangzeb spent fortunes to subdue rebels, there were fewer sources of

Portrait of a Great Mogol, *a drawing of Aurangzeb from a seventeenth-century English "Voyage to East India."*

revenue and the mansab holders found that the system could no longer work for them. Moreover, where the Moghul government maintained direct control, it reduced cultivators to misery by attempts to extract higher taxes. On Aurangzeb's death the mansab holders fell to quarreling with one another and supported rival Moghul pretenders.

Older Hindu lineages such as the Rajputs, Marathas, and Jats, and the newer non-Muslim adherents of the Sikh religion asserted their right to autonomy. Like the Muslim-ruled areas around Hyderabad and Oudh, they became self-contained governments. The breakdown of political unity led to disorder in the countryside, a situation that allowed European trading stations to become semi-independent states. By 1764 the British, who had driven the French and Dutch from most of

India a few years earlier, had uncontested control of the Bengal and Bihar, which they ruled as nominal governors of the powerless Moghuls. A surprising feature of this political scene was that many participants in the hurly-burly of Indian politics maintained the fiction that a Moghul empire still existed. This attitude continued right up to the great rebellion of 1857–1858, often called the Sepoy Rebellion, against the British, who were then in overwhelming control. During this uprising the Delhi rebels declared the Moghul ruler Bahadur Shah II emperor of India. The British consequently deposed him and put an end to all vestiges of Moghul rule. The Moghuls represented a claim that the subcontinent was an interrelated system with a center; they also represented the memory that the center had once been the carrier of a high court culture toward which all directed their gaze. That claim and that memory had sustained the twilight of Moghul rule for a remarkably long time.

Society and Culture in the Seventeenth and Eighteenth Centuries

The apparent decline of the four Islamic empires in the late seventeenth and eighteenth centuries can be explained only in part by the internal weaknesses of those empires. Earlier empires—even earlier phases of these early modern Islamic empires—had gone through periods of decentralization and then pulled themselves together. But the military and economic onslaught of Europe had brought about an altogether new situation. It was not only that Europeans were gobbling up the edges of Islamic regimes, but there was a growing awareness among Muslims that the Islamic world could no longer unthinkingly believe itself to be the central civilization of mankind. From the Treaty of Karlowitz in 1699 there were permanent European embassies in Istanbul. All Islamic powers became enmeshed in European patterns of diplomatic relations, hitherto alien, in large part so that they could use the rivalry of European powers to survive.

The Europeans used these diplomatic relations to good advantage in advancing European commercial penetration. Following a Byzantine custom, the Ottomans and other empires issued special rights to foreigners to trade and to govern their own traders abroad in treaties called "regimes of capitulation," which initiated a growing loss of trade to Europeans and—with the growth of foreign trader communities—a loss of sovereignty. Moreover, non-Muslim minorities often had trading partners of the same religious and ethnic affiliation throughout Europe and the Middle East. For example, the Armenians developed a network of trade in Persian

Suleiman receives the Austrian ambassador. Not until 1683 was the Turkish threat removed from Vienna.

silks that extended from India to Amsterdam. These minorities often knew European languages and acted as middle men in the trade between Europeans and the Islamic empires. By the eighteenth century European missionaries had come to educate Middle Eastern Christians, and the Greeks and Armenians of Istanbul often sent their children to the University of Padua in Italy. The rise of non-Muslim trading elites was yet another sign of the degree that the Islamic world was becoming enmeshed in a world economy.

This sense of no longer being in control of their destinies had a different effect on royal courts than it had on the ulama. The courts experienced a great vogue for European objects such as eyeglasses, telescopes, and pocket watches. But the growing gap in scientific development meant that technology could not be imported so easily. The Ottomans and Moghuls were still striving to make huge cannons at a time when Europeans were developing more mobile and accurate cannons. The trade in luxury objects was turning in favor of Europe.

Nevertheless, European objects were one of the important influences on many of the minor arts of the Islamic world, which reached their greatest sophistication in the seventeenth and eighteenth centuries.

Although taste in architecture and miniature painting often degenerated into a cloying cuteness and sentimentality in the eighteenth century, the everyday possessions of the wealthy—such as hair scissors, pen cases, and formal clothing—were of a sumptuous and yet not gaudy beauty. Similarly, some of the less-grandiose buildings of the period, such as the summer houses of the Ottoman nobility along the Bosporus, reflect a uniquely happy marriage of traditional Ottoman style with European rococo taste. Interestingly, while the older literatures of the Middle East, Arabic and Persian, produced few memorable works in this period, Ottoman Turkish poetry, as well as the poetry of newly written languages such as Pushtu and Urdu, produced lyrics of great beauty, in part because this poetry was closer to living vernaculars.

The ulama by and large reacted to European encirclement by becoming more hostile to European influence. In this they partly reflected the mood of the Muslim masses. They also reflected the disgust of many Muslims at the debauchery of the court. Selim II (1566–74), the son and successor of Suleiman the Magnificent, who bore the sobriquet "the Sot," was not the only drunkard among Muslim rulers. All four Safavid rulers who ruled from 1629 to 1722 were enthusiastically given to drinking—forbidden, of course, by Islamic law. Not only did they drink, but many of these seventeenth- and eighteenth-century rulers were patrons of miniature painting of great sensuality, which endeared them even less to the guardians of religion. When in 1727 an Ottoman statesman opened the first printing press owned by a Muslim in the Ottoman Empire, he wisely chose to print only books related to secular matters such as geography and the natural sciences. In the seventeenth century some of the Ottoman ulama waged a war against popular practices such as the use of tobacco and coffee, which was then becoming enshrined in the coffeehouses that would become a basic feature of local life in the Middle East. But in this instance the "consensus of the community," a principle of Islamic law, overwhelmed learned opposition and the ulama acquiesced.

Other influences, not necessarily related to European presence, also profoundly affected the orientation of Muslim religious thought in the eighteenth century. Many Muslims, both Sunni and Shi'ite, both ulama and lay believers, reacted against the highly scholastic Islamic sciences taught in madrasas and called for a renewal of direct imitation of the piety of the Prophet through a study of his sayings. Many Muslims also suggested the pious should take direct action to restore piety and not wait for governments to do so. One such movement to rid Islam of "false" accretions, called

The Islamic World Under the Turkish Dynasties and the Early Modern Empires

998–1030	Mahmud of Ghazna raids over half of the Indian subcontinent
11th–15th c.	Tribes of Turkish nomads enter the Middle East
13th–14th c.	Mongol empire under Genghis Khan and his descendants, the Il-Khans in Iran and the Golden Horde in Russia
1212	Defeat of Muslims at Las Navas de Tolosa begins their loss of Iberia to the Spanish and Portuguese
1260	Mamluks defeat Mongols at Ain Jalut in Syria
end of 14th c.	Tamerlane reconstitutes empire of the Il-Khans
1389	Battle at Kosovo Polje in Serbia
1492	Fall of Granada; expulsion of Muslims and Jews from Spain
1453	Ottoman sultan Mehmed II takes Constantinople from the Byzantines
1501	Safavid ruler Isma'il assumes title Shah of Iran and later proclaims Twelver Shi'ism the only acceptable form of Islam in his empire
1516	Babur founds Moghul dynasty in India
1517	Ottomans defeat Mamluks at Marj Dabiq in Syria
1520–66	Height of the Ottoman Empire under Suleiman the Magnificent
1550	Sharifian leader Muhammad al-Mahdi captures Fez in Moroccan interior
1571	Spanish and Venetians defeat Ottomans at battle of Lepanto
1587–1629	Safavid dynasty reaches apogee under Shah Abbas I
1590	Sharifians conquer Timbuktu
1672–1727	Reign of Alawi Sharifian leader Moulay Isma'il, who expels Christian powers from port cities of Morocco
1683	Ottomans besiege Vienna but are repulsed
1722	Afghans march unopposed to the Safavid capital Isfahan
1699	Treaty of Karlowitz
1658–1707	Aurangzeb extends Moghul control to virtually all of the Indian subcontinent as well as the Hindu Kush and The Himalaya
1730s	Nader Shah reconstitutes Safavid empire, defeats Moghuls, sacks Delhi
1774	Treaty of Kuchuk Kainarji

Wahhabism after its leader Muhammad 'Abd al-Wahhab (1703–92), grew steadily in political power in Arabia and in intellectual influence throughout the Islamic world, where its austerity was seen as an answer to corruption and decline. Sufi leaders also adapted to the more activist climate of the eighteenth century and took a direct role in politics. The vigor and hope created by these pietistic movements was to persist well into the nineteenth century.

Broadly viewed, the decline of the great empires may have been accompanied by an impoverishment of their peoples and much local disorder, but this by no means meant a decay of the social order. Without doubt, in the eighteenth century the rulers of the great empires lost control of many of their provinces for long periods. Even the Ottomans, the stablest of the empires,

had only a hazy control of Egypt and Iraq, which were effectively ruled by local Mamluks. However, all of these early modern Islamic empires, though not states in the modern sense, created or reinforced local structures that persisted through periods of weak central rule and maintained their collective existence even without government supervision. Somehow, the Islamic world emerged from the eighteenth century with its constituent social communities alive and intact.

The important changes that transformed the governments of the Middle Eastern and Islamic world in the period from the Mongol invasions in the thirteenth century to the eve of European colonization in the late eighteenth century were only partly responsible for changes in society and culture. Governments were more central-ized, more accustomed to maintaining a body of royal law, more inclined to interfere in the application of Islamic law, and more prone to exact stock taking and exploita-tion of the resources of their domains. Governments moved toward creating institutions that might have an impersonal life apart from the ruler or his representatives. But government remained largely personal, and neither the reconfiguration of "fiefs" nor the restructuring of military slavery produced categories of people—even in the hearts of these empires—who felt permanently in-vested in maintaining the central governments' control.

Nevertheless, the empires helped define cultural ar-eas that continued long after central governments failed. Moreover, many aspects of cultural life, in particular ma-terial culture, reached their highest development during this period. This high development was due not only to court patronage but also to the activity of certain catego-ries of the population, such as traders and the ulama, who continued to form international elites. In this sense of belonging to an international community, they were joined by ordinary Muslims who felt less encapsulated in imperially defined "states" and more a part of a world-wide Islamic community. Therefore, while some aspects of what in Europe would be considered the "state" had emerged in these empires, by and large society looked to itself and not to its ruling centers for its identity. These early modern empires had respectably long lives—from two centuries among the Safavids to five centuries among the Ottomans. But even when the empires broke down, society proved remarkably resilient, perhaps because society and government, although closer in this period than in earlier periods of Islamic history, were still living together without being married.

SUGGESTIONS FOR FURTHER READING

GENERAL READING

* P. M. Holt, A. K. S. Lambton, and B. Lewis, eds., *Cambridge History of Islam* (Cambridge: Cambridge University Press, 1970). Excellent chapters on each of the early modern Islamic empires along with good surveys of major topics; a standard book in the field and a useful place to find basic historical facts.
* Ira M. Lapidus, *A History of Islamic Societies* (Cambridge: Cambridge University Press, 1988). A fine survey of Islamic history with good chapters on the early modern empires and thoughtful consideration of the role of Islam in shaping Is-lamic societies.

Francis Robinson, *Atlas of the Islamic World Since 1500* (New York: Facts on File, 1982). Not only an atlas but also a very imaginatively conceived social and cultural history of the pe-riod with magnificent illustrations.

THE ISLAMIC WORLD BEFORE THE EARLY MODERN EMPIRES

Ibn Battuta, *The Travels of Ibn Battuta* (Cambridge: Hakluyt Society, 1958–62). A translation—still not complete—of the memoirs of this fourteenth-century world traveler, which gives an unmatched view of the world of Islamic courts, col-leges, holy men, and merchants.
* R. Stephen Humphreys, *Islamic History: A Framework For Inquiry* (Princeton: Princeton University Press, 1990). An astute guide to the major themes and problems facing historians of this subject with an expert review of bibliography of the field.

THE ISLAMIC WORLD DIVIDES INTO FOUR EMPIRES

R. M. Savory, *Iran Under the Safavids* (Cambridge: Cam-bridge University Press, 1980). The best book on the Safavids, with extensive treatment of cultural subjects such as literature.
S. A. A. Rizvi, *The Wonder That Was India*, Vol. II (London: Sidgwick and Jackson, 1987). While waiting for the new vol-ume on the Moghuls in the *Cambridge History of Islam*, this study, which treats the entire subcontinent from 1200 to 1700, gives a useful panorama of most aspects of Moghul history.
Halil Inalcik, *The Ottoman Empire: The Classical Age 1300–1600* (London: Weidenfeld and Nicolson, 1973). A masterly treat-ment by the doyen of specialists on the Ottomans, strong on administration, trade, learning, and royal law.
* Jamil M. Abun-Nasr, *A History of the Maghrib* (Cambridge: Cambridge University Press, 1975). The standard history of the Maghrib and Andalus with good chapters on the Sa'dians, Alawis, and Ottoman provinces, and a helpful bibliography.

POLITICAL DECLINE AND TRANSFORMATION IN THE SEVENTEENTH AND EIGHTEENTH CENTURIES

Annemarie Schimmel, *The Mystical Dimension of Islam* (Chapel Hill: The University of North Carolina Press, 1975). The best general treatment of Sufism, which was probably the religious orientation of most Muslims during the period covered, with excellent chapters on its intellectual and literary traditions.
Thomas Naff and Roger Owen, eds., *Studies in Eighteenth Century Islamic Society* (Carbondale, IL: Southern Illinois Uni-versity Press, 1987). A pioneering collection of articles that show that the old paradigm of decline does not fit the con-tinuing vitality of Islamic society in the eighteenth century.

* Indicates paperback edition available.

CHAPTER 16

Nation Building and War: Europe, 1450–1650

THE MASSACRE OF THE INNOCENTS

"War is one of the scourges with which it has pleased God to afflict men," wrote Cardinal Richelieu (1585–1642), the French minister who played no small part in spreading the scourge. War was a constant of European society and penetrated to its very core. It dominated all aspects of life. It enhanced the power of the state, it defined gender roles, it consumed lives and treasure and commodities ravenously. War affected every member of society from combatants to civilians. There were no innocent bystanders. Grain in the fields was destroyed because it was food for soldiers; houses were burned because they provided shelter for soldiers. Civilians were killed for aiding the enemy or holding out against demands for their treasure and supplies. Able-bodied men were taken forcibly to serve as conscripts, leaving women to plant and harvest as best as they could.

Neither the ancient temple nor the Roman costume can conceal the immediacy of the picture on the facing page. It is as painful to look at now as it was when it was created over 350 years ago. Painted by Nicolas Poussin (1594–1665) at the height of the Thirty Years' War, the *Massacre of the Innocents* remains a horrifying composition of power, terror, and despair. The cruel and senseless slaughter of the innocent baby that is about to take place is echoed throughout the canvas. Between the executioner's legs can be seen a mother clasping her own child tightly and anticipating the fall of the sword. In the background on the right another mother turns away from the scene and carries her infant to safety. In the foreground strides a mother holding her dead child. She tears at her hair and cries in anguish. To a culture in which the image of mother and child—of Mary and Jesus—was one of sublime peacefulness and inexpressible joy, the contrast could hardly be more shocking.

The picture graphically displays the cruelty of the soldier, the helplessness of the child, and the horror of the mother. By his grip on the mother's hair and his foot on the baby's throat, the warrior shows his brute power. The mother's futile effort to stop the sword illustrates her powerlessness. She scratches uselessly at the soldier's back. Naked, the baby boy raises his hands as if to surrender to the inevitable, as if to reinforce his innocence.

To study Europe at war, we must enter into a world of politics and diplomacy, of issues and principles, of judgment and error. There can be no doubt that the future of Europe was decisively shaped by the century of wholesale slaughter from 1555 to 1648, during which dynastic and religious fervor finally ran its course. The survival of Protestantism, the disintegration of the Spanish empire, the rise of Holland and Sweden, the collapse of Poland and Muscovy, the fragmentation of Germany—these were all vital transformations whose consequences would be felt for centuries. We cannot avoid telling this story, untangling its causes, narrating its course, revealing its outcome. But neither should we avoid facing its reality. Look again at the painting by Poussin.

The Formation of States

The early sixteenth century was the age of the prince, the first great stage of nation building that would last for the next three hundred years. The New Monarchies, as they are sometimes called, consolidated territories that were divided culturally, linguistically, and historically. The states of Europe are political units and they were forged by political means: by diplomacy, by marriage, and most commonly by war.

It was Machiavelli who identified the prince as the agent of change in the process of state formation. He believed that the successful prince could bring unity to his lands, security to his borders, and prosperity to his subjects. The unsuccessful prince brought nothing but ruin.

A process as long and as complex as the formation of nations is not subject to the will of individuals, even princes. Factors as diverse as geography, population, and natural resources are all decisive. So too are the structures of human activity. The ways in which families are organized and wealth is transmitted from generation to generation can result in large estates with similar customs or small estates with varying ones. The manner in which social groups are formed and controlled can mean that power is centralized or dispersed. The beliefs of ordinary people and the way they practice them can define who is a part of a community and who is apart from it. All these elements and many others influence the way European states began to develop from medieval monarchies at the end of the fifteenth century. Despite these complexities, we should not lose sight of the simple truth of Machiavelli's observations. In the first stages of the consolidation of European nations, the role of the prince was crucial.

Indeed, in the middle of the fifteenth century there were many factors working against the formation of large states in Europe. The most obvious involved simple things like transportation and communication. The distance that could be covered quickly was very small. In wet and cold seasons travel was nearly impossible. Large areas were difficult to control and to defend. Communication was subject not only to the hazards of travel but also to the distinct languages or dialects of small states. Separate languages meant separate cultures. Customary practices, common ancestry, and shared experiences helped define a sense of community through which small states defined themselves.

In addition to these natural forces that governed the existence of small units of government, there were invented ones. To succeed, a prince had to establish supremacy over a number of rivals. For the most part, states were inherited. In some places it was customary to follow the rule of primogeniture, inheritance by the eldest son. In others, estates were split among sons, or among children of both sexes. Some traditions, like the French, excluded inheritance through women; others, like the Castilian, treated women's claims as equal to men's. Short lives meant prolonged disputes about inheritance. Rulers had to defend their thrones from rivals with strong claims to legitimacy.

So, too, did rulers have to defend themselves from the ambitions of their mightiest subjects. The constant warfare of the European nobility was one of the central features of the later Middle Ages. To avoid resort to arms, princes and peers entered into all manner of alliances, using their children as pawns and the marriage bed as the chessboard. Rulers also faced independent institutions within their states, powerful organizations that had to be won over or crushed. By the end of the fifteenth century, the long process of taming the Church was about to enter a new stage. Fortified towns presented a different problem. They possessed both the manpower and wealth necessary to raise and maintain armies. They also jealously guarded their privileges. Rulers who could not tax their towns could not rule their state. Finally, most kingdoms had assemblies representing the propertied classes, especially in matters of taxation. Some, like the English Parliament and the Spanish Cortes, were strong; others, like the Imperial Diet and the French Estates-General, were weak. But everywhere they posed an obstacle to the extension of the power of princes.

In combination, these factors slowed and shaped the process of state formation. But neither separately nor together were they powerful enough to overcome it. The fragmentation of Europe into so many small units of government made some consolidation inevitable. The practice of dynastic marriage meant that smaller states were continually being inherited by the rulers of larger ones. If the larger state was stable, it absorbed the smaller one. If not, the smaller state would split off again to await its next predator or protector. As the first large states took shape, the position of smaller neighbors grew ever more precarious.

This was especially true by the end of the fifteenth century because of the increase in the destructive power of warfare. Technological advances in cannonry and in the skills of gunners and engineers made medieval fortifications untenable. Gunpowder decisively changed battlefield tactics. It made heavy armor obsolete and allowed for the development of a different type of warfare. Lightly armored horses and riders could not only inflict more damage upon one another, but they were now mobile enough to be used against infantry. Infantry armed with long pikes or small muskets became the crucial components of armies that were growing ever larger. What could not be inherited, or married, could be conquered.

Eastern Configurations

The interplay of factors that encouraged and inhibited the formation of states is most easily observed in the eastern parts of Europe. There the different paths taken by Muscovy and Poland-Lithuania stand in contrast. At the beginning of the sixteenth century, the principality of Muscovy was the largest European political unit. Muscovy had established itself as the heir to the ancient state of Russia through conquest, shrewd political alli-

The sixteenth century saw the introduction of new and powerfully destructive weapons. Many felt that these "murderous engines" would destroy the virtues of chivalry. In this woodcut from 1521, the bows and arrows, lances, and heavy armor of the Middle Ages are challenged by the new cannon.

ances, and the good fortune of its princes to be blessed with long reigns. Muscovy's growth was phenomenal. Under Ivan III, "the Great" (1462–1505), Muscovy expanded to the north and west, annexing Novgorod and large parts of Livonia and Lithuania. Its military successes were almost unbroken, but so too were its diplomatic triumphs. Between 1460 and 1530, Muscovy increased its territory by 1.5 million square miles.

A number of factors led to the rise of Muscovy. The deterioration of the Mongol empire and the fall of Constantinople significantly diminished external threats. And internally, Ivan the Great was fortunate in having no competitors for his throne. He was able to extend power to others to administer the new Muscovite territories without fear of setting up rivals to power. Ivan expanded the privileges of his nobility and organized a military class who received land as a reward for their fidelity. He also extended his sovereignty to cover all lands to which there was an ancient Russian claim and combined it with the religious authority of the Orthodox church. Both he and his successors ruled with the aid of able Church leaders who were normally part of the prince's council.

What made the expansion of Muscovy so impressive is that land once gained was never lost. The military and political achievements of Ivan the Great were furthered by his son Vasili and his more famous grandson Ivan IV, "the Terrible" (1533–84). Ivan IV defeated the Mongols on his southeastern border and incorporated the entire Volga basin into Muscovy. But his greatest ambition was to gain a Livonian port on the Baltic Sea and establish a northern outlet for commerce. Nearly three decades of warfare between Muscovy and Poland-Lithuania, with whom Livonia had allied itself, resulted in large territorial gains, but never the prized Baltic port. And Ivan's northern campaigns seriously weakened the defense of the south. In 1571 the Crimean Tartars advanced on Muscovy's southwestern border and inflicted a powerful blow when they burned the city of Moscow. Although the Tartars were eventually driven off Muscovite soil, expansion in both north and south was at an end for the next seventy-five years.

By the reign of Ivan IV, Muscovite society was divided roughly into three groups: the hereditary landed nobility known as the boyars, the military service class, and the peasantry who were bound to the land. There was no large mercantile presence in Muscovy and its urban component remained small. The boyars inherited their lands and owed little to the tsar. Members of the military class, however, depended on the success of the crown for the possession of their estates, which were granted out of lands gained through territorial expansion.

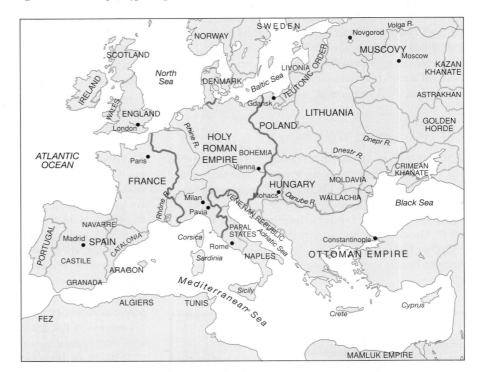

Europe, ca. 1500

Gradually the new military service class grew in power and prestige, largely at the expense of the older boyars. Ivan IV used members of the military service class as legislative advisors and elevated them in his parliamentary council (the Zemsky Sobor), which also contained representatives of the nobility, clergy, and towns.

Unlike his grandfather, Ivan IV had an abiding mistrust of the boyars. They had held power when he was a child and it was rumored that they had poisoned his mother. It was in his treatment of the boyars that he earned the nickname "the Terrible." During his brutal suppression of supposed conspiracies, several thousand boyar families were massacred by Ivan's orders, and thousands more were forcibly relocated. This practice made the boyars' situation similar to that of the military service class, who owed their fortunes to the tsar.

All of these measures contributed to the breakdown of local networks of influence and power and to a disruption of local governance. But they also made possible a system of central administration, one of Ivan IV's most important achievements. He created departments of state to deal with the various tasks of administration, such as revenues and the military. He created new boyars, who owed their positions and loyalty to him. Both boyars and the military benefited from Ivan's policy of binding the great mass of people to the land. Russian

peasants had few political or economic rights in comparison to western peasants, but during the early sixteenth century even their meager rights were curtailed. Binding the peasants in serfdom to the land made possible the prolonged absence of military leaders from their estates and contributed to the creation of the military service class. But in the long term, serfdom retarded economic development by removing incentive from large landholders to make investments in commerce or to improve agricultural production.

Following the death of Ivan the Terrible in 1584, the Muscovite state began to disintegrate. Ivan had murdered his heir in a fit of anger and left his half-witted son to inherit the throne. This led to a vacuum of power at the center as well as a struggle for the spoils of government that lasted for thirty years. When Michael Romanov (1613–45) was chosen tsar by an assembly of landholders, he only gradually restored order.

The growth of an enlarged and centralized Muscovy stands in contrast to the experiences of Poland-Lithuania during the same period. At the end of the fifteenth century Casimir IV (1447–92) ruled the kingdom of Poland and the grand duchy of Lithuania. His son Vladislav II ruled Bohemia (1471–1516) and Hungary (1490–1516). Had the four states been permanently consolidated, they could have become an effective barrier to Ottoman

A delegation of Russian boyars bearing gifts visited the Holy Roman Emperor Maximilian II in 1576 to seek his aid against Poland-Lithuania.

expansion in the south and Russian expansion in the east. But the union of crowns had never been the union of states. It had taken place over the previous century by political alliances, diplomatic marriages, and the consent of the nobility. Such arrangements kept peace among the four neighbors, but it kept any one of them from becoming a dominant partner.

There were many reasons why a unified state did not appear in east central Europe as it did in Muscovy. In the first place, external forces disrupted territorial and political arrangements. Wars with the Ottomans and the Russians absorbed resources. Second, the princes faced internal rivals to their crowns. Though Casimir IV was able to place his son on the thrones of both Bohemia and Hungary, his success necessitated concessions to leading citizens, which decreased the ability of the princes to centralize their kingdoms or to effect real unification among them. The nobility of Hungary, Bohemia, and Poland-Lithuania all developed strong local interests that increased over time. In Bohemia, Vladislav II was king in name only, and even in Poland the nobility won confirmation of its rights and privileges from the monarchy.

Until the end of the sixteenth century, Poland-Lithuania was the dominant power in the eastern part of Europe. The permanent union of the two separate states in 1569 made it economically healthy and militarily powerful. Through its Baltic ports, especially Gdansk, Poland played a central role in international commerce and was a leader in the northern grain trade. Matters of war and peace, of taxation, and of reform were placed under the strict supervision of the Polish Diet, a parliamentary body that represented the landed elite. But the failure of the Jagiellon monarchy in Poland to produce an heir ended that nation's most successful line of kings and forced the Polish nobility and gentry to peddle their throne among the princes of Europe. Successively, a French duke, a Hungarian prince, and finally in 1587 the heir to the Swedish throne, Sigismund III (1587–1632), were elected. As in Muscovy, the absence of strong rule led to military and economic decline by the beginning of the seventeenth century.

The Western Powers

Just as in the east, there was no single pattern to the consolidation of the large western European states. They, too, were internally fragmented and externally imperiled. While England had to overcome the ruin of decades of civil war, France and Spain faced the challenges of invasion and occupation. Western European princes struggled against powerful institutions and individuals within their states. Some they conquered, others they absorbed. Each nation formed its state differently: England by administrative centralization, France by good fortune, and Spain by dynastic marriage. Yet in 1450 few imagined that any one of these states would succeed.

The Taming of England. England was the only European state that suffered no threat of foreign invasion during the fifteenth century. This island fortress might easily have become the first consolidated European state were it not for the ambitions of the nobility and the weakness of the Crown. For thirty years the English aristocracy fought over the spoils of a helpless monarch. The Wars of the Roses (1455–85), as they came to be called, were as much a free-for-all among the English peerage as they were a contest for the throne between the houses of Lancaster and York. At their center was an attempt by the dukes of York to wrest the crown from the mad and ineffective Lancastrian king Henry VI (1422–61). All around the edges was the continuation of local and family feuds that had little connection to the dynastic struggle.

Three decades of intermittent warfare virtually destroyed the houses of Lancaster and York. Edward IV (1461–83) succeeded in gaining the crown for the House of York, but he never wore it securely. When he died, his children, including his heir, Edward V (1483), were placed in the protection of their uncle Richard III (1483–85). The two boys disappeared, reputedly murdered in the Tower of London, and Richard declared himself king. Richard's usurpation led to civil war, and he was killed by the forces of Henry Tudor at the battle of Bosworth Field in 1485. By the end of the Wars of the Roses the monarchy had lost both revenue and prestige, and the aristocracy had stored up bitter memories for the future.

Henry Tudor picked up the pieces of the kingdom, as legend has it he picked up the crown off a bramble bush. The two chief obstacles to his determination to consolidate the English state were the power of the nobility and the poverty of the monarchy. No English monarch had held secure title to the throne for over a century. Henry Tudor, as Henry VII (1485–1509), put an end to this dynastic instability at once. He married Elizabeth of York, and their children were indisputable successors to the crown. He also began the long process of taming his overmighty subjects. Traitors were hung and turncoats rewarded. He and his son Henry VIII (1509–47) adroitly created a new peerage, who owed their titles and loyalty to the Tudors. They were favored with offices and spoils and were relied upon to suppress both popular and aristocratic rebellions.

The financial problems of the English monarchy were not so easily overcome. An English king was supposed to live "of his own," that is, off the revenues from his own estates. Only in extraordinary circumstances were the king's subjects required to contribute to the maintenance of government. This principle was defended through the representative institution, the Parliament. When the kings of England wanted to tax their subjects, they first had to gain the assent of Parliament. Though Parliaments did grant requests for extraordinary revenue, especially for national defense, they did so grudgingly. The English landed elites were not exempt from taxation, but they were able to control the amount of taxes they paid.

The inability of the Crown to extract its living from its subjects fostered the efficient management of the royal estates. Thus English state building depended upon the growth of centralized institutions that could oversee royal lands and collect royal customs. Gradually, medieval institutions like the Exchequer were supplanted by newer organs that were better able to adjust to modern methods of accounting, record keeping, and enforcement. Whether Henry's reputation for greed and rapacity was warranted, it was undeniable that he squeezed as much as possible from a not very juicy inheritance. His financial problems limited both domestic and foreign policy.

Not until the middle of the next reign was the English monarchy again solvent. As a result of his dispute with the papacy, Henry VIII confiscated the enormous wealth of the Catholic church, and with one stroke solved the Crown's monetary problems (see chapter 13). But the real contribution that Henry and his chief minister, Thomas Cromwell (ca. 1485–1540), made to forming an English state was the way in which this windfall was administered. Cromwell accelerated the centralization of government that had begun under Edward IV. He created separate departments of state to handle the various administrative functions—record keeping, revenue collection, law enforcement, etc. Each had a distinct jurisdiction and a permanent, trained staff. Cromwell coordinated the work of these departments by expanding the power of the Privy Council, which included the heads of these administrative bodies and which came to serve as the king's executive.

ANNE BOLEYN'S SPEECH FROM THE SCAFFOLD (1536)

■ *Anne Boleyn was the second wife of Henry VIII and the mother of Elizabeth I. Henry's desire to have a son and his passion for Anne resulted in his divorce from Catherine of Aragon and England's formal break with the Roman Catholic church. When Anne bore only a daughter she too became dispensable. She was convicted of adultery and incest and executed in 1536. Here are her last words.*

Good friends, I am not come here to excuse or to justify myself, for as much as I know full well that aught that I could say in my defense doth not appertain unto you, and that I could draw no hope of life from the same. But I come here only to die, and thus to yield myself humbly to the will of the King my Lord. And if in my life I did ever offend the King's grace, surely with my death I do now atone for the same. And I blame not my judges, nor any other manner of person, nor anything save the cruel law of the land by which I die. But be this, and be my faults as they may, I beseech you all, good friends, to pray for the life of the King my sovereign lord and yours, who is one of the best princes on the face of the earth, and who hath always treated me so well that better could not be; wherefore I submit to death and with a good will, humbly asking pardon of the world.

Holbein's last portrait of Henry VIII, 1542. Henry made England into one of the world's greatest naval powers but embroiled the kingdom in a series of costly foreign wars. He married six times in an effort to produce a legitimate male heir.

of the pretensions of the monarchy and fiercely loyal to their province and its local customs and institutions. And France was splintered by profound regional differences. The north and south were divided by culture and by language (the *langue d'oc* in the south and the *langue d'oïl* in the north).

The first obstacles that were overcome were the external threats to French security. For over a century the throne of France had been contested by the kings of England. The so-called Hundred Years' War (1337–1453) originated in a dispute over the inheritance of the French crown and English possessions in Gascony in southern France (see chapter 10).

The problems posed by the Hundred Years' War were not just those of victory and defeat. The struggle between the kings of England and the kings of France allowed French princes and dukes, who were nominally vassals of the king, to enhance their autonomy by making their own alliances with the highest bidder. When the English were finally driven out of France in the middle of the fifteenth century, the kings of France came into a weakened and divided inheritance.

Nor was England the only threat to the security of the French monarchy. On France's eastern border, in a long arching semicircle, were the estates of the dukes of Burgundy. The dukes of Burgundy and the kings of France shared a common ancestry; both were of the House of Valois. Still, the sons of brothers in one generation were only cousins in the next, and the two branches of the family grew apart. The original Burgundian inheritance was in the southeast, centered at Dijon. A good marriage and good fortune brought to the first duke the rich northern province of Flanders. For the next hundred years, by marriage and through force, the dukes of Burgundy managed to unite their divided estates in one long unbroken string. But it was a string stretched taut. The power of Burgundy threatened its neighbors in all directions. Both France and the Holy Roman Empire were too weak to resist its expansion, but the confederation of Swiss towns to the southwest of Burgundy was not. In a series of stunning military victories Swiss forces repelled the Burgundians from their lands and demolished their armies. Charles the Bold, the last Valois duke of Burgundy, fell at the battle of Nancy in 1477. His estates were quickly dismembered. France recovered its ancestral territories, including Burgundy itself, and through no effort of its own was now secure on its eastern border.

The king most associated with the consolidation of France was Louis XI (1461–83). He inherited an estate exhausted by warfare and civil strife. More by chance

Cromwell also saw the importance of Parliament as a legislative body. Through Parliament, royal policy could be turned into statutes that had the assent of the political nation. If Parliament was well managed, issues that were potentially controversial could be defused. Laws passed by Parliament were more easily enforced locally than were proclamations issued by the king.

The Unification of France. Perhaps the most remarkable thing about the unification of France is that it took place at all. The forces working against the consolidation of a French state were formidable. France was surrounded by aggressive and powerful neighbors with whom it was frequently at war. Its greatest nobles were semi-independent princes who were constant rivals for the throne and consistent opponents of the extension of royal power. The French people were deeply suspicious

than by plan he vastly extended the territories under the dominion of the French crown and, more importantly, subdued the nobility. Louis XI was as cunning as he was peculiar. In an age in which royalty was expressed through magnificence, Louis sported an old felt hat and a well-worn coat. His enemies constantly underestimated his abilities, which earned him the nickname "the Spider." But gradually during the course of his reign, Louis XI won back what he had been forced to give away. Years of fighting both the English and each other depleted the ranks of the French aristocracy and the stocks of fathers and sons ran low. Estates with no male heirs fell forfeit to the king. In this manner the crown absorbed Anjou and Maine in the northwest and Provence in the south. And by brilliant political marriages for his son and daughter, Louis XI ultimately obtained control of the two greatest independent fiefs, Brittany and Orléans. When in 1527 the lands of the duke of Bourbon fell to the crown, the French monarch ruled a unified state.

The consolidation demonstrated how a state could be formed without the designs of a great leader. Neither Louis XI nor his son Charles VIII (1483–98) were nation builders. Louis's main objective was always to preserve his estate. And considerable good fortune saved him from the consequences of many ill-conceived policies. But no amount of luck could make up for Louis's failure to obtain the Burgundian Low Countries for France after the death of Charles the Bold in 1477. The marriage of his daughter and heir Mary of Burgundy to Maximilian of Habsburg initiated the struggle between France and Spain for control of the Low Countries that endured for over two centuries.

These long years of war established the principle of royal taxation, which was so essential to the process of state building in France. This enabled the monarchy to raise money for defense and for consolidation. Because of the strength of the nobles, most taxation fell only on the commoners, the so-called third estate. The *taille* was a direct tax on property, from which the nobility and clergy were exempt. The *gabelle* was a consumption tax on the purchase of salt in most parts of the kingdom, and the *aide* was a tax on a variety of commodities including meat and wine. These consumption taxes were paid by all members of the third estate no matter how poor they might be. In spite of complaints, the French monarchy established a broad base for taxation and a high degree of compliance long before any other European nation.

Along with money went soldiers, fighting men necessary to repel the English and to defend the crown against rebels and traitors. Again the French monarchy established a first, the principle of a national army,

raised and directed from the center but quartered and equipped regionally. Originally towns were required to provide artillery, but constant troubles with the nobility had led the kings of France to establish their own store of heavy guns. The towns supplied small arms, pikes, and swords and later pistols and muskets. By the beginning of the sixteenth century the French monarch could raise and equip an army of his own.

Taxation and military obligation demanded the creation and expansion of centralized institutions of government. This was the most difficult development in the period of state formation in France. The powers of royal agents were constantly challenged by the powers of regional nobles. It is easy to exaggerate the extent of the growth of central control and to underestimate the enduring hold of regional and provincial loyalties. Even the crown's absorption of estates did not always end local privileges and customs. But despite continued regional autonomy, a beginning had been made.

The Marriages of Spain. Before the sixteenth century there was little prospect of a single nation emerging on the Iberian Peninsula. North African Muslims called Moors occupied the province of Granada in the south, while the stable kingdom of Portugal dominated the western coast. The Spanish peoples were divided among a number of separate states. The two most important were Castile and Aragon. Three religions and four languages (not including dialects) widened these political divisions. And the different states had different outlooks. Castile was, above all, determined to subjugate the last of Islamic Spain and to convert its large Jewish population to Christianity. Aragon played in the high-stakes game for power in the Mediterranean. It claimed sovereignty over Sicily and Naples and exercised it whenever it could.

A happy teenage marriage brought together the unhappy kingdoms of Castile and Aragon. When Ferdinand of Aragon and Isabella of Castile secretly exchanged wedding vows in 1469, both their homelands were rent by civil war. In Castile, Isabella's brother Henry IV (1454–74) struggled unsuccessfully against the powerful Castilian nobility. In Aragon, Ferdinand's father, John II (1458–79), faced a revolt by the rich province of Catalonia on one side and the territorial ambitions of Louis XI of France on the other. Joining the heirs together increased the resources of both kingdoms. Ferdinand took an active role in the pacification of Castile, while Castilian riches allowed him to defend Aragon from invasion. In 1479 the two crowns were united and the Catholic monarchs, as they were called,

An idealized portrait of Ferdinand and Isabella shows the Catholic monarchs reigning in Renaissance style surrounded by richly costumed courtiers.

The reconquista helped create a national identity for the Christian peoples of Spain. In order to raise men and money for the war effort, Ferdinand and Isabella mobilized their nobility and town governments and created a central organization to oversee the invasion. The conquered territories were used to reward those who had aided the effort, though the crown maintained control and jurisdiction over most of the province. But the idea of the holy war also had a darker side and an unanticipated consequence. The Jewish population that had lived peacefully in both Castile and Aragon became another object of hostility. Many Jews had risen to prominence in government and in skilled professions. Others, who had accepted conversion to Christianity and were known as *conversos*, had become among the most powerful figures in the Church and the state.

Both groups were now attacked. The conversos fell prey to a special Church tribunal created to examine their sincere devotion to Catholicism. This was the Spanish Inquisition which, though it used traditional judicial practices—torture to gain confessions, public humiliation to show contrition, and burnings at the stake to maintain purity—used them on a scale never before seen. Thousands of conversos were killed and many more families had their wealth confiscated to be used for the reconquista. In 1492 the Jews themselves were expelled from Spain. Though the reconquista and the expulsion of the Jews inflicted great suffering upon victims and incalculable loss to the Castilian economy, both events enhanced the prestige of the Catholic monarchs.

In many ways, Ferdinand and Isabella trod the paths of the medieval monarchy. They relied upon personal contact with their people more than upon the use of a centralized administration. They frequently dispensed justice personally, sitting in court and accepting petitions from their subjects. Queen Isabella was venerated in Castile, where women's right to inheritance remained strong. Ferdinand's absences from Aragon were always a source of contention between him and the Cortes of the towns. Yet he was careful to provide regents to preside in his absence and regularly returned to visit his native kingdom.

Ferdinand and Isabella consciously sought to bring about a permanent union. Ferdinand made Castilian the official language of government in Aragon and even appointed Castilians to Aragonese posts. He and Isabella actively encouraged the intermarriage of the two aristocracies and the expansion of the number of wealthy nobles who held land in both kingdoms. Nevertheless, these measures did not unify Spain or erase the centuries-long tradition of hostility among the diverse Iberian peoples.

ruled the two kingdoms jointly. But the unification of the crowns of Castile and Aragon was not the same as the formation of a single state. Local privileges were zealously guarded, especially in Aragon, where the representative institutions of the towns, the Cortes, were aggressively independent. The powerful Castilian nobility never accepted Ferdinand as their king and refused him the crown after Isabella's death.

But Ferdinand and Isabella (1479–1516) took the first steps toward forging a Spanish state. Their most notable achievement was the final recovery of the lands that had been conquered by the Moors. For centuries the Spanish kingdoms had fought against the North African Muslims who had conquered large areas of the southern peninsula. The *reconquista* was characterized by short bursts of warfare followed by long periods of wary coexistence. The final stages of the reconquista began in 1482 and lasted for a decade. It was waged as a holy war and was financed in part by grants from the pope and the Christian princes of Europe. It was a bloody undertaking, but in 1492 Granada, the only remaining Moorish stronghold, finally fell and the province was absorbed into Castile.

Heroic portrait of the Emperor Charles V by Titian, 1547. The emperor is shown at the battle of Mühlberg, which paved the way for the Peace of Augsburg of 1555.

Yet neither his personal efforts to rule as a Spanish monarch, nor those of his able administrators were the most important factor in uniting the Spanish kingdoms of Iberia. Rather it was the fact that Charles V brought Spain to the forefront of European affairs in the sixteenth century. Spanish prowess, whether in arms or in culture, became a source of national pride that helped erode regional identity. Gold and silver from the New World helped finance Charles's great empire. In Italy he prosecuted Aragonese claims to Sicily and Naples; in the north he held on firmly to the kingdom of Navarre, which had been annexed by Ferdinand and which secured Spain's border with France. In the south he blocked off Ottoman and Muslim expansion. The reign of Charles V ushered in the dawn of Spain's golden age.

The process by which European kingdoms became states was long and involved. The first steps were taken all over the continent at the end of the fifteenth century. Inheritance, dynastic marriages, and wars of conquest expanded territory under the domination of a single monarch. Bureaucracy, the spread of legal jurisdiction, and the extraction of resources through taxation expanded the monarch's internal control. In kingdoms as diverse as Muscovy and Spain, Poland-Lithuania, and England a similar process was under way, a process that would define European history for centuries to come.

It was left to the heirs of Ferdinand and Isabella to forge together the Spanish kingdoms, and the process was a painful one. The hostility to a foreign monarch increased dramatically at the accession of their grandson, who became the emperor Charles V (1516–56) and who had been born and raised in the Low Countries, where he ruled over Burgundy and the Netherlands. Through a series of dynastic accidents, Charles was heir to the Spanish crown with its possessions in the New World and to the vast Habsburg estates that included Austria. Charles established his rule in Spain gradually. For a time he was forced to share power in Castile and to suppress a disorganized aristocratic rebellion.

Because of his foreign obligations, Charles was frequently absent from Spain. During those periods he governed through regents and royal councils that helped centralize administration. Charles V realized the importance of Spain, especially of Castile, in his empire. He established a permanent bureaucratic court, modeled on that of Burgundy, and placed able Spaniards at the head of its departments. This smoothed over the long periods when Charles was abroad.

The Dynastic Struggles

The formation of large states throughout Europe led inevitably to conflicts among them. Thus the sixteenth century was a period of almost unrelieved warfare that took the whole Continent as its theater. Advances in technology made war more efficient and more expensive. They also made it more horrible. The use of artillery against infantry increased the number of deaths and maiming injuries, as did the replacement of the arrow by the bullet. As the size of armies increased, so did casualties.

Power and Glory

The frequency of offensive war in the sixteenth century raises a number of questions about the militaristic values of the age. Valor remained greatly prized—a Renaissance virtue inherited from the crusading zeal and chivalric ideals of the Middle Ages—and princes sought to do valiant deeds. Ferdinand of Aragon and Francis I

(1515–47) of France won fame for their exploits in war. Charles the Bold and Louis II of Hungary were less fortunate. Their battlefield deaths led to the breakup of their states. Wars were fought to further the interests of princes rather than the interests of national sovereignty or international Christianity. They were certainly not fought in the interests of their subjects. States were an extension of a prince's heritage; what rulers sought in battle was a part of their historical and familial rights, which defined themselves and their subjects. The wars of the sixteenth century were dynastic wars.

Along with desire came ability. The New Monarchs were capable of waging war. The very definition of their states involved accumulating and defending territories. Internal security depended upon locally raised forces or hired mercenaries. Both required money, which was becoming available in unprecedented quantities as a result of the increasing prosperity of the early sixteenth century and the windfall of gold and silver from the New World. Professional soldiers, of whom the Swiss and Germans were the most noteworthy, sold their services to the highest bidders. Developments in transport and supply meant campaigns could take place far from the center of a state. Finally, communications were improving. The need to know about potential rivals or allies strengthened the European system of diplomacy. Princes installed agents in all the European capitals, and their dispatches were the most reliable sources of information about the strengths of armies or the weaknesses of governments, about the birth of heirs or the death of princes.

Personality also influenced the international warfare of the early sixteenth century. The three most consistent protagonists, Charles V, Francis I, and Henry VIII, were of similar age and outlook. Each came unexpectedly to his throne in the full flush of youth, eager for combat and glory. The three were self-consciously rivals. Henry VIII and Francis I held wrestling bouts when they met in 1520. Francis I challenged Charles V to single combat

after the French king's humiliating imprisonment in Madrid in 1526. As the three monarchs aged, their youthful wars of conquest matured into strategic warfare designed to maintain a Continental balance of power.

Habsburg and Valois

The struggle for supremacy in Europe in the sixteenth century pitted the French House of Valois against the far-flung estates of the Habsburg empire. In order for one house or the other to succeed, it was necessary to construct alliances among the various Italian city-states and most especially with England, whose aid both Charles and Francis sought in the early 1520s. Henry VIII was eager to reconquer France and cut a figure on the European scene. Despite the fact that his initial Continental adventures had emptied his treasury without fulfilling his dreams, Henry remained hungry for war. Charles V made two separate trips to London, while Henry crossed the Channel in 1520 to meet Francis I in one of the gaudiest displays of conspicuous consumption that the century would witness, appropriately known as the Field of the Cloth of Gold.

The result of these diplomatic intrigues was an alliance between England and the Holy Roman Empire. English and Burgundian forces would invade northern France while Spanish and German troops would attempt to dislodge the French forces from Italy. The strategy worked better than anyone could have imagined. In 1523 Charles's forces gained a foothold in Milan by taking the heavily fortified town of Pavia. Two years later Francis was ready to strike back. At the head of his own royal guards, he massed Swiss mercenaries and French infantry outside Pavia and made ready for a swift assault. Instead, a large imperial army arrived to relieve the town, and in the subsequent battle the French suffered a shattering defeat. Francis I was captured.

The Field of the Cloth of Gold, the lavish setting for the meeting between Henry VIII and Francis I in June 1520. The fountain in the foreground provides free wine for all.

Portrait of Mary, Queen of Scots.

*T*he Monstrous Regiment of Women

"To promote a woman to bear rule, superiority, dominion or empire above any realm, nation, or city is repugnant to nature, contumely to God, and the subversion of good order, of all equity and justice." So wrote the Scottish theologian John Knox (1513-72) in *The First Blast of the Trumpet Against the Monstrous Regiment of Women* (1558). Though he made his points more emphatically than many others, Knox was only repeating the commonplace notions of his day. He could quote Aristotle and Aquinas as well as a host of secular authorities to demonstrate female inadequacies:

"Nature, I say, doth paint them forth to be weak, frail, impatient, feeble, and foolish." He could quote Saint Paul along with the ancient Fathers of the Church to demonstrate the "proper" place of women—"Man is not of the woman, but the woman of the man."

But no stacking up of authorities, no matter how numerous or revered, could erase the fact that all over Europe in the sixteenth century women could and did rule. In the Netherlands Mary, Queen of Hungary (1531–52) and Margaret of Parma (1559–67) were successful regents. Jeanne d'Albret

(1562–72) was queen of the tiny state of Navarre, territory claimed by both France and Spain but kept independent by this remarkable woman. Catherine de Médicis (1560–89), wife of one king of France and mother of three others, was the effective ruler of that nation for nearly thirty years. Mary, Queen of Scots (1542–87) was the nominal ruler of Scotland almost from her birth. England was ruled by two very different women, the Catholic Mary I (1553–58) and her Protestant half-sister Elizabeth I (1558–1603).

The problems faced by this long list of queens and regents were more than just the ordinary cares of government. The belief that women were inherently inferior in intelligence, strength, and character was so pervasive that for men like Knox, a woman ruler was almost a contradiction in terms.

Yet this was not the view taken by everyone, and female rule had its defenders as well as its detractors. One set of objections was overcome by the traditional medieval theory of the two bodies of the monarch. This argument was developed to reconcile the divine origins and functions of monarchs with their very real human frailties. In the theory of the two bodies, there was the body natural and the body politic. Both were joined together in the person of the ruler but the attributes of each could be separated. Rule of a woman did nothing to disrupt this notion. In fact, it made it easier to argue that the frailties of the body natural of a woman were in no way related to the strengths of the body politic of a monarch.

While such ideas might help a female ruler to be accepted by her subjects, they did little to invigorate her own sense of her role. Female rulers often strained against the straitjacket that definitions of gender placed them in. When angered, Elizabeth I would proclaim that she had more courage than her father, Henry VIII, "though I am only a woman." Mary, Queen of Scots, once revealed that her only regret was that she "was not a man to know what life it was to lie all night in the fields or to walk with a buckler and a broadsword." Some queens assumed masculine traits, riding in armor or leading forces to battle. Other women rulers mixed together characteristics that were usually separated by gender definitions. Margaret of Parma was considered one of the most accomplished horse riders of her day. After leading her courtiers through woods and fields at breakneck speed, she would then attend council meetings and work on her needlepoint. Mary, Queen of Scots, loved hawking, a traditional kingly sport in the Scottish wilds. After relishing the hawk's destruction of its prey, she liked to negotiate matters of state by beginning with tears and entreaties and ending with accusations and threats. The effect was more than discomforting.

Women were no more nor less successful as rulers than were men. Women's achievements, like men's, depended upon strength of character and the circumstances of the times. All the women rulers of the sixteenth century had received outstanding educations. Whether raised Catholic or Protestant, each was trained in Latin as well as modern languages, in the liberal arts, and in fine arts.

Mary, Queen of Scots, was the only one of these female rulers born to rule. She was the sole survivor of her father, who died shortly after her birth. Mary and Elizabeth Tudor came to their thrones after the death of their younger brother Edward VI; Mary of Hungary and Margaret of Parma came to theirs as princesses of the House of Habsburg. The rule of Catherine de Médicis was the most unexpected of all. Her vigorous husband, Henry II, died during a jousting tournament and her eldest son, Francis II, husband of Mary, Queen of Scots, died the following year. Instead of retirement as a respected queen dowager—the widow of a previous king—Catherine de Médicis was forced into the vortex of French politics to protect the rights of her ten-year-old son, Charles IX.

Unfortunately, the accomplishments of women rulers did little to dispel prejudices against women as a whole or to alter the definition of gender roles. Except for Mary, Queen of Scots, whose principal achievement was to provide an heir to the English throne, all the queens and regents of the sixteenth century were successful rulers. Margaret of Parma steered the careful middle course in the conflict between Spain and the Netherlands. She opposed the intervention of the Duke of Alba, and had her advice been followed, the eighty years of war between Spain and the Netherlands might have been avoided. Catherine de Médicis held the crown of France on the heads of her sons, navigated the treacherous waters of civil war, and provided the model for religious toleration that finally was adopted in the Edict of Nantes. Elizabeth I of England became one of the most beloved rulers in that nation's history. A crafty politician who learned to balance the factions at her court and who turned the aristocracy into a service class for the crown, she brought nearly a half-century of stability to England at a time when the rest of Europe was in flames.

The victory at Pavia in 1525 occurred on Charles V's twenty-fifth birthday and seemingly made him master of all of Europe. His ally Henry VIII urged an immediate invasion and dismemberment of France and began raising an army to spearhead the attack. But Charles's position was much less secure than it appeared. The Ottomans threatened his Hungarian territories, and the Protestants threatened his German lands. He could not afford a war of conquest in France. His hope now was to reach an agreement with Francis I for a lasting European peace, and for this purpose the French king was brought in captivity to Madrid.

It is doubtful that there was ever any real chance for peace between Habsburg and Valois after the battle of Pavia. Francis's personal humiliation and Charles's military position were both too strong to allow for a permanent settlement in which Habsburgs ruled in Milan and Naples. Charles demanded that Burgundy be returned to him. Though Francis was hardly in a position to bargain, he held out on this issue for as long as possible and he secretly prepared a disavowal of the final agreement before it was made. By the Treaty of Madrid in 1526, Francis I yielded Burgundy and recognized the Spanish conquest of Navarre and Spanish rule in Naples. The agreement was sealed by the marriage of

Francis to Charles's sister, Eleanor of Portugal. But marriage was not sufficient security for such a complete capitulation. To secure his release from Spain, Francis was required to leave behind as hostages his seven- and eight-year-old sons until the treaty was fulfilled. For three years the children languished in Spanish captivity.

No sooner had he set foot upon French soil than Francis I renounced the Treaty of Madrid. He even gained the sanction of the pope for violating his oath. Setting France on a war footing, he began seeking new allies. Henry VIII, disappointed with the meager spoils of his last venture, switched sides. Most importantly, Francis I entered into an alliance with the Ottoman sultan, Suleiman the Magnificent (1520–66), whose armies were pressing against the southeastern borders of the Holy Roman Empire. In the year following Pavia, the Ottomans secured an equally decisive triumph at Mohács, captured Budapest, and threatened Vienna, the eastern capital of the Habsburg lands. Almost overnight Charles V had been turned from hunter into hunted. The Ottoman threat demanded immediate attention in Germany, the French and English were preparing to strike in the Low Countries, and the Italian wars continued. In 1527 Charles's unpaid German mercenaries

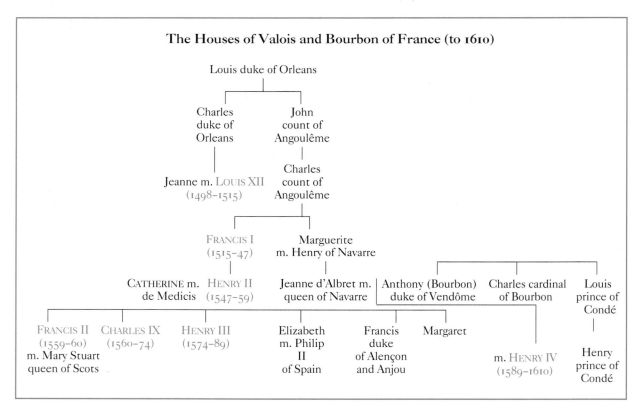

The Houses of Valois and Bourbon of France (to 1610)

stormed through Rome, sacked the papal capital, and captured the pope. Christian Europe was mortified.

The struggle for European mastery ground on for decades. The Treaty of Cateau-Cambrésis in 1559 brought to a close sixty years of conflict that had accomplished little. The great stores of silver that poured into Castile from the New World were consumed in the fires of Continental warfare. In 1557 both France and Spain declared bankruptcy to avoid foreclosures by their creditors. For the French, the Italian wars were disastrous. They seriously undermined the state's financial base, eroded confidence in the monarchy, thinned the ranks of the ruling nobility, and brought France nearly to ruin. The fiasco ended with fitting irony. After the death of Francis I, his son Henry II (1547–59) continued the struggle. Henry never forgave his father for abandoning him in Spain, and he sought revenge on Charles V, who had been his jailer. He celebrated the Treaty of Cateau-Cambrésis with great pomp and pageantry. Among the feasts and festivities were athletic competitions. Henry II entered the jousting tournament and there was killed.

In 1555 Charles abdicated all of his titles and retired to a monastery to live out his final days. He split apart his empire and granted to his brother, Ferdinand I (1558–64), the Austrian and German lands and the mantle of the Holy Roman Empire. To his son, Philip II (1556–98), he ceded the Low Countries, Spain and the New World, Naples, and his Italian conquests. The cares of an empire that once stretched from Peru to Vienna were lifted from his shoulders. On 21 September 1558, he died in his bed.

The wars for European supremacy between France and Spain dominated the politics of the first half of the sixteenth century. The quest for glory involved the Continent's two greatest kingdoms in unrelenting warfare, warfare that bankrupted both fiscally and emotionally. The humiliation of Francis I in prison in Madrid was ultimately matched by that of Charles V fleeing across the Alps as the Ottomans advanced on his German territories. For decades the two states poured all of their resources into warfare and made it a more deadly and more expensive venture than ever before.

The Crises of the European States

In the sixteenth century, society was an integrated whole, equally dependent upon monarchical, ecclesiastical, and civil authority for its effective survival. A Eu-

ropean state could no more tolerate the presence of two churches than it could the presence of two kings. But the Reformation had created two churches. The coexistence of both Catholics and Protestants in a single realm posed a stark challenge to accepted theory and traditional practice.

The problem proved intractable because it admitted only one solution: total victory. There could be no compromise for several reasons. Religious beliefs were profoundly held, and religious controversy was a struggle between everlasting life and eternal damnation. The practical solution of toleration was still unacceptable. To the modern mind, toleration seems so logical that it is difficult to understand why it took over a century of bloodshed before it came to be grudgingly accepted by those countries most bitterly divided. But toleration was not a practical solution in a society that admitted no principle of organization other than one king, one faith.

The French Wars of Religion

Protestantism came late to France. It was not until after Calvin reformed the church in Geneva and began to export his brand of Protestantism that French society began to divide along religious lines. By 1560 there were over two thousand Protestant congregations in France, whose membership totaled nearly 10 percent of the French population. Calvin and his successors had their greatest success among the middle ranks of urban society, merchants, traders, and craftsmen. They also found a receptive audience among aristocratic women, who eventually converted their husbands and their sons.

The wars of religion, however, were brought on by more than the rapid spread of Calvinism. Equally important was the vacuum of power that had been created when Henry II (1547–59) died in a jousting tournament. Surviving Henry were his extraordinary widow, Catherine de Médicis, three daughters, and four sons, the oldest of whom, Francis II (1559–60), was only fifteen. Under the influence of his beautiful young wife, Mary, Queen of Scots, Francis allowed the noble Guise family to dominate the great offices of state and to exclude their rivals from power. The Guises controlled the two most powerful institutions of the state—the army and the Church.

The Guises were staunchly Catholic and among their enemies were the Bourbons, a family with powerful Protestant members and a direct claim to the French throne. The revelation of a Protestant plot to remove the king from Paris provided the Guises with an opportunity to eliminate their most potent rivals. The Bourbon Duc de Condé, the leading Protestant peer of the realm, was sentenced to death. But five days before Condé's execution, Francis II died and Guise power evaporated. The new king, Charles IX (1560–74), was only ten years old and firmly under the grip of his mother, Catherine de Médicis, who now declared herself regent of France. (See Special Feature, "The Monstrous Regiment of Women," pp. 484–485.)

Condé's death sentence convinced him that the Guises would stop at nothing to gain their ambitions. Force would have to be met with force. Protestants and Catholics alike raised armies and in 1562 civil war ensued. Once the wars began, the leading Protestant peers fled the court, but the position of the Guises was not altogether secure. Henry Bourbon, king of Navarre, was the next in line to the throne should Charles IX and his two brothers die without male heirs. Henry had been raised in the Protestant faith by his mother, Jeanne d'Albret, whose own mother, Marguerite of Navarre, was among the earliest protectors of the Huguenots, as the French Calvinists came to be called.

The early battles were inconclusive, but the assassination of the Duc de Guise in 1563 by a Protestant fanatic added a personal vendetta to the religious passions of the Catholic leaders. They encouraged the slaughter of Huguenot congregations and the murder of Huguenot leaders. Protestants gave as good as they got. In open defiance of Valois dynastic interests, the Guises courted support from Spain, while the Huguenots imported Swiss and German mercenaries to fight in France. Noble factions and irreconcilable religious differences were together pulling the government apart.

By 1570 Catherine was ready for reconciliation. She announced her plans for a marriage between her daugh-

The French Wars of Religion

1559	Death of Henry II
1560	Protestant Duc de Condé sentenced to death
1562	First battle of wars of religion
1563	Catholic Duc de Guise assassinated
1572	Saint Bartholomew's Day massacre
1574	Accession of Henry III
1576	Formation of Catholic League
1584	Death of Duc d'Anjou makes Henry of Navarre heir to throne
1585	War of the three Henrys
1588	Henry Guise murdered by order of Henry III
1589	Catherine de Médicis dies; Henry III assassinated
1594	Henry IV crowned
1598	Edict of Nantes

ter Margaret and Henry of Navarre, a marriage that would symbolize the spirit of conciliation between the crown and the Huguenots. The marriage was to take place in Paris during August 1572. The arrival of Huguenot leaders from all over France to attend the marriage ceremony presented an opportunity of a different kind to the Guises and their supporters. If leading Huguenots could be assassinated in Paris, the Protestant cause might collapse and the truce that the wedding signified might be turned instead into a Catholic triumph.

Saint Bartholomew was the apostle that Jesus described as a man without guile. Ironically it was on his feast day that the Huguenots who had innocently come to celebrate Henry's marriage were led like lambs to the slaughter. On 24 August 1572 the streets of Paris ran red with Huguenot blood. Though frenzied, the slaughter was inefficient. Henry of Navarre and a number of other important Huguenots escaped the carnage and returned to their urban strongholds. In the following weeks the violence spread from Paris to the countryside and thousands of Protestants paid for their beliefs with their lives.

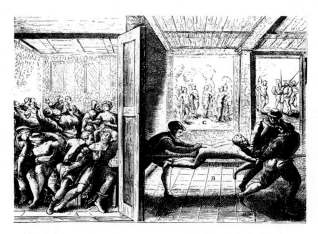

This scene depicts the mistreatment of French Catholics by the Protestants in the town of Angoulême. They were deprived of all nourishment, dragged over a taut rope, and then slowly roasted at the stake.

After Saint Bartholomew's Day, a genuine revulsion against the massacres swept the nation. A number of Catholic peers now joined with the Huguenots to protest the excesses of the crown and the Guises. These Catholics came to be called the *politiques* from their desire for a practical settlement of the wars. They were led by the Duc d'Anjou, next in line to the throne when Charles IX died in 1574 and Henry III (1574–89) became king. Against them, in Paris and a number of other towns, the Catholic League was formed, a society that pledged its first allegiance to religion. The League took up the slaughter of Huguenots where the Saint Bartholomew's Day massacre left off. Matters grew worse in 1584 when the Huguenot Henry of Navarre became next in line for the throne. Catholic Leaguers talked openly of altering the royal succession and began to develop theories of lawful resistance to monarchical power. By 1585, when the final civil war began—the war of the three Henrys, named for Henry III, Henry Guise, and Henry of Navarre—the crown was in the weakest possible position. Paris and the Catholic towns were controlled by the League, the Protestant strongholds by Henry of Navarre. King Henry III could not abandon his capital or his religion, but neither could he gain control of the Catholic party. The extremism of the Leaguers kept the politiques away from court, and without the politiques, there could be no settlement.

In December 1588 Henry III took matters into his own hands. He summoned Henry Guise and Guise's brother to a meeting in the royal bedchamber. There they were murdered in an attempt to destroy the League. The politiques were blamed for the murders—revenge was taken on a number of them—and Henry III was forced to flee his capital. He made a pact with Henry of Navarre and together royalist and Huguenot forces besieged Paris. Only the arrival of a Spanish army prevented its fall. In 1589 a fanatic priest avenged the murder of the Guises by assassinating Henry III.

Now Henry of Navarre came into his inheritance. But after nearly thirty years of continuous civil war it was certain that a Huguenot could never rule France. If Henry was to become king of all France, he would have to become a Catholic king. It is not clear when Henry made the decision to accept the Catholic faith—"Paris is worth a mass," he reportedly declared—but he did not announce his decision at once. Rather he strengthened his forces, tightened his bonds with the politiques, and urged his countrymen to expel the Spanish invaders. He finally made his conversion public and in 1594 was crowned Henry IV (1589–1610). In 1598 Henry proclaimed the Edict of Nantes, which granted limited toleration to the Huguenots. It was the culmination of decades of attempts to find a solution to the existence of two religions in one state.

The World of Philip II

By the middle of the sixteenth century Spain was the greatest power in Europe. The dominions of Philip II (1556–98) of Spain stretched from the Atlantic to the Pacific: his Continental territories included the Netherlands in the north and Milan and Naples in Italy. In 1580 Philip became king of Portugal, uniting all the states of the Iberian Peninsula. With the addition of Portugal's Atlantic ports and its sizable fleet, Spanish maritime power was now unsurpassed. Philip saw himself as a Catholic monarch fending off the spread of heresy. He was particularly hostile toward England,

FROM THE EDICT OF NANTES

■ *The Edict of Nantes (1598) was a milestone in the development of religious toleration in Europe. It was granted by King Henry IV to the Huguenots at the end of the French wars of religion. The Edict of Nantes established the rights of Protestants and was in effect for nearly a century.*

We ordain that the Catholic, Apostolic and Roman religion shall be restored and re-established in all places and districts of this our kingdom and the countries under our rule, where its practice has been interrupted, so that it can be peacefully and freely practiced there, without any disturbance or hindrance. We forbid very expressly all persons of whatever rank, quality or condition they may be, under the aforesaid penalties, to disturb, molest or cause annoyance to clerics in the celebration of the Divine worship.

where he had briefly been married to the Catholic Queen Mary I (1553–58). But her Protestant successor, Queen Elizabeth I (1558–1603), encouraged piracy against Spanish treasure ships and covertly aided both French and Dutch Protestants. Finally in 1588 Philip decided upon invasion.

He assembled a fleet of over 130 ships, many of them the pride of the Spanish and Portuguese navies. The ships of the Spanish Armada were bigger and stronger than anything possessed by the English, whose forces were largely merchant vessels hastily converted for battle. But the English ships were faster and more maneuverable in the unpredictable winds of the English Channel. They also contained guns that could readily be reloaded for multiple firings, while the Spanish guns were designed to discharge only one broadside before hand-to-hand combat ensued. With these advantages the English were able to prevent the Armada from reaching port in the Netherlands and to destroy many individual ships as they were blown off course. The

defeat of the Spanish Armada was less a military than a psychological blow to Philip II. He could more easily replace ships than restore confidence in Spanish power.

That confidence was to be shaken more thoroughly by the greatest crisis of his reign: the revolt of the Netherlands. Though Philip's father, Charles V, amassed a great empire, he had begun only as the duke of Burgundy. Charles's Burgundian inheritance encompassed a diverse territory in the northwestern corner of Europe. The seventeen separate provinces of this territory were called the Netherlands or the Low Countries because of the flooding that kept large portions of them under water. The Netherlands was one of the richest and most populous regions of Europe, an international leader in manufacturing, banking, and commerce. The heavy concentration of urban populations in the Low Countries provided the natural habitat for Calvinist preachers, who made converts across the entire social spectrum. As Holy Roman Emperor, Charles V may have made his peace with Protestants, but as king of Spain he

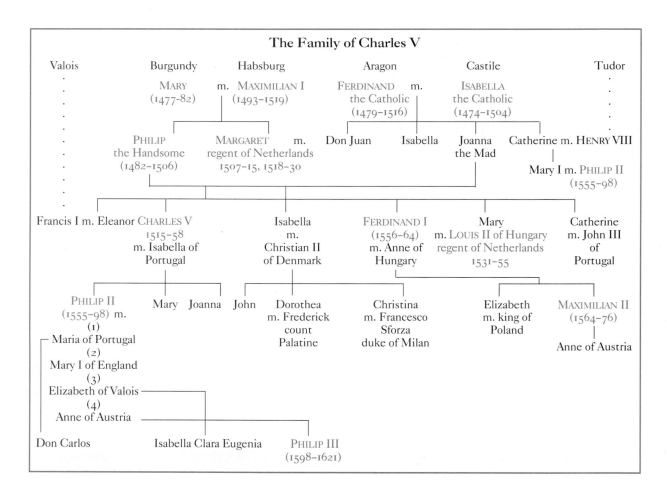

The Spanish and the English Fleets Engaged, 1588, *by an unknown artist, ca. 1590. In the foreground, two English warships flank a Spanish ship bearing the standard of the pope.*

had not. Charles V had maintained the purity of the Spanish Catholic church through a sensible combination of reform and repression.

Philip II intended to pursue a similar policy in the Low Countries. With papal approval he initiated a scheme to reform the hierarchy of the Church by expanding the numbers of bishops, and he invited the Jesuits to establish schools for orthodox learning. The

Protestants sought the protection of their local nobility who, Catholic or Protestant, had their own reasons for opposing the strict enforcement of heresy laws. Provincial nobility and magistrates resented both the substance of Philip's policies and the fact that they disregarded local autonomy. Town governors and noblemen refused to cooperate in implementing the new laws.

The Revolt of the Netherlands

The passive resistance of nobles and magistrates was soon matched by the active resistance of the Calvinists. Unable to enforce Philip's policy, Margaret of Parma, his half-sister, whom Philip had made regent, agreed to a limited toleration. But in the summer of 1566, before it could be put into effect, bands of Calvinists violently attacked Catholic property, breaking stained glass windows and statues of the Virgin and the saints, which they claimed were idolatrous. Local authorities could not protect Church property and open revolt ensued. Fearing social rebellion, even the leading Protestant noblemen helped suppress these riots.

In Spain, the events in the Netherlands were treated for what they were: open rebellion. Philip II was determined to punish the rebels and enforce the heresy laws. He sent a large military force from Spain under the

The Revolt of the Netherlands

Revolt of the Netherlands

1559	Margaret of Parma named regent of the Netherlands
1566	Calvinist iconoclasm begins revolt
1567	Duke of Alba arrives in Netherlands
1572	Protestants capture Holland and Zeeland
1576	Sack of Antwerp Pacification of Ghent
1581	Catholic and Protestant provinces split
1609	Twelve Years' Truce

command of the Duke of Alba (1507–82). Alba fulfilled his mission with a vengeance, executing leading Protestant noblemen, harshly punishing participants in the rebellion, and destroying towns implicated in the revolt. As many as sixty thousand Protestants fled north beyond Alba's jurisdiction. By the end of 1568 royal policy had gained a sullen acceptance in the Netherlands, but for the next eighty years, with only occasional truces, Spain and the Netherlands were at war.

Alba's policies had driven Protestants into rebellion, and this forced the Spanish government to maintain its army by raising taxes from those southern provinces that had remained loyal. Soon the loyal provinces too were in revolt, not over religion, but over taxation and local autonomy. Alba was unprepared for the series of successful assaults Protestants launched in the northern provinces during 1572. The Protestant generals established a permanent base in the northwestern provinces of Holland and Zeeland. By 1575 they had gained a stronghold that they would never relinquish. Prince William of Orange assumed the leadership of the two provinces, which were now united against the tyranny of Philip's rule.

Spanish government was collapsing all over the Netherlands. William ruled in the north, and the States-General, a parliamentary body composed of representatives from the separate provinces, ruled in the south. No one was in control of the Spanish army. The soldiers, who had gone years with only partial pay, now roamed the southern provinces looking for plunder. Brussels and Ghent both were targets, and in 1576 the worst atrocities of all occurred when mutinous Spanish troops sacked Antwerp. Over seven thousand people were slaughtered and nearly a third of the city burned to the ground.

The "Spanish fury" in Antwerp effectively ended Philip's rule over his Burgundian inheritance. The Protestants had established a permanent home in the north. The States-General had established its ability to rule in the south, and Spanish policy had been totally discredited. To achieve a settlement, the Pacification of Ghent of 1576, the Spanish government conceded local autonomy in taxation, the central role of the States-General in legislation, and the immediate withdrawal of all Spanish troops from the Low Countries. This rift among the provinces was soon followed by a permanent split. In 1581 one group of provinces voted to depose Philip II while a second group decided to remain loyal to him. Philip II refused to accept the dismemberment of his inheritance and refused to recognize the independent

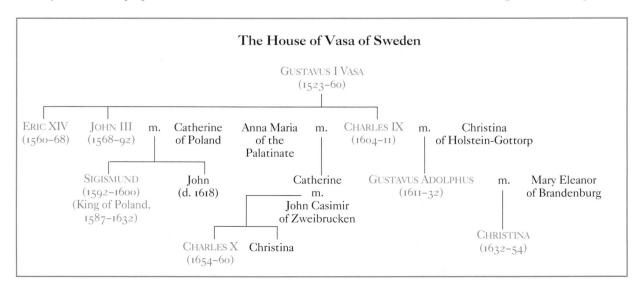

The House of Vasa of Sweden

Dutch state that now existed in Holland. Throughout the 1580s and 1590s military expeditions attempted to reunite the southern provinces and to conquer the northern ones. In 1609 Spain and the Netherlands concluded the Twelve Years' Truce, which tacitly recognized the existence of the state of Holland. By the beginning of the seventeenth century Holland was not only an independent state, it was one of the greatest rivals of Spain and Portugal.

The Thirty Years' War, 1618-1648

Though there was nothing new about warfare in Europe, the fighting that set the Continent ablaze from 1555 to 1648 brought together the worst of dynastic and religious conflicts. These wars were fought on a larger scale, were more brutal and more expensive, and claimed more victims, civilians and combatants alike. During this century war extended throughout the Continent. Dynastic strife, rebellion, and international rivalries joined together with the ongoing struggle over religion. Ambition and faith were an explosive mixture. The French endured forty years of civil war; the Spanish eighty years of fighting with the Dutch. The battle for hegemony in the east led to dynastic strife for decades on end, as Poles, Russians, and Swedes pressed their rival claims to each other's territory until the Swedes emerged victorious. Finally, in 1618, these separate theaters of war came together in one of the most brutal and terrifying episodes of destruction in European history, the Thirty Years' War.

The Rise of Sweden

Sweden's aggressive foreign policy began accidentally when the Baltic seaport of Reval requested Swedish protection. After some hesitation, Sweden fortified Reval in 1560. A decade later, Swedish forces captured Narva, farther to the east, and consolidated their hold on the Livonian coast, where they controlled a sizable portion of the Muscovite trade. As the Swedes secured the northern Livonian ports, more of the Muscovy trade moved to the south and passed through Riga, which would have to be captured or blockaded if the Swedes were to control commerce in the eastern Baltic. At the beginning of the seventeenth century the powerful Swedish navy blockaded Riga and entered into war against Poland.

A Livonian peasant. Livonia was conquered by Ivan the Terrible in his campaign of 1563, but was soon reclaimed by the Poles. In 1660 Livonia became part of the Swedish empire. Livonia was originally inhabited by the Livs, a Finnish people.

The blockade of Riga and the assembly of a large Swedish fleet in the Baltic threatened Denmark. The Danes claimed sovereignty over Sweden and now took the opportunity of the Polish-Swedish conflict to reassert it. In 1611, under the energetic leadership of the Danish king Christian IV (1588–1648), Denmark invaded Sweden from both the east and the west, threatening to take Stockholm. In the same year, during the Danish war, Sweden's king Charles IX died and was succeeded by his son Gustavus Adolphus (1611–32). Gustavus's greatest skills were military, and the calamitous wars inherited from his father occupied him during the early years of his reign. He was forced to conclude a humiliating peace with the Danes in 1613. For most of the next decade he rebuilt his armies and nursed his grievances. Then in 1621 he struck. He landed a force in Livonia and in two weeks he captured Riga, the capstone of Sweden's Baltic ambitions. Occupation of Riga increased Swedish control of the Muscovy trade and it deprived Denmark of a significant portion of its customs duties. Gustavus now claimed Riga as a Swedish port and successfully demanded that ships sailing from there pay tolls to Sweden rather than Denmark.

THE DESTRUCTION OF MAGDEBURG

■ No event of the Thirty Years' War had a greater effect on public opinion than the annihilation of the Protestant city of Magdeburg in 1631. Dozens of pamphlets and woodcuts detailed the slaughter of civilians and the devastation of property. It was commonly believed that neither a human nor an animal escaped the destruction.

Thus it came about that the city and all its inhabitants fell into the hands of the enemy, whose violence and cruelty were due in part to their common hatred of the adherents of the Augsburg Confession, and in part to their being imbittered by the chain shot which had been fired at them and by the derision and insults that the Magdeburgers had heaped upon them from the ramparts.

Then was there naught but beating and burning, plundering, torture, and murder. Most especially was every one of the enemy bent on securing much booty. When a marauding party entered a house, if its master had anything to give he might thereby purchase respite and protection for himself and his family till the next man, who also wanted something, should come along. . . .

Thus in a single day this noble and famous city, the pride of the whole country, went up in fire and smoke; and the remnant of its citizens, with their wives and children, were taken prisoners and driven away by the enemy with a noise of weeping and wailing that could be heard from afar, while the cinders and ashes from the town were carried by the wind to Wanzleben, Egeln, and still more distant places.

The rise of Sweden had two dramatic effects in the reorganization of power politics in northeastern Europe. In the first place, it signalled the permanent eclipse of Poland-Lithuania in the region. Once a territorial giant with pretensions of dominating all of eastern Europe, Poland-Lithuania now saw its territories shrink and its power diminish. With the Swedish capture of Riga, dominance over the Muscovy trade passed out of Polish hands, never to return. Secondly, and most importantly for the immediate future of Europe, the rise of Sweden created a Protestant counterbalance to the power of the Austrian Habsburgs. Sweden's domination of the Baltic ports placed its future firmly on German soil at just the moment that Germany was to explode into warfare.

Bohemia Revolts

The Peace of Augsburg had served the German states well. The principle that the religion of the ruler was the religion of the state complicated the political life of the Holy Roman Empire, but it also pacified it. Though rulers had the right to enforce uniformity on their subjects, in practice many of the larger states tolerated more than one religion. By the beginning of the seventeenth century Catholicism and Protestantism had achieved a rough equality within the German states, symbolized by the fact that of the seven electors who chose the Holy Roman Emperor, three were Catholic, three Protestant, and the seventh was the emperor himself, acting as king of Bohemia. This situation was not unwelcome to the leaders of the Austrian Habsburg family, who succeeded Emperor Charles V and who were more tolerant than their Spanish kinfolk. The head of their house was elected king of Bohemia and king of Hungary, both states with large Protestant populations.

In 1617 Mathias, the childless Holy Roman Emperor, began making plans for his cousin, Ferdinand Habsburg, to succeed him. Ferdinand was Catholic, very devout and very committed. In order to ensure a Catholic majority among the electors, the emperor relinquished his Bohemian title and pressed for Ferdinand's election as the new king of Bohemia. The Protestant nobles of Bohemia forced the new king to accept strict limitations upon his political and religious powers, but once elected Ferdinand had no intention of honoring them. His opponents were equally strong-willed. When Ferdinand violated Protestant religious liberties, a group of noblemen marched to the royal palace in Prague in May 1618, found two of the king's chief advisers, and hurled them out of an upper-story window.

The Defenestration of Prague, as this incident came to be known, initiated a Protestant counteroffensive throughout the Habsburg lands. Fear of Ferdinand's policies led to Protestant uprisings in Hungary as well as

Bohemia. Those who seized control of the government declared Ferdinand deposed and the throne vacant. But they had no candidate to accept their crown. When Emperor Mathias died in 1619, Ferdinand succeeded to the imperial title as Ferdinand II (1619–37) and Frederick V, one of the Protestant electors, accepted the Bohemian crown.

Frederick was a sincere but weak Calvinist whose credentials were much stronger than his abilities. He ruled a geographically divided German state known as the Palatinate. One hundred miles separated the two segments of his lands, but both were strategically important. The Lower Palatinate bordered on the Catholic Spanish Netherlands and the Upper Palatinate on Catholic Bavaria.

Once Frederick accepted the Bohemian crown, he was faced with a war on three fronts. Ferdinand II had no difficulty enlisting allies to recover the Bohemian crown, since he could pay them with the spoils of Frederick's lands. Spanish troops from the Netherlands occupied the Lower Palatinate, and Bavarian troops occupied the Upper Palatinate. Frederick, on the other hand, met rejection wherever he turned. Neither the Dutch nor the English would send more than token aid—both had advised him against breaking the imperial peace. The Lutheran princes of Germany would not enter into a war between Calvinists and Catholics, especially after Ferdinand II promised to protect the Bohemian Lutherans.

At the battle of the White Mountain in 1620, Ferdinand's Catholic forces annihilated Frederick's army. Frederick and his wife fled to Denmark, and Bohemia was left to face the wrath of Ferdinand, the victorious king and emperor. The retribution was horrible. Mercenaries who had fought for Ferdinand II were allowed to sack Prague for a week. Elective monarchy was abolished and Bohemia became part of the hereditary Habsburg lands. Free peasants were enserfed and subjected to imperial law. Those nobles who had supported Frederick lost their lands and their privileges. Calvinism was repressed and thoroughly rooted out, consolidating forever the Catholic character of Bohemia. Frederick's estates were carved up and his rights as elector transferred to the Catholic duke of Bavaria. The battle of the White Mountain was a turning point in the history of central Europe, for it forced all Protestant nations to arm for war.

The War Widens

For the Habsburgs, religious and dynastic interests were inseparable. Ferdinand II and Philip III of Spain (1598–1621) fought for their beliefs and for their patrimony. Their victory gave them more than they could have expected. Ferdinand swallowed up Bohemia and strengthened his position in the empire. Philip gained possession of a vital link in his supply route between Italy and the Netherlands. Spanish expansion threatened France. The occupation of the Lower Palatinate placed a ring of Spanish armies around France from the Pyrenees to the Low Countries.

Frederick, now in Holland, refused to accept the judgment of battle. He lobbied for a grand alliance to repel the Spaniards from the Lower Palatinate and to restore the religious balance in the empire. Though his personal cause met with little sympathy, his political logic was impeccable, especially after Spain again declared war upon the Dutch in 1621. A grand Protestant alliance—secretly supported by the French—brought together England, Holland, a number of German states, and Denmark. It was the Danes who led this potentially powerful coalition. In 1626 a large Danish army under the command of King Christian IV engaged imperial forces on German soil. But Danish forces could not match the superior numbers and the superior leadership of the Catholic mercenary forces under the command of the ruthless and brilliant Count Albrecht

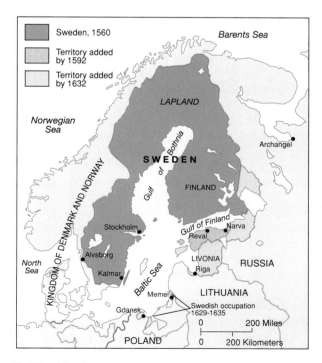

The Rise of Sweden

von Wallenstein (1583–1634). In 1629 the Danes withdrew from the empire and sued for peace.

If the Catholic victory at the White Mountain in 1620 threatened the well-being of German Protestantism, the Catholic triumph over the Danes threatened its survival. More powerful than ever, Ferdinand II determined to turn the religious clock back to the state of affairs that had existed when the Peace of Augsburg was concluded in 1555. He demanded that all lands that had then been Catholic but had since become Protestant must now be returned to the fold. He also proclaimed that as the Peace of Augsburg made no provision for the toleration of Calvinists, they would no longer be tolerated in the empire. These policies together constituted a virtual revolution in the religious affairs of the German states, and they proved impossible to impose. Ferdinand succeeded in only one thing—he united Lutherans and Calvinists against him.

In 1630 King Gustavus Adolphus of Sweden decided to enter the German conflict to protect Swedish interests. While Gustavus Adolphus struggled to construct his alliance, imperial forces continued their triumphant progress. In 1631 they besieged, captured, and put to the torch the town of Magdeburg—a turning point in Protestant fortunes. Brandenburg and Saxony joined Gustavus Adolphus, not only enlarging his forces, but allowing him to open a second front in Bohemia. In the autumn of 1631 this combination overwhelmed the imperial armies. Gustavus won a decisive triumph at Breitenfeld, while the Saxons occupied Prague.

Gustavus Adolphus lost no time in pressing his advantage. The Swedes marched west to the Rhine, easily conquering the richest of the Catholic cities and retak-

The Thirty Years' War

1618	Defenestration of Prague
1619	Ferdinand Habsburg elected Holy Roman Emperor Frederick of the Palatinate accepts the crown of Bohemia
1620	Catholic victory at battle of the White Mountain
1621	End of Twelve Years' Truce; war between Spain and Netherlands
1626	Danes form Protestant alliance under Christian IV
1627	Spain declares bankruptcy
1630	Gustavus Adolphus leads Swedish forces into Germany
1631	Sack of Magdeburg Protestant victory at Breitenfeld
1632	Protestant victory at Lutzen; death of Gustavus Adolphus
1635	France declares war on Spain
1643	Battle of Rocroi; French forces repel Spaniards
1648	Peace of Westphalia

ing the Lower Palatinate. In early 1632 Protestant forces plundered Bavaria, but Wallenstein chose to chase the Saxons from Bohemia rather than the Swedes from Bavaria. Not until the winter of 1632 did the armies of Gustavus and Wallenstein finally meet. At the battle of Lutzen the Swedes won the field but lost their beloved king. In less than two years Gustavus Adolphus had decisively transformed the course of the war and the course of Europe's future. Protestant forces now occupied most of central and northern Germany.

The final stages of the war involved the resumption of the century-old struggle between France and Spain. When the Twelve Years' Truce expired in 1621, Spain again declared war upon the Dutch. Dutch naval power was considerable and the Dutch took the war to the far reaches of the globe, attacking Portuguese settlements in Brazil and in the East and harassing Spanish shipping on the high seas. In 1628 the Dutch captured the entire Spanish treasure fleet as it sailed from the New World. Spain had declared bankruptcy in 1627, and the loss of the whole of the next years' treasure from America exacerbated an already catastrophic situation.

The siege of Magdeburg, 1631. The sack of the city by the Imperial troops of Tilly's army was one of the most barbarous incidents of a brutal war.

Allegorical painting celebrating the Treaty of Westphalia. The shattered weapons of war lie in the foreground; at the right, the ship of peace carries the news to the capitals of Europe.

These reversals, combined with the continued successes of Habsburg forces in central Europe, convinced Louis XIII and his chief minister, Cardinal Richelieu, that the time for active involvement in European affairs was now at hand. Throughout the early stages of the war, France had secretly aided anti-Habsburg forces. Gustavus Adolphus's unexpected success dramatically altered French calculations. Now it was evident that the Habsburgs could no longer combine their might, and Spanish energies would be drained off in the Netherlands and in central Europe. The time had come to take an open stand. In 1635 France declared war on Spain.

France took the offensive first, invading the Spanish Netherlands. In 1636 a Spanish army struck back, pushing to within twenty-five miles of Paris before it was repelled. Both sides soon began to search for a settlement, but pride prevented them from laying down their arms. Spain toppled first. Its economy in shambles and its citizens in revolt over high prices and higher taxes, it could no longer maintain its many-fronted war. In 1643 Spain gambled once more on a knockout blow against the French. But at the battle of Rocroi, exhausted French troops held out and the Spanish invasion failed.

By now the desire for peace was universal. Most of the main combatants had long since perished: Philip III, ever optimistic, in 1621; Frederick V, an exile to the end, in 1632; Gustavus Adolphus, killed at Lutzen in the same year; Wallenstein, murdered by order of Ferdinand II in 1634; Ferdinand himself in 1637; and Louis XIII in 1643, five days before the French triumph at Rocroi. Those who succeeded them had not the same passions, and after so many decades the longing for peace was the strongest emotion on the Continent.

In 1648 a series of agreements, collectively known as the Peace of Westphalia, established the outlines of the political geography of Europe for the next century. Its focus was on the Holy Roman Empire and it reflected Protestant successes in the final two decades of war. Sweden gained further territories on the Baltic, making it master of the north German ports. France, too, gained

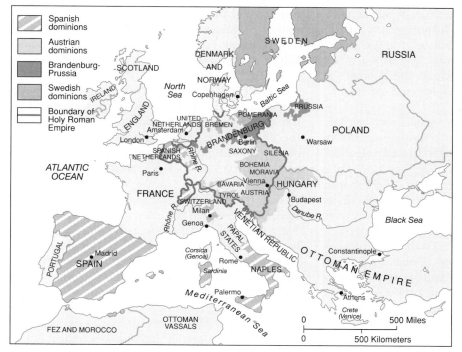

The Peace of Westphalia

THE HORRORS OF THE THIRTY YEARS' WAR

■ *No source has better captured the brutality of the Thirty Years' War than the novel* Simplisissimus. *In a series of loosely connected episodes, the hero (whose name means "the simplest of the simple") is snatched from his village to serve in marauding armies whose confrontations with local villagers are usually more horrifying than the episode narrated here.*

These troopers were even now ready to march, and had the pastor fastened by a rope to lead him away. Some cried, "Shoot him down, the rogue!" Others would have money from him. But he, lifting up his hands to heaven, begged, for the sake of the Last Judgment, for forbearance and Christian compassion, but in vain; for one of them rode him down and dealt him such a blow on the head that he fell flat, and commended his soul to God. Nor did the remainder of the captured peasants fare any better. But even when it seemed these troopers, in their cruel tyranny, had clean lost their wits, came such a swarm of armed peasants out of the wood, that it seemed a wasps'-nest had been stirred. And these began to yell so frightfully and so furiously to attack with sword and musket that all my hair stood on end; and never had I been at such a merry-making before: for the peasants of the Spessart and the Vogelsberg are as little wont as are the Hessians and men of the Sauerland and the Black Forest to let themselves be crowed over on their own dunghill. So away went the troopers, and not only left behind the cattle they had captured, but threw away bag and baggage also, and so cast all their booty to the winds lest themselves should become booty for the peasants: yet some of them fell into their hands. This sport took from me well-nigh all desire to see the world, for I thought, if 'tis all like this, then is the wilderness far more pleasant.

From Hans von Grimmelhausen, *Simplisissimus* (1669).

in territory and prestige. It kept the vital towns in the Lower Palatinate through which Spanish men and material had moved and, though it did not agree to come to terms with Spain immediately, France's fear of encirclement was at an end. The Dutch gained statehood through official recognition by Spain and through the power they had displayed in building and maintaining an overseas empire.

Territorial boundaries were reestablished as they had existed in 1624, giving the Habsburgs control of both Bohemia and Hungary. The independence of the Swiss cantons was now officially recognized as were the rights of Calvinists to the protection of the Peace of Augsburg, which again was to govern the religious affairs of the empire. Two of the larger German states were strengthened as a counterweight to the emperor's power. Bavaria was allowed to retain the Upper Palatinate, and Brandenburg, which ceded some of its coastal territory to Sweden, gained extensive territories in the east. The emperor's political control over the German states was also weakened. German rulers were given independent authority over their states and the imperial diet, rather than the emperor, was empowered to

settle disputes. Thus weakened, future emperors ruled in the Habsburg territorial lands with little ability to control, or influence, or even arbitrate German affairs. The judgment that the Holy Roman Empire was neither holy, Roman, nor an empire was now irrevocably true.

The Peace of Westphalia put back together the pieces of the map of European states. Protestantism and Catholicism now coexisted and there was to be little further change in the geography of religion. The northwest of Europe—England, Holland, Scandinavia, and the north German states—was Protestant; the south was Catholic. The empire of the German peoples was now at an end, the Austro-Hungarian empire at a beginning. Holland and Sweden had become international powers; Spain and Denmark faded from prominence. Muscovy began a long period of isolation from the west, attempting to restore a semblance of government to its people. But if the negotiators at Westphalia could resolve the political and religious ambitions that gave rise to a century of nearly continuous warfare, they could do nothing to eradicate the effects of war itself. The devastation of humanity in the name of God with which the reform of religion had begun was now exhausted. The costs were horrific. The population of Germany fell from 15 million in 1600 to 11 million in 1650. The armies brought destruction of all kinds in their wake. Plague again raged in Europe—the town of Augsburg lost 18,000 inhabitants in the early 1630s. Famine, too, returned to a continent that fifty years earlier had been self-sufficient in grain. The war played havoc with all of the economies that it touched. Inflation, devaluation of coinage, huge public and private debts were all directly attributable to the years of fighting. And the toll taken on the spirit of those generations that never knew peace is incalculable.

SUGGESTIONS FOR FURTHER READING

GENERAL READING

* J. H. Elliott, *Europe Divided 1559-1598* (New York: Harper & Row, 1968). An outstanding synthesis of European politics in the second half of the sixteenth century.

* Geoffrey Parker, *Europe in Crisis 1598-1648* (London: William Collins and Sons, 1979). The best introduction to the period.

* William Doyle, *The Old European Order* (Oxford: Oxford University Press, 1978). An important synthetic essay bristling with ideas.

* Jan de Vries, *The European Economy in an Age of Crisis* (Cambridge: Cambridge University Press, 1976). A comprehensive study of economic development, including long-distance trade and commercial change.

THE FORMATION OF STATES

J. H. Shennan, *The Origins of the Modern European State 1450-1725* (London: Hutchinson, 1974). An analytic account of the rise of the state.

Bernard Guenée, *States and Rulers in Later Medieval Europe* (London: Basil Blackwell, 1985). An engaging argument about the forces that helped shape the state system in Europe.

* Norman Davies, *God's Playground: A History of Poland, Vol. 1. The Origins to 1795* (New York: Columbia University Press, 1982). The best treatment in English of a complex history.

* Richard Pipes, *Russia Under the Old Regime* (London: Widenfeld and Nicolson, 1974). A magisterial account.

* Robert O. Crummey, *The Formation of Muscovy 1304-1613* (London: Longman, 1987). The best one-volume history.

* J. R. Lander, *Government and Community, England 1450-1509* (Cambridge, MA: Harvard University Press, 1980). A comprehensive survey of the late fifteenth century.

* S. B. Chrimes, *Henry VII* (Berkeley, CA: University of California Press, 1972). A traditional biography of the first Tudor king.

* C. D. Ross, *The Wars of the Roses* (London: Thames and Hudson, 1976). The best one-volume account.

* G. R. Elton, *Reform and Reformation, England 1509-1558* (Cambridge, MA: Harvard University Press, 1977). An up-to-date survey by the dean of Tudor historians.

Richard Vaughan, *Valois Burgundy* (Hampden, CT: Shoe String Press, 1975). An engaging history of a vanished state.

* Paul M. Kendall, *Louis XI: The Universal Spider* (New York: Norton, 1971). A highly entertaining account of an unusual monarch.

* R. J. Knecht, *French Renaissance Monarchy* (London: Longman, 1984). A study of the nature of the French monarchy and the way it was transformed in the early sixteenth century.

* J. H. Elliot, *Imperial Spain 1469-1716* (New York: Mentor, 1963). Still worth reading for its insights and examples.

THE DYNASTIC STRUGGLES

* J. R. Hale, *War and Society in Renaissance Europe* (Baltimore: Johns Hopkins University Press, 1986). Assesses the impact of war on the political and social history of early modern Europe.

M. E. Alvarez, *Charles V* (London: Thames and Hudson, 1975). An accessible biography of the most remarkable man of the age.

* R. J. Knecht, *Francis I* (Cambridge: Cambridge University Press, 1982). A compelling study by the leading scholar of sixteenth-century France.

* J. J. Scarisbrick, *Henry VIII* (Berkeley, CA: University of California Press, 1968). The definitive biography.

THE CRISES OF THE EUROPEAN STATES

J. H. M. Salmon, *Society in Crisis* (New York: St. Martin's Press, 1975). The best single-volume account of the French civil wars; difficult but rewarding.

Robert Kingdon, *Myths About the St. Bartholomew's Day Massacres 1572-76* (Cambridge, MA: Harvard University Press, 1988). A study of the impact of a central event in the history of France.

* Mark Greengrass, *France in the Age of Henri IV* (London: Longmans, 1984). An important synthesis of French history in the early seventeenth century.

Geoffrey Parker, *Philip II* (Boston: Little, Brown, 1978). The best introduction.

* Garrett Mattingly, *The Armada* (Boston: Houghton Mifflin, 1959). Still the classic account despite recent reinterpretations.

* Henry Kamen, *Spain 1469-1714* (London: Longmans, 1983). A recent survey with up-to-date interpretations.

* Geoffrey Parker, *The Dutch Revolt* (London: Penguin Books, 1977). An outstanding account of the tangle of events that comprised the revolts of the Netherlands.

W. E. Reddaway et al., eds., *The Cambridge History of Poland to 1696* (Cambridge: Cambridge University Press, 1950). A difficult but thorough narrative of Polish history.

Michael Roberts, *Gustavus Adolphus and the Rise of Sweden* (London: English Universities Press, 1973). A highly readable account of Sweden's rise to power.

THE THIRTY YEARS' WAR

* C. V. Wedgwood, *The Thirty Years' War* (New York: Doubleday, 1961). A heroic account; the best narrative history.

* Peter Limm, *The Thirty Years' War* (London: Longmans, 1984). An excellent brief survey with documents.

* Indicates paperback edition available.

CHAPTER 17

The Royal State System of Seventeenth-Century Europe

FIT FOR A KING

Behold Versailles: the greatest palace of the greatest king in seventeenth-century Europe. Everything about it was stupendous, a reflection of the grandeur of Louis XIV and of France. Sculptured gardens in dazzling geometric forms stretched for acres, scenting the air with exotic perfumes. Nearly as beautiful as the grounds were the 1,400 fountains, especially the circular basins of Apollo and Latona, the sun god and his mother. The hundreds of water jets that sprayed at Versailles defied nature as well as the senses, for the locale was not well irrigated and the water had to be pumped through elaborate mechanical works all the way from the Seine. Gardens and fountains provided the setting for the enormous palace with its hundreds of rooms for both use and show. Five thousand people, a tenth of whom served the king alone, inhabited the palace. Thousands of others flocked there daily. Most lived in the adjacent town, which had grown from a few hundred to over forty thousand in a single generation. The royal stables quartered twelve thousand horses and thousands of carriages. The cost of all of this magnificence was equally astounding. Fragmentary accounts indicate that construction costs were over 100 million French pounds. Louis XIV ordered the official receipts burned.

Like the marble of the palace, nature itself was chiseled to the requirements of the king. Forests were pared to make leafy avenues or trimmed to conform to the geometric patterns of the gardens. In spring and summer groves of orange trees grown in tubs were everywhere; in winter and fall they were housed indoors at great expense. Life-size statues and giant carved urns lined the carefully planned walkways that led out to breathtaking views or in to sheltered grottoes. A cross-shaped artificial canal, over a mile long, dominated the western end of the park. Italian gondolas skimmed along its surface, carrying visitors to the zoo and aviary on one side or to the king's private château on the other.

But this great pile of bricks and stone, of marble and precious metals expressed the contradictions of its age as well as its grandeur. The seventeenth century was a time when the monarchical state expanded its power and prestige even as it faced the grave challenge of balancing the monarch's right to rule with the subjects' duty to obey. As royal government wrapped itself in the mantle of the theory of absolute monarchy, it was challenged by civil wars and revolutions. Thus it was fitting that this prodigious monument was uncomfortable to live in, so unpleasant that Louis had a separate château built on the grounds as a quiet retreat. His wife and mistresses complained constantly of accommodations in which all interior comforts had been subordinated to the external facade of the building. Versailles was a seat of state as well as the home of the monarch, and it is revealing that the private was sacrificed to the public.

The Duc de Saint-Simon, who passed much of his time at Versailles, was well aware of the contradictions. "The beautiful and the ugly were sewn together, the vast and the constricted." Soldiers, tradesmen, and the merely curious clogged the three great avenues that led from Paris to the palace. When the king dined in public, hordes of Parisians drove out for the spectacle, filing past the monarch as if he were an exhibit at a museum. The site itself was poorly drained. "Its mud is black and stinking with a stench so penetrating that you can smell it for several leagues around." The orange groves and the stone urns filled with flower petals were more practical than beautiful: they masked the stench of sewage that was particularly noxious in the heat and rain. Even the gardens were too vast to be enjoyed. In the planted areas, the smell of flowers was overpowering while the acres of mown lawn were less than inviting to an aristocracy little given to physical exercise. "The gardens were admired and avoided," Saint-Simon observed acidly. In these contrasts of failure amid achievement Versailles stands as an apt symbol of its age: a gaudy mask to hide the wrinkles of the royal state.

The Rise of the Royal State

The religious and dynastic wars that dominated the early part of the seventeenth century had a profound impact upon the western European states. Not only did they cause terrible suffering and deprivation but they also demanded efficient and better-centralized states to conduct them. War was both a product of the European state system and a cause of its continued development. As armies grew in size, the resources necessary to maintain them grew in volume. As the battlefield spread from state to state, defense became government's most important function. More and more power was absorbed by the monarch and his chief advisers, more and more of the traditional privileges of aristocracy and of towns were eroded. At the center of these rising states, particularly in western Europe, were the king and his court. In the provinces were tax collectors and military recruiters.

Divine Kings

"There is a divinity that doth hedge a king," wrote Shakespeare. Never was that hedge more luxuriant than in the seventeenth century. In the early sixteenth century, monarchs treated their states and their subjects as personal property. Correspondingly, rulers were praised in personal terms, for their virtue, their wisdom, or their strength. By the early seventeenth century, the monarchy had been transformed into an office of state. Now rulers embodied their nation and, no matter what their personal characteristics, they were held in awe because they were monarchs.

Thus as rulers lost direct personal control over their patrimony, they gained indirect symbolic control over their nation. This symbolic power was everywhere to be seen. By the beginning of the seventeenth century, monarchs had permanent seats of government attended by vast courts of officials, place seekers, and servants. They no longer moved from place to place with their vast entourages. The idea of the capital city emerged, with Madrid, London, and Paris as the models. Here, the grandiose style of the ruler stood proxy for the wealth and glory of the nation. Great display bespoke great pride, and great pride was translated into great strength.

Portraits of rulers in action and in repose conveyed the central message. Elizabeth I was depicted bestriding a map of England or clutching a rainbow and wearing a gown woven of eyes and ears to signify her power to see and hear her subjects. The Flemish painter Sir Anthony van Dyck (1599–1641) created powerful images of three generations of Stuart kings of England. He was court painter to Charles I, whose qualities he portrayed with great sympathy and not a little exaggeration. Diego Velázquez (1599–1660) was court painter to Philip IV of Spain. His series of equestrian portraits of the Habsburgs—kings, queens, princes, and princesses—exude the spirit of the seventeenth-century monarchy, the grandeur and pomp, the power and self-assurance. Peter Paul Rubens (1577–1640) represented twenty-one separate episodes in the life of Marie de Médicis, queen regent of France.

Queen Elizabeth I of England. This portrait was commissioned by Sir Henry Lee to commemorate the Queen's visit to his estate at Ditchley. Here the queen is the very image of Gloriana—ageless and indomitable.

The themes of artists were no different from those of writers. Monarchy was glorified in a variety of forms of literary representation. National history, particularly of recent events, enjoyed wide popularity. Its avowed purpose was to draw the connection between the past and the present glories of the state. One of the most popular French histories of the period was entitled *On the Excellence of the Kings and the Kingdom of France.* Francis Bacon (1561–1626), who is remembered more as a philosopher and scientist, wrote a laudatory history of England's Henry VII, founder of the Tudor dynasty.

In England it was a period of renaissance. Poets, playwrights, historians, and philosophers by the dozens gravitated to the English court. One of the most remarkable of them was Ben Jonson (1572–1637). He began life

as a bricklayer, fought against the Spanish in Flanders, and then turned to acting and writing. His wit and talent brought him to court, where he made his mark by writing and staging masques, light entertainment that included music, dance, pantomime, and acting. Jonson's masques were distinguished by their lavish productions and exotic costumes and the inventive set designs of the great architect Inigo Jones (1573–1652). They were frequently staged at Christmastime and starred members of the court as players. The masques took for their themes the grandeur of England and its rulers.

The role of William Shakespeare (1564–1616) in the celebration of monarchy was more ambiguous. Like Jonson, Shakespeare came from an ordinary family, had little formal education, and began his astonishing career as an actor and producer of theater. He soon began to write as well as direct his plays and his company, the King's Players, received royal patronage. He set many of his plays at the courts of princes and even comedies like *The Tempest* (1611) and *Measure for Measure* (1604) centered on the power of the ruler to dispense justice and to bring peace to his subjects. Both were staged at court. His history plays focused entirely on the character of kings. In *Richard II* (1597) and *Henry VI* (3 parts, 1591–94) Shakespeare exposed the harm that weak rulers inflicted on their states, while in *Henry IV* (2 parts, 1598–1600) and *Henry V* (1599) he highlighted the benefits to be derived from strong rulers. Shakespeare's tragedies made this point in a different way. The tragic flaw in the personality of rulers exposed the world around them to ruin. In *Macbeth* (1606) this flaw was ambition. Macbeth killed to become a king and had to keep on killing to remain one. In *Hamlet* (1602) the tragic flaw was irresolution. The inability of the "Prince of Denmark" to act decisively and reclaim the crown that was his by right brought his state to the brink of collapse. Shakespeare's plays were viewed in London theaters by members of all social classes, and his concentration on the affairs of rulers helped reinforce their dominating importance in the lives of all of their subjects.

The political theory of the divine right of kings further enhanced the importance of monarchs. This theory held that the institution of monarchy had been created by God, and the monarch functioned as God's representative on earth. One clear statement of divine right theory was actually written by a king, James VI of Scotland, who later became King James I of England (1603–25). In *The True Law of Free Monarchies* (1598) James reasoned that God had placed kings on earth to rule, and he would judge them in heaven for their transgressions.

The idea of divine origin of monarchy was uncontroversial, and it was espoused not only by kings. One of the few things that the French Estates-General actually agreed upon during its meeting in 1614—the last for over 175 years—was the statement that "the king is sovereign in France and holds his crown from God only." This sentiment echoed the commonplace view of French political theorists. The greatest writer on the subject, Jean Bodin (1530–96), called the king "God's image on earth." In *The Six Books of the Commonwealth* (1576), Bodin defined the essence of the monarch's power: "The principal mark of sovereign majesty is essentially the right to impose laws on subjects generally without their consent."

Though at first glance the theory of the divine right of kings appears to be a blueprint for arbitrary rule, in fact it was yoked together with a number of principles that restrained the conduct of the monarch. As James I pointed out, God had charged kings with the obligations "to minister justice; to establish good laws; and to procure peace."

Kings were bound by the law of nature and the law of nations. They could not deprive their subjects of their lives, their liberties, or their property without due cause established by law. As one French theorist held, "while the kingdom belongs to the king, the king also belongs to the kingdom." Wherever they turned, kings were instructed in the duties of kingship. In tracts, in letters, and in literature they were lectured on the obligations of their office. "A true king should be first in government, first in council, and first in all the offices of state."

The Court and the Courtiers

For all of the bravura of divine-right theory, far more was expected of kings than they could possibly deliver. The day-to-day affairs of government had grown beyond the capacity of any monarch to handle them. The expansion in the powers of the western states absorbed more officials than ever. At the beginning of the sixteenth century the French court of Francis I employed 622 officers; at the beginning of the seventeenth century the court of

THE DIVINE ORIGINS OF MONARCHY IN HUMAN SOCIETY

■ *Sir Robert Filmer's* Patriarcha *is one of the clearest statements of the divine origins of monarchy in human society. Filmer believed that Adam, the first father, was monarch of the universe and that his children owed him absolute obedience.* Patriarcha *was written a half century before it was published in 1680.*

In all kingdoms or commonwealths in the world, whether the prince be the supreme father of the people or but the true heir of such a father . . . there is, and always shall be continued to the end of the world, a natural right of a supreme father over every multitude, although, by the secret will of God, many at first do most unjustly obtain the exercise of it.

To confirm this natural right of regal power, we find in the decalogue that the law which enjoins obedience to kings is delivered in the terms of 'honour thy father' [Exodus, xx, 12] as if all power were originally in the father. If obedience to parents be immediately due by a natural law, and subjection to princes but by the mediation of an human ordinance, what reason is there that the law of nature should give place to the laws of men . . . ?

If we compare the natural duties of a father with those of a king, we find them to be all one, without any difference at all but only in the latitude or extent of them. As the father over one family, so the king, as father over many families, extends his care to preserve, feed, clothe, instruct and defend the whole commonwealth. His wars, his peace, his courts of justice and all his acts of sovereignty tend only to preserve and distribute to every subordinate and inferior father, and to their children, their rights and privileges, so that all the duties of a king are summed up in an universal fatherly care of his people.

From Sir Robert Filmer, *Patriarcha,* 1680.

LIFE AT VERSAILLES

■ *Louis de Rouvroy, Duc de Saint-Simon, spent much of his career at the court of Louis XIV. His* Memoires *provide a fascinating study of life at Versailles as well as poison-pen portraits of the king and his courtiers.*

He always took great pains to find out what was going on in public places, in society, in private houses, even family secrets, and maintained an immense number of spies and tale-bearers. These were of all sorts; some did not know that their reports were carried to him; others did know it; there were others, again, who used to write to him directly, through channels which he prescribed; others who were admitted by the backstairs and saw him in his private room. Many a man in all ranks of life was ruined by these methods, often very unjustly, without ever being able to discover the reason; and when the King had once taken a prejudice against a man, he hardly every got over it . . .

No one understood better than Louis XIV the art of enhancing the value of a favour by his manner of bestowing it; he knew how to make the most of a word, a smile, even of a glance. If he addressed any one, were it but to ask a trifling question or make some commonplace remark, all eyes were turned on the person so honored; it was a mark of favour which always gave rise to comment . . .

He loved splendour, magnificence, and profusion in all things, and encouraged similar tastes in his Court; to spend money freely on equipages and buildings, on feasting and at cards, was a sure way to gain his favour, perhaps to obtain the honour of a word from him. Motives of policy had something to do with this; by making expensive habits the fashion, and, for people in a certain position, a necessity, he compelled his courtiers to live beyond their income, and gradually reduced them to depend on his bounty for the means of subsistence.

From Duc de Saint-Simon, *Memoires.*

Henry IV employed over 1,500. Yet the difference was not only in size. Members of the seventeenth-century court were becoming servants of the state as well as of the monarch.

Expanding the court was one of the ways in which monarchs co-opted potential rivals within the aristocracy. In return, those who were favored enhanced their power by royal grants of titles, lands, and income. As the court expanded so did the political power of courtiers. Royal councils—a small group of leading officeholders who advised the monarch on state business—grew in significance. Not only did the council assume the management of government, it also began to advocate policies for the monarch to adopt.

Yet, like everything else in seventeenth-century government, the court revolved around the monarch. The monarch appointed, promoted, and dismissed officeholders at will. As befit this type of personal government, most monarchs chose a single individual to act as a funnel for private and public business. This was the "favorite," whose role combined varying proportions of best friend, right-hand man, and hired gun. Some favorites, like the French Cardinal Richelieu and the Spanish Count-Duke Olivares, were able to transform themselves into chief ministers with a political philosophy and a vision of government. Others, like the English Duke of Buckingham, simply remained royal companions. Favorites walked a not very tight rope. They could retain their balance only as long as they retained their influence with the monarch. Richelieu claimed that it was "more difficult to dominate the four square feet of the king's study than the affairs of Europe." The parallel careers of Richelieu, Olivares, and Buckingham neatly illustrate the dangers and opportunities of the office.

Cardinal Richelieu (1585–1642) was born into a French noble family of minor importance. A younger son, he trained for the law and then for a position that his family owned in the Church; he was made a cardinal in 1622. After skillful participation in the meeting of the Estates-General of 1614, Richelieu was given a court post through the patronage of Queen Marie de Médicis, mother of Louis XIII. The two men made a good match. Louis XIII hated the work of ruling and Richelieu loved little else.

Though Richelieu received great favor from the king—he became a duke and amassed the largest private fortune in France—his position rested upon his managerial abilities. Richelieu never enjoyed a close personal relationship with his monarch, and he never felt that his position was secure. In 1630, Marie de Médicis turned against him and he was very nearly ousted from office. His last years were filled with suppressing plots to undermine his power or to take his life.

The Count-Duke Olivares (1587–1645) was a younger son of a lesser branch of a great Spanish noble family. By the time he was twenty he had become a courtier with a title, a large fortune, and most unusually, a university education. Olivares became the favorite of King Philip IV (1621–65). He was elevated to the highest rank of the nobility and lost no time consolidating his position.

Olivares used his closeness to the monarch to gain court appointments for his relatives and political supporters, but he was more interested in establishing political policy than in building a court faction. His objective was to maintain the greatness of Spain, whose fortunes, like the Count-Duke's moods, waxed and waned. Like Richelieu, Olivares attempted to further the process of centralizing royal power, which was not very advanced in Spain. Olivares's plans for a nationally recruited and financed army ended in disaster. His efforts at tax reform went unrewarded. He advocated the aggressive foreign policy that mired Spain in the Thirty Years' War and the eighty years of war in the Netherlands. As domestic and foreign crises mounted, Philip IV could not resist the pressure to dismiss his chief minister. In 1643 Olivares was removed from office and two years later, physically exhausted and mentally deranged, he died.

This portrait of Richelieu by Philippe de Champaigne shows the cardinal's intellectual power and controlled determination.

The Spanish master Diego Velázquez painted this portrait of the Count-Duke Olivares.

The Duke of Buckingham (1592–1628) was also a younger son, but not of the English nobility. He received the aimless education of a country gentleman, spending several years in France learning the graces of fashion and dancing. Reputedly one of the most handsome men in Europe, Buckingham hung about the fringes of the English court until his looks and charm brought him to the attention of Queen Anne, James I's wife. She recommended him for a minor office that gave him frequent access to the king. Buckingham quickly caught the eye of James I, and his rise was meteoric. In less than seven years he went from commoner to duke, the highest rank of the English nobility.

Along with his titles, Buckingham acquired political power. He assumed a large number of royal offices, among them Admiral of the Navy, and placed his relatives and dependents in many others. Buckingham took his obligations seriously. He began a reform of naval administration, for example, but his rise to power was so sudden that he found enemies at every turn. These increased dramatically when James I died in 1625. But he succeeded where so many others had failed by becoming the favorite and chief minister of the new king, Charles I (1625–49). His accumulation of power and patronage proceeded unabated, as did the enmity he aroused. But Charles I stood firmly behind him. In 1628 a discontented naval officer finally accomplished what the most powerful men in England could not: Buckingham was assassinated. While Charles I wept inconsolably at the news, ordinary Londoners drank to the health of his killer.

The Drive to Centralize Government

Richelieu, Olivares, and Buckingham met very different ends. Yet in their own ways they shared a common goal, to extend the authority of the monarch over his state and to centralize his control over the machinery of governance.

George Villiers, duke of Buckingham. The royal favorite virtually ruled the country between 1618 and 1628. The general rejoicing at his death embittered the king and helped bring about the eleven years' rule without Parliament.

One of the chief means by which kings and councilors attempted to expand the authority of the state was through the legal system. Administering justice was one of the sacred duties of the monarchy. The complexities of ecclesiastical, civil, and customary law gave trained lawyers an essential role in government. As legal experts and the demands for legal services increased, royal law courts multiplied and expanded. In France, the Parlement of Paris, the main law court of the state, became a powerful institution that contested with courtiers for the right to advise the monarch. In Spain the *letrados*— university-trained lawyers who were normally members of the nobility—were the backbone of royal govern-

ment. Formal legal training was a requirement for many of the administrative posts in the state. In Castile members of all social classes frequently used the royal courts to settle personal disputes. The expansion of a centralized system of justice thus joined the interests of subjects and the monarchy.

In England the legal system expanded differently. Central courts situated in the royal palace of Westminster grew and the lawyers and judges who practiced in them became a powerful profession. They were especially active in the House of Commons of the English Parliament, which along with the House of Lords had extensive advisory and legislative powers. More important than the rise of the central courts, however, was the rise of the local ones. The English Crown extended royal justice to the counties by granting legal authority to members of the local social elite. These justices of the peace, as they were known, became agents of the Crown in their own localities. Justices were given power to hear and settle minor cases and to imprison those who had committed serious offenses until the assizes, the semi-annual sessions of the county court.

Assizes combined the ceremony of rule with its process. Royal authority was displayed in a great procession to the courthouse that was led by the judge and the county justices, followed by the grand and petty juries of local citizens who would hear the cases, and finally by the carts carrying the prisoners to trial. Along with the legal business that was performed, assizes were occasions for edifying sermons, typically on the theme of obedience. Their solemnity, marked by the black robes of the judge, the Latin of the legal proceedings, and the public executions with which assizes invariably ended, all served to instill a sense of the power of the state in the throngs of ordinary people who witnessed them.

Efforts to integrate center and locality extended to more than the exercise of justice. The monarch also needed officials who could enforce royal policy in those localities where the special privileges of groups and individuals remained strong. The best strategy was to appoint local leaders to royal office. But with so much of the aristocracy resident at court, this was not always an effective course. By the beginning of the seventeenth century, the French monarchy began to rely on new central officials known as *intendants* to perform many of the tasks of the provincial governors. Cardinal Richelieu expanded the use of the intendants and by the middle of the century they had become a vital part of royal government.

The Lords Lieutenant were a parallel institution created in England. Unlike every other European state,

England had no national army. Every English county was required to raise, equip, and train its own militia. Lords Lieutenant were in charge of these trained bands. Since the aristocracy was the ancient military class in the state, the lieutenants were chosen from the greatest nobles of the realm. But they delegated their work to members of the gentry, large local landholders who took on their tasks as a matter of prestige rather than profit. Perhaps not surprisingly, the English military was among the weakest in Europe and nearly all its foreign adventures ended in disaster.

Efforts to centralize the affairs of the Spanish monarchy could not proceed so easily. The separate regions over which the king ruled maintained their own laws and privileges. Attempts to apply Castilian rules or implant Castilian officials always drew opposition from other regions. Olivares frequently complained that Philip IV was the king of Castile only and nothing but a thorough plan of unification would make him the king of Spain. This he proposed in 1625 to attempt to solve the dual problems of military manpower and military finance. After 1621, Spain was again deeply involved in European warfare. Fighting in the Netherlands and in Germany demanded large armies and larger sums of money. Olivares launched a plan for a Union of Arms to which all the separate regions of the empire, including Mexico and Peru in the west, Italy in the east, and the separate regions in Iberia would contribute. Not all of the Iberian provinces were persuaded to contribute. Catalonia stood upon its ancient privileges and refused to grant either troops or funds. But Olivares was able to establish at least the principle of unified cooperation.

The Taxing Demands of War

More than anything else, the consolidation of the state was propelled by war. Whether offensive or defensive, continuous or intermittent, successful or calamitous, war was the irresistible force of the seventeenth-century monarchy. War taxation was its immovable object. Perhaps half of all revenue of the western states went to finance war. To maintain its armies and navies, its fortresses and outposts, the state had to squeeze every penny from its subjects. Old taxes had to be collected more efficiently, new taxes had to be introduced and enforced. On the other side, the unprecedented demands for money on the part of the state were always resisted. The privileged challenged the legality of levying taxes, the unprivileged did whatever they could to avoid paying them.

The economic hardships caused by the ceaseless military activity touched everyone. Those in the direct path of battle had little left to feed themselves, let alone to provide to the state. The disruption of the delicate cycle of planting and harvesting devastated local communities. Armies plundered ripened grain and trampled seedlings as they moved through fields. The conscription of village men and boys removed vital skills from the community and upset the gender-based division of labor. Peasants were squeezed by the armies for crops, by the lords for rents, and by the state for taxes.

In fact, the inability of the lower orders of European society to finance a century of warfare was clear from the beginning. In Spain and France, the principal problem was that so much of the wealth of the nation was beyond the reach of traditional royal taxation. The nobility and many of the most important towns had long achieved exemption from basic taxes on consumption and wealth. European taxation was regressive, falling most heavily upon those least able to pay. Rulers and subjects alike recognized the inequities of the European system of taxation. Regime after regime began with plans to overhaul the national system of taxation

The oppression of the peasantry is the theme of this engraving published in the mid-seventeenth century: "This noble is the spider and the peasant the fly." The poor man is handing over goods and money to the fat milord, who says, "You must pay or serve." The peasant replies, "To all masters, all honors."

before settling for propping up new emergency levies against the rotting foundations of the old structure. Nevertheless, the fiscal crisis that the European wars provoked did result in an expansion of state taxation.

Though uninvolved in the European conflicts, England was not immune from military spending. War with Ireland in the 1590s and with Spain between 1588 and 1604 depleted the reserves that the crown had obtained when Henry VIII dissolved the monasteries. Disastrous wars against France and Spain in the 1620s provoked fiscal crisis for a monarchy that had few direct sources of revenue. While the great wealth of the kingdom was in land, the chief sources of revenue for the Crown were in trade. In the early seventeenth century customs duties, or impositions, became a lucrative source of income when the judges ruled that the king could determine which commodities could be taxed and at what rate.

Because so much of the Crown's revenues derived from commerce and because foreign invasion could only come from the sea, the most pressing military need of the English monarchy was for naval defense. Even during the Armada crisis, the largest part of the English fleet had been made up of private merchant ships pressed into service through the emergency tax of Ship Money. This was a tax on each port town to hire a merchant ship and fit it out for war. In the 1630s, Charles I revived Ship Money and extended it to all English localities.

War finance was like an all-consuming monster. No matter how much new revenue was fed into it, its appetite grew for more. New taxes and increased rates of traditional taxation created suffering and a sense of grievance throughout the western European states. Opposition to taxation was not based on greed. The state's right to tax was not yet an established principle. Monarchs received certain forms of revenue in return for grants of immunities and privileges to powerful groups in their state. The state's efforts to go beyond these restricted grants was viewed as theft of private property. In the Ship Money case challengers argued that the king had no right to what belonged to his subjects except in a case of national emergency. This was a claim that the king accepted, arguing that such an emergency existed in the presence of pirates who were attacking English shipping. But if Charles I did not make a convincing claim for national emergency, the monarchs of France and Spain, the princes of Germany, and the rulers of the states of eastern Europe all did.

Throughout the seventeenth century, monarchy solidified itself as a form of government. The king's authority came from God, but his power came from his people. By administering justice, assembling armies, and extracting resources through taxation, the monarch ruled as well as governed. The richer the king and the more powerful his might, the more potent was his state. Europeans began to identify themselves as citizens of a nation and to see themselves in distinction to other nations.

The Crises of the Royal State

The expansion of the functions, duties, and powers of the state in the early seventeenth century was not universally welcomed in European societies. The growth of central government came at the expense of local rights and privileges held by corporate bodies like the Church and the towns or by individuals like provincial officials and aristocrats. The state proved a powerful competitor, especially in the contest for the meager surplus produced on the land. As rents and prices stabilized in the early seventeenth century, after a long period of inflation, taxation increased, slowly at first and then at a pace with the gathering momentum of the Thirty Years' War. State exactions burdened all segments of society. Peasants lost the small benefit that rising prices had conferred upon producers. The surplus that parents had once passed on to children was now taken by the state. Local officials, never altogether popular, came to be seen as parasites and were easy targets for peasant rebellions. Larger landholders, whose prosperity depended upon rents and services from an increasingly impoverished peasantry, suffered along with their tenants. Even the great magnates were appalled by the state's insatiable appetite.

It was not only taxation that aroused opposition. Social and economic regulation meant more laws. More laws meant more lawyers and agents of enforcement. State regulation may have been more efficient—though many believed it was more efficient only for the state—but it was certainly disruptive. It was also expensive at a time when the fragile European economy was in a phase of decline. The early seventeenth century was a time of hunger in most of western Europe. Subtle changes in climate reduced the length of growing seasons and the size of crops. Bad harvests in the 1620s and 1640s left disease and starvation in their wake. And the wars ground on. Armies brought misery to those who were forcibly recruited to fight, those who were taxed into destitution, and those who simply had the misfortune to live in the path of destruction.

By the middle of the seventeenth century, a Europe-wide crisis was taking shape, though its timing and its forms differed from place to place. Rural protests, like grain riots and mob assaults on local institutions, had a long history in all of the European states. Popular revolt was not the product of mindless despair, but rather the natural form of political action for those who fell outside the institutionalized political process. Bread riots and tax revolts became increasingly common in the early seventeenth century. More importantly, as the focus of discontent moved from local institutions to the state, the forms of revolt changed. So, too, did the participants. Members of the political elite began to formulate their own grievances against the expansion of state power. If revolts were not new, their justification was. A theory of resistance, first developed in the French wars of religion, came to be applied to political tyranny, and posed a direct challenge to the idea of the divine right of kings. By the 1640s all of these forces converged and rebellion exploded across the Continent. In Spain the ancient kingdoms of Catalonia and Portugal asserted their independence from Castilian rule; in France members of the aristocracy rose against a child monarch and his regent. In Italy, revolts rocked Naples and Sicily. In England, a constitutional crisis gave way to civil war and then to the first political revolution in European history.

The Need to Resist

Europeans lived more precariously in the seventeenth century than in any period since the Black Death. One benchmark of crisis was population decline. In the Mediterranean, Spanish population fell from 8.5 to 7 million and Italian population from 13 to 11 million. The ravages of the Thirty Years' War were most clearly felt in central Europe. Germany lost nearly a third of its people, Bohemia nearly half. Northwestern Europe—that is, England, the Netherlands, and France—was hardest hit in the first half of the century and only gradually recovered by 1700. Population decline had many causes and, rather remarkably, direct casualties from warfare were a very small component. The indirect effects of war, the disruption of agriculture, and the spread of disease were far more devastating. Spain alone lost one half million people at the turn of the century and another half million between 1647 and 1652. Severe outbreaks in 1625 and in 1665 hit England, while France endured three consecutive years of epidemics from 1629 to 1631.

All sectors of the European economy from agriculture to trade stagnated or declined in the early seventeenth century. Not surprisingly, peasants were hardest

The Plague in Milan, *a painting by Caspar Crayer of the seventeenth-century Flemish school. The victims of the epidemic are shown being consoled by a priest.*

hit. The surplus from good harvests did not remain in rural communities to act as a buffer for bad ones. Tens of thousands died during the two great subsistence crises in the late 1620s and the late 1640s.

Predictably, acute economic crisis led to rural revolt. As the French peasants reeled from visitations of plague, frost, and floods, the French state was raising the *taille*, the tax on basic commodities that fell most heavily upon the lower orders. A series of French rural revolts in the late 1630s focused on opposition to tax increases. The Nu-Pieds—the barefooted—rose against changes in the salt tax, others rose against new levies on wine. These revolts began in the same way, with the murder of a local tax official, the organization of a peasant militia, and the recruitment of local clergy and notables. The rebels forced temporary concessions from local authorities, but they never achieved lasting reforms. Each revolt ended with the reimposition of order by the state. In England the largest rural protests, like the Midland Revolt of 1607, centered upon opposition to the enclosure of grain fields and their conversion to pasture.

The most spectacular popular uprisings occurred in Spanish-occupied Italy. In the spring of 1647 the Sicilian city of Palermo exploded under the pressure of a disastrous harvest, rising food prices, and relentless taxation. As grain prices rose, the city government subsidized the price of bread, running up huge debts in the process. When the town governors could no longer afford the subsidies, they decided to reduce the size of the loaf rather than increase its price. The women of the city rioted when the first undersized loaves were placed on sale, and soon the entire city was in revolt. Commoners who were not part of the urban power structure led the revolt, and for a time they achieved the abolition of Spanish taxes on basic foodstuffs. Their success provided the model for a similar uprising in Naples, the largest city in Europe. The revolt began in 1647 after the Spanish placed a tax on fruit. A crowd gathered to protest the new imposition, burned the customs house, and murdered several local officials. The protesters were led first by a fisherman and then by a blacksmith, and again the rebels achieved the temporary suspension of Spanish taxation. But neither of the Italian urban revolts could attract support from the local governors or the nobility. Both uprisings were eventually crushed.

The Right to Resist

Rural and urban revolts by members of the lower orders of European society were doomed to failure. Not only did the state control vast military resources, but it could count upon the loyalty of the governing classes to suppress local disorder. It was only when local elites rebelled and joined their social and political discontent to the economic grievances of the peasants that the state faced a genuine crisis. Traditionally, aristocratic rebellion centered upon the legitimacy rather than the power of the state. Claimants to the throne initiated civil wars for the prize of the crown. By the early seventeenth century, however, hereditary monarchy was too firmly entrenched to be threatened by aristocratic rebellions. When Elizabeth I of England died without an heir, the throne passed to her cousin, James I, without even a murmur of discontent. The assassination of Henry IV in 1610 left a child on the French throne, yet it provoked little more than intrigue over which aristocratic faction

would advise him. The principles of hereditary monarchy and the divine right of kings laid an unshakable foundation for royal legitimacy. But if the monarch's right to rule could no longer be challenged, was the method of rule equally unassailable? Were subjects bound to their sovereign in all cases whatsoever?

Luther and Calvin had preached a doctrine of passive obedience. Magistrates ruled by divine will and must be obeyed in all things, they argued. Both left a tiny crack in the door of absolute submission, however, by recognizing the right of lesser magistrates to resist their superiors if divine law was violated. It was during the French civil wars that a broader theory of resistance began to develop. In attempting to defend themselves from accusations that they were rebels, a number of Huguenot writers responded with an argument that accepted the divine right of kings but that limited royal power. They claimed that kings were placed on earth by God to uphold piety and justice. When they failed to do so, lesser magistrates were obliged to resist them. As God would not institute tyranny, oppressive monarchs could not be acting by divine right. Therefore, the king who violated divine law could be punished. In the most influential of these writings, *A Defense of Liberty Against Tyrants* (1579), Philippe Duplessis-Mornay (1549–1623) took the critical next step and argued that the king who violated the law of the land could also be resisted.

In the writings of both the French Huguenots and the Dutch Protestants there remained strict limits to this right to resist. These authors accepted all the premises of divine right theory and restricted resistance to other divinely ordained magistrates. Obedience tied society together at all levels. Loosening any of the knots might unravel everything. In fact, one crucial binding had already come loose when the arguments used to justify resistance in matters of religion came to be applied to matters of state. Logic soon drove the argument further. If it was the duty of lesser magistrates to resist monarchical tyranny, why was it not the duty of all citizens to do so? This was a question posed not by a Protestant rebel, but by a Jesuit professor, Juan de Mariana (1536–1624). In *The King and the Education of the King* (1598), Mariana described how human government developed from the need of individuals to have leaders to act for their convenience and well-being. These magistrates were first established by the people and then legitimated by God. Magistrates were nothing other than the people's representatives, and if it was the duty of magistrates to resist the tyranny of monarchs, then it must also be the duty of every individual citizen. "If the sacred fatherland is falling into ruins, he who tries to kill the tyrant will be acting in no ways unjustly."

In his defense of the English Revolution, the great English poet John Milton (1608–74) built upon traditional resistance theory as it had developed over the previous fifty years. Kings were instituted by the people to uphold piety and justice. Lesser magistrates had the right to resist monarchs. An unjust king forfeited his divine right and was to be punished as any ordinary citizen. In *The Tenure of Kings and Magistrates* (1649), Milton expanded upon the conventional idea that society was formed by a covenant, or contract, between ruler and ruled. The king in his coronation oath promised to uphold the laws of the land and to rule for the benefit of his subjects. The subjects promised to obey. Failure to meet obligations—by either side—broke the contract.

By the middle of the seventeenth century, resistance theory provided the intellectual justification for a number of quite different attacks upon monarchical authority. In 1640 simultaneous rebellions in the ancient kingdoms of Portugal and Catalonia threatened the Spanish monarchy. The Portuguese successfully dissolved the rather artificial bonds that had been created by Philip II and resumed their separate national identity. Catalonia, the easternmost province of Spain, which Ferdinand of Aragon had brought to the union of crowns in the fifteenth century, presented a more serious challenge. Throughout the 1620s, Catalonia, with its rich Mediterranean city of Barcelona, had consistently rebuffed Olivares's attempts to consolidate the Spanish provinces. The Catalan Cortes—the representative institution of the towns—refused to make even small contributions to the Union of Arms or to successive appeals for emergency tax increases. Catalonian leaders feared that these demands were only the thin edge of the wedge. They did not want their province to go the way of Castile, where taxation was as much an epidemic as was plague.

Catalonia relied upon its ancient laws to fend off demands for contributions to the Spanish military effort. But soon the province was embroiled in the French war and Olivares was forced to bring troops into Catalonia. The presence of the soldiers and their conduct inflamed the local population. In the spring of 1640 an unconnected series of peasant uprisings took place. Soldiers and royal officials were slain, and the Spanish viceroy of the province was murdered. But the violence was not only directed against outsiders. Attacks upon wealthy citizens raised the specter of social revolt.

It was at this point that a peasant uprising broadened into a provincial rebellion. The political leaders of Bar-

celona not only decided to sanction the rebellion, they decided to lead it. They declared that Philip IV had violated the fundamental laws of Catalonia and that in consequence their allegiance to the crown of Spain was dissolved. Instead they turned to Louis XIII of France, offering him sovereignty if he would preserve their liberties. In fact, the Catalonians simply exchanged a devil they knew for one they did not. The French happily sent troops into Barcelona to repel a Spanish attempt to crush the rebellion. Now two armies occupied Catalonia. The Catalan rebellion lasted for twelve years. When the Spanish finally took Barcelona in 1652, both rebels and ruler were exhausted from the struggle.

The revolt of the Catalans posed a greater external threat to the Spanish monarchy than it did an internal one. In contrast, the French Fronde, an aristocratic rebellion that began in 1648, was more directly a challenge to the underlying authority of the state. It too began in response to fiscal crises brought on by war. Throughout the 1640s the French state had tottered on the edge of bankruptcy. It had used every means of creative financing that its ministers could devise, mortgaging as much of the future as anyone would buy. Still it was necessary to raise traditional taxes and to institute new ones. The first tactic revived peasant revolts, especially in the early years of the decade; the second led to the Fronde.

The Fronde was a rebellion against the regency government of Louis XIV (1643–1715), who was only four years old when he inherited the French throne. His mother, Anne of Austria (1601–66), ruled as regent with the help of her Italian advisor, Cardinal Mazarin (1602–61). In the circumstances of war, agricultural crisis, and financial stringency, no regency government was going to be popular, but Anne and Mazarin made the worst of a bad situation. They initiated new taxes on officeholders, Parisian landowners, and the nobility. Soon all three united against them, led by the Parlement of Paris, the highest court in the land, in which new decrees of taxation had to be registered. When the Parlement refused to register a number of the new taxes proposed by the government and soon insisted upon the right to control the crown's financial policy, Anne and Mazarin struck back by arresting a number of leading members of the Parlement. But in 1648 barricades went up in Paris, and the court, along with the nine-year-old king, fled the capital. Quickly the Fronde—which took its name from the slingshots that children used to hurl stones at carriages—became an aristocratic revolt aimed not at the king, but at his advisers. Demands for Mazarin's resignation, the removal of the new taxes, and greater

An episode from the second Fronde, one of the two French civil wars that occurred during the minority of Louis XIV.

participation in government by nobles and Parlement were coupled with profuse statements of loyalty to the king.

The Duc de Condé, leader of the Parisian insurgents, courted Spanish aid against Mazarin's forces, and the cardinal was forced to make concessions to prevent a Spanish invasion of France. The leaders of the Fronde agreed that the crown must overhaul its finances and recognize the rights of the administrative nobility to participate in formulating royal policy. But they had no concrete proposals to accomplish either aim. Nor could they control the deteriorating political situation in Paris and a number of provincial capitals where urban and rural riots followed the upper-class attack upon the state. The catastrophic winter of 1652, with its combination of harvest failure, intense cold, and epidemic disease, brought the crisis to a head. Louis XIV was declared old enough to rule and his forces recaptured Paris, where he was welcomed as a savior. Born of frustration, fear, and greed, the Fronde accomplished little. It demonstrated only that the French aristocracy remained an independent force in politics. Like the Catalonian revolt, it revealed the fragility of the absolute state on the one hand, yet its underlying stability on the other.

The English Civil Wars

On the surface, it is difficult to understand why the most profound challenge to monarchical authority in the seventeenth century took place in England. Among the nations of Europe, England alone enjoyed peace in the early seventeenth century. Except for a brief period around 1620, the English economy sputtered along. The monarchy itself was stable. In 1603 James I had succeeded his cousin Elizabeth I without challenge and already had as many children as the Tudors had produced in nearly a century.

James I was not a lovable monarch but he was capable, astute, and generous. His principal difficulties were that he succeeded a legend and he was Scottish. There was little he could do about either. Elizabeth I had ruled England successfully for over forty years. As the economy soured and the state tilted toward bankruptcy in the 1590s, the queen remained above criticism. She sold off royal lands worth thousands of pounds and ran up huge debts at the turn of the century. Yet the gleaming myth of the glorious virgin queen tarnished not the least bit, and when she died, the general population wept openly.

At first, James I endeared himself to the English gentry and aristocracy by showering them with the gift of social elevation. On his way to London from Scotland, the first of the Stuart kings knighted thousands of gentlemen. But he showered favor equally on his own countrymen, members of his royal Scottish court who accompanied him to England. A strong strain of ethnic prejudice combined with the disappointed hopes of English courtiers to generate immediate hostility to the new regime. Though he relied upon Elizabeth's most trusted ministers to guide state business, James was soon plunged into financial and political difficulties. He never escaped from either.

His financial problems resulted directly from the fact that the tax base of the English monarchy was undervalued. For decades the monarchy had staved off a crisis by selling lands that had been confiscated from the Church in the mid-sixteenth century. But this solution reduced the Crown's long-term revenues and made it dependent upon extraordinary grants of taxation from Parliament. Royal demands for money were met by parliamentary demands for political reform. The most significant, in 1628, during the reign of Charles I, led to the formulation of the Petition of Right, which restated the traditional English freedoms from arbitrary arrest and imprisonment (habeas corpus), from nonparliamentary taxation, and from the confiscation of property by martial law.

Religious problems mounted on top of economic and political difficulties. Demands were made for thoroughgoing church reforms by groups and individuals who had little in common other than the name given to them by their detractors: Puritans. One of the most contentious issues raised by some Puritans was the survival in the Anglican church of the Catholic hierarchy of archbishops and bishops. These Puritans demanded the abolition of this episcopal form of government and its replacement with a presbyterial system similar to that in Scotland, in which congregations nominated their own representatives to a national assembly. Neither James I nor his son, Charles I, opposed religious reform, but to achieve their reforms they strengthened episcopal power. In the 1620s Archbishop William Laud (1573–1645) rose to power in the English church by espousing a Calvinism so moderate that many denied it was Calvinism at all. Laud preached the beauty of holiness and strove to reintroduce decoration in the church and a formal decorum in the service. One of Laud's first projects after he was appointed archbishop of Canterbury was to establish a consistent divine service in England and Scotland by creating new prayer books.

It fell to the unfortunate dean of St. Giles Cathedral in Edinburgh to introduce the new Scottish prayer book in 1637. The reaction was immediate: someone threw a stool at his head and dozens of women screamed that "popery" was being brought to Scotland. There were riots by citizens and resistance to the use of the new prayer book by clergy and the nobility. To Charles I the opposition was rebellion and he began to raise forces to suppress it. But Scottish soldiers were far more determined to preserve their religious practice than were English soldiers to impose the king's. By the end of 1640 an army of Charles's Scottish subjects had successfully invaded England.

Now the fiscal and political problems of the Stuart monarchs came into play. For eleven years Charles I had managed to do what he was in theory supposed to do, live from his own revenues. He had accomplished this by a combination of economy and the revival of ancient feudal rights that struck hard at the governing classes. He levied fines for unheard-of offenses, expanded traditional taxes, and added a brutal efficiency to the collection of revenue. While these expedients sufficed during peacetime, now that an army had to be raised and a war fought, Charles I was again dependent upon grants from Parliament, which he reluctantly summoned in 1640.

The Long Parliament, which met in November 1640 and sat for thirteen years, saw little urgency in levying taxes to repel the Scots. After all, the Scots were resisting Laud's religious innovations and there were many

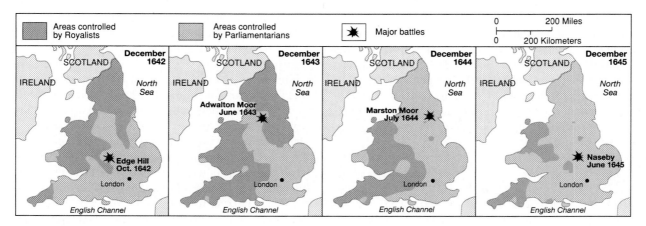

The English Civil War

Englishmen who believed that they should be resisted. Parliament proposed a number of constitutional reforms that Charles I reluctantly accepted. The Long Parliament would not be dismissed without its own consent. In the future Parliaments would be summoned once in every three years. Due process in common law would be observed, and the ancient taxes that the Crown had revived would be abolished.

At first Charles I could do nothing but bide his time and accept these assaults upon his power and authority. Once he had crushed the Scots he would be able to bargain from a position of strength. But as the months passed it became clear that Parliament had no intention of providing him with money or forces. Rather, the members sought to negotiate with the Scots themselves and to continue to demand concessions from the king as long as the Scottish threat remained. By the end of 1641 Charles's patience had worn thin. He bungled an attempt to arrest the leaders of the House of Commons, but he successfully spirited his wife and children out of London. Then he too left the capital and headed north where, in the summer of 1642, he raised the royal

AN EYEWITNESS ACCOUNT OF THE EXECUTION OF CHARLES I

■ *Charles I was executed at Westminster on a bitter January afternoon in 1649. This excerpt comes from an eyewitness account of his last moments. He was accompanied on the scaffold by the bishop of London and discovered that the chopping block was very short so that he could be held down if he resisted.*

And to the executioner he said, "I shall say but very short prayers, and when I thrust out my hands—"

Then he called to the bishop for his cap, and having put it on, asked the executioner, "Does my hair trouble you?" who desired him to put it all under his cap; which, as he was doing by the help of the bishop and the executioner, he turned to the bishop, and said, "I have a good cause, and a gracious God on my side."

The bishop said, "There is but one stage more, which, though turbulent and troublesome, yet is a very short one. You may consider it will soon carry you a very great way; it will carry you from earth to heaven; and there you shall find to your great joy the prize you hasten to, a crown of glory."

The king adjoins, "I go from a corruptible to an incorruptible crown; where no disturbance can be, no disturbance in the world."

The bishop. "You are exchanged from a temporal to an eternal crown,—a good exchange."

Then the king asked the executioner, "Is my hair well?" . . . and looking upon the block, said, "You must set it fast."

The executioner. "It is fast, sir."

King. "It might have been a little higher."

Executioner. "It can be no higher, sir."

King. "When I put out my hands this way, then—"

Then having said a few words to himself, as he stood, with hands and eyes lift up, immediately stooping down he laid his neck upon the block; and the executioner, again putting his hair under his cap, his Majesty, thinking he had been going to strike, bade him, "Stay for the sign."

Executioner. "Yes, I will, an it please your Majesty."

After a very short pause, his Majesty stretching forth his hands, the executioner at one blow severed his head from his body; which, being held up and showed to the people, was with his body put into a coffin covered with black velvet and carried into his lodging.

His blood was taken up by divers persons for different ends: by some as trophies of their villainy; by others as relics of a martry; and in some hath had the same effect, by the blessing of God, which was often found in his sacred touch when living.

A satirical print depicting Cromwell dissolving the Long Parliament in 1653. Symbolic animals include an owl that cannot see despite glasses and a candle, and a tiny dog mimicking the British lion. The sign on the wall says, "This House is to let."

standard and declared the leaders of Parliament rebels and traitors. England was plunged into civil war.

There were strong passions on both sides. Parliamentarians believed that they were fighting to defend their religion, their liberties, and the rule of law. Royalists believed they were fighting to defend their monarch, their church, and social stability. After nearly three years of inconclusive fighting, in June 1645 Parliament won a decisive victory at Naseby and brought the war to an end the following summer. The king was in captivity, bishops had been abolished, a Presbyterian church had been established, and limitations were placed on royal power. All that remained necessary to end three years of civil war was the king's agreement to abide by the judgment of battle.

But Charles I had no intention of surrendering either his religion or his authority. Despite the rebels' suc-

cesses, they could not rule without him, and he would concede nothing as long as opportunities to maneuver remained. In 1647 there were opportunities galore. The war had proved ruinously expensive to Parliament. It owed enormous sums to the Scots, to its own soldiers, and to the governors of London. Each of these elements had its own objectives in a final settlement of the war and they were not altogether compatible. London feared the parliamentary army, unpaid and camped dangerously close to the capital. The Scots and the English Presbyterians in Parliament feared that the religious settlement already made would be sacrificed by those known as Independents, who desired a more decentralized church. The Independents feared that they would be persecuted just as harshly by the Presbyterians as they had been by the king. In fact, the war had settled nothing.

The English Revolutions

Charles I happily played both ends against the middle until the army decisively ended the game. In June 1647 parliamentary soldiers kidnaped the king and demanded that Parliament pay their arrears, protect them from legal retribution, and recognize their service to the nation. Those in Parliament who opposed the army's intervention were impeached, and when London Presbyterians rose up against the army's show of force, troops moved in to occupy the city. The civil war, which had come so close to resolution in 1647, had now become a military revolution. Religious and political radicals flocked to the army and encouraged the soldiers to support their programs and to resist disbandment. New fighting broke out in 1648 as Charles encouraged his supporters to resume the war. But forces under the command of Sir Thomas Fairfax (1612–71) and Oliver Cromwell (1599–1658) easily crushed the royalist uprisings in England and Scotland. The army now demanded that Charles I be brought to justice for his treacherous conduct both before and during the war. When the majority in Parliament refused, still hoping against hope to reach an accommodation with the king, the soldiers again acted decisively. In December 1648 army regiments were sent to London to purge the two houses of Parliament of those who opposed the army's demands. The remaining members, contemptuously called the Rump Parliament, voted to bring the king to trial for his crimes against the liberties of his subjects. On 30 January 1649, Charles I was executed and England was declared to be a commonwealth. (See Special Feature, "King Charles's Head," pp. 518–519.) The monarchy and the House of Lords were abolished and the nation was to be governed by what was left of the membership of the House of Commons.

For four years the members of the Rump Parliament struggled with proposals for a new constitution while balancing the demands of moderate and radical reformers and an increasingly hostile army. It achieved little other than to raise the level of frustration. In 1653 Oliver Cromwell, with the support of the army's senior officers, forcibly dissolved the Rump and became the leader of the revolutionary government. At first he ruled along with a Parliament handpicked from among the supporters of the commonwealth. When Cromwell's Parliament proved no more capable of governing than had the Rump, a written constitution, The Instrument of Government (1653), established a new polity. Cromwell was given the title Lord Protector and he was to rule along with a freely elected Parliament and an administrative body known as the council of state.

Cromwell was able to hold the revolutionary cause together through the force of his own personality. A member of the lesser landed elite who had opposed the arbitrary policies of Charles I, he was a devout Puritan who believed in a large measure of religious toleration for Christians. As both a member of Parliament and a senior officer in the army, he had been able to temper the claims of each when they conflicted.

Though many urged him to accept the crown of England and begin a new monarchy, Cromwell steadfastly held out for a government in which fundamental authority resided in Parliament. Until his death he defended the achievements of the revolution and held its conflicting constituents together.

But a sense that only a single person could effectively rule a state remained too strong for the reforms of the revolutionary regimes to have much chance of success. When Cromwell died in 1658 his eldest son Richard was proposed as the new Lord Protector, but Richard had very little experience in either military or civil affairs. Nor did he have the sense of purpose that was his father's greatest source of strength. Without an individual to hold the movement together, the revolution fell apart. In 1659 the army again intervened in civil affairs, dismissing the recently elected Parliament and calling for the restoration of the monarchy, to provide stability to the state. After a period of negotiation in which the king agreed to a general amnesty with only a few exceptions, the Stuarts were restored when Charles II (1649–85) took the throne in 1660.

Twenty years of civil war and revolution had their effect. Parliament became a permanent part of civil government and now had to be managed rather than ignored. Royal power over taxation and religion was curtailed, though in fact Parliament proved more vigorous in suppressing religious dissent than the monarchy ever was. England was to be a reformed Protestant state, though there remained much dispute about what constituted reform. Absolute monarchy had become constitutional monarchy with the threat of revolution behind the power of Parliament and the threat of anarchy behind the power of the Crown.

Both threats proved potent in 1685 when James II (1685–88) came to the throne. A declared Catholic, James attempted to use his power of appointment to foil the constraints that Parliament imposed upon him. He elevated Catholics to leading posts in the military and in the central government and began a campaign to pack a

A fanciful rendition of the execution of Charles I by a contemporary Flemish painter. At the top are portraits of Charles and his executioner. Below are scenes of Charles on his way to execution and of people dipping their handkerchiefs in his blood after the beheading.

King Charles's Head

They could have killed him quietly: the executioners slipping away silently in the night, unauthorized, unknown. It was the quickest way and it would end all doubts. Since June 1647, Charles I had been a prisoner of the parliamentary army, and there had been more than one moment in which his elimination would have settled so many vexing problems. They could have let him escape. Let him live out his life in exile. Dangerous, perhaps, but still he would be gone and a new government in the name of the people could get on with creating a new order. They could have done it quietly.

Instead the leaders of Parliament and the army decided on a trial, a public presentation of charges against the king, a public judgment of his guilt. A high court of justice, enforcing the laws of

England, would try its king for treason against the state. The logic was simple: if Parliament had fought for the preservation of the liberties of all Englishmen, then they could only proceed against the king by law. If they followed any other course, they were open to the charge that they were usurpers, that they ruled by the power of might rather than by the power of law. But if the logic was simple, everything else was hopelessly complex. English law was a system of precedents, one case stacking upon another to produce the weighty judgments of what was and was not lawful. Never had there been a treason case like this one. Indeed, how could the king commit treason, how could he violate his own allegiance? Always before, the king acted as prosecutor, the

king's judges had rendered decisions, and the king's executioner had carried out sentences. Not one of these precedents was now in the least way useful.

Nor was it clear what court had jurisdiction over this unprecedented case. The royal judges would have no part of it; neither would the House of Lords. The House of Commons was forced to create its own high court of justice, 135 supporters of the parliamentary cause drawn from its own members, from the army, and from among the leading citizens of London. Barely half attended any of the sessions. Judge John Bradshaw, who presided over two provincial royal courts, was chosen to preside at the king's trial after several of his more distinguished colleagues tactfully declined the post. Bradshaw took the precaution of lining his hat with lead against the chance that he would be shot from the galleries rather than the floor.

These shortcomings did not deter the leaders of the parliamentary cause. These were unprecedented times and the ossified procedures of lawyers and law courts could not be allowed to detract from the undeniable justice of their cause. Charles I had committed treason against his nation. He had declared war on his people. He had brought Irish and Scottish armies into England to repress Parliament, and when that had failed he had negotiated with French, Danish, and Dutch troops for the same purpose. Even when he had been defeated in battle, when the judgment of God was clear for all to see, even then he plotted and he tricked. His lies were revealed by his own hand, his captured correspondence detailing how he intended to double-cross those to whom he swore he would be faithful. Cromwell called him "a man against whom the Lord has witnessed," and the prosecution needed no better testimony than that. If there were no precedents, then this trial would set one.

Nevertheless, the makeshift nature of the court provided the king with his line of attack. If there was to be a public display, then Charles I was determined to turn it to his advantage. Even as his royal palace was being converted into a courtroom and an execution platform was being hastily erected on one of its balconies, even now the king could not conceive that the nation could be governed without him. Royal government had guided England for a millennium and for all he could see would do so for another. Rather he feared that he would be deposed and replaced, and against that eventuality he

had secured the escape of his two elder sons. They were safe in France and only his youngest child was in the hands of these savage parliamentarians.

About the trial itself, he worried not at all. There could be no court in the land that could try its king, no authority but his own that could determine a charge of treason. When it was read out that he was a tyrant and traitor, he burst out laughing. "Remember, I am your king, your lawful king and what sins you bring upon your heads and the judgment of God upon this land, think well upon it," he told his accusers.

The trial began on Saturday, 20 January 1649. Armed soldiers in battle dress cleared the floor of the large chamber. Curious onlookers packed the galleries. The king wore the enormous golden star of the Order of the Garter on his cloak but was allowed no other symbol of royalty to overawe his accusers.

The charge of "treason and high misdemeanors" had been carefully prepared. When the resounding indictment concluded, all eyes turned toward Charles I. Now he would have to answer the charge, guilty or not guilty. But rather than answer the charge, he questioned the authority of the court. "I would know by what power I am called hither, a king cannot be tried by any superior jurisdiction here on earth." This was the weakest point of the parliamentary strategy. Judge Bradshaw could only assert that the court represented the free people of England. But Charles was relentless. He demanded precedents and refused

to be silenced by the assertion that his objections were overruled.

In English law, a defendant who refused to plead was presumed guilty. Thus the king's trial ended as soon as it had begun. After three fruitless sessions and much behind-the-scenes maneuvering, it was decided that the king should be condemned and sentenced to die. On 27 January, Judge Bradshaw appeared in the scarlet robes of justice and issued the sentence. Charles had prepared a statement for maximum effect and waited patiently to deliver it. Now it was the king's turn to be surprised. After pronouncing sentence, Bradshaw and the commissioners rose from the bench. "Will you not hear me a word, sir," called a flustered Charles I. "No," replied the judge. "Guards, withdraw your prisoner."

Tuesday, 30 January, dawned cold and clear. Charles put on two shirts so that if he trembled from the cold it would not be interpreted as fear. In fact he made a very good end. The chopping block had been set very low and great iron staples were driven in the platform to pin down the king's arms if he attempted to resist his fate. But Charles was more than ready to accept his fate. He spoke briefly and to the point, denying he had acted against the true interests and rights of his subjects. Then he lay down on the platform, and prayed. As the axe fell, one witness recorded, "such a groan as I never heard and hope never to hear again," broke forth from the crowd. The English Revolution had begun.

new Parliament with his supporters. This proved too much for the governing classes, who entered into negotiations with William, Prince of Orange, husband of Mary Stuart, James's eldest daughter. In 1688 William landed in England with a small force. Without support, James II fled to France, the English throne was declared vacant, and William and Mary were proclaimed king and queen of England. There was little bloodshed in England and little threat of social disorder, and the event soon came to be called the Glorious Revolution. Its achievements were set down in the Declaration of Rights (1689), which was presented to William and Mary before they took the throne. The Declaration reasserted the fundamental principles of constitutional monarchy as they had developed over the previous half-century. Security of property and the regularity of Parliaments were guaranteed. The Toleration Act (1689) granted religious freedom to nearly all groups of Protestants. The liberties of the subject and the rights of the sovereign were to be in balance.

The events of 1688 in England reversed a trend toward increasing power on the part of the Stuarts. This second episode of resistance resulted in the development of a unique form of government which, a century later, spawned dozens of imitators. John Locke (1632–1704) was the theorist of the Revolution of 1688. He was heir to the century-old debate on resistance and he carried the doctrine to a new plateau. In *Two Treatises on Civil Government* (1690), Locke developed the contract theory of government. Political society was a compact that individuals entered into freely for their own well-being. It was designed to maintain each person's natural rights—life, liberty, and property. Natural rights were inherent in individuals; they could not be given away. The contract between rulers and subjects was an agreement for the protection of natural rights. "Arbitrary power cannot consist with the ends of society and government. Men would not quit the freedom of the state of nature were it not to preserve their lives, liberties, and fortunes and by stated rules to secure their peace and happiness." When rulers acted arbitrarily, they were to be deposed by their subjects, preferably in the relatively peaceful manner in which James II had been replaced by William III.

The efforts of European monarchies to centralize their power came at the expense of the church, the aristocracy, and the localities. It was a struggle that took place over decades and was not accomplished easily. In France the Fronde was an aristocratic backlash; in Spain the revolt of the Catalans pitted the Castilian crown against a proud ethnic province. In England a civil war fought to prevent the encroachments of the Crown against the rights of the community gave way to a bloody revolution that combined religious and constitutional grievances. The excesses of monarchy were succeeded by the excesses of parliamentary rule. But the lesson learned by the English ruling elites was that for a nation to enjoy the benefits of a powerful central authority, it was necessary to restrain it. The Revolution of 1688 helped create a constitutional balance between ruler and ruled.

The Zenith of the Royal State

The mid-century crises tested the mettle of the royal states. Over the long term, the seventeenth-century crises had two different consequences. First they provided a check to the exercise of royal power. Fear of recurring rebellions had a chilling effect upon policy, especially taxation. Reforms of financial administration, long overdue, were one of the themes of the later seventeenth century. Even as royal government strengthened itself, it remained concerned about the impact of its policies. On the other hand, the memory of rebellion served to control the ambitions of factious noblemen and town oligarchies.

A 1689 engraving by de Hooghe and C. Allard shows William and Mary as the champions of parliamentary liberty and the Bill of Rights.

If nothing else, these episodes of opposition to the rising royal states made clear the universal desire for stable government, which was seen as the responsibility of both subjects and rulers. By the second half of the seventeenth century, effective government was the byword of the royal state. The natural advantages of monarchy had to be merged with the interests of the citizens of the state and their desires for wealth, safety, and honor. After so much chaos and instability, the monarchy had to be elevated above the fray of day-to-day politics, elevated to become a symbol of the power and glory of the nation.

In England, Holland, and Sweden a form of constitutional monarchy developed in which rulers shared power, in varying degrees, with other institutions of state. In England it was Parliament, in Holland the town oligarchies, and in Sweden the nobility. But in most other states in Europe there developed a pure form of royal government known as absolutism. Absolute monarchy revived the divine right theories of kingship and added to them a cult of the personality of the ruler. Absolutism was practiced in states as dissimilar as Denmark, Brandenburg-Prussia, and Russia. It reached its zenith in France under Louis XIV, the most powerful of the seventeenth-century monarchs.

The Nature of Absolute Monarchy

Locke's theory of contract provided one solution to the central problem of seventeenth-century government: how to balance the monarch's right to command and the subjects' duty to obey. By establishing a constitutional monarchy, in which power was shared between the ruler and a representative assembly of subjects, England found one path out of this thicket. But it was not a path that many others could follow.

The English solution was most suited to a state that was largely immune from invasion and land war. Constitutional government required a higher level of political participation of citizens than did an absolute monarchical one. Greater participation in turn meant greater freedom of expression, greater toleration of religious minorities, and greater openness in the institutions of government. All were dangerous. The price that England paid was a half-century of governmental instability.

The alternative to constitutional monarchy was absolute monarchy. It, too, found its greatest theorist in England. Thomas Hobbes (1588–1679) in his greatest work, *Leviathan* (1651), argued that before civil society had been formed, humans lived in a savage state of nature, "in a war of every man against every man." This

The title page of the first edition of Thomas Hobbes's Leviathan, *published in 1651. The huge figure composed of many tiny human beings symbolizes the surrender of individual human rights to those of the state.*

was a ghastly condition without morality or law—"the notions of right and wrong, of justice and injustice have there no place." People came together to form a government for the most basic of all purposes: for self-preservation. Without government they were condemned to a life that was "solitary, poor, nasty, brutish, and short." To escape the state of nature, individuals pooled their power and granted it to a ruler. The terms of the Hobbesian contract were simple. Rulers agreed to rule; subjects agreed to obey. When the contract was intact, people ceased to live in a state of nature. When it was broken, they returned to it. With revolts, rebellions, and revolutions erupting in all parts of Europe, Hobbes's state of nature never seemed very far away.

For most states of Europe in the later seventeenth century, absolute monarchy became not only a necessity but an ideal. The consolidation of power in the hands of the divinely ordained monarch who, nevertheless, ruled according to principles of law and justice, was seen as the perfect form of government.

The main features of absolute monarchy were all designed to extend royal control. As in the early seventeenth century, the person of the monarch was revered. Courts grew larger and more lavish in an effort to enhance the glory of the monarchy and thereby of the state. *L'etat, c'est moi*—"I am the state"—Louis XIV was supposed to have said. No idea better expresses absolutism's connection between governor and governed. As the king grew in stature, his competitors for power all shrank. Large numbers of nobles were herded together at court under the watchful eye of monarchs who now ruled rather than reigned. The king shed the cloak of his favorites and rolled up his own sleeves to manage state affairs. Representative institutions, especially those that laid claim to control over taxation, were weakened or cast aside for obstructing efficient government and endangering the welfare of the state. Monarchs needed standing armies, permanent forces that could be drilled and trained in the increasingly sophisticated arts of war. Thus the military was expanded and made an integral part of the machinery of government. The military profession developed within nations, gradually replacing mercenary adventurers who had fought for booty rather than for duty.

Yet the absolute state was never as powerful in practice as it was in theory. Nor did it ever exist in its ideal shape. Absolutism was always in the making, never quite made. Its success depended upon a strong monarch who knew his own will and could enforce it. It depended upon unity within the state, upon the absence or ruthless suppression of religious or political minorities. The absolute ruler needed to control information and ideas, to limit criticism of state policy. Ultimately, the absolute state rested upon the will of its citizens to support it. The seventeenth-century state remained a loose confederation of regions, many acquired by conquest and whose loyalty was practical rather than instinctive. There were no state police to control behavior or attitudes, no newspapers or mass communication to spread propaganda. Censorship might restrict the flow of forbidden books, but it could do little to dam up the current of ideas.

Absolutism in the East

Frederick William, the Great Elector of Brandenburg-Prussia (1640–88), was one of the European princes who made the most effective use of the techniques of absolutism. In 1640 he inherited a scattered and ungovern-

able collection of territories. The nobility, known as *die Junker*, enjoyed immunity from almost all forms of direct taxation, and the towns had no obligation to furnish either men or supplies for military operations beyond their walls.

When Frederick William attempted to introduce an excise—the commodity tax on consumption that had so successfully financed the Dutch Revolt and the English Revolution—he was initially rebuffed. But military emergency overcame legal precedents. By the 1650s Frederick William had established the excise in the towns though not on the land.

With the excise as a steady source of revenue, the Great Elector could now create one of the most capable standing armies of the age. The strictest discipline was maintained in the new army, and the Prussian army developed into a feared and efficient fighting machine. Frederick William organized one of the first departments of war to oversee all of the details of the creation of his army, from housing and supplies to the training of young officer candidates. This department was also responsible for the collection of taxes. By integrating military and civilian government, Frederick William was able to create an efficient state bureaucracy that was particularly responsive in times of crisis. The creation of the Prussian army was the force that led to the creation of the Prussian state.

The same materials that forged the Prussian state led to the transformation of Russia. Soon after the young Tsar Peter I, known later as "the Great" (1682–1725) came to the throne, he realized that he could compete with the western states only by learning to play their game.

Like those of Frederick William, Peter's greatest reforms were military. Peter realized that if Russia was to flourish in a world dominated by war and commerce it would have to reestablish its hold on the Baltic ports. This meant dislodging the Swedes from the Russian mainland and creating a fleet to protect Russian trade. Neither goal seemed likely. The Swedes were one of the great powers of the age, constant innovators in battlefield tactics and military organization. Peter studied their every campaign. His first wars against the Swedes ended in humiliating defeats, but with each failure came a sharper sense of what was needed to succeed.

First Peter introduced a system of conscription that resulted in the creation of a standing army. Conscripts were branded to inhibit desertion, and a strict discipline was introduced to prepare the soldiers for battle. Peter unified the military command at the top and stratified it in the field. He established promotion based on merit.

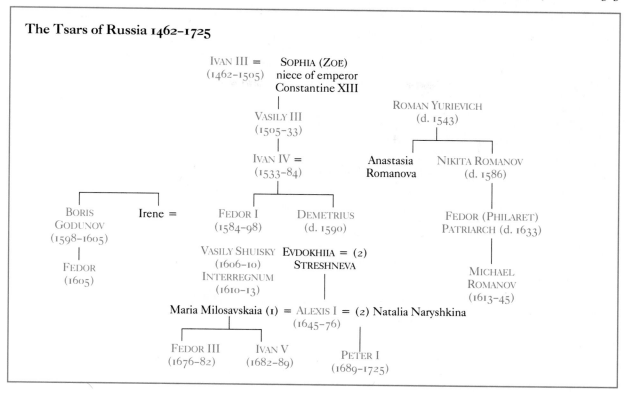

The Tsars of Russia 1462-1725

IVAN III = SOPHIA (ZOE)
(1462-1505) niece of emperor
Constantine XIII

ROMAN YURIEVICH
(d. 1543)

VASILY III
(1505-33)

IVAN IV =
(1533-84)

Anastasia   NIKITA ROMANOV
Romanova   (d. 1586)

BORIS   Irene =   FEDOR I   DEMETRIUS   FEDOR (PHILARET)
GODUNOV   (1584-98)   (d. 1590)   PATRIARCH (d. 1633)
(1598-1605)

FEDOR   VASILY SHUISKY   EVDOKHIIA = (2)   MICHAEL
(1605)   (1606-10)   STRESHNEVA   ROMANOV
                   INTERREGNUM   (1613-45)
                   (1610-13)

Maria Milosavskaia (1) = ALEXIS I = (2) Natalia Naryshkina
                         (1645-76)

FEDOR III   IVAN V   PETER I
(1676-82)   (1682-89)   (1689-1725)

For the first time Russian officers were given particular responsibilities to fulfill during both training and battle. Peter created military schools to train cadets for the next generation of officers.

Finally in 1709 Peter realized his ambitions. At the battle of Poltava the Russian army routed the Swedes, wounding King Charles XII, annihilating his infantry, and capturing dozens of his leading officers. That night Peter toasted the captured Swedish generals. He claimed that everything he knew about warfare he had learned from them and he congratulated them on their success as teachers. After the battle of Poltava, Russia gradually replaced Sweden as the dominant power in the Baltic.

Like everything else about him, Peter the Great's absolutism was uniquely his own. But though Peter's power was unlimited, it was not uncontested. He secularized the Russian Orthodox church, subjecting it to the control of state power and confiscating much of its wealth in the process. He broke the old military service class, which attempted a coup d'etat when he was abroad in the 1690s. By the end of his reign, the Russian monarchy was among the strongest in Europe.

The Origins of French Absolutism

Nowhere was absolutism as successfully implanted as in France. Louis XIII (1610-43) was only eight years old when he came to the throne, and he grew slowly into his role under the tutelage of Cardinal Richelieu. It was Richelieu's vision that stabilized French government. As chief minister, Richelieu saw clearly that the prosperity and even the survival of France depended upon strengthening royal power. He preached a doctrine of *raison d'etat*—reason of state—in which he placed the needs of the nation above the privileges of its most important groups. Richelieu saw three threats to stable royal government, "the Huguenots shared the state, the nobles conducted themselves as if they were not subjects, and the most powerful governors in the provinces acted as if they were sovereign in their office."

Richelieu took measures to control all three. The power of the nobles was the most difficult to attack. The nobles' long tradition of independence from the crown had been enhanced by the wars of religion. Perhaps more importantly, the ancient aristocracy, the

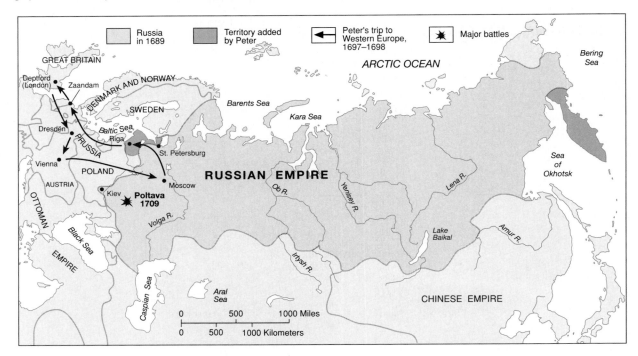

Russia Under Peter the Great

nobility of the sword, felt themselves in a particularly vulnerable position. Their world was changing and their traditional roles were becoming obsolete. Professional soldiers replaced them at war; professional administrators at government. Mercantile wealth threatened their economic superiority, the growth of the nobility of the robe—lawyers and state officials—threatened their social standing. They were hardly likely to take orders from a royal minister like Richelieu.

To limit the power of local officials, Richelieu used intendants to examine their conduct and to reform their administration. He made careful appointments of local governors and brought more regions under direct royal control. Against the Calvinists, who were called Huguenots in France, Richelieu's policy was more subtle. He was less interested in challenging their religion than their autonomy. In 1627 when the English sent a force to aid the Huguenots against the government, Richelieu and Louis XIII abolished the Huguenots' privileges altogether. They were allowed to maintain their religion but not their special status. Finally, in 1685 Louis XIV revoked the Edict of Nantes, which had guaranteed civil and religious rights to the Huguenots. All forms of Protestant worship were outlawed and the ministers who were not hunted down and killed were forced into exile. Despite a ban on Protestant emigration,

over two hundred thousand Huguenots fled the country, many of them carrying irreplaceable skills with them to Holland and England in the west and to Brandenburg in the east.

Richelieu's program was a vital prelude to the development of absolute monarchy in France. But the cardinal was not a king. While it is clear that Richelieu did not act without the full support of Louis XIII, and clear that the king initiated many reforms for which the cardinal received credit, there can be no doubt that Richelieu was the power behind the throne. Louis XIII hated the business of government and even neglected his principal responsibility of providing the state with an heir. For years he and his wife slept in separate palaces and only a freak rainstorm in Paris forced him to spend a night with the queen, Anne of Austria, in 1637. It was the night of the conception of Louis XIV. Louis XIII and Richelieu died within six months of each other in 1642–43, and the nation again endured the turmoil of a child king.

Louis le Grande

Not quite five years old when he came to the throne, Louis XIV was tutored by Cardinal Jules Mazarin (1602–61), Richelieu's successor as chief minister. If anything,

This Hyacinthe Rigaud portrait of Louis XIV in his coronation robes shows the splendor of the Roi Soleil (Sun King), who believed himself to be the center of France as the sun is the center of the solar system.

Mazarin was more ruthless and less popular than his predecessor. Like Richelieu, whom he emulated, Mazarin was an excellent administrator who had learned well the lessons of *raison d'etat*. At the conclusion of the Thirty Years' War, for example, Mazarin refused to make peace with Spain, believing that the time was ripe to deliver a knockout blow to the Spanish Habsburgs.

In order to pacify the rebellious nobility of the Fronde, who opposed Mazarin's power, Louis XIV was declared to have reached his majority at the age of thirteen. But it was not until Mazarin died ten years later in 1661 that the king began to rule. Louis was blessed with able and energetic ministers. The two central props of his state—money and might—were in the hands of dynamic men, Jean-Baptiste Colbert (1619–83) and the Marquis de Louvois (1639–91). Colbert, to whom credit belongs for the building of the French navy, the reform of French legal codes, and the establishment of national academies of culture, was Louis's chief minister for finance. Colbert's fiscal reforms were so successful that in less than six years a debt of 22 million French pounds

had become a surplus of 29 million. Colbert achieved this astonishing feat not by raising taxes but by increasing the efficiency of their collection. Until Louis embarked upon his wars, the French state was solvent.

To Louvois, Louis's minister of war, fell the task of reforming the French army. During the Fronde, royal troops were barely capable of defeating the makeshift forces of the nobility. By the end of the reign, the army had grown to 400,000 and its organization had been thoroughly reformed.

Louis XIV furthered the practice of relying upon professional administrators to supervise the main departments of state and to offer advice on matters of policy. He built upon the institution of the intendant that Richelieu had developed with so much success. Intendants were now a permanent part of government, and their duties expanded from their early responsibilities as coordinators and mediators into areas of policing and tax collection. It was through the intendants that the wishes of central government were made known in the provinces.

Though Louis XIV was well served, it was the king himself who set the tone for French absolutism. "If he was not the greatest king he was the best actor of majesty that ever filled the throne," wrote an English observer. The acting of majesty was central to Louis's rule. His residence at Versailles was the most glittering court of Europe, renowned for its beauty and splendor. It was built on a scale never before seen, and Louis took a personal interest in making sure it was fit for a king. When the court and king moved there permanently in 1682, Versailles became the envy of the Continent. But behind the imposing facade of Versailles stood a well-thought-out plan for domestic and international rule.

Louis XIV attempted to tame the French nobles by requiring their attendance at his court. Louis established a system of court etiquette so complex that constant study was necessary to prevent humiliation. While the nobility studied decorum, they could not plot rebellion. Leading noblemen of France rose at dawn so that they could watch Louis be awakened and hear him speak his first words. Dozens followed him from hall to gallery and from gallery to chamber as he washed, dressed, prayed, and ate. There was no greater concern than the king's health, unless it was the king's mood, which was as changeable as the weather.

During Louis's reign, France replaced Spain as the greatest nation in Europe. Massive royal patronage of art, science, and thought brought French culture to new heights. The French language replaced Latin as the universal European tongue. France was the richest and most populous European state, and Louis's absolute rule finally harnessed these resources to a single purpose. France became a commercial power rivaling the Netherlands, a naval power rivaling England, and a military power without peer. It was not only for effect that Louis took the image of the sun as his own. In court, in the nation, and throughout Europe everything revolved around him.

Louis XIV made his share of mistakes, which were magnified by the awe in which his opinions were held. His aggressive foreign policy ultimately bankrupted the crown. But without doubt, his greatest error was to persecute the Huguenots. As an absolute ruler, Louis believed that it was necessary to have absolute conformity and obedience. The existence of the Huguenots, with their separate communities and distinct forms of worship, seemed an affront to his authority.

Supporters of the monarchy celebrated the revocation of the Edict of Nantes in 1685 as an act of piety. Religious toleration in seventeenth-century Europe was still a policy of expediency rather than of principle. Even the English, who prided themselves on developing the concept, and the Dutch, who welcomed Jews to Amsterdam, would not officially tolerate Catholics. But the persecution of the Huguenots was a social and political disaster for France. Those who fled to other Protestant states spread the stories of atrocities that stiffened European resolve against Louis. Those who remained became an embittered minority who pulled at the fabric of the state at every chance. Nor did the official abolition of Protestantism have much effect upon its existence. Against these policies, the Huguenots held firm to their beliefs. There were well over one million French Protestants, undoubtedly the largest religious minority in any state. Huguenots simply went underground, practicing their religion secretly and gradually replacing their numbers. No absolutism, however powerful, could succeed in eradicating religious beliefs.

Louis XIV gave his name to the age that he and his nation dominated, but he was not its only towering figure. The Great Elector, Peter the Great, Louis the Great: so they were judged by posterity, kings who had forged nations for a new age. Their style of rule showed the royal state at its height, still revolving around the king but more and more dependent upon permanent institutions of government that followed their own imperatives. The absolute state harnessed the economic and intellectual resources of the nation to the political

will of the monarch. It did so to ensure survival in a dangerous world. But while monarchs ruled as well as reigned, they did so by incorporating vital elements of the state into the process of government. In England the importance of the landholding classes was recognized in the constitutional powers of Parliament. The rights of the monarch were balanced against the liberties of the subject. In Prussia the military power of *die Junker* was asserted through command in the army, the most important institution of the state. In France, Louis XIV co-opted many nobles at his court, while he made use of a talented pool of lawyers, clergymen, and administrators in his government. A delicate balance existed between the will of the king and the will of the state, a balance that would soon lead these Continental powers into economic competition and military confrontation.

SUGGESTIONS FOR FURTHER READING

GENERAL READING

* Thomas Munck, *Seventeenth Century Europe, 1598–1700* (New York: St. Martin's Press, 1990). The most up-to-date survey.

* William Doyle, *The Old European Order* (Oxford: Oxford University Press, 1978). An important synthetic essay bristling with ideas.

* Geoffrey Parker, *Europe in Crisis 1598–1648* (London: William Collins and Sons, 1979). The best introduction to the period.

Perry Anderson, *Lineages of the Absolutist State* (London: NLB Books, 1974). A sociological study of the role of absolutism in the development of the western world.

THE RISE OF THE ROYAL STATE

* Graham Parry, *The Golden Age Restor'd* (New York: St. Martin's Press, 1981). A study of English court culture in the reigns of James I and Charles I.

J. H. Elliott and Jonathan Brown, *A Palace for a King* (New Haven, CT: Yale University Press, 1980). An outstanding work on the building and decorating of a Spanish palace.

* J. N. Figgis, *The Divine Right of Kings* (Cambridge: Cambridge University Press, 1914). Still the classic study of this central doctrine of political thought.

* J. H. Elliott, *Richelieu and Olivares* (Cambridge: Cambridge University Press, 1984). A brilliant dual portrait.

* Roger Lockyer, *Buckingham* (London: Longman, 1984). A stylish biography of the favorite of two monarchs.

THE CRISES OF THE ROYAL STATE

* Quentin Skinner, *The Foundations of Modern Political Thought*, 2 vols. (Cambridge: Cambridge University Press, 1978). A seminal work on the history of ideas from Machiavelli to Calvin.

* Perez Zagoin, *Rebels and Rulers*, 2 vols. (Cambridge: Cambridge University Press, 1982). A good survey of revolutions, civil war, and popular protests throughout Europe.

* Trevor Aston, ed., *Crisis in Europe 1600–1660* (Garden City, NY: Doubleday, 1967). Essays on the theme of a general crisis in Europe by distinguished historians.

G. Parker and L. Smith, eds., *The General Crisis of the Seventeenth Century* (London: Routledge & Kegan Paul, 1978). A collection of essays on the problem of the general crisis.

* Lawrence Stone, *The Causes of the English Revolution* (New York: Harper & Row, 1972). A vigorously argued explanation of why England experienced a revolution in the mid-seventeenth century.

* Ann Hughes, *The Causes of the English Civil War* (New York: St. Martin's Press, 1991). A lucid introduction to the scholarship of a vast subject.

* D. E. Underdown, *Pride's Purge* (London: Allen and Unwin, 1985). The most important work on the politics of the English Revolution.

THE ZENITH OF THE ROYAL STATE

* H. W. Koch, *A History of Prussia* (London: Longman, 1978). A comprehensive study of Prussian history with an excellent chapter on the Great Elector.

* Paul Dukes, *The Making of Russian Absolutism* (London: Longman, 1982). A thorough survey of Russian history in the seventeenth and eighteenth centuries.

* Vasili Klyuchevsky, *Peter the Great* (Boston: Beacon Press, 1984). A classic work, still the best study of Peter.

* W. E. Brown, *The First Bourbon Century in France* (London: University of London Press, 1971). A good introduction to French political history.

* William Beik, *Absolutism and Society in Seventeenth Century France* (Cambridge: Cambridge University Press, 1985). The single best study of the government of a French province in the seventeenth century.

Peter Burke, *The Fabrication of Louis XIV* (New Haven, CT: Yale University Press, 1992). A compelling account of a man and a myth.

* John Wolf, *Louis XIV* (New York: Norton, 1968). An outstanding biography of the Sun King.

* Indicates paperback edition available.

CHAPTER 18

Science and Commerce in Europe, 1550–1700

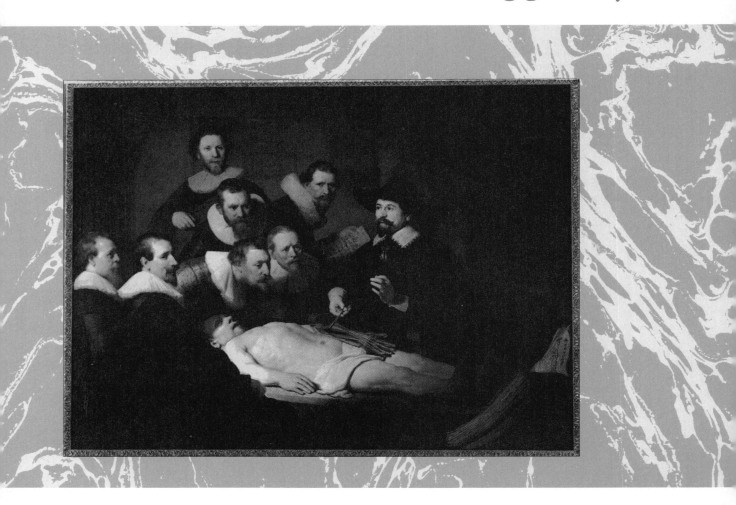

REMBRANDT'S LESSONS

By the early seventeenth century interest in scientific investigation had spread out from narrow circles of specialists to embrace educated men and women. One of the more spectacular demonstrations of new knowledge was public dissection, by law performed only on the corpses of criminals. Here the secrets of the human body were revealed both for those who were in training as physicians and for those who had the requisite fee and strong stomach. Curiosity about the human body was becoming a mark of education. New publications, both scientific and popular, spread ancient wisdom as well as the controversial findings of the moderns. Pictures drawn on the basis of dissections filled the new medical texts like the one on the stand at the feet of the corpse in *The Anatomy Lesson of Dr. Nicolaes Tulp* (1632) by Rembrandt van Rijn (1606–69).

Dr. Tulp's anatomy lesson was not meant for the public. In fact, those gathered around him in various poses of concentration were not students at all. They were members of the Amsterdam company of surgeons, the physicians' guild of the early seventeenth century. The sitters had commissioned the picture, which was a celebration of themselves as well as of the noted Professor Tulp. They hired the young Rembrandt to compose the picture with the assurance that each of the sitters (whose names are written on the paper one of them holds in his hand) would appear as if he alone were the subject of a portrait. Rembrandt succeeded beyond expectation. Each individual was given his due. The expressions on their faces as much as their physical characteristics mark each one out from the group. Yet the portraits were only one part of the painting. The scene that Rembrandt depicted unified them. They became a group by

their participation in the anatomy lesson. Rembrandt has chosen a moment of drama to stop the action. Dr. Tulp is demonstrating how the gesture he is making with his left hand looks in the dissected arm of the gruesome cadaver. The central figures of the group are rapt in attention though only one of them is actually observing the procedure of the anatomy. Each listens to Tulp, comparing his own experience and knowledge to that of the professor and the text that stands open.

The Anatomy Lesson established the twenty-five-year-old Rembrandt as one of the most gifted and fashionable painters in Amsterdam. If any people could be said to be consumers of art in seventeenth-century Europe, it was the Dutch. Artists flourished and pictures abounded. Travelers were struck by the presence of artwork in both public and private places and in the homes of even moderately prosperous people. The group portrait, which Rembrandt brought to new levels of expression, was becoming a favorite genre. It was used to celebrate the leaders of Dutch society who, unlike the leaders of most other European states, were not princes and aristocrats, but rather merchants, guild officials, and professionals. Rembrandt captured a spirit of civic pride in his group portraits. Here it was the surgeons' guild; later it would be the leaders of the cloth merchants' guild, another time a militia company.

Like the leaders of the surgeons' guild who commissioned their own portrait, which hung in their company's hall, the Dutch Republic swelled with pride in the seventeenth century. Its long war with Spain was finally over, and it was time to celebrate the birth of a new state. The Dutch were a trading people, and their trade flourished as much in times of war as in times of peace. Their ships traveled to all parts of the globe, and after a century of conflict they dominated the great luxury trades of the age. Bankers and merchants were the backbone of the Dutch Republic. Yet this republic of merchants was also one of the great cultural centers of the Continent. Intellectual creativity was cultivated in the same manner as was a trading partner. In the burgeoning port of Amsterdam, the fastest growing city in Europe, artists, philosophers, and mathematicians lived in close proximity. The free exchange of ideas made Amsterdam home to those exiled for their beliefs. The Dutch practiced religious toleration as did no one else. Catholics, Protestants, and Jews all were welcomed to the Republic and found that they could pursue their own paths without persecution. Freedom of thought and freedom of expression helped develop a new spirit of scientific inquiry, like that portrayed in *The Anatomy Lesson of Dr. Nicolaes Tulp*.

The New Science

"And new Philosophy calls all in doubt,/ The element of fire is quite put out;/ The sun is lost and the earth, and no man's wit/ Can well direct him where to look for it." So wrote the English poet John Donne (1572–1631) about one of the most astonishing yet perplexing moments in the history of Western thought: the emergence of the new science. It was astonishing because it seemed truly new. The discoveries of the stargazers, like those of the sea explorers, challenged people's most basic assumptions and beliefs. Men dropping balls from towers or peering at the skies through a glass claimed that they had disproved thousands of years of certainty about the nature of the universe. But it was perplexing because it seemed to loosen the moorings of everything that educated people thought they knew about their world. Nothing could be more disorienting than to challenge common sense. One needed to do little more than wake up in the morning to know that the sun moved from east to west while the earth stood still. But mathematics, experimentation, and deduction were needed to understand that the earth was in constant motion and that it revolved around the sun.

The scientific revolution was the opening of a new era in European history. After two centuries of classical revival, European thinkers had finally come against the limits of ancient knowledge. Ancient wisdom had served Europeans well, and it was not to be discarded lightly. But one by one, the certainties of the past were being called into question. The explanations of the universe and the natural world that had been advanced by Aristotle and codified by his followers no longer seemed adequate. There were too many contradictions between theory and observation, too many things that did not fit. Yet breaking the hold of Aristotelianism was no easy task. A full century was to pass before even learned people would accept the proofs that the earth revolved around the sun. Even then, the most famous of them —Galileo—had to recant these views or be condemned as a heretic.

The two essential characteristics of the new science were that it was materialistic and mathematical. Its materialism was contained in the realization that the universe is composed of matter in motion. This meant that the stars and planets were not made of some perfect ethereal substance but of the same matter that was found on earth. They were thus subject to the same rules of motion as were earthly objects. The mathematics of the new science was contained in the realization that calculation had to replace common sense as the basis for understanding the universe. Mathematics itself was transformed with the invention of logarithms, analytic geometry, and calculus. More importantly, scientific experimentation took the form of measuring repeatable phenomena. When Galileo attempted

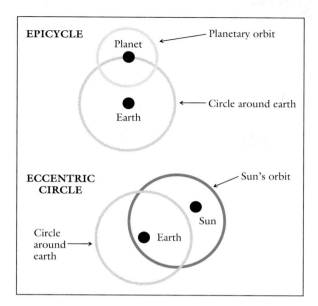

one. The heavens were unchangeable and therefore they were better than the earth. The sun, moon, and planets were all faultless spheres, unblemished and immune from decay. Their motion was circular because the circle was the perfect form of motion. The earth was at the center of the universe because it was the heaviest planet and because it was at the center of the great chain of being, between the underworld of spirits and the upperworld of gods. The second advantage to the Aristotelian worldview was that it was easily incorporated into Christianity. Aristotle's description of the heavens as being composed of a closed system of crystalline rings that held the sun, moon, and planets in their circular orbits around the earth left room for God and the angels to reside just beyond the last ring.

There were, of course, problems with Aristotle's explanation of the universe as it was preserved in the work of Ptolemy, the greatest of the Greek astronomers. For one thing if the sun revolved in a perfect circle around the earth, then why were the seasons not perfectly equal? If the planets all revolved around the earth in circles, then why did they look nearer or farther, brighter or darker at different times of the year? To solve these problems, a host of ingenious hypotheses were advanced. Perhaps the sun revolved around the earth in an eccentric circle, that is, a circle not centered on the earth. This would account for the differing lengths of seasons. Perhaps the planets revolved in circles that

to develop a theory of acceleration, he rolled a brass ball down an inclined plane and recorded the time and distance of its descent one hundred times before he was satisfied with his results.

The new science was also a Europe-wide movement. The spirit of scientific inquiry flourished everywhere. The main contributors to astronomy were a Pole, a Dane, a German, and an Italian. The founder of medical chemistry was Swiss, the best anatomist was Belgian. England contributed most of all—the founders of modern chemistry, biology, and physics. By and large, these scientists operated outside the traditional seats of learning at the universities. Though most were university-trained and not a few taught the traditional Aristotelian subjects, theirs was not an academic movement. Rather it was a public one made possible by the printing press. Once published, findings became building blocks for scientists throughout the Continent and from one generation to the next. Many discoveries were made in the search for practical solutions to ordinary problems, and what was learned fueled advances in technology and the natural sciences. The new science gave seventeenth-century Europeans a sense that they might finally master the forces of nature.

Heavenly Revolutions

There was much to be said for Aristotle's understanding of the world, for his cosmology. For one thing, it was harmonious. It incorporated a view of the physical world that coincided with a view of the spiritual and moral

This chart of the heavens was engraved by Andreas Cellarius in 1660. It portrays the heliocentric universe described by Nicolaus Copernicus and accepted by Galileo. Earth and Jupiter are shown with moons orbiting them.

COPERNICUS ON THE REVOLUTIONS OF HEAVENLY SPHERES

■ *Nicolaus Copernicus was born in Poland and educated at the University of Kraków, which had one of the greatest mathematics faculties of the age. He prepared for a career in the Church, but his abiding interest was the study of astronomy. Through observation and calculation, Copernicus worked out a heliocentric view of the universe in which Earth revolved on an axis and orbited the Sun. His path-breaking work was not published until the year of his death, and he was fully aware of the implications of his discovery.*

I was induced to think of a method of computing the motions of the spheres by nothing else than the knowledge that the Mathematicians are inconsistent in these investigations.

For, first, the mathematicians are so unsure of the movements of the Sun and Moon that they cannot even explain or observe the constant length of the seasonal year. Secondly, in determining the motions of these and of the other five planets, they use neither the same principles and hypotheses nor the same demonstrations of the apparent motions and revolutions. . . . Nor have they been able thereby to discern or deduce the principal thing—namely the shape of the Universe and the unchangeable symmetry of its parts . . .

Thus assuming motions, which in my work I ascribe to the Earth, by long and frequent observations I have at last discovered that, if the motions of the rest of the planets be brought into relation with the circulation of the Earth and be reckoned in proportion to the circles of each planet, not only do their phenomena presently ensue, but the orders and magnitudes of all stars and spheres, nay the heavens themselves, become so bound together that nothing in any part thereof could be moved from its place without producing confusion of all the other parts of the Universe as a whole.

---

rested on a circle around the earth. Then when the planet revolved within the larger circle, it would seem nearer and brighter, and when it revolved outside it, it would seem farther away and darker. This was the theory of epicycles.

In the 1490s, Nicolaus Copernicus (1473–1543) came to the Polish University of Kraków, which had one of the leading mathematical faculties in Europe. There they taught the latest astronomical theories and vigorously debated the existence of eccentric circles and epicycles. Copernicus came to Kraków for a liberal arts education before pursuing a degree in Church law. He became fascinated by astronomy and puzzled by the debate over planetary motion. Copernicus believed, like Aristotle, that the simplest explanations were the best. If the sun was at the center of the universe and the earth simply another planet in orbit, then many of the most elaborate explanations of planetary motion were unnecessary. "At rest, in the middle of everything is the sun," Copernicus wrote in *On the Revolutions of the Heavenly Spheres* (1543). "For in this most beautiful temple who would place this lamp in another or better position than that from which it can light up the whole thing at the same time?" Because Copernicus accepted most of the rest of the

traditional Aristotelian explanation, especially the belief that the planets moved in circles, his sun-centered universe was only slightly better at predicting the position of the planets than the traditional earth-centered one, but Copernicus's idea stimulated other astronomers to make new calculations.

Under the patronage of the king of Denmark, Tycho Brahe (1546–1601) built a large observatory to study planetary motion. In 1572, Brahe discovered a nova, a brightly burning star that was previously unknown. This discovery challenged the idea of an immutable universe composed of crystalline rings. In 1577 the appearance of a comet cutting through the supposedly impenetrable rings punched another hole into the old cosmology. Brahe's own views were a hybrid of old and new. He believed that all planets but the earth revolved around the sun and that the sun and the planets revolved around a fixed earth. To demonstrate this theory, Brahe and his students compiled the largest and most accurate mathematical tables of planetary motion yet known. From this research, Brahe's pupil, Johannes Kepler (1571–1630), one of the great mathematicians of the age, formulated laws of planetary motion. Kepler discovered that planets orbited the sun in an elliptical rather than a

THE STARRY MESSENGER

■ *No single individual is as much associated with the scientific revolution as Galileo. He made formative contributions to mathematics, physics, and astronomy, but he also served as a lightning rod for the dissemination of the newest ideas. He popularized the work of Copernicus and was condemned by the Catholic church for his views and publications. He ended his life under house arrest. Among his other accomplishments, Galileo was the first to use a telescope to make scientific observations.*

About ten months ago a report reached my ears that a certain Fleming had constructed a spyglass by means of which visible objects, though very distant from the eye of the observer, were distinctly seen as if nearby. Of this truly remarkable effect several experiences were related, to which some persons gave credence while others denied them. A few days later the report was confirmed to me in a letter from a noble Frenchman at Paris, Jacques Badovere, which caused me to apply myself wholeheartedly to inquire into the means by which I might arrive at the invention of a similar instrument. This I did shortly afterwards, my basis being the theory of refraction. First I prepared a tube of lead, at the ends of which I fitted two glass lenses, both plane on one side while on the other side one was spherically convex and the other concave. Then placing my eye near the concave lens I perceived objects satisfactorily large and near, for they appeared three times closer and nine times larger than when seen with the naked eye alone. Next I constructed another one, more accurate, which represented objects as enlarged more than sixty times. Finally, sparing neither labor nor expense, I succeeded in constructing for myself so excellent an instrument that objects seen by means of it appeared nearly one thousand times larger and over thirty times closer than when regarded with our natural vision.

It would be superfluous to enumerate the number and importance of the advantages of such an instrument at sea as well as on land. But forsaking terrestrial observations, I turned to celestial ones, and first I saw the moon from as near at hand as if it were scarcely two terrestrial radii . . . Let us speak first of that surface of the moon which faces us. For greater clarity I distinguish two parts of this surface, a lighter and a darker; the lighter part seems to surround and to pervade the whole hemisphere, while the darker part discolors the moon's surface like a kind of cloud, and makes it appear covered with spots . . . From observation of these spots repeated many times I have been led to the opinion and conviction that the surface of the moon is not smooth, uniform, and precisely spherical as a great number of philosophers believe it (and the other heavenly bodies) to be, but is uneven, rough, and full of cavities and prominences, being not unlike the face of the earth, relieved by chains of mountains and deep valleys.

From Galileo, *The Starry Messenger.*

---

circular path. This accounted for their movements nearer and farther from the earth. More importantly, he demonstrated that there was a precise mathematical relationship between the speed with which a planet revolved and its distance from the sun. Kepler's findings supported the view that the solar system was heliocentric and that the heavens, like the earth, were made of matter that was subject to physical laws.

What Kepler demonstrated mathematically, the Italian astronomer Galileo Galilei (1564-1642) confirmed by observation. Creating a telescope by using magnify-

ing lenses and a long tube, Galileo saw parts of the heavens that had never been dreamt of before. In 1610 he discovered four moons of Jupiter, proving conclusively that not all heavenly bodies revolved around the earth. He observed the landscape of the earth's moon and described it as full of mountains, valleys, and rivers. It was of the same imperfect form as the earth itself. He even found spots on the sun, which suggested that it, too, was composed of ordinary matter. Many of Galileo's scientific discoveries had to do with motion—he was the first to posit a law of inertia—but his greatest

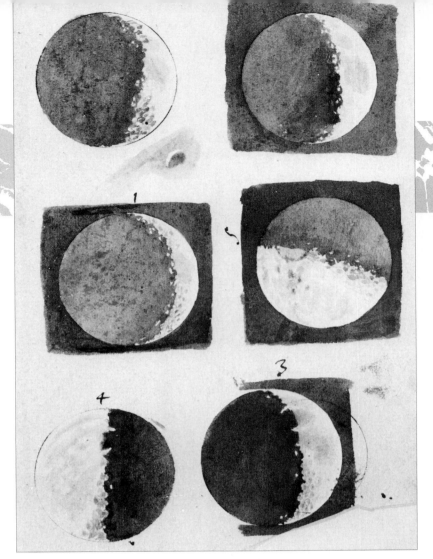

These drawings of Galileo's moon observations accompanied the first draft of the Starry Messenger. *Galileo correctly interpreted the bright spots that appear on the dark part of the moon as mountain peaks.*

*T*he Trials of Galileo

For eight years he had held his peace. Since 1616 he had bided his time, waiting for a change in the attitudes of the Catholic authorities or, as he believed, waiting for reason to prevail. For a time he had even abandoned his astronomical investigations for the supposedly safer fields of motion and physics. Even there Aristotle had been wrong. No matter what he touched, his reason showed him that the conclusions of Aristotle, the conclusions adopted and supported by the Roman Catholic church, were wrong. Now finally, with the accession of Pope Urban VIII, old Cardinal Barbarini, who was himself a mathematician, Galileo felt confident that he could resume his writing and publishing.

Galileo's rebellion began early, when he decided to study mathematics rather than medicine. Galileo was fascinated with the manipulation of numbers and by the age of twenty-five was teaching at the University of Pisa. There he began to conduct experiments to measure rates of motion. Galileo was soon in trouble with his colleagues and was forced to leave Pisa for Padua.

It was in Padua that his real difficulties began. After seeing a small prototype made in Holland, Galileo developed a telescope that could magnify objects to thirty times their size, which made it possible to see clearly the stars and planets that had been only dimly perceptible before. In 1610 Galileo had looked at the moon and discovered that its properties were similar to those of the earth. He had seen four moons of Jupiter, the first conclusive proof that there were heavenly bodies that did not revolve around the earth. Even before he had gazed at the stars, Galileo was persuaded that Copernicus must be right in arguing that the earth revolved around the sun. Now he believed he had irrefutable proof, the proof of his own eyes. From the publication of the *Starry Messenger* in 1610, Galileo became the most active and best known advocate of the Copernican universe.

In 1616 he was called to Rome and warned about his opinions. Belief in the theories of Copernicus was heresy, he was told. If Galileo held or maintained them, he would incur a heavy penalty. The Church accepted unequivocally the Ptolemaic explanations of the structure of the universe and could cite innumerable passages in the Bible to support them. It was willful and stubborn to oppose official doctrine, doctrine that had been frequently and fully examined. At first it looked like Galileo would be silenced, but the erudite Cardinal Bellarmine, to whom the case had been assigned, wished only to caution him. Galileo might still examine the Copernican hypotheses, he might still discuss them with his learned colleagues, as long as he did not hold or maintain them to be true.

For eight years he kept his peace. When he decided to write again, it was with the belief that things were changing. He created a dialogue between a Ptolemaist and a Copernican. Let the one challenge the other on the most basic points just as if they were in formal academic dispute. How did each explain the most difficult things that there were to explain, the existence of spots on the sun or the movement of the tides. Especially the tides. If the earth stood still and the sun moved, why were there tides in the seas that moved with such regularity that they could be predicted?

Galileo was no heretic. He had no desire to challenge the Church. He would not print his tract anonymously in a Protestant country. Rather he would create a true dialogue, one with which not even the most narrow-minded censor of the Roman church could find fault. He submitted his book to the official censor in Rome for approval, then to the official censor in Florence. The censors struck out passages, changed some words, and deleted others. They demanded a new preface, even a new title: *A Dialogue Between the Two Great Systems of the World*. Finally, in 1632 the book went to press and it was an immediate success.

Indeed it was a success that could not be ignored. The Jesuits, who regarded learning and education as their special mission, demanded that action be taken against Galileo. Their teachings had been held up to ridicule; their official astronomers had been challenged; their doctrines had been repudiated. There was much at stake. Galileo's book had not been the vigorous academic dispute that he promised and it had not concluded with the triumph of Church doctrine over the speculations of Copernicus. No, it had been advocacy. Anyone could see where the author's true sympathies lay. The character chosen to speak the part of Aristotle was not named Simplicio for nothing. Though this was the name of an ancient Aristotelian, it was also a perfect description for the arguments that the speaker advanced. Especially in the matter of the tides, Galileo had reduced the Aristotelian position to nonsense. The Jesuits brought their case directly to the pope and won an investigation, an investigation that they knew would end with Galileo's condemnation.

Though initially Pope Urban VIII was reluctant to prosecute the seventy-year-old astronomer, "the light of Italy," ultimately he had no choice. The great war to stamp out heresy was going badly for the Church. The pope needed the support of the Jesuits in Vienna and in Madrid much more than he needed the support of a scientist who had seen the moons of Jupiter. Nevertheless, when the case was turned over to the Inquisition, it proved weak in law. Galileo had only to present the book itself to show that he had received the official sanction of not one, but two censors of the Roman Catholic church. If there was still anything in his book that offended, could the fault be his alone? The argument stymied the prosecutors, who were forced to find evidence where none existed. Resurrecting the agreement between Galileo and Bellarmine, they attempted to make it say that Galileo was under an absolute ban from even discussing the Copernican theories. Either Galileo would agree to recant his views, admit his errors, and beg the forgiveness of the Church or he would be tried and burned as a heretic. But though he could be forced to recant his view that the earth orbits the sun, Galileo could not be forced to change his mind.

After his recantation, Galileo was sentenced to live out his days under house arrest. Five years after his death in 1642, his greatest scientific work, *The Two New Sciences*, was smuggled out of Italy and printed anonymously in Holland in 1648.

contribution to the new science was his popularization of the Copernican theory.

As news of his experiments and discoveries spread, Galileo became famous throughout the Continent, and his support for heliocentrism became a celebrated cause. In 1616 the Roman Catholic church cautioned him against promoting his views. In 1633, a year after publishing his *A Dialogue Between the Two Great Systems of the World*, Galileo was tried by the Inquisition and forced specifically to recant the idea that the earth moves. He spent the rest of his life under house arrest. But Galileo insisted that there was nothing in the new science that was anti-Christian. He rejected the view that his discoveries refuted the Bible, arguing that the Bible was often difficult to interpret and that nature was another way in which God revealed himself. (See Special Feature, "The Trials of Galileo," pp. 534–535.)

The Natural World

The new science originated from a number of traditions that were anything but scientific. Inquiry into nature and the environment grew out of the discipline of natural philosophy and was nurtured by spiritual and mystical traditions. Much of the most useful medical knowledge had come from the studies of herbalists; the most reliable calculations of planetary motion had come from astrologers. Though the first laboratories and observatories were developed in aid of the new science, practice in them was as much magical as experimental. For those attempting to unlock the mysteries of the universe, there was no separation between magic and science. Some of the most characteristic features of modern science, such as the stress on experimentation and empirical observation, developed only gradually. What was new about the new science was the determination to develop systems of thought that could help humans understand and control their environment. Thus there was a greater openness and spirit of cooperation about discoveries than in the past, when experiments were conducted secretly and results were kept hidden away.

Aristotelianism was not the only philosophical system to explain the nature and composition of the universe. During the Renaissance the writings of Plato attracted a number of Italian humanists, most notably Marsilio Ficino (1433–99) and Pico della Mirandola (1463–94). In Florence, they taught Plato's theory that the world was composed of ideas and forms, which were hidden by the physical properties of objects. These Neoplatonic humanists believed that the architect of the universe possessed the spirit of a geometrician and

that the perfect disciplines were music and mathematics. These elements of Neoplatonism created an impetus for the mathematically based studies of the new scientists. They were especially important among the astronomers, who used both calculation and geometry in exploring the heavens. But they served as well to bolster the sciences of alchemy and astrology. Alchemy was the use of fire in the study of metals, an effort to find the essence of things through their purification. While medieval alchemists mostly attempted to find gold and silver as the essence of lead and iron, the new experimentation focused on the properties of metals in general. Astrology was the study of the influence of the stars on human behavior, calculated by planetary motion and the harmony of the heavenly spheres. Astrologers made careful calculations based on the movement of the planets and were deeply involved in the new astronomy. The Neoplatonic emphasis upon mathematics also accorded support for a variety of mystical sciences based on numerology. These were efforts to predict events from the combination of particular numbers.

The most influential of these mystical traditions was that associated with Hermes Trismegistus (Thrice Greatest), an Egyptian who was reputed to have lived in the second century C.E. and to have known the secrets of the universe. A body of writings mistakenly attributed to Hermes was discovered during the Renaissance and formed the basis of a Hermetic tradition. The core of Hermetic thinking centered on the idea of a universal spirit that was present in all objects and that spontaneously revealed itself. Kepler was one of many of the new scientists influenced by Hermeticism. His efforts to understand planetary motion derived from his search for a unifying spirit.

A combination of Neoplatonic and Hermetic traditions was central to the work of one of the most curious of the new scientists, the Swiss alchemist Paracelsus (1493–1541). Paracelsus studied with a leading German alchemist before following in his father's footsteps by becoming a physician. Though he worked as a doctor, his true vocation was alchemy, and he conducted innumerable experiments designed to extract the essence of particular metals. Paracelsus taught that all matter was composed of combinations of three principles: salt, sulfur, and mercury. This view replaced the traditional belief in the four elements of earth, water, fire, and air.

The Paracelsian system transformed ideas about chemistry and medicine. Paracelsus rejected the theory that disease was caused by an imbalance in the humors of the body, the standard view of Galen, the great Greek physician of the second century C.E. Instead, Paracelsus

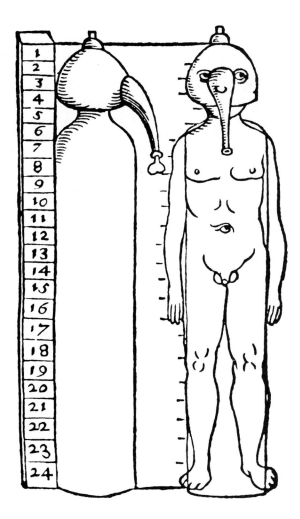

Paracelsus devised this "anatomical furnace" in which a patient's urine was distilled in a measuring cylinder, the parts of which correspond in length and width to those of the human body. Thus the body was "chemically dissected" for the benefit of the patient.

argued that each disease had its own cause, which could be diagnosed and remedied. Where traditional doctors treated disease by bloodletting or sweating to correct the imbalance of humors, Paracelsus prescribed the ingestion of particular chemicals, especially distilled metals like mercury, arsenic, and antimony, and he favored administering them at propitious astrological moments.

Although established physicians and medical faculties rejected Paracelsian cures and methods, his influence spread among ordinary practitioners. It ultimately had a profound impact on the studies of Robert Boyle (1627–91), an Englishman who helped establish the basis of the science of chemistry. Boyle devoted his ener-

gies to raising the study of medical chemistry above that of merely providing recipes for the cure of disease. He worked carefully and recorded each step in his experiments. Boyle's first important work, *The Sceptical Chymist* (1661), attacked both the Aristotelian and Paracelsian views of the basic components of the natural world. Boyle rejected both the four humors and the three principles. Instead he favored an atomic explanation in which matter "consisted of little particles of all sizes and shapes." Changes in these particles, which would later be identified as the chemical elements, resulted in changes in matter. Boyle's most important experiments were with gases—a word invented by Paracelsus. He formulated the relationship between the volume and pressure of a gas (Boyle's Law), and he invented the air pump.

The new spirit of scientific inquiry also affected medical studies. The study of anatomy through dissection had helped the new scientists reject many of the descriptive errors in Galen's texts. The Belgian doctor Andreas Vesalius (1514–64) published the first modern set of anatomical drawings in 1543. But accurate knowledge of the composition of the body did not mean better understanding of its operation. Dead bodies didn't easily yield the secrets of life. Much of what was known about matters as common as reproduction was an inadequate combination of ancient wisdom and the practical experiences of midwives and doctors.

One of the greatest mysteries was the method by which blood moved through the vital organs. It was generally believed that the blood originated in the liver, traveled to the right side of the heart, and then passed to the left side through invisible pores. William Harvey (1578–1657), an Englishman who had received his medical education in Italy, offered an entirely different explanation. Harvey's main interest was in studying the anatomy of the heart. He examined hearts in more than forty species before concluding that the heart worked like a pump or, as he put it, a water bellows. Harvey observed that the valves of the heart chambers allowed the blood to flow in only one direction. He thus concluded that the blood was pumped by the heart and circulated throughout the entire body.

The greatest of all English scientists was the mathematician and physicist Sir Isaac Newton (1642–1727). It was Newton who brought together the various strands of the new science. He made a great study of Hermetic writings and from them revived the mystical notions of attraction and repulsion. He merged the materialists and Hermeticists, the astronomers and astrologers, the chemists and alchemists. Newton was the first to

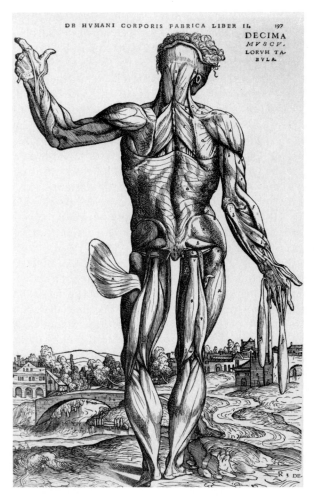

DE HVMANI CORPORIS FABRICA LIBER II.   197

DECIMA
MVSCV.
LORVM TA.
BVLA.

Tenth "Muscle plate" from Andreas Vesalius's De Humani Corporis Fabrica (Concerning the Fabric of the Human Body), *published in 1543. The muscles of the back of the body are laid bare.*

lated the concept of force and his famous laws of motion: (1) that objects at rest or in uniform linear motion remain in such a state unless acted upon by an external force; (2) that changes in motion are proportional to force; and (3) that for every action there is an equal and opposite reaction. From these laws of motion, Newton advanced one step further. If the world was no more than matter in motion and if all motion was subject to the same laws, then the movement of the planets could be explained in the same way as the movement of an apple falling from a tree. There was a mathematical relationship between attraction and repulsion, a universal gravitation as Newton called it, that governed the movement of all objects. Newton's theory of gravity joined Kepler's astronomy and Galileo's physics. The mathematical, materialistic world of the new science was now complete.

Science Enthroned

By the middle of the seventeenth century, the new science was firmly established throughout Europe. Royal and noble patrons supported the enterprise by paying some of the costs of equipment and experimentation. Royal observatories were created for the astronomers, colleges of physicians for the doctors, laboratories for the chemists. Both England and France established royal societies of learned scientists to meet together and discuss their discoveries. The French Académie des Sciences (1666) was composed of twenty salaried scientists and an equal number of students, divided among the different branches of scientific learning. The English Royal Society (1662) boasted some of the greatest minds of the age. It was there that Newton first made public his most important discoveries. Scientific bodies were also formed outside the traditional universities. These were the so-called mechanics colleges, like Gresham College in London, where the practical applications of mathematics and physics were taught.

The establishment of learned scientific societies and practical colleges fulfilled part of the program advocated by Sir Francis Bacon (1561–1626), one of the leading supporters of scientific research in England. In *The Advancement of Learning* (1605), Bacon proposed a scientific method through inductive, empirical experimentation. Bacon believed that experiments should be carefully recorded so that results were both reliable and repeatable, and in his numerous writings he stressed the practical impact of scientific discovery.

Bacon's support for the new science contrasts markedly with the stance taken by the Roman Catholic

understand the composition of light, the first to develop a calculus, the first to build a reflecting telescope. He made stunning contributions to the sciences of optics, physics, astronomy, and mathematics, and his magnum opus, *Mathematical Principles of Natural Philosophy* (1687), is one of a handful of the most important scientific works ever composed. Most importantly, Newton solved the single most perplexing problem: if the world was composed of matter in motion, what was motion?

Though Galileo had first developed a theory of inertia, the idea that a body at rest stays at rest, most materialists believed that motion was inherent in objects. In contrast, Newton believed that motion was the result of the interaction of objects and that it could be calculated mathematically. From his experiments he formu-

church. Embattled by the Reformation and the wars of religion, the Church had taken the offensive in preserving the core of its heritage. By the early seventeenth century the missionary work of the Jesuits had won many reconversions and had halted the advance of Protestantism. Now the new science appeared to be another heresy. Not only did it confound ancient wisdom and contradict Church teachings, but it was also a lay movement that was neither directed nor controlled from Rome. The trial of Galileo slowed the momentum of scientific investigation in Catholic countries and starkly posed the conflict between authority and knowledge. But the stand taken by the Church was based on more than narrow self-interest. Ever since Copernicus had published his views, a new skepticism had emerged among European intellectuals. Every year new theories competed with old ones, and dozens of contradictory explanations for the most common phenomena were advanced and debated. The skeptics concluded that nothing was known and nothing was knowable. Their position led inevitably to the most shocking of all possible views: atheism. But there was no necessary link between the new science and an attack upon established religion. So Galileo had argued all along. Few of the leading scientists saw a contradiction between their studies and their faith. Still by the middle of the century attacks upon the Church were increasing and some blamed the new science for them. Thus it was altogether fitting that one of the leading mathematicians of the day should provide the method for harmonizing faith and reason.

René Descartes (1596–1650) was trained in one of the best Jesuit schools in France before taking a law degree in 1616. He entered military service in the Dutch Republic and after the outbreak of the Thirty Years' War, in the Duke of Bavaria's army. Descartes was keenly interested in mathematics, and during his military travels he met and was tutored by a leading Dutch mathematician. For the first time he learned of the new scientific discoveries and of the advances made in mathematics. In 1619 he dreamt of discovering the scientific principles of universal knowledge. After this dream, Descartes returned to Holland and began to develop his system. He was on the verge of publishing his views when he learned of Galileo's condemnation. Reading Galileo's *Dialogue Between the Two Great Systems of the World* (1632), Descartes discovered that he shared many of the same opinions and had worked out mathematical proofs for them, but he refrained from publishing until 1637, when he brought out the *Discourse on Method*.

In the *Discourse on Method*, Descartes demonstrated how skepticism could be used to produce certainty. He began by declaring that he would reject everything that could not be clearly proven beyond doubt. Thus he rejected the material world, the testimony of his senses, all known or imagined opinions. He was left only with doubt. But what was doubt, if not thought, and what was thought, if not the workings of his mind? The only thing of which he could be certain, then, was that he had a mind. Thus, his famous formulation: "I think, therefore I am." From this first certainty came another, the knowledge of perfectibility. He knew that he was imperfect and that a perfect being had to have placed that knowledge within him. Therefore, a perfect being—God—existed.

Descartes's philosophy, known as Cartesianism, rested on the dual existence of matter and mind. Matter was the material world subject to the incontrovertible laws of mathematics. Mind was the spirit of the creator. Descartes was one of the leading mechanistic philosophers, believing that all objects operated in accord with natural laws. He invented analytic geometry and made important contributions to the sciences of optics and physics upon which Newton would later build. Yet it was in his proof that the new science could be harmonized with the old religion that Descartes made his greatest contribution.

Astronomy, chemistry, biology, and physics all had their modern origins in the seventeenth century. Because thinking about the natural world was integrated, the discoveries in one discipline made possible breakthroughs in another. The mathematical calculations of Kepler, the observational astronomy of Galileo, and the experimental biology of Harvey fed upon an atmosphere of intellectual curiosity and disciplined scientific enquiry. Though many of the breakthrough discoveries of the new scientists would not find practical use for centuries, the spirit of discovery was to have great impact in an age of commerce and capital. The quest for mathematical certainty and prime movers led directly to improvements in agriculture, mining, navigation, and industrial activity. The new sense of control over the material world provided a new optimism for generations of Europeans.

Empires of Goods

Under the watchful eye of the European states, a worldwide marketplace for the exchange of commodities had been created. First the Dutch and then the English had established monopoly companies to engage in exotic trades in the East. The Spanish and Portuguese, then the English and French had established colonial dependencies in the Atlantic, which they carefully nurtured in hope of economic gain. Protected trade had flourished beyond the wildest dreams of its promoters. Luxury commodities became staples; new commodities became luxuries. Trade enhanced the material life of all European peoples, though it came at great cost to the Asians, Africans, and Latin Americans whose labor and raw materials were converted into the new crazes of consumption.

Though long-distance trade was never as important to the European economy as was inland and intracontinental trade, its development in the seventeenth and eighteenth centuries had a profound impact upon lifestyles, economic policy, and ultimately on warfare. It was the Dutch who became the first great commercial power. Their achievements were based on innovative techniques, rational management, and a social and cultural environment that supported mercantile activities. Dutch society was freer than any other, open to new capital, new ventures, and new ideas. The Dutch innovated in the organization of trade by developing the concept of the entrepôt, a place where goods were brought for storage before being exchanged. They pioneered in finance by establishing the Bank of Amsterdam. They led in shipbuilding by developing the flyboat, a long flat-hulled vessel designed specifically to carry bulky cargoes like grain. They traded around the globe with the largest mercantile fleet yet known. It was not until the end of the seventeenth century that England and France surpassed the Dutch. This reversal owed less to new innovations than it did to restrictions on trade. Because the Dutch dominated the European economy, the French and English began to pass laws to eliminate Dutch competition. The English banned imports carried in Dutch ships; the French banned Dutch products. Both policies cut heavily into the Dutch superiority and both ultimately resulted in commercial warfare.

The Marketplace of the World

By the seventeenth century, long-distance trade had begun to integrate the regions of the world into a single marketplace. Slaves bought in Africa mined silver in South America. The bullion was shipped to Spain, where it was distributed across Europe. Most went to Amsterdam to settle Spanish debts, Dutch bankers having replaced the Italians as the paymasters of Europe. From Holland the silver traveled east to the Baltic Sea, the Dutch lifeline where vital stores of grain and timber were purchased for home consumption. By the 1630s over five hundred Dutch ships a year called at Gdansk,

The Geographer *by Jan Vermeer van Delft, 1669. a Dutch cartographer, holding dividers, is shown surrounded by charts, a globe, and other paraphernalia of his craft. Such cartographers combined the skills of artist and mathematician.*

the largest of the Baltic ports. From there the silver was transported to the interior of Poland and Russia, the great storehouses of European raw materials. Even more of this African-mined Spanish silver, traded by the Dutch, was carried to Asia to buy spices in the South Sea Islands, cottons in India, or silk in China. Millions of ounces flowed from America to Asia via the European trading routes. On the return voyage, brightly colored Indian cottons were traded in Africa to purchase slaves for the South American silver mines.

The remarkable fact about the expansion of European trade in the seventeenth and eighteenth centuries is that it took place as a result of the ingenuity of traders rather than because of technological or geographical discoveries. By the sixteenth century all the major trading routes had already been opened. The Spanish moved back and forth across the Atlantic; the Dutch and Portuguese sailed around the tip of Africa to the Indian Ocean. The Baltic trade connected the eastern and western parts of Europe as Danes, Swedes, and Dutch exchanged Polish and Russian raw materials for English and French manufactured goods. The Mediterranean, which had dominated world trade for centuries, was still a vital artery of intercontinental trade, but its role was

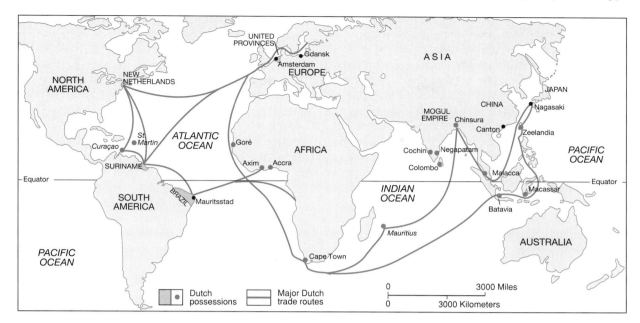

Dutch Trading Routes, ca. 1650

diminishing. In 1600 almost three-quarters of the Asian trade was still land-based, much of it carried through the Middle East to the Mediterranean. A century later nearly all Asian trade was carried directly to western Europe by Dutch and English vessels. Commercial power was shifting to the northern European states just as dramatically as was military and political power.

The technology associated with commerce achieved no breakthroughs to compare with the great transformations of the fifteenth century, when new techniques of navigation made transatlantic travel possible. It is certainly true that there continued to be improvements. The astronomical findings of the new science were a direct aid to navigation, as were the recorded experiences of so many practiced sea travelers. The materials used to make and maintain ships improved with the importation of pitch and tar from the east and with the greater availability of iron and copper from Scandinavia. It was the Dutch who made the single most important innovation in shipbuilding. To gain maximum profit from their journeys to the Baltic, the Dutch designed the so-called flyboats. Flyboats sacrificed speed and maneuverability, but they were cheap to build and could be manned by small crews. They carried no heavy armaments and were thus well adapted to the serene Baltic trade.

It was unspectacular developments like the flyboat that had such an impact on seventeenth- and eighteenth-century transcontinental trade. Innovation, organization, and efficient management were the principal elements of what historians have called the commercial revolution. Concerted efforts to maximize opportunities and advantages accounted for the phenomenal growth in the volume and value of commercial exchange. One of the least spectacular and most effective breakthroughs was the replacement of bilateral with triangular trade. In bilateral trade, the surplus commodities of one community were exchanged for those of another. This method, of course, restricted the range of trading partners to those with mutually desirable surplus production: England and Italy were unlikely to swap woolens or Sicily and Poland to trade grain. For those with few desirable commodities, bilateral trade meant the exchange of precious metals for goods, and throughout much of the sixteenth and early seventeenth centuries bullion was by far the most often traded commodity. Triangular trade created a larger pool of desirable goods. British manufactured goods could be traded to Africa for slaves, the slaves could be traded in the West Indies for sugar, and the sugar could be consumed in Britain. Moreover, the merchants involved in shifting these goods from place to place could achieve profits on each exchange. Indeed their motive in trading could now change from dumping surplus commodities to matching supply and demand.

Equally important were the changes made in the way trade was financed. As states, cities, and even individuals could stamp their own precious metal, there were hundreds of different European coins with different nominal and metallic values. The influx of American silver further destabilized an already unstable system of exchange. The Bank of Amsterdam was created in 1609 to establish a uniform rate of exchange for the various currencies traded in that city. From this useful function a second developed, transfer, or giro, banking, a system that had been invented in Italy. In giro banking, various merchant firms held money on account and issued bills of transfer from one to another. This transfer system meant that merchants in different cities did not have to transport their precious metals or endure long delays in having their accounts settled.

Giro banking also aided the development of bills of exchange, an early form of checking. Merchants could conclude trades by depositing money in a given bank or merchant house and then having a bill drawn for the sum they owed. Bills of exchange were especially important in international trade as they made large-scale shipments of precious metals to settle trade deficits unnecessary. By the end of the seventeenth century, bills of exchange had become negotiable, that is, they could pass from one merchant to another without being redeemed. Thus a Dutch merchant could buy French wines in Bordeaux with a bill of exchange drawn on an account in the Bank of Amsterdam. The Bordeaux merchant could then purchase Spanish oranges and use the same bill of exchange as payment. There were two disadvantages to this system: ultimately the bill had to return to Amsterdam for redemption, and when it

did the account on which it was drawn might be empty. The establishment of the Bank of England in 1694 overcame these difficulties. The Bank of England was licensed to issue its own bills of exchange, or bank notes, which were backed by the revenue from specific English taxes. This security of payment was widely sought after, and the Bank of England soon became a clearing house for all kinds of bills of exchange. The Bank would buy in bills at a discount, paying less than their face value, and pay out precious metal or their own notes in exchange.

The effects of these and many other small-scale changes in business practice helped fuel prolonged growth in European commerce. It was the European merchant who made this growth possible, accepting the risks of each individual transaction, building up small pools of capital from which successive transactions could take place. Most mercantile ventures were conducted by individuals or families and were based on the specialized trade of a single commodity. Trade offered high returns because it entailed high risks. The long delays in moving goods and their uncertain arrival, the unreliability of agents and the unscrupulousness of other traders, and the inefficiencies in transport and communication all weighed heavily against success. Those who succeeded did so less by luck than by hard work. They used family members to receive shipments. They lowered shipping costs by careful packaging. They lowered protection costs by securing their trade routes. Financial publications lowered the costs of information. Ultimately, lower costs meant lower prices. For centuries luxury goods dominated intercontinental trade. But by the eighteenth century European merchants had

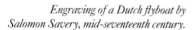
Engraving of a Dutch flyboat by Salomon Savery, mid-seventeenth century.

created a world marketplace in which the luxuries of the past were the common fare of the present.

Consumption Choices

As long-distance trade became more sophisticated, merchants became more sensitive to consumer tastes. Low-volume, high-quality goods like spices and silks could not support the growing merchant communities in the European states. These goods were the preserve of the largest trading companies and, more importantly, they had reached saturation levels by the early seventeenth century. The price of pepper, the most used of all spices, fell nearly continuously after 1650. Moreover, triangular trade allowed merchants to provide a better match of supplies and demands. The result was the rise to prominence of a vast array of new commodities, which not only continued the expansion of trade but also reshaped diet, lifestyles, and patterns of consumption. New products came from both east and west. Dutch and English incursions into the Asian trade provoked competition with the Portuguese and expanded the range of commodities that were shipped back to Europe. An aggressive Asian triangle was created in which European bullion bought Indonesian spices that were exchanged for Persian silk and Chinese and Japanese finished goods. In the Atlantic, the English were quick to develop both home and export markets for a variety of new or newly available products.

The European trade with Asia had always been designed to satisfy consumer demand rather than to exchange surplus goods. Europeans manufactured little that was desired in Asia, and neither merchants nor governments saw fit to attempt to influence Asian tastes in the way they did those of Europeans. The chief commodity imported to the East was bullion, tons of South American silver, perhaps a third of all that was produced. In return came spices, silk, coffee, jewels, jade, porcelain, dyes, and a wide variety of other exotic goods. By the middle of the seventeenth century the Dutch dominated the spice trade, obtaining a virtual monopoly over cinnamon, cloves, nutmeg, and mace and carrying the largest share of pepper. Each year Europeans consumed perhaps one million pounds of the four great spices and seven million pounds of pepper. Both Dutch and English competed for preeminence in the silk trade. The Dutch concentrated on Chinese silk, which they used mostly in trade with Japan. The English established an interest in lower quality Indian silk spun in Bengal and even hired Italian silk masters to try to teach European techniques to the Indian spinners.

A Chinese porcelain copy of a vase from the famous pottery works at the Dutch town of Delft. The Delft vase itself had been copied from a Chinese original. The date is probably early eighteenth century.

The most important manufactured articles imported from the East to Europe were the lightweight, brightly colored Indian cottons known as calicoes. It was the Dutch who first realized the potential of the cotton market. Until the middle of the seventeenth century cotton and cotton blended with silk were used in Europe only for wall hangings and table coverings. Colorful Asian chintz contained floral patterns that Europeans still considered exotic. But the material was also soft and smooth to the touch, and it soon replaced linen for use as underwear and close-fitting garments among the well-to-do. The fashion quickly caught on and the Dutch began exporting calicoes throughout the Continent. The English and French followed suit, establishing their own trading houses in India and bringing European patterns and designs with them for the Asians to copy.

Along with the new apparel from the East came new beverages. Coffee, which was first drunk in northern Europe in the early seventeenth century, became a fashionable drink by the end of the century. Coffeehouses sprang up in the major urban areas of northern Europe.

Detail of an Indian textile from the Madras region, ca. 1650. Calicut gave its name to the cotton cloth called calico. This is an example of a "painted Calicut" wall hanging.

There political and intellectual conversation was as heady as the strong Middle Eastern brew that was served.

As popular as coffee became among the European elites, it paled in comparison to the importance of tea as both an import commodity and a basic beverage. While coffee drinking remained the preserve of the wealthy, tea consumption spread throughout European society. It was probably most important in England, where the combination of China tea and West Indian sugar created a virtual revolution in nutrition. The growth in tea consumption was phenomenal. In 1706 England imported 100,000 pounds of tea. By the end of the century the number had risen to over 15 million pounds. The English imported most of this tea directly from China, where an open port had been established at Canton. Originally just one of a number of commodities that was carried on an Asian voyage, tea soon became the dominant cargo of the large English merchant ships. Some manufactured goods would be brought to India on the outward voyage, to fill as much cargo space as possible, but once the ships had loaded the green and black teas, they sailed directly home. Almost all tea was purchased with bullion as the Chinese had even less use for Euro-

pean goods than did other Asians. It was not until the discovery that the Chinese consumed large quantities of opium, which was grown in India and Southeast Asia, that a triangular trade developed.

The success of tea was linked to the explosive growth in the development of sugar in Europe's Atlantic colonies. The Portuguese had attempted to cultivate sugar in the Azores at the end of the fifteenth century, but it was not until the settlement of Brazil, whose hot, humid climate was a natural habitat for the cane plants, that widespread cultivation began. The island of Barbados became the first English sugar colony. Barbados turned to sugar production accidentally when its first attempts to market tobacco failed. The planters modeled their development on Brazil, where African slaves were used to plant, tend, and cut the giant canes from which the sugar was extracted. Hot, sweet tea became a popular drink for the lower orders of English society, a drink that, unlike beer, provided a quick burst of energy. By 1700 the English were sending home over 50 million pounds of sugar besides what they were shipping directly to the North American colonies.

The triangular trade of manufactures—largely reexported calicoes—to Africa for slaves, who were exchanged in the West Indies for sugar, became the dominant form of English overseas trade. Colonial production depended upon the enforced labor of hundreds of thousands of Africans. Gold and silver, tobacco, sugar, rice, and indigo were all slave crops. Africans were enslaved by other Africans and then sold to Europeans to be used in the colonies. Over six million black slaves were imported into the Americas during the course of the eighteenth century. While rum and calicoes were the main commodities exchanged for slaves, the Africans that dominated the slave trade organized a highly competitive market. Every colonial power participated in this lucrative trade. Over three million slaves were imported into the Portuguese colony of Brazil; by the end of the eighteenth century there were 500,000 slaves and only 35,000 French inhabitants of the sugar island of Saint Domingue. But it was the English with their sugar colonies of Barbados and Jamaica and their tobacco colonies of Virginia and Maryland who ultimately came to control the slave trade. The prosperity of Newport, Rhode Island, in North America and the port of Liverpool in Lancashire were built entirely upon the slave trade, as were hundreds of plantation fortunes. The sweet tooth of Europe was fed by the sweat of black Africans.

Sugar was by far the dominant commodity of the colonial trade but it was not the only one. Furs and fish

Nineteenth-century engraving of a tobacco plantation. Slaves labor while masters take their ease. In the background, ships wait to take the barrels of tobacco to far-off markets.

had first driven Europeans toward North America and both remained important commodities. Beaver and rabbit skins were the most common materials for making headgear in an age in which everyone wore a hat. The Canadian cod schools were among the richest in the world, and the catch was shipped back either salted ordried. The English established what amounted to a manufacturing industry on the Newfoundland coast, where they dried the tons of fish that they caught. In the eighteenth century, rice was grown for export in the southern American colonies, particularly South Carolina. Tobacco was the first new American product to come into widespread use in Europe, and its popularity—despite various official efforts to ban its use as dirty and unhealthy—grew steadily. American tobacco was grown principally in the colonies of Virginia and Maryland and shipped across the ocean, where it was frequently blended with European varieties. Although the English were the principal importers, it was the Dutch who dominated the European tobacco trade, making the most popular blends.

The new commodities flooded into Europe from all parts of the globe. By the middle of the eighteenth century tea, coffee, cocoa, gin, and rum were among the most popular beverages. These were all products that had been largely unknown a century earlier. New habits were created as new demands were satisfied. Tea and sugar passed from luxury to staple in little more than a generation and the demand for both products continued to increase. To meet it, the European trading powers needed to create and maintain a powerful and efficient mercantile system.

Dutch Masters

For the nearly eighty years between 1565 and 1648 that the Dutch were at war, they grew ever more prosperous. While the economies of most other European nations were sapped by warfare, the Dutch seemed to draw strength from their interminable conflict with the Spanish empire. They did have the advantage of fighting defensively on land and offensively on sea. Land war was terribly costly to the aggressor, who had to raise large armies, transport them to the site of battles or sieges, and feed them while they were there. The defender simply had to fortify strong places, keep its water routes open to secure supplies, and wait for the weather to change. Sea war—or piracy, depending on one's viewpoint—required much smaller outlays for men and material and promised the rewards of captured prizes. The Dutch became expert at attacking the Spanish silver fleets, hunting like a lion against a herd by singling out the slower and smaller vessels for capture. The Dutch also benefited from the massive immigration into their provinces of Protestants who had lived and worked in the southern provinces. They brought with them vital skills in manufacturing and large reserves of capital for investment in Dutch commerce.

The Dutch East India Company's trading station on the Hooghly River in Bengal, 1665. The station was one of a network of bases the Company established throughout its eastern trading empire.

The Dutch grounded their prosperity on commerce. Excellent craftsmen, they took the lead in the skilled occupations necessary for finishing cloth, refining raw materials, and decorating consumer goods. They were also successful farmers, especially given the small amounts of land with which they had to work and the difficult ecological conditions in which they worked it. But their greatest abilities were in trade.

Though the Dutch Republic comprised seven separate political entities, with a total population of about two million, the province of Holland was preeminent among them. Holland contained more than a quarter of this population, and its trading port of Amsterdam was one of the great cities of Europe. The city had risen dramatically in the seventeenth century, growing from a mid-sized urban community of 65,000 in 1600 to a metropolis of 170,000 fifty years later. The port was one of the busiest in the world, for it was built to be an entrepôt. Vast warehouses and docks lined its canals. Visitors were impressed by the bustle, the cleanliness, and the businesslike appearance of Amsterdam. There were no great public squares and few recognizable monuments. The central buildings were the Bank and the Exchange, testimony to the dominant activities of the residents.

The Dutch dominated all types of European trade. They carried more English coal than England, more French wine than France, more Swedish iron than Sweden. Dutch ships outnumbered all others in every important port of Europe. Goods were brought to Amsterdam to be redistributed throughout the world. Dutch prosperity rested first upon the Baltic trade. Even after it ceased to expand in the middle of the seventeenth century, the Baltic trade composed over one quarter of all of Holland's commercial enterprise. The Dutch also

were the leaders in the East Indian trade throughout the seventeenth century. They held a virtual monopoly on the sale of exotic spices and the largest share of the pepper trade. Their imports of cottons and especially of porcelain began new consumer fads that soon resulted in the development of European industries. Dutch potteries began to produce china, as lower quality ceramic goods came to be known. Dutch trade in the Atlantic was of less importance, but the Dutch did have a colonial presence in the New World, controlling a number of small islands and the rapidly growing mainland settlement of New Netherland. Yet the Dutch still dominated the secondary market in tobacco and sugar, becoming the largest processor and refiner of these important commodities.

In all of these activities the Dutch acted as merchants rather than as consumers. Unlike most other Europeans they regarded precious metal as a commodity like any other and took no interest in accumulating it for its own sake. This attitude enabled them to pioneer triangular trading and develop the crucial financial institutions necessary to expand their overseas commerce. The Dutch were not so much innovators as improvers. They saw the practical value in Italian accounting and banking methods and raised them to new levels of efficiency. They made use of marine insurance to help diminish the risks of mercantile activity. Their legal system favored the creation of small trading companies by protecting individual investments. The European stock and commodity markets were centered in Amsterdam. By the 1670s over 500 commodities were traded on the Amsterdam exchange, and even a primitive futures market evolved for those who wished to speculate.

There were many explanations for the unparalleled growth of this small maritime state into one of the greatest of European trading empires. Geography and climate provided one impetus, the lack of sufficient foodstuffs another. Yet there were cultural characteristics as well. One was the openness of Dutch society. Even before the struggle with Spain, the northern provinces had shown a greater inclination toward religious toleration than had most parts of Europe. Amsterdam became a unique center for religious and intellectual exchange. European Jews flocked there, as did Catholic dissidents like Descartes. They brought with them a wide range of skills and knowledge along with capital that could be invested in trade. There was no real social nobility among the Dutch and certainly no set of values that prized investment in land over investment in trade. The French and Spanish nobility looked with scorn upon their mercantile classes and shunned any form of commercial investment, and the English, though more open to industry and trade, sank as much of their capital as possible into landed estates and country houses. The Dutch economic elite invested in trade. By the middle of the seventeenth century the Dutch Republic enjoyed a reputation for cultural creativity that was the envy of the Continent. A truly extraordinary school of Dutch artists led by Rembrandt celebrated this new state born of commerce with vivid portrayals of its people and its prosperity.

Mercantile Organization

Elsewhere in Europe, trade was the king's business. The wealth of the nation was part of the prestige of the monarch and its rise or fall part of the crown's power. Power and prestige were far more important to absolute rulers than was the profit of merchants. Indeed, in all European states except the Dutch Republic, the activities of merchants were scorned by both the landed elite and the salaried bureaucrats. Leisure was valued by the one and royal service by the other. The pursuit of wealth by buying and selling somehow lacked dignity. Yet the activities of the mercantile classes took on increasing importance for the state for two reasons. First, imported goods, especially luxuries, were a noncontroversial target for taxation. Customs duties and excise taxes grew all over Europe. Representative assemblies composed of landed elites were usually happy to grant them to the monarch, and merchants could pass them on to consumers in higher prices. Secondly, the competition for trade was seen as a competition between states rather than individual merchants. Trading privileges involved special arrangements with foreign powers,

arrangements that recognized the sovereign power of European monarchs. In this way, trade could bring glory to the state.

The competition for power and glory derived from the theory of mercantilism, a set of assumptions about economic activity that were commonly held throughout Europe and that guided the policies of almost every government. There were two interrelated ideas. One was that the wealth of a nation resided in its stock of precious metal, and the other was that economic activity was a zero-sum game. There was thought to be a fixed amount of money, a fixed amount of commodities, and a fixed amount of consumption. Thus what one country gained, another lost. If England bought wine from France and paid £100,000 in precious metal for it, then England was £100,000 poorer and France £100,000 richer. If one was to trade profitably, it was absolutely necessary to wind up with a surplus of precious metal. Therefore it was imperative that governments regulate trade so that the stocks of precious metal were protected from the greed of the merchants. The first and most obvious measure of protection, then, was to prohibit the export of coin except by license, a prohibition that was absolutely unenforceable and was violated more often by government officials than by merchants.

These ideas about economic activity led to a variety of forms of economic regulation. The most common was the monopoly, a grant of special privileges in return for both financial considerations and an agreement to abide by the rules set out by the state. In the context of the seventeenth-century economy, there were a number of advantages to monopolies. First, of course, were those that accrued to the crown. There were direct and indirect revenues: monopolists usually paid considerable fees for their rights, and their activities were easy to monitor for purposes of taxation. The crown could use the grant of monopoly to reward past favors or to purchase future support from powerful individuals. There were also advantages for the monopolists. They could make capital investments with the expectation of long-term gains. This advantage was especially important in attracting investors for risky and expensive ventures like long-distance trade. Indeed, there were even benefits for the economy as a whole, as monopolies increased productive investment at a time when most capital was being used to purchase land, luxury goods, or offices.

Two monopoly companies, the English and the Dutch East India companies, dominated the Asian trade. The English East India Company, founded in 1600 with a capital of £30,000, was given the exclusive

EARLY HISTORY OF THE DUTCH EAST INDIA COMPANY

▪ The Dutch East India Company was the most important of the monopoly trading companies that were founded in the early seventeenth century. It was organized as a stock company and its shares traded on the Amsterdam bourse. Merchants could purchase portions of its ships' cargoes for both imports and exports, and the company was given total control over the eastern spice trade. It was also given political and diplomatic powers in the areas in which it traded, and its overseas members behaved as much as foreign ambassadors as merchants. This excerpt is from an early history of the company and provides details of its original charter.

After various private merchants joined with others in the 1590s and after the turn of the century to form companies, first in Amsterdam and then in other cities of Holland and Zeeland, to open up and undertake travel and trade with the East Indies, and from time to time equipped and sent out many ships, which returned, on the average, with no small success, the States General came to the conclusion that it would be more useful and profitable not only for the country as a whole but also for its inhabitants individually, especially all those who had undertaken and shared in navigation and trade, that these companies should be combined and this navigation and trade be placed and maintained on a firm footing, with order and political guidance. After much argument and persuasion, this union was worked out by Their High Mightinesses [the government of the United Provinces], in their own words, to advance the prosperity of the United Netherlands, to conserve and increase its industry and to bring profit to the Company and to the people of the country.

The Company's charter authorized it to make alliances with princes and potentates east of the Cape of Good Hope and beyond the Straits of Magellan, to make contracts build fortresses and strongholds, name governors, raise troops, appoint officers of justice, and perform other necessary services for the advancement of trade; to dismiss the said governors and officers of justice if their conduct was found to be harmful and disloyal, provided that these governors or officers could not be prevented from returning here to present such grievances or complaints as they think they might have.

The inhabitants of this country were permitted to invest as much or as little as they pleased in shares of the Company.

The subscription had to be made before September 1, 1602. . . .

. . . When the time for this investment or subscription had expired, various competent persons in different places presented requests in person or by sealed letter to the assembly of the XVII, asking that they be permitted to join the Company with the investment of certain sums of money; it was decided that no one else should be permitted to join in violation of the charter and to the detriment of the shareholders who had paid in their subscriptions before the expiration of the date fixed, and that the subscribed capital should be neither increased nor reduced.

right to the Asian trade and immediately established itself throughout the Indian Ocean. The Dutch East India Company was formed two years later with ten times the capital of its English counterpart. By the end of the century the Dutch company employed over twelve thousand people. Both companies were known as joint-stock companies, an innovation in the way in which businesses were organized. Subscribers owned a percentage of the total value of the company, based on the number of shares they bought, and were entitled to a distribution of profits on the same basis. Initially, the English company determined profits on single voyages and was to distribute all of its assets to its shareholders after a given period. But changes in legal practice gave the company an identity separate from the individuals that held the shares. Now shares could be exchanged without the breakup of the company as a whole. Both Amsterdam and London soon developed stock markets to trade the shares of monopoly companies.

Both East India companies were remarkably good investments. The Dutch East India Company paid an average dividend of 18 percent for over two hundred years. The value of English East India Company shares rose fivefold in the second half of the seventeenth century alone. Few other monopoly companies achieved a record comparable to that of the East India companies. The English Royal African Company, founded in 1672 to provide slaves for the Spanish colonies, barely recouped costs and was soon superseded by private trade. Even the French East Indian and African companies, which were modeled on the Dutch and English, were forced to abandon their monopolies. The Dutch and English companies were successful not because of their special privileges but because they were able to lower the costs of protecting their ships and cargoes.

Monopolies were not the only form of regulation in which seventeenth-century government engaged. For those states with Atlantic colonies, regulation took the form of restricting markets rather than traders. In the 1660s the English government, alarmed at the growth of Dutch mercantile activity in the New World, passed a series of Navigation Acts designed to protect English shipping. Colonial goods—primarily tobacco and sugar—could be shipped to and from England only in English boats. If the French wanted to purchase West Indian sugar, they could not simply send a ship to the English colony of Barbados loaded with French goods and exchange them for sugar. Rather, they had to make their purchases from an English import-export merchant and the goods had to be unloaded in an English port before they could be reloaded to be shipped to France. As a result, the English reexport trade skyrocketed. In the year 1700 reexports amounted to nearly 40 percent of all English commerce. With such a dramatic increase in trading, all moved in English ships, shipbuilding boomed. English coastal towns enjoyed heightened prosperity as did the great colonial ports of Bristol and Liverpool. For a time, colonial protection proved effective.

French protectionism was as much internal as colonial. The French entered the intercontinental trade later than their North Atlantic rivals, and they were less dependent upon trade for their subsistence. Of all the states of Europe, only France could satisfy its needs from its own resources. But to achieve such self-sufficiency required coordination and leadership. In the 1670s Louis XIV's finance minister, Jean-Baptiste Colbert (1619–83) developed a plan to bolster the French economy by protecting it against European imports. First Colbert followed the English example of restricting the reexport trade by requiring that imports come to France either in French ships or in the ships of the country from which the goods originated. In addition, he used tariffs to make imported goods unattractive in France. He sponsored a drive to increase French manufacturing, especially of textiles, tapestries, linens, glass, and furniture. To protect the investments in French manufacturing, enormous duties were placed on the import of similar goods manufactured elsewhere. The Venetian glass industry, for example, suffered a serious blow from Colbert's tariffs. English woolen manufacturers were also damaged and the English sought retaliatory measures. But in fact, the English had already begun to imitate this form of protection. In the early eighteenth century England attempted to limit the importation of cotton goods from India to prevent the collapse of the domestic clothing industry.

The Navigation Acts and Colbert's program of protective tariffs were directed specifically against Dutch reexporters. The Dutch were the acknowledged leaders in all branches of commerce in the seventeenth century. There were many summers when there were more Dutch vessels in London Harbor than there were English ships. In the 1670s the Dutch merchant fleet was probably larger than the English, French, Spanish, Portuguese, and German fleets combined. Restrictive navigation practices were one way to combat an advantage that the Dutch had built through heavy capital investment and by breaking away from the prevailing theories about the relationship between wealth and precious metals. The English and French Navigation Acts cut heavily into the Dutch trade and ultimately both the English and French overtook them. But protectionism had its price. Just as the dynastic wars were succeeded by the wars of religion, so were the wars of religion succeeded by the wars of commerce.

"The discovery of America and that of a passage to the East Indies by the Cape of Good Hope are the two greatest and most important events in the history of mankind." So wrote the great Scottish economist Adam Smith (1723–90) in *The Wealth of Nations* (1776). For Smith and his generation, the first great age of commerce was coming to an end. The innovations of the Dutch had given way to a settled pattern of international long-distance trade. States now viewed commerce as a part of their national self-interest. They developed overseas empires, which they protected as markets for their goods and sources for their raw materials. These were justified by the theory of mercantilism and the demands of a generation of consumers who saw the luxuries of the past as the necessities of the present.

The Wars of Commerce

The belief that there was a fixed amount of trade in the world was still strong in the late seventeenth century. One country's gains in trade were another's losses. There was not more than enough to go around and it could not be easily understood how the expansion of one country's trade could benefit all countries. Competition for trade was the same as competition for territory or subjects, part of the struggle by which the state grew powerful. It was not inevitable that economic competition would lead to warfare, only that restrictive competition would.

Thus the scramble for colonies in the seventeenth century led to commercial warfare in the eighteenth. As the English gradually replaced the Dutch as the leading commercial nation, so the French replaced the English as the leading competitor. Hostility between the English and the French had existed for centuries, and it was not without cause that the commercial wars of the eighteenth century should be likened to the territorial wars of the Middle Ages. The greed of merchants and the glory of princes fueled a struggle for the dominance of world markets that brought European warfare to every corner of the globe.

The Mercantile Wars

Commercial warfare in Europe began between the English and the Dutch in the middle of the seventeenth century. Both had established aggressive overseas trading companies in the Atlantic and in Asia. In the early seventeenth century the Dutch were the undisputed leaders, their carrying capacity and trade monopolies the greatest in the world. But the English were rising quickly. Their Atlantic colonies began to produce valuable new commodities like tobacco and sugar, and theirAsian trade was expanding decade after decade. Conflict was inevitable, and the result was a series of three naval wars fought between 1652 and 1674.

The Dutch had little choice but to strike out against English policy, but they also had little chance of overall success. Their spectacular naval victory in 1667, when the Dutch fleet surprised many English warships at port and burned both ships and docks at Chatham, obscured the fact that Dutch commercial superiority was slipping. In 1664 the English conquered New Netherland on the North American mainland and renamed it New York. With this defeat, the Dutch lost their largest colonial possession. The wars were costly to both states, nearly bankrupting the English Crown in 1672. Anglo-Dutch rivalry was finally laid to rest after 1688, when William of Orange, stadtholder of Holland, became William III (1689-1702), king of England.

The Anglo-Dutch commercial wars were just one part of a larger European conflict. Dutch commerce was as threatening to France as it was to England, though in a different way. Under Colbert, France pursued a policy of economic independence. The state supported internal industrial activity through the financing of large workshops and the encouragement of new manufacturing techniques. To protect French products, Colbert levied a series of punitive tariffs on Dutch imports, which severely depressed both trade and manufacture in Holland. Though the Dutch retaliated with restrictive tariffs of their own—in 1672 they banned the import of all French goods for an entire year—the Dutch economy depended upon free trade. The Dutch had much more to lose than did France in a battle of protective tariffs.

But the battle that Louis XIV had in mind was to be more deadly than one of tariffs. Greedily he eyed the Spanish Netherlands—to which he had a weak claim through his Habsburg wife—and believed that the Dutch stood in the way of his plans. The Dutch had entered into an alliance with the English and Swedes in 1668 to counter French policy, and Louis was determined to crush them in retaliation. He successfully bought off both of Holland's supposed allies, providing cash pensions to the kings of England and Sweden in return for England's active participation and Sweden's passive neutrality in the impending war. In 1672 Louis's army, over one hundred thousand strong, invaded the Low Countries and swept all before them. Only the opening of the dikes prevented the French from entering the province of Holland itself.

The French invasion coincided with the third Anglo-Dutch war, and the United Provinces found themselves besieged on land and sea. Their international trade was disrupted, their manufacturing industries were in ruins,

ADAM SMITH, *THE WEALTH OF NATIONS*

■ *Adam Smith was a Scottish political theorist whose* The Wealth of Nations *was the first great work of economic analysis in European history. Smith had wide-ranging interests and wrote with equal authority about manufacturing, population, and trade. He was the first to develop the doctrine of free trade, which he called "laissez-faire." Smith argued that the government that governed least governed best, and he was an early critic of protective tariffs and monopolies.*

Every individual necessarily labours to render the annual revenue of the society as great as he can. He generally, indeed, neither intends to promote the public interest, nor knows how much he is promoting it. By preferring the support of domestic to that of foreign industry, he intends only his own security; and by directing that industry in such a manner as its produce may be of the greatest value, he intends only his own gain, and he is in this, as in many other cases, led by an invisible hand to promote an end which was no part of his intention. Nor is it always the worse for the society that it was no part of it. By pursuing his own interest he frequently promotes that of the society more effectually than when he really intends to promote it. I have never known much good done by those who affected to trade for the public good . . .

Each nation has been made to look with an invidious eye upon the prosperity of all the nations with which it trades, and to consider their gain as its own loss. Commerce, which ought naturally to be, among nations as among individuals, a bond of union and friendship, has become the most fertile source of discord and animosity. The capricious ambition of kings and ministers has not, during the present and the preceding century, been more fatal to the repose of Europe, than the impertinent jealousy of merchants and manufacturers. The violence and injustice of the rulers of mankind is an ancient evil, for which, I am afraid, the nature of human affairs can scarce admit of a remedy. But the mean rapacity, the monopolizing spirit of merchants and manufacturers, who neither are, nor ought to be, the rulers of mankind, though it cannot perhaps be corrected, may very easily be prevented from disturbing the tranquillity of anybody but themselves . . .

The natural advantages which one country has over another in producing particular commodities are sometimes so great, that it is acknowledged by all the world to be in vain to struggle with them . . . Very good grapes can be raised in Scotland, and very good wine too can be made of them at about thirty times the expense for which at least equally good can be brought from foreign countries. Would it be a reasonable law to prohibit the importation of all foreign wines merely to encourage the making of claret and burgundy in Scotland?

From Adam Smith, *The Wealth of Nations*, 1776.

and their military budget skyrocketed. Only able diplomacy and skillful military leadership prevented total Dutch demise. A separate peace was made with England, and Spain, whose sovereign territory had been invaded, entered the war on the side of the Dutch as did a number of German states. Louis's hope for a lightning victory faded, and the war settled into a series of interminable sieges and reliefs of fortified towns. The Dutch finally persuaded France to come to terms in the Treaty of Nijmegen (1678–79). While Louis XIV retained a number of the territories he had taken from Spain, his armies withdrew from the United Provinces and he agreed to lift most of the commercial sanctions against Dutch goods. The first phase of mercantile warfare was over.

The Wars of Louis XIV

It was Louis XIV's ambition to restore the ancient Burgundian territories to the French crown and to provide secure northern and eastern borders for his state. Pursuit of these aims involved him in conflicts with nearly every other European state. Spain had fought for eighty years to preserve the Burgundian inheritance in the Low

Countries. By the Peace of Westphalia (1648), the northern portion of this territory became the United Provinces, while the southern portion remained loyal to the crown and became the Spanish Netherlands. This territory provided a barrier between Holland and France that both states attempted to strengthen by establishing fortresses and bridgeheads at strategic places. In the east, Louis eyed the duchies of Lorraine and Alsace and the large swath of territory farther south known as Franche-Comté. The Peace of Westphalia had granted France control of a number of imperial cities in these duchies, and Louis aimed to link them together. All of these territories were ruled by Habsburgs: Alsace and Lorraine by the Austrian Holy Roman Emperor, Franche-Comté by the Spanish king.

In the late seventeenth century, ambassadors and ministers of state began to develop the theory of a balance of power in Europe. This was a belief that no state or combination of states should be allowed to become so powerful that its existence threatened the peace of the others. Behind this purely political idea of the balance of power lay a theory of collective security that knit together the European state system. French expansion in either direction not only threatened the other states directly involved but also posed a threat to European security in general.

Louis showed his hand clearly enough in the Franco-Dutch war that had ended in 1679. Though he withdrew his forces from the United Provinces and evacuated most of the territories he had conquered, by the Treaty of Nijmegen France absorbed Franche-Comté as well as portions of the Spanish Netherlands. Louis began plotting his next adventure almost as soon as the treaty was signed. Over the next several years, French troops advanced steadily into Alsace, ultimately forcing the city of Strasbourg, a vital bridgehead on the Rhine, to recognize French sovereignty. Expansion into northern Italy was similarly calculated. Everywhere Louis looked, French engineers rushed to construct fortresses and magazines in preparation for another war.

It finally came in 1688 when French troops poured across the Rhine to seize Cologne. A united German empire led by Leopold I, archduke of Austria, combined with the maritime powers of England and Holland, led by William III, to form the Grand Alliance, the first of the great balance of power coalitions. In fact, the two sides proved so evenly matched that the Nine Years' War (1688-97) settled very little, but it demonstrated that a successful European coalition could be formed against France. It also signified the permanent shift in alliances that resulted from the Revolution of 1688 in England. Although the English had allied with France against the Dutch in 1672, after William became king he persuaded the English Parliament that the real enemy was France. Louis's greatest objective, to secure the borders of his state, had withstood its greatest test. He might have rested satisfied but for the vagaries of births, marriages, and deaths.

Like his father, Louis XIV had married a daughter of the king of Spain. Philip IV had married his eldest

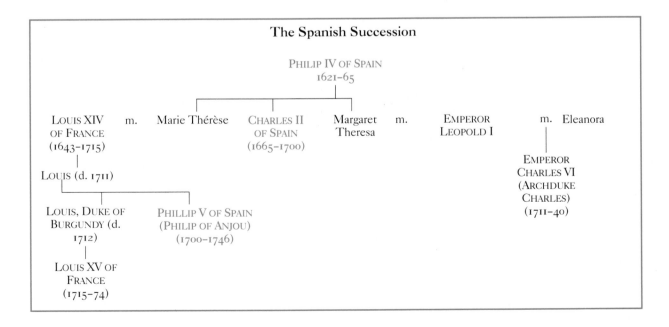

The Spanish Succession

PHILIP IV OF SPAIN
1621-65

LOUIS XIV   m.   Marie Thérèse   CHARLES II   Margaret   m.   EMPEROR   m.   Eleanora
OF FRANCE   OF SPAIN   Theresa   LEOPOLD I
(1643-1715)   (1665-1700)

LOUIS (d. 1711)   EMPEROR
                                                                                             CHARLES VI
LOUIS, DUKE OF   PHILLIP V OF SPAIN   (ARCHDUKE
BURGUNDY (d.   (PHILIP OF ANJOU)   CHARLES)
1712)   (1700-1746)   (1711-40)

LOUIS XV OF
FRANCE
(1715-74)

War and Peace, 1648–1763

1648	Peace of Westphalia
1652–54	First Anglo-Dutch War
1665–67	Second Anglo-Dutch War
1672	Franco-Dutch war
1672–74	Third Anglo-Dutch war
1678–79	Treaty of Nijmegen
1688	Revolution of 1688; William of Orange becomes William III of England Grand Alliance formed
1688–97	Nine Years' War (France vs. Grand Alliance)
1702–14	War of the Spanish Succession
1713–14	Treaty of Utrecht
1756–63	Seven Years' War
1763	Peace of Paris

daughter to Louis XIV and a younger one to Leopold I of Austria, who subsequently became the Holy Roman Emperor (1658–1705). Before he died, Philip finally fathered a son, Charles II (1665–1700), who attained the Spanish crown at the age of four but was mentally and physically incapable of ruling his vast empire. For decades it was apparent that there would be no direct Habsburg successor to an empire which, despite its recent losses, still contained Spain, South America, the Spanish Netherlands, and most of Italy. Louis XIV and Leopold I both had legitimate claims to an inheritance that would have irreversibly tipped the European balance of power.

As Charles II grew increasingly feeble, efforts to find a suitable compromise to the problem of the Spanish succession were led by William III who, as stadtholder of Holland, was vitally interested in the fate of the Spanish Netherlands and, as king of England, in the fate of the Spanish American colonies. In the 1690s two treaties of partition were drawn up. The first achieved near universal agreement but was nullified by the death of the German prince who was to inherit the Spanish crown. The second, which would have given Italy to Louis's son and everything else to Leopold's son, was opposed by Leopold, who had neither naval nor commercial interests and who claimed most of the Italian territories as imperial fiefs.

All of these plans had been made without consulting the Spanish. If it was the aim of the European powers to partition the Spanish empire in order to prevent any one state from inheriting too much of it, it was the aim of the Spanish to maintain their empire intact. To this end, they devised a brilliant plan. Charles II bequeathed his entire empire to Philip of Anjou, the younger grandson of Louis XIV, with two stipulations. First that Philip renounce his claim to the French throne, and second that he accept the empire intact, without partition. If he—or more to the point, if his grandfather Louis XIV—did not accept these conditions then the empire would pass to Archduke Charles, the younger son of Leopold I. Such provisions virtually assured war between France and the empire unless compromise between the two powers could be reached. But before terms could even be suggested, Charles II died and Philip V (1700–46) was proclaimed king of Spain and its empire.

Thus the eighteenth century opened with the War of the Spanish Succession (1702–14). Emperor Leopold rejected the provisions of Charles's will and sent his troops to occupy Italy. Louis XIV confirmed the worst fears of William III when he provided his grandson with French troops to "defend" the Spanish Netherlands. William III revived the Grand Alliance and initiated a massive land war against the combined might of France and Spain. The allied objectives were twofold: to prevent the unification of the French and Spanish thrones and to partition the Spanish empire so that both Italy and the Netherlands were ceded to Austria. The objective of Louis XIV was simply to preserve as much as possible of the Spanish inheritance for the house of Bourbon.

William III died in 1702 and was succeeded by Anne (1702–14). John Churchill (1650–1722), duke of Marlborough and commander in chief of the army, continued William's policy. England and Holland again provided most of the finance and sea power, but in addition the English also provided a land army nearly seventy thousand strong. Prussia joined the Grand Alliance, and disciplined Prussian troops helped offset the addition of the Spanish army to Louis's forces. In 1704 Churchill defeated French forces at Blenheim in Germany and in 1706 at Ramillies in the Spanish Netherlands. France's military ascendancy was over.

Efforts to negotiate a peace settlement took longer than the war itself. The Austrians had taken control of Italy, the English and Dutch had secured the Spanish Netherlands, and the French had been driven back beyond the Rhine. The Allies believed that they could now enforce any treaty they pleased upon Louis XIV and

KING

♠

stop thief

All Europ's Riveted in this Belief,
My Grandfather before me was a Thief,
I'll steal Spains Crown &Jewels n^{ch} its pelf
And be at last a Nominal king my self

An eighteenth-century English playing card showing Philip of Anjou, the grandson of Louis XIV, stealing the Spanish crown.

in the Nine Years' War and the War of the Spanish Succession did not result in large territorial gains but it did result in an enormous increase in English power and prestige. Over the next thirty years England would assert its own imperial claims.

The Colonial Wars

The Treaty of Utrecht (1713–14) ushered in almost a quarter century of peace in western Europe. Austrian rule in the Netherlands and Italy remained a major irritant to the Spanish but Spain was too weak to do more than sulk and snarl. The death of Louis XIV in 1715 quelled French ambitions for a time and even led to an Anglo-French accord, which guaranteed the preservation of the settlement reached at Utrecht. Peace allowed Europe to rebuild its shattered economy and resume the international trade that had been so severely disrupted over the last forty years. The Treaty of Utrecht had resolved a number of important trading issues, all in favor of Great Britain, as England was known after its union with Scotland in 1707. In addition to receiving Gibraltar and Minorca from Spain, Britain was also granted the monopoly to provide slaves to the Spanish American colonies and the right to send

along with concessions from France attempted to oust his grandson, Philip V, from the Spanish throne. This proved impossible to achieve though it took more than five years to learn the lesson. By then the European situation had taken another strange twist. Both the Emperor Leopold and his eldest son had died. Now Leopold's younger son, Archduke Charles, inherited the empire as Charles VI (1711–40) and raised the prospect of an equally dangerous combined Austrian-Spanish state. Between 1713 and 1714 a series of treaties at Utrecht settled the War of the Spanish Succession. Spanish possessions in Italy and the Netherlands were ceded to Austria; France abandoned all its territorial gains east of the Rhine and ceded its North American territories of Nova Scotia and Newfoundland to England. England also acquired from Spain Gibraltar on the southern coast of Spain and the island of Minorca in the Mediterranean. Both were strategically important to English commercial interests. English intervention

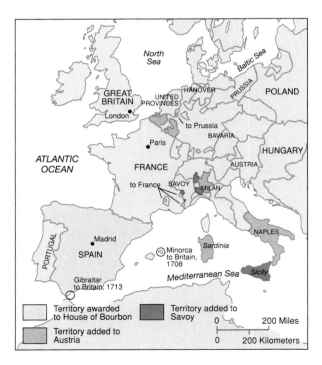

Treaty of Utrecht

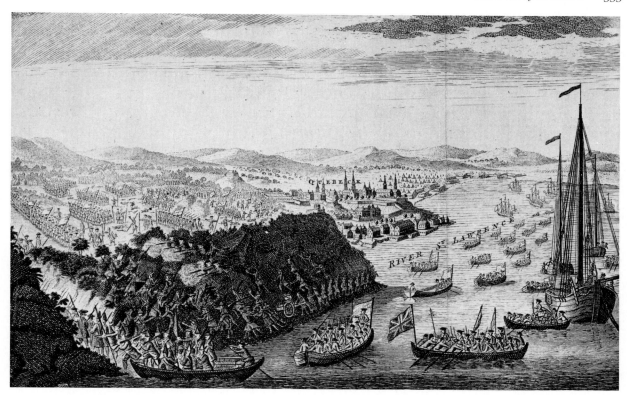

The storming of Quebec by British forces in 1759. The capture of the first city of New France was a major British victory in the North American theater of the Seven Years' War.

one trading ship a year to them. In east and west, Britain was becoming the dominant commercial power in the world.

At least some of the reason for Britain's preeminence was the remarkable growth of the Atlantic colonies. The colonial economy was booming and consumer goods that were in demand in London, Paris, and Amsterdam were also in demand in Boston, Philadelphia, and New York. Like every other colonial power, the British held a monopoly on their colonial trade. They were far less successful than were the Spanish and French in enforcing the notion that colonies existed only for the benefit of the parent country, but the English Parliament continued to pass legislation aimed at restricting colonial trade with other nations and other nations' colonies. Like almost all other mercantile restrictions, these efforts were stronger in theory than in practice. Tariffs on imports and customs duties on British goods provided a double incentive for smuggling.

France emerged as Britain's true colonial rival. In the Caribbean, the French had the largest and most profitable of the West Indian sugar islands, Saint Domingue (modern-day Haiti). In North America France held not only Canada but laid claim to the entire continent west of the Ohio River. The French did not so much settle their colonial territory as occupy it. They surveyed the land, established trading relations with the Native Americans, and built forts at strategic locations. The English, in contrast, had developed fixed communities, which grew larger and more prosperous by the decade. France determined to defend its colonies by establishing an overseas military presence. Regular French troops were shipped to Canada and installed in Louisburg, Montreal, and Quebec. The British responded with troops of their own and sent an expeditionary force to clear the French from the Ohio River Valley. This action was the immediate cause of the Seven Years' War (1756–63).

Although the Seven Years' War had a bitter Continental phase, it was essentially a war for empire between the English and the French. There were three main theaters: the North American mainland, the West Indian sugar plantations, and the eastern coast of India. All over the globe, the British won smashing victories. The British navy blockaded the water route to Canada, inflicting severe hardship on French settlers in

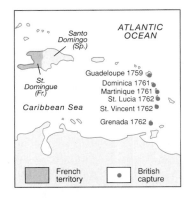

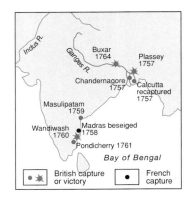

Seven Years' War

Montreal and Quebec. British forces ultimately captured both towns. After some initial successes, the French were driven back west across the Mississippi River and their line of fortresses in the Ohio Valley fell into English hands. The English also succeeded in taking all the French sugar islands except Saint Domingue. British success in India was equally complete. The French were chased from their major trading zone and English dominance was secured.

By the end of the Seven Years' War, Britain had become a global imperial power. In the Peace of Paris (1763) France ceded all of Canada in exchange for the return of its West Indian islands. British dominion in the East Indian trade was recognized and led ultimately to British dominion of India itself. In less than a century the ascendancy of France was broken and Europe's first modern imperial power had been created.

European commercial expansion was the first step in a long process that would ultimately transform the material life of all human beings. The quest for new commodities led to the sophistication of transportation, marketing, and distribution, all vital developments for agricultural changes in the future. The ability to move large quantities of goods from place to place and to exchange them between different parts of the globe laid the foundation for organized manufacturing. The practical impact of scientific discovery, as yet only dimly glimpsed, would soon spur the transformation of handicrafts into industries. In the eighteenth century the material world was still being conquered and the most unattractive features of this conquest were all too plainly visible. Luxuries for the rich were won by the labors of the poor. The pleasures of sugar and tobacco were purchased at the price of slavery for millions of Africans. The greed of merchants and the glory of princes was an unholy alliance that resulted in warfare

around the globe. But it was a shrinking globe, one whose peoples were becoming increasingly interdependent, tied together by the goods and services that they could provide to each other.

SUGGESTIONS FOR FURTHER READING

GENERAL READING

* A. Rupert Hall, *The Revolution in Science 1500–1750* (London: Longman, 1983). The best introduction to the varieties of scientific thought in the early modern period. Detailed and complex.

* Jan de Vries, *The European Economy in an Age of Crisis* (Cambridge: Cambridge University Press, 1976). A comprehensive study of economic development, including long-distance trade and commercial change.

* K. H. D. Haley, *The Dutch in the Seventeenth Century* (London: Thames and Hudson, 1972). A well-written and illustrated history of the golden age of Holland.

* Derek McKay and H. M. Scott, *The Rise of the Great Powers 1648–1815* (London: Longman, 1983). An outstanding survey of diplomacy and warfare.

* Jeremy Black, *The Rise of the European Powers 1679–1793* (New York: Edward Arnold, 1990). A new look at diplomatic history from an English point of view.

THE NEW SCIENCE

* Margaret C. Jacob, *The Cultural Meaning of the Scientific Revolution* (New York: Knopf, 1988). Scientific thought portrayed in its social context.

* Stillman Drake, *Galileo* (New York: Hill and Wang, 1980). A short but engaging study of the great Italian scientist.

* Allen Debus, *Man and Nature in the Renaissance* (Cambridge: Cambridge University Press, 1978). An especially good account of the intellectual roots of scientific thought.

Charles Webster, *The Great Instauration: Science, Medicine, and Reform* (London: Duckworth, 1975). A complicated but rewarding analysis of experimental science and the origins of scientific medicine.

* Frank E. Manuel, *Sir Isaac Newton: A Portrait* (Cambridge, MA: Harvard University Press, 1968). A readable account of one of the most complex intellects in European history.

EMPIRES OF GOODS

* Ralph Davis, *The Rise of the Atlantic Economies* (Ithaca, NY: Cornell University Press, 1973). A nation-by-nation survey of the colonial powers.

K. N. Chaudhuri, *The Trading World of Asia and the English East India Company* (Cambridge: Cambridge University Press, 1978). A brilliant account of the impact of the Indian trade on both Europeans and Asians.

* Sidney Mintz, *Sweetness and Power* (New York: Viking Press, 1985). An anthropological examination of the lure of sugar and its impact upon Western society.

* Philip Curtin, *The Atlantic Slave Trade* (Madison, WI: University of Wisconsin Press, 1969). A study of the importation of African slaves into the New World with the best estimates of the numbers of slaves and their destinations.

* Simon Schama, *The Embarrassment of Riches* (New York: Knopf, 1987). A social history of the Dutch Republic, which explores the meaning of commerce in Dutch society.

* Holden Furber, *Rival Empires of Trade in the Orient 1600–1800* (Minneapolis: University of Minnesota Press, 1976). A comprehensive survey of the battle for control of the Asian trade in the seventeenth and eighteenth centuries.

THE WARS OF COMMERCE

A. C. Carter, *Neutrality or Commitment: The Evolution of Dutch Foreign Policy 1667–1795* (London: Edward Arnold, 1975). A tightly written study of the objectives and course of Dutch diplomacy.

Charles Wilson, *Profit and Power* (London: Longman, 1957). Still the best study of the Anglo-Dutch wars of the mid-seventeenth century.

Paul Langford, *The Eighteenth Century 1688–1815* (New York: St. Martin's Press, 1976). A reliable guide to the growth of British power.

Ragnhild Hatton, ed., *Louis XIV and Europe* (London: Macmillan, 1976). An important collection of essays on French foreign policy in its most aggressive posture.

Richard Pares, *War and Trade in the West Indies 1739–63* (Oxford: Oxford University Press, 1936). A blow-by-blow account of the struggle for colonial supremacy in the sugar islands.

* Indicates paperback edition available.

CHAPTER 19
Africa and the Middle East,
1600–1800

A Surprise from Benin

It is 18 February 1897 in Benin City, in the southwestern part of Nigeria. A British force under Admiral Sir Harry Rawson has just entered the abandoned city. By now the colonial takeover of Africa is in its last stages, and this action is seen as something of a mopping-up operation. But this campaign turns out to be somewhat different. Upon entering the palace of the king (*oba*) of Benin, the British troops encounter something that perplexes and astonishes them. All around them, in every corner of the palace, are over two thousand plaques and statues made of brass, ivory, iron, and wood. Although doubtful that Africans could have made such striking artifacts, Rawson is nonetheless pleased to have some curios to send back to the British Museum as spoils of war and to parcel out to his men as souvenirs of their participation in the campaign. Two days after the fall of the city, on 20 February, a fire sweeps through Benin City, a fittingly apt symbol for the end of Benin's independence.

The dynasty that was overthrown by the British on that February day in 1897 was extraordinary. Occupying a strategically important position in the coastal hinterland, the obas, local big men, had been able to expand their small city-state gradually before 1300. Between 1325 and 1380 they began to have themselves memorialized in brass and ivory. In subsequent decades the power of the obas' state increased with its expansion, and the obas themselves became increasingly regarded as powerful rulers.

As kings, they realized that there were always tendencies for states in Africa to disintegrate. Therefore, they did everything possible to ensure that this fate did not befall Benin. Control was the essence of continued power, and the obas established control wherever possible. Religious ceremonies gave the oba spiritual control, and whenever the oba appeared in public, he was surrounded by the trappings of majesty and power. Guilds of artisans were all headed by the oba, thereby giving him economic control. The army was expanded, giving the oba political control. The thrust for control extended to the arts as well, and all artists who worked in brass were forbidden, under threat of death, to work for anyone outside the royal court. By 1485, under the oba's rule, Benin City had become one of Africa's largest and most prosperous cities.

While Benin was a strictly African phenomenon, based on trade within the region and on specifically African political and religious ideas and institutions, it was drawn into the wider world economy after 1485, initially through trade with the Portuguese. The obas of Benin, like many other African leaders, were wise enough not to equate independence with isolation from strangers, realizing that the powers they already had could be increased through contacts with the world beyond Africa. And so the obas vigorously encouraged Europeans to establish trading centers in Benin's territory, making sure all the time, however, that they monopolized the trade. Local people traded ivory, beads, pepper, cloth, and slaves to the Europeans. In return, the obas received various European luxury goods, brass and iron, and, most importantly, guns and ammunition, and even, at times, cavalry horses. With a steady supply of Western imports, the obas were able to expand their state and maintain their independence until the fateful British attack on 18 February 1897.

Throughout this long period of over five hundred years, the obas decorated their palace with brass plaques, such as the one illustrated here, both because they were beautiful in themselves and because they attested to their power. In this plaque, dating from the last half of the sixteenth century, power is the central theme. The oba is much bigger than his retainers. He carries a shield and a spear, symbols of military power. A naked retainer carries a huge sword. The oba wears the royal crown and the distinctive collar, or choker, made of coral. This coral was imported to Benin over the trans-Saharan trade routes from the Balearic Islands and its use was restricted to the powerful. Significantly, in the upper corners there are two floating figures depicting Portuguese traders with whom the oba dealt. It is appropriate that they appear on the plaque, for they represent another source of the oba's powers, this drawn from beyond Africa and fittingly symbolized by their lack of local roots.

When the British troops returned home from Africa in 1897, some sold the curios they had acquired. Some of the most elaborate plaques fetched a price of about $100. During the twentieth century, however, things began to change. The racism of the nineteenth century, which devalued all things made by Africans, began to erode. Great Western artists such as Pablo Picasso began to draw inspiration from African art. Art critics began to take African creativity seriously. And the price of Benin plaques responded, starting to rise in the 1930s and continuing upward. Were the descendants of one of the British troops in the campaign of 1897 to find a "souvenir" such as the one depicted in an attic trunk today, they would be lucky indeed. At auction, the plaque that sold for $100 in 1900 would today probably go for $500,000. The obas clearly had good artistic taste as well as political and economic power.

Africa in the Era of Rising European Capitalism

In the seventeenth century, several increasingly powerful competitors successfully challenged the Portuguese's position as the principal Europeans dealing with Africa. Seeking both a part of the profits made from supplying slaves to the expanding plantations of America and a share of the Indian Ocean trade, English, Dutch, and French traders increased European involvement with Africa and brought ever wider areas of it into deeper relations with the world economy. Such intervention contributed to changes in many African societies, especially in West Africa, where Europeans functioned primarily as traders, and in South Africa, where they settled.

During the last third of the eighteenth century, at the very height of the slave trade, criticism of it grew, especially in Britain, which was entering the first stages of the Industrial Revolution. Abolitionists not only demanded the end of the slave trade but also called for the establishment of a new relationship between Europe and Africa to be based solely on a trade in commodities other than slaves. The effort to expand this so-called "legitimate trade" was a slow and uncertain process and was marred by the persistence of the slave trade. By 1860, however, the West African slave trade had largely ended and the region entered into a new type of relationship with Europeans.

European Mercantilism and the Growth of Sugar Consumption

In 1580 Spain invaded Portugal and brought it under the Spanish crown, apparently confirming itself as the world's most powerful state. By 1600, however, the unified Iberian monarchy was in decline for two important reasons. The first was a shift in fiscal and economic power to the cities of Antwerp and Amsterdam because of Portugal's balance of payments deficit with its Asian trading partners and the persistent inflation in Spain caused by the inflow of large amounts of silver from America. The second reason for the decline of the Iberian monarchy was a parallel shift in political balance toward the countries of northwest Europe at a time when Holland, England, and France were emerging as nation-states able to challenge Spanish hegemony. The well-known destruction of the Spanish Armada in 1588 was, for example, merely one incident in a long conflict between Elizabethan England and Spain that lasted from 1585 to 1604. This rivalry between the new nation-states and Spain led to Spain's gradual defeat.

With Spain's decline and its conclusion in 1609 of the Twelve Years' Truce with the United Provinces, a new world power, Holland, came into prominence, growing ever stronger as the seventeenth century passed. The Dutch economy was based on a wide range of activities ranging from fishing and shipbuilding to sugar refining and agriculture, and its rulers sought to play an active role in world trade. Holland's rise to power coincided with important structural changes in Europe's economy. During the fifteenth and sixteenth centuries the European economy as a whole had expanded rapidly, drawing Africa, the Caribbean, Brazil, and the Indian Ocean basin more and more deeply into its orbit. At the start of the seventeenth century, however, much of the economy entered a period of sluggishness that continued until 1750 and brought a declining standard of living to rural Europe and a slowing of industrial growth.

After 1600, then, the combination of the growing Dutch political and economic threat and the persistent economic lethargy of the rest of Europe severely challenged the states of western Europe. In response, a new economic ideology known as mercantilism became widely accepted. Put simply, this was the idea that every nation-state should have its own colonies and that these would exchange their raw materials for manufactured goods from the home country. Mercantilism's aim was to create a closed system that would help insulate the home country's economy from outside influences. Between 1600 and 1750, mercantilism came to be the established economic orthodoxy for most of Europe's leaders, prompting them to build navies and seek colonies throughout the world, especially those already in Spanish and Portuguese control. In the wild scramble for colonies that occurred in the first half of the seventeenth century, the French seized Guadeloupe and Martinique and the English occupied many of the Caribbean islands, including Barbados, and also British Guiana (now Guyana), on the coast of South America. The Dutch seized Curaçao, Aruba, and Dutch Guiana (now Suriname), which remained Dutch until the twentieth century, as well as briefly occupying the

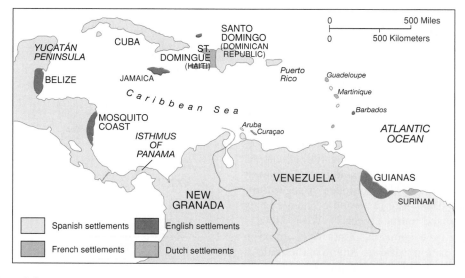

Caribbean Colonies, 17th Century

thriving Portuguese sugar colony of Brazil. In Africa, the Dutch for a short while also occupied Angola, from which most slaves for America's plantations were then obtained, and seized the old Portuguese trading fortress of Elmina, on the Lower Guinea Coast, where gold was still traded.

To the disappointment of their new owners, many of the Caribbean colonies initially seemed useless, with failed early attempts to grow cotton and tobacco with white European indentured laborers. Gradually, however, the new colonial powers decided that sugar, the one major crop that had already proven a success in America's tropics, might be suitable for their Caribbean colonies. This changeover to sugar production prompted a shift to using black African slaves, for it was widely believed that only slaves could provide the large, cheap, and disciplined workforce the plantation owners required. A 40 per cent drop in the prices of slaves from the Kongo-Angola area in the middle decades of the seventeenth century because of chronic warfare there encouraged them to expand this use of slaves.

Changing patterns of sugar consumption soon ratified the shift to sugar production in the Caribbean. For the most part, sugar had been used mostly as a medicine, condiment, and preservative. Between 1650 and 1675, however, just as increased production in America was lowering its price, its use as a sweetener sharply increased. At that time three new beverages—chocolate, tea, and coffee—were coming into fashion. All are naturally bitter and benefit from the addition of sugar. The growing middle classes of Europe particularly relished the new beverages, especially when sweetened, and provided a ready market for all four commodities as their prices fell. In short, a situation developed in which all the sugar that could be produced in the world would be consumed. In the third quarter of the seventeenth century sugar consumption accelerated with each passing year, ensuring both the further expansion of America's sugar plantations and fresh demands for African slaves.

In effect, then, the combination of mercantilist economic policies that demanded the creation of colonial empires and a seemingly unrelievable European sweet tooth that demanded endless supplies of sugar drew Africa ever more firmly into the world economy. Many areas of Africa—and most especially West Africa—became locked into economic relations that centered on the trade of slaves from Africa to America, the trade of sugar from America to Europe, and the trade of manufactured goods from Europe to Africa and America.

The New World's Demands on Africa: The West African Slave Trade

In the last half of the sixteenth century, English and Dutch merchants had sporadically challenged Portuguese domination of the West African trade. Although mortality rates from disease were high among Europeans, profits were also high, and, to the great disappointment of the Portuguese, in the seventeenth century British and Dutch companies established permanent trading stations along the West African coast. These companies enthusiastically traded for gold, pepper, ivory, gums, and other tropical products as well as for slaves.

After 1650, this situation gradually changed. Now possessing their own colonies in America and having improved their trade links with Asia, Europeans could obtain tropical products cheaper and with less loss of life from disease than they could from Africa. As a result, an African trade deficit with Europe began to become evident along the West African coast. Africans were now being asked to pay gold, a commodity rare outside the Gold Coast, for the imported goods they purchased, not trade other items they produced. This change presented a dilemma to African traders and politicians who depended on the import-export trade. How could they obtain the cloth and metal goods from Europe upon which they had come to depend? The question boiled

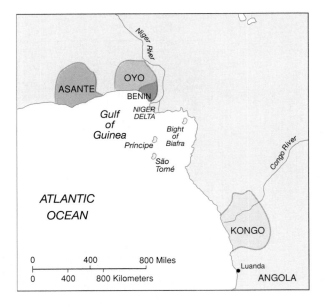

The Lower Guinea Coast

down to whether or not they could find a substitute for gold that would satisfy European traders.

Certain powerful Africans in certain areas responded to their fiscal problems by marketing the one remaining item that Europeans were eager to purchase from Africa in larger and larger quantities. That item was slaves. The worldwide demand for slaves was growing with the plantation system, and these West African leaders believed that, if they were to maintain their positions of power and wealth, they had no choice but to increase the supply of slaves. As they increased their efforts to meet the demand, and during the eighteenth century especially, armaments became more important in the mix of imports from Europe as certain leaders consolidated their military power and turned it on less powerful neighbors specifically to produce war captives whom they could then sell.

As demand grew, the main source of African slaves gradually shifted from the Portuguese-dominated Kongo-Angola area northward to the Lower Guinea Coast. During the late eighteenth century, at the height of the transatlantic slave trade, the great majority of slaves—as many as 65 per cent in any one year—came from this relatively small stretch of territory. This was so for two reasons. First, this region had dense populations near the coast from which slaves could be drawn. Sec-

ond, sturdy trading infrastructures were already in place that could increase the numbers of slaves available as fast as demand rose.

In the western part of the Lower Guinea Coast it was the leaders of such powerful states as Benin, Asante, Oyo, and Dahomey who, at different times, became active in the trade. They had access to coastal trading ports and were also strong enough to dominate the trade routes to the interior, from which most slaves were obtained.

Oyo, a Yoruba-speaking state located in the south central area of Nigeria, provides one example of how the trade worked. Oyo had long traded salt, kola nuts, and high quality cotton cloth produced in its own cities northward to the Sudanic region. In exchange it received horses, which it used to outfit a cavalry corps. Using this powerful cavalry, in the late seventeenth century Oyo's leaders expanded to the south and southwest, through a tsetse-free corridor of land, all the way to the coast, defeating neighboring Yoruba- and Aja-speaking peoples whom they encountered and taking many prisoners. These war captives were then sold into the ever receptive Atlantic slave trade, with many of the manufactured items acquired from Europe then traded north to the Sudanic zone for more horses. By building up its cavalry in this way, in the early eighteenth century

This drawing of the oba *in great state was published in 1668 in a report of a visit to Benin by the Dutch traveler O. Dapper.*

Oyo came to dominate the inland zones of a large part of the Lower Guinea Coast, using the Portuguese fortress of Ouidah (Whydah) as its main coastal outlet for slaves.

The eastern part of the Lower Guinea Coast, the Niger Delta and Bight of Biafra areas, produced slaves in a manner different from the western sector's. Here slaves were seldom captured in warfare or raiding carried out by states but rather came from kidnapping, small-scale skirmishing, and through the manipulation of judicial and religious institutions. The political organization of the area's Igbo and Ibibio speakers was on a small scale, taking the form of city-states or even villages. Nonetheless, big men whose fortune and power rested on trade were powerful in these societies, and they had formed alliances among themselves to create merchant castes protected by mercenaries. Religious leaders who supervised the oracles that adjudicated disputes and prophesied the future worked with these castes to produce slaves. False accusations of witchcraft became common, and religious officials demanded human sacrifices as compensation. Payments to the oracle for foretelling the future could also be made in the form of human beings. The victims so obtained were delivered to the merchants, who then disposed of them into the transatlantic trading system.

By employing existing legal and religious institutions, the violence of warfare and raiding common to the west was largely avoided. Yet the area's silent violence, which was so effective at producing slaves, sorely tested the ideology of kinship, with "family" becoming defined in ever more restricted terms and with the former assimilation of pawns, criminals, and war captives into the extended family largely forgotten. The turmoil that resulted as leaders sought to meet the increased demand for slaves in America could not but erode old cultural values and stimulate new ones.

Clearly, the slave-producing systems that operated on the Lower Guinea Coast in the late seventeenth and eighteenth centuries were complex. But there was also a unity of purpose evident. Throughout the area slaves were produced for the single overriding reason that powerful political leaders and wealthy merchants saw the trade as essential to maintaining themselves in their positions of power, especially when rising prices for slaves encouraged more exports. It was the work of an elite and its agents, not of the ordinary people, who remained for the most part engaged in subsistence production at the village level and who were not major consumers of the goods obtained from abroad. While important overall, the slave trade had few direct links with the village-level local economy.

An African slave is immobilized by a heavy forked log as he awaits shipment to the New World.

Several questions arise from the existence of the slave trade. First, how many people were transported across the Atlantic? For the entire period of trade across the Atlantic, from 1444, when the Portuguese began it at Arguin, to the late nineteenth century, scholars estimate that some 13 to 14 million Africans from all parts of Africa were transported, with, of course, substantial numbers of war captives and other victims dying either before leaving Africa or on shipboard during the dreaded "Middle Passage." During the period of the peak of the trade, between 1700 and 1810, West Africa alone exported 3,250,000 slaves, most of whom were carried in British, French, and Portuguese vessels.

That such large numbers of people were removed raises the further question of how Africa could, with its chronic labor shortage, "afford" to send away so many millions of its young and productive men and women. In trying to answer this question one must take certain facts into account. First, since a free market in labor did not exist, Africa was exporting a commodity that had already been ideologically devalued. Most victims of the trade were war captives from outside the society that actually traded them and were considered "surplus." As a consequence, at times of great availability of supply, prices for slaves reached astonishingly low figures on the coast.

Moreover, the draining of people does not seem to have depopulated Africa as a whole. This may have been because the population was growing naturally. Or it may have been because most people taken were young men, with women left behind to bear children in Africa. Scholars have also suggested that the introduction from

A SLAVE'S EXPERIENCE OF THE MIDDLE PASSAGE, 1755

■ Although the slave trade was a central factor in relations between Europeans and Africans for centuries, there are few descriptions by those enslaved of their experiences. One exception is the autobiography of Olaudah Equiano, an Igbo boy sold into slavery at the age of ten, transported to Barbados, and eventually freed in 1766. His book was published in 1789 as part of the Abolitionist campaign to end the slave trade. This passage describes his experiences on the slave ship that took him from Africa.

The stench of the hold while we were on the coast was so intolerably loathsome that it was dangerous to remain there for any time, and some of us had been permitted to stay on the deck for fresh air; but now that the whole ship's cargo were confined together it became absolutely pestilential. The closeness of the place and the heat of the climate, added to the number in the ship, which was so crowded that each had scarcely room to turn himself, almost suffocated us. This produced copious perspirations, so that the air became unfit for respiration from a variety of loathsome smells, and brought on a sickness among the slaves, of which many died, thus falling victim to the improvident avarice of their purchasers. This wretched situation was again aggravated by the galling of the chains, now become insupportable, and the filth of the necessary tubs, into which the children often fell and were almost suffocated. The shrieks of the women and the groans of the dying rendered the scene of horror almost inconceivable.

One day, when we had a smooth sea and moderate wind, two of my wearied countrymen who were chained together, preferring death to such a life of misery, somehow made through the nettings and jumped into the sea: immediately another quite dejected fellow, who on account of his illness was suffered to be out of irons, also followed their example; and I believe many more would soon have done the same if they had not been prevented by the ship's crew, who were instantly alarmed.

America of maize and cassava, crops that could feed more people per unit of land than earlier ones had done, supported a population growing enough to match the drain of the slave trade. In any case, however, had the slave trade never occurred, Africa's population would probably have been substantially greater than it was at the time the trade was finally ended.

Yet statements regarding the impact of the slave trade on Africa as a whole are largely irrelevant. In terms of the trade, Africa was *not* a whole, but a set of parts and regions and peoples, each with its own experience. When the trade affected a single area for a short and intense period—which was usual, since warfare was one of the major ways slaves were produced—then that area suffered greatly, not merely because slaves were taken from it, but because the violence destroyed local infrastructure and drove away people as refugees.

Finally, there is the issue of the extent to which the slave trade injured the underlying social structures in the affected areas. As we have seen, most African societies involved in the slave trade had already become differentiated into rulers and governed, rich and poor, powerful and powerless during the period when the luxury trade in gold and spices and other commodities was in its heyday, from the fifteenth through the mid-seventeenth centuries. Clearly, the slave trade benefited the rich and powerful who participated in it and who viewed it as a necessary, if regrettable, part of economic and political life once European traders decided that they did not want other African products. Clearly also, it injured the defeated or raided societies, such as the Aja or Yoruba, and greatly victimized people who were kidnapped within societies such as the Igbo.

The Abolitionist Movement and the Decline of Slavery's Viability

In 1800, the transatlantic slave trade raged stronger than ever. The American plantation economies that had originally sparked it had grown, and slaves were working now to produce not only sugar, but tobacco and cotton, with coffee soon to be added to the list. Yet by 1860 the

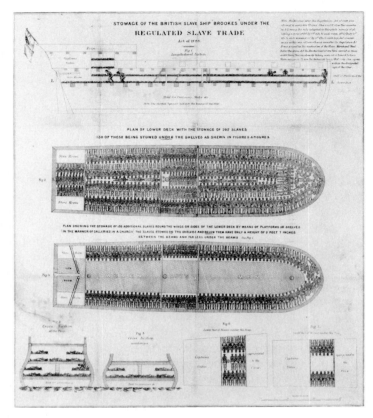

This diagram shows how slaves were packed into cargo holds for the notorious Middle Passage to the Americas. The plan was a model of efficiency as slave traders sought to maximize profits.

slave trade had virtually ended, and Africa was poised to enter a new phase of its history having little to do with that trade. The ending of the slave trade was not merely a natural occurrence brought about by changes in the world economy. Rather, it was also directly due to the success of the Abolitionist movement, which grew up in many countries in the last third of the eighteenth century.

Until the 1760s, most Europeans—indeed, most so-cieties—felt that slavery was both normal and accept-able. Periodic criticisms of it were regarded as little more than manifestations of crankiness. Yet major changes occurred in the late eighteenth century that, when combined, undermined the slave trade's accept-ability. The first was a complex change in ideas about the nature of humanity that occurred throughout all western Europe. Some of these ideas arose from the French Enlightenment and proclaimed the revolution-ary message that all people were created equal at birth and should have equal opportunity in this life. Intellec-tuals such as the Baron Montesquieu (1689–1755) and Jean-Jacques Rousseau (1712–78) specifically argued that Western civilization had been basically corrupted

by its pursuit of profits from such endeavors as growing sugar on plantations with slave labor and its denial of equality to slaves. The literature of the time depicted slaves as people who, although enslaved, preserved their original human dignity and their love of liberty in a world almost wholly corrupted by European greed and selfishness.

Buttressing the French Enlightenment's critique were arguments made by Scottish intellectuals, who argued against slavery from two perspectives. First, they said that it was immoral because of the suffering it caused and that no amount of reasonable, logical argu-mentation demonstrating its economic rationality could justify slavery. Adam Smith (1723–90), perhaps the most famous of Scottish intellectuals of the time, went further, arguing that slavery was not only morally repug-nant but also economically irrational because free labor-ers worked harder than slaves. Slavery and the slave trade were, then, both ethically evil and economically stupid.

Finally, changes in Christianity also prompted at-tacks on the slave trade. Most Christians had long ac-cepted that it was natural to have slaves at the bottom of the social hierarchy. Yet in the seventeenth and eighteenth centuries many Protestants began to make the radical claim that human equality in heaven should somehow be reflected by equality on earth, and they singled out slavery as an inherently sinful phenomenon because it denied human equality. Quakers and Methodists especially equated slavery with sin and asserted that slaveholders and slave traders were the very agents of Satan. Atonement for this sin required the ending of slavery and the slave trade. By the 1780s these three strains of criticism had merged to provide people with the intellectual ammunition for a generalized attack on both evils. The campaign that followed was known as Abolitionism.

As early as 1772 Britain's chief justice had declared that any slave who walked on English soil automatically became free. Then, in 1783, a group of Quakers organized a committee to petition the British Parliament to end the slave trade abroad. This initiative occurred simultaneously with great public shock and rage about one of the most hideous atrocities in the trade's whole atrocious history. The owners of the slave ship *Zong* had filed an insurance claim for a payment for lost property for 132 slaves who had been thrown into the Atlantic because, they claimed, the ship's provisions were running out. Such an action was legal, because slaves were viewed as property. At the enquiry, however, it was discovered that dysentery had broken out on the ship and that the 132 slaves who were thrown overboard were actually ill. Because insurance did not cover loss through illness, the owners fabricated the story about food running out as they sought to have their insurance cover their losses.

The inhumanity demonstrated by the *Zong* incident galvanized British opinion, and the Quakers soon found themselves with many allies. In 1787 the Quaker committee became the Society for the Abolition of the Slave Trade. In 1788 Parliament established a committee to investigate the slave trade, and in 1789 Olaudah Equiano published his *Travels* as part of the ongoing campaign against it. The British slave trade's seemingly imminent day of reckoning was postponed, however. The uncertainties produced by the French Revolution of 1789 and the horror of social chaos that the British felt when the slaves of Haiti, led by Toussaint L'Ouverture (ca. 1743–1803), successfully rebelled in 1791 and expelled the French colonial masters from the country, made British leaders reluctant to tamper with any type of property relations for some twenty years.

By the first years of the nineteenth century, however, the economic situation within the British Empire had altered, and those with vested interests in the slave trade had become too weak to mount an effective resistance to the Abolitionist arguments. British colonial sugar plantation owners, undercut in the mid- and late eighteenth century by competition from Martinique, Guadeloupe, and Haiti, had advocated tariff protection in keeping with the mercantilist notions of the time. By the start of the next century, however, leading figures in British economic life were moving to end mercantilist protectionism. As industrialization took hold in Britain, free trade became more and more attractive and mercantilism was seen as little more than an anachronistic excuse for sugar tariffs, slavery, and other evils. Protection seemed all the more pointless now that Britain had seized from France West Indian islands, such as Dominica, that produced cheaper sugar than Trinidad or British Guiana. The slave trade, an intrinsic part of the mercantilist system, came to be viewed as having outlived its usefulness, and it was accepted that both slavery and the slave trade, the immoral enemies of progress, should end. This was the age of liberalism (see chapter 25), and to be liberal meant to be against slavery.

In 1805 Britain outlawed the slave trade to its newly acquired colonies; in 1806 the ban was extended to include colonies of foreign countries; and in 1807 all slave trading by British subjects was outlawed. In the following year the United States passed a similar law. In 1814 the Netherlands acted similarly, and in 1815 France followed suit. Britain pressured Portugal, whose nationals were among those most deeply involved in the trade, to outlaw the trade as well. But, as ideas of liberalism and free trade had not yet penetrated to mercantilist Portugal, it refused. Only under great pressure did it agree to restrict the trade to areas south of the equator. To enforce these laws and agreements, the British established an anti-slave-trade patrol to arrest any ships caught in the trade, with special attention given to the main area of the trade, the West African coast.

Settler Society in South Africa

The impact of an expansive Europe after 1600 was by no means restricted to West Africa. In the process of meeting the growing seventeenth-century European demand for tea, coffee, and the various products of Asia, the Dutch East India Company, almost accidentally and certainly without intention, drastically changed the history of South Africa. The company's ships, sailing from Holland to the Far East, needed places to stop for fresh provisions. One such strategically important place had been the Cape of Good Hope, at the southern tip of Africa, where they took on fresh water and traded iron

This romanticized version of the partnership between England and the African kingdoms was rendered after the Congress of Vienna condemned the slave trade in 1815.

for meat. The Africans with whom the Dutch dealt there were the Khoi people, descendants of the hunters and gatherers who had once inhabited all of Africa south of the equator and who had been largely displaced when Bantu speakers occupied the subcontinent. As the Cape had a Mediterranean-type climate, however, it was unsuitable for the crops the Bantu grew and they had, therefore, left the Khoi in possession of the land, on which they raised sheep and cattle.

In the middle of the seventeenth century the Dutch East India Company decided that the Cape could also produce fresh fruit and vegetables for passing ships as well as supply water and meat. Having had good relations with the Khoi for decades and having recently been expelled by the Portuguese from their occupancy of Angola, in 1652 the company established a much-needed station at the Cape. As it was a private, capitalist company, its aim was to trade, not to govern people, and the very last thing it wanted was to have warfare eat up its profits. A small way station with well-defined boundaries and peaceful relations with the Khoi was the company's aim when it established Cape Town.

Unlike tropical Africa, where Europeans lacked immunity to local fevers and draft animals died, the Cape had neither malaria nor tsetse fly. Its climate was pleasant and its soils were good. The Khoi, sparsely settled on the land, did not threaten. As a consequence, in 1657, the company made a decision, the effects of which are still present in southern Africa. It released a group of its employees from their contracts, assigned them land, and told them to start producing food. These people came to be known as "free burghers." In response, the Khoi attempted to drive the Dutch out by waging guerrilla wars in 1659–60 and between 1673 and 1677. One by one, however, the Dutch forced the Khoi groups to come to terms. Many became propertyless laborers in Cape Town, working for the free burghers, and many others disappeared into the interior to join other groups of Khoi. After 1670 the company's representatives, seeking more meat and draft animals, pushed deeper into the interior and forced the Khoi there to trade their animals at prices the company set. Coming at a time of recurrent drought and cattle diseases, the company's persistent new demands pushed the Khoi into a pattern of social disintegration by the 1690s. Cattle, the wealth of the Khoi, were disappearing from their society and they were going bankrupt.

By 1713, just sixty years after Cape Town was founded, the majority of the Khoi had become manual laborers in the colony. Then fell the final blow. In February 1713 a ship carrying smallpox put into the harbor. By April an epidemic had broken out in the town. The Khoi died in large numbers. To escape the epidemic, many fled to seek refuge with their relatives in the interior. As a result, they carried smallpox into the interior. Over half the Khoi population died. The Khoi never recovered from this catastrophe, and after 1713 they gradually faded away, with their genes becoming merged in a general "coloured" population, which also included slaves imported from east Africa and Malaysia to do manual labor for the white settlers. By the end of the eighteenth century, the Khoi had lost their own specific identity.

While such changes were destroying Khoi society, other changes affecting the free burghers were making them into a wholly new one. In the first thirty years of their agriculturally oriented settlement, which was based on production carried out largely by slaves and Khoi workers, the European population had grown only slowly. Then, in 1685, in far-distant France, King Louis XIV revoked the Edict of Nantes, which had guaranteed religious freedom to French Protestants. Many thousands of Protestant Huguenots fled France and many of these came to the Cape, bringing with them the specialized skills needed to make local society viable. With wheelwrights, carpenters, engineers, glassmakers, and other skilled artisans now present, it became a largely self-sufficient society based on wheat and wine production and vegetable growing.

By 1700 it was clear that the increased settler population was exceeding the company's own limited requirements. Yet, with its mercantilist attitudes, it refused to allow the settlers to produce commodities for the wider world market. Finding themselves at an economic dead-end, many settlers decided to abandon farming, move away from Cape Town, and become cattle and sheep ranchers, occupying the niche that the now-fading Khoi had occupied in the local economy and forcibly displacing the San hunters and gatherers from the land onto which they moved. As the company wanted meat, it granted these settlers so-called loan farms on which to raise animals. Most of these loan farms were situated in dry areas of the interior, where the number of animals a unit of land could support was

limited. As there was no shortage of land, the loan farms tended to be very large, in the neighborhood of 6,000 acres or even more. Because the farms and ranches were so large, European expansion eastward across South Africa proceeded quickly.

During this period of expansion, the free burghers formed a new rural society. Sometimes called the Boers ("farmers"), they differed greatly from their cousins who had remained as farmers in the western Cape area, near Cape Town and even more greatly from their distant cousins in faraway Holland. Theirs was a semisubsistence pastoral existence and they depended for their survival on their cattle and sheep, trading meat, cattle hides, or wool when they needed to purchase goods. Wealth for them came to be seen as cattle and sheep, not as money or land. In religion they were all Calvinist Protestants and remained far from the leavening influence of the Enlightenment. The settlers founded no real cities as they expanded eastward nor did they produce intellectuals. Although they generally could read and write some Dutch, their spoken language began to change, picking up words and terms from local Khoi or from their slaves, gradually becoming a new language which was later to be called Afrikaans.

Significantly, their society was organized on strictly hierarchical lines that were congruent with race. On top were whites, the possessors of wealth. Below them were low-paid Khoi and "coloured" farm laborers who were considered dependents of the settlers. Finally, at the bottom, almost every Afrikaner had a slave or two, imported either from the East Indies or from East Africa. The perpetuation of this racial hierarchy entrenched among settlers attitudes of disdain and exploitation towards people of color.

As they left Cape Town farther and farther behind, these settlers became increasingly independent of the Dutch East India Company and developed their own distinct goals that conflicted with the company's. Their rapid eastward expansion continued until, in the 1770s, they reached the Bantu-speaking, black-skinned, cattle-raising agriculturalists who lived in the Eastern Cape. These were people who spoke the Xhosa language. Initially, in the late 1760 and early 1770s, the Xhosa and the settlers traded peacefully with one another. When missionaries ventured into Xhosa country, they were usually allowed to remain and some Xhosa even converted to Christianity. Some Xhosa worked on Afrikaner ranches. Some settlers went to dwell in Xhosa society, marry Xhosa women, become part of the group, and raise families.

A seventeenth-century engraving shows an idyllic scene of peaceful, mutually beneficial trade between the Khoi people and European sailors. In reality, the Europeans more often killed the Khoi and took what they wanted.

By the late 1770s, however, the westernmost Xhosa and the leading edge of the expanding population of settlers found themselves in increased competition for limited summer pasture lands. Cattle rustling on both sides further soured relations. As competition grew, the earlier peaceful relationships between settlers and Xhosa deteriorated and the first of a series of frontier wars broke out (1779–81). Unlike the Khoi, however, the Xhosa did not crumble or fade away.

These problems caused the Dutch East India Company great apprehensions. Its purpose was to make money, not fight wars. And so it promulgated a series of laws intended to keep the European settlers away from the Africans and thus reduce friction. The settlers ignored the company's efforts, however, and conflict grew. Finally, in 1793, after a great drought had made summer pastureland even more valuable, the Second Frontier War broke out. The company rushed troops to the area, but, instead of attacking the Xhosa, its troops forced the settlers to withdraw westward, hoping that physical separation would produce peace in the Eastern Cape. In February 1795 some settlers rebelled against the company, justifiably claiming that it was preoccupied with its profits and unconcerned with their interests. They demanded the right to administer local affairs and to have unlimited access to guns and ammunition.

The British Takeover of the Cape and the Great Trek

It was at this point, in 1795, that European events caught up with the settlers. Engaged in the early stages of the Napoleonic wars, Britain wanted to strangle France's world trade. Because France had occupied the Netherlands, the British seized the Cape of Good Hope from the Dutch East India Company in 1795. The new British administration was uncertain as to how long it would remain. The British wanted to keep Cape Town because of its strategic importance on the route to India and were willing to administer the Western Cape area because it was peaceful, but they feared involvement in costly wars with the Xhosa in the Eastern Cape for the sake of a scattering of settler stock raisers. Repeated British attempts to fix a firm boundary line between Xhosa and settlers, including the Third Frontier War (1799–1803), all failed, and the uncertainties of the Eastern Cape continued as before.

In 1811, however, this situation, which had dragged on for some thirty-five years or so, changed suddenly. The British, increasingly aware that the economic power given to them by the Industrial Revolution at home and the political power garnered by successive defeats of the French abroad had made them the world's most powerful nation, decided to use their power to establish order in the Eastern Cape. The British victory in the Fourth Frontier War (1811–12) ended the balance

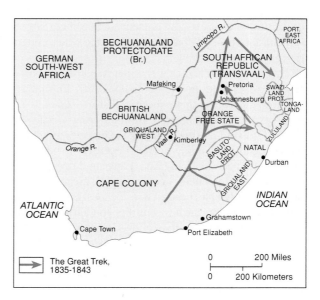

The Great Trek

THE DUTCH EAST INDIA COMPANY'S ATTITUDE TO THE XHOSA, 1794

■ *In business to make profits, not war, the Dutch East India Company desired peace with the Xhosa people on the Eastern Cape frontier. After the war of 1793 between the Xhosa and the Afrikaner settlers, the company asked for a report of its causes. In this report, the company's agent in the Eastern Cape suggests how the Xhosa should be treated if peace is to be maintained.*

Whoever has even an average knowledge of our country and the nature of the [Xhosa] nation will quickly understand that the discord with them must bring about the most disastrous consequences for the colony and its inhabitants. The colony is already being plagued by the vexations of the Bushmen (San people) who have now eventually been reduced to a wild and savage nation, staying alive through theft alone, so that the inhabitants of the colony are hardly able to protect themselves and their possessions against them. And who does not then realize that hostilities with the [Xhosa], who are so powerful people and of whom—as experience has taught—even a small part can throw the country into tumult, will produce the most fatal consequences for this colony.

I am convinced that these consequences cannot be countered, nor can peace and quiet be preserved, by other means than by lenient and moderate measures. Such measures, as I have often found, can have a great influence on the [Xhosa] nation, as a people susceptible to reason and jealous of their freedom. Yet these are also measures so alien to the way of thinking of many of our inhabitants that I must add, though it grieves me greatly to do so, that in continuing with these measures, I am meeting with the most extreme opposition and have difficulty in keeping some of the inhabitants from violence against this nation . . . [D]iscord with these [Xhosa] should at all times be counteracted with the most lenient measures. At the least, one should in no cases resort to extreme measures, but only do so when it is essential as a means of defence, and all other more humane measures have been tried without success.

From Report of H. C. D. Maynier to Commissary A. J. Sluysken, 31 March 1794.

that had existed between settlers and Xhosa and resulted in the expulsion eastward of some 8,000 Xhosa people, with many killed in the process. From that time the military advantage was unmistakably on the side of the Europeans.

The British determined to act against the white settlers as well. Intent upon introducing a wholly new form of colonialism based on bureaucratic efficiency and concern for due process of law, they soon gave the settlers a full catalog of grievances. One area of contention was labor relations. The large group of mixed-race offspring of the settlers and Khoi, San, Malay, Xhosa, or slave concubines were not themselves slaves, but settler law curtailed their rights to own property, compelled them to carry identity documents known as "passes," and forced them to work for the settlers for low wages. The British asserted that anyone not a slave was free and should have the rights of a free man. As a consequence,

the British took a series of steps to liberate the settlers' dependents, culminating in 1828 with the promulgation of Ordinance 50. This law reinforced earlier laws, ended peonage absolutely, and freed people from the obligation of having to carry passes. It also permitted them to own land in their own right, and it regulated working conditions for the first time. In effect, the British had dissolved the ties of dependency between the settlers and their clients.

A wide-ranging British attack on settler culture and institutions also provoked resentment. Pursuing a policy of anglicization, the British decreed that only English was to be used in the courts. English was also encouraged in the schools, and the British even found a group of Scottish Calvinist clergymen to fill the pulpits of the Calvinist Dutch Reformed Church, the settlers' church. In 1820 over 5,000 British settlers were introduced to the Eastern Cape to dilute the

Dutch presence. The cultural assault was increased in 1827, when the British replaced the system of local government and courts that the settlers had established with new English-speaking local magistrates and new British-staffed courts. Local political power was, thus, finally removed from local settlers to Cape Town.

Another grievance focused on the economy. Although the economy had grown after the British take-over, the major beneficiaries were the new English settlers, with the Dutch settlers remaining embedded in a sleepy subsistence economy. They felt that the British were unfairly dominating the economy and that they had been left behind in poverty. Finally, the straw

A young man of mixed Khoi and European ancestry poses in Western garb. African children of mixed blood often adopted Western manners and dress.

that broke the camel's back was the British policy on slavery. In 1834 slavery was abolished throughout the British Empire. The settlers were embittered both by what they saw as a violation of their property rights and by an inadequate compensation for their lost property.

Chafing under such policies, a group of settlers decided that if they were to remain true to their cultural heritage, they would have to leave British control. In 1835 some 4,000 of them, together with several thousand of their African and mixed-race retainers, left the Cape Colony on what became known as the Great Trek, moving north of the Orange River into the interior to escape the British. The interior had been affected during the 1820s by a series of wars known as the *Mfecane*, and many of its Tswana- and Sotho-speaking inhabitants were too weak to resist the migrants effectively. The powerful Zulu state, the one power that might have blocked their invasion of the interior, was itself defeated in 1838 at the battle of Blood River, one of the turning points in the history of South Africa, and the settlers were able to establish their new societies.

The Great Trek became the defining event in the history of Dutch settlement in South Africa. The settlers staked out huge ranches and farms of between 6,000 and 12,000 acres, forced defeated Africans to become farm laborers, and set up their own independent governments. Seeing them occupying only the barren interior, the British decided not to expend the money or effort that would be required to undo this movement of settler independence. Locked away in the interior, the British believed, the settlers could do little harm and they were thus given the opportunity to develop further into a unique people that came to be known as the Afrikaners.

"Legitimate Trade" and the Slave Trade in West Africa After 1807

At the end of the eighteenth century approximately 90 per cent of the value of the exports from sub-Saharan Africa was in the form of slaves. The outlawing of the slave trade could not but change radically the structure of African societies and their economies. What the British hoped was that the slave trade, now considered evil and illegitimate, would be replaced by a major expansion of what they termed the "legitimate trade." The expansion of European industrialization had produced a growing demand for vegetable oils to lubricate industrial machinery, to be manufactured into candles by which the newly literate classes could read, and, especially, to be made into soap. Peanuts grew well along the

Upper Guinea Coast, while along the Lower Guinea Coast palm trees produced palm nuts and palm oil in abundance. Traders eager to purchase these products soon arrived on the West Coast in ever larger numbers.

The expansion of this "legitimate trade" brought important changes to the coastal societies. First, new classes were given the opportunity to participate in the trade. While the production of slaves had been mostly controlled by large-scale merchants, aristocrats, and kings, producing peanuts and palm oil could be done by ordinary people using family labor and traditional tools. The new trade gave ordinary people the opportunity to earn money and brought about the creation of a new African peasantry willing and even eager to produce for the world economy.

At the same time, it opened the way for new middle classes to emerge by prompting a change in the system of labor mobilization. Up to then labor for subsistence cultivation had been mobilized either through kinship or, where possible, domestic slavery. These old ways were, however, inadequate to meet growing demands for oil products. The result was a commercialization of labor in West Africa, with certain people using the money they obtained from the new trade to hire either local poor people or migrant workers from the north for

A Xhosa fighter armed with traditonal weapons. The Xhosa were the first Bantu speakers to clash with the British and the Boers in southern Africa.

more production or even to purchase people as slaves to work locally. These increasingly well-off people, with their own ideas about progress, joined the social structure between the elite above and the poor peasants, subsistence producers, and slaves below.

The nature of imports also changed. The slave trade had involved imports of textiles, tobacco, rum, luxury goods for the elite, guns, and gunpowder. Ordinary people were uninterested in large quantities of guns and gunpowder, and traders now brought larger quantities of textiles, tobacco, hardware, salt, and other goods intended for mass consumption, thereby developing a mass market in West Africa for the first time.

Changes in pricing in the decades before 1860 greatly strengthened the growth of the new type of trade. As competition to buy African vegetable oils increased, their prices rose by over 100 per cent in forty years. At the same time, the prices of imported manufactured goods decreased steadily because of technological strides in Europe. This meant that producers were able to obtain more and more manufactured goods per unit of their oil products. In other words, between 1810 and 1860, the terms of trade were very much in Africa's favor, improving with each decade and stimulating even more production.

Yet despite these remarkable changes, the slave trade from West Africa continued. The Portuguese legally traded slaves south of the equator, using Angola and Mozambique as principal sources. Yet even in the parts of West Africa where the new "legitimate trade" was taking root and growing, those with vested interests in the slave trade on both sides of the Atlantic resisted British attempts to suppress it. In Cuba and Brazil, for example, as well as in areas of the American South, the importance of slaves in plantation agriculture increased in the early nineteenth century as demand for sugar, coffee, and cotton grew steadily. Thus, when Brazil became independent from Portugal in 1822, it renounced even Portugal's half-hearted restrictions on the slave trade and vigorously continued it. Slavery endured in Brazil until 1888.

When the British moved to abolish the trade in 1807, African rulers and merchants were astonished that Europeans should suddenly be denouncing what they had been clamoring for for so many centuries. Once they had recovered from their astonishment, however, most determined that they would continue the trade if at all possible. It had been the source of the arms and luxury goods that they had come to depend upon for their political and economic survival, and they would not willingly let it die. The income from peanut and palm oil production seemed a poor substitute for the wealth derived from the slave trade, particularly as it was difficult to tax peasant producers.

But the African leaders needed partners, and with demand for slaves still strong in America, people eager to take up that role soon appeared. European nationals generally obeyed their countries' laws and abandoned the slave trade. But when the price of slaves on the West African coast fell to about half of what it had been before 1807, a group of Brazilians moved to the Bight of Benin to handle the trade. By 1820, it had revived and an estimated 80,000 slaves, many drawn illegally from West Africa, were shipped annually across the Atlantic.

This reinvigorated trade was clandestine and illegal but it was nonetheless real. British attempts at blockading it were far from effective. The nearness of the Lower Guinea Coast to the equator meant that a ship flying the Portuguese or Brazilian flag could drop quickly into the Southern Hemisphere, where the trade was still legal in international law. Also, the limitations of poor communications in the days before radio and the slow sail-powered ships in the British antislavery patrol resulted in the British being simply unable to stop slavers even when they detected them north of the equator, for the slave traders used the most advanced American-built ships, which could outrun the antiquated British naval vessels. The West African coast itself also had many lagoons and estuaries in which the slave traders' ships could hide until their cargo was completed, at which time they would make a break when signals were given that, literally, the coast was clear of the British navy. Finally, the Portuguese rented their flag to the ships of other nations, thereby protecting them from seizure. As Britain's foreign minister in the mid-1830s, Lord Palmerston, aptly remarked, "The ships of Portugal now prowl about the oceans, pandering to the crimes of other nations; and, where her own ships are not sufficiently numerous for the purpose, her flag is lent as a shield to protect the misdeeds of foreign pirates."

So successfully had the Brazilians been in eluding the British that in 1850 the commander of the British anti-slave-trade squadron reported that the profits of the traders were as high as ever and that the export of slaves from the Bight of Benin area was actually increasing to meet the demand for slaves that a recent expansion of Cuban sugar production and Brazilian coffee production had produced. As a result of all these problems, it is estimated that only one out of every sixteen slaves—or 160,000 people in all—sent across the Atlantic after 1807 were actually rescued and freed by the British patrols.

The Development of South African Society to 1852

1652	Dutch East India Company establishes Cape Town as a way station between Holland and the East Indies
1657	The company releases workers from their contracts, creating a class of European settlers known as "free burghers"
ca. 1700	Expansion of European settlement eastward from Cape Town as free burghers become sheep farmers and cattle ranchers on "loan farms"
1713	Smallpox epidemic destroys over half of Khoi people
ca. 1770	Settlers expanding eastward encounter Xhosa people in Eastern Cape in neighborhood of the Great Fish River
1795	Britain takes over the Cape from the Dutch during Napoleonic wars
1811	British military expels Xhosa beyond the Great Fish River in effort to establish a border
1818	Shaka becomes leader of Mthethwa and begins Zulu expansion
1820	Arrival of 5,000 British settlers in the Eastern Cape
1828	Ordinance 50 restructures relationships between Afrikaners and their dependents
1834	British abolition of slavery in the Cape angers Afrikaners
1835–38	Many Afrikaners leave Cape on their Great Trek into the interior, where they create their own states beyond British control
1838	Battle of Blood River, in which Afrikaners defeat the Zulu armies
1852–54	Britain grants level recognition to Afrikaner republics in the interior

The final end of the transatlantic slave trade came abruptly. In 1856, accepting the argument that the trade was a crime against humanity, the British government threatened war against Brazil. Brazil capitulated immediately. Once the demand was turned off, the trade that had characterized relations between Europe and Africa to a lesser or greater extent since 1444 trickled out speedily.

Mid-nineteenth-century Africa was very different from the Africa of 1600. In large measure this difference was the result of the impact that Europeans had as Africa entered into an expanding world economy through the nexus of trade. Aside from the intensive white settlements in South Africa and the far weaker influence of the Portuguese in Angola and Mozambique, Africa was still politically independent, with many states having profited from the centuries of trade with Europe and strengthened themselves. In 1860 there seemed to be no reason why this independence should not continue. Yet within two decades a new era had begun. It was to be far more exploitative than the one that had ended in around 1860. This was the era of imperialism and colonial takeover.

The Middle East and the World System

Tsar Nicholas II of Russia called it the "sick man of Europe"; British prime minister William Gladstone referred to it as "the unspeakable Turk." Indeed, to most nineteenth-century European observers, the Ottoman Empire appeared to be an empire in decline, a petrified shell of its former grand self.

The evidence for such a view of not only the Ottoman Empire, but also of Egypt (which, although autonomous during this century, was legally a part of the Ottoman Empire), and of Persia was clearly discernible to contemporary observers. Although during the nineteenth century the leaders of these states attempted to build the infrastructure necessary to maintain their territorial integrity and transform their societies, the boundaries that separated the Ottoman Empire and Persia from Europe were continuously pushed back. By the first decades of the twentieth century, the Ottoman Empire would be forced out of most of its European territories, French and Italian settlers and armies would be entrenched in North Africa, and Great Britain would occupy Egypt, where its troops would remain until 1956.

In terms of economics, over the course of the nineteenth century the Ottoman Empire, Egypt, and Persia became increasingly dependent on international markets, which set the prices for the agricultural goods they sold: Cotton from Egypt fed the mills of Lancashire, while raw silk from Lebanon was exported to France. In return, the empires of the Middle East imported manufactured goods and borrowed money from Europe to finance internal improvements. The trade imbalances and debts became so severe that both the Ottoman Empire and Egypt were forced to declare bankruptcy in 1876.

Integration of the Middle East into the World Economy

The relationship between the Middle East and Europe in the nineteenth century was the culmination of a process that had begun three centuries earlier when European voyages of discovery, the commercial revolution, and the rise of the Atlantic economies placed western Europe at the center of a new world economic and political system, integrating other regions of the world into the system in a subordinate role.

The discovery of large quantities of gold and silver in the Americas in the sixteenth century affected the Middle East as well as Africa. The influx of precious metals inflated prices in Europe, so Europeans turned to the Ottoman Empire for agricultural products and raw materials such as wheat, wool, raw silk, and metals. Further, to offset their trade deficits, governments of European trading states encouraged their merchants

The European Great Powers, especially Russia, had designs on Ottoman territory. This cartoon shows the British lion, the German and Austrian eagles, and the Russian bear closing in on a hapless turkey, which represents the "sick man of Europe."

to produce and export manufactured goods, such as textiles, for overseas markets. Such goods, sold in Middle Eastern markets, undercut local craftsmen and crippled local production. By the mid-eighteenth century, imports into the Ottoman Empire exceeded exports.

If the Ottoman Empire, Egypt, or Persia had been able to raise the level of import tariffs or create monopolies to guarantee local production, perhaps they could have resisted the subordination of the Middle East to the Atlantic economies. But because of their political and military weakness, neither the Ottoman Empire, Egypt, nor Persia was able to do so. Thus, an unequal trade relationship developed and continued between Europe and the Middle East, a relationship not without its ironies. Between 1840 and 1914, for example, cotton textiles represented about one-third of the Middle East's imports, while during the first decade of the twentieth century raw cotton made up 90 percent of Egypt's exports and about 20 percent of the exports from the Ottoman Empire and Persia.

Thus, during the nineteenth century, the pace and scope of the political and economic incorporation of the Middle East into the world system accelerated and widened. This process affected all aspects of social, economic, and political life in the region.

The Near Eastern Question

The Treaty of Kuchuk Kainarji in 1774 between Russia and the Ottoman Empire marked a turning point in the history of Ottoman-European relations. The Ottoman state was clearly no longer, in the words of one seventeenth-century English observer, "the present terror of the world." As the eighteenth and nineteenth centuries progressed, European statesmen no longer worried about how to defend against Ottoman expansion. Instead, they pondered how to deal with the problem of an increasingly enfeebled Ottoman state whose decay threatened to create a power vacuum in southeastern Europe and the eastern Mediterranean—a power vacuum that would threaten the balance of power in Europe. This problem became known as the Near Eastern Question.

There were two parts to the Near Eastern Question in the nineteenth century—one external to the region, one internal. After the Russian state had been consolidated under Tsar Peter the Great in the eighteenth century, it began to expand southward, threatening the Ottoman Empire in the southwest and Persia in the southeast. The Russian advance south in search of a

warm-water outlet to the sea could be made only at the expense of the Ottoman Empire.

At the same time, to protect its lifeline to India and to ensure a European balance of power favorable to its interests, Great Britain had to prevent the Russian advance. British foreign secretary Lord Palmerston, reacting to one in a series of Middle Eastern crises that focused the attention of his nation on the region, enunciated a policy to which British governments adhered until 1914: "His majesty's government attach great importance to the maintenance of the integrity of the Ottoman Empire, considering that state to be a material element in the general balance of power in Europe." Britain and Russia remained at loggerheads over the Ottoman Empire throughout the century. Farther east, the Russian attempt to expand at the expense of Persia threatened British India and sparked a rivalry between the two powers that was called by Rudyard Kipling the Great Game.

Over the course of the nineteenth century, the Near Eastern Question was complicated by the activities of other European powers, which frequently intervened in the region to protect their interests. After France lost control of the Atlantic to the British in the Seven Years' War (1756–63), for example, it turned to the Mediterranean as an area from which to sell manufactured goods. French economic and strategic concerns in the region led to their invasion of Egypt in 1798 and conquest of Algeria in 1830. After unification, Germany also looked to the Middle East as an area for commercial expansion, and became a major promoter of Ottoman railroad construction, even proposing a line from Berlin to Baghdad.

The integrity of the Ottoman Empire was further threatened by two internal factors. The first factor was the rise of nationalism among the Balkan peoples of the Ottoman Empire, who desired independence and often sought the assistance of their fellow Orthodox Christians in Russia to obtain it. The second factor was the inability of the Ottoman government to control local governors in the Middle East and North Africa, such as Muhammad 'Ali, the viceroy of Egypt, who sought autonomy or independence with increasing success.

Defensive Modernization

Confronted by both foreign and internal challenges, Middle Eastern leaders responded by attempting to centralize and expand their authority in order to strengthen their states and make them more efficient. In the Ottoman Empire, Egypt, and Persia, leaders concentrated their first efforts on military matters. To

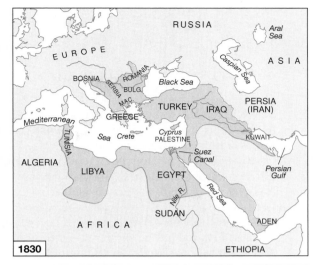

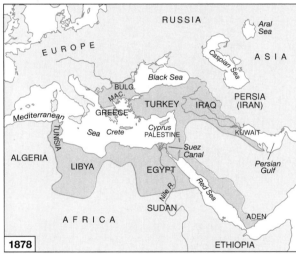

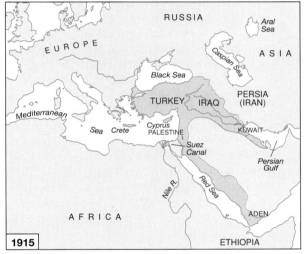

The Decline of the Ottoman Empire

resist foreign encroachment, they sought to reconstruct their armies along Western lines. Military reform was expensive, however, and to support these new armies they encouraged the cultivation of cash crops and tried to rationalize taxation and increase tax revenues. The Ottoman Empire eliminated middlemen such as tax farmers—private individuals who purchased from the state the right to collect and pocket taxes from the local peasantry. Further, staffing the modern armies and government bureaus required educated personnel. This meant building new educational institutions and teaching subjects such as mathematics, engineering, and foreign languages. This process is known as defensive modernization.

The most striking example of defensive modernization took place in Egypt, where a dynasty established in 1807 by a former Albanian soldier in the Ottoman service, Muhammad 'Ali, took power during the chaos that followed the French invasion. For Muhammad 'Ali, military reform was essential for two reasons: not only did he want to maintain internal stability and protect Egypt's near total autonomy in the Ottoman Empire, but he wanted to expand the area under his control to ensure the supply of essential raw materials and to monopolize east-west trade routes.

Thus, in 1831, Muhammad 'Ali's son, Ibrahim, led a military expedition into Syria to gain access to trade routes that passed through the eastern Mediterranean

LAMENT ON THE FRENCH CONQUEST OF ALGIERS

■ *The following is an excerpt from a lament written by Shaykh ʻAbd al-Qadir, a witness to the French conquest of Algiers in 1830. It later became a part of Algerian oral tradition.*

May your servants regain peace, may all their grief be ended
And may this oppression which crushes the Muslims cease!
Let us cry over the *muftis,* over the *qadis,*
Over the *ulama* of the city, those guides of the religion.
Let us cry over the mosques and their sermons
And over their pulpits of elevated marble.
Let us weep over their *minarets*[1] and the calls of the *muezzins;*[2]
and over the classes of their teachers and over their cantors of the Qur'an.
Let us lament the private chapels whose doors have been locked
And which have sunk today, yes Sir, into oblivion.
Alas where are the precious trinkets of the city, where are its houses?
Where are their low apartments and the elevated rooms for the eunuchs?
They are no longer but a parade ground and their traces have disappeared.
So much does that cursed one breathe to plague us!
The Christians have installed themselves in the city;
Its appearance has changed;
It no longer has seen anything but impure people.
The *janissaries'* houses! They have razed their walls;
They have torn down its marble and its sculptured balustrades,
The iron grills which protected the windows
Have been put to pieces by those impious ones, enemies of the Religion.
Likewise, they have named that Qaisariya "the Square",
Where the Books and their binders were formerly found.
The Magnificent Mosque which was next to it
Has been destroyed by them simply in order to spite the Muslims.

[1]*Minaret:* slender tower attached to mosques. Balconies on the minaret are the place from where people are called to prayer.
[2]*Muezzin:* Muslim official who calls the faithful to prayer (from the minaret).

region, acquire raw materials such as timber, and monopolize the Syrian silk trade. Egypt continued to occupy this area for ten years until the Ottoman government, with British assistance, was able to reassert control. During that time, the Egyptians introduced policies into the region typical of defensive modernizers: conscription, direct taxation, public works, the cultivation of cash crops that could be sold abroad to earn foreign exchange, and measures to increase public security and expand trade.

To support his military adventures abroad, Muhammad ʻAli undertook new economic policies at home. He confiscated lands that had been held by the previous Mamluk rulers of Egypt. He placed lands that had been under the control of tax farmers directly under the control of the Egyptian government. His government attempted to control all aspects of agriculture. The government encouraged the planting of cash crops, particularly cotton. It set up a monopoly that bought cotton from cultivators to sell to European agents, and it invested in industries associated with cotton, such as ginning and spinning. These changes had important social consequences: They put women to work spinning and weaving in factories while their husbands were recruited to the corvee (forced labor) digging irrigation ditches.

Muhammad 'Ali, shown here meeting with the British colonel Patrick Campbell and French engineers, called upon foreign experts to help in the modernization of Egypt.

Muhammad 'Ali's encouragement of cotton cultivation further integrated Egypt into the world economic system, and Egyptian revenues became directly dependent on the price of cotton in the international marketplace. In 1800, for example, more than 50 percent of Egypt's trade was with the Ottoman Empire, and 14 percent was with Europe; by 1823, these figures were reversed.

Cotton production proved to be both a blessing and a curse for Egypt. During the American Civil War, the Northern blockade of Southern ports cut off Europe's supply of Confederate cotton and drove cotton prices up. As a result, both Egyptian revenues and dependency on cotton cultivation increased. Muhammad 'Ali's successors, anticipating a lasting boom, borrowed heavily from European bankers to finance internal improvements and prestige projects, such as an opera house in Cairo. When the American crop went on the market again, the price of cotton plummeted, Egyptian revenues collapsed, and the government was forced to declare bankruptcy.

It is ironic that the policy originally intended to ensure political and economic independence had the opposite effect. For Egypt, defensive modernization led to borrowing, borrowing led to bankruptcy, and bankruptcy led in 1882 to a British occupation that would last more than three-quarters of a century. While in Egypt, the British encouraged the continued cultivation of cotton to feed their mills and discouraged investment in industries that might compete with those in Britain. British direction hindered the social and political devel-

opment of Egypt as well. For example, the first British consul general, Lord Cromer, discouraged expenditures on education because he feared the creation of a class of disaffected, unmanageable intellectuals.

In other parts of the Middle East, defensive modernization, called by the Ottomans the *Tanzimat* ("reorderings"), also had mixed results. The Ottoman Empire of the eighteenth century had been virtually decentralized; instead of power being concentrated in Istanbul, local notables ruled their provinces with little control from the central government. Even in those regions where the state could exercise power, however, it often did not do so, allowing the population to organize its own affairs through guilds and informal networks of authority.

Under the nineteenth-century Tanzimat sultans, the state not only attempted to curb the powers of local leaders, but it also expanded its own authority into areas where governments had never before intruded, such as education and social welfare. The Tanzimat sultans abolished the Janissary corps and replaced it with a conscript army. They legislated against tax-farming, restructured the central bureaucracy along European lines, and established provincial councils based on representative principles. They extended the authority of secular law. In an attempt to unify the empire, they built railroads and established *rushdiyye* schools, which took children after Qur'an training and prepared them for Western-style colleges.

The effects of the Tanzimat, however, were uneven. As in the case of Egypt, the cost of defensive modernization eventually led to bankruptcy and to European supervision of Ottoman finances. The size and diversity of the empire also complicated the centralization and rationalization of the government and the economy. Whereas, by contrast, the homogeneity of the land and population of Egypt made the mandating of a cotton-based economy relatively easy, such was not the case in the Ottoman Empire, which included the Balkans, North Africa, and the Arab Middle East.

Furthermore, the traditional Ottoman state had been built on informal networks, the predominance of Islamic institutions, and local autonomy. Many groups resisted centralization. For peasants, the restructuring often meant the potential for more efficient taxation and conscription; for ulama who were not attached to the central bureaucracy, it meant loss of prestige and limitations on their educational and judicial functions; for local notables, it meant loss of power.

Because of this local resistance, many of the regulations had effects different from those intended. For

INAUGURATION DU CANAL DE SUEZ. — *Te Deum* chanté à Port-Saïd en présence de LL. MM. l'Empereur d'Autriche et l'Impératrice des Français. — D'après un croquis de M. Auguste Marc.

The ceremony for the opening of the Suez Canal in 1869.

Linking the Seas

Building a canal to link the Mediterranean Sea with the Red Sea and Indian Ocean had been a dream since the times of the Egyptian pharaohs. With the shift in the center of the European economy away from the Mediterranean toward the Atlantic, beginning in the sixteenth century, the benefits to be derived from such a canal increased. A canal, cut through the Isthmus of Suez, would reduce by half the distance that merchant ships traveled from London to Bombay.

According to an apocryphal story still told in Egypt, history owes the construction of the Suez Canal to macaroni. Muhammad 'Ali, the founder of a dynasty that ruled Egypt for more than 150 years, was a soldier who hated the corpulence of his son, Sa'id. Muhammad 'Ali forced Sa'id to take exercise every morning, but while out riding, Sa'id would meet up with Ferdinand de Lesseps, a junior member of the French diplomatic mission in Egypt, and the two would return to the embassy to lunch on pasta. When, years later, de Lesseps returned to Egypt with a plan to dig the Suez Canal, Sa'id could not refuse him.

Whatever the truth to this story, it is well-known that Sa'id had a passion for grand public works and was very susceptible to the flattery of anyone who had a project to promote. He could hardly have been unmoved by de Lesseps' memorandum in which the wily promoter wrote,

The names of the Egyptian sovereigns who erected the pyramids, those monuments of human pride, remain unknown. The name of the Prince who opens the great maritime canal will be blessed from century to century, down to the most distant posterity.

De Lesseps thus acquired the backing of the viceroy for his project.

Sa'id obligated the Egyptian government to purchase 64,000 of the 400,000 public shares of de Lesseps' Suez Canal Company. When, by 1858, only half the stock issue had been sold, de Lesseps persuaded the Egyptian government to take up the remainder. In addition, Sa'id promised de Lesseps that he would provide a corvee (forced labor) of 20,000 laborers each year to dig the canal. At times, the number of forced laborers exceeded 40,000, contributing the equivalent of over 1 million days of labor. The conditions under which these laborers worked, equated by the British press to the worst conditions of slavery, caused a furor in Europe. In a public exchange of letters, an outraged de Lesseps accused the British of hypocrisy, comparing, without any hint of irony, conditions among the laborers on the canal to that of the unemployed poor of London or the lowest classes in British India.

De Lesseps understood that the British government based its concern for the plight of the Egyptian fellah (peasant) on the fact that it felt that "Egypt is the key to our house in India." Because of this, the British naturally opposed a French-initiated canal project straddling the route to their most important colony. If a canal was to be built, Britain would have to control it. As Prime Minister Lord Palmerston put it,

We do not want Egypt or wish it for ourselves, any more than any rational man with an estate in the north of England and a residence in the south would have wished to possess the inns on the road. All he could want would have been that the inns should be well-kept, always accessible, and furnishing him, when he came, with mutton-chops and post-horses.

Thus, in 1875, with the canal an established fact, the British government purchased the Suez Canal Company stock owned by an Egyptian government which, in the wake of the collapse of cotton prices, was heavily in debt and facing bankruptcy. With this purchase, the British government became the largest single shareholder of the canal company's stock. The protection of this vital interest became a major British strategic concern and was one of the reasons for the British invasion and occupation of Egypt in 1882.

Canal construction continued for ten years. Sa'id's successor, Isma'il, planned a huge celebration for the opening of the canal in 1869: a procession of ships, led by Empress Eugénie of France aboard the imperial yacht, sailed down the canal. The viceroy commissioned the Italian composer Giuseppe Verdi to write an opera with an Egyptian theme, *Aida*, for the event. When one Egyptian minister complained to a European guest about the cost of the festivities, saying "We are eating up the Pyramids stone by stone," his guest summed up European relations with Egypt by replying, "Never mind, Your Excellency, you can borrow money from us and then you can buy from us the cement to replace them."

The opening to the Suez Canal had major repercussions for international and regional trade. The cost of shipping goods from Europe to India and vice versa was substantially cut, and the opening of the canal proved to be a boon to fragile steamboats, which could not weather the Cape route. The canal had major repercussions for the Middle Eastern economy as well. While trade between Iraq and Europe grew, and the value of Iraqi exports, such as grain and wool, increased by 350 percent during the period 1870–75, the importance of cities dependent on the overland caravan trade, such as Damascus, declined. Ironically, with the opening of the canal, the Egyptian government lost revenues from the overland transit of goods and mail from Alexandria, on the Mediterranean, to the Red Sea ports.

In 1876, the Turkish statesman Midhat Pasha (1822–83) proclaimed a constitution for the Ottoman Empire, culminating an era of reform based on western European ideas. However, the constitution did not survive the succession of the Sultan Abdülhamid II (1876).

example, the 1858 Ottoman Land Code was designed to increase agricultural production and end tax farming by giving peasants the right to register the lands they were working in their own names. Peasants were often suspicious of the motives of the Ottoman government. Fearing that this "gift" of land was made merely to increase their tax burden and that registration would lead to conscription, many either fled their land or signed it over to urban-based notables, becoming, in the process, tenant farmers.

In Persia, the effects of defensive modernization were different from either Egypt or the rest of the Ottoman Empire. Three situations explain this difference. First, the dynasty that governed the country, the Qajar dynasty, did not have strong roots among the population and, having little effective control outside the capital of Tehran, ruled indirectly through tribal leaders, local families, and the indigenous bureaucracy. Second, as a result of the Great Game, both Britain and Russia discouraged the Persian government from seeking technical assistance or loans from its rival. Finally,

the Shi'i ulama of Persia, who conceived of themselves as defenders of Persian Shi'i tradition against foreign domination and autocratic rule, were not only well organized and financially independent, but they also were allied with other urban-based strata, such as merchants, an alliance that increased their influence in society.

After half-hearted attempts at military reform early in the century had failed, and after only limited success in fostering institutions necessary for defensive modernization, successive Persian governments attempted to generate revenues and hasten development by granting concessions to European financiers—that is, selling them the right to produce, market, and export a commodity or commodities. For example, in 1872 the Persian shah granted to Julius de Reuter, a British subject, the exclusive right to build streetcars and railroads, extract minerals, establish a national bank, and exploit the national forests in exchange for a modest down payment and the promise of future royalties. A similar concession in 1889 to the Imperial Tobacco Company allowed the company to control the cultivation, sales, distribution, and export of all Persian tobacco and tobacco products. In the wake of protests led by ulama, both of these agreements had to be cancelled.

The overall effects of the attempts at defensive modernization in Egypt, the Ottoman Empire, and Persia were ambiguous. If measured by the success in centralization and the spread of governmental authority into previously unregulated areas of society, then it is possible to claim that defensive modernization succeeded in Egypt, had mixed results in the Ottoman Empire, and had very modest success in Persia. But the purpose of defensive modernization was to defend Middle Eastern states from Western political and economic intrusion, and this effort failed. During the nineteenth century, the Ottoman Empire lost most of its Balkan and North African territories, Britain occupied Egypt, and, in 1907, Britain and Russia announced plans to divide Persia into spheres of influence. Economically, some measures actually facilitated Western economic penetration of the region. Among these were the encouragement of cultivation of cash crops, foreign borrowing, and the construction of networks of communication and transportation, as well as educational and governmental institutions that more closely corresponded with those of Europe.

Overall, integration of the Middle East into the world system and changes brought about as a result of defensive modernization affected, either directly or indirectly, almost every aspect of life in the region. As a result, both social institutions and the relationship between state and society in the Middle East were substantially different at the close of the nineteenth century from those at the beginning of the century.

The Transformation of Society and Culture in the Middle East

In the nineteenth century, the Middle East was defined to a great extent by its integration into the world system and by the reaction of national leaders to this integration. However, to view Middle Eastern history in this era as only decline and subordination to Europe would be a mistake. Dramatic changes took place: new social classes were created, urban centers were reconstructed, and the responsibilities of government and citizenry were redefined.

Accompanying the institutional changes that transformed the Middle East in the nineteenth century were corresponding cultural changes. European penetration of the region influenced the content of the intellectual movements, both directly and indirectly, while defensive modernization fostered a stratum of intellectuals who would be both the primary producers and primary consumers of many of the new intellectual trends.

The Reconstruction of Urban Life

Urban-based civilizations have inhabited the Middle East for thousands of years. Indeed, the residents of such cities as Damascus and Jericho still demonstrate civic pride by claiming that their cities are the oldest continuously inhabited places on earth. Until the nineteenth century, however, Middle Eastern cities had differed from European and American cities in several ways. Unlike their Western counterparts, for example, Middle eastern cities were not independent, corporate entities, nor did they foster such entities. Autonomous municipal governments with responsibility for providing public services simply did not exist. Instead, residents themselves took responsibility for endowing public works such as fountains, parks, and mosques, and for providing the limited public services, such as the policing of residential areas.

In the nineteenth century, European economic penetration and defensive modernization transformed urban life and municipal structures in several ways. First, as the Middle East became more tightly integrated into the world economic system, coastal cities such as Alexandria in Egypt, Jaffa in Palestine, and Beirut in Lebanon became the centers for the export of agricultural products and the import of manufactured goods from Europe. These cities grew dramatically over the course of the nineteenth century. In 1800, the population of Beirut was approximately 6,000; on the eve of World War I, the population had reached 130,000. Moreover, cities such as Ismailia on the Suez Canal were founded in response to new trade routes, population shifts, and new export products.

To ensure rapid and widespread shipment of goods, railroads linked coastal cities to the interior. Rail networks were constructed connecting Beirut and Damascus, Alexandria and Cairo, Jaffa and Jerusalem, spreading the economic and social transformation inland. Interior towns such as Zahle along the Beirut-Damascus rail line took on new importance, while farmers in the grain-producing Hauran region that had supplied Damascus began cultivating crops for foreign consumption. In Iraq, new steam-powered riverboats plying the Tigris and Euphrates rivers served the same function as railroads did in other parts of the empire and proved to have such potential for transporting grain that, on the eve of the First World War, British planners envisioned using Mesopotamia as a huge plantation to supply India with agricultural products.

Cities were rebuilt as a result of new technologies, foreign investment, or imported conceptions of municipal order. The new city of Ismailia was laid out according to a checkerboard pattern, and the viceroy of Egypt, Isma'il, and the shah of Persia, Nasr ed-Din, were so impressed by late nineteenth-century Paris that they rebuilt parts of their capitals in imitation, with wide boulevards, public parks, and landscaped roads.

The destruction of old quarters, the leveling of narrow cul-de-sacs, and the construction of wide streets and public transportation fostered a new civic identity among the populace, whose lives were no longer confined to a bounded quarter. This civic sense was further enhanced by new civic institutions. By the late nineteenth century, cities such as Damascus, which had been governed by a single locally-chosen governor, were governed by municipal councils that dealt with local administrative, financial, and judicial affairs. The new councils were neither autonomous nor democratically elected; members were appointed by the Ottoman government from among various notable families. Nonetheless, they represented an important step in the integration of the city as a whole.

The integration of the Middle East into the world economy, compounded by Ottoman attempts to strengthen centralized control over the population, sparked the transformation of other urban institutions as well. For centuries associations of artisans of the same profession, called guilds, had been influential urban structures. At times their functions included everything from providing for the welfare of their members and their members' families to ensuring high standards of artisanal production. By the nineteenth century, however, locally produced goods could not compete with mass-produced European goods, and the guild system began to decay. To fill the void, the Ottoman state itself assumed responsibility for many of the guilds' social welfare functions.

Economic integration and defensive modernization affected social relations in other ways. A new class of Christian merchants, based in coastal cities such as Beirut and Alexandria, acted as middlemen between European companies and Middle Eastern consumers or producers. These merchants, who were familiar with European commercial practices and European languages, and who frequently had connections abroad, were often granted special status by European consulates. This status enabled them to engage in foreign trade while paying the same low tariffs as foreign nationals. Their privileges gave them an advantage over Muslim merchants, and, as a result, the evolution of the Christian communities in the Middle East often followed a different path from that of their Muslim neighbors, sometimes precipitating tension or violence between the two communities.

Defensive modernization was the most important factor behind the emergence of another stratum in Middle Eastern society, one that would have far more political importance than the Christian merchant class. These were the professionals, trained military officers and intellectuals who were graduates of modern, secular educational systems that had been established as a result of defensive modernization. As the product of societies in which government responsibilities had expanded dramatically in the previous half century, these professionals generally shared the attitude that deficiencies in society could be overcome by the intervention of an activist government.

By the early twentieth century, individuals from the professional stratum would lead the agitation for constitutional rule in the Ottoman Empire, participate in the Iranian Constitutional Revolution of 1906, and found the first political parties in Egypt. Their agitation for constitutional and parliamentary rule was not rooted in a belief in democracy, but rather in the fact that they were part of an emergent, yet unrepresented, social group seeking access to political participation. It would be from this group that much of the post-World War I leadership in the Middle East would arise.

Cities and Countryside: Connections and Conflicts

In the Middle East, city and hinterland had always been interconnected. In the nineteenth century, advances in transportation, the cultivation of cash crops for export, the spread of the use of money and usury, and changing patterns of land tenure all contributed further to binding the two areas together.

As mentioned, urban notables in the Ottoman Empire increasingly took control over surrounding lands,

A study of Syrian Bedouins by Bonfils, a French photographer.

sometimes as an unforeseen result of the 1858 Ottoman Land Code, sometimes as a result of peasants defaulting on loans, sometimes merely because land provided a profitable opportunity for investment. The holdings were often quite extensive; by the first decade of the twentieth century, for example, each of the wealthiest families of the cities of Homs and Hama in Syria owned from forty-five to sixty villages in the surrounding plain. Thus, urban notables dominated the grain trade, frequently set grain prices, and had the power to dictate which crops would be cultivated. Similarly, in Egypt, agriculture was dominated by wealthy landlords, often descendants of the family and retainers of Muhammad 'Ali. Having confiscated lands that had been held by the Mamluk rulers of Egypt, Muhammad 'Ali distributed them to his family and associates, sometimes forcing the beneficiaries to pay "back taxes" in exchange.

The boundaries between city and village were permeable, and during periods of rural insecurity and famine, peasants frequently sought shelter in nearby cities. Because artisanal trades in Ottoman cities at the beginning of the nineteenth century were regulated by guilds, and because guilds attempted to keep prices high by restricting production, most peasants found it difficult to enter the trades and so ended up in lower-class quarters, frequently outside the city wall, where they engaged in husbandry and "unclean" professions such as tanning.

Migration also took place in the opposite direction. During the first half of the nineteenth century, many peasants living in Damascus and Aleppo returned to their original villages. There were two causes for this migration: not only was the Ottoman government temporarily able to ensure rural security, but employment opportunities in the important weaving industry declined as a result of the importation of cheap, European-made textiles. During this period, the populations of Damascus and Aleppo dropped from highs of approximately 120,000 and 150,000, respectively, to 80,000 each. In addition to migration, temporary labor exchanges also took place. In times of emergency, a city's population might be mobilized to help with the harvest or to beat off infestations of locusts, a situation that occurred in Palestine and Syria during the First World War.

The immediate countryside around most urban concentrations in the Ottoman Empire stretched no further than about thirty miles. The area outside this limit was often the equivalent of a frontier, sometimes inhabited by Bedouin. The romantic image of Bedouin life is that of independent nomads grouped together into small family-based units. This image is mistaken on several counts. Bedouin were not necessarily isolated groups of primitives. Indeed, during the nineteenth century, tribal confederations sometimes contained as many as 250,000 members. Tribes were often made up of settled cultivators, or seasonal cultivators, or even migrant workers who hired out to work fields during harvest or planting seasons. Bedouin depended on the cities for certain commodities, sometimes sought permanent or semipermanent employment in urban areas, and borrowed money from urban-based usurers. Thus, the cities, the surrounding agricultural hinterland, and the deserts were linked demographically and economically, and the relationship between tribe and village or tribe and city ran the gamut from hostile to interdependent.

While the states in the Fertile Crescent that had preceded the Ottoman state had often attempted to integrate the Bedouin by granting tribal leaders land in exchange for tribute or loyalty, by the end of the sixteenth century the Ottoman government felt strong enough to attempt to crowd the Bedouin out—both by using force and by placing economic embargoes on the tribes. In the seventeenth century, large-scale tribal migrations into the Fertile Crescent foiled the Ottoman plan. As a result, the Ottoman government changed its strategy, hoping to integrate tribes into the Ottoman system by settling them along major communication routes, or by employing them to escort and/or provision both commercial caravans and the yearly Hajj caravan to Mecca.

Throughout the eighteenth and nineteenth centuries, the balance between the state and the Bedouin in frontier areas tipped first in one direction, then the other. In the period following the Crimean War (1854–56), the Ottoman government implemented a policy of forced settlement of the Bedouin throughout the Fertile Crescent. By the late nineteenth century, children of Bedouin *sheikhs* could attend a special school set up for them in Istanbul.

Because of the widespread cultivation of cash crops and advances in land reclamation, Bedouin leaders and urban notables could work together profitably. Tribal leaders offered their tribes as cheap agricultural labor to work on marginal lands, while the urban notables provided financial backing. Marriages were even arranged among the families of urban notables and those of tribal leaders.

The relationship between the central authority and the Bedouin varied from place to place throughout the Middle East. In Egypt, where life can be sustained only in a small area on the banks of the Nile River, Muhammad 'Ali had little trouble settling large numbers of indigenous Bedouin. In Iraq, on the other hand, the "Bedouin problem" was not resolved until well into the twentieth century, when the Iraqi government was able to call on the technical assistance of the British Royal Air Force to forcibly settle tribes that resisted control by the state.

Moral Reconstruction: Purifying Islam

The eighteenth century was marked by political and social turmoil in the Ottoman Empire. Local notables effectively challenged the authority of the central government. European armies consistently pushed back the boundaries of the empire. Peasants, who could no longer count on the government to ensure rural security, fled to the cities. Artisans were displaced as a result of the sale of cheap European manufactured products.

These circumstances engendered a feeling of malaise and a yearning for moral reconstruction among both intellectuals and the urban masses. There was a feeling that something had gone drastically wrong, and this feeling was accompanied by the search for the causes of the decline and for a model upon which society could be reconstructed. That model—one readily accessible to Muslims—was the original Islamic community in Medina, which had been founded and guided by Muhammad in the year 622.

The desire for reconstruction was combined with a form of organization that could overcome the feeling of rootlessness of the displaced peasant, artisan, or merchant—the Sufi *tariqa* (literally, "path"). Sufism has been previously described as Islamic mysticism. Like Western mysticism, most Sufi paths tended toward pantheism, the loss of the individual identity and its absorption into God. In the eighteenth century, however, many Sufi *turuq* (the plural of *tariqa*) focused on providing guidance for individuals who did not seek to escape the world. These turuq emphasized the need for individuals to live their lives in accord with the rules and regulations established by Muhammad and his companions in the original Islamic community.

Sufi turuq proliferated and spread throughout the Middle East. These organizations took diverse forms. They might be informal clubs organized by merchants to study the pronouncements of the Prophet about the rules of trade, or they might be more formal. They were very popular: by the beginning of the nineteenth century almost every male of every social class in Cairo, for example, belonged to a tariqa.

Increasingly, in the eighteenth century, turuq became the vehicles for purification and renewal. Since different turuq or Sufi masters might be based in different cities, merchants and ulama traveled from city to city, cross-fertilizing ideas from one part of the Middle East with ideas from another—from Istanbul to Damascus to Mecca and Medina to, of course, Cairo, with its great Islamic university, al-Azhar.

In outlying areas of the empire, movements associated with moral reconstruction—either associated with turuq or organized along other lines—took openly political forms. The most famous of these movements, Wahhabism, has already been discussed (see Chapter 15). In the heart of the empire, movements took a less political form, but the message was the same—moral reconstruction based on the principles of a purified Islam, an Islam without the accretions of eleven hundred years of local custom and medieval scholasticism.

The university of al-Azhar in Cairo, founded in the tenth century, is one of the world's oldest.

Islamic Modernism: Reinterpreting Islam

Thus, an overwhelming majority of Muslims in the Ottoman Empire found indigenous Islamic answers to problems raised by the events of the eighteenth and early nineteenth centuries. Among the ruling elites, however, successive military defeats brought a different response, a response engendered by the educational policies associated with defensive modernization.

Middle Eastern leaders such as Muhammad 'Ali sent students to Europe to learn Western science and technology. Although these students and elites recognized the need to restructure the Ottoman Empire or Egypt by adopting certain mechanical, military, or administrative techniques, they were equally certain that Islamic/Ottoman culture was inherently superior to the culture of Christian Europe. But as the century progressed and the West pulled further ahead of the Middle East, that confidence was shaken.

Whereas at the beginning of the nineteenth century intellectuals might merely assert Muslim superiority, by 1850 they increasingly took up the cause of moral reconstruction. In reply to Western polemics, intellectuals argued from two premises. First, they argued that the Islam of their day *was* in a deplorable state. This had occurred because pure, true Islam, which had once inspired the conquest of the area between Afghanistan and Spain, had been corrupted and was therefore inadequate to maintain order even in the heart of the empire.

This argument was not new. But these intellectuals added a new twist to moral reconstructionism. They argued that the Islam that had preserved Greek philosophy during Europe's Dark Ages was not incompatible with science and reason. If Islam would shed its superstitious additions and root itself in reason, it could act as the foundation for a Middle Eastern scientific and industrial revolution.

Those who argued that true Islam was compatible with Western progress and modern ideas were called "Islamic modernists." Islamic modernists had usually been exposed to Western ideas and frequently were acquainted with either English or French. In addition, they usually advocated reform through education, not through direct political confrontation. Although they were united by the same general ideas and tactical

ISLAMIC MODERNIST STATEMENT ON THE UNIVERSALITY OF SCIENCE

■ *In a speech delivered at Albert Hall, Calcutta, India, in 1882, the Islamic modernist Jamal ad-Din al-Afghani stated the following:*

The strangest thing of all is that our ulama these days have divided science into two parts. One they call Muslim science, and one European science. Because of this they forbid others to teach some of the useful sciences. They have not understood that science is that noble thing that has no connection with any nation, and is not distinguished by anything but itself. Rather, everything that is known is known by science, and every nation that becomes renowned becomes renowned through science. Men must be related to science, not science to men.

How very strange it is that the Muslims study those sciences that are ascribed to Aristotle with the greatest delight, as if Aristotle were one of the pillars of the Muslims. However, if the discussion relates to Galileo, Newton, and Kepler, they consider them infidels. The father and mother of science is proof, and proof is neither Aristotle nor Galileo. The truth is where there is proof, and those who forbid science and knowledge in the belief that they are safeguarding the Islamic religion are really the enemies of that religion. The Islamic religion is the closest of religions to science and knowledge, and there is no incompatibility between science and knowledge and the foundation of the Islamic faith.

approaches for changing society and although sharing many of the same experiences, details of the programs of groups of Islamic modernists differed according to time and place.

An illuminating example of Islamic modernism lay in the heart of the Ottoman Empire. There, a diffuse group of intellectuals known as the Young Ottomans argued that the Tanzimat had failed—that while it strengthened the powers of the sultan, it did not stop the European penetration of the Ottoman Empire. What was needed, they argued, was a political system that could guarantee and inspire the loyalty of all citizens of the empire. Such a system should be based on authentic Islamic principles, particularly the principle of *shura*, government by consultation. The Young Ottoman message thus laid the ideological groundwork for the Ottoman constitution of 1876.

In other parts of the Ottoman Empire, Islamic modernism took different forms. One of the first important propagators of the Islamic modernist message was Jamal ad-Din al-Afghani (1838–97). As a teenager, al-Afghani had spent time in India during the Indian Mutiny of 1857. The mutiny, actually a revolt against British rule, was endorsed by Muslim leaders as *jihad* (holy war). From this experience, according to his biographers, al-Afghani took three ideas. First, he developed a fierce hatred of imperialism, particularly British imperialism. Second, because of the strength of the West, he believed that the battle against imperialism would be successful only if it involved all Muslims. Because he called for the unity of all Muslims against the West, al-Afghani has been considered the father of modern pan-Islamism. Finally, al-Afghani believed that to defeat imperialism, Muslims would have to adopt both the technology of the West and the method to obtain that technology—the scientific method. Like the moral reconstructionists and Wahhabis before him, he argued that Muslims had to stop following the dictates of the medieval scholastics, who were ignorant of the world around them, and instead apply reason to solve modern problems. Muslims must base their moral lives on the first generation of Muslims, the salaf-al-salih (*pious ancestors*). Because he took his inspiration from this period, the Islamic modernist movement which al-Afghani founded has been called the Salafiyya movement.

Al-Afghani's influence was spread by his students. His students, however, borrowed selectively from their teacher's ideas. For example, Muhammad 'Abduh (1849–1905), who would hold the highest judicial post in Egypt, Grand Mufti, and who also was rector of al-Azhar, borrowed al-Afghani's passion for reason and re-

The Transformation of the Middle East in the Nineteenth Century

1774	Treaty of Kuchuk Kainarji between Russia and the Ottoman Empire
1798	Invasion of Egypt by Napoleon Bonaparte
1805–49	Rule of Muhammad 'Ali in Egypt
1830	French conquest of Algeria
1831–41	Egyptian occupation of Syria
1839–76	Era of the Tanzimat reforms of the Ottoman Empire
1858	Ottoman Land Code grants peasants right to register in their own names the land they work
1826	End of the Ottoman Janissary Corps
1838–97	Jamal ad-Din al-Afghani, the father of modern pan-Islamism
1856–80	Forced settlement of Bedouin by Ottoman government
1866	Founding of Syrian Protestant College in Beirut, later renamed American University
1869	Opening of the Suez Canal
1872	Persian shah grants railroad, mineral, banking, and forestry concession to Julius de Reuter
1876	Ottoman constitution
1882	Declaration of bankruptcy by Egyptian government leads to British occupation of Egypt

form, ignoring his teacher's political radicalism. One of 'Abduh's students, the Syrian-born Rashid Rida (1865–1935), followed a different path. He, like al-Afghani, was a political activist who believed in pan-Islamism. He therefore encouraged the Ottoman sultan to stand at the head of the international Islamic community as caliph, the spiritual leader of the Muslims, and to lead a united Islam in the struggle against the West. Like 'Abduh, Rida also held high office, becoming the president of the Syrian General Congress in the immediate aftermath of the First World War.

The Revival of Arabic Culture

While Islamic modernists attempted to reinterpret Islamic symbols and values to conform to the aspirations of their social class and to modern conditions, other mid- to late-nineteenth-century intellectuals propounded secular modernist ideas. These intellectuals, mainly Syrian and Lebanese Christians from Beirut and Damascus, and Syrian and Lebanese émigrés in such far-flung places as Europe and the Americas, participated in a literary revival to resurrect the Arabic language and culture. This emerging stratum of intellectuals undertook language reform and often adopted Western literary forms to write Arabic-language poetry, short stories, and even, in one case, epics to be used as libretti for Arabic-language opera. Typical of these intellectuals were the activities of playwrights and theatrical producers in Egypt and Syria during the latter half of the nineteenth century. Writers such as Farah Antun and Khalil Matran translated into Arabic the works of Sophocles, Molière, and Shakespeare and produced them on stage in an effort to forge a new Arabic literary culture. Others disseminated their ideas and works through newspapers and literary salons that proliferated in Beirut, Cairo, and Istanbul. Both newspapers and literary salons became increasingly common when censorship was lifted in the wake of the Ottoman Constitutional Restoration of 1908.

It should come as no surprise that westernized Christians, members of the aforementioned rising Christian bourgeoisie, would prefer to adopt modernism in a secular rather than Islamic form. Many of these Christians were trained in Western mission schools, such as the American missionary-sponsored Syrian Protestant College in Beirut, now called the American University in Beirut, founded in 1866. These Arab Christians saw in an Arabic language and cultural rebirth a means of forging a common secular Arab identity with their Muslim neighbors.

Also participating in a cultural revival were young Arab Muslims who had graduated from one of the centers of higher education in Istanbul or one of the preparatory schools in the Arab provinces of the empire. Their abandonment of Islamic themes was in part rooted in their secular training and in the declining status and opportunities for those trained in the religious sciences in a post-Tanzimat Ottoman Empire—an Ottoman Empire in which education and judicial affairs had increasingly come under secular authority.

The economic and political changes that took place in the Middle East in the nineteenth century affected every aspect of life, from the creation of new social classes and the redefinition of urban space to the evolution of new intellectual and literary movements. These changes set the course for the twentieth century as well, for those Arabs, Turks, and Persians who came of age in the late nineteenth century would be the state builders in the aftermath of the First World War.

SUGGESTIONS FOR FURTHER READING

AFRICA IN THE ERA OF RISING EUROPEAN CAPITALISM

Philip D. Curtin, *The Atlantic Slave Trade: A Census* (Madison, WI: University of Wisconsin Press, 1969). A classic, seminal work on the question of how many people were sent to the New World as slaves.

Joseph C. Miller, *Way of Death: Merchant Capitalism and the Angolan Slave Trade, 1730–1830* (Madison, WI: University of Wisconsin Press, 1988). A magisterial study of the Angolan slave trade to Brazil.

* Paul E. Lovejoy, *Transformations in Slavery: A History of Slavery in Africa* (New York: Cambridge University Press, 1983). A comprehensive survey of the place slavery and the slave trade have held in African history.

* Patrick Manning, *Slavery and African Life: Occidental, Oriental, and African Slave Trades* (New York: Cambridge University Press, 1990). A recent summary of what is known about the trade and stimulating suggestions as to its impact on African societies.

Roger Anstey, *The Atlantic Slave Trade and British Abolition, 1760–1810* (London: Macmillan, 1975). An old but still useful analysis of the British abolitionist movement in the late eighteenth century.

* David Eltis, *Economic Growth and the Ending of the Transatlantic Slave Trade* (New York: Oxford University Press, 1987). A dense and closely argued analysis of the motives, costs, and effects of the British Abolitionist effort down to 1860.

* A. G. Hopkins, *An Economic History of West Africa* (London: Longman, 1973). A controversial but immensely stimulating assessment of changes in West African trade patterns.

* Leonard Thompson, *A History of South Africa* (New Haven, CT: Yale University Press, 1990). A comprehensive overview of South African history.

Richard Elphick, *Kraal and Castle: Khoikhoi and the Founding of White South Africa* (New Haven, CT: Yale University Press, 1977). A classic discussion of the downfall of Khoi society in the Cape of Good Hope.

* Richard Elphick and Hermann Giliomee, eds., *The Shaping of South African Society, 1652–1840* (Middletown, CT: Wesleyan University Press, 1989). A lengthy and highly detailed discussion of South Africa's development before 1840.

Gender and Culture

DEPARTURE FROM THE ISLE OF CYTHERA

Figure 1

The recognition of love and the pursuit of affection are standard subjects in the visual arts. They also offer insight into the codes of culture and the habits of society. Images of courtship and flirtation have remarkable similarities that span time and location, misleading us to think that love is expressed in a universal language. The characteristic actions—the exchange of glances, the holding of hands, the sharing of kisses—are easy to identify in a work of art. However, these seemingly natural gestures have ritual importance that varies from culture to culture. Similarly, there seem to be set roles for men and women. The active male pursues his love, while the passive female serves as the inspiration for his affection. Yet these are nuanced roles, given to subtle reversals. Interpreting the imagery of romantic love is simultaneously easy and complex, for it represents a message of culturally specific ideas in a deceptively familiar language.

Antoine Watteau's *Departure From the Isle of Cythera* (1717, France; Figure 1) idealizes romantic love. On the island of Venus, elegant couples meet, exchange their vows, and share their affections in an atmosphere of peace and pleasure. The men carry staffs and traveler's pouches, revealing that this journey is a pilgrimage, to pay tribute to the goddess of love. But, details of the painting reveal that this perfect moment will soon end. At the far right, is a statue of Venus, adorned with rose garlands. It takes the form of a "term," a

LOVERS ENTERTAINED BY MUSICIANS AND DANCERS   *Figure 2*

pedestal topped with a half-length statue, traditionally used to mark the termination of a road. The three couples in the foreground rise to join their companions for the journey home. Their gestures and responses tell a poignant story. In each case, the man leads the woman back to the mundane life and, in each case, she is reluctant to go. Watteau's golden vision is fleeting, revealing that the perfect moment of love always passes and it is always bittersweet.

The Persian miniature painting *Lovers Entertained by Musicians and Dancers*, attributed to Sultan-Muhammad (ca. 1533, Persia; Figure 2), offers an intimate glimpse of royal courtship. One of five illustrations in the Diwan of Hafiz manuscript, it is believed to depict the son of Shah Isma'l, a notable patron of the arts. He has spared no expense to please his graceful lover. Seated in the shade of a fine, brocade canopy, they watch lithe dancers play castanets and move to the rhythm of drums and tambourines. They are serenaded by singers and served tea by a silent servant. Courtly love is an elaborate affair, involving gifts and rituals, available only to the privileged few.

In another Persian painting, the roles of pursuer and pursued seem to be reversed. The beautiful women depicted in this miniature from the *Anthology of Iskandar Sultan* (1410, Persia; Figure 3), beckon to the men on the shore to join them in their frolic in the water. Their gestures are bold. Lifting their hands above the waves, they reach out to the objects of their desire. One man has taken the challenge, and embraces the woman as he joins her in the water. The other men keep to the shore, but are drawn to the irresistible call. These are not natural women, but sirens, and like Ulysses and his mariners, Iskandar and his men are enchanted by the unearthly song and risk their lives for a glance at a beautiful femme fatal.

ANTHOLOGY OF ISKANDAR SULTAN

Figure 3

THE SWING

Figure 4

The Swing, by Jean Honoré Fragonard (1766, France; Figure 4), portrays a lively and flirtatious young woman. She is the picture of energy and joy, delighting in the simple, vigorous activity. Her girlish hat, her flushed cheeks, and the way she kicks off her shoe suggest a childlike ingenuity. In actuality, the subtext of this picture is anything but innocent. The Baron de Saint-Julien commissioned this painting directly from the artist and dictated its particular content. He requested a portrait of his mistress, amusing herself on a swing. He instructed Fragonard to paint him as well, positioned "to observe the legs of this charming girl." The Baron even used the scene to make fun of the clergy. A bishop works the pulls of the swing in the background, unaware of the flirtation he facilitates. Fragonard inserted his own joke. The little statue of Cupid, based on a well-known work by Falconet, presses his finger to his lips, warning the viewer not to reveal the secret.

THE MIDDLE EAST AND THE WORLD SYSTEM

S. N. Fisher, *The Middle East: A History* (New York: Alfred A. Knopf, 1959). Good overview; a bit simplistic.

J. C. Hurewitz, *The Middle East and North Africa in World Politics*, Vol. 1: 1535–1914 (New Haven, CT: Yale University Press, 1975). Collection of source documents in diplomatic history.

Charles Issawi, *The Economic History of the Middle East 1800–1914* (London: Methuen, 1981). An interesting selection of source documents in economic history.

Peter Mansfield, *A History of the Middle East* (New York: Penguin Books, 1991). Similar to S. N. Fisher's book but more up-to-date.

M. E. Yapp, *The Making of the Modern Near East, 1792–1923* (London: Longman, 1987). The most detailed and probably the best of the general histories on this list.

THE TRANSFORMATION OF SOCIETY AND CULTURE IN THE MIDDLE EAST

M. S. Anderson, *The Eastern Question, 1774–1923* (New York: St. Martin's Press, 1966). Perhaps the best general survey of international diplomacy in the Middle East.

Niyazi Berkes, *The Development of Secularism in Turkey* (Montreal: McGill University Press, 1961). Account of defensive modernization in Turkey from the eighteenth century through the establishment of the republic.

L. Carl Brown, *International Politics and the Middle East* (Princeton, NJ: Princeton University Press, 1984). Traces the Near Eastern Question from its inception to the present day.

Moshe Ma'oz, *Ottoman Reform in Syria and Palestine* (Oxford: Oxford University Press, 1968). Study of the local effects of defensive modernization.

Afaf Lutfi as-Sayyid Marsot, *Egypt in the Reign of Mohammad 'Ali* (Cambridge: Cambridge University Press, 1984). Well-written narrative of life and policies of Egypt's first defensive modernizer.

Roger Owen, *The Middle East in the World Economy, 1800–1914* (London: Methuen, 1981). The standard work on political economy in the nineteenth century.

Sevket Pamuk, *The Ottoman Empire and European Capitalism, 1820–1913* (Cambridge: Cambridge University Press, 1987). Detailed study of the effects of integration and peripheralization on the Middle East.

W. R. Polk and R. L. Chambers, *The Beginnings of Modernization in the Middle East* (Chicago: University of Chicago Press, 1968). A strong collection of essays on the Tanzimat.

Hamid Algar, *Religion and State in Iran 1785–1906* (Berkeley, CA: University of California Press, 1969). Emphasizes the role of the Shi'i ulama in shaping modern Iran.

Gabriel Baer, *Fellah and Townsman in the Middle East* (London: Frank Cass and Co., 1982). Collection of essays, including superlative essays on urban history from the sixteenth to twentieth centuries, urban and rural revolts, and Turkish guilds.

Gabriel Baer, *Studies in the Social History of Modern Egypt* (Chicago: University of Chicago Press, 1969). Excellent collection on selected topics in Egyptian social history.

Edmond Bosworth and Carole Hillenbrand, *Qajar Iran* (Costa Mesa, CA: Mazda Publishers, 1992). Contains more than twenty essays, divided into sections on political and cultural history.

Nikki R. Keddie, *Scholars, Saints, and Sufis* (Berkeley, CA: University of California Press, 1972). Essays on the role of the ulama in Middle Eastern society.

Donald Quataert, *Social Disintegration and Popular Resistance in the Ottoman Empire, 1881–1908* (New York: New York University Press, 1983). Innovative study of social/political movements in the late Ottoman Empire.

Linda Schilcher, *Families in Politics* (Stuttgart: Franz Steiner Verlag Wiesbaden GMBH, 1985). Detailed account of elite family politics in Damascus, Syria, in the eighteenth and nineteenth centuries.

David Dean Commins, *Islamic Reform* (New York: Oxford University Press, 1990). Study of the intellectual origins of the Salafiyya movement in Syria.

Albert Hourani, *Arabic Thought in the Liberal Age, 1798–1939* (Cambridge: Cambridge University Press, 1962). Best introduction to modernist thinking in the Middle East.

Nikki R. Keddie, *An Islamic Response to Imperialism* (Berkeley, CA: University of California Press, 1968). Good introduction to the life and works of Jamal ad-Din al-Afghani, including his writings.

Bernard Lewis, *The Emergence of Modern Turkey* (London: Oxford University Press, 1961). Although the book covers all aspects of Ottoman/Turkish history, it is strongest when describing intellectual life.

Serif Mardin, *The Genesis of Young Ottoman Thought* (Princeton, NJ: Princeton University Press, 1962). A detailed study of the doctrines and members of the Young Ottoman movement.

John Obert Voll, *Islam: Continuity and Change in the Modern World* (Boulder, CO: Westview Press, 1982). Traces Islamic responses to economic, political, and social changes from the eighteenth through twentieth centuries.

* Indicates paperback edition available.

CHAPTER 20

The Balance of Power in Eighteenth-Century Europe

CALLING THE TUNE

Frederick the Great loved music. During his youth it was one of his private passions that so infuriated his father. Mathematics, political economy, modern languages, even dreaded French—these were the subjects that a future king of Prussia should learn. But music, never. Rather the boy should be at the hunt watching the dogs tear apart a stag, or on maneuvers with the Potsdam guards, a troop of soldiers all nearly seven feet tall. This was the regimen King Frederick William I prescribed for his son. It was no longer enough to reign over one's subjects; to be a successful monarch in the power politics of the eighteenth century, a king had to be a soldier.

But Frederick the Great loved music. He secretly collected all the books and manuscripts he could find on the subject, outspending his tiny allowance in the process. He had Johann Quantz (1697–1773), the greatest flutist of the day, placed on his staff to teach him and to conspire with him against his father. At night, while the old king drank himself into a stupor—an activity he warmly recommended to his son—Frederick powdered his hair, put on a jacket of the latest French style, and regaled his friends with his newest compositions. A lookout guarded the door in case the king wandered by unexpectedly. Once the musicians were almost discovered and Frederick's fine new jacket was tossed on the fire, but the flutes and musical scores remained safely hidden.

After he became king Frederick the Great could indulge his passion more openly. Yet he preferred to hold his concerts, usually small gatherings, at the Palace of San Souci, which he built in Potsdam. A special music room was designed for the king's use and he lavished attention on it. The great chandelier, lit by a circle of candles, illuminated the center of the room and highlighted the soloist. The entire palace reflected Frederick's personal taste. Unlike most great palaces of state, it was small, functional, and beautiful. Here Frederick could escape the mounting cares of governing one of the most powerful states in Europe by reading, corresponding with eminent French intellectuals, and playing the flute. In this picture, *Das Flötenkonzert* (the Flute Concert), Frederick is portrayed performing in his great music room. Before a small audience of courtiers and intimates, he plays to the accompaniment of cello, violins, and piano.

Frederick's talent was real enough. A British visitor to Sans Souci, who had little reason to flatter the king, reported: "I was much pleased and surprised with the neatness of his execution. His performance surpassed anything I had ever heard among the dilettanti or even professors." This judgment is reinforced when one studies the expressions of the three men in the left-hand corner of the painting. They are taking genuine pleasure in the music they are hearing (all the more genuine in that the king's back is to them). So, too, are the musicians who are accompanying the king. There is as much joy as concentration upon their faces.

Frederick's musical accomplishment was not unique among eighteenth-century monarchs. Joseph II of Austria was also a skilled flutist. But it was not so much music as accomplishment that was coming to be valued among the monarchs of the new European powers. Catherine the Great of Russia corresponded with philosophers; Frederick the Great brought the great French intellectual Voltaire (1698–1778) to his court—though they quickly took a dislike to each other. The acquisition of culture seemed

593

to matter more and more as the century wore on. Museums, opera houses, great art collections were established all over the Continent. The Hermitage in Saint Petersburg was stocked with the works of Dutch and English masters. The British Museum was founded in London with the support of King George II, who deposited his great library there. Whether this veneer of culture did anything to lessen the brutality of warfare and power politics is a matter of opinion. But as a veneer it was as highly polished as the flute that Frederick the Great is so delicately pressing to his mouth.

Europe in 1714

Within a relatively short span of time at the beginning of the eighteenth century, two treaties brought about a considerable reorganization of the political geography of Europe. The Treaty of Utrecht (1713–14) created a new Europe in the west. The Treaty of Nystad (1721) created a new Europe in the east. Both agreements reflected the dynamics of change that had taken place over the previous century. The rise of France on the Continent and of Britain's colonial empire around the globe were facts that could no longer be ignored. The decline of Sweden and Poland and the emergence of Russia as a great power were the beginning of a long-term process that would continue to dominate European history.

All of this could be seen on a map of Europe in the early eighteenth century. France's absorption of Alsace and encroachments into Lorraine would be bones of contention between the French and Germans for two centuries and ultimately contributed to the outbreak of World Wars I and II. The political footballs of the Spanish Netherlands and Spanish Italy, now temporarily Austrian, continued to be kicked about until the nationalist movements of the nineteenth century gave birth to Belgium, Luxembourg, and a united Italy. The emergence of Brandenburg-Prussia on the north German coast and the gradual decline in the power of the Holy Roman Emperor were both vital to the process that created a unified Germany and a separate Austria. In the southeast, the slow but steady reconquest of the Balkans from Ottoman dominion restored the historic southern border of the Continent. The inexorable expansion of Russia was also already apparent.

Expansion in the West

Perhaps the most obvious transformation in the political geography of western Europe was the expansion of European power around the globe. In the Atlantic, Spain remained the largest colonial power. Through its viceroyalty system it controlled all of Mexico and Central America, the largest and most numerous of the Caribbean islands, North America from Colorado to California (as well as Florida), and most of South America. The other major colonial power in the region was Portugal, which shared dominion over the South American continent. In the Portuguese colony of Brazil, production of sugar, dyestuffs, timbers, and exotic commodities amply repaid the meager investment the Portuguese had made.

In North America the French and British shared the eastern half of the continent. The French controlled most of it. They had landed first in Canada and then slowly made their way down the Saint Lawrence River. New France, as their colonial empire was called, was a trading territory and it expanded along the greatest of the waterways, the Great Lakes, and the Ohio, Missouri, and Mississippi rivers. French settlements had sprung up as far south as the Gulf of Mexico. France also claimed the territory of Louisiana, named for Louis XIV, which stretched from New Orleans to Montana. The British settlements were all coastal, stretching from

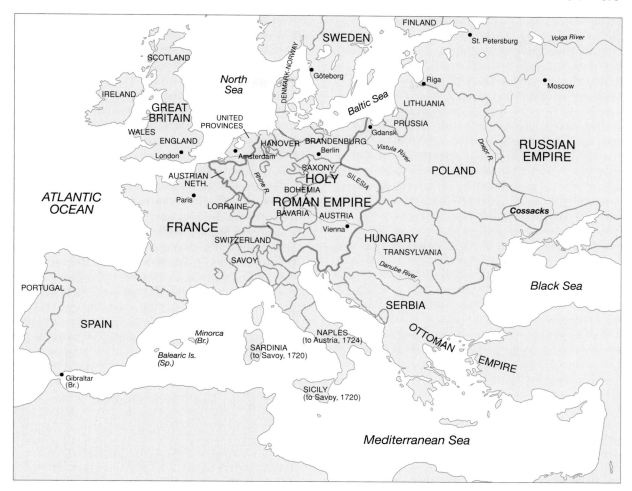

Europe, ca. 1714

Maine to Georgia on the Atlantic seaboard. Unlike the French, the British settled their territory and were only interested in expansion when their population, which was doubling every twenty-five years, outgrew its resources. By the early eighteenth century the ports of Boston, New York, Philadelphia, and Charleston were thriving commercial centers.

Europeans managed their eastern colonial territories differently than they did those in the Atlantic. Initially the Portuguese and the Dutch had been satisfied with establishing trading factories—coastal fortresses in Africa and Asia that could be used as warehouses and defended against attack. But in the seventeenth century, the European states began to take control of vital ports and lucrative islands. Here the Dutch were the acknowledged leaders, replacing the Portuguese who had begun the process at the end of the sixteenth cen-

tury. Holland held by force or in conjunction with local leaders all the Spice Islands in the Pacific. The Dutch also occupied both sides of the Malay Peninsula and nearly all the coastal areas of the islands in the Java Sea. Dutch control of Ceylon was strategically important for its Indian trade. Compared to the Dutch Republic, all other European states had only a minor territorial presence in the East, with the exception of Spain, which still controlled the Philippines. The British had limited their eastern outposts to trading establishments. Through these they maintained a significant presence in India. During the eighteenth century the British began to colonize the Indian subcontinent directly.

Imperial expansion was the most obvious change in the geopolitical boundaries of Europe, but it was not the only one. A brief tour of the western states after the Treaty of Utrecht reveals some others. In 1707 England

European Colonial Powers in America

Since the accession of Louis XIV, France had plucked small pieces from the territories that had been contested between France and Spain since the fifteenth century. Between French aggression and the Dutch occupation of such important places as Ghent and Ypres, the ability of the southern provinces to maintain a separate identity suffered a grave blow. But not as grave as that formalized at Utrecht, when sovereignty over this territory was assigned to Austria, ostensibly because the emperor was a Habsburg, but really because the balance of power in western Europe demanded it.

To the south lay France, still the most powerful nation in Europe despite its losses in the War of the Spanish Succession. By 1714 Louis XIV had broken forever the danger of Spanish encirclement that had been the worry of every French king since Francis I in the early sixteenth century. Louis had methodically set out to occupy those territories that were strategically necessary to defend his state from invasion by the Dutch, the Spanish, the British, or the emperor. In the northeast he absorbed the Duchy of Bar. In the north he absorbed a healthy portion of Flanders including Dunkirk on the English Channel and the prosperous clothing town of Lille. He pushed the eastern boundary of his state to the Rhine by overrunning Alsace and parts of Lorraine. Strasbourg remained French under the settlement of 1714, testimony to the fact that it was possible to hold France only at the western banks of the Rhine. Finally, farther to the south Louis had won and held Franche-Comté, once the center of Burgundy. In 1714 France was larger, stronger, and better able to defend its borders than ever before. It was also exhausted.

and Scotland formally joined together to form Great Britain. In addition to its eastern and western colonies, Britain had also gained control of Gibraltar at the foot of Spain and the island of Minorca in the Mediterranean. Both territories were strategically important to British commerce.

Across the English Channel were the Low Countries, now permanently divided between the United Provinces in the north, led by Holland, and those provinces in the south that had remained loyal to the Spanish crown in the sixteenth century. By 1714 the golden age of the Dutch was over. Though the Dutch continued as a colonial and maritime power, their small numbers and meager natural resources eventually outweighed their abilities as innovators and managers. They lost their eastern empire to Britain, their predominance in European trade to France. What the Dutch gained at Utrecht was the right to maintain their forces in the towns along the border between France and the old Spanish Netherlands. The Spanish Netherlands, the original Burgundian inheritance, were now being slowly dismembered.

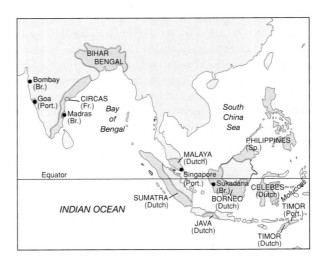

European Colonial Powers in the East Indies

As France expanded, so Spain contracted. Less than two centuries earlier a Spanish king had dreamed of being monarch over all of Europe. Now a French Bourbon sat on the great Habsburg throne and Spain was slowly being sliced to pieces. By 1714 the European territories of the Spanish empire had been reduced to Iberia itself. But the loss of its European empire was to prove a blessing in disguise for Spain, which now entered upon a new and unexpected phase of growth and influence.

The center of Europe remained occupied by the agglomeration of cities, bishoprics, principalities, and small states known collectively as the Holy Roman Empire, but now more accurately called the German empire. There were still over three hundred separate jurisdictions, most of them vulnerable to preying neighbors such as Louis XIV. Bavaria in the south, and Saxony, Brandenburg, and Hanover in the north were among the most important of the large states with the added twist that Hanover was now ruled by the king of Great Britain. The emperor, now officially prohibited from interference in the internal administration of the large states, was less dominant in German affairs than he had been before the Thirty Years' War.

Increasingly, Habsburg power centered on Austria, Bohemia, and Hungary. This was especially true during the reign of Leopold I (1655–1705). Withstanding threats on all sides, Leopold was able to expand his state both to the west and to the south and to bring Austria into the ranks of the great European powers. Such an outcome could hardly have been foreseen in the middle of the seventeenth century, when the Ottomans made their last great thrust into the interior of Europe. In 1683 the Ottomans besieged Vienna itself, and only the arrival of seventy thousand Polish-led troops saved it from falling. But from that time forward, Austrian forces scored stunning victories. By 1699 almost all of Hungary had been retaken by Austria; with the Treaty of Passarowitz in 1718 Austria gained the rest of Hungary and Serbia. When the Treaty of Utrecht granted Austria control of the Netherlands, Lombardy, and Naples, the Austrian Habsburgs became rulers of a European empire.

Austria's Italian possessions included the vast southern territories of Naples (including Sicily after 1720) and the rich industrial area surrounding Milan in the north. Alongside the Austrian territories a number of independent city-states continued to flourish on the Italian peninsula. Both Venice and Genoa remained prosperous and independent. The Grand Duchy of Tuscany, with its great city of Florence, and the Papal States had expanded over the course of the seventeenth century, absorbing their smaller neighbors until both were

Composite view of the siege of Vienna, 1683, when the invading Turks were repelled in this, their last great advance in Europe.

large consolidated territories. To the west of the Italian states was the Duchy of Savoy. Savoy had pursued a flexible foreign policy, pleasing whichever of its powerful neighbors was most dangerous and accepting the patronage of whichever seemed most friendly. Client of the Spanish, French, and Austrians, Savoy grew and prospered. After the War of the Spanish Succession Savoy was counted among the victors, though it fought on both sides. Duke Victor Amadeus II became a king when he received the island of Sicily, which he exchanged with Austria for Sardinia in 1720.

Thus the Treaty of Utrecht signaled a new configuration of political power. England, France, Prussia, and Austria were the ascending powers, Holland and Spain the declining ones. Italy and the southern Netherlands were the bones over which the biggest dogs fought, sometimes playfully, sometimes in deadly earnest.

Realignment in the East

This was western Europe in 1714. In the east, it was the Treaty of Nystad (1721) ending the Great Northern War (1700–21) that fixed the political geography. Here the emerging powers were Russia and Prussia, those in decline were Sweden and Poland. The critical factor in eastern European politics remained access to the sea. Outlets to the Baltic Sea in the north and the Black Sea in the south were the vital lifeline for this part of the Continent, and control of these outlets was the central motivation for the long years of war fought among the eastern states.

The expansion of Russia is one of the central events in European history, and the early eighteenth century is its pivotal period. During the long years of social and economic recovery after the death of Ivan the Terrible in 1584, Russia had been easy prey for its powerful neighbors Sweden and Poland. Through a series of wars and political pacts, Russia had ceded most of its Baltic territories to Sweden while it had relinquished land and population in the west to Poland. Peter the Great (1682–1725) set out to reclaim what had been lost. As a result of the Great Northern War, Russia regained the eastern Baltic coastline from the southeastern end of Finland to Riga in the west. Russia now controlled all of the vital Baltic ports in the east. Peter built a new capital on the Gulf of Finland. In this new city, named Saint Petersburg, he laid the foundation for the Russian navy.

What Russia gained, Sweden lost. At the height of its power in the middle of the seventeenth century, Sweden had dominated the Baltic. It occupied all of Finland, controlled the important eastern coast of Norway, and had gained a foothold in Germany. Most importantly, Sweden had captured the southern tip of its own peninsula from the Danes, making the mainland portion of its state whole. But Sweden's century-long rise to power was followed by a rapid period of decline. The small and relatively poor population could not long succeed in governing an empire. The Great Northern War ended whatever pretensions Sweden had left. It lost all of its German territories: those on the North Sea went to Hanover, those on the Baltic to Prussia. Livonia, Estonia, and the eastern provinces were returned to Russia, but Sweden was able to hold on to its vital gains from the Danes. Sweden had built its own window to the west at Göteborg on the North Sea, and from there it could carry on a direct trade with Britain and the Netherlands.

Since the end of the Thirty Years' War, Brandenburg-Prussia had been steadily growing. A strange configuration of a state with its geographical heart in Brandenburg, it was one of the domains of the Holy Roman Empire. From the capital at Berlin the princes of Brandenburg directed the accumulation of small neighboring German lands: Magdeburg and Halle to the southwest, a piece of Pomerania to the northeast. But while Brandenburg expanded in every direction, it could do little to join itself to the kingdom of Prussia. A huge swath of Poland, cutting between the two, stood in the way. This division of Brandenburg-Prussia was its most important geopolitical feature. In the eighteenth century, the determination to expand to the east dominated Prussian history.

This aim meant, of course, eventual conflict with Poland. Despite its political weakness, Poland was one of the largest landmasses in Europe. On its southern

This portrait of Peter the Great by his court painter Louis Caravaque pays homage to Peter's intense interest in naval matters. Ships flying English, Dutch, Danish, and Russian flags prepare for maneuvers under his command.

border it held back Ottoman expansion, on its eastern border it held back the Russians. Its great port of Gdansk on the Baltic dominated the grain and timber trade with northern Europe as well as local Baltic commerce between Scandinavia and the mainland. Sweden and Russia, the eastern powers, controlled Poland politically, helping nominate its elected kings and ensuring that its decentralized form of aristocratic government kept Poland weak. Poland served as a useful counterweight in the balance of power in eastern Europe. Except for its Baltic territories, Poland was not yet seen as a great prize to be fought over. But by the beginning of the eighteenth century it was a helpless giant ready to be toppled.

Thus a potent Prussia and Russia and a prostrate Poland characterized the realignment of the eastern portion of Europe. Most importantly, the separation between east and west was narrowing. Prussia's German orientation and the westernization of Russia led to closer ties with the west.

The Rise of Russia

At the beginning of the eighteenth century, Russia was scarcely known about or cared about in the rest of Europe. Peter the Great changed all that. The Treaty of Nystad had confirmed the magnitude of his victory over the Swedes in the Great Northern War, both in territory and prestige. The change created consternation in the courts of Europe. Just a quarter century before, no one had cared very much what the king of Russia called himself. In fact, little was known for sure about the Russian ruler or his state. What little mercantile contact there was between Russia and the west was conducted entirely by westerners. Foreign merchants were allowed to live in Moscow in a separate ghetto called "Germantown." Their letters were the main source of western knowledge about the vast Muscovite empire.

Peter the Great brought Europe to Russia and Russia to Europe. Twice he visited Europe to discover the secrets of western prosperity and might. He arranged marriages between the closest heirs to his throne, including his son Alexis, and the sons and daughters of German princes and dukes. By 1721 he had established twenty-one separate foreign embassies. The sons of the Russian gentry and nobility were sent west—sometimes forcibly—to further their education and to learn to adapt to western outlooks. Peter recruited Europeans to fill the most important skilled positions in the state: foreign engineers and gunners to serve in the army; foreign architects to build the new capital at Saint Petersburg; foreign scholars to head the new state schools; foreign administrators to oversee the new departments of state. Peter borrowed freely and adapted sensibly. If necessary, he would drag his countrymen kicking and screaming into the modern world.

By 1721 Russia was recognized all over Europe as an emerging power. The military defeat of the seemingly invincible Swedes had made monarchs from Louis XIV to William III sit up and take notice. And the great Russian victory over Sweden at Poltava in 1709 was no fluke. Peter's forces followed it up with several strong campaigns which proved that Russia could organize, equip, finance, and train an up-to-date military force. Moreover, Peter's absorption of Sweden's Baltic territories made Russia a power in the north. The Russian navy, built mostly by foreigners, was now capable of protecting Russian interests and defending important ports such as Riga and Saint Petersburg. Even the Dutch, who had long plotted the decline of Swedish might, now became nervous. Thus it was unsettling that Peter wished to be recognized as emperor.

The Reforms of Peter the Great

Peter the Great was not the first Russian tsar to attempt to borrow from western developments. The process had been under way for decades. The opening of the northern port of Archangel in 1584 led to direct contact with British and Dutch traders, who brought with them new ideas and useful products, which were adapted to Russian needs and conditions. Russia was a vast state and Europe was only one of its neighbors. Its religion had come from Byzantium rather than Rome, thus giving Russian Christianity an eastern flavor. Its Asian territories mixed the influence of Mongols and Ottomans; its southern borders met Tartars and Cossacks. While most European states were racially and ethnically homogeneous, Russia was a loose confederation of diverse peoples. Yet it was the western states that posed the greatest threat to Russia in the seventeenth century, and it was to the west that Peter, like his father before him, turned his attention.

It would be wrong to see Peter's westernizing innovation as a systematic program. More to the point, nearly all of his reforms—economic, educational, administrative, social, military—were done to enhance military efficiency rather than civil progress. In his thirty years of active rule there was only one year—1724—during which he was not at war. Vital reforms like the poll tax (1724), which changed the basis of taxation from the household to the individual adult male, had enormous social consequences. The new policy of taxing individuals officially erased whole social classes. A strict census taken (and retaken) to inhibit tax evasion became the basis for further governmental encroachments on the tsar's subjects. Yet the poll tax was not designed for any of these purposes. It was instituted to increase tax revenue for war. Similarly, the establishment of compulsory, lifetime military service required of the landowning classes (the nobility and gentry) was undertaken to provide officers and state servants for an expanding military machine.

Yet if Peter's reforms were not systematic and developed from little other than military necessity, nevertheless they constituted a fundamental transformation in the life of all Russian people. The creation of a gigantic standing army and an entirely new navy meant conscription of the Russian peasantry on a grand scale. In a ten-year period of the Great Northern War the army absorbed 330,000 conscripts, most of whom never returned to their homes. Military service was not confined to the peasantry. Traditionally, the rural gentry raised and equipped the local conscript forces and gave them what training they could. Most gentry lived on estates that had been granted to them along with the resident peasants as a reward for their military contributions. Peter the Great intensified the obligations of the gentry. Not only were they to serve the state for life, but they were to accompany their regiments to the field and lead them in battle. When too old for active military service, they were to perform administrative service in the new departments of state.

The expansion of military forces necessitated an expansion of military administration as well. Peter's first innovation was the creation of the Senate, a group of nine senior administrators who were to oversee all aspects of military and civil government. The Senate became a permanent institution of government led by an entirely new official, the Procurator-General, who presided over its sessions and could propose legislation as well as oversee administration. From the Senate emanated five hundred officials known as the fiscals, who traveled throughout the state looking for irregularities in tax assessment and collection. They quickly developed into a hated and feared internal police force.

Peter's efforts to reorganize his government went a step further in 1722, when he issued the Table of Ranks. This was an official hierarchy of the state that established the social position or rank of individuals. It was divided into three categories—military service, civil service, and owners of landed estates. Each category contained fourteen ranks, and it was decreed that every person who entered the hierarchy did so at the bottom and worked his way up. The creation of the Table of Ranks was significant in a number of ways. It demonstrated Peter's continued commitment to merit as a criterion for advancement. This standard had been shown in the military, where officers were promoted on the basis of service and experience rather than birth or background. Equally important was Peter's decision to make the military service the highest of the three categories. This reversed the centuries-old position of the landed aristocracy and the military service class. Though the old nobility also served in the military and continued to dominate state service, the Table of Ranks opened the way for the infusion of new elements into the Russian elite.

Many of those who were able to advance in the Table of Ranks did so through attendance at the new institutions of higher learning that Peter founded. His initial

Peter the Great was a precocious child. He began his education at the age of two, using a book similar to the illustrated Russian speller whose "Z" page is seen above.

educational establishments were created to further the military might of the state. The colleges of Mathematics, Engineering, and Artillery, which became the training grounds for his army officers, were all founded during the Great Northern War. But Peter was interested in liberal education as well. He had scores of western books translated into Russian. He had a press established in Moscow to print original works, including the first Russian newspaper. He decreed that a new, more westernized alphabet replace that used by the Russian Orthodox church and that books be written in the language that the people spoke rather than in the formal literary language of religious writers. He also introduced Arabic numerals into official accounting records.

Peter's reforms of government and society were matched by his efforts to energize the economy. No state in Europe had as many natural resources as did

Russia, yet manufacturing barely existed there. As with everything else he did, Peter took a direct hand in establishing factories for the production of textiles, glass, leather, and most importantly, iron and copper. The state directly owned about half of these establishments, most of them on a larger scale than any known in the west. By 1726 more than half of all Russian exports were manufactured goods and Russia had become the largest producer of iron and copper in the world.

In all of these ways and more, Peter the Great transformed Russia. But the changes Peter wrought did not come without cost. The traditions of centuries were not easily broken. Intrigue against Peter led first to confrontation with the old military elite and later to conflict with his only son, Alexis. It remains unclear if the plot with which Alexis was connected actually existed or was a figment of Peter's imagination, but it is abundantly clear that Alexis's death from torture plunged the state into a succession crisis in 1725. Finally, the great costs of westernization were paid by the masses of people who benefited little from the improvement in Russia's international standing or from the social and economic changes that affected the elites.

Life in Rural Russia

At the beginning of the eighteenth century nearly 97 percent of the Russian people lived on the land and practiced agriculture. Farming techniques and agrarian lifestyles had changed little for centuries. Most of the country's soil was poor. Harsh climate and low yields characterized Russian agriculture. Thirty-four of the one hundred Russian harvests during the eighteenth century can be termed poor or disastrous, yet throughout the century state taxation was making larger and larger demands upon the peasantry. During Peter's reign alone, direct taxation increased by 500 percent.

The theory of the Russian state was one of service, and the role of Russian peasants was to serve their master. Beginning in the mid-seventeenth century, the peasantry had undergone a change in status. The law code of 1649 formalized a process that had been under way for over a century whereby peasants were turned into the property of their landlords. During the next century laws curtailed the ability of peasants to move freely from one place to another, eliminated their right to hold private property, and abolished their freedom to petition the tsar against their masters. At the same time that landlords increased their hold over peasants, the state increased its hold over landlords. They were made responsible for the payment of taxes owed by their peasants and for the military service due from them. By the middle of the eighteenth century over half of all peasants—6.7 million adult males by 1782—had thus become serfs, the property of their masters, without any significant rights or legal protection.

Private landlords reckoned their wealth in the number of serfs they owned. But in fact most owned only a small number, fewer than fifty in the middle of the eighteenth century. This resulted from the common practice whereby a father divided his estate among all of his surviving sons. Most gentry were small landholders, constantly in debt and rarely able to meet their financial and service obligations to the state. This life of poverty at the top was, of course, magnified at the bottom. The vast majority of serfs lived in small villages where they divided up their meager surplus to pay their taxes and drew lots to see who would be sent for military service. When the debts of their lords became too heavy, it was the serfs who were foreclosed upon.

If serfs made up the bottom half of the Russian peasantry, there were few advantages to being in the top half among the state peasants. State peasants lived on lands owned by the monarchy itself. Like the serfs, they were subject to the needs of the state for soldiers and workers. The use of forced labor was a feature of each of Peter's grandiose projects. Saint Petersburg was built by the backbreaking labor of peasant conscripts. From 1709, when the project began, perhaps as many as 40,000 laborers a year were forced to work on the various sites. The unhealthy conditions of the swampy environment from which the new capital rose claimed the lives of thousands of these workers, as did the appalling conditions of overwork and undernourishment in which they lived.

Many Russian peasants developed a philosophy of submission and a rich folk culture that valued a stubborn determination to endure. For those who would no longer bend to the knout—the heavy leather whip that was the omnipresent enforcer of obedience—there was only flight or rebellion. Hundreds of thousands of serfs fled to state-owned lands in hope of escaping the cruelties of individual landlords. Although severe penalties were imposed for aiding runaway serfs, in fact most state overseers and many private landlords encouraged runaways to settle on their lands. In their social and economic conditions, eighteenth-century Russian peasants were hardly distinguishable from medieval European serfs.

The Enlightened Empress Catherine

Of all the legacies of Peter the Great, perhaps the one of most immediate consequence was that government could go on without him. During the next thirty-seven years, six tsars ruled Russia, "three women, a boy of twelve, an infant, and a mental weakling," as one commentator acidly observed. More to the point, each succession was contested, as there were no direct male heirs to the throne in this period. Nevertheless, despite turmoil at the top, government continued to function smoothly and Peter's territorial conquests were largely maintained. Russia also experienced a remarkable increase in numbers during this period. Between 1725 and 1762 the population increased from 13 to 19 million, a jump of nearly one-third in a single generation. This explosion of people dramatically increased the wealth of the landholding class, who reckoned their status by the number of serfs they owned.

The expansion of the economic resources of the nobility was matched by a rise in legal status and political power. This was the period sarcastically dubbed "the emancipation of the nobility," a phrase that captures not only the irony of the growing gap between rich and poor but also the contrast between the social structures of Russia and those of western Europe. In return for their privileges and status, Peter the Great extended the duties the landowning classes owed to the state. By granting unique rights, like the ownership of serfs, to the descendants of the old military service class, Peter had forged a Russian nobility. Lifetime service, however, was the price of nobility.

In order to gain and hold the throne, each succeeding tsar had to make concessions to the nobility to gain their loyalty. At first it was a few simple adjustments. The sons of wealthy landowners who completed a course of education at one of the state academies were allowed to enter the Table of Ranks in the middle of the hierarchy rather than at the bottom. Then life service was commuted to a term of twenty-five years, still a long time in a world of short lives and sudden deaths. But these concessions were not enough.

Twenty-five years of service did not solve the problem of estate management, especially as the tasks of management grew along with the population of serfs. Thus the next capitulation was that a single son could remain on the estate and escape service altogether. The births of younger sons were concealed; owners of multiple estates claimed the exemption of one son for each. Most decisively, the talented remained at home to serve the family while the wastrels were sent to serve the

state. Finally in 1762, the obligation for state service by the nobility was abolished entirely.

The abolition of compulsory service was not the same as the abolition of service itself. In fact the end of compulsory service enabled Catherine II, the Great (1762–96), to enact some of the most important reforms of her reign. (See Special Feature, "Catherine Before She Was Great," pp. 604–605.) At first, Catherine's accession seemed nothing more than a continuation of monarchical instability—her first two acts were to have her husband Peter III murdered and to lower the salt tax. Each bought her a measure of security.

Catherine was a dynamic personality who alternately captivated and terrified those with whom she came into contact. Her policies were as complex as her personality, influenced on the one hand by the new French ideas of social justice and the nobility of the human race and on the other by the traditional Russian ideas of absolute rule over an enserfed and subhuman population. Catherine handled these contrasting dimensions of her rule masterfully, gaining abroad the reputation as the most enlightened of European monarchs and at home the sincere devotion of her people.

The most important event in the early years of Catherine's reign was the establishment of a legislative commission to review the laws of Russia. Catherine herself wrote the *Instruction* (1767) by which the elected commissioners were to operate. She borrowed her theory of law from the French jurist Baron de Montesquieu (1689–1755) and her theory of punishment from the Italian reformer Cesare Beccaria (1738–94). Among other things, Catherine advocated the abolition of capital punishment, torture, serf auctions, and the breakup of serf families by sale. Few of these radical reforms were ever put into practice.

But in 1775 Catherine did restructure local government. Russia was divided into fifty provincial districts, each with a population of between 300,000 and 400,000 inhabitants. Each district was to be governed by both a central official and elected local noblemen. This reform was modeled upon the English system of justices of the peace. Previous local reforms had failed because of the absence of a resident local nobility. The abolition of compulsory service finally made possible the establishment of local institutions. In 1785, Catherine issued the Charter of the Nobility, a formal statement of the rights and privileges of the noble class. The Charter incorporated all the gains the nobility had made since the death of Peter the Great, but it also instituted the requirements for local service that had been the basis of Catherine's reforms. District councils with the

MEMOIRS OF THE EARLY YEARS OF CATHERINE THE GREAT

■ *Catherine the Great has left a fascinating account of her early years that is in sharp contrast to her reputation for ruthlessness as a ruler.*

My father, whom I saw very seldom, considered me to be an angel, my mother did not bother much about me. She had had, eighteen months after my birth, a son whom she passionately loved, whereas I was merely tolerated and often repulsed with violence and temper, not always with justice. I was aware of all this, but not always able to understand what I really felt about it.

At the age of seven I was suddenly seized with a violent cough. It was the custom that we should kneel every night and every morning to say our prayers. One night as I knelt and prayed I began to cough so violently that the strain caused me to fall on my left side, and I had such sharp pains in my chest that they almost took my breath away.

Finally, after much suffering, I was well enough to get up and it was discovered, as they started to put on my clothes, that I had in the meantime assumed the shape of the letter Z; my right shoulder was much higher than the left, the backbone running in zigzag and the left side falling in.

right to petition directly to the tsar became the centerpiece of Russian provincial government.

In order to train the local nobility for government service, Catherine introduced educational reforms. Peter had established military schools for the nobility and had staffed them with foreigners. The University of Moscow had been founded in 1755, and its faculty too was dominated by European emigrants. Catherine saw the need to broaden the educational system. Borrowing from the Austrian system, she established provincial elementary schools to train the sons and daughters of the local nobility. To staff these, Catherine created teachers' colleges so that the state would have its own educators. Though the program called for the equal educationof women, except in Saint Petersburg and Moscow few women attended either elementary or high schools.

Catherine's reforms did little to enhance the lives of the vast majority of her people. Though she often spoke in the terms of the French philosophers who saw the enserfment of fellow humans as a blot on civilization, Catherine took no effective action either to end serfdom or to soften its rigors. In fact, by grants of state land Catherine gave away 800,000 state peasants, who became serfs. So, too, did millions of Poles who became her subjects after the partition of Poland in 1793 and 1795.

The most significant uprising of the century, Pugachev's revolt (1773–75), took place during Catherine's reign. Emelyan Pugachev (1726–75) was a Cossack who in his youth had been a military adventurer.

Chained but undaunted, Emelyan Pugachev awaits punishment for leading a peasant rebellion in the southern Urals.

Portrait of Catherine the Great.

Catherine Before She Was Great

Catherine the Great wasn't always called the Empress of all the Russias. In fact, she wasn't always called Catherine. Sophie of Anhalt-Zerbst was the daughter of a petty German prince whose estates were too poor to provide for his family. He hired himself out as a military officer to the kings of Prussia and became governor of the dreary Baltic port of Stettin. Here Sophie passed her childhood.

By far the most significant event of Sophie's childhood was the sudden sickness that overtook her at the age of seven. She was seized by coughing, fevers, and fits that incapacitated her for weeks. For a time her life was in danger. Then one morning she awoke without fever and without the racking cough that had seared through her body. But in its place had come a physical change. Weeks of lying on her side had deformed her physique: "I had assumed the shape of a letter Z," she later recalled. Doctors were sought for advice, but none could help until at last a veterinarian who practiced on the limbs of horses and cows built a body frame for Sophie that was designed to reshape her deformity. She wore this for four years until she regained her former posture.

Sophie's father was a strict Lutheran who prescribed a regimen for the education of his children that was to be precisely followed. At the age of seven, just after her recovery, tutors were brought in to teach Sophie history and geography, and a Lutheran minister was deputed to train her in religion. Though Sophie did not have a close relationship with her mother—in later years they quarreled incessantly—it was her mother who showed her the world outside Stettin. Joanna of Holstein-Gottorp had grown up surrounded by courtly pomp rather than military rigor, and every year she visited her relations in Brunswick. When Sophie began to accompany her mother on these trips, they became for her the principal means to escape the boredom of life in Stettin. On one visit to Berlin she was introduced to Frederick William I, king of Prussia. These trips to Brunswick and Berlin opened Sophie's eyes to the possibility of a life different than the one she had expected, the possibility of life with one of the crown princes of Europe.

As it happened, Sophie had little need to wish. By a strange twist of fate, another of her mother's innumerable cousins had recently been declared heir to the throne of Russia. This was Peter, soon to be duke of Holstein-Gottorp and ultimately to be Peter III of Russia. Empress Elizabeth of Russia was childless and Peter was her nearest relative. She determined to have him married to an eligible German princess, and after much casting about, the choice fell on Sophie. In 1744 Sophie was summoned to Russia.

Princely marriages were matters of international diplomacy. In the case of Russia, Frederick the Great of Prussia took more than a neighborly interest. It was he who pushed the claims of a daughter of one of his own military dependents and it was he who enlisted Joanna to become an agent of Prussia at the Russian court. No one asked Sophie what she thought, since her opinion hardly mattered.

The journey to Russia was a trip that Sophie would never forget. On the journey to the east, carriages gave way to sleighs, and her heavy cloth clothing to sable. Sophie and Joanna huddled together for warmth, covering their faces and hands from the bitter arctic winds. It took nearly four weeks to reach Saint Petersburg, and when they arrived they were informed that they must hurry to join the royal court at

Moscow. There they were received with unusual warmth as it was the sixteenth birthday of the new heir to the throne and all of Russian society was eager to see his bride-to-be.

Sophie's earliest meetings with her fiancé were not entirely satisfactory. In a strange land she might have expected strange customs, but Peter was a German like herself. Thus she was unprepared for their first interview, in which Peter professed his passionate love for one of the ladies of the court. Sophie was only fifteen and, by her own account at least, innocent in sexual matters. Peter's frank confession, which was accompanied by assurances that he would marry Sophie anyhow, caused her as much confusion as it did anger and resentment. She resolved to keep her own counsel and to attempt to please the empress if not the heir. Sophie spent the days before her marriage learning both the Russian language and the Eastern Orthodox religion. She would have to convert to the old faith before she could be betrothed. As part of her conversion, she had to take a Russian name and thus she came to be called Catherine. Whether her change of religion was sincere or not, it was required. Sophie was shrewd enough to realize the importance of the Church, and she won many admirers at court when, after being taken ill, she asked for an Ortho-

dox priest rather than a Lutheran minister or a doctor.

Sophie's marriage took place in 1745. By then she knew that she was alone in the world. She had fought bitterly with her mother, who had became a political liability after she bungled her role as an agent for Frederick the Great. Sophie shared nothing with her new husband—including the marriage bed. The household set up for her was composed entirely of spies for the empress and even her correspondence was monitored. She spent the next fifteen years supplementing the education that she had received as a child. She read everything that she could get. She devoured the classics, especially history and philosophy, and for the first time became acquainted with the works of the new European writers whose reputations had reached as far as Russia.

She also developed a passion for the handsome guardsmen who inhabited the palace. Perhaps in revenge for her husband's conduct, perhaps in return for his neglect, she took the first of more than twenty lovers. When she became pregnant in 1754, it was almost certainly not Peter's child. Eight years later the private life of Sophie of Anhalt-Zerbst ended. Then Empress Elizabeth died, the half-mad Peter III acceded to the throne, and Sophie, now known to the world as Catherine, began her remarkable public career.

Disappointed in his career, he made his way to the Ural mountains, where he recruited Asian tribesmen and laborers forced to work in the mines. By promising freedom and land ownership, he drew peasants to his cause. In 1773 Pugachev declared himself to be Tsar Peter III, the murdered husband of Catherine II. He began with small raiding parties against local landlords and military outposts and soon had gained the allegiance of tens of thousands of peasants. In 1774, with an army of nearly twenty thousand, Pugachev took the city of Kazan and threatened to advance on Moscow. It was another year before state forces could effectively control the rebellion. Finally, Pugachev was betrayed by his own followers and sent to Moscow, where he was executed.

During the reigns of Peter and Catherine the Great, Russia was transformed into an international power. Saint Petersburg, a window to the west, was a capital worthy of a potent monarch, and during the course of the eighteenth century it attracted many of Europe's leading luminaries. At court French was spoken, the latest fashions were worn, and the newest ideas for economic and educational reform were aired. The Russian nobility mingled comfortably with its European counterparts, while the military service class developed into bureaucrats and administrators. But if life glittered at court, it remained the same dull regimen in the country. Millions of peasants were owned either by the state or by private landlords, and their quality of life was no different at the end of the campaign of westernization than it had been at the beginning.

The Two Germanies

The Thirty Years' War, which ended in 1648, initiated a profound transformation of the Holy Roman Empire. Warfare had devastated imperial territory. It was decades before the rich imperial lands recovered, and then the political consequences of the war had taken effect. There were now two empires, a German and an Austrian, though both were ruled by the same person. In the German territories, whether Catholic or Protestant, the Holy Roman Emperor was more a constitutional monarch than the absolute ruler he was in Austria. The larger states like Saxony, Bavaria, and Hanover made their own political alliances despite the jurisdictional control that the emperor claimed to exercise. Most decisively, so did Brandenburg-Prussia. By the beginning of the eigh-

teenth century, the electors of Brandenburg had become the kings of Prussia, and Prussia's military power and efficient administrative structure became the envy of its German neighbors.

The Austrian empire was composed of Austria and Bohemia, the Habsburg hereditary lands, and as much of Hungary as could be controlled. In Austria, the Habsburgs clung tightly to their power. For decades Austria was the center of the still-flourishing Counter-Reformation, and the power and influence of the Jesuits was as strong here as it was in Spain. The War of the Spanish Succession, which gave the Habsburgs control of the southern Netherlands and parts of Italy, brought Austria an enhanced role in European affairs. Austria remained one of the great powers of Europe and the leading power in the Holy Roman Empire despite the rise of Prussia. Indeed from the middle of the eighteenth century the conflict between Prussia and Austria was the defining characteristic of central European politics.

The Rise of Prussia

The transformation of Brandenburg-Prussia from a petty German principality to a great European power was one of the most significant and least expected developments of the eighteenth century. Frederick William, the Great Elector (1640–88), had begun the process of forging Brandenburg-Prussia into a power in its own right by building a large and efficient military machine. At the beginning of the eighteenth century Prussia was on the winning side in both the War of the Spanish Succession and the Great Northern War. When the battlefield dust had settled, Prussia found itself in possession of Pomerania and the Baltic port of Stettin. It was now a recognized power in eastern Europe.

Frederick William I (1713–40) and his son Frederick II, the Great (1740–86), turned this promising beginning into an astounding success. A devout Calvinist, Frederick William I deplored waste and display as much on moral as on fiscal grounds. The reforms he initiated were intended to subordinate both aristocracy and peasantry to the needs of the state and to subordinate the needs of the state to the demands of the military.

Because of its geographical position, Prussia's major problem was to maintain an efficient and well-trained army during peacetime. Defense of its exposed territories required a constant state of military preparedness, yet the relaxation of military discipline and the desertion of troops to their homes inevitably followed the cessation of hostilities. Frederick William I solved this problem by integrating the economic and military structures of his state. First he appointed only German officers to command his troops, eliminating the mercenaries who sold their services to the highest bidders. Then he placed these noblemen at the head of locally recruited regiments. Each adult male in every district was required to register for military service in the regiment of the local landlord. These reforms dramatically increased the effectiveness of the army by shifting the burden of recruitment and training to the localities.

Yet despite all the attention that Frederick William I lavished on the military—by the end of his reign nearly 70 percent of state expenditures went to the army—his foreign policy was largely pacific. In fact, his greatest achievements were in civil affairs, reforming the bureaucracy, establishing a sound economy, and raising state revenues. Through generous settlement schemes and by welcoming Protestant and Jewish refugees, Frederick William was able to expand the economic potential of these eastern territories. Frederick William I pursued an aggressive policy of land purchase to expand the royal domain, and the addition of so many new inhabitants in Prussia further increased his wealth. While the major western European powers were discovering deficit financing and the national debt, Prussia was running a surplus.

Financial security was vital to the success of Frederick the Great. Father and son had quarreled bitterly throughout Frederick's youth—not only about music—and most observers expected that out of spite Frederick would tear down all that his father had built up. In fact father and son were cast in the same mold, with the unexpected difference that the son was the more ruthless and ambitious. With his throne, Frederick II inherited the fourth largest army in Europe and the richest treasury. He wasted no time in putting both to use. His two objectives were to acquire the Polish corridor of West Prussia that separated his German and Prussian territories and the agriculturally and industrially rich Austrian province of Silesia to the southeast of Berlin. Just months after his coronation, Frederick conquered Silesia, increasing the size of Prussia by nearly a quarter. Within a decade the province dominated the Prussian economy, outproducing and outconsuming all other areas of Frederick's state.

It was Frederick's military prowess that earned him the title "the Great." But this was only a part of his

DEFINITION OF AN ENLIGHTENED DESPOT

■ *Frederick the Great wrote philosophical and military tracts and composed dozens of compositions for the flute. Here is his definition of the enlightened despot.*

The sovereign is attached by indissoluble ties to the body of the state; hence it follows that he, by repercussion, is sensible to all the ills which afflict his subjects; and the people, in like manner, suffer from the misfortunes which affect their sovereign. There is but one general good, which is that of the state. . . . The sovereign represents the state; he and his people form but one body, which can only be happy as far as united by concord. The prince is to the nation he governs what the head is to the man; it is his duty to see, to think, and act for the whole community, so that he may procure it every advantage of which it is capable. . . . Such are in general the duties imposed upon a prince, from which, in order that he may never depart, he ought often to recollect that he himself is but a man, like the least of his subjects. If he be the first general, the first minister of the realm, it is not so that he should shelter in the shadow of authority, but that he should fulfil the duties of such titles. He is only the first servant of the state, who is obliged to act with probity and prudence; and to remain as totally disinterested as if he were each moment liable to render an account of his administration to his fellow citizens.

From: Frederick the Great, *An Essay on Forms of Government.*

Prussian infantry officers display their uniforms in this painting from the late eighteenth century. Distinctive, colorful, and elaborate uniforms, different for each regiment, were common in European armies before the field-gray and khaki era of the twentieth century.

Austria Survives

Austria was the great territorial victor in the War of the Spanish Succession, acquiring both the Netherlands and parts of Italy. Austrian forces recaptured a large part of Hungary from the Turks, thereby expanding their territory to the south and the east. Hereditary ruler of Austria and Bohemia, king of Hungary, and Holy Roman Emperor of the German nation, Charles VI (1711–40) was recognized as one of Europe's most potent rulers. But appearances were deceptive. The apex of Austrian power and prestige had already passed. Austria had benefited from balance-of-power politics, not so much from its own strength as from the leverage it could give to others. With the rise of Russia and Prussia there was now more than one fulcrum to power in eastern Europe.

The difficulties facing Austria ran deep. The Thirty Years' War had made the emperor more an Austrian monarch than an imperial German ruler. On the Austrian hereditary estates, the Catholic Counter-Reformation continued unabated, bringing with it the benefits of Jesuit education, cultural revival, and the religious unity necessary to motivate warfare against the Ottomans. But these benefits came at a price. Perhaps as many as two hundred thousand Protestants fled Austria and Bohemia, taking with them their skills and capital. For centuries the vision of empire had dominated Habsburg rule. This meant that the Austrian monarchy was a multiethnic confederation of lands loosely tied together by loyalty to a single head. The components preserved a high degree of autonomy: Hungary elected the Habsburg emperor its king in a separate ceremony. Local autonomy continually restricted the imposition of central policy, and never were the localities more autonomous than in the matter of taxation. Thus it was hard for Austria to centralize in the same way as had Prussia.

Austria was predominantly rural and agricultural. Less than 5 percent of the population lived in towns of ten thousand or more; less than 15 percent lived in towns at all. On the land the local aristocracy, whether nobility or gentry, exploited serfs to the maximum. Not only were serfs required to give labor service three days a week (and up to six during planting and harvest times), but the nobility maintained a full array of feudal privileges including the right to mill all grain and brew all beer. When serfs married, when they transferred property, even when they died, they paid taxes to their lord. As a result they had little left to give the state. In consequence, the Austrian army was among the smallest and the poorest of the major powers despite the fact that it had the most active enemies along its borders.

achievement. More than his father, Frederick II forged an alliance with the Prussian nobility, integrating them into a unified state. A tightly organized central administration, which depended upon the cooperation of the local nobility, directed both military and bureaucratic affairs. At the center, Frederick worked tirelessly to oversee his government. Where Louis XIV had proclaimed, "I am the state," Frederick the Great announced "I am the first servant of the state." He codified the laws of Prussia, abolished torture and capital punishment, and instituted agricultural techniques imported from the states of western Europe. By the end of Frederick's reign, Prussia had become a model for bureaucratic organization, military reform, and enlightened rule.

REVERIES UPON THE ART OF WAR

■ *Herman Maurice de Saxe was the illegitimate son of the king of Poland. He had extensive military experience in both eastern and western Europe. He ultimately achieved the office of Marshal of France, where he was celebrated as a military reformer. He modeled many of his reforms on the Prussian army.*

Would it not be much better to establish a law obliging men of all conditions of life to serve their king and country for the space of five years? A law, which could not reasonably be objected against, as it is both natural and just for people to be engaged in the defense of that state of which they constitute a part, and in choosing them between the years of twenty and thirty, no manner of inconvenience can possibly be the result; for those are years devoted, as it were, to libertinism; which are spent in adventures and travels, and, in general, productive of but small comfort to parents. An expedient of this kind could not come under the denomination of a public calamity, because every man, at the expiration of his five years service, would be discharged. It would also create an inexhaustible fund of good recruits, and such as would not be subject to desertion. In course of time, everyone would regard it as an honor rather than a duty to perform his task; but to produce this effect upon a people, it is necessary that no sort of distinction should be admitted, no rank or degree whatsoever excluded, and the nobles and rich rendered, in a principal manner, subservient to it. This would effectually prevent all murmur and repining, for those who had served their time, would look upon such, as betrayed any reluctance, or dissatisfaction at it, with contempt; by which means, the grievance would vanish insensibly, and every man at length esteem it an honor to serve his term. The poor would be comforted by the example of the rich; and the rich could not with decency complain, seeing themselves on a footing with the nobles.

Lack of finance, lack of human resources, and lack of governmental control were the underlying problems of Austria, but they were not the most immediate difficulties facing Charles VI. With no sons to succeed him, Charles feared that his hereditary and elective states would go their separate ways after his death and that the great Habsburg monarchy would end. For twenty years his abiding ambition was to gain recognition for the principle that his empire would pass intact to his daughter, Maria Theresa. He expressed the principle in a document known as the Pragmatic Sanction, which stated that all Habsburg lands would pass intact to the eldest heir, male or female. Charles VI made concession after concession to gain acceptance of the Pragmatic Sanction. But the leaders of Europe licked their lips at the prospect of a dismembered Austrian empire.

Maria Theresa (1740–80) inherited the imperial throne in 1740 and quickly discovered what it was like to be a woman in a man's world. In 1740 Frederick of Prussia invaded the rich Austrian province of Silesia and attracted allies for an assault upon Vienna. Faced with Bavarian, Saxon, and Prussian armies, Maria Theresa might well have lost her inheritance had she not shown her remarkable capacities so early in her reign. She appeared before the Hungarian estates, accepted their crown, and persuaded them to provide her with an army capable of halting the allied advance. Though she was unable to reconquer Silesia, Hungarian aid helped her hold the line against her enemies.

The loss of Silesia, the most prosperous part of the Austrian domains, signaled the need for fundamental reform. The new eighteenth-century idea of building a state replaced the traditional Habsburg concern with maintaining an empire. Maria Theresa and her son Joseph II (1780–90) began the process of transformation. For Austria, state building meant first the reorganization of the military and civil bureaucracy to clear the way for fiscal reform. As in Prussia, a central directory was created to oversee the collection of taxes and the disbursement of funds. Maria Theresa personally persuaded her provincial estates both to increase taxation and to extend it to the nobles and the clergy. While her success was limited, she finally established royal control over the raising and collection of taxes.

Maria Theresa and her family. Eleven of Maria Theresa's sixteen children are posed with the empress and her husband, Francis of Lorraine. Standing next to his mother is the future emperor Joseph II.

The second element in Maria Theresa's reform program involved the condition of the Austrian peasantry. Maria Theresa established the doctrine that the "peasant must be able to support himself and his family and pay his taxes in time of peace and war." She limited labor service to two days per week and abolished the most burdensome feudal dues. Joseph II ended serfdom altogether. The new Austrian law codes guaranteed peasants' legal rights and established their ability to seek redress through the law. Joseph II hoped to extend reform even further. In the last years of his life he abolished obligatory labor service and ensured that all peasants kept one-half of their income before paying local and state taxes. Such a radical reform met a storm of opposition and was ultimately abandoned at the end of the reign.

The reorganization of the bureaucracy, the increase in taxation, and the social reforms that created a more productive peasantry revitalized the Austrian state. The efforts of Maria Theresa and Joseph II to overcome provincial autonomy worked better in Austria and Bohemia than in Hungary. The Hungarians declined to contribute at all to state revenues, and Joseph II took the unusual step of refusing to be crowned king of Hungary so that he would not have to make any concessions to Hungarian autonomy. He even imposed a tariff on Hungarian goods sold in Austria. More seriously, parts of the empire already had been lost before the process of reform could begin. Prussia's seizure of Silesia was the hardest blow of all. Yet in 1740, when Frederick the Great and his allies swept down from the north, few would have predicted that Austria would survive.

The Politics of Power

Frederick the Great's invasion of Silesia in 1740 was callous and cynical. Since the Pragmatic Sanction bound him to recognize Maria Theresa's succession, Frederick cynically offered her a defensive alliance in return for which she would simply hand over Silesia. It was an offer she should not have refused. Though Frederick's action initiated the War of the Austrian Succession, he was not alone in his desire to shake loose parts of Austria's territory. Soon nearly the entire Continent became embroiled in the conflict.

The War of the Austrian Succession (1740–48) resembled a pack of wolves stalking its injured prey. It quickly became a major international conflict involving Prussia, France, and Spain on one side and Austria, Britain, and Holland on the other. Spain joined the fighting to recover its Italian possessions, Saxony claimed Moravia, France entered Bohemia, and the Bavarians moved into Austria from the south. With France and Prussia allied, it was vital that Britain join with Austria to maintain the balance of power. Initially the British did little more than subsidize Maria Theresa's forces, but once France renewed its efforts to conquer the Netherlands, both Britain and the Dutch Republic joined in the fray. That the British cared little about the fate of the Habsburg empire was clear from the terms of the treaty that they dictated at Aix-la-Chapelle (Aachen) in 1748. Austria recognized Frederick's conquest of Silesia, as well as the loss of parts of its Italian territories to Spain. France, which the British had always regarded as the real enemy, withdrew from the Netherlands in return for the restoration of a number of colonial possessions. The War of the Austrian Succession made Austria and Prussia permanent enemies and gave Maria Theresa a crash course in international diplomacy. She learned firsthand that self-interest rather than loyalty underlay power politics. This lesson was reinforced in 1756 when Britain and Prussia entered into a military accord at the beginning of the Seven Years' War (1756–63). Prussian expansion and duplicity had already alarmed both Russia and France, and Frederick II feared that he would be squeezed from east and west. He could hardly expect help from Maria Theresa, so he extended overtures to the British, whose interests in protecting Hanover, the hereditary estates of their German-born king, outweighed their prior commitments to Austria. Frederick's actions drove France into the arms of both the Austrians and the Russians, and an alliance that included the German state of Saxony was formed in defense. Thus was initiated a diplomatic revolution in which France and Austria became allies after three hundred years as enemies.

Once again, Frederick the Great took the offensive and once again, he won his risk against the odds. His attack on Saxony and Austria in 1756 brought a vigorous response from the Russians, who interceded on Austria's behalf with a massive army. Three years later, at the battle of Kunersdorf, Frederick suffered the worst military defeat of his career when the Russians shattered his armies. In 1760 his forces were barely a third of the size of those massed by his opponents, and it was only a matter of time before he was fighting defensively from within Prussia.

In 1762 Empress Elizabeth died. She was succeeded by her nephew, the childlike Peter III, a German by birth who worshiped Frederick the Great. When Peter came to the throne, he immediately negotiated peace with Frederick, abandoning not only his allies but also the substantial territorial gains that the Russian forces had made within Prussia. It was small wonder that the Russian military leadership joined in the coup d'état that brought Peter's wife, Catherine, to the throne in 1762. With Russia out of the war, Frederick was able to fend off further Austrian offensives and to emerge with his state, including Silesia, intact.

The Seven Years' War did little to change the boundaries of the German states, but it had two important political results. The first was to establish beyond doubt the status of Prussia as a major power and a counterbalance to Austria in central Europe. The existence of the dual Germanies, one led by Prussia and the other by Austria, was to have serious consequences for German unification in the nineteenth century and for the two world wars in the twentieth. The second result of the Seven Years' War was to initiate a long period of peace in eastern Europe. Both Prussia and Austria were financially exhausted from two decades of fighting. Both states needed a breathing spell to initiate administrative and economic improvements, and the period following the Seven Years' War witnessed the sustained programs of internal reforms for which Frederick the Great, Maria Theresa, and Joseph II were famous in the decades following 1763.

Peace among the eastern European powers did not mean that they abandoned their territorial ambitions.

First Partition, 1772	Second Partition, 1793	Third Partition, 1795
To Prussia	To Prussia	To Prussia
To Russia	To Russia	To Russia
To Austria		To Austria
Poland in 1772	Poland in 1793	

Partition of Poland

All over Europe absolute rulers reformed their bureaucracies, streamlined their administrations, increased their sources of revenue, and built enormous standing armies. All over Europe except in Poland. There the autonomous power of the nobility remained as strong as ever. No monarchical dynasty was ever established, and each elected ruler not only confirmed the privileges of the nobility but usually was forced to extend them. In the Diet, the Polish representative assembly, small special-interest groups could bring legislative business to a halt by exercising their veto power. Given the size of Poland's borders, its army was pathetically inadequate for the task it had to face. The Polish monarchy was helpless to defend its subjects from the destruction on all sides.

In 1764 Catherine the Great and Frederick the Great combined to place one of Catherine's former lovers on

This engraving by Le Mire is called The Cake of the Kings: First Partition of Poland, 1773. *The monarchs of Russia, Austria, and Prussia join in carving up Poland. The Polish king is clutching his tottering crown.*

the Polish throne and to turn Poland into a weak dependent. Russia and Prussia had different interests in Poland's fate. For Russia, Poland represented a vast buffer state that kept the German powers at a distance from Russia's borders. It was more in Russia's interest to dominate Polish foreign policy than to conquer its territory. For Prussia, Poland looked like another helpless flower, "to be picked off leaf by leaf," as Frederick observed. Poland seemed especially appealing because Polish territory, including the Baltic port of Gdansk, separated the Prussian and Brandenburg portions of Frederick's state.

By the 1770s the idea of carving up Poland was being actively discussed in Berlin, Saint Petersburg, and Vienna. Austria, too, had an interest in a Polish partition, especially to maintain its power and status with the other two states, and perhaps to use Polish territory as a potential bargaining chip for the return of Silesia. Finally, in 1772, the three great eastern powers struck a deal. Russia would take a large swath of the grain fields

of northeast Poland, which included over one million people, while Frederick would unite his lands by seizing West Prussia. Austria gained both the largest territories, including Galicia, and the greatest number of people, nearly two million Polish subjects.

In half a century the balance of power in central Europe had shifted decisively. Prussia's absorption of Silesia and parts of Poland made it a single geographical entity as well as a great economic and military power. Austria, despite its lost territory, proved capable of surviving the accession of a female ruler and of fighting off an attempt to dismember its empire. Its participation in the partition of Poland strengthened its role in the politics of the eastern powers, while its alliance with France fortified its role in the west. From one empire there were now two states, and the relationship between Prussia and Austria would dominate central Europe for the next century.

The Greatness of Great Britain

By the middle of the eighteenth century, Great Britain had become the leading power of Europe. It had won its spurs in Continental and colonial wars. Britain was unsurpassed as a naval power, able to protect its far-flung trading empire and to make a show of force in almost any part of the world. Perhaps more impressively for a nation that did not support a large standing army, British soldiers had won decisive victories in the European land wars. Until the American Revolution, Britain came up a winner in every military venture it undertook. But might was only one part of British success. Economic preeminence was every bit as important. British colonial possessions in the Atlantic and Indian oceans poured consumer products into Britain for export to the European marketplaces. Growth in overseas trade was matched by growth in home production. British advances in agricultural technique had transformed Britain from an importer to an exporter of grain. The manufacturing industries that other European states attempted to create with huge government subsidies flourished in Britain through private enterprise.

British military and economic power was supported by a unique system of government. In Britain the nobility served the state through government. The British constitutional system, devised in the seventeenth century and refined in the eighteenth, shared power between the monarchy and the ruling elite through the institution of Parliament. Central government integrated monarch and ministers with chosen representatives from the localities. Such integration not only provided the Crown with the vital information necessary to formulate national policy, but it eased acceptance and enforcement of government decisions. Government was seen as the rule of law which, however imperfect, was believed to operate for the benefit of all.

The parliamentary system gave Britain some of its particular strengths, but they came at a cost. Politics was a national pastime rather than the business of an elite of administrators and state servants. Decentralization of decision making led to half-measures designed to placate competing interests. Appeals to public opinion, especially by candidates for Parliament, often played upon fears and prejudices that divided rather than united the nation. Moreover, the relative openness of the British system hindered diplomatic and colonial affairs, in which secrecy and rapid changes of direction were often the monarch's most potent weapons. These weaknesses came to light most dramatically during the struggle for independence waged by Britain's North American colonists. There the clash of principle and power was most extreme and the strengths and weaknesses of parliamentary rule were ruthlessly exposed.

The British Constitution

The British Constitution was a patchwork of laws and customs that was gradually sewn together to form a workable system of government. Many of its greatest innovations came about through circumstance rather than design, and circumstance continued to play an essential role in its development in the eighteenth century. At the apex of the government stood the king, not an absolute monarch like his European counterparts, but not necessarily less powerful for having less arbitrary power. The British people revered monarchy and the monarch. The theory of mixed government depended upon the balance of interests represented by the monarchy in the Crown, the aristocracy in the House of Lords, and the people in the House of Commons. Less abstractly, the monarch was still regarded as divinely ordained and a special gift to the nation. The monarch was the actual and symbolic leader of the nation as well as the "Supreme Head" of the Church of England. Allegiance to the Anglican church, whether as a political creed among the elite or as a simple matter of devotion among the populace, intensified allegiance to the king.

The partnership between Crown and representative body was best expressed in the idea that the British government was composed of King-in-Parliament. Parliament consisted of three separate organs: monarch, lords, and commons. Though each existed separately as a check upon the potential excesses of the others, it was only when the three functioned together that parliamentary government could operate. The king was charged with selecting ministers, initiating policy, and supervising administration. The two houses of Parliament were charged with raising revenue, making laws, and presenting the grievances of subjects to the Crown.

There were 558 members of the House of Commons after the union with Scotland in 1707. Most members of the lower house were nominated to their seats. The largest number of seats were located in small towns where a local oligarchy, or neighboring patron, had a customary right to make nominations that were invariably accepted by the electorate. Even in the largest cities, influential citizens made arrangements for nominating members in order to avoid the cost and confusion of an actual election. Campaigns were ruinously expensive for the candidates—an election in 1754 cost the losing candidates £40,000—and potentially dangerous to the local community, where bitter social and political divisions boiled just below the surface.

The British gentry dominated the Commons, occupying over 80 percent of the seats in any session. Most of these members also served as unpaid local officials in the counties, as justices of the peace, captains of the local militias, or collectors of local taxes. They came to Parliament not only as representatives of the interests of their class, but as experienced local governors who understood the needs of both Crown and subject.

Nevertheless, the Crown had to develop methods to coordinate the work of the two houses of Parliament and facilitate the passage of governmental programs. The king and his ministers began to use the deep royal pockets of offices and favors to bolster their friends in Parliament. Not only were those employed by the Crown encouraged to find a place in the House of Commons, but those who had a place in Parliament were encouraged to take employment from the Crown. Despite its potential for abuse, this was a political process that integrated center and locality, and at first it worked rather well. Those with local standing were brought into central offices. There they could influence central policy making while protecting their local constituents. These officeholders, who came to be called *placemen*, never constituted a majority of the members of Parliament.

The interior of the British House of Commons in the 1700s. The arrangement of the benches and galleries is much the same as that seen today in the London parliamentary chamber.

They formed the core around which eighteenth-century governments operated but it was a core that needed direction and cohesion. It was such leadership and organization that was the essential contribution of eighteenth-century politics to the British Constitution.

Parties and Ministers

Though parliamentary management was vital to the Crown, it was not the Crown that developed the basic tools of management. Rather these techniques originated within the political community itself and their usefulness was only slowly grasped by the monarchy. The first and, in the long term, most important tool was the party system. Political parties initially developed in the late seventeenth century around the issue of the Protestant succession. Those who opposed James II because he was a Catholic attempted to exclude him

from inheriting the crown. They came to be called by their opponents Whigs, which meant "Scottish horse thieves." Those who supported James's hereditary rights but who also supported the Anglican church came to be called by their opponents Tories, which meant "Irish cattle rustlers." The Tories cooperated in the Revolution of 1688 that placed William and Mary on the throne because James had threatened the Anglican church by tolerating Catholics and because Mary had a legitimate hereditary right to be queen. After the death of Queen Anne in 1714, the Tories supported the succession of James III, James II's Catholic son who had been raised in France, rather than of George I (1714–27), prince of Hanover and Protestant great-grandson of James I. An unsuccessful rebellion to place James III on the throne in 1715 discredited the leadership of the Tory party, but did not weaken its importance in both local and parliamentary politics.

The Whigs supported the Protestant succession and a broad-based Protestantism. They attracted the allegiance of large numbers of dissenters, heirs to the Puritans of the seventeenth century who practiced forms of Protestantism different from the Anglican church. The struggle between Whigs and Tories was less a struggle for power than it was for loyalty to their opposing viewpoints. As the Tories opposed the Hanoverian succession and the Whigs supported it, it was no mystery which party would find favor with George I. Moreover, as long as there was a pretender to the British throne—another rebellion took place in Scotland in 1745 led by the grandson of James II—the Tories continued to be tarred with the brush of disloyalty.

The division of political sympathies between Whigs and Tories helped create a set of groupings to which parliamentary leadership could be applied. A national, rather than a local or regional outlook, could be used to organize support for royal policy as long as royal policy conformed to that national outlook. The ascendancy of the Whigs enabled George I and his son George II (1727–60) to govern effectively through Parliament, but at the price of dependence upon the Whig leaders. Though the monarch had the constitutional freedom to choose his ministers, realistically he could choose only Whigs, and practically none but the Whig leaders of the House of Commons. Happily for the first two Georges, they found a man who was able to manage Parliament but desired only to serve the Crown.

Sir Robert Walpole (1676–1745) came from a long-established gentry family in Norfolk. Walpole was an early supporter of the Hanoverian succession and an early victim of party warfare. But once George I was

Sir Robert Walpole addressing the cabinet.

securely on the throne, Walpole became an indispensable leader of the House of Commons. His success rested upon his extraordinary abilities: he was an excellent public speaker; he relished long working days and the details of government; and he understood better than anyone else the intricacies of state finance. Walpole became First Lord of the Treasury, a post that he transformed into first minister of state. From his treasury post, Walpole assiduously built a Whig parliamentary party. He carefully dispensed jobs and offices, using them as bait to lure parliamentary supporters. Walpole's organization paid off both in the passage of legislation desired by the Crown and at the polls, where Whigs were returned to Parliament time and again.

From 1721 to 1742 Walpole was the most powerful man in the British government. He refused an offer of a peerage so that he could continue to lead the House of Commons. Walpole's long tenure in office was as much a result of his policies as of his methods of governing. He brought a measure of fiscal responsibility to government by establishing a fund to pay off the national debt. In foreign policy he pursued peace with the same fervor that both his predecessors and successors pursued war. The long years of peace brought prosperity to both the landed and merchant classes, but they also brought crit-

icism of Walpole's methods. The way in which he used government patronage to build his parliamentary party was attacked as corruption. So too were the ways in which the pockets of Whig officeholders were lined. During his last decade in office Walpole struggled to survive. His attempt to extend the excise tax on colonial goods nearly led to his loss of office in 1733. His refusal to respond to the clamor for continued war with Spain in 1741 finally led to his downfall.

Walpole's twenty-year rule established the pattern of parliamentary government. The Crown needed a "prime" minister who was able to steer legislation through the House of Commons. It also needed a patronage broker who could take control of the treasury and dispense its largess in return for parliamentary backing. Walpole's personality and talents had combined these two roles. Hereafter they were divided. Those who had grown up under Walpole had learned their lessons well. The Whig monopoly of power continued unchallenged for nearly another twenty years. The patronage network Walpole had created was vastly extended by his Whig successors. Even minor posts in the customs or the excise offices were now exchanged for political favor, and only those approved by the Whig leadership could claim them. The cries of corruption grew louder not only in the country houses of the long-disenfranchised Tories, but in the streets of London, where a popular radicalism developed in opposition to the Whig oligarchy. They were taken up as well in the North American colonies, where two million British subjects champed at the bit of imperial rule.

America Revolts

Britain's triumph in the Seven Years' War (1756–63) had come at great financial cost to the nation. At the beginning of the eighteenth century, the national debt stood at £14 million; in 1763 it had risen to £130 million despite the fact that Walpole's government had been paying off some of it. Then, as now, the cost of world domination was staggering. George III (1760–1820) came to the throne with a taste for reform and a desire to break the Whig stranglehold on government. He was to have limited success on both counts, though not for want of trying. In 1763 the king and his ministers agreed that reform of colonial administration was long overdue. Such reform would have the twin benefit of shifting part of the burden of taxation from Britain to North America and of making the commercial side of colonization pay.

This was sound thinking all around, and in due course Parliament passed a series of duties on goods imported into the colonies, including glass, wine, coffee, tea, and most notably sugar. The so-called Sugar Act (1764) was followed by the Stamp Act (1765), a tax on printed papers such as newspapers, deeds, and court documents. Both acts imposed taxes in the colonies similar to those that already existed in Britain. Accompanying the acts were administrative orders designed to cut into the lucrative black market trade. The government instituted new rules for searching ships and transferred authority over smuggling from the local colonial courts to Britain's Admiralty courts. Though British officials could only guess at the value of the new duties imposed, it was believed that with effective enforcement £150,000 would be raised. All this would go to pay the vastly greater costs of colonial administration and security.

British officials were more than perplexed when these mild measures met with a ferocious response. Assemblies of nearly every colony officially protested the Sugar Act. They sent petitions to Parliament begging for repeal and warning of dire economic and political consequences. Riots followed passage of the Stamp Act. Tax collectors were hounded out of office, their resignations precipitated by threats and acts of physical violence. In Massachusetts mobs that included political leaders in the colony razed the homes of the collector and the lieutenant-governor. However much the colonists might have regretted the violence that was

done, they believed that an essential political principle was at stake. It was a principle of the freedom of an Englishman.

At their core, the protests of the American colonists underscored the vitality of the British political system. The Americans argued that they could not be taxed without their consent and that their consent could come only through representation in Parliament. Since there were no colonists in Parliament, Parliament had no jurisdiction over the property of the colonists. Taxation without representation was tyranny. There were a number of subtleties to this argument that were quickly lost as political rhetoric and political action heated up. In the first place, the colonists did tax themselves through their own legislatures and much of that money paid the costs of administration and defense. Secondly, as a number of pamphleteers pointed out, no one in the colonies had asked the British government to send regiments of the army into North America. The colonists had little reason to put their faith in British protection. Hard-fought colonial victories were tossed away at European negotiating tables, while the British policy of defending Indian rights in the Ohio Valley ran counter to the interests of the settlers. When defense was necessary, the colonists had proven themselves both able and cooperative in providing it. A permanent tax meant a permanent army, and a standing army was as loathed in Britain as it was in the colonies.

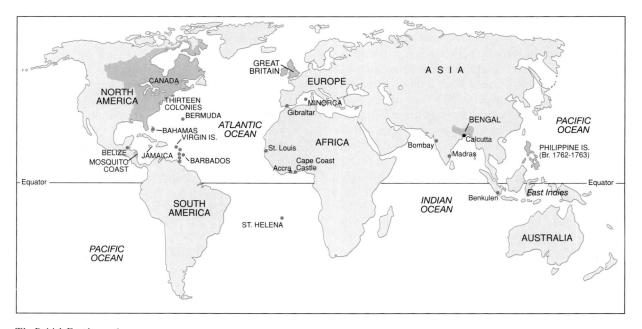

The British Empire, 1763

From *The Declaration of Independence*

■ *The* Declaration of Independence *succinctly summarized the principles upon which the American colonists were to build a new form of democratic government. It was written by Thomas Jefferson.*

We hold these truths to be self-evident, that all men are created equal, that they are endowed by their Creator with certain inalienable Rights, that among these are Life, Liberty and the pursuit of Happiness. That to secure these rights, Governments are instituted among Men, deriving their just powers from the consent of the governed, That whenever any Form of Government becomes destructive of these ends, it is the Right of the People to alter or to abolish it, and to institute new Government, laying its foundation on such principles and organizing its powers in such form, as to them shall seem most likely to effect their Safety and Happiness. Prudence, indeed, will dictate that Governments long established should not be changed for light and transient causes; and accordingly all experience hath shown, that mankind are more disposed to suffer, while evils are sufferable, than to right themselves by abolishing the forms to which they are accustomed. But when a long train of abuses and usurpations, pursuing invariably the same Object, evinces a design to reduce them under absolute Despotism, it is their right, it is their duty, to throw off such Government, and to provide new Guards for their future security.

Colonists also tried to draw a distinction between internal and external taxation in opposing the Stamp Act. They deemed regulation of overseas commerce a legitimate power of Parliament but argued that the regulation of internal exchange was not. But this distinction was lost once the issue of parliamentary representation was raised. If the colonists had not consented to British taxation, then it made no difference whether taxation was internal or external. The passion generated in the colonies was probably no greater than that generated in Britain. The British government also saw the confrontation as a matter of principle, but for Britain the principle was parliamentary sovereignty. This, above all, was the rock upon which the British Constitution had been built over the last century. Parliament had entered into a partnership with the Crown. The Crown had surrendered—willingly or not—many of its prerogatives. In return, Parliament had bound the people to obedience. There were well-established means by which British subjects could petition Parliament for redress of grievances against the monarch, but there were no channels by which they could question the sovereignty of Parliament.

Once the terms of debate had been so defined, it was difficult for either side to find a middle ground. Parliamentary moderates managed repeal of the Stamp Act and most of the clauses of the Sugar Act, but they also joined in passing the Declaratory Act (1766), which stated unequivocally that Parliament held sovereign jurisdiction over the colonies "in all cases whatsoever." This was a claim that became more and more difficult to sustain as colonial leaders began to cite the elements of resistance theory that had justified the Revolution of 1688. Then the protest had been against the tyranny of the king, now it was against the tyranny of Parliament. American propagandists claimed that a conspiracy existed to deprive the colonists of their property and rights, to enslave them for the benefit of special interests and corrupt politicians.

The techniques of London radicals who opposed parliamentary policy were imported into the colonies. Newspapers were used to whip up public support; boycotts brought ordinary people into the political arena; public demonstrations like the Boston Tea Party (1774) were carefully designed to intimidate; mobs were occasionally given free rein. Though the government had faced down these tactics when they were used in London to support John Wilkes (1725–97), an ardent critic of royal policy, they were less successful when the crisis lay an ocean away. When, in 1770, British troops fired upon a Boston mob, American propagandists were provided with empirical evidence that Britain intended to enslave the colonies. Violence was met by violence, passion by passion. In 1775 full-scale fighting was under

An engraving by Paul Revere showing the Boston Massacre on March 5, 1770, in which five rioters were killed by British soldiers sent to Boston to enforce British tax laws. This incident became one of the landmark events on the way to revolution in the British North American colonies.

The New European Powers

1707	England and Scotland unite to form Great Britain
1713–14	Treaty of Utrecht ends War of the Spanish Succession (1702–14)
1714	British crown passes to House of Hanover
1721	Treaty of Nystad ends Great Northern War (1700–21)
1721–42	Sir Robert Walpole leads British House of Commons
1722	Peter the Great of Russia creates Table of Ranks
1740	Frederick the Great of Prussia invades Austrian province of Silesia
1748	Treaty of Aix-la-Chapelle ends War of the Austrian Succession (1740–48)
1756–63	Seven Years' War pits Prussia and Britain against Austria, France, and Russia
1773–75	Pugachev's Revolt in Russia
1774	Boston Tea Party
1775	American Revolution begins
1786	Catherine the Great of Russia issues Charter of the Nobility

way. Eight years later Britain withdrew from a war it could not win, and the American colonies were left to govern themselves.

By the end of the third quarter of the eighteenth century, Europe had a new political configuration. A continent once dominated by a single power—Spain in the sixteenth century and France in the seventeenth—was now dominated by a state system in which alliances among several great powers held the balance. Despite the loss of its American colonies, Great Britain had proved the most potent of the states. Its victories over the French in the Seven Years' War and over France and Prussia in the War of the Austrian Succession secured its position. But it was a position that could be maintained only through alliances with the German states, either with Prussia or Austria. The rise of Prussia provided a counterweight to French domination of the Continent. Though these two states became allies in the middle of the century, the ambitions of their rulers made them natural enemies, and it would not be long before French and Prussian armies were again pitted against each other. France, still the wealthiest and most populous of European states, had slumbered through the eighteenth-century reorganization. The legacies of Louis XIV took a long time to reach fruition. He had claimed glory for his state, giving the French people a sense of national identity and national destiny, but mak-

ing them pay an enormous price in social and economic dislocation. Thus the mid-eighteenth century was to be an age of the greatest literary and philosophical achievement for France, but the late eighteenth century was to be an age of the greatest social upheaval that Europe had ever known.

SUGGESTIONS FOR FURTHER READING

GENERAL READING

* Olwen Hufton, *Europe: Privilege and Protest 1730–1789* (Ithaca, NY: Cornell University Press, 1980). An excellent survey of the political and social history of the mid-eighteenth century.

* Leonard Krieger, *Kings and Philosophers 1689–1789* (New York: Norton, 1970). A brilliant depiction of the personalities and ideas of eighteenth-century Europe.

* M. S. Anderson, *Europe in the Eighteenth Century 1713–1783* (London: Longman, 1976). A country-by-country survey of political developments.

Nicholas Riasanovsky, *A History of Russia* (New York: Oxford University Press, 1984). The best one-volume history of Russia.

EUROPE IN 1714

* Derek McKay and H. M. Scott, *The Rise of the Great Powers* (London: Longman, 1983). An outstanding survey of diplomacy and warfare.

THE RISE OF RUSSIA

* Paul Dukes, *The Making of Russian Absolutism 1613–1801* (London: Longman, 1982). An extensive survey of the Russian monarchy in its greatest period.

* B. H. Sumner, *Peter the Great and the Emergence of Russia* (New York: Collier Books, 1962). A short and readable study; the best introduction.

* M. S. Anderson, *Peter the Great* (London: Thames and Hudson, 1978). A well-constructed, comprehensive biography.

* Jerome Blum, *Lord and Peasant in Russia* (New York: Columbia University Press, 1961). The best work on the social life of Russians.

* Isabel de Madariaga, *Catherine the Great, a Short History* (New Haven, CT: Yale University Press, 1990). The best brief life.

THE TWO GERMANIES

* H. W. Koch, *A History of Prussia* (London: Longman, 1978). An up-to-date study of the factors that led to Prussian dominance of Germany.

* Gerhard Ritter, *Frederick the Great* (Berkeley: University of California Press, 1974). A classic biography; short and readable.

* Walther Hubatsch, *Frederick the Great of Prussia* (London: Thames and Hudson, 1975). A full account of the reign of Prussia's greatest leader.

* Ernst Wangermann, *The Austrian Achievement* (New York: Harcourt Brace Jovanovich, 1973). The most readable study of Austrian politics, culture, and society in the eighteenth century.

* T. C. W. Blanning, *Joseph II and Enlightened Despotism* (London: Longman, 1970). Displays the relationship between new ideas, reform policies, and the practical necessities of government.

C. A. Macartney, *Maria Theresa and the House of Austria* (Mystic, CT: Verry Inc., 1969). Still the best introductory study.

THE GREATNESS OF GREAT BRITAIN

*J. C. D. Clark, *English Society 1688–1832* (Cambridge: Cambridge University Press, 1985). A bold reinterpretation of the most important features of English society.

* J. H. Plumb, *The Origins of Political Stability, England 1675–1725* (Boston: Houghton Mifflin, 1967). A comprehensive account of the contributions of Walpole to the establishment of the British Constitution.

Ragnhild Hatton, *George I Elector and King* (Cambridge, MA: Harvard University Press, 1978). An outstanding biography that shows the German side of a British monarch.

* John Brewer, *The Sinews of Power* (New York: Alfred A. Knopf, 1989). A brilliant account of the rise of Britain.

* Ian Christie and Benjamin W. Labaree, *Empire or Independence 1760–1777* (New York: Norton, 1977). Surveys the American troubles from the British point of view.

* Bernard Bailyn, *The Ideological Origins of the American Revolution* (Cambridge, MA: Harvard University Press, 1967). A brilliant interpretation of the underlying causes of the break between Britain and the North American colonies.

* Edward Countryman, *The American Revolution* (New York: Hill & Wang, 1985). A readable, up-to-date narrative of the events of the American Revolution.

* Indicates paperback edition available.

CHAPTER 21

Culture and Society in Eighteenth-Century Europe

HAPPY FAMILIES

"Happy families are all alike," wrote Lev Tolstoy in the nineteenth century when the idea of a happy family was already a cliché. Such an idea would never have occurred to his eighteenth-century forebears. For them the happy family was doubly new—new in the change in the relationships within the family, new in the stress upon happiness itself. Personal happiness was an invention of the Enlightenment, the result of novel attitudes about human aspirations and human capabilities. "Happiness is a new idea in Europe," wrote Louis de Saint-Just (1767–94). It emerged in response to the belief that what was good brought pleasure and what was evil brought pain. Happiness, both individual and collective, became the yardstick by which life was measured. This meant a reorientation in personal conduct and most of all a reorientation of family life. Especially for those with an economic cushion, a pleasurable family life was essential. Husbands and wives were to become companions, filled with romantic love for each other and devoted to domestic bliss. Children, the product of their affection, were to be doted upon, treated not as miniature adults to be lectured and beaten, but as unfilled vessels into which all that was good was to be poured.

Were ever a couple more in love than the husband and wife depicted in *A Visit to the Wet Nurse* by Jean-Honoré Fragonard (1732–1806)? The man clasps his wife's arm to his cheek, she lays her hand on his shoulder. Their sighs are almost audible! Together they admire the fruit of their love, the baby asleep in the cradle. It is hard to guess which parent dotes more, the mother with her rapturous expression or the father with his intensity. He kneels on a cushion in almost religious devotion, his hands folded as if in prayer. Who can doubt their companionship or their love for their babe? They have come together to see how the wet nurse is caring for their child. Doubtless it was they who provided the rather opulent bassinet, which contrasts sharply with the other furniture in the room, and the linens and pillows into which the baby has nestled.

At the beginning of the eighteenth century, the use of a wet nurse was still common among the families of the French bourgeoisie, the class to which this couple—judging from their clothes—undoubtedly belongs. As time moved on, however, more and more mothers began to nurse their babies themselves. In part this change was a response to the higher mortality rate among infants sent out to wet nurses. The unsanitary environment of the towns ran a close race with the neglect that many wet nurses showed their charges. But a wet nurse who could be supervised, that is one who lived near enough to be visited, but far enough away from the town to enjoy wholesome air, might be the best of both worlds. This is just what the couple here has found, and today they come, with their other child (the boy in the hat), to see their baby sleeping peacefully, the wet nurse sitting attentively at the infant's side.

But there are two families in this picture, and they are hardly alike. At first glance, the wet nurse looks like an old woman, perhaps even an aging nanny. She sits with her distaff in her hand, for the arrival of her clients has interrupted her spinning. It is shocking to realize that she cannot be much older than thirty, an age beyond which wealthy families would not hire her for fear either she would not have much milk or that it would be sour. The two younger children are undoubtedly hers, the youngest

621

probably just weaned so that all of her milk would go to the baby. No adoring husband sits beside the wet nurse. Her husband, if he is still alive, is hard at work with no leisure time for visits. Not only does the wet nurse have to sell her milk, but she also spins, to keep her family clothed and to earn a little extra to put away for hard times. The newest fads of the age have passed her family by. While the child in the cradle will be spoiled by toys manufactured especially for children—puzzles, games, rocking horses and balls—the children of the wet nurse must make do with household objects and their own imagination. A ball of yarn thrown to the cat helps the elder child while away the hours. Like much else in the eighteenth century, the world of the family was divided between high and low.

The Nobility

Eighteenth-century society was a hybrid of old and new. It remained highly stratified. Birth and occupation determined wealth, privilege, and quality of life as much as they had in the past. There were now more paths toward the middle and upper classes, more wealth to be distributed among those above the level of subsistence, but at the top of society the nobility remained the privileged order in every European state.

Nobles were defined by their legal rights. They had the right to bear arms, the right to special judicial treatment, the right to tax exemptions. In Russia only nobles could own serfs; in Poland only nobles could hold government office. In France and Britain the highest court positions were always reserved for noblemen. Nobles dominated the Prussian army. The Spanish nobility rich or poor, shunned all labor as a right of their heritage. Swedish and Hungarian noblemen had their own legislative chambers, just as the British had the House of Lords.

Though all who enjoyed these special rights were noble, not all nobles were equal. In many states the noble order was subdivided into easily identifiable groups. The Spanish grandees, the upper nobility, were numbered in the thousands; the Spanish *hidalgos*, the lower nobility, in the hundreds of thousands. In Hungary out of 400,000 noblemen only about 15,000 belonged to the "landed" nobility who held titles and were exempt from taxes. In England the elite class was divided between the peerage and the gentry. The peerage held titles, were members of the House of Lords, and had a limited range of judicial and fiscal privileges. In the mid-eighteenth century there were only 190 British peers. The gentry, which numbered over 20,000, dominated the House of Commons and local legal offices but were not strictly members of the nobility. The French nobility was informally distinguished among the small group of peers known as the *Grandes*, whose ancient lineage, wealth, and power set them apart from all others; a rather larger service nobility whose privileges derived in one way or another from municipal or judicial service; and what might be called the country nobility, whose small estates and local outlook made their exemption from taxes vital to their survival.

These distinctions among the nobilities of the European states masked a more important one: wealth. As the saying went, "all who were truly noble were not wealthy, but all who were truly wealthy were noble." In the eighteenth century, despite the phenomenal increase in mercantile activity, wealth was still calculated in profits from the ownership of land, and it was the wealthy landed nobility who set the tone of elite life in Europe.

All That Glitters

For the wealthy, aristocracy was becoming an international status. The influence of Louis XIV and the court of Versailles lasted for well over a century and spread to town and country life. Most nobles maintained multiple residences. The new style of aristocratic entertainment required more public space on the first floor, while the increasing demand for personal and familial privacy necessitated more space in the upper stories. The result was larger and more opulent homes. Here the British elite led all others. Over one hundred fifty country houses were built in the early eighteenth century alone, including Blenheim Palace, which was built for John Churchill, duke of Marlborough, at a cost of £300,000. To the expense of architecture was added the expense of decoration. New materials, like West Indian mahogany, occasioned new styles, and both drove up costs. The high-quality woodwork and plastering made fashionable by the English Adam brothers was quickly imitated on the Continent. Only the Spanish nobility shunned country estates, preferring to reside permanently in towns.

The building of country houses was only one part of the conspicuous consumption of the privileged orders. Improvements in travel, both in transport and roads, permitted increased contact between members of the national elites. The stagecoach linked towns, and canals linked waterways. Both made travel quicker and more enjoyable. The grand tour of historical sites continued to be used as a substitute for formal education. The grand tour was a means of introducing the European aristocracies to each other and also a means of communicating taste and fashion among them. Whether it was a Russian noble in Germany, or a Briton in Prussia, all spoke French and shared a common cultural outlook.

Decorative architecture, especially interior design, reflected the increasing sociability of the aristocracy. Entertainment became a central part of aristocratic life, losing its previous formality. In this atmosphere music became one of the passions of noble culture. The string quartet made its first appearance in the eighteenth century and chamber music enjoyed unparalleled popularity.

Musical entertainments in European country houses were matched by the literary and philosophical entertainments of the urban salons. The salons, especially in Paris, blended the aristocracy and bourgeoisie with the leading intellectuals of the age. At formal meetings, papers on scientific or philosophical topics were read and discussed. At informal gatherings new ideas were examined and exchanged. There were to be found the most influential thinkers of the day presenting the ideas of the Enlightenment, a new European outlook on religion, society, and politics. The Enlightenment was not an aristocratic movement; indeed, many Enlightenment ideas were profoundly anti-aristocratic. But it was the nobility who had the leisure to read, write, and discuss, and many of the nobility were actively engaged in the intellectual and social changes that the Enlightenment brought in its wake. Though enlightened thinkers sought the improvement of life for the many, they pitched their appeal to the few. "Taste is thus like philosophy," Voltaire opined. "It belongs to a very small number of privileged souls."

The Enlightenment

The Enlightenment was less a set of ideas than it was a set of attitudes. At its core was criticism, a questioning of traditional institutions, customs, and morals. In 1762 the French philosopher Jean-Jacques Rousseau (1712–78) published one of the most important works on social theory, *The Social Contract*, which opened with the gripping maxim "Man is born free and everywhere he is in chains." But most of the great thinkers of the Enlightenment were not so much philosophers as savants, knowledgeable popularizers whose skills were in simplifying and publicizing a hodgepodge of new views.

In France Enlightenment intellectuals were called *philosophes* and claimed all the arts and sciences as their purview. The *Encyclopedia* (35 volumes, 1751–80), edited by Denis Diderot (1713–84), was one of the greatest achievements of the age. Entitled the *Systematic Dictionary of the Sciences, Arts, and Crafts*, it attempted to summarize all acquired knowledge and to dispel all imposed superstitions. There was no better definition of a *philosophe* than that given them by one of their enemies. "Just what is a *philosophe?* A kind of monster in society who feels under no obligation towards its manners and morals, its proprieties, its politics, or its religion. One may expect anything from men of their ilk."

The influence of French counterculture on enlightened thought was great, but the Enlightenment was by no means a strictly French phenomenon. Its greatest figures included the Scottish economist Adam Smith (1723–90), the Italian legal reformer Cesare Beccaria (1738–94), and the German philosopher Immanuel Kant (1724–1804). In France it began among anti-establishment critics; in Scotland and the German states it flourished in the universities; and in Prussia, Austria, and Russia it was propagated by the monarchy. The Enlightenment began in the 1730s and was still going strong a half-century later when its attitudes had been absorbed into the mainstream of European thought.

No brief summary can do justice to the diversity of enlightened thought in eighteenth-century Europe.

THE PURPOSE OF AN ENCYCLOPEDIA

■ *The* Encyclopedia *was one of the great collaborative ventures of the new spirit of reason that so characterized the Enlightenment. Following is the* Encyclopedia's *entry on itself, the purpose of compiling human knowledge in book form.*

Encyclopedia . . . In truth, the aim of an *encyclopedia* is to collect all the knowledge scattered over the face of the earth, to present its general outlines and structure to the men with whom we live, and to transmit this to those who will come after us, so that the work of past centuries may be useful to the following centuries, that our children, by becoming more educated, may at the same time become more virtuous and happier, and that we may not die without having deserved well of the human race . . .

I have said that it could only belong to a philosophical age to attempt an *encyclopedia;* and I have said this because such a work constantly demands more intellectual daring than is commonly found in [less courageous periods]. All things must be examined, debated, investigated without exception and without regard for anyone's feelings . . . We must ride roughshod over all these ancient puerilities, overturn the barriers that reason never erected, give back to the arts and sciences the liberty that is so precious to them . . . We have for quite some time needed a reasoning age when men would no longer seek the rules in classical authors but in nature.

From Denis Diderot, *The Encyclopedia* (1751–72).

Because it was an attitude of mind rather than a set of shared beliefs, there are many contradictory strains to follow. In his famous essay *What Is Enlightenment?* (1784) Immanuel Kant described it simply as freedom to use one's own intelligence. "I hear people clamor on all sides: Don't argue! The officer says: Don't argue, drill! The tax collector says: Don't argue, pay. The pastor says: Don't argue, believe." To all of them Kant replied: "Dare to know! Have the courage to use your own intelligence."

The Spirit of the Enlightenment.   In 1734 there appeared in France a small book entitled *Philosophical Letters Concerning the English Nation*. Its author, Voltaire (1694–1778) had spent two years in Britain and while there he made it his business to study the differences between the peoples of the two nations. In a simple but forceful style Voltaire demonstrated time and again the superiority of the British. They practiced religious toleration and were not held under the sway of a venal clergy. They valued people for their merits rather than their birth. Their political constitution was a marvel— "The English nation is the only one on earth that has succeeded in controlling the power of kings by resisting

them." They made national heroes of their scientists, their poets, and their philosophers. In all of this Voltaire contrasted British virtue with French vice. He attacked the French clergy and nobility directly, the French monarchy implicitly. Not only did he praise the genius and accomplishments of Sir Isaac Newton above those of René Descartes, but he also graphically contrasted the Catholic church's persecution of Descartes with the British state's celebration of Newton. "England, where men think free and noble thoughts," Voltaire enthused.

It is difficult now to recapture the psychological impact that the *Philosophical Letters* had on the generation of educated Frenchmen who first read them. The book was officially banned and publicly burned, and a warrant was issued for Voltaire's arrest. The *Letters* dropped like a bombshell upon the moribund intellectual culture of the Church and the universities and burst open the complacent, self-satisfied Cartesian worldview. The book ignited in France a movement that would soon be found in nearly every corner of Europe.

Born in Paris in 1694 into a bourgeois family with court office, François-Marie Arouet, who later took the pen name Voltaire, was educated by the Jesuits, who encouraged his poetic talents and instilled in him an enduring love of literature. He was a difficult student, especially as he had already rejected the core of the Jesuits' religious doctrine. He was no less difficult as he grew and began a career as a poet and playwright. It was not long before he was imprisoned in the Bastille for penning verses that maligned the honor of the regent of France. Released from prison, he insulted a nobleman, who retaliated by having his servants publicly beat Voltaire. Voltaire issued a challenge for a duel, a greater insult than the first, given his low birth. Again he was sent to the Bastille and was only released on the promise that he would leave the country immediately.

Thus Voltaire found himself in Britain, where he spent two years learning English, writing plays, and enjoying his celebrity free from the dangers that celebrity entailed in France. When he returned to Paris in 1728, it was with the intention of popularizing Britain to Frenchmen. He wrote and produced a number of plays and began writing the *Philosophical Letters*, a work that not only secured his reputation but also forced him into exile at the village of Cirey, where he moved in with the Marquise du Châtelet (1706–49).

The Marquise du Châtelet, though only twenty-seven at the time of her liaison with Voltaire, was one of the leading advocates of Newtonian science in France. She built a laboratory in her home and introduced Voltaire to experimental science. While she undertook the immense challenge of translating Newton into French, Voltaire worked on innumerable projects: poems, plays, philosophical and anti-religious tracts (which she wisely kept him from publishing), and histories. It was one of the most productive periods of his life, and when the Marquise du Châtelet died in 1749, Voltaire was crushed.

Now past 50 years old, Voltaire began his travels. He was invited to Berlin by Frederick the Great, who admired him most of all the intellectuals of the age. The relationship between these two great egotists was predictably stormy and resulted in Voltaire's arrest in Frankfurt. Finally allowed to leave Prussia, Voltaire eventually settled in Geneva, where he quickly became

Painting of a lively conversation among philosophers, who are conveniently identified by number. Voltaire, with raised arm, is shown seated to the left of Diderot.

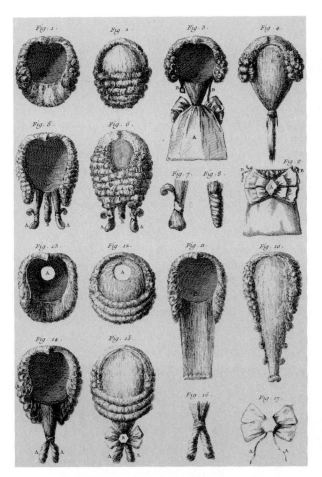

This illustration from Diderot's Encyclopedia *details the many types of wigs and tonsorial accessories worn by men in the eighteenth century. The tradition of wig-wearing lingers on in British law courts.*

questioned his own paternity and the morals of his mother; he lived openly with the Marquise du Châtelet and her husband; and he spoke as slightingly of kings and aristocrats as he did of his numerous critics. At the height of the French Revolution, Voltaire's body was removed from its resting place in Champagne and taken in great pomp to Paris, where it was interred in the Panthéon, where the heroes of the nation were put to rest. "Voltaire taught us to be free," was the slogan that the Parisian masses chanted during the funeral procession. It was an ending perhaps too solemn and conventional for one as irreverent as Voltaire. When the monarchy was restored after 1815, his bones were unceremoniously dumped in a lime pit.

Some enlightened thinkers based their critical outlook on skepticism, the belief that nothing could be known for certain. When the Scottish philosopher David Hume (1711–76) was accused of being an atheist, he countered the charge by saying he was too skeptical to be certain that God did not exist. Hume's first major philosophical work, *A Treatise of Human Nature* (1739), made absolutely no impression upon his contemporaries. For a time he took a post as a merchant's clerk; then he served as a tutor; and finally he found a position as a private secretary. During the course of these various employments he continued to write, publishing a series of essays on the subject of morality and rewriting his treatise into *An Enquiry Concerning Human Understanding* (1748), his greatest philosophical work.

embroiled in local politics and was none too politely asked to leave. He was tired of wandering and tired of being chased. His youthful gaiety and high spirits, which remained in Voltaire long past youth, were dealt a serious blow by the tragic earthquake in Lisbon in 1755, when thousands of people attending church services were killed.

Optimism in the face of such a senseless tragedy was no longer possible. His black mood was revealed in *Candide* (1759), which was to become his enduring legacy. *Candide* introduced the ivory-tower intellectual Dr. Pangloss, the overly optimistic Candide, and the very practical philosophy, "everyone must cultivate their own garden." It was Voltaire's capacity to challenge all authority that was probably his greatest contribution to Enlightenment attitudes. He held nothing sacred. He

Voltaire.

David Hume.

Hume made two seminal contributions to Enlightenment thought. He exploded the synthesis of Descartes by arguing that neither matter nor mind could be proved to exist with any certainty. Only perceptions existed, either as impressions of material objects or as ideas. If human understanding was based on sensory perception rather than on reason, then there could be no certainty in the universe. Hume's second point launched a frontal attack upon established religion. If there could be no certainty, then the revealed truths of Christian religion could have no basis. In his historical analysis of the origins of religion Hume argued that "religion grows out of hope or fear." He attacked the core of Christian explanations based on either Providence or miracles by arguing that to anyone who understood the basis of human perception it would take a miracle to believe in miracles.

In 1749 Hume received in the mail a work from an admiring Frenchman, entitled *The Spirit of the Laws*. The sender was Charles-Louis de Secondat, Baron Montesquieu (1689–1755). Born in Bordeaux, he ultimately inherited both a large landed estate and the office of president of the Parlement of Bordeaux. His novel *Persian*

Letters (1721) was a brilliant satire of Parisian morals, French society, and European religion all bound together by the story of a Persian despot who leaves his harem to learn about the ways of the world. The use of the Persian outsider allowed Montesquieu to comment on the absurdity of European customs in general and French practices in particular. The device of the harem allowed him to titillate his audience with exotic sexuality.

After this success, Montesquieu decided to sell his office and make the grand tour. He spent nearly two years in England for which, like Voltaire, he came to have the greatest admiration. Back in Bordeaux, Montesquieu began to assemble his thoughts for what he believed would be a great work of political theory. The two societies that he most admired were ancient Rome and present-day Britain, and he studied the forms of their government and the principles that animated them. *The Spirit of the Laws* was published in 1748, and despite its gargantuan size and densely packed examples, it was immediately recognized as a masterpiece. Catherine the Great of Russia kept it at her bedside, and it was the single most influential work for the framers of the United States Constitution.

In both the *Persian Letters* and *The Spirit of the Laws* Montesquieu explored how liberty could be achieved and despotism avoided. He divided all forms of government into republics, monarchies, and despotisms. Each form had its own peculiar spirit: virtue and moderation in republics, honor in monarchies, and fear in despotisms. Like each form, each spirit was prone to abuse and had to be restrained if republics were not to give way to vice and excess, monarchies to corruption, and despotisms to repression. Montesquieu classified regimes as either moderate or immoderate, and through the use of extensive historical examples attempted to demonstrate how moderation could be maintained through rules and restraints, through the spirit of the law.

For Montesquieu, a successful government was one in which powers were separated and checks and balances existed within the institutions of the state. As befit a provincial magistrate, he insisted upon the absolute separation of the judiciary from all other branches of government. The law needed to be independent and impartial and it needed to be just. Montesquieu advocated that law codes be reformed and reduced mainly to regulate crimes against persons and property. Punishment should fit the crime but should be humane. He was one of the first to advocate the abolition of torture. Like most Europeans of his age, he saw monarchy as the only realistic form of government, but he argued that for

VOLTAIRE'S DEFINITION OF EVIL

■ *More than anyone, Voltaire symbolized the new thinking of the Enlightenment. Witty, ironic, irreverent, and penetrating, his writings provoked howls of protest and squeals of delight. Among the most widely read was his philosophical dictionary, from which this definition of evil is drawn.*

People clamor that human nature is essentially perverse, that man is born the child of the devil, and of evil. Nothing is more ill-advised; for, my friend, in preaching at me that everybody is born perverse, you warn me that you were born that way, that I must distrust you as I would a fox or a crocodile . . . It would be much more reasonable, much nobler, to say to me: "You were all born good; see how frightful it would be to corrupt the purity of your being." We should treat mankind as we should treat all men individually . . .

Man is not born evil; he becomes evil, as he becomes sick . . . Gather together all the children of the universe; you will see in them nothing but innocence, gentleness, and fear . . .

If men were essentially evil, if they were all born the subjects of a being as malevolent as it is unhappy, who inspired them with all this frenzy to avenge his own torment, we would see husbands murdered by their wives, and fathers by their children every morning.

From Voltaire, *The Philosophical Dictionary* (1764).

---

a monarchy to be successful, it needed a strong and independent aristocracy to restrain its tendency toward corruption and despotism. He based his arguments on what he believed was the case in Britain, which he praised as the only state in Europe in which liberty resided.

Enlightened thinkers attacked established institutions, above all the Church. Most were deists who believed in the existence of God on rational grounds only. Following the materialistic ideas of the new science, deists believed that nature conformed to its own material laws and operated without divine intervention. God, in a popular Enlightenment image, was like a clock-maker who constructed the elaborate mechanism, wound it, and gave the pendulum its first swing. After that the clock worked by itself. Deists were accused of being anti-Christian and they certainly opposed the ritual forms of both Catholic and Protestant worship. They also opposed the role of the Church in education, for education was the key to an enlightened view of the future. This meant, above all, conflict with the Jesuits. "Let's eat a Jesuit," was Voltaire's half-facetious comment.

Jean-Jacques Rousseau attacked the educational system. His tract on education, disguised as the romantic novel *Emile* (1762), argued that children should be taught by appealing to their interests rather than with strict discipline. Education was crucial because the Enlightenment was dominated by the idea of the British philosopher John Locke (1632–1704) that the mind was blank at birth, a *tabula rasa*—"white paper void of all characters"—and that it was filled up by experience. Contrary to the arguments of Descartes, Locke wrote in *An Essay Concerning Human Understanding* (1690) that there were no innate ideas and no good or evil that was not conditioned by experience. For Locke, as for a host of thinkers after him, good and evil were defined as pleasure and pain. We do good because it is pleasurable and we avoid evil because it is painful. Morality was a sense experience rather than a theological one. It was also relative rather than absolute. This was an observation that derived from increased interest in non-European cultures. The *Persian Letters* of Baron Montesquieu was the most popular of a genre that described non-European societies that knew nothing of Christian morality.

By the middle of the eighteenth century the pleasure/pain principle enunciated by Locke had come to be applied to the foundations of social organization. If personal good was pleasure, then social good was happiness. The object of government, in the words of the Scottish moral philosopher Francis Hutcheson (1694–1746), was "the greatest happiness of the greatest number." This

The frontispiece from Montesquieu's The Spirit of the Laws *has a medallion of the author surrounded by allegorical figures, including blind justice. In the lower left corner are copies of the authors works.*

of liberation from the weight of centuries of traditions. "This is the best of all possible worlds and all things turn out for the best," was the satirical slogan of Voltaire's Candide. But if Voltaire believed that enlightened thinkers had taken optimism too far, others believed that it had to be taken further still.

Progress, an idea that not all enlightened thinkers shared, was another invention of the age. It was expressed most cogently by the French philosopher the Marquis de Condorcet (1743–94) in *The Progress of the Human Mind* (1795), in which he developed an almost evolutionary view of human development from a savage state of nature to a future of harmony and international peace.

The Impact of the Enlightenment. As there was no single set of Enlightenment beliefs, so there was no single impact of the Enlightenment. Its general influence was felt everywhere, even seeping to the lowest strata of society. Its specific influence is harder to gauge. Paradoxically, enlightened political reform took firmer root in eastern Europe, where the ideas were imported, than in western Europe, where they originated. It was absolute rulers who were most successful in borrowing Enlightenment reforms.

It is impossible to determine what part enlightened ideas and what part practical necessities played in the

principle was at the core of *Crimes and Punishments* (1764), Cesare Beccaria's pioneering work of legal reform. Laws were instituted to promote happiness within society. They had to be formulated equitably for both criminal and victim. Punishment was to act as a deterrent to crime rather than as retribution. Therefore Beccaria advocated the abolition of torture to gain confessions, the end of capital punishment, and the rehabilitation of criminals through the improvement of penal institutions. By 1776 happiness was established as one of the basic rights of man, enshrined in the American Declaration of Independence as "life, liberty, and the pursuit of happiness."

It was in refashioning the world through education and social reform that the Enlightenment revealed its orientation toward the future. *Optimism* was a word invented in the eighteenth century to express this feeling

Jean-Jacques Rousseau.

THE STRENGTHS OF REPUBLICAN GOVERNMENT

■ *Baron de Montesquieu's* Spirit of the Laws *was one of the most important political works of the Enlightenment. It analyzed the various forms of government and estimated their strengths and weaknesses. Montesquieu provided inspiration for the American Declaration of Independence and the Constitution.*

OF THE REPUBLICAN GOVERNMENT, AND THE LAWS IN RELATION TO DEMOCRACY

In a democracy the people are in some respects the sovereign, and in others the subject. There can be no exercise of sovereignty but by their suffrages, which are . . . fundamental to this government. And indeed it is as important to regulate in a republic, in what manner, by whom, to whom, and concerning what suffrages are to be given, as it is in a monarchy to know who is the prince, and after what manner he ought to govern . . .

The people are extremely well qualified for choosing those whom they are to intrust with part of their authority . . . They can tell when a person has fought many battles, and been crowned with success . . . They can tell when a judge is assiduous in his office, gives general satisfaction, and has never been charged with bribery . . . But are they capable of conducting an intricate affair, of seizing and improving the opportunity and critical moment of action? No; this surpasses their abilities . . .

As most citizens have sufficient ability to choose, though unqualified to be chosen, so the people, though capable of calling others to an account for their administration, are incapable of conducting the administration themselves.

From Montesquieu, *Spirit of the Laws* (1750).

---

eastern European reform movement that began around mid-century. In at least three areas the coincidence between ideas and actions was especially strong: law, education, and the extension of religious toleration. Law was the basis of Enlightenment views of social interaction, and the influence of Montesquieu and Beccaria spread quickly. In Prussia and Russia the movement to codify and simplify the legal system did not reach fruition in the eighteenth century, but in both places it was well under way. The Prussian jurist Samuel von Cocceji (1679–1755) initiated the reform of Prussian law and legal administration. Cocceji's project was to make the enforcement of law uniform throughout the realm, to prevent judicial corruption, and to produce a single code of Prussian law. The code, finally completed in the 1790s, reflected the principles of criminal justice articulated by Beccaria. In Russia, the Law Commission summoned by Catherine the Great in 1767 never did complete its work. Nevertheless, profoundly influenced by Montesquieu, Catherine attempted to abolish torture and to introduce the Beccarian principle that the accused was innocent until proven guilty. In Austria, Joseph II presided over a wholesale

reorganization of the legal system. Courts were centralized, laws codified, and torture and capital punishment abolished.

Enlightenment ideas also underlay the efforts to improve education in eastern Europe. The religious orders, especially the Jesuits, were the most influential educators of the age, and the Enlightenment attack upon them created a void that had to be filled by the state. Efforts at compulsory education were first undertaken in Russia under Peter the Great, but these were aimed at the compulsory education of the nobility. It was Catherine who extended the effort to the provinces, attempting to educate a generation of Russian teachers. She was especially eager that women receive primary schooling, although the prejudice against educating women was too strong to overcome. Austrian and Prussian reforms were more successful in extending the reach of primary education, even if its content remained weak.

Religious toleration was the area in which the Enlightenment had its greatest impact in Europe, though again it was in the eastern countries that this was most visible. Freedom of worship for Catholics was barely whispered about in Britain, while neither France nor Spain were moved to tolerate Protestants. Nevertheless, within these parameters there were some important changes in the religious makeup of the western European states. In Britain, Protestant dissenters were no longer persecuted for their beliefs. By the end of the eighteenth century the number of Protestants outside the Church of England was growing, and by the early nineteenth century discrimination against Protestants was all but eliminated. In France and Spain relations between the national church and the papacy were undergoing a reorientation. Both states were asserting more independence—both theologically and financially—from Rome. The shift was symbolized by disputes over the role of the Jesuits, who were finally expelled from France in 1764 and from Spain in 1767.

In eastern Europe, enlightened ideas about religious toleration did take effect. Catherine the Great abandoned persecution of a Russian Orthodox sect known as the Old Believers. Prussia had always tolerated various Protestant groups, and with the conquest of Silesia it acquired a large Catholic population. Catholics were guaranteed freedom of worship, and Frederick the Great even built a Catholic church in Berlin to symbolize this policy. Austria extended furthest enlightened ideas about toleration. Maria Theresa was a devout Catholic and actually increased religious perse-

cution in her realm. But Joseph II rejected his mother's dogmatic position. In 1781 he issued the Patent of Toleration, which granted freedom of worship to Protestants and members of the Eastern Orthodox church. The following year he extended this toleration to Jews. Joseph's attitude toward toleration was as practical as it was enlightened. He believed that the revocation of the Edict of Nantes—which had granted limited toleration to Protestants—at the end of the seventeenth century had been an economic disaster for France, and he encouraged religious toleration as a means to economic progress.

A science of economics was first articulated during the Enlightenment. A group of French thinkers known as the *physiocrats* subscribed to the view that land was wealth and thus argued that agricultural activity, especially improved means of farming and livestock breeding, should take first priority in state reforms. As wealth came from land, taxation should be based only on land ownership, a principle that was coming into increased prominence, despite the opposition of the landowning class. Physiocratic ideas combined a belief in the sanctity of private property with the need for the state to increase agricultural output. Ultimately the physiocrats, like the great Scottish economic theorist Adam Smith, came to believe that government should cease to interfere with private economic activity. They articulated the doctrine *laissez faire, laissez passer*—"let it be,

THE INDESTRUCTIBILITY OF THE GENERAL WILL

■ *Jean-Jacques Rousseau's* The Social Contract *was one of the greatest visionary tracts of the eighteenth century. In it Rousseau envisioned a harmonious society capable of eliminating want and controlling evil. Here he discusses his famous idea of the general will.*

As long as men united together look upon themselves as a single body, they have but one will relating to the common preservation and general welfare. Then all the energies of the state are vigorous and simple; its maxims are clear and luminous; there are no mixed contradictory interests; the common prosperity shows itself everywhere, and requires only good sense to be appreciated. Peace, union, and equality are enemies of political subtleties. Upright, honest men are difficult to deceive, because of their simplicity; decoys and pretexts do not impose upon them, they are not cunning enough to be dupes. When we see among the happiest people in the world troops of peasants regulating the affairs of state under an oak, and conducting themselves wisely, can we help despising the refinements of other nations, who make themselves illustrious and miserable with so much art and mystery?

From Jean-Jacques Rousseau, *The Social Contract* (1762).

Major Works of the Enlightenment

1690	*An Essay Concerning Human Understanding* (Locke)
1721	*Persian Letters* (Baron Montesquieu)
1734	*Philosophical Letters Concerning the English Nation* (Voltaire)
1739	*A Treatise of Human Nature* (Hume)
1740	*Pamela* (Richardson)
1748	*An Enquiry Concerning Human Understanding* (Hume) *The Spirit of the Laws* (Baron Montesquieu)
1751–80	*Encyclopedia* (Diderot)
1759	*Candide* (Voltaire)
1762	*Emile; The Social Contract* (Rousseau)
1764	*Crimes and Punishments* (Beccaria)
1784	*What Is Enlightenment?* (Kant)
1795	*The Progress of the Human Mind* (Marquis de Condorcet)
1798	*An Essay on the Principles of Population* (Malthus)

let it go." The ideas of Adam Smith and the physiocrats ultimately formed the basis for nineteenth-century economic reform.

If the Enlightenment did not initiate a new era, it did offer a new vision, whether in Hume's psychology, Montesquieu's political science, Rousseau's sociology, or Smith's economic theory. All of these subjects, which have such a powerful impact on contemporary life, had their modern origins in the Enlightenment. As the British poet Alexander Pope (1688–1744) put it: "Know then thyself, presume not God to scan/ The proper study of mankind is man." Enlightened thinkers challenged existing ideas and existing institutions. A new emphasis on self and on pleasure led to a new emphasis on happiness. All three fed into the distinctively Enlightenment idea of self-interest. Happiness and self-interest were values that would inevitably corrode the old social order, which was based upon principles of self-sacrifice and corporate identity. It was only a matter of time.

The Bourgeoisie

Bourgeois is a French word, and it carried the same tone of derision in the eighteenth century that it does today. The bourgeois was a man on the make, scrambling after money or office or title. He was neither well born nor well bred, or so said the nobility. Yet the bourgeoisie served vital functions in all European societies. They dominated trade, both nationally and internationally. They made their homes in cities and did much to improve the quality of urban life. They were the civilizing influence in urban culture, for unlike the nobility they were permanent denizens of the city. Perhaps most importantly, the bourgeoisie provided the safety valve between the nobility and those who were acquiring wealth and power but who lacked the advantages of birth and position. By developing their own culture and class identity, the bourgeoisie provided successful individuals with their own sense of pride and achievement and eased the explosive buildup of social resentments.

In the eighteenth century the bourgeoisie was growing in both numbers and importance. An active commercial and urban life gave many members of this group new social and political opportunities and many of them passed into the nobility through the purchase of land or office. But for those whose aspirations or abilities were different, this social group began to define its own values, which centered on the family and the home. A new interest in domestic affairs touched both men and women of the European bourgeoisie. Their homes became a social center for kin and neighbors and their outlook on family life reflected new personal relationships.

Marriages were made for companionship as much as for economic advantage. Romantic love between husbands and wives was newly valued. So were children, whose futures came to dominate familial concern. Childhood was recognized as a separate stage of life and the education of children as one of the most important of parental concerns. The image of the affectionate father replaced that of the hard-bitten businessman; the image of the doting mother replaced that of the domestic drudge.

The Dutton Family *by John Zoffany. This eighteenth-century painting shows the comforts enjoyed by the British upper middle class.*

Urban Elites

In the society of orders, nobility was the acid test. The world was divided into the small number of those who had it and the large number of those who did not. At the apex of the non-noble pyramid was the bourgeoisie, the elites of urban Europe whose place in the society of orders was ambiguous. Bourgeois, or burgher, simply meant "town dweller," but as a social group it had come to mean "wealthy town dweller." The bourgeoisie was strongest where towns were strongest: in western rather than in eastern Europe, in northern rather than southern Europe, with the notable exception of Italy. Holland was the exemplar of a bourgeois republic. More than half of the Dutch population lived in towns and there was no significant aristocratic class to compete for power. The Regents of Amsterdam were the equivalent of a European court nobility in wealth, power, and prestige, though not in the way in which they had accumulated their fortunes. The size of the bourgeoisie in various European states cannot be absolutely determined. At the end of the eighteenth century the British middle classes probably constituted around 15 percent of the population, the French bourgeoisie less than 10 percent. By contrast, the Russian or Hungarian urban elites were less than 2 percent of the population of those states.

Like the nobility, the bourgeoisie constituted a diverse group. At the top were great commercial families engaged in the expanding international marketplace and reaping the profits of trade. In wealth and power they were barely distinguishable from the nobility. At the bottom were the so-called petit-bourgeois; shopkeepers, craftsmen, and industrial employers. The solid core of the bourgeoisie was employed in trade, exchange, and service. Most were engaged in local or national commerce. Trade was the lifeblood of the city, for by itself the city could neither feed nor clothe its inhabitants. Most bourgeois fortunes were first acquired in trade. Finance was the natural outgrowth of commerce, and another segment of the bourgeoisie accumulated or preserved their capital through the sophisticated financial instruments of the eighteenth century. While the very wealthy loaned directly to the central government or bought shares in overseas trading companies, most bourgeois participated in government credit markets. They purchased state bonds or lifetime annuities and lived on the interest. The costs of war flooded the urban credit markets with high-yielding and generally stable financial instruments. Finally, the bourgeoisie were members of the burgeoning professions that provided services for the rich. Medicine, law, education, and the bureaucracy were all bourgeois professions, for the cost of acquiring the necessary skills could be borne only by those already wealthy.

During the course of the eighteenth century, this combination of occupational groups was expanding both in numbers and in importance all over Europe. So was the bourgeois habitat. The urbanization of Europe continued steadily throughout the eighteenth century. A greater percentage of the European population were living in towns and a greater percentage were living in large towns of over 10,000 inhabitants which, of necessity, were developing complex socioeconomic structures. In France alone there were probably over a hundred such towns, each requiring the services of the bourgeoisie and providing opportunities for their expansion. And the larger the metropolis the greater the need. In 1600 only twenty European cities contained as many as 50,000 people; in 1700 that number had risen to thirty-two; and by 1800 to forty-eight. London, the largest city, had grown to 865,000, a remarkable feat considering that in 1665 over a quarter of the London population died in the Great Plague. In such cities the demand for lawyers and doctors, for merchants and shopkeepers was almost insatiable.

Besides wealth, the urban bourgeoisie shared another characteristic: mobility. The aspiration of the bourgeoisie was to become noble, either through office or by acquiring rural estates. In Britain, a gentleman was still defined by lifestyle. "All are accounted gentlemen in England who maintain themselves without manual labor." Many trading families left their wharves and countinghouses to acquire rural estates, live off rents, and practice the openhanded hospitality of a gentleman. In France and Spain, nobility could still be purchased, though the price was constantly going up. For the greater bourgeoisie, the transition was easy; for the lesser, the failure to move up was all the more frustrating for being just beyond their grasp. The bourgeoisie did not only imagine their discomfort, they were made to feel it at every turn. They were the butt of jokes, of theater, and of popular songs. They were the first victims in the shady financial dealings of the crown and court, the first casualties in urban riots. Despised from above, envied from below, the bourgeoisie were uncomfortable with the present yet profoundly conservative about the future. The one consolation to their perpetual misery was that as a group they got richer and richer. And as a group they began to develop a distinctive culture that reflected their qualities and aspirations.

Bourgeois Values

Many bourgeoisie viewed their condition as temporary and accepted the pejorative connotations of the word itself. They had little desire to defend a social group out of which they fervently longed to pass. Others, whose aspirations were lower, were nevertheless uncomfortable with the status that they had already achieved. They had no ambition to wear the silks and furs reserved for the nobility or to attend the opening night at the opera decked in jewels and finery. In fact, such ostentation was alien to their existence and to the success that they had achieved. There was a real tension between the values of noble and bourgeois. The ideal noble was idle, wasteful, and ostentatious; the ideal bourgeois was industrious, frugal, and sober. Voltaire, who made his fortune as a financial speculator rather than a man of letters, aped the lifestyle of the nobility. But he could never allow himself to be cheated by a tradesman, a mark of his origins. When Louis XVI tried to make household economies in the wake of a financial crisis, critics said that "he acts like a bourgeois."

Even if the bourgeoisie did not constitute a class, they did share certain attitudes that constituted a culture. The wealthy among them participated in the new world of consumption, whether they did so lavishly or frugally. For those who aspired to more than their birth allowed, there was a loosening of the strict codes of dress that reserved certain fabrics, decorative materials, and styles to the nobility. Merchants and bankers could now be seen in colored suits or with pipings made of cloth of gold; their wives could be seen in furs and silks. They might acquire silverware, even if they did not go so far as the nobility and have a coat of arms engraved upon it. Coaches and carriages were also becoming common among the bourgeoisie, to take them on the Sunday rides through the town gardens or to their weekend retreats in the suburbs. Parisian merchants, even master

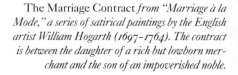
The Marriage Contract *from "Marriage à la Mode," a series of satirical paintings by the English artist William Hogarth (1697–1764). The contract is between the daughter of a rich but lowborn merchant and the son of an impoverished noble.*

craftsmen like clockmakers, were now acquiring suburban homes although they could not afford to retire to them for the summer months.

But more and more, the bourgeoisie was beginning to travel. In Britain whole towns were established to cater to leisure travelers. The southwestern town of Bath, which was rebuilt in the eighteenth century, was the most popular of all European resort towns, famous since Roman times for the soothing qualities of its waters. Bath was soon a social center as notable for its marriage market as for its recreations. Brighton, a seaside resort on the south coast, quadrupled in size in the second half of the eighteenth century. Bathing—what we would call swimming—either for health or recreation, became a middle-class fad, displacing traditional fears of the sea.

The leisure that wealth bestowed on the bourgeoisie quickly became, in good bourgeois fashion, commercialized. Theater and music halls for both light and serious productions proliferated. Voltaire's plays were performed before packed houses in Paris, with the author himself frequently in attendance to bask in the adulation of the largely bourgeois audiences who attended them. In Venice it was estimated that over 1,200 operas were produced in the eighteenth century. Public concerts were a mark of bourgeois culture, for the court nobility was entertained at the royal palaces or at great country houses.

Theater and concert going were part of the new attitude toward socializing that was one of the greatest contributions of the Enlightenment. Enlightened thinkers spread their views in the salons, and the salons soon spawned the academies, local scientific societies which, though led and patronized by provincial nobles, included large numbers of bourgeois members. The academies sponsored essay competitions, built up libraries, and became the local center for intellectual interchange. A less structured form of sociability took place in the coffeehouses and tearooms that came to be a feature of even small provincial towns. In the early eighteenth century there were over two thousand London coffee shops where men—for the coffeehouse was largely a male preserve—could talk politics, read the latest newspapers and magazines, and indulge their taste for this still-exotic beverage. Parisian clubs, called *sociétés*, covered a multitude of diverse interests. Literary *sociétés* were the most popular, maintaining their purpose by forbidding drinking, eating, and gambling on their premises.

Above all, bourgeois culture was literate culture. Wealth and leisure led to mental pursuits—if not always to intellectual ones. The proliferation of relatively cheap printed material had an enormous impact on the lives of those who were able to afford it. Holland and Britain were the most literate European societies and

A caricature by an unknown artist shows Lloyd's, the famous London coffeehouse, in the 1790s.

also, because of the absence of censorship, the centers of European printing. This was the first great period of the newspaper and the magazine. The first daily newspaper appeared in London in 1702; eighty years later, thirty-seven provincial towns had their own newspapers, while the London papers were read all over Britain. Then as now, the newspaper was as much a vehicle for advertisement as for news. News reports tended to be bland, avoiding controversy and concentrating on general national and international events. Advertising, on the other hand, tended to be lurid, promising cures for incurable ills, and the most exquisite commodities at the most reasonable prices.

For entertainment and serious political commentary, the British reading public turned to magazines, of which

Lady leaving a lending library with a book, a colored mezzotint by J. R. Smith, 1781.

there were over 150 separate titles by the 1780s. The most famous were *The Spectator*, which ran in the early part of the century and did much to set the tone for a cultured middle-class life, and the *Gentleman's Magazine*, which ran in the mid-century and was said to have had a circulation of nearly fifteen thousand. The longest-lived of all British magazines was *The Ladies Diary*, which continued in existence from 1704 to 1871 and doled out self-improvement, practical advice, and fictional romances in equal proportion.

The Ladies Diary was not the only literature aimed at the growing number of leisured and lettered bourgeois woman. Though enlightened thinkers could be ambivalent about the place of women in the new social order, they generally stressed the importance of female education and welcomed women's participation in intellectual pursuits. Whether it was new ideas about women or simply the fact that more women had leisure, a growing body of both domestic literature and light entertainment was available to them. This included a vast number of teach-yourself books aimed at instructing women how best to organize domestic life or how to navigate the perils of polite society. Moral instruction, particularly on the themes of obedience and sexual fidelity, was also popular. But the greatest output directed toward women was in the form of fanciful romances, from which a new genre emerged. The novel first appeared in its modern form in the 1740s. Samuel Richardson (1689–1761) wrote *Pamela* (1740), the story of a maidservant who successfully resisted the advances of her master until he finally married her. It was composed in long episodes, or chapters, that developed Pamela's character and told her story at the expense of the overt moral message that was Richardson's original intention.

Family Life

In the eighteenth century a remarkable transformation in home life was under way, one that the bourgeoisie shared with the nobility. In the pursuit of happiness encouraged by the Enlightenment, one of the newest joys was domesticity. The image—and sometimes the reality—of the happy home, where love was the bond between husband and wife and care between parents and children, came to dominate both the literary and visual arts. Only those wealthy enough to afford to dispense with women's work could partake of the new domesticity, only those touched by Enlightenment ideas could attempt to make the change. But where it occurred, the transformation in the nature of family life was one of the most profound alterations in eighteenth-century culture.

The first step toward the transformation of family relationships was in centering the conjugal family in the home. In the past, the family was a less important structure for most people than the social groups to which they belonged or the neighborhood in which they lived. Marriage was an economic partnership at one end and a means to carry on lineage at the other. Individual fulfillment was not an object of marriage and this attitude could be seen among the elites in the high level of arranged marriages, the speed with which surviving spouses remarried, and the formal and often brutal personal relationships between husbands and wives.

Patriarchy was the dominant value within the family. Husbands ruled over wives and children, making all of the crucial decisions that affected both the quality of their lives and their futures. As late as the middle of the eighteenth century a British judge established the "rule of thumb," which asserted that a husband had a legal right to beat his wife with a stick, but the stick should be no thicker than a man's thumb. It was believed that children were stained with the sin of Adam at birth and that only the severest upbringing could clean some of it away. Children were sent out first for wet-nursing, then at around the age of seven for boarding, either at school or in a trade, and finally into their own marriages.

There can be no doubt that this profile of family life began to change, especially in western Europe, during the second half of the eighteenth century. Though the economic elements of marriage remained strong—newspapers actually advertised the availability of partners and the dowries or annual income that they would bring to the marriage—other elements now appeared. Fed by an unending stream of stories and novels and a new desire for individual happiness, romantic and sexual attraction developed into a factor in marriage. Potential marriage partners were no longer kept away from each other or smothered by chaperons. Perhaps more importantly, the role of potential spouses in choosing a partner appears to have increased. Even in earlier centuries parents did not simply assign a spouse to their children, but by the eighteenth century adolescents themselves searched for their own marriage partners and exercised a strong negative voice in identifying unsuitable ones.

The quest for compatibility, no less than the quest for romantic love, led to a change in personal relationships between spouses. The extreme formality of the

Motherhood, *an oil painting by Marguerite Gérard (1761–1837).*

past was gradually breaking down. Husbands and wives began spending more time with each other, developing common interests and pastimes. Their personal life began to change. For the first time houses were built to afford the couple privacy from their children, their servants, and their guests. Rooms were designed for specific functions and were set off by hallways. This new design allowed for an intimate life that earlier generations did not find necessary and which they could not, in any case, put into practice.

Couples had more time for each other because they were beginning to limit the size of their families. There were a number of reasons for this development, which again pertained only to the upper classes. For one thing, child mortality rates were declining among wealthy social groups. Virulent epidemic diseases like the plague, which knew no class lines, were gradually disappearing. Moreover, though there were few medical breakthroughs in this period, sanitation was improving. Bearing fewer children had an enormous impact on the lives of women, reducing the danger of death and disablement in childbirth and giving them leisure time to pursue domestic tasks. This is not to say that the early part of a woman's marriage was not dominated by children; in fact, because of new attitudes toward child rearing it may have been so dominated more than ever. Many couples appear to have made a conscious decision to space births, though success was limited by the fact that the most common technique of birth control was *coitus interruptus*, or withdrawal.

The transformation in the quality of relationships between spouses was mirrored by an even greater transformation in attitudes toward children. There were many reasons why childhood now took on a new importance. Decline in mortality rates had a profound psychological impact. Parents could feel that their emotional investment in their children had a greater chance of fulfillment. But equally important were the new ideas about education, especially Locke's belief that the child enters into the world a blank slate whose personality is created through early education. This view not only placed a new responsibility upon parents but also gave them the concept of childhood as a stage through which individuals passed. This idea could be seen in the commercial sphere as well as in any other. In 1700 there was not a single shop in London that sold children's toys exclusively; by the 1780s there were toyshops everywhere. There were also shops that sold clothes specifically designed for children, no longer simply adult clothes in miniature. Most important of all was the development of materials for the education of children. This took place in two stages. At first so-called children's books were books whose purpose was to help adults teach children. Later came books directed at children themselves with large print, entertaining illustrations, and nonsensical characters, usually animals who taught moral lessons.

The commercialization of childhood was, of course, directed at adults. The new books and games that were designed to enhance a child's education not only had to be purchased by parents but had to be used by them as well. More and more mothers were devoting their time to their children. Among the upper classes the practice of wet nursing began to decline. Mothers wanted to nurture their infants both literally by breast-feeding and figuratively by teaching them. Children became companions to be taken on outings to the increasing number of museums or shows of curiosities.

The emergence of the bourgeoisie was one of the central social developments of the eighteenth century. Their culture, which emphasized a fulfilling homelife, leisure pursuits, and literacy, soon came to dominate the values of society in general. But this transformation of family life could not be shared by the population at large. Working women could afford neither the cost of instructional materials for their children nor the time to use them. Ironically, they now began using wet nurses,

once the privilege of the wealthy, for increasingly a working woman's labor was the margin of survival for her family. Working women enjoyed no privacy in the hovels in which they lived with large families in single rooms. Wives and children were still beaten by husbands and fathers and were unacquainted with enlightened ideas of the worth of the individual and the innocence of the child. By the end of the eighteenth century two distinct family cultures coexisted in Europe, one based on companionate marriage and the affective bonds of parents and children, the other based on patriarchal dominance and the family as an economic unit.

The Masses

The paradox of the eighteenth century was that for the masses life was getting better by getting worse. More Europeans were surviving than ever before, more food was available to feed them; there was more housing, better sanitation, even better charities. Yet for all of this, there was more misery. Those who would have succumbed to disease or starvation a century before now survived from day to day, beneficiaries—or victims—of increased farm production and improved agricultural marketing. The market economy organized a more effective use of land, but it created a widespread social problem. The landless agrarian laborer of the eighteenth century was the counterpart of the sixteenth-century wandering beggar. In the cities, the plight of the poor was as desperate as ever. Even the most open-hearted charitable institutions were unable to cope with the massive increase in the poor. Thousands of mothers abandoned their children to the foundling hospitals, hoping they would have a better chance of survival, even though hospital death rates were near 80 percent.

Not all members of the lower orders succumbed to poverty or despair. In fact, many were able to benefit from existing conditions to lead a more fulfilling life than ever before. The richness of popular culture, signified by a spread of literacy into the lower reaches of European society, was one indication of this change. So too were the reforms urged by enlightened thinkers to improve basic education and to improve the quality of life in the cities. For that segment of the lower orders that could keep its head above water, the eighteenth century offered new opportunities and new challenges.

Beggar Feeding a Child, *by Giacomo Ceruti. Every eighteenth-century European city had its legion of beggars. This man has done well enough to be able to feed himself and his little daughter for one more day.*

Breaking the Cycle

Of all the legacies of the eighteenth century, none was more fundamental than the steady increase in European population that began around 1740. This was not the first time that Europe had experienced sustained population growth, but it was the first time that such growth was not checked by a demographic crisis. Breaking the cycle of population growth and crisis was a momentous event in European history despite the fact that it went unrecorded at the time and unappreciated for centuries after.

The figures tell one part of the story. In 1700 European population is estimated to have been 120 million. By 1800 it had grown 50 percent to over 180 million. And the aggregate hides significant regional variations. While France, Spain, and Italy expanded between 30 and 40 percent, Prussia doubled and Russia and Hungary may have tripled in number. Britain increased by 80 percent from about 5 to 9 million, but the rate of growth was accelerating. In 1695 the English population stood

at 5 million. It took 62 years to add the next million and 24 years to add the million after that. In 1781 the population was 7 million, but it took only 13 years to reach 8 million and only 10 more years to reach 9 million. Steady population growth had continued without significant checks for well over half a century.

Ironically, the traditional pattern of European population found its theorist at the very moment that it was about to disappear. In 1798 Thomas Malthus (1766–1834) published *An Essay on the Principles of Population*. Reflecting on the history of European population, Malthus observed the cyclical pattern by which growth over one or two generations was checked by a crisis that significantly reduced population. From these lower levels new growth began until it was checked and the cycle repeated itself. Because people increased more quickly than did food supplies, the land could sustain only a certain level of population. When that level was near, population became prone to a demographic check. Malthus divided population checks into two categories, positive and preventive. Positive checks were war, disease, and famine, all of which Malthus believed were natural, although brutal, means of population control. Famine was the obvious result of the failure of food supplies to keep pace with demand; war was the competition for scarce resources; and disease often accompanied both. It was preventive checks that most interested Malthus. These were the means by which societies could limit their growth to avoid the devastating consequences of positive checks. Celibacy, late marriages, and sexual abstinence were among the choices of which Malthus approved, though abortion, infanticide, and contraception were also commonly practiced.

In the sixteenth and seventeenth centuries, the dominant pattern of the life cycle was high infant and child mortality, late marriages, and early death. All controlled population growth. Infant and child mortality rates were staggering: only half of all those born reached the age of ten. Late marriage was the only effective form of birth control—given the strong social taboos against sexual relations outside marriage—for a late marriage reduced a woman's childbearing years. Women in western Europe generally married between the ages of twenty-four and twenty-six; they normally ceased bearing children at the age of forty. But not all marriages lasted this fourteen or sixteen-year span, as one or the other partner died. On average, the childbearing period for most women was between ten and twelve years, long enough to endure six pregnancies, which would result in three surviving children. (See Special Feature, "Giving Birth to the Eighteenth Century," pp. 640–641.)

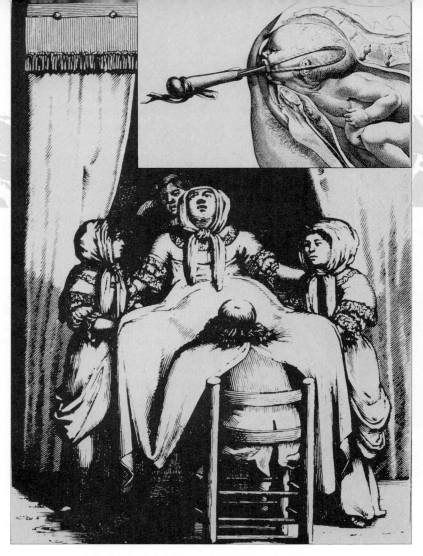

A woman being delivered by a man midwife is covered by a sheet to protect her modesty. The inset is a model drawing showing a delivery using forceps.

Giving Birth to the Eighteenth Century

"In sorrow thou shalt bring forth children." Such was Eve's punishment for eating of the forbidden tree, and that sorrow continued for numberless generations. Childbirth was painful, dangerous, and all too often, deadly. Though successful childbirth needed no outside intervention whatsoever—there were no obstetricians in caves—without the accumulated wisdom of the ages, babies and mothers routinely perished. That wisdom was passed from mother to daughter and finally was accumulated by skilled women who practiced the craft of midwifery. Every village, no matter how small, had women who were capable of assisting others in childbirth.

Midwives, who until the late seventeenth century were always women, were part of the support group that attended a woman during her labor. Typically, childbirth was a social occasion for women. Along with the midwife would be a wet nurse and female kin and neighbors, who would offer encouragement, bring refreshments, and tend to the ordinary chores that the pregnant woman would otherwise have performed herself. Without chemicals to induce contractions and without the ability to intervene in the delivery, labor was usually a long-drawn-out affair. Ordinarily it did not take place in bed, but rather in a room or a part of a room set aside for the occasion. By the eighteenth century, at least in larger urban areas, poor women, who had no separate space for labor, could give birth in lying-in hospitals. Within the birthing room, the conclave of women was much like a social gathering. The pregnant woman was advised to adopt any positions that made her feel comfortable; standing and walking were favored in the belief that the effects of gravity helped the baby move downward. The woman might sit on a neighbor's lap or on a birthing stool, a chair open at the bottom, during contractions and delivery.

By the seventeenth century manuals for midwives began to be published, some of them written by women, but most by male doctors whose surgical experiences provided them with ideas and information that were valuable to childbearing. Midwives and doctors were always at daggers drawn. No matter how skilled, midwives were denied access to medical training that might have enabled them to develop lucrative practices on their own. Thus they had no intention of letting male doctors into their trade. For a time the compromise was the handbooks, which contained guides to anatomy, descriptions of the most common complications, and the direst warnings to call trained physicians when serious problems arose.

By the beginning of the eighteenth century the "man-midwife," medically trained and usually experienced in other forms of surgery, had made his appearance in western Europe. The emergence of the man-midwife led to a number of breakthroughs in increasing the safety of childbirth. But at the same time, the social experience of childbirth changed dramatically. What had been a female rite of passage, experienced by and with other women, now became a private event experienced by an individual woman and her male doctor. As female midwives were still excluded from medical training and licensing, their ability to practice their trade eroded in the face of new techniques and information to which they were denied access.

The man-midwife's first task was to ascertain that the fetus was in the proper position to descend. In order to do this, however, he had to make an examination that was socially objectionable. Though advanced thinkers could face their man-midwife with the attitude "I considered that through modesty I was not to give up my life"—as one English noblewoman reasoned—many women and more husbands were unprepared for the actual practice of a man. Thus students were taught that they were not to examine the patient unless there was another person present in the room. They were not to ask direct questions, and they were not to face the patient during any of their procedures. They were taught to keep a linen cloth on top of the woman's abdomen and to make the examination only by touch. If the fetus was in the correct position, nothing further would be done until the delivery itself. It was only when the fetus was in what was labeled an "unnatural" position that the skill of the physician came into play.

For the most part, a child that could not be delivered head first and face down was in serious risk of being stillborn, and the mother was in serious risk of dying in labor. This was the problem to which physicians addressed themselves in the eighteenth century and for which they found remarkable solutions. The first advance was the realization that the fetus could be turned while still in the womb. Pressure applied on the outside of the stomach, especially in the early stages of labor, could help the fetus drop down correctly. A baby who emerged feet first had to be turned face down before it was pulled through the birth canal.

For babies who could not be manually manipulated, the greatest advance of the eighteenth century was the invention of the forceps. or the *tire-tête* as the French called them. With forceps the physician could pull the baby by force when the mother was incapable of delivery. Forceps were used mostly in breech births but were also a vital tool when the baby was too large to pass through the cervix by contraction. The forceps were invented in Britain in the middle of the seventeenth century. In the eighteenth century they came into general use when the Scotsman William Smellie (1697-1765) developed a short, leather-covered instrument that enabled the physician to do as little damage as possible to either mother or child. Obstetrics now emerged as a specialized branch of medical practice. If neither the pain nor the sorrow of childbirth could be eliminated, its dangers could be lessened.

Three surviving children for every two adults would, of course, have resulted in a 50 percent rise in population in every generation. Celibacy was one limiting factor, cities were another. Perhaps as much as 15 percent of the population in western Europe remained celibate either by entering religious orders that imposed celibacy or by lacking the personal or financial attributes necessary to make a match. Rural migrants accounted for the appallingly high urban death rates in cities. When we remember that the largest European cities were continuously growing—London from 200,000 in 1600 to 675,000 in 1750; Paris from 220,000 to 576,000; Rome from 105,000 to 156,000; Madrid from 49,000 to 109,000; Vienna from 50,000 to 175,000—then we can appreciate how many countless thousands of immigrants perished from disease, famine, and exposure before marriage. If urban perils were not enough, there were still the positive checks. Plagues carried away hundreds of thousands, wars halved populations of places in their path, and famine overwhelmed the weak and the poor.

The late seventeenth and early eighteenth centuries was a period of population stagnation if not actual decline. It was not until the third or fourth decade of the eighteenth century that another growth cycle began. It rapidly gained momentum throughout the Continent and showed no signs of abating after two full generations. More importantly, this upward cycle revealed unusual characteristics. In the first place fertility was increasing. This had several causes. In a few areas, most notably in Britain, women were marrying younger, thereby increasing their childbearing years. This pattern was also true in eastern Europe where women traditionally married younger. Sexual activity outside marriage was also rising. Illegitimacy rates, especially in the last decades of the century, were spurting everywhere.

But increasing fertility was only part of the picture. More significant was decreasing mortality. The positive checks of the past were no longer as potent. European warfare not only diminished in scale after the middle of the century, it changed location as well. Rivalry for colonial empires removed the theater of conflict from European communities. So did the increase in naval warfare. The damage caused by war had always been more by aftershock than by actual fighting. The destruction and pillage of crops and the wholesale slaughter of livestock created food shortages that weakened local populations for the diseases that came in train with the armies. As the virulence of warfare abated, so did that of epidemic disease. The plague had all but disappeared from western Europe by the middle of the eighteenth century. The widespread practice of quarantine, especially in Hungary, which had been the crucial bridge between eastern and western epidemics, went far to eradicate the scourge of centuries.

Without severe demographic crises to maintain the cyclical pattern, the European population began a gentle but continuous rise. Urban sanitation, at least for permanent city dwellers, was becoming more effective. Clean water supplies, organized waste and sewage disposal, and strict quarantines were increasingly part of urban regulations. The use of doctors and trained midwives helped lower the incidence of stillbirth and decreased the number of women who died in childbirth. Almost everywhere levels of infant and child mortality were decreasing. More people were being born, more were surviving the first ten dangerous years, and thus more were marrying and reproducing. Increased fertility and decreased mortality could have only one result: renewed population growth. No wonder Malthus was worried.

Daily Bread

In the past, if warfare or epidemic diseases failed to check population growth, famine would have done the job. How the European economy conquered famine in the eighteenth century is a complicated story. There was no single breakthrough that accounts for the ability to feed the tens of millions of additional people who now inhabited the Continent. Holland and Britain, at the cutting edge of agricultural improvement, employed dynamic new techniques that would ultimately provide the means to support continued growth, but most European agriculture was still mired in the time-honored practices that had endured for centuries. Still,

Agricultural techniques are illustrated in this plate from Diderot's Encyclopedia. *In the foreground, a man steers a high-wheeled, horse-drawn plow while a woman operates a hopper device to sow seeds.*

not everyone could be fed or fed adequately. Widespread famine might have disappeared, but slow starvation and chronic undernourishment had not. It is certainly the case that hunger was more common at the end of the eighteenth century than at the beginning and that the nutritional content of a typical diet may have reached its lowest point in European history.

Nevertheless, the capacity to sustain rising levels of population can be explained only in terms of agricultural improvement. Quite simply, European farmers were now producing more food and marketing it better. In the most advanced societies this was a result of conscious efforts to make agriculture more efficient. In traditional open-field agriculture, communities quickly ran up against insurmountable obstacles to growth. The three-field crop rotation system left a significant proportion of land fallow each year, while the concentration on subsistence cereal crops progressively eroded the land that was in production. Common farming was only as strong as the weakest member of the community. There was little incentive for successful individuals to plow profits back into the land, either through the purchase of equipment or the increase of livestock.

Livestock was a crucial variable in agricultural improvement. As long as there was only enough food for humans to eat, only essential livestock could be kept

alive over the winter. Oxen, which were still the ordinary beasts of burden, and pigs and poultry, which required only minimal feed, were the most common. But few animals meant little manure and without manure the soil could not easily be regenerated.

It was not until the middle of the seventeenth century that solutions to these problems began to appear. The first change was consolidation of landholdings so that traditional crop rotations could be abandoned. A second innovation was the introduction of fodder crops, some of which—like clover—added nutrients to the soil, while others—like turnips—were used to feed livestock. Better grazing and better winter feed increased the size of herds, while new techniques of animal husbandry, particularly crossbreeding, produced hardier strains. It was quite clear that the key to increased production lay in better fertilization, and by the eighteenth century some European farmers had broken through the "manure barrier." Larger herds, the introduction of clover crops, the use of human waste from towns, and even the first experiments with lime as an artificial fertilizer were all part of the new agricultural methods.

Along with the new crops that helped nourish both soil and animals came new crops that helped nourish people. Indian corn, or maize, was a staple crop for Native Americans and gradually came to be grown in most parts of western Europe. Maize not only had higher nutritional value than most other cereals, it also yielded more food per acre than traditional grains. So, too, did the potato, which also entered the European diet from the New World. The potato grew in poor soil, required less labor, and yielded an abundant and nutritious harvest. It rapidly took hold in Ireland and parts of Prussia, from which it spread into eastern Europe. The potato allowed families to subsist on smaller amounts of land and with less capital outlay.

It must be stressed, however, that these new developments involved only a very narrow range of producers. The new techniques were expensive and knowledge of the new crops spread slowly. Change had to overcome both inertia and intransigence. With more mouths to feed, profits from agriculture soared without landowners having to lift a finger. Only the most ambitious were interested in improvement. At the other end, peasant farmers were more concerned with failure than success. An experiment that did not work could devastate a community; one that did only meant higher taxes. Thus the most important improvements in agricultural production were more traditional ones. Basically, there was an increase in the amount of land that was utilized for

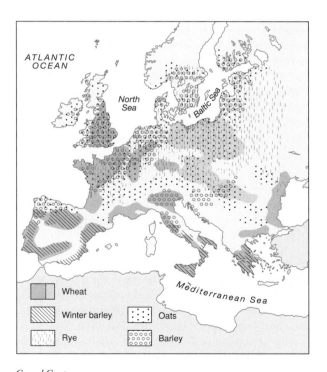

Cereal Crops

growing. In Russia, Prussia, and Hungary hundreds of thousands of new acres came under the plow, while in the west, drainage schemes and forest clearance expanded productive capacity.

There was also an upswing in the efficiency with which agricultural products were marketed. From the seventeenth century onward, market agriculture was gradually replacing subsistence agriculture in most parts of Europe. Market agriculture had the advantage of allowing specialization on farms. Single-crop farming enabled farmers to benefit from the peculiarities of their own soil and climate. They could then exchange their surplus for the range of crops they needed to subsist. Market exchange was facilitated by improved transportation and communication and above all by the increase in the population of towns, which provided demand. The new national and international trade in large quantities of grain evened out regional variations in harvests and went a long way toward reducing local grain shortages. The upkeep of roads, the building of canals, and the clearing of waterways created a national lifeline for the movement of grain.

Finally, it is believed that the increase in agricultural productivity owed something to a change in climate that took place in the late eighteenth century. The European climate is thought to have been unusually cold and wet during the seventeenth century, and it seems to have gradually warmed during the eighteenth century. Even moderate climatic change, when combined with new techniques, new crops, expanded cultivation, and improved marketing, would go a long way toward explaining how so many more people were being fed at the end of the eighteenth century.

The Plight of the Poor

"Of every ten men one is a beggar, five are too poor to give him alms, three more are ill at ease, embarrassed by debts and lawsuits, and the tenth does not represent a hundred thousand families." So observed an eighteenth-century Frenchman about the distribution of wealth in his country. There can be no doubt that the most serious social problem of the eighteenth century centered on the dramatic population increase of poor people throughout Europe. There was grim irony in the fact that advances in the production and distribution of food and the retreat of war and plague allowed more people to survive from hand to mouth than ever before. Where their ancestors had succumbed to quick death from disease or starvation, they eked out a miserable

existence of constant hunger and chronic pain with death at the end of a seemingly endless corridor.

It is impossible to gauge the number of European poor or to separate them into categories of greater and greatest misery. The truly indigent, the starving poor, probably composed 10 to 15 percent of most societies, perhaps as many as 20 million people throughout the Continent. They were most prevalent in towns but were an increasing burden on the countryside, where they wandered in search of agricultural employment. The wandering poor had no counterpart in eastern Europe, where serfdom kept everyone tied to the land, but the hungry and unsheltered certainly did. Yet the problem of poverty was not to be seen only among the destitute. In fact, the uniqueness of the poor in the eighteenth century is that they were drawn from social groups that even in the hungry times of the early seventeenth century had been successful subsistence producers.

It was easy to see why poverty was increasing. The relentless advance of population drove up the price of food and drove down the price of wages. In the second half of the eighteenth century, the cost of living in France rose by over 60 percent while wages rose only by 25 percent. In Spain the cost of living increased by 100 percent while wages rose only 20 percent. Only in Britain did wages nearly keep pace with prices. Rising prices made land more valuable. At the beginning of the eighteenth century, as the first wave of population expansion hit western Europe, smallholdings began to decrease in size. The custom of partible inheritance, by which each son received a share of land, shrank the average size of a peasant holding below that necessary to sustain an average-size family, let alone one that was growing larger. In one part of France it was estimated that thirty acres was a survival plot of land in good times. At the end of the seventeenth century 80 percent of the peasants there owned less than twenty-five acres.

As holdings contracted, the portion of the family income derived from wage labor expanded. In such circumstances males were more valuable than females, either as farmers or laborers, and there is incontrovertible evidence that European rural communities practiced female infanticide. In the end, however, it became increasingly difficult for the peasant family to remain on the land. Small freeholders were forced to borrow against future crops until a bad harvest led to foreclosure. Many were allowed to lease back their own lands, on short terms and at high rents, but most swelled the ranks of agricultural laborers, migrating during the planting and harvest seasons, suffering cruelly during winter and summer.

Emigration was the first logical consequence of poverty. In places where rural misery was greatest, like Ireland, whole communities pulled up stakes and moved to America. Frederick the Great attracted hundreds of thousands of emigrants to Prussia by offering them land. But most rural migrants did not move to new rural environments. Rather they followed the well-trodden paths to the cities. Many traditional domestic crafts were evolving into industrial activities. In the past, peasants supplemented their family income by processing raw materials in the home. Spinning, weaving, and sewing were common cottage industries in which the workers took in the work, supplied their own equipment, and were paid by the piece. Now, especially in the cloth trades, a new form of industrial activity was being organized. Factories, usually located in towns or larger villages, assembled workers together, set them at larger and more efficient machines, and paid them for their time rather than for their output. Families unable to support themselves from the land had no choice but to follow the movement of jobs.

Neither state nor private charities could cope with the flood of poor immigrants. Hospitals, workhouses, and more ominously, prisons were established or expanded to deal with them. Hospitals were residential asylums rather than places for health care. They took in the old, the incapacitated, and increasingly, the orphaned young. Workhouses existed for those who were capable of work but incapable of finding it. They were supposed to improve the values of the idle by keeping them busy, though in most places they served only to improve the profits of the industrialists, who rented out workhouse inmates at below-market wages. Prisons grew with crime. There were spectacular increases in crimes against property in all eighteenth-century cities and despite severe penalties that could include hanging for petty theft, more criminals were incarcerated than executed. Enlightened arguments for the reform of prisons and punishment tacitly acknowledged the social basis of most crime. As always, the victims of crime were mostly drawn from the same social backgrounds as the perpetrators. Along with all of their other troubles, it was the poor who were most commonly robbed, beaten, and abused.

Popular Culture

However depressing is this story of the unrelieved misery of the poor, we should not think of the masses of eighteenth-century society only as the downtrodden victims of social and economic forces beyond their control. For the peasant farmer about to lose his land or the urban artisan without a job, security was an overwhelming concern. While many were to endure such fates, many others lived comfortably by the standards of the age and almost everyone believed that things were better now than they had ever been before. Popular culture was a rich mixture of family and community activities that provided outlets from the pressures of work and the vagaries of fortune. It was no less sustaining to the population at large than was the purely literate culture of the elite, no less vital as a means of explanation for everyday events than the theories of the philosophers or the programs of the *philosophes*.

In fact, the line between elite and popular culture in the eighteenth century is a thin one. For one thing, there was still much mixing of social classes in both rural and urban environments. Occasions of display, like festivals, village fairs, or religious holidays, brought entire communities together and reinforced their collective identities. Moreover, there were many shared elements between the two cultures. All over Europe, literacy was increasing, the result of primary education, of new business techniques, and of the millions of books that were available in editions tailored to even the most modest purse. Nearly half of the inhabitants of France were literate by the end of the eighteenth century, perhaps 60 percent of those in Britain. Men were more likely to have learned to read than women, as were those who lived in urban areas. More than a quarter of French women could read, a number that had doubled over the century. As the rates of female literacy rose, so did overall rates, for women took the lead in teaching children.

Popular literacy spawned popular literature in remarkable variety. Religious tracts aimed at the populace were found throughout Europe. They contained stories of the saints in Catholic countries or of the martyrs in Protestant ones, proverbs intended to increase spirituality, and prayers to be offered for all occasions. Romances were the staple of lending libraries, which were also becoming a common feature of even small towns. These books were usually published in inexpensive installments spaced according to the time working families needed to save the pennies to purchase them. Yet the best-selling popular fiction, at least in western Europe, was melodramatic tales of knights and ladies from the age of chivalry. These themes had seeped into popular consciousness after having fallen out of favor among the elites.

Nevertheless, literate culture was not the dominant form of popular culture. Traditional social activities continued to reflect the violent and even brutal nature of day-to-day existence. Village festivals were still the safety valve of youth gangs who enforced sexual morals by shaming husbands whose wives were unfaithful or women whose reputations were sullied. Many holidays were celebrated by sporting events that pitted inhabitants of one village against those of another. These almost always turned into free-for-alls in which broken bones were common and deaths not unknown.

Even more popular were the so-called blood sports, which continued to be the most common form of popular recreation. These were brutal competitions in which, in one way or another, animals were maimed or slaughtered. Dog- and cock-fighting are among those that still survive today. Less attractive to the modern mind were bearbaiting or bullrunning, in which the object was the slaughter of a large beast over a prolonged period of time. Blood sports were certainly not confined to the masses—foxhunting and bullfighting were pastimes for the very rich—but they formed a significant part of local social activity.

So too did the tavern or alehouse, which in town or country was the site for local communication and recreation, where staggering amounts of alcohol were consumed. The increased use of spirits—gin, brandy, rum, and vodka—changed the nature of alcohol consumption in Europe. Wine and beer had always been drunk in quantities that we would find astounding, but these beverages were also an important part of diet. The nutritional content of spirits was negligible. People drank spirits to get drunk. The level to which drunkenness rose in the eighteenth century speaks volumes about the changes in social and economic life that the masses of European society were now experiencing.

Eighteenth-century Europe was a society of orders gradually transforming itself into a society of classes. At the top, as vigorous as ever, was the nobility. But the bourgeoisie was growing in both numbers and importance. An active commercial and urban life gave many members of this group new social and political opportunities and many of them passed into the nobility through the purchase of land or office. Opulence and poverty increased in step as the fruits of commerce and land enriched the upper orders while rising population impoverished the lower ones. The rise of the new science and of Enlightenment ideas highlighted the contradictions. The attack on traditional authority, especially the Roman Catholic church, was an attack on a conservative, static worldview. Enlightenment thinkers looked to the future, to a new world shaped by reason and knowledge, a world ruled benevolently for the benefit of all human beings. Government, society, the individual—all could be improved if only the rubble of the past was cleared away. They could hardly imagine how potent their vision would become.

The Cockpit *(ca. 1759) by William Hogarth. The central figure is a blind nobleman who was said never to have missed an important cockfight. The steel spurs on the birds' legs enabled them to inflict serious damage in the heat of battle.*

SUGGESTIONS FOR FURTHER READING

GENERAL READING

* Olwen Hufton, *Europe: Privilege and Protest 1730–1789* (Ithaca, NY: Cornell University Press, 1980). An excellent survey of the political and social history of the mid-eighteenth century.

* Leonard Krieger, *Kings and Philosophers 1689–1789* (New York: Norton, 1970). A brilliant depiction of the personalities and ideas of eighteenth-century Europe.

* Isser Woloch, *Eighteenth Century Europe, Tradition and Progress, 1715–89* (New York: Norton, 1982). Especially strong on social movements and popular culture.

* William Doyle, *The Old European Order 1660–1800* (Oxford: Oxford University Press, 1978). An important essay on the structure of European societies and the ways in which they held together.

* Raymond Birn, *Crisis, Absolutism, Revolution: Europe 1648-1789/91* (New York: Dryden Press, 1977). A reliable survey with especially good chapters on the Enlightenment.

THE NOBILITY

Michael Bush, *Noble Privilege* (New York: Holmes & Meier, 1983). A good analytic survey of the rights of European nobles.

J. V. Beckett, *The Aristocracy in England* (London: Basil Blackwell, 1986). A comprehensive study of a tightly knit national aristocracy.

* Albert Goodwin, ed., *The European Nobility in the Eighteenth Century* (New York: Harper & Row, 1967). Separate essays on national nobilities, including those of Sweden, Poland, and Spain.

* Norman Hampson, *The Enlightenment* (London: Penguin Books, 1982). The best one-volume survey.

* Peter Gay, *The Enlightenment: An Interpretation*, 2 vols. (New York: Knopf, 1966–69). A difficult but rewarding study by one of the leading historians of the subject.

Carolyn Lougee, *Le Paradis des Femmes: Women, Salons, and Social Stratification* (Princeton, NJ: Princeton University Press, 1976). A study of the foundation of the French salons and the role of women in it.

* Judith Sklar, *Montesquieu* (Oxford: Oxford University Press, 1987). A concise, readable study of the man and his work.

Theodore Besterman, *Voltaire* (Chicago: University of Chicago Press, 1976). The best of many biographies of an all-too-full life.

* John G. Gagliardo, *Enlightened Despotism* (New York: Thomas Y. Crowell, 1967). A sound exploration of the impact of Enlightenment ideas on the rulers of Europe, with most emphasis on the east.

THE BOURGEOISIE

Jan de Vries, *European Urbanization 1500-1800* (Cambridge, MA: Harvard University Press, 1984). An important, though difficult study of the transformation of towns into cities with the most reliable estimates of size and rates of growth.

* P. J. Corfield, *The Impact of English Towns 1700-1800* (Oxford: Oxford University Press, 1982). A thorough survey of the role of towns in English social and economic life.

* Elinor Barber, *The Bourgeoisie in Eighteenth Century France* (Princeton, NJ: Princeton University Press, 1955). Still the best study of the French bourgeoisie.

* Simon Schama, *The Embarrassment of Riches* (Berkeley: University of California Press, 1987). The social life of Dutch burghers richly portrayed.

* Ian Watt, *The Rise of the Novel* (Berkeley: University of California Press, 1957). An important essay on the relationship between literature and society in the eighteenth century.

David Garrioch, *Neighborhood and Community in Paris, 1740-90* (Cambridge: Cambridge University Press, 1986). A good microstudy of Parisian neighborhoods and of the people who inhabited them.

George Sussman, *Selling Mothers' Milk: The Wet-Nursing Business* (Bloomington: Indiana University Press, 1982). A study of buyers and sellers in this important social marketplace.

Samia Spencer, *French Women and the Age of Enlightenment* (Bloomington, IN: Indiana University Press, 1984). A survey of the role of women in French high culture.

* Lawrence Stone, *The Family, Sex and Marriage in England 1500-1800* (New York: Harper & Row, 1979). A controversial but extremely important argument about the changing nature of family life.

* Jean Louis Flandrin, *Families in Former Times* (Cambridge: Cambridge University Press, 1979). Strong on family and household organization.

THE MASSES

* Michael W. Flinn, *The European Demographic System* (Baltimore: Johns Hopkins University Press, 1981). The best single-volume study, especially for the nonspecialist reader.

E. A. Wrigley and R. S. Schofield, *The Population History of England* (Cambridge, MA: Harvard University Press, 1981). The most important reconstruction of a national population by a team of researchers.

Olwen Hufton, *The Poor in Eighteenth Century France* (Oxford: Oxford University Press, 1974). A compelling study of the life of the poor.

* Roy Porter, *English Society in the Eighteenth Century* (London: Penguin Books, 1982). A breezy, entertaining survey of English social life.

* J. M. Beattie, *Crime and the Courts in England* (Princeton, NJ: Princeton University Press, 1986). A difficult but sensitive analysis of crime and criminal justice.

* Peter Burke, *Popular Culture in Early Modern Europe* (New York: Harper & Row, 1978). A wide survey of practices throughout the Continent.

Robert Muchembled, *Popular Culture and Elite Culture in France, 1400-1750* (Baton Rouge, LA: Louisiana State University Press, 1985). A complex but richly textured argument about the relationship between two cultures.

* Robert Malcolmson, *Popular Recreation in English Society, 1700-1850* (Cambridge: Cambridge University Press, 1973). Sport and its role in society.

* Indicates paperback edition available.

CHAPTER 22

The French Revolution and the Napoleonic Era, 1750–1815

"Let Them Eat Cake"

The Queen of France was bored. Try as she might, Marie Antoinette (1755–93) found insufficient diversion in her life at the great court of Versailles. When she was fourteen, she had married the heir to the French throne, the future Louis XVI. By the age of nineteen, she was queen of the most prosperous state in continental Europe. Still she was bored. Her life, she complained to her mother, Empress Maria Theresa of Austria, was futile and meaningless. Maria Theresa advised the unhappy queen to suffer in silence or risk unpleasant consequences. Sometimes mothers know best.

Unpopular as a foreigner from the time she arrived in France, Marie Antoinette suffered a further decline in her reputation as gossip spread about her gambling and affairs at court. The public heard exaggerated accounts of the fortunes she spent on clothing and jewelry. In 1785 she was linked to a cardinal in a nasty scandal over a gift of a diamond necklace. In spite of her innocence, rumors of corruption and infidelity surrounded her name. Dubbed "Madame Deficit," she came to represent all that was considered decadent in royal rule.

She continued to insist, "I am afraid of being bored." To amuse herself, she ordered a life-size play village built on the grounds of Versailles, complete with cottages, a chapel, a mill, and a running stream. Then, dressed in the silks and muslins intended as the royal approximation of a milkmaid's garb, she whiled away whole days with her friends and children, all pretending they were inhabitants of this picturesque "hamlet." Her romantic view of country life helped pass the time, but it did little to bring her closer to the struggling peasants who made up the majority of French subjects.

Marie Antoinette's problems need not have mattered much. Monarchs before her had been considered weak and extravagant. The difference was that her foibles became public in an age when the opinion of the people affected political life. Rulers, even those believed to be divinely appointed, were subjected to a public scrutiny all the more powerful because of the growth of the popular press. Kings, their ministers, and their spouses were held accountable—a dangerous phenomenon for an absolute monarchy.

This Austrian-born queen may not have been more shallow or spendthrift than other queens, but it mattered that people came to see her that way. The queen's reputation sank to its nadir when it was reported that she dismissed the suffering of her starving subjects with the haughty retort: "Let them eat cake." What better evidence could there be of the queen's insensitivity than this heartless remark?

Marie Antoinette never said, "Let them eat cake," but everyone thought she did. This was the kind of callousness that people expected from the monarchy in 1789. Marie Antoinette understood the plight of her starving subjects, as her correspondence indicates. Probably a courtier at Versailles was the real source of the brutal retort, but the truth didn't matter. Marie Antoinette and her husband were being indicted by the public for all the political, social, and fiscal crises that plagued France.

In October 1793, Marie Antoinette was put on trial by the Revolutionary Tribunal and found guilty of treason. She was stripped of all the trappings of monarchy and forced to don another costume. Dressed as a poor working woman, her hair shorn, the former queen mounted the guillotine, following in the footsteps of her husband, who had been executed earlier that year. The monarchy did not fall because of a spendthrift queen with too much time on her hands. Nor did it fall because of the mistakes of the well-meaning but inept king. The monarchy had ceased to be responsive to the profound changes that shook France. It fell because of a new concern in the land for royal accountability in words and deeds. A rising democratic tide carried with it ideas about political representation, participation, and equality. If a queen could change places with a milkmaid, why should not a milkmaid be able to change places with a queen?

The Crisis of the Old Regime in France, 1715-1788

France in the eighteenth century, the age of the Enlightenment, was a state invigorated by new ideas. It was also a world dominated by tradition. The traditional institutions of monarchy, Church, and aristocracy defined power and status. Talk of reform, progress, and perfectibility coexisted with the social realities of privileges and obligations determined by birth. The eighteenth century was a time when old ways prevailed even as a new view of the world was taking shape.

The tensions generated by the clash of continuity and change made the end of the eighteenth century an exciting and complex period in both Britain and France. In France, reformers talked of progress while peasants still used wooden plows. The *philosophes* glorified reason in a world of violence, superstition, and fear. The great crisis of eighteenth-century France, the French Revolution, destroyed the *ancien régime* (old regime). But the Revolution was as much a product of continuities and traditions as it was a product of change and the challenge of new ideas.

Louis XV's France

When Louis XV (1715-74) died, he was a hated man. His legacy was well captured in the expression erroneously attributed to him, *aprés moi le déluge*—"after me, the flood." In his fifty-nine-year reign, he managed to turn the public against him. He was denounced as a tyrant who was trying to starve his people, a slave to the mistresses who ruled his court, and a pleasure-seeker dominated by evil ministers. Louis XV's apathy and ineptitude contributed to his poor image. The declining fortunes and the damaged prestige of the monarchy, however, reflected more than the personality traits of an ineffectual king: they reflected structural challenges to fiscal solvency and absolutist rule that the monarchy was unable to meet.

Louis XV, like his great-grandfather Louis XIV, laid claim to rule as an absolute monarch. He insisted that "the rights and interests of the nation . . . are of necessity one with my own, and lie in my hands only." Such claims failed to mask the weaknesses of royal rule. Louis XV lacked a sufficiently developed bureaucracy to administer and tax the nation in an evenhanded fashion. By the beginning of the eighteenth century, the absolute monarchy had extended royal influence into the new areas of policing, administration, lawmaking, and taxation. But none of this proved sufficient to meet the growing needs of the state.

The growing tensions between the monarch and the aristocracy found expression in various institutions, especially the *parlements*, the thirteen sovereign courts in the French judicial system, with their seats in Paris and a dozen provincial centers. The magistrates of each parlement were members of the nobility, some of them nobles of recent origin and others of long standing, depending on the locale. The king needed the parlements to record royal decrees before they could become law.

This recording process conferred real political power on the parlements, which could withhold approval for the king's policies by refusing to register his decrees. When the king attempted to make new laws, the magistrates could refuse to endorse them. When decrees involved taxation, they often did. Because magistrates purchased their offices in the parlements, the king found it difficult to control the courts. His fiscal difficulties prevented him from buying up the increasingly valuable offices in order to appoint his own men. Stripping magistrates of their positions was considered tantamount to the theft of property. By successfully challenging the king, the parlements became a battleground between the elite, who claimed that they represented the nation, and the king, who said the nation was himself.

The king repeatedly attempted to neutralize the power of the parlements by relying instead on his own state bureaucracy. His agents in the provinces, called *intendants*, were accountable directly to the central government. The intendants, as the king's men, and the magistrates who presided in the parlements represented contradictory claims to power. As the king's needs increased in the second half of the eighteenth century, the situation was becoming intolerable for those exercising power and those aspiring to rule in the name and for the good of the nation.

The nadir of Louis XV's reign came in 1763 with the French defeat in the Seven Years' War on the Continent and in the French and Indian War in the American colonies. In the Treaty of Paris, France ceded territory, including its Canadian holdings, to Great Britain. France lost more than lands; it lost its footing in the competition with its chief rival Great Britain, which had been pulling ahead of France in international affairs since the early eighteenth century. The war was also a financial debacle, paid for by loans secured against the guarantee of victory. The defeat not only left France barren of funds, it also promoted further expenditures for strengthening the French navy against the superior British fleet. New taxation was the way out of the financial trap in which the king now found himself.

Louis XV's revenue problem was not easily solved. In order to raise taxes, the king had to turn to the recording function of the parlements. Following the costly Seven Years' War, the parlements chose to exercise the power of refusal by blocking a proportional tax to be imposed on nobles and commoners alike. The magistrates resisted taxation with an argument that confused liberty with privilege: the king, the magistrates asserted, was attacking the liberty of his subjects by attempting to tax those who were exempt by virtue of their privileged status.

René Nicolas Charles Augustin de Maupeou (1714–92), Louis XV's chancellor from 1768 to 1774, decided that the political power of the parlements had to be curbed. In 1770, in an attempt to coerce the magistrates into compliance with the king's wishes, he engineered the overthrow of the Parlement of Paris, the most important of the high courts. Those magistrates who remained obdurate were sent into exile. New courts whose membership was based on appointment instead of the sale of offices took their place amid much public criticism. Ultimately, Maupeou's attempt did nothing to improve the monarch's image, and it did less to solve the fiscal problems of the regime.

In 1774 Louis XV died suddenly of smallpox. His unprepared twenty-year-old grandson, Louis XVI (1774–92), a young man who amused himself by hunting and pursuing his hobby as an amateur locksmith, was left to try to stanch the flood.

Louis XVI and the National Debt

Louis XV left to his heir Louis XVI the legacy of a disastrous deficit. From the beginning of his reign, Louis XVI was caught in the vicious circle of excessive state spending—above all, military spending—followed by bouts of heavy borrowing. Borrowing at high rates required the government to pay out huge sums in interest and service fees on the loans that were keeping it afloat. These outlays in turn piled the state's indebtedness ever higher, requiring more loans, and threatening to topple the whole financial structure and the regime itself.

In inheriting this trouble-ridden fiscal structure, Louis XVI made his own contribution to it. Following in the footsteps of his grandfather, Louis XVI involved France in a costly war, the War of American Independence (1775–83), by supporting the thirteen colonies in their revolt against Great Britain. The involvement brought the French monarchy to the brink of bankruptcy. Contrary to public opinion, most of the state's expenditures did not go toward lavishing luxuries on the royal court and the royal family at Versailles. They went to pay off loans. More than half of the state budget in the 1780s represented interest on loans taken to pay for foreign military ventures.

As one of the first acts of his reign, in 1775 Louis XVI had restored the magistrates to their posts in the

This cartoon from 1789 depicts Necker (at left) showing the king how to conceal the size of the deficit from the estates. On the wall, a list of royal loans is headed "New ways to revive France"—but the total is "Deficit."

more than a drop compared to the vast ocean of debt that threatened to engulf the state.

The existing tax structure proved hopelessly inadequate to meet the state's needs. The *taille*, a direct tax, was levied, either on persons or on land, according to region. Except for those locales where the taille was attached to land, the nobility was always exempt from direct taxation. Members of the bourgeoisie could also avoid the direct tax as citizens of towns enjoying exemption. That meant that the wealthy, those best able to pay, were often exempt. Indirect taxes, like those on salt (the *gabelle*) and on food and drink (the *aide*), and internal and external customs taxes were regressive taxes that hit hardest those least able to pay. The peasantry bore the brunt of the nation's tax burden, and Louis XVI knew all too well that a peasantry too weighted down would collapse—or rebel.

Louis XVI appointed Anne-Robert-Jacques Turgot (1727–81) as his first controller-general. Turgot's reformist economic ideas were influenced by Enlightenment *philosophes*. In order to generate revenues, Turgot reasoned, France needed to prosper economically. The government was in a position to stimulate economic growth by eliminating regulations, by economizing at court, and by improving the network of roads through a tax on landowners. Each of Turgot's reforms offended established interests, thereby ensuring his early defeat. Emphasis on a laissez-faire economy outraged the guilds; doing away with the forced labor of peasants on the roads (the *corvée*) threatened privileged groups who had never before been taxed. As the king was discovering, divine right did not bring with it absolute authority or fiscal solvency.

As he floundered about for a solution to his economic difficulties, the king turned to a new adviser, Jacques Necker (1732–1804), a Swiss-born Protestant banker. Necker applied his accounting skills to measuring—for the first time—the total income and expenditures of the French state. Instead of raising taxes, Necker committed his ministry to eliminating costly inefficiencies. He promised to abolish venal offices that drained revenues from the crown. He next set his sights on the contracts of the farmers-general, collectors of the indirect salt taxes. But the budget that Necker produced was based on disastrous miscalculations, and he was forced to resign in 1781.

Charles Alexandre de Calonne (1734–1802), appointed controller-general in 1783, had his own ideas of how to bail out the ship of state. He authored a program of reforms that would have shifted the tax burden off those least able to pay and onto those best able to

parlements, treating their offices as a form of property of which they had been deprived. By 1776 the Parlement of Paris was again obstructing royal decrees. The privileged elite persisted in rejecting the crown's attempts to tax them. But to those who could afford to purchase them, the king continued to sell offices that carried with them titles, revenues, and privileges. He also relied on the sale of annuities that paid high interest rates and that attracted speculators, large and small. The crown had leased out its rights to collect the salt tax in return for large lump-sum advances from the Royal General Farms, a syndicate of about one hundred wealthy financier families. But the combined revenues collected by the king through these various stratagems were little

support the state. He proposed a tax on land proportional to land values, a measure that would have most seriously affected the land-rich nobility. In addition, taxes that affected the peasantry were to be lightened or eliminated. Finally, Calonne proposed the sale of Church lands for revenues. In an attempt to bypass the recalcitrant parlements, Calonne advised the crown in 1787 to convene an Assembly of Notables made up of 150 individuals from the magistracy, the Church hierarchy, the titled nobility, and municipal bodies, for the purpose of enlisting their support for reforms. Louis listened to Calonne, who was denounced by the Assembly of Notables for attacking the rights of the privileged. He too was forced to resign. All of Louis XVI's attempts to persuade the nobility to agree to tax reforms had failed.

In the 1780s, almost 50 percent of annual expenditures went to servicing the accumulated national debt of 4 billion livres and paying interest. The new controller-general, Archbishop Loménie de Brienne (1727–94) recommended emergency loans. The crown once again disbanded the Parlement of Paris, which was now threatening to block loans as well as taxes. Aristocratic magistrates now insisted on a constitution, in which their own right to govern would be safeguarded and the accountability of the king would be defined. In opposing the royal reforms, nobles spoke of the "rights of man" and used the term *citizen*. The nobility had no sympathy for tax programs that would have resulted in a loss of privilege and what some nobles were beginning to consider an attack on individual freedom.

Louis XVI was a desperate man in 1788, so desperate that he yielded to the condition placed on him by the Parlement of Paris: he agreed to convene the Estates-General, a medieval body that had not met since 1614 and that had been considered obsolete with the rise of a centralized bureaucratic government. In the 1614 voting of the Estates-General, the three orders—clergy, nobility, commoners—were equally weighted. This arrangement favored the nobility, who controlled the first two estates and thus were not worried by the prospect of the Estates-General deciding the tax reform program. Many were sure that a new age of liberty was at hand.

The Three Estates

The Estates-General included representatives from the three "estates" of the clergy, nobility, and commoners. About two hundred thousand subjects belonged to the

first two estates. The Third Estate was composed of all those members of the realm who enjoyed a common identity only in their lack of privilege—over 23 million French people. In the second half of the eighteenth century, these traditional groups no longer reflected social realities—a situation that proved to be a source of serious problems for the Estates-General. The piety of the first order had been called into doubt as religious leaders were criticized for using the vast wealth of the Church for personal benefit instead of public worship. The protective military function of the second order had ceased to exist with the rise of the state and the changing nature of war. The bourgeoisie, those who worked with their heads, not their hands, shared privileges with the nobility and aspired to a noble lifestyle, in spite of their legal and customary presence in the ranks of the Third Estate.

The vast majority of French subjects who constituted the Third Estate certainly were identified by

Cartoon showing the plight of the French peasants. An old farmer is bowed down under the weight of the privileged aristocracy and clergy while birds and rabbits, protected by unfair game laws, eat his crops.

work, but the vast array of mental and physical labor—and lack of work—splintered the estate into myriad occupations, aspirations, and identities. All power flowed upward in this arrangement, with the First and Second Estates dominating the social and political universe.

The king continued to stand at the pinnacle of the eighteenth-century social pyramid. Traditionally revered as the "father" of his subjects, he claimed to be divinely appointed by God. Kingship in this era had a dual nature. The king was both supreme overlord from feudal times, and he was absolute monarch. As supreme overlord he dominated the aristocracy and the court. As absolute monarch he stood at the head of the state and society. Absolutism required a weakened nobility and a bureaucracy strong enough to help the monarchy to adjust to changes. After the death of Louis XIV in 1715, Louis XV and Louis XVI faced a resurgent aristocracy without the support of a state bureaucracy capable of successfully challenging aristocratic privilege or of solving fiscal problems.

While the system of orders set clear boundaries of social status, distinctions within estates created new hierarchies. The clergy, a privileged order, contained both commoners and nobles, but leadership in the Church depended on social rank. The aristocracy retained control of the bishoprics, even as an activist element among the lower clergy agitated for reforms and better salaries. In a state in which the king claimed to rule by God's will, Catholicism, virtually the state religion, was important in legitimizing the divine claims of the monarchy.

The nobility experienced its own internal tensions, generated by two groups: the older nobility of the sword, who claimed descent from medieval times; and the more recent nobility of the robe, who had acquired their position through the purchase of offices that conferred noble status. By increasing the numbers of the nobility of the robe, Louis XIV hoped to undermine the power of the aristocracy as a whole and to decrease its political influence. But aristocrats rallied and closed ranks against the dilution of their power. As a result, both Louis XV and Louis XVI faced a reviving rather than a declining aristocracy. Nobles had succeeded in restoring their economic and social power. A growing segment of the aristocracy, influenced by Enlightenment ideas and the example of English institutions, was intent on increasing the political dominance of the aristocracy too.

The nobility strengthened their powers in two ways. First, they monopolized high offices and closed access to nonnobles. They took over posts in ministries, the Church, and the army. Second, the nobility benefited greatly from the doubling in land values brought on by the increase in the value of crops. Those aristocrats who controlled sizable holdings profited greatly from higher dues paid to them, as they reaped increased incomes from crops. In addition, many aristocrats revived feudal claims to ancient seigneurial, or lordly, privileges. They hired lawyers to unearth old claims and hired agents to collect dues.

Although technically prevented from participating in trade by virtue of their titles and privileges, an active group among the nobility succeeded in making fortunes in metallurgy, glassmaking, and mining. These nobles were an economically dynamic and innovative segment of the aristocracy. In spite of the obsolete aspect of their privileges, aristocrats were often responsible for the introduction of modern ideas and techniques in the management of estates and in the bookkeeping involved with collection of rents. These nobles formed an elite partnership with forward-looking members of the bourgeoisie.

Common people, that is, those who did not enjoy the privileges of the nobility, embraced a broad range of the French populace. The peasantry was by far the largest group, joined in the designation as "commoners" by the middle class, or bourgeoisie, and by workers in both cities and rural areas. Most French peasants were free, no longer attached to the soil as serfs were in a feudal system. Yet all peasants endured common obligations placed on them by the crown and the privileged classes. Peasants owed the tithe to the Church, land taxes to the state, and seigneurial dues and rents to the landlord. A bewildering array of taxes afflicted peasants. Dues affected almost every aspect of rural life, including harvests and the sale of property. In addition, indirect taxes like that on salt (the hated gabelle) were a serious burden for the peasantry.

The precariousness of rural life and the increase in population in the countryside contributed to the permanent displacement and destitution of a growing sector of rural society. Without savings and destroyed by poor harvests, impoverished rural inhabitants wandered the countryside looking for odd jobs and eventually begging to survive. Many peasants with small plots were able to work for wages. Peasant women sought employment in towns and cities as seamstresses and servants in order to send money back home. Children, too, added their earnings to the family pot. But in spite of various strategies for survival, more and more families were disrupted by the end of the eighteenth century.

Bourgeoisie—as the term was used in the eighteenth century—meant those members of the middle class who lived on income from investments. Yet the term really embraced within it a whole hierarchy of professions from bankers and financiers to businessmen, merchants, entrepreneurs, lawyers, shopkeepers, and craftsmen. Along with the nobility, wealthy bourgeois formed the urban elites that administered cities and towns. Prestigious service to the state or the purchase of offices that carried with them noble status enabled the wealthiest members of the bourgeoisie to move into the ranks of the nobility.

Like the rest of the social universe, the world of artisans and workers was shaded with various gradations of wealth and status. Those who owned their own shops and perhaps employed other workers stood as an elite among the working class. In spite of their physical proximity, there was a vast difference between those who owned their own shops and those who earned wages or were paid by the piece. Wage earners represented about 30 percent of the population of cities and towns. And their numbers were swelling, as craftsmen were pushed out of their guilds and peasants were pushed off their land.

Those who worked in crafts were a labor elite, and guilds were intended to protect the corporations of masters, journeymen, and apprentices through monopolistic measures. Guilds insisted that they were best able to ensure the quality of goods. But the emphasis on free trade and the expansion of markets in the eighteenth century weakened the hold of the guilds. Merchants often took them over and paid workers by the piece. The effect was a reduction in the wages of skilled workers. By the 1780s, most journeymen who hoped to be masters knew that their dream would never be realized. Frustration and discontent touched workers in towns and cities who may not have shared a common work experience. But they did share a common anger about the high cost of bread.

In August 1788 Louis XVI announced that the Estates-General would meet in May 1789. In desperate straits, the king hoped that the clergy, nobility, and commoners from the three estates who were to assemble at Versailles would solve all of his problems. The Estates-General was to achieve what the king's ministers could not—fiscal solvency and a strengthened monarchy. Yet each of the estates had its own ideas about proper solutions and its own grievances. The stage was set for a confrontation of social groups whose political values were riven by conflicting ideas about justice, social status, and economic well-being.

The First Stage of the French Revolution, 1789-1792

The French Revolution, or the Great Revolution, as it was known to contemporaries, was a time of creation and discovery. The ten years from 1789 to 1799 were punctuated by genuine euphoria and democratic transformations. From the privileged elites who initiated the overthrow of the existing order to peasants and workers, women and men, who united against tyranny, the Revolution touched every segment of society.

The Revolution achieved most in the area of politics. The overthrow of absolutist monarchy brought with it new social theories, new symbols, and new behavior. The excitement of anarchy was matched by the terror of repression. Revolutionary France had to contend with a Europe-wide war. The Revolution had its dark side of violence and instability, and in its wake came internal discord, civil war, and violent repression. In the search for a new order, political forms followed one upon the other in rapid succession: constitutional monarchy, republic, oligarchy. The creation of Napoleon's dictatorship at the end of the century was the act that signified that the Revolution had come to an end.

Revolutionary incidents flared up throughout Europe in the second half of the eighteenth century—in the Netherlands, Belgium, and Ireland. Absolute authority was challenged and sometimes modified. Across the Atlantic, American colonists concerned with the principle of self-rule had thrown off the yoke of the British in the War of Independence. But none of these events, including the American Revolution, was so violent in breaking with the old order, so extensive in involving millions of men and women in political action, and so consequential for the political futures of other European states, as was the French Revolution. The triumphs and contradictions of the revolutionary experiment in democracy mark the end of the old order and the beginning of modern history. Politics would never be the same.

Taking Politics to the People

Choosing representatives for the Estates-General in March and April 1789 stirred up hope and excitement in every corner of France. The call for national elections set in motion a politicizing process the king could not control. From the very beginning, there were warning signs that a more astute monarch might have noticed.

Members of the Third Estate, traditionally excluded from political and social power, were presented with the opportunity of expressing their opinions on the state of government and society. In an increasingly literate age, pamphlets, broadsides, and political tracts representing every political persuasion blanketed France. Farmhands and urban laborers realized that they were participating in the same process as their social betters. And they believed they had a right to speak and be heard. Taxes could be discussed and changed; the state bureaucracy could be reformed—or better, abolished.

Intellectuals discussed political alternatives in the salons of the wealthy. Nobles and bourgeois met in philosophical societies dedicated to enlightened thought. Commoners gathered in cafes to drink and debate. The poor fell outside this network of communication, but they were not immune to the ideas that emerged. In the end, people of all classes had opinions, and they were more certain than ever of their right to express their ideas. Absolutism was in trouble, although Louis XVI did not know it, as people began to forge a shared idea of politics. People now had a forum—the Estates-General—and a focus—the politics of taxation. But most important, they had the elections. The message of the elections,

and of the representative principle on which they were based, was that one could compete for power.

In competing for power, some members of the Third Estate were well aware of their vast numerical superiority over the nobility. Because of it, they demanded greater representation than the three hundred members per estate defined according to the practices of 1614. At the very least, they argued, the number of representatives of the Third Estate should be doubled to six hundred members, giving commoners equality in numbers with nobles and priests together. Necker, recalled as director-general of finance in August 1788, agreed to the doubling in the size of the Third Estate as a compromise but left unresolved the additional demand of vote by head rather than by order. If voting was to be left as it was, in accordance with the procedures of 1614, the nobility who controlled the First and Second Estates would determine all outcomes. With a voting procedure by head instead of by order, however, the deputies of the Third Estate could easily dominate the Estates-General.

In conjunction with this political activity and in scheduled meetings, members of all three estates drew up statements of their problems. This took place in a variety of forums, including guilds and village and town meetings. The people of France set down their grievances in notebooks—known as *cahiers de doléances*—that were then carried to Versailles by the deputies elected to the Estates-General. This was the first national poll of opinion commissioned by the crown, and it involved every level of society. It was a tool of political education as the mass of French people were being given the impression for the first time that they were part of the policy-making process.

The cahiers expressed the particular grievances of each estate. These notebooks contained a collective outpouring of problems and they are important for two major reasons. First, they made clear the similarity of grievances shared throughout France. Second, they indicated the extent to which a common political culture, based on a concern with political reform, had permeated different levels of French society. Both the privileged and the nonprivileged identified a common enemy in the system of state bureaucracy to which the monarch was so strongly tied. Although the king was still addressed with respect, new concerns with liberty, equality, property, and the rule of law were voiced. People were questioning their traditional roles and now had elected deputies who would represent them before the king. In the spring of 1789 a severe economic crisis swept through France heightening

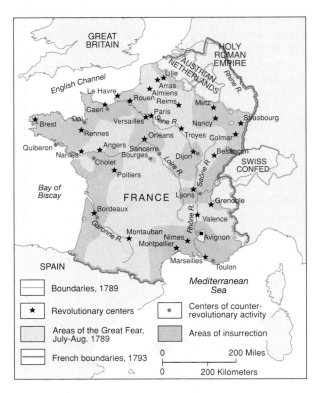

Revolutionary France

political uncertainty. For a king expected to save the situation, time was running out.

Convening the Estates-General

The elected deputies arrived at Versailles at the beginning of May 1789, carrying in their valises and trunks the grievances of their estates. The opening session of the Estates-General took place in a great hall especially constructed for the event. The 1,248 deputies presented a grand spectacle as they filed to their assigned places to hear speeches by the king and his ministers. Contrasts among the participants were immediately apparent. Seated on a raised throne under a canopy at one end of the hall, Louis XVI was vested in full kingly regalia. On his right sat the archbishops and cardinals of the First Estate, dramatically clad in the pinks and purples of their offices. On his left were the richly and decorously attired nobility. Facing the stage sat the 648 deputies of the Third Estate, dressed in plain black suits, stark against the colorful and costly costumes of the privileged. Fired by the hope of equal treatment and an equal share of power, they had come to Versailles to make a constitution.

The tension between commoners and privileged was aggravated by the unresolved issue of how the voting was to proceed. The Third Estate was adamant in its demand for vote by head. The privileged orders were equally adamant in insisting on vote by order. Paralysis set in, as days dragged into weeks and the Estates were unable to act. The body that was to save France from fiscal collapse was hopelessly deadlocked.

Two men in particular, whose backgrounds made them unlikely heroes, emerged as leaders of the Third Estate. One, the Abbé Emmanuel-Joseph Sieyès (1748–1836), was a member of the clergy who frequented Parisian salons. The other, the comte Honoré Gabriel Victor de Mirabeau (1749–91), a black sheep among the nobility, had spent time in prison because of his father's charges that he was a defiant son who led a misspent, debauched, and profligate youth. In spite of his nobility, Mirabeau appeared at Versailles as a deputy for Aix and Marseilles to the Third Estate. His oratory and presence commanded attention from the start. As a consummate politician, Mirabeau combined forces with Sieyès, who had already established his reputation as a firebrand reformer with his eloquent pamphlet, "What Is the Third Estate?"

Sieyès and Mirabeau reminded members of the Third Estate of the reformist consensus that characterized their ranks. Under their influence, the Third

The French Revolution

August 1788	Louis XVI announces meeting of Estates-General to be held in May 1789
5 May 1789	Estates-General convenes
17 June 1789	Third Estate declares itself the National Assembly
20 June 1789	Oath of the Tennis Court
14 July 1789	Storming of the Bastille
20 July 1789	Revolution of peasantry begins
26 August 1789	*Declaration of the Rights of Man and Citizen*
5 October 1789	Parisian women march to Versailles; force Louis XVI to return to Paris
November 1789	Church property nationalized
February 1790	Monasteries, convents dissolved
July 1790	Civil Constitution of the Clergy
June 1791	Louis XVI and family attempt to flee Paris; are captured and returned
June 1791	*Declaration of Rights of Woman and Citizen*
April 1792	France declares war on Austria
10 August 1792	Storming of the Tuileries
21 September 1792	Abolition of monarchy
22 September 1792	Creation of the First Republic; day one of revolutionary calendar (implemented in 1793)
January 1793	Louis XVI executed
July 1793	Robespierre assumes leadership of Committee of Public Safety
1793–94	Reign of Terror
1794	Robespierre guillotined
1794–95	Thermidorian Reaction
1795–99	Directory
1799	Napoleon overthrows the Directory and seizes power

"WHAT IS THE THIRD ESTATE?"

■ As an ambitious clergyman from Chartres, the site of one of France's most stunning Gothic cathedrals, the Abbé Sieyès was a member of the First Estate. In the elections for the Estates-General, Sieyès was elected a deputy from the Third Estate on the basis of his attacks on aristocratic privilege. He participated in the writing and editing of the great documents of the early Revolution: the Oath of the Tennis Court and the Declaration of the Rights of Man and Citizen. *His most famous revolutionary document, the pamphlet for which he is immortalized in revolutionary lore, was his daring "What Is the Third Estate?" Written in January 1789, it boldly confronted the bankruptcy of the system of privilege of the Old Regime and threw down the gauntlet to those who ruled France. In this document the Revolution found its rallying point.*

1st. What is the third estate? Everything.
2nd. What has it been heretofore in the political order? Nothing.
3rd. What does it demand? To become something therein.

Who, then, would dare to say that the third estate has not within itself all that is necessary to constitute a complete nation? It is the strong and robust man whose one arm remains enchained. If the privileged order were abolished, the nation would not be something less but something more. Thus, what is the third estate? Everything; but an everything shackled and oppressed. What would it be without the privileged order? Everything; but an everything free and flourishing. Nothing can progress without it; everything would proceed infinitely better without the others. It is not sufficient to have demonstrated that the privileged classes, far from being useful to the nation, can only enfeeble and injure it; it is necessary, moreover, to prove that the nobility does not belong to the social organization at all; that, indeed, it may be a *burden* upon the nation, but that it would not know how to constitute a part thereof.

The third estate, then, comprises everything appertaining to the nation; and whatever is not the third estate may not be regarded as being of the nation. What is the third estate? Everything!

From Abbé Emmanuel-Joseph Sieyès, "What Is the Third Estate?"

Estate decided to proceed with its own meetings. On 17 June 1789, the Third Estate, joined by some sympathetic clergy, changed its name to the National Assembly as an assertion of its true representation of the French nation. Three days later, members of the new National Assembly found themselves locked out of their regular meeting room by the king's guard. Outraged by this insult, they moved to a nearby indoor tennis court, where they vowed to stay together for the purpose of writing a constitution. This event, known as the Oath of the Tennis Court, marked the end of the absolutist monarchy and the beginning of a new concept of the state that power resided in the people. The Revolution had begun.

The drama of Versailles, a staged play of gestures, manners, oaths, and attire, also marked the beginning of a far-reaching political revolution. Although it was a drama that took place behind closed doors, it was not one unknown to the general public. Throughout

May and June 1789, Parisians trekked to Versailles to watch the deliberations. Then they brought news back to the capital. Deputies wrote home to their constituents to keep them abreast of events. Newspapers that reported daily on these wranglings and pamphleteers who analyzed them spread the news throughout the nation. Information, often conflicting, stirred up anxiety; news of conflict encouraged action.

The frustration and the stalemate of the Estates-General threatened to put the spark to the kindling of urban unrest. The people of Paris had suffered through a harsh winter and spring under the burdens of high prices (especially of bread), limited supplies, and relentless tax demands. The rioting of the spring had for the moment ceased, as people waited for their problems to be solved by the deputies of the Estates-General. The suffering of the urban poor was not new, but their ability to connect economic hardships with the politics at Versailles and to blame the government was. As hopes began to dim with the news of political stalemate, news broke of the creation of the National Assembly.

The Storming of the Bastille

The king, who had temporarily withdrawn from sight following the death of his son at the beginning of June, reemerged to meet with the representatives of each of the three estates and propose reforms, including a constitutional monarchy. But Louis XVI refused to accept the now popularly supported National Assembly as a legitimate body, choosing instead to rely on the three estates for advice. He simply did not understand that the choice was no longer his to make. He summoned troops to Versailles and began concentrating soldiers in Paris. Urban dwellers recognized the threat of repression that the troops represented, and crowds decided to meet force with force. To do so, they needed arms themselves, and they knew where to get them.

On 14 July 1789, irate citizens of Paris stormed the Bastille, a royal armory that also served as a prison for a handful of debtors. The storming of the Bastille has become the great symbol in the revolutionary legend of the overthrow of the tyranny and oppression of the old

regime. But it is significant for another reason. It was an expression of the power of the people to take politics into their own hands. Parisians were following the lead of their deputies in Versailles. They had formed a citizen militia, known as the National Guard, and were prepared to defend their concept of justice and law.

The people who stormed the Bastille were not the poor, the unemployed, the criminals, or the urban rabble, as they were portrayed by their detractors. They were bourgeois and petit bourgeois, shopkeepers, guild members, family men and women, who considered it their right to seize arms to protect their interests. The Marquis de Lafayette (1757-1834), a noble beloved of the people because of his participation in the American Revolution, helped organize the National Guard. Under his direction, the militia adopted the tricolor flag as their standard, replacing the fleur-de-lis of the Bourbons.

The king could no longer dictate the terms of the constitution. By their actions, the people in arms had ratified the National Assembly. Louis XVI was forced to yield. Similar uprisings erupted in cities and towns throughout France. National guards in provincial cities modeled themselves after the Parisian militia. Government officials fled their posts and abandoned their responsibilities. Commoners stood ready to fill the power

This painting of the Oath of the Tennis Court is by the Revolution's leading artist, Jacques Louis David. Sieyès sits at a table on which Bailly stands reading the oath. Robespierre is seen clutching his breast in the group behind Sieyès.

This lively amateur painting of the fall of the Bastille is by Claude Cholat, one of the attackers. Tradition has it that Cholat is manning the cannon in the background. The inscription proclaims that the painting is by one of the "Conquerors of the Bastille."

vacuum that now existed. But the Revolution was not just an urban phenomenon. The peasantry had their own grievances and their own way of making a revolution.

The Revolution of the Peasantry

In the spring and early summer of 1789, food shortages drove bands of armed peasants to attack manor houses throughout France. In the areas surrounding Paris and Versailles, peasants destroyed game and devastated the forests where the king and his nobles hunted. The anger reflected in these seemingly isolated events was suspended as the hope grew that the proceedings at Versailles would produce results. Remote as peasant involvement in the drawing up of the cahiers might have been, peasants everywhere expected that aid was at hand.

News of the events of Versailles and then of the revolutionary action in Paris did not reassure rural inhabitants. By the end of June the hope of deliverance from crippling taxes and dues was rapidly fading. The news of the Oath of the Tennis Court and the storming of the Bastille terrified country folk, who saw the actions as evidence of an aristocratic plot that threatened sorely needed reforms. As information moved along postal routes in letters from delegates to their supporters, or news was repeated in the Sunday market gatherings, distortions and exaggerations crept in. It seemed to rural inhabitants that their world was falling apart. Some peasants believed that Paris was in the hands of brigands and that the king and the Estates-General were victims of an aristocratic plot.

This state of affairs was aggravated as increasing numbers of peasants had been pushed off the land to seek employment as transient farm laborers, moving from one area to another with the cycles of sowing and harvesting. Throughout the 1780s the number of peasants without land was increasing steadily. Filthy, poorly dressed, and starving men, women, and children were frightening figures to villagers who feared that the same fate would befall them with the next bad harvest.

Hope gave way to fear. Beginning on 20 July 1789, peasants in different areas of France reacted with a kind of collective hysteria, spreading false rumors of a great conspiracy. Fear gripped whole villages, and in some areas spawned revolt. Just as urban workers had connected their economic hardships to politics, so too did desperate peasants see their plight in political terms. They banded together and marched to the residences of the local nobility, breaking into the chateaus with a single mission in mind: to destroy all legal documents by which nobles claimed payments, dues, and services from local peasants. They drove out the lords and in some cases burned their chateaus, putting an end to the tyranny of the privileged over the countryside.

The overthrow of privileges rooted in a feudal past was not as easy as that. Members of the National Assembly were aghast at the eruption of rural violence. They knew that to stay in power they had to maintain peace. They also knew that to be credible they had to protect property. Peasant destruction of seigneurial claims posed a real dilemma for the bourgeois deputies directing the Revolution. If they gave in to peasant demands, they risked losing aristocratic support and undermining their own ability to control events. If they gave in to the aristocracy, they risked a social revolution in the countryside, which they could not police or repress. Liberal members of the aristocracy cooperated with the bourgeois leaders in finding a solution.

In a dramatic meeting that lasted through the night of 4–5 August 1789, the National Assembly agreed to abolish the principle of privilege. The peasants had won—or thought they had. In the weeks and months ahead, rural people learned they had lost their own prerogatives—the rights to common grazing and gathering—and were expected to buy their way out of their feudal services.

Women on the March

Women participated with men in both urban and rural revolutionary actions. Acting on their own, women were responsible for the most dramatic event of the early years of the Revolution: in October 1789 they forced the king and the royal family to leave Versailles for Paris to deal in person with the problems of the bread supply, high prices, and starvation. Women milling about in the marketplaces of Paris on the morning of 5 October were complaining bitterly about the high cost and shortages of bread. The National Assembly was in session and the National Guards were patrolling the streets of Paris. But these trappings of political change had no impact on the brutal realities of the marketplace.

On the morning of 5 October 1789, six thousand Parisian women marched out of the city toward Versailles. Women, who were in charge of buying food for their families, were most directly in touch with the state of provisioning the capital. When they were unable to buy bread because of shortages or high prices, the situation became intolerable. They were taking their problem to the king with the demand that he solve it. Later in the day, Lafayette, sympathetic to the women's cause, led the Parisian National Guard to Versailles to mediate events. The women were armed with pikes, the simple weapon available to the poorest defender of the Revolution, and they were prepared to use them.

The battle came early the next morning, when the women, tired and cold from waiting all night at the gates of the palace, invaded the royal apartments and chased Marie Antoinette from her bedroom. Several members of the royal guards, hated by the people of Paris for

This engraving from the late eighteenth century shows French country houses ablaze while speeding carriages carry their frightened owners to safety. The peasants attacked and looted the houses of the gentry and burned the rolls of feudal duties.

A contemporary print of the women of Paris advancing on Versailles. The determined marchers are shown waving pikes and dragging an artillery piece. The women were hailed as heroines of the Revolution.

alleged insults against the tricolor cockade, were killed by the angry women, who decapitated them and mounted their heads on pikes. A shocked Louis XVI agreed to return with the crowd to Paris. The crowd cheered Louis' decision, which briefly reestablished his personal popularity. But as monarch, he had been humiliated at the hands of women of the capital. "The baker, the baker's wife, and the baker's son" were forced to return to Paris that very day. Louis XVI was now captive to the Revolution, whose efforts to form a constitutional monarchy he purported to support.

The Revolution Threatened

The disciplined deliberations of committees intent on fashioning a constitutional monarchy replaced the passion and fervor of revolutionary oratory. The National, or Constituent, Assembly divided France into new administrative units—*départements*—for the purpose of establishing better control over municipal governments. Along with new administrative trappings, the government promoted its own rituals. On 14 July 1790, militias

from each of the newly created eighty-three départements of France came together in Paris to celebrate the first anniversary of the storming of the Bastille. A new national holiday was born and with it a sense of devotion and patriotism for the new France liberated by the Revolution. In spite of these unifying elements, however, the newly achieved revolutionary consensus showed signs of breaking down.

On 2 November 1798 Church lands were nationalized. Three months later, legislation dissolved all monasteries and convents, except for those that provided aid to the poor or that served as educational institutions. As the French church was stripped of its lands, Pope Pius VI (1775–99) denounced the principles of the Revolution. In July 1790 the government approved the Civil Constitution of the Clergy: priests now became the equivalent of paid agents of the state. By requiring an oath of loyalty to the state from all practicing priests, the National Assembly created a new arena for dissent: Catholics were forced to choose to embrace or reject the Revolution. Many "nonjuring" priests who refused to take the oath went into hiding.

The wedge driven between the Catholic church and revolutionary France allowed a mass-based counterrevolution to emerge. Aristocratic émigrés who had fled the country because of their opposition to the Revolution were languishing because of lack of a popular base. From his headquarters in Turin, the king's younger brother, the comte d'Artois, was attempting to incite a civil war in France. When the revolutionaries decided to attack the Church, not just as a landed and privileged institution but also as a religious one, the counterrevolution rapidly expanded.

The Constitution of 1791, completed after over two years of deliberations, established a constitutional monarchy with a ministerial executive power answerable to a legislative assembly. Louis XVI, formerly the divinely anointed ruler of France, was now "Louis, by the grace of God and the constitutional law of the state, King of the French." In proclaiming his acceptance of the constitution, Louis expressed the sentiments of many when he said, "The end of the revolution is come. It is time that order be reestablished so that the constitution may receive the support now most necessary to it; it is time to settle the opinion of Europe concerning the destiny of France, and to show that French men are worthy of being free."

The Constitution of 1791 marked the triumph of the principles of the Revolution. But months before the ink was dry on the final document, the actions of the king doomed the new constitution to failure. To be successful, constitutional monarchy required a king worthy of honor and respect. Louis XVI seemed to be giving the revolutionaries what they wanted by cooperating with the framers of the constitution. Yet late one night in June 1791, Louis XVI, Marie Antoinette, and their children disguised themselves as commoners, crept out of the royal apartments in the Tuileries Palace, and fled Paris. Louis intended to leave France to join foreign forces opposing the Revolution at Metz. He got as far as Varennes, where he was captured by soldiers of the National Guards and brought back to a shocked Paris. The king had abandoned the Revolution. Although he was not put to death for another year and a half, he was more than ever a prisoner of the Revolution. The monarchy was effectively finished as part of a political solution and with its demise went liberal hopes for a constitutional settlement. The defection of the king was certainly serious, but other problems plagued the revolutionary government, notably the fiscal crisis coupled with inflation, and foreign war.

In order to establish its seriousness and legitimacy, the National Assembly had been willing in 1789 to absorb the debts of the old regime. The new government could not sell titles and offices, as the king had done to deal with financial problems, but it did confiscate

The fleeing Louis XVI and his family were apprehended at Varennes in June 1791.

Church property. In addition, it issued treasury bonds in the form of *assignats* in order to raise money. The assignats soon assumed the status of banknotes, and by spring 1790 they became compulsory legal tender. Initially they were to be backed by land confiscated from the Church and now being sold by the state. But the need for money soon outran the value of the land available and the government continued to print assignats according to its needs. Depreciation of French currency in international markets and inflation at home resulted. The revolutionary government found itself in a situation that in certain respects was worse than that experienced by Louis XVI before the calling of the Estates-General. Assignat-induced inflation produced a sharp decline in the fortunes of bourgeois investors living on fixed incomes. Rising prices meant increased misery for workers and peasants.

New counterrevolutionary groups were becoming frustrated with revolutionary policies. Throughout the winter and spring of 1791–92 people rioted and demanded that prices be fixed, as the assignat dropped to less than half of its face value. Peasants refused to sell their crops for the worthless paper. Hoarding further drove up prices. Angry crowds turned to pillaging, rioting, and murders, which became more frequent as the value of the currency declined and prices rose.

Foreign war beginning in the fall of 1791 also challenged stability. Some moderate political leaders welcomed war as a blessing in disguise, since it could divert the attention of the masses away from problems at home and could promote loyalty to the Revolution. Others envisioned war as a great crusade to bring revolutionary principles to oppressed peoples throughout Europe. The king and queen, trapped by the Revolution, saw war as their only hope of liberation. Louis XVI could be rightfully restored as the leader of a France defeated by the sovereigns of Europe. Others opposed the war, believing it would destabilize the Revolution. France must solve its problems at home, they argued, before fighting a foreign enemy. Louis, however, encouraged those ministers and advisers eager for battle. In April 1792, France declared war against Austria.

The first stage of the French Revolution ended in the summer of 1792 with the prospect of increased violence both from abroad in international war and at home in mounting civil strife. In its first three years, however, the Revolution had accomplished great things by abolishing aristocratic privilege, by affirming the political principles of liberty, equality, and fraternity, and by asserting constitutional prerogatives of royal accountability. The attempt at constitutional monarchy had failed, but the contours of a new political universe took shape according to bourgeois definitions of political participation, property, and civil liberties. As women and men of all classes discovered between 1789 and 1792, there was little certainty about what political solutions lay ahead, but there was no doubt there could be no turning back.

Experimenting with Democracy: The Revolution's Second Stage, 1792–1799

The French Revolution was a school for the French nation. A political universe populated by individual citizens replaced the eighteenth-century world of subjects loyal to their king. This new construction of politics in which all individuals were equal ran counter to prevailing ideas about collective identities defined in guilds and orders. People on all levels of society learned politics by doing it. In the beginning, experience helped. The elites, both noble and bourgeois, had served in government and administration. But the rules of the game under the old regime had been very different, with birth determining power.

After 1789, all men were declared free and equal, in opportunity if not in rights. Men of ability and talent, who had served as middlemen for the privileged elite under the old regime, now claimed power as their due. Many of them were lawyers, educated in the rules and regulations of the society of orders. They experienced firsthand the problems of the exercise of power in the old regime and had their own ideas about reform. But the school of the Revolution did not remain the domain of a special class. Women demanded their places. Workers seized their rights. And because of the inherent contradictions of representation and participation, experimenting with democracy led to outcomes that did not look very democratic at all.

Declaring Political Rights

The Constitution of 1791 was a statement of faith in a progressive constitutional monarchy. A king accountable to an elected parliamentary body would lead France into a prosperous and just age. The constitution acknowledged the people's sovereignty as the source of political power. It also enshrined the principle of property by making voting rights dependent on property ownership. All men might be equal before the law, but by the Constitution of 1791 only wealthy men had the right to vote for representatives and hold office.

All titles of nobility were abolished. In the early period of the Revolution, civil liberties were extended to Protestants and Jews, who had been persecuted under the old regime. Previously excluded groups were granted freedom of thought and worship and full civil liberties. More reluctantly, slavery in the colonies was outlawed in 1794. Slave unrest in Saint Domingue (modern-day Haiti) had coincided with the political conflicts of the Revolution and exploded in rebellion in 1791, driving the revolutionaries in Paris to support black independence although it was at odds with French colonial interests. Led by Toussaint L'Ouverture (1743–1803), black rebels worked to found an independent Haitian state, which was declared in 1804. But the concept of equality with regard to race remained incompletely integrated with revolutionary principles, and Napoleon reestablished slavery in the French colonies in 1802.

Men were the subject of these newly defined rights. No references to women or their rights appear in the constitutions or the official Declaration of Rights. But women were critical actors in the Revolution from its very inception, and their presence shaped and directed the outcome of events, as the women's march to Versailles in 1789 made clear. The Marquis de Condorcet (1743–94), elected to the Legislative Assembly in 1791, was one of the first to chastise the revolutionaries for overlooking the political rights of women who, he pointedly observed, were half of the human race. "Either no individual of the human race has genuine rights, or else all have the same; and he who votes against the right of another, whatever the religion, color, or sex of that other, has henceforth abjured his own." Condorcet argued forcefully but unsuccessfully for the right of women to be educated. Women's talents, he warned, were slumbering under the ignorance of neglect.

The revolutionaries had declared that liberty was a natural and inviolable right, a universal right that was extended to all with the overthrow of a despotic monarch and a privileged elite. The principle triumphed in religious toleration. Yet the revolutionary concept of liberty foundered on the divergent claims of excluded groups of workers, women, and slaves, who demanded full participation in the world of politics. In 1792 revolutionaries confronted the contradictions inherent in their political beliefs of liberty and equality now challenged in the midst of social upheaval and foreign war. In response, the Revolution turned to more radical measures in order to survive.

The Second Revolution: The Revolution of the People

The first revolution of 1789 through the beginning of 1792 was based on liberty—the liberty to compete, to own, and to succeed. The second revolution, which began in 1792, took equality as its rallying cry. This was the revolution of the working people of French cities. The popular movement that spearheaded political action in 1792 was committed to equality of rights in a way not characteristic of the leaders of the Revolution of 1789. Urban workers were not benefiting from the Revolution, but they had come to believe in their own power as political beings. Organized on the local level into sections, craft workers in cities identified themselves as

Slaves revolting against the French in Saint Domingue in 1791. Napoleon sent an army to restore colonial rule in 1799, but yellow fever decimated the French soldiers and the rebels defeated the weakened French army in 1803.

DECLARATION OF THE RIGHTS OF MAN AND CITIZEN

■ *Sounding a refrain similar to the American Declaration of Independence (1776), the* Declaration of the Rights of Man and Citizen *was adopted by the National Assembly on 26 August 1789. The document amalgamated a variety of Enlightenment ideas drawn from the works of political philosophy, including those of Locke and Montesquieu. The attention to property, which was defined as "sacred and inviolable," rivaled liberty as a "natural" and "imprescriptible" right of man.*

1. Men are born and remain free and equal in rights. Social distinctions may be founded only upon the general good.

2. The aim of all political association is the preservation of the natural and imprescriptible rights of man. These rights are liberty, property, security, and resistance to oppression.

3. The principle of all sovereignty resides essentially in the nation. No body nor individual may exercise any authority which does not proceed directly from the nation.

4. Liberty consists in the freedom to do everything which injures no one else; hence the exercise of the natural rights of each man has no limits except those which assure to the other members of the society the enjoyment of the same rights. These limits can only be determined by law.

5. Law can only prohibit such actions as are hurtful to society. Nothing may be prevented which is not forbidden by law, and no one may be forced to do anything not provided for by law.

6. Law is the expression of the general will. Every citizen has a right to participate personally, or through his representative, in its formation. It must be the same for all, whether it protects or punishes. All citizens, being equal in the eyes of the law, are equally eligible to all dignities and to all public positions and occupations, according to their abilities, and without distinction except that of their virtues and talents.

7. No person shall be accused, arrested, or imprisoned except in the cases and according to the forms prescribed by law. Any one soliciting, transmitting, executing, or causing to be executed, any arbitrary order, shall be punished. But any citizen summoned or arrested in virtue of the law shall submit without delay, as resistance constitutes an offense.

8. The law shall provide for such punishments only as are strictly and obviously necessary . . .

9. As all persons are held innocent until they shall have been declared guilty, if arrest shall be deemed indispensable, all harshness not essential to the securing of the prisoner's person shall be severely repressed by law.

10. No one shall be disquieted on account of his opinions, including his religious views, provided their manifestation does not disturb the public order established by law.

11. The free communication of ideas and opinions is one of the most precious of the rights of man. Every citizen may, accordingly, speak, write, and print with freedom, but shall be responsible for such abuses of this freedom as shall be defined by law.

12. The security of the rights of man and of the citizen requires public military forces. These forces are, therefore, established for the good of all and not for the personal advantage of those to whom they shall be intrusted.

13. A common contribution is essential for the maintenance of the public forces and for the cost of administration. This should be equitably distributed among all the citizens in proportion to their means.

14. All the citizens have a right to decide, either personally or by their representatives, as to the necessity of the public contribution; to grant this freely; to know to what uses it is put; and to fix the proportion, the mode of assessment and of collection and the duration of the taxes.

15. Society has the right to require of every public agent an account of his administration.

Declaration of the Rights of Man and Citizen

16. A society in which the observance of the law is not assured, nor the separation of powers defined, has no constitution at all.

17. Since property is an inviolable and sacred right, no one shall be deprived thereof except where public necessity, legally determined, shall clearly demand it, and then only on condition that the owner shall have been previously and equitably indemnified.

sans-culottes, literally those who did not wear knee breeches, to distinguish themselves from the privileged elite.

On 10 August 1792, the people of Paris invaded the Tuileries Palace, chanting their demands for "Equality!" and "Nation!" Love and respect for the king had vanished. What the people of Paris demanded now was universal manhood suffrage and participation in a popular democracy. The self-designated sans-culottes were the working men and women of Paris. Some were wealthier than others, some were wage earners, but all shared a common identity as consumers in the marketplace. They wanted government power to be decentralized, with neighborhoods ruling themselves through sectional organizations. When they invaded the Tuileries, the sans-culottes did so in the name of the people. They saw themselves as patriots whose duty it was to brush the monarchy aside. The people were now a force to be reckoned with and feared.

"Terror Is the Order of the Day"

Political factions characterized revolutionary politics from the start. The terms *Left* and *Right*, which came to represent opposite ends of the political spectrum, originated in a description of where people sat in the Assembly in relation to the podium. Political designations were refined in successive parliamentary bodies. The Convention was the legislative body elected in September 1792, which succeeded the Legislative Assembly by the latter's own decree and had as its charge determining the best form of government after the collapse of the monarchy. On 21 September 1792, monarchy was abolished in France; the following day the Republic, France's first, came into being. Members of the Convention conducted the trial of Louis XVI for treason and

pronounced the death sentence for his execution on the guillotine in January 1793.

The various political factions of the Convention were described in terms borrowed from geography. The Mountain, sitting in the upper benches on the left, was made up of members of the Jacobin Club (named for its meeting place in an abandoned monastery). The Jacobins were the most radical element, supporting democratic solutions and speaking in favor of the cause of people in the streets. The Plain held the moderates, who were concerned with maintaining public order against popular unrest. Many members of the Plain came to be called Girondins in the mistaken belief that they originated in the Gironde département of France.

Both Girondins and Jacobins were from the middle ranks of the bourgeoisie, and both groups were dedicated to the principles of the Revolution. At first the two groups were more similar than different. Although controlling the ministries, the Girondins began to lose their hold on the Revolution and the war. The renewed European war fragmented the democratic movement, and the Girondins, unable to control violence at home, saw political control slipping away. They became prisoners of the Revolution when eighty thousand armed Parisians surrounded the National Convention in June 1793.

Girondin power had been eroding in the critical months between August 1792 and June 1793. A new leader was working quietly and effectively behind the scenes to weld a partnership between the popular movement of sans-culottes and the Jacobins. He was Maximilien Robespierre (1758–94), leader of the Mountain and the Jacobin Club. Robespierre was typical of the new breed of revolutionary politicians. Only 31 years old in 1789, he wrote mediocre poems and attended the local provincial academy to discuss the latest

DECLARATION OF THE RIGHTS OF WOMAN AND CITIZEN

■ *"Woman, wake up!" In such a manner did Olympe de Gouges (d. 1793), the daughter of a butcher and a self-educated playwright, address French women in 1791. Aware that women were being denied the new rights of liberty and property extended to all men by the* Declaration of the Rights of Man and Citizen, *Gouges composed her own* Declaration of the Rights of Woman and Citizen, *modeled article for article on the 1789 document. In addition to defending the political rights of women, Gouges spoke out for the freedom of slaves. Persecuted for her political beliefs, she foreshadowed her own demise at the hands of revolutionary justice in article 10 of her* Declaration: *". . . woman has the right to mount the scaffold; she must equally have the right to mount the rostrum, provided her demonstrations do not disturb the legally established public order." The Declaration of the Rights of Woman and Citizen became an important document in women's demands for political rights in the nineteenth century, and Gouges herself became a feminist hero.*

Article I
Woman is born free and lives equal to man in her rights. Social distinctions can be based only on the common utility.

Article II
The purpose of any political association is the conservation of the natural and imprescriptible rights of woman and man; these rights are liberty, property, security, and especially resistance to oppression.

Article III
The principle of all sovereignty rests essentially with the nation, which is nothing but the union of woman and man; no body and no individual can exercise any authority which does not come expressly from it [the nation].

Article IV
Liberty and justice consist of restoring all that belongs to others; thus, the only limits on the exercise of the natural rights of woman are perpetual male tyranny; these limits are to be reformed by the laws of nature and reason.

Article V
Laws of nature and reason proscribe all acts harmful to society; everything which is not prohibited by these wise and divine laws cannot be prevented, and no one can be constrained to do what they do not command.

Article VI
The law must be the expression of the general will; all female and male citizens must contribute either personally or through their representatives to its formation; it must be the same for all: male and female citizens, being equal in the eyes of the law, must be equally admitted to all honors, positions, and public employment according to their capacity and without other distinctions besides those of their virtues and talents.

Article VII
No woman is an exception; she is accused, arrested, and detained in cases determined by law. Women, like men, obey this rigorous law.

Article VIII
The law must establish only those penalties that are strictly and obviously necessary. . . .

Article IX
Once any woman is declared guilty, complete rigor is [to be] exercised by the law.

Article X
No one is to be disquieted for his very basic opinions; woman has the right to mount the scaffold; she must equally have the right to mount the rostrum, provided that her demonstrations do not disturb the legally established public order.

Article XI
The free communication of thoughts and opinions is one of the most precious rights of woman, since that liberty assures the recognition of children by their fathers. Any female citizen thus may say freely, I am the mother of a child which belongs to you, without being forced by a barbarous prejudice to hide the truth; [an exception may be made] to respond to the abuse of this liberty in cases determined by the law.

DECLARATION OF THE RIGHTS OF WOMAN AND CITIZEN

Article XII

The guarantee of the rights of woman and the female citizen implies a major benefit; this guarantee must be instituted for the advantage of all, and not for the particular benefit of those to whom it is entrusted.

Article XIII

For the support of the public force and the expenses of administration, the contributions of woman and man are equal; she shares all the duties [*corvées*] and all the painful tasks; therefore, she must have the same share in the distribution of positions, employment, offices, honors and jobs [*industrie*].

Article XIV

Female and male citizens have the right to verify, either by themselves or through their representatives, the necessity of the public contribution. This can only apply to women if they are granted an equal share, not only of wealth, but also of public administration, and in the determination of the proportion, the base, the collection, and the duration of the tax.

Article XV

The collectivity of women, joined for tax purposes to the aggregate of men, has the right to demand an accounting of his administration from any public agent.

Article XVI

No society has a constitution without the guarantee of rights and the separation of powers; the constitution is null if the majority of individuals comprising the nation have not cooperated in drafting it.

Article XVII

Property belongs to both sexes whether united or separate; for each it is an inviolable and sacred right; no one can be deprived of it, since it is the true patrimony of nature, unless the legally determined public need obviously dictates it, and then only with a just and prior indemnity.

ideas, when he was not practicing law in his hometown of Arras. Elected to the Estates-General, he joined the Jacobin Club and quickly rose to become its leader. He was willing to take controversial stands on issues. Unlike most of his fellow members of the Mountain, including his rival, the popular orator Georges-Jacques Danton (1759–94), he opposed the war in 1792. Although neither an original thinker nor a compelling orator, Robespierre discovered with the Revolution that he was a stunning political tactician. He gained a following and learned how to manipulate it. It was he who engineered the Jacobin replacement of the Girondins as leaders of the government.

Robespierre's chance for real power came when he assumed leadership of the Committee of Public Safety in July 1793. Due to the threat of internal anarchy and external war, the elected body, the National Convention, yielded political control to the twelve-man Committee of Public Safety that ruled dictatorially under Robespierre's direction. The Great Committee, as it was known at the time, orchestrated the Reign of Terror (1793–94), a period of systematic state repres-

sion that meted out justice in the people's name. Summary trials by specially created revolutionary tribunals were followed by the swift execution of the guilty under the blade of the guillotine. (See Special Feature, "The Guillotine and Revolutionary Justice," pp. 670–671.)

Influenced by the *Social Contract* (1762) and other writings of Jean-Jacques Rousseau, Robespierre believed that sovereignty resided with the people. For him individual wills and even individual rights did not matter when faced with the will of the nation. As head of the Great Committee, Robespierre oversaw a revolutionary machinery dedicated to economic regulation, massive military mobilization, and a punitive system of revolutionary justice characterized by the slogan, "Terror is the Order of the Day." Militant revolutionary committees and revolutionary tribunals were established in the départements to identify traitors and to mete out the harsh justice that struck hardest against those members of the bourgeoisie who were perceived as opponents of the government. The civil war, which raged most violently in the Vendée in the west of France, consisted often of primitive massacres that sent

In this portrayal of the execution of Louis XVI, one of the executioners displays the erstwhile king's severed head to the crowd.

*T*he Guillotine and Revolutionary Justice

In the sultry summer days of 1792, Parisians found a new way to entertain themselves. They attended executions. French men, women, and children were long accustomed to watching criminals being tortured and put to death in public view. During the old regime, spectators could enjoy the variety of a number of methods: drawing and quartering, strangling, or hanging. Decapitation, reputedly a less painful death, was a privilege reserved for nobles sentenced for capital crimes. The Revolution extended this formerly aristocratic privilege to all crimi-

nals condemned to death. What especially attracted people into public squares in the third year of the Revolution was the introduction of a novel method of decapitation. In 1792 the new instrument of death, the guillotine, became the center of the spectacle of revolutionary justice.

The guillotine promised to eliminate the suffering of its victims. Axes, swords, and sabers—the traditional tools of decapitation and dismemberment—were messy and undependable, producing slow and bloody ordeals when inept and drunken executioners missed their

mark or victims flinched at the fatal moment. The design of the guillotine took all of this into account. On its easel-like wooden structure, victims, lying on their stomachs, were held in place with straps and a pillory. Heavy pulleys guaranteed that the sharp blade would fall efficiently from its great height. A basket was placed at the base of the blade to catch the severed head; another was used to slide the headless body for removal through the base of the scaffolding. In place of unintended torture and gore, the guillotine was devised as a humanitarian instrument to guarantee swift and painless death.

It should have been called the Louisette, after its inventor, Dr. Antoine Louis. In what now seems a dubious honor, the new machine was named instead after its greatest supporter, Dr. Joseph Ignace Guillotin, a delegate to the National Assembly. Both Guillotin and Louis were medical doctors, men of science influenced by Enlightenment ideas and committed to the Revolution's elimination of the cruelty of older forms of punishment. In the spirit of scientific experimentation, Louis' invention was tested on sheep, cadavers, and then convicted thieves. In 1792 it was used for the first time against another class of offenders, political prisoners.

Early in the Revolution, the Marquis de Condorcet, philosophe and mathematician, had opposed capital punishment with the argument that the state did not have the right to take life. Ironically, Maximilien Robespierre, future architect of the Reign of Terror, was one of the few revolutionaries who agreed with Condorcet. But those who favored justice by execution of the state's enemies prevailed. The revolutionary hero and associate of the radical Jacobins, Jean Paul Marat (1743–93), who was himself stabbed to death in his bathtub, advocated the state's use of violence against its enemies: "In order to ensure public tranquillity, 200,000 heads must be cut off." By the end of 1792, as revolution and civil war swept over France, eighty-three identical guillotines were constructed and installed in each of the départements of France. For the next two years, the guillotine's great blade was rhythmically raised and lowered daily in public squares all over France. In the name of the Revolution, the "axe of the people" dispatched over 50,000 victims.

Although intended as a humanitarian instrument, the guillotine became the symbol of all that was arbitrary and repressive about a revolution run amok. Day and night in Paris, the Revolutionary Tribunal delivered the death sentence to the "enemies of the people." Most of those executed were members of what had been the Third Estate: members of the bourgeoisie, workers, peasants. Only 15 percent of the condemned were nobles and priests. During the Terror, the guillotine was sometimes used to settle old scores. Sans-culottes turned in their neighbors, sometimes over long-standing grievances that owed more to spite than politics. The most fanatical revolutionaries had fantasies that guillotines were about to be erected on every street corner to dispense with hoarders and traitors. Others suggested that guillotines be made portable so that by putting justice on wheels, it could be taken directly to the people.

As usual, Paris set the style. The most famous of the guillotines stood on the Place du Carrousel, deliberately placed in front of the royal palace of the Tuileries. It was eventually moved to the larger Place de la Révolution in order to accommodate the growing numbers of spectators. Famous victims drew especially large crowds. The revolutionary drama took on the trappings of a spectacle, as hawkers sold toy guillotines, miniature pikes, and liberty caps as souvenirs, along with the usual food and drink. Troops attended these events, but not to control the crowd. Members of the National Guard in formation, their backs to the people, faced the stage of the scaffold. They, like the citizenry, were there to witness the birth of a new nation and, by their presence, to give legitimacy to the event. The crowd entered into the ritual, cheering the victim's last words and demanding that the executioner hold high the severed head. In the new political culture death was a festival.

For two centuries, Western societies have debated the legitimacy of the death sentence and have periodically considered the relative merits of the guillotine, the gas chamber, and the electric chair. For the French, the controversy temporarily ceased in 1794, when people were convinced that justice had gotten out of hand and that they had had enough. For the time being, the government put an end to capital punishment. The guillotine would return. But at the height of its use between 1792 and 1794, it had played a unique role in forging a new system of justice: the guillotine had been the great leveler. In the ideology of democracy, people were equal—in death as well as in life. The guillotine came to be popularly known as the "scythe of equality." It killed king and commoner alike.

In this German caricature (1814), called the "Corpse Head," Napoleon's face is composed of his prisoners, living and slain. The epaulet is his own blood-stained hand.

year at the Military Academy in Paris, and received a commission as a second lieutenant of artillery in January 1786.

The Revolution changed everything for him. It made new posts available when aristocratic generals defected and crossed over to the enemy side both before and after the execution of the king. The Revolution also created great opportunities for military men to test their mettle.

Foreign war and civil war required military leaders devoted to the Revolution. Forced to flee Corsica because he had sided with the Jacobins, Bonaparte crushed Parisian protesters who rioted against the Directory in 1795. The revolutionary wars had begun in 1792 as wars to liberate humanity in the name of liberty, equality, and fraternity. Yet concerns for power, territory, and riches replaced earlier French concerns with defense of the nation and of the Revolution. This aggrandizement was nowhere more evident than in the Egyptian campaign of 1798, in which Napoleon Bon-

aparte headed an expedition whose goal was to enrich France by hastening the collapse of the Turkish Empire, crippling British trade routes, and handicapping Russian interests in the region. With Napoleon's highly publicized campaigns in Egypt and Syria, the war left the European theater and moved to the east, leaving behind the original revolutionary ideals.

The Egyptian campaign, which was in reality a disaster, made Napoleon a hero at home. Above all, his victories in the Italian campaign in 1796–97 launched his political career. As he extended French rule into central Italy, he became the embodiment of revolutionary values and energy. In 1799 he readily joined a conspiracy that pulled down the Directory, the government he had earlier preserved, and became the First Consul of a triumvirate of consuls.

Napoleon set out to secure his position of power by eliminating his enemies on the Left and weakening those on the Right. He guaranteed the security of property acquired in the Revolution, a move that undercut the royalists, who wanted to return property to its original owners. Through policing forces and special criminal courts, law and order prevailed and civil war subsided. The First Consul promised a balanced budget and appeared to deliver it. Bonaparte spoke of healing the nation's wounds, especially those opened by religious grievances caused by dechristianization during the Revolution. Realizing the importance of religion in maintaining domestic peace, Napoleon reestablished relations with the pope in 1801 in the Concordat, which recognized Catholicism as the religion of the French and restored the Roman Catholic hierarchy.

Napoleon's popularity as First Consul flowed from his military and political successes and his religious reconciliation. He had come to power in 1799 by appealing for the support of the army. In 1802 Napoleon decided to extend his power by calling for a plebiscite in which he asked the electorate to vote him First Consul for life. Public support was overwhelming. An electoral landslide gave Napoleon greater political power than any of his Bourbon predecessors.

War and More War

Napoleon was at war or preparing for war during his entire reign. His military successes, real and apparent, before 1799 had been crucial in his bid for political power. By 1802, he had signed favorable treaties with both Austria and Great Britain. He appeared to deliver a lasting peace and to establish France as the dominant power in Europe. But the peace was short-lived. In 1803 France embarked on an eleven-year period of continuous war. Under Napoleon's command, the French army delivered defeat after defeat to the European powers. Austria fell in 1805, Prussia in 1806, and the Russian armies of Alexander I were defeated at Friedland in 1807. In 1808 Napoleon invaded Spain in order to drive out British expeditionary forces intent on invading France. Spain became a satellite kingdom of France although the conflict continued.

Britain was the one exception to the string of Napoleonic victories. Napoleon initially considered sending a French fleet to invade the island nation. Lacking the strength necessary to achieve this, he turned to economic warfare and blockaded European ports against British trade. Beginning in 1806, the Continental System, as the blockade was known, erected a structure of protection for French manufactures in all continental European markets. The British responded to the tariff walls and boycotts with a naval blockade that succeeded in cutting French commerce off from its Atlantic markets. The Continental System did not prove to be the decisive policy that Napoleon had planned: the British economy was not broken and the French economy did not flourish when faced with restricted resources and the persistence of a black market in smuggled goods.

Still, by 1810 the French leader was master of the Continent. French armies had extended revolutionary reforms and legal codes outside France and brought with them civil equality and religious toleration. They had also drained defeated countries of their resources and had inflicted the horrors of war with armies of occupation, forced billeting, and pillage. Napoleon's empire extended across Europe, with only a diminished Austria, Prussia, and Russia remaining independent. He placed his relatives and friends on the thrones of the new satellite kingdoms of Italy, Naples, Westphalia, Holland, and Spain.

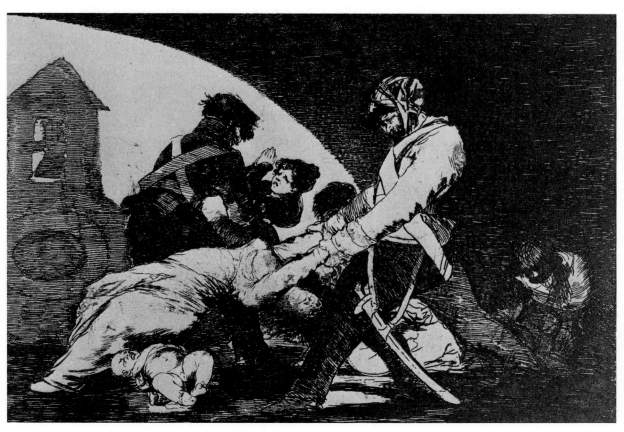

This engraving, from the series "Disasters of War" by Francisco Goya, depicts the horrors of war. The series was inspired by Napoleon's invasion and occupation of Spain from 1808 to 1813.

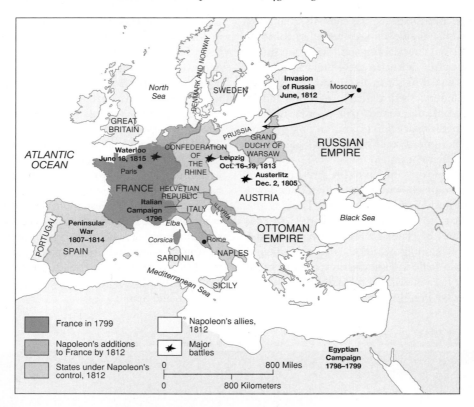

Napoleon's Empire

Peace at Home

Napoleon measured domestic prosperity in terms of the stability of his reign. Through the 1802 plebiscite that voted him First Consul for life, he maintained the charade of constitutional rule, while he ruled as virtual dictator. In 1804, he abandoned all pretense and had himself proclaimed emperor of the French. He staged his own coronation and that of his wife Josephine at the cathedral of Notre Dame de Paris.

Secure in his regime, surrounded by a new nobility that he created based on military achievement and talent, and that he rewarded with honors, Napoleon set about implementing sweeping reforms in every area of government. He recognized the importance of science for both industry and war. The Revolution had removed an impediment to the development of a national market by creating a uniform system of weights and measures—the metric system, which was established by 1799. But Napoleon felt the need to go further. To assure French predominance in scientific research and application, Napoleon became a patron of science, supporting important work in the areas of physics and

chemistry. Building for the future, Napoleon made science a pillar in the new structure of higher education.

The Directory had restored French prosperity through stabilization of the currency, fiscal reform, and support of industry. Napoleon's contribution to the French economy was the much needed reform of the tax system. He authorized the creation of a central banking system. French industries flourished under the protection of the state. The blockade forced the development of new domestic crops like beet-sugar and indigo, which became substitutes for colonial products. Napoleon extended the infrastructure of roads so necessary for the expansion of national and European markets.

Perhaps his greatest achievement was the codification of law, a task begun under the Revolution. Combined with economic reforms, the new Napoleonic Code facilitated trade and the development of commerce by regularizing contractual relations and protecting property rights and equality before the law. The civil laws of the new code carved out a family policy characterized by hierarchy and subordination.

Married women were neither independent nor equal to men in ownership of property, custody of children, and access to divorce. Women also lacked political rights. In the Napoleonic Code, women, like children, were subjected to paternal authority. The Napoleonic philosophy of woman's place is well captured in an anecdote told by Madame Germaine de Staël (1766–1817), a leading intellectual of her day. As the daughter of Jacques Necker, the Swiss financier and adviser to Louis XVI at the time of the Revolution, she had been educated in Enlightenment ideas from an early age. On finding herself seated next to Napoleon at a dinner party, she asked him what was very likely a self-interested question: whom did he consider the greatest woman, alive or dead? Napoleon had no name to give her but he responded without pausing, "The one who has had the most children."

Napoleon turned his prodigious energies to every aspect of French life. He encouraged the arts, while creating a police force. He had monuments built but did not forget about sewers. He organized French administrative life in a fashion that has endured. In place of the popular democratic movement, he offered his own singular authority. In place of elections, clubs, and free associations, he gave France plebiscites and army service. To be sure, Napoleon believed in constitutions but he thought they should be "short and obscure." For Napoleon the great problem of democracy was its unpredictability. His regime solved that problem by eliminating choices.

Decline and Fall

Militarily, Napoleon went too far. The first cracks in the French facade began to show in the Peninsular War (1808–14) with Spain, as Spanish guerrilla tactics proved costly for French troops. But Napoleon's biggest mistake, the one that shattered the myth of his invincibility, occurred when he decided to invade Russia in June 1812. Having decisively defeated Russian forces in 1807, Napoleon entered into a peace treaty with Tsar Alexander I that guaranteed Russian allegiance to French policies. But Alexander repudiated the Continental System in 1810 and appeared to be preparing for his own war against France. Napoleon seized the initiative, sure that he could defeat Russian forces once again. With an army of 500,000 men, Napoleon moved deep into Russia in the summer of 1812. The tsar's troops fell back in retreat, and when Napoleon and his men entered Moscow in September, they found a city in flames. The people of Moscow had destroyed their own city to deprive the French troops of winter quarters. Napoleon's men found themselves facing a severe Russian winter without overcoats, without supplies, and without food. The starving and frostbitten French army was forced into retreat. Fewer than 100,000 men made it back to France.

The empire began to crumble. Britain, unbowed by the Continental System, remained Napoleon's sworn enemy. Prussia joined Great Britain, Sweden, Russia, and Austria in opposing France anew. In the Battle of Nations at Leipzig in October 1813, France was forced to retreat. Napoleon refused a negotiated peace and fought on until the following March, when the victorious allies marched down the streets of Paris and occupied the French capital. Deserted by his allies, Napoleon abdicated in April 1814, in favor of his young son, the titular king of Rome (1811–32). When the allies

The Reign of Napoleon

1799	Napoleon establishes consulate; becomes First Consul
1801	Napoleon reestablishes relations with pope; restores Roman Catholic hierarchy
1802	Plebiscite declares Napoleon First Consul for life
1804	Napoleon proclaims himself Emperor of the French
1806	Continental System implemented
1808–14	France engaged in Peninsular War with Spain
June 1812	Napoleon invades Russia
September 1812	French army reaches Moscow, is trapped by Russian winter
October 1813	Napoleon defeated at Battle of Nations at Leipzig
March 1814	Napoleon abdicates and goes into exile on island of Elba
March 1815	Napoleon escapes Elba and attempts to reclaim power
15 June 1815	Napoleon is defeated at Waterloo and exiled to island of Saint Helena

This 1835 painting by De Boisdenier depicts the suffering of Napoleon's Grand Army on the retreat from Moscow. The Germans were to meet a similar fate over one hundred years later when they invaded Russia without adequate supplies for the harsh winter.

refused to accept the young "Napoleon II," the French called upon the Bourbon Louis XVIII and crowned him king. Napoleon was then exiled to the Mediterranean island of Elba.

Still it was not quite the end for Napoleon. While the European heads of state sat in Vienna trying to determine the future of Europe and France's place in it, Napoleon returned from his exile on Elba. On 15 June 1815, Napoleon once again and for the final time confronted the European powers in one of the most famous battles in history—Waterloo. With 125,000 loyal French forces, Napoleon seemed within hours of reestablishing the French empire in Europe, but the defeat of his forces was decisive. Napoleon's return proved brief—it lasted only one hundred days. He was exiled to the island of Saint Helena in the South Atlantic. For the next six years, Napoleon wrote his memoirs under the watchful eyes of his British jailors. He died on 5 May 1821.

The period of revolution and empire from 1789 to 1815 radically changed the face of France. A new, more cohesive elite of bourgeois and nobles emerged, sharing power based on wealth and status. Ownership of land remained a defining characteristic of both old and new elites. A new state bureaucracy, built on the foundations of the old, expanded and centralized state power.

The people as sovereign now legitimated political power. Napoleon at his most imperial never doubted that he owed his existence to the people. In this sense, Napoleon was the king of the Revolution—an apparently contradictory fusion of old forms and new ideology. Napoleon channeled democratic forces into enthusiasm for empire. He learned his lessons from the failure of the Bourbon monarchy and the politicians of the Revolution. For sixteen years Napoleon successfully reconciled the old regime with the new France. Yet he could not resolve the essential problem of democracy: the relationship between the will of the people and the exercise of political power. The picture in 1815 was not dramatically different from the situation in 1789. The Revolution might be over, but changes fueled by the revolutionary tradition were just beginning. The struggle for a workable democratic culture recurred in France for another century and elsewhere in Europe through the twentieth century.

SUGGESTIONS FOR FURTHER READING

THE CRISIS OF THE OLD REGIME IN FRANCE, 1715–1788

C. B. A. Behrens, *Society, Government, and the Enlightenment* (New York: Harper & Row, 1985). A comparative study of eighteenth-century France and Prussia, focusing on the relationship between government and the ruling classes, that explains how pressures for change in both countries led to different outcomes, revolution in France, and reform in Prussia.

* Roger Chartier, *The Cultural Origins of the French Revolution*, trans. Lydia G. Cochrane (Durham, NC: Duke University Press, 1991). Argues for the importance of the rise of critical modes of thinking in the public sphere in the eighteenth century and of long-term dechristianization in shaping the desire for change in society and politics.

Olwen Hufton, *The Poor in Eighteenth-Century France, 1750–1789* (Oxford: Clarendon, 1974). Examines the lives of the poor before the Revolution and the institutions that attempted to deal with the problem of poverty.

* Daniel Roche, *The People of Paris* (Berkeley, CA: University of California Press, 1987). An essay on popular culture in the eighteenth century, in which the author surveys the lives of the Parisian popular classes—servants, laborers, and artisans—and examines their housing, furnishing, dress, and leisure activities.

Isser Woloch, *Eighteenth-Century Europe: Tradition and Progress, 1715–1789* (New York: Norton, 1982). A discussion of eighteenth-century Europe, comparing social, economic, political, and intellectual developments elsewhere in Europe to the French experience, with special attention to cultural aspects, such as popular beliefs and religion.

THE FIRST STAGE OF THE FRENCH REVOLUTION, 1789–1792

* Georges Lefebvre, *The Great Fear of 1789* (New York: Pantheon Books, 1973). This classic study analyzes the rural panic that swept through parts of France in the summer of 1789. The Great Fear is presented as a distinct episode in the opening months of the Revolution, with its own internal logic.

François Furet and Denis Richet, *The French Revolution* (New York: Macmillan, 1970). Two experts on the French Revolution present a detailed overview of the period from 1789 to 1798, when Bonaparte returned to Paris.

Colin Lucas, ed., *Rewriting the French Revolution* (Oxford: Clarendon Press, 1991). Responding to the historiographic challenge of the bicentenary of the French Revolution, eight scholars present new interpretations in the areas of social development, ideas, politics, and religion.

* Michel Vovelle, *The Fall of the French Monarchy* (Cambridge: Cambridge University Press, 1984). A social history of the origins and early years of the Revolution, beginning with a brief examination of the old regime and paying special attention to social and economic changes initiated by the Revolution, the role of the popular classes, and the creation of revolutionary culture.

EXPERIMENTING WITH DEMOCRACY: THE REVOLUTION'S SECOND STAGE, 1792–1799

* François Furet, *Interpreting the French Revolution* (Cambridge: Cambridge University Press, 1981). A series of essays challenging many of the assumptions concerning the causes and outcome of the Revolution and reviewing the historiography of the Revolution. The author argues that political crisis, not class conflict, was the Revolution's primary cause and that revolutionary ideas concerning democracy are central to an understanding of the Terror.

Carla Hesse, *Publishing and Cultural Politics in Revolutionary Paris, 1789–1810* (Berkeley, CA: University of California Press, 1991). Reconstructs the publishing world that emerged from the revolutionary struggles of publishers and printers of Paris; and examines the political, legal, and socioeconomic forces shaping the new cultural politics between 1789 and 1810.

* Lynn Hunt, *Politics, Culture, and Class in the French Revolution* (Berkeley, CA: University of California Press, 1984). A study of the Revolution as the locus of the creation of modern political culture. The second half of the book examines the social composition and cultural experiences of the new political class that emerged in the Revolution.

* Lynn Hunt, *The Family Romance of the French Revolution* (Berkeley, CA: University of California Press, 1992). Studies recurrent images of the family in French revolutionary politics to understand the gendered nature of revolutionary and republican politics.

* Joan B. Landes, *Women and the Public Sphere* (Ithaca, NY: Cornell University Press, 1988). Landes examines the genesis of the modern notion of the public sphere from a feminist perspective and argues that within the revolutionary process women were relegated to the private sphere of the domestic world.

* Sara E. Melzer and Leslie W. Rabine, eds., *Rebel Daughters: Women and the French Revolution* (New York: Oxford University Press, 1992). Contributors from a variety of disciplines examine the integral relationship of women and the French Revolution, with special attention to the political exclusion of women from the new politics.

* Albert Soboul, *The Sans-Culottes* (New York: Anchor, 1972). An exhaustive study of the artisans who composed the core of popular political activism in revolutionary Paris. The political demands and ideology of the sans-culottes are examined with the composition, culture, and actions of the popular movement during the Revolution.

THE REIGN OF NAPOLEON, 1799–1815

* Louis Bergeron, *France Under Napoleon* (Princeton, NJ: Princeton University Press, 1981). An analysis of the structure of Napoleon's regime, its social bases of support, and its opponents.

Isser Woloch, *The French Veteran From the Revolution to the Restoration* (Chapel Hill, NC: University of North Carolina Press, 1979). Examines the social impact of revolutionary and Napoleonic policies by concentrating on the changing fortunes of war veterans.

* Indicates paperback edition available.

CHAPTER 23

States and Societies in East Asia, 1600–1800

RITUALS AND REALITIES OF CHINESE IMPERIAL RULE

Hidden from view in his palanquin, shouldered by thirty-six soldiers, the Qianlong emperor (1736–95) took his place in the stately procession from his palace to the Temple of Heaven. There he, like Ming (1368–1643) and Qing (1644–1911) emperors before him, annually made sacrifices to Heaven at the winter solstice. Flanked by swordsmen with a rear guard of archers, the emperor's palanquin came near the end of a magnificent display that included carriages drawn by teams of white horses and others pulled by elephants. Colorful banners and flags identified different officials who walked alongside.

Whenever the emperor moved from his palace chambers on a formal occasion, he was accompanied by an armed honor guard. The Song emperor Shenzong (1067–85) reportedly had some 22,000 attendants accompany him on the most important occasions. In contrast, the early Qing emperors kept very small honor guards. At times only fourteen people were in attendance—six men carrying banners, two with parasols, and six armed guards. In 1748 the Qianlong emperor announced new regulations to expand his honor guard, the size of the entourage growing with the importance of the ceremony from 104 to 660 attendants.

The annual sacrifices at the Temple of Heaven required the most lavish presentation of imperial grandeur to affirm the emperor's august authority. His 660 attendants were part of a much larger procession painted on the scroll we view here, which measures a majestic 56 feet in length. From this scroll of the 1748 sacrifices, we know that more than 3,700 participants to this event witnessed the emperor perform his sol-

emn duty of informing Heaven of the past year's important events.

The grandeur depicted here does not tell the whole story of imperial rule, however, for the observance of ritual occasions was but one important part of the emperor's duties. Equally crucial during this period were the bureaucracy's administrative duties, which some emperors guided more effectively than others. In contrast to the late Ming emperors, who ruled before the Manchu takeover, three early Qing emperors— the Kangxi emperor (1661–1722), the Yongzheng emperor (1723–35), and the Qianlong emperor (1736–95)—fulfilled ritual functions as well as promoting active bureaucratic rule of the empire. The Kangxi emperor personally led military campaigns to consolidate the empire's expanded borders; for civilian administration, he approved new procedures for evaluating official performance and for managing state finances. His son, the Yongzheng emperor, allocated more resources to local officials to help them meet the challenges of maintaining local social order; he also streamlined bureaucratic communication among different levels of the administration, and centralized imperial control over important decision making.

In his early years, the Qianlong emperor continued to implement policies that promoted popular welfare—for example, a vast granary system provided famine relief, and river and canal maintenance reduced flooding possibilities and improved transportation. By the 1780s, however, the limitations of the bureaucracy became increasingly evident. Officials often had too few fiscal and human resources to meet their responsibilities. By the late eighteenth century, toward the end of the Qianlong emperor's long reign, the expansion of the empire—territorially, demographically, and economically—greatly complicated the bureaucratic task of sustaining political order. As a result, the limits to China's imperial rule, not apparent in the ritual performances of this scroll, were becoming clearer to officials of the day. But these problems were themselves the products of political successes. Without the creation of major institutions to promote popular welfare and social stability, their maintenance could not have become an issue.

This century of rule stands out in late imperial Chinese history, not simply for the grandeur of its rituals, but more importantly for its political successes. These were more imposing than those of their late Ming predecessors in the seventeenth century but less obvious than the political failures of their late Qing successors in the nineteenth century.

Late Imperial China, 1600–1800

In 1600 China was the world's most populous country, as it had been for centuries and has continued to be until the present. With an expanding commercial economy based on agricultural and rural handicraft production, the society had as strong an economic foundation as any across Eurasia. But the imperial state revealed growing weaknesses domestically and in foreign relations, leading the country into a period of turmoil similar in some ways to the crises challenging European states and societies during this same century.

For China, the resolution of political conflicts and social unrest was the fall of the Ming dynasty (1368–1644) and its replacement by the Qing dynasty (1644–1911). After consolidating its domestic rule by the 1680s, the Qing guided the country through a century of general social stability and relative material security. The empire's territory and population virtually doubled, and the agrarian commercial economy expanded dramatically. The state attempted to guide these processes of change.

The Experience of Daily Life in Late Imperial China

Most of the 150 million to 175 million people alive in China in 1600 lived in villages and spent much of their time working the land. These peasants exceeded in numbers the total population of all of Europe, which at the time numbered roughly 100 million people. Beneath the massive weight of the numbers, we can discover dramatic variety in the local conditions of Chinese peasant life. Speaking mutually unintelligible dialects, peasants in north China could not understand those in the area along the Yangzi River. Those living along the southeast coast spoke dialects different from those in north China and Guangdong. Living in very different ecologies, ranging from semitropical forest in the southwest to semiarid plateaus in the northwest, China's peasants planted different crops to meet the possibilities and limitations of distinct environments. South of the Yangzi River, the areas of paddy rice agriculture were gradually extended; in the north, dry fields planted in some combination of wheat, buckwheat, and millet provided the staple grains, which were often made into noodles or porridge. In China's northwest, peasants fashioned homes out of the caves in the windswept hillsides of a dry and difficult terrain; on the North China Plain, surrounding the capital city of Beijing, peasants built their homes of bricks fired in small kilns. To provide heat during the chilly winters, these homes in the north relied upon the *kang*, an elevated bed platform made of earthen bricks that radiated heat supplied by the flues connected to cooking stoves. To the south of the Yangzi River, peasants enjoyed a broader variety of building materials, including timber and bamboo. Throughout China, rural homes were usually rectangular and their layouts had a strong sense of symmetry.

The Chinese family ideal was to have many generations living under a single roof. This goal led to the addition of rooms to form courtyards to house married sons and their families. With the great importance attached to filial piety and respect for the ancestors, most rural life centered on the family household. In some villages of seventeenth-century China, families belonged to larger kinship groups, or lineages, that traced their origins to a common male ancestor of several generations before. But extended families and lineages were more important as a Confucian ideal than as a common social reality. Most families were in fact small and many did not belong to lineages.

Women generally left their villages of birth to live with their husbands. In only a few parts of seventeenth-century China did many women routinely get beyond the household gate or the fields. Their social horizon was bounded by kinship relations. For peasant men the social universe was a bit larger, often extending to a nearby market town, where peasants sold their cash crops and handicrafts, sipped tea in teahouses, and discussed local social affairs. More prominent in the market towns were the gentry, who achieved high social status by earning degrees from passing civil service examinations. They were joined by other literati who were equally educated but less successful at the exams. Some of the gentry, many of whom were large landowners, lived in the market towns alongside other rich landlords and merchants, while others continued to live in the countryside. The gentry met in teahouses as well as at each others' homes, to discuss local politics, to learn about prices in distant markets, to write each other poetry, and to enjoy fine food and wine. While there were certainly differences in wealth and status in late imperial China, there was no sharp separation of urban and rural classes or between rich and poor. All pursued their lives in a society increasingly influenced by a cash economy.

Commercialization in an Agrarian Society

In late imperial China market exchange played some role in virtually everyone's life. Few people lived in households where all their food, clothing, and other daily needs were met solely by their own family's efforts. The region along the lower reaches of the Yangzi River made the most dramatic advances in cash cropping, handicrafts, and trade, sustaining its position as China's most prosperous area, an achievement it has largely maintained from the tenth century to the present day. The expansion of cash crops and handicrafts—cotton and silk textiles, tobacco, indigo for dyeing cotton cloth blue, paper products, straw mats—spread along the Yangzi River, creating new markets and agricultural centers of production in both the middle and upper Yangzi regions. Beyond the Yangzi watershed, significant agricultural and handicraft developments took place in Guangdong and along the southeast coast. In north China, less favored by nature with riverine transportation possibilities, commercialization was most pronounced along the Grand Canal and in the hinterlands of larger cities.

By 1600 the lower Yangzi region had developed a considerable network of specialized market towns.

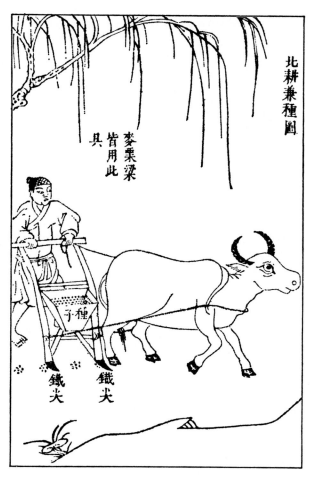

Farmer operating a combination plow and seeder pulled by a water buffalo.

Other parts of the empire had less sophisticated networks, but trade itself continued to expand. These urban developments continued in the eighteenth century. But China's overall population did not become more urbanized, as was the case in Europe beginning in the late eighteenth century, because the countryside's population also continued to grow. Rural areas supported continued commercialization, making much of the Chinese countryside among the most market-oriented in the world.

Two major merchant groups dominated trade between the sixteenth and eighteenth centuries. First were the Shanxi merchants, who initially made their money in the Ming dynasty from government contracts to provision troops stationed along China's north and northwest borders. In exchange for supplying grain to the frontiers they received licenses to sell salt, a commodity with state-determined prices from which merchants could make large profits. Salt was an easy commodity for the state to control because its production was limited to a few places and it was important to everyone's food supply, both to preserve and to season food. Shanxi merchants entered other trades, developed a financial network, and dominated commerce in the northern half of the empire. The second group, the Huizhou merchants, initially made their money in grain, cloth, and timber. They established commercial operations in all the major cities and market towns in the southern half of the empire, much as Shanxi merchants did in the north.

Merchants never developed an exclusively urban orientation. They were city sojourners who usually maintained agricultural lands in their native places. Some of their sons managed those lands, while others helped out with the urban businesses. But the most prestigious work was to study successfully for the civil service examinations. Status was based on ideals defined by the political system and the landowning elite. As a consequence, the urban lifestyle developed by Chinese merchants, unlike those in Japan and Europe, never achieved much autonomy from the ideals typical of other social groups. Chinese merchant wealth could support sumptuous feasts, the collection of pottery and painting, and new themes in literature, but it did not generate a distinctive view of the material and social worlds that would displace older visions of political and social order. Gentry and landed elites nevertheless worried that the profits from trade would entice too many people with extravagant lifestyles. But the value of owning land and living in a restrained manner retained its attractions.

Official fears that merchant wealth would lure people away from agriculture were exaggerated. Vulnerability to poor harvests was a more constant possibility than the dangers of extravagant living. Along with their counterparts across Eurasia, Chinese peasants shared a basic dependence on weather and climate that made their lives intimately enmeshed with the seasons. In any one year, flood and drought could spell disaster, and a series of harsh years made survival extremely tenuous. When human disruptions—peasant rebellions or war—compounded the impact of natural disasters, peasant life was in great peril indeed. Such circumstances seriously threatened the political life of the dynasty, as happened in the first half of the seventeenth century.

From the Ming Dynasty to the Qing Dynasty

Traditional Chinese historians believed in a dynastic cycle. When a dynasty was young and vigorous, the emperor ruled benevolently and the people prospered. As a dynasty grew old, corruption crept into the bureaucracy and emperors became feeble leaders. The seventeenth-century political scene conforms to many elements of this belief. For decades a faction-ridden bureaucracy had made decisions without meaningful guidance or even participation by the emperors. Struggle in the government raged between two factions—one led by eunuchs who served in large numbers in the Imperial Household Administration, the other led by a group of officials known as the Donglin ("Eastern Forest"), movement. These officials criticized the eunuchs' control over the government and proposed reforms to give themselves more power. Nonetheless, factionalism proved easier to deal with than the mounting fiscal problems. In spite of tax reform begun in the sixteenth century, the need for additional resources grew steadily because of military expenditures along the northern border, where China was vulnerable to attack by the Manchus. To raise additional funds, the government levied new taxes, which prompted popular protests. In one dramatic instance in 1601, the imposition of a tax on Suzhou weavers brought the industry to a halt as weavers protested what they perceived to be unwarranted and illegitimate taxes. The government quelled the disturbance and made arrests. But when one of the leaders was released more than a decade later he was still remembered as a local hero.

In the seventeenth century, the Chinese state, like its European counterparts, had difficulties raising revenues to meet crises, often of military origin. Domestic

ZHANG YING'S ADVICE TO HIS SON

■ *"Remarks on real estate" by Zhang Ying (1638–1708) was initially addressed to this official's six sons during a home leave from Court, probably around 1697. In this long essay filled with historical allusions and contemporary anecdotes, Zhang stresses the importance of investing in land. Land does not depreciate in value, nor can it be stolen. It can, however, be passed on to one's descendants and form the basis of family security for generations into the future. Zhang recognizes that higher returns can be made from investments in usury or commerce, but he believes the dangers of losing profits kept in cash through poor investment or extravagant spending make the lower returns from landownership more prudent. In a period of increasing commercialization and the pursuit of material pleasures in market towns and cities, Zhang promoted the virtues of scholarship and frugal living in the countryside.*

Only land is a commodity which even after a hundred or a thousand years is always as good as new. Even if agricultural labour is not intensive, if the land is poor and the produce meagre, as soon as it is manured and irrigated it will be renewed. Even if the land is gone to waste and the homestead is covered with weeds, once it is reclaimed it will be renewed. If you construct many ponds, poor land can be enriched, and if you vigorously uproot the weeds then barren soil can be made fertile. From ancient times to the present day there has never been any fear that it will decay or fall into ruin, nor anxiety lest it abscond or suffer attrition. This is really something to be treasured!

In the present age the young men in a family have elegant clothing and spirited horses and are always dancing and carousing . . .

If the young men have a modicum of good sense they will not tolerate things being thrown away extravagantly. How can they live sheltered lives knowing what it is like to have full stomachs and warm clothing, but paying no attention whatever to the conservation of resources and indeed casting them away in the mire?

Thus failure to regulate expenditure is undoubtedly the major reason for incurring debts and selling property. Apart from this, however, gambling, depravity and wastefulness also lead unquestionably to ruin. Again, there are those who sell their property because of marriage expenses, which is absolutely ridiculous. As long as there are men and women there will always be marriages, but you should measure your resources and regulate the style of the affair on the basis of a good year's savings. Why should you sell something which has been the mainstay of the family for generations in order to make a fine show on one particular occasion?

For a family the two words 'wealth' and 'honour' signify merely transient glory. To raise their sons and grandsons they rely ultimately on agriculture and study.

When finally you succeed in your studies and are given an official appointment you may live in the city. Thus you move back to the city, but after one or two generations it is proper once more to live in the country, so you again move to the country to live. In this way agriculture and study, country and city life succeed each other in cycles and may be great and long-lasting. What a fine and auspicious thing this is!

disorder compounded state fiscal problems and led to profound political uncertainty. The Ming Court faced the double challenge of the Manchus poised for attack from the north and domestic peasant rebellions. Between 1627 and 1631, Li Zicheng, an unemployed post-station attendant who had previously served as an iron-worker's apprentice and worked in a wineshop, organized peasants for raiding in the northwestern province of Shanxi. The scale of raiding grew in a second period between 1631 and 1636, as rebel groups roamed

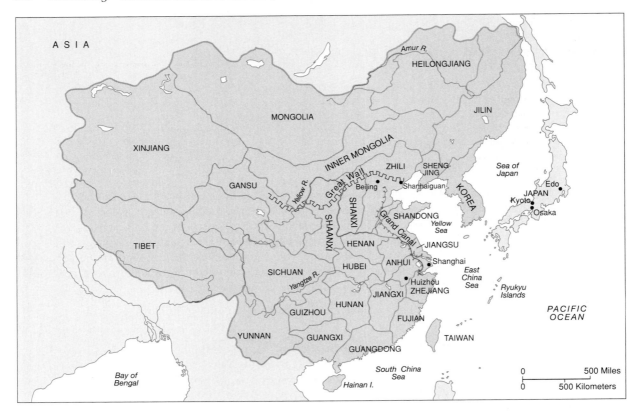

East Asia, ca. 1800

the forested border areas of Hubei, Henan, and Shanxi. In a third stage, Li Zicheng and a second major rebel leader, Zhang Xianzhong, organized more formal armies, and after 1641 these armies seriously challenged the state and brought down the government. In the fourth and final stage, marked by Li's entrance into Beijing, the Manchus quickly followed his rebel armies to proclaim themselves the restorers of social order. They routed the rebels and defeated the Ming dynasty. As the Manchus proclaimed their Qing dynasty in 1644, they made their appeal to Beijing residents in the language and logic of earlier Chinese rulers, not as some northern barbarians ignorant of Chinese ways. They were able to do so because for many decades the Manchus had been building their power in the northeast and preparing for the day they might enter China proper.

The Manchus were one of two different kinds of people living to the north of the Great Wall. The first, of whom the most famous were the Mongols, were nomadic and seminomadic peoples who lived on the steppe and depended on livestock grazing and trade

with sedentary peoples. The second, represented by the Manchus, lived to the northeast in heavily forested areas and depended upon hunting, agriculture, and trade. Their hunting tradition provided the Manchus with the martial values and skills to conquer other peoples in the northeast. To consolidate their rule in this region, the Manchus developed new forms of organization; from Chinese institutions they borrowed certain principles that they combined with their own to form a government that centralized Manchu forces. Thus, before even entering China proper, the Manchus had a far better sense of China than had the Mongols who preceded them in forming a Chinese dynasty some four hundred years earlier. But Manchu understanding of Chinese customs did not make important elites any friendlier to them. In order to gain their support and help with local rule, the new regime had to accommodate elite interests on subjects like tax reform.

Creating domestic order through a combination of intimidation and accommodation proved less dramatic a challenge than facing the military power of generals farther south, who had been rewarded for their service to the Manchus during the defeat of the Ming with large estates of land and control over bureaucratic appointments. The most famous of these was Wu Sangui (1612–78), the general who had let the Manchus through the Shanhaiguan pass to enter China proper. As the Qing moved to reduce their power, Wu and his colleagues mounted a counteroffensive known as the Revolt of the Three Feudatories, which lasted from 1673 to 1681, when Qing troops defeated the rebel generals. Two years later the last rebels, who had fled to the island of Taiwan, were defeated and the island was incorporated into the southeast coastal province of Fujian. In contrast to conventional images of a peaceful government, the Qing state in fact continued to be an active military power for the next century, giving battle to groups across the northern and northwestern frontiers as well as making forays into Southeast Asia. Qing defeats by the Vietnamese and Burmese in the 1780s marked the end of a century of military successes.

As they established their dynasty, the Qing adopted most of the bureaucratic institutions of the Ming, with the central government divided into Six Boards and a vertically integrated territorial administration of provinces, prefectures, and counties. To the Ming system of government the Qing added a system to register all Manchus, as well as some Chinese and Mongolians. Known in English as the banner system, this organizational format was the basis for the Qing's military forces. In addition, even Manchus who were not ac-

tively serving in military service were organized into banners through which they were allotted land to cultivate. The Qing made other changes, including streamlined bureaucratic communication with the throne, and the creation of a new high-level body known as the Grand Council to handle the most important reports or memorials.

As a minority, the Manchus were acutely aware that China proper contained a diverse population. The Han Chinese dominated as the principal ethnic group, but many other small populations of ethnically or culturally distinct people were important in different areas. Some groups were ethnically and linguistically related to populations in Southeast Asia such as the Miao (Hmong) and Tai. In the northwest and southwest, there was a considerable religious minority of ethnic Han who had converted to Islam, mostly after the sixteenth century. Finally, there were groups of Han Chinese who suffered friction with local Han Chinese residents. The largest such group, called Hakka, or "guest people," was in south China and had a distinct dialect, customs, and cuisine. Qing rulers were sensitive to the problems of minorities. Often the government regulated Han settlement in minority areas to protect minority people's livelihoods. At the same time, however, the government sought to incorporate the minority groups politically. Through a shift from native chieftain rule to standard bureaucratic administration during the Yongzheng reign, the government began to incorporate remote areas with indigenous ethnic minorities.

The Hall of Prayer for Good Harvests in Beijing, built originally in 1420 on the spot where Ming emperors came to pray for good harvests. The complex was enlarged and rebuilt by the Qianlong emperor, and it remains an emblem of China's enduring civilization to this day.

Complementing political integration was sinification, the effort to make the entire population thoroughly Chinese. The government insisted that Chinese language and customs were the standard for civilization and created the category of "Chinese" as a cultural rather than a racial designation. A "Chinese" was someone who spoke, dressed, and ate in the manner of a Chinese; a "Chinese" was one who was married and buried according to Chinese customs. One could become Chinese, and conversely one could potentially become "barbarian" by adopting the customs of some minority people. To achieve stability across an agrarian empire, the Qing sought to create a Chinese cultural order. An expanding empire with a distinctive agrarian political economy supported this goal.

The Political Economy of Eighteenth-Century China

The initial establishment of Qing political control was quickly followed by the resettlement of lands abandoned during the peasant rebellions of the late Ming. Resettlement of fertile areas was followed by migration to ecologically less favored frontier regions in the southwest and northwest. The government supported these movements through a homesteading policy that granted tax holidays of three to five years to peasants opening unclaimed land. In some cases the government made loans of seed grain and provided help with buying draft animals. By the eighteenth century more than seven million acres of newly reclaimed land were added to the tax registers, and the total amount of reclaimed land was even greater due to new fields that escaped registration. This expansion supported the growth of China's population from 175 million to 350 million during the eighteenth century.

This dramatic population growth was also stimulated by continued intensification of land use and expanded commercial exchange. Increased use of organic fertilizers, coupled with seed improvements and expanded irrigation facilities, made higher yields possible in many locales across China. New trade patterns—such as north China soybean fertilizer exchanged for cloth produced in the lower Yangzi region—were established. Peasant families also turned to handicraft production to create new sources of income. In addition to expanding cotton textile production, activities like mat weaving

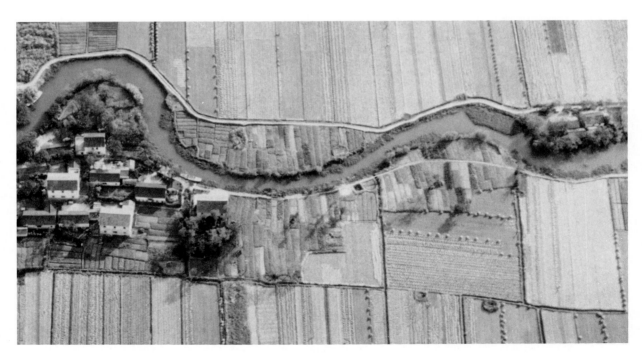

The Grand Canal, shown here winding through farmland, is one of the world's longest artificial waterways, extending 1200 miles from Beijing to Hangzhou.

or silkworm raising involved members of the household in different agricultural and handicraft activities—all carried out within the family's dwelling.

Unlike European states, which paid little attention to peasants other than as a source of tax revenues, the Qing state demonstrated considerable concern for peasant welfare, motivated by the Confucian belief that a starving peasantry would rise up in rebellion and bring down the dynasty. Officials monitored market prices, and bought and sold grain to dampen seasonal and annual fluctuations in harvest supplies. These policies complemented efforts to promote agricultural production and migration to frontiers.

Contrary to stereotypes, the Chinese state was not anticommercial in any serious sense. The state actively supported merchants' movement of goods over long distances and envisioned its own role as most important in those areas of the empire most poorly served by the commercial economy. In other words, the state was most active in storing grain, promoting land clearance, and creating infrastructure for the agrarian economy in areas where commerce mattered relatively little. Officials were committed to the policies of "practical learning," or the statecraft necessary to sustain these efforts successfully.

The eighteenth-century Chinese state's achievements were remarkable. Chinese grain prices fluctuated far less than European prices in the same centuries, while life expectancy in China was at least as high as in Europe. Dwarfing efforts made by European states to affect the economic conditions of peasants, the Qing dynasty was able to oversee a dramatic demographic expansion supported by economic developments that confirmed China's position of preeminence in Asia. Taking advantage of the positive functions that merchants and literati elites could perform, the state succeeded in managing a broad and diverse empire. The state's capacity to span varied scenarios and integrate them into an agrarian empire depended in part upon the state's promotion and control over a common culture.

Chinese Culture and the State

For centuries the Chinese state took an active role in defining acceptable belief and behavior. In Europe organized religion was the institutional source of moral belief and guidelines for proper behavior. Compared to the Chinese state, European states had much less to say about such matters in the seventeenth and eighteenth centuries. At the center of the Chinese state's influence over elite perspectives was the examination system. Study for the civil service examinations committed would-be degree holders to mastering a canon of general beliefs about politics and society, more specific strategies for good government, and concrete methods to deal with particular problems. But literati culture, the culture of the educated elite, extended well beyond studying for exams. To live up to the amateur ideal of someone skilled in the cultural arts, for example, a proper gentleman would always be able to compose a poem at a fine banquet or upon parting from friends.

Fiction and drama appealed to the tastes and curiosities of a broader audience. Martial heroes, heartless lovers, reunited couples, thieves and tricksters filled romances and stories of court cases. Other tales were filled with ghosts and spirits. Dramas were performed for a variety of occasions. Some were held during annual festivals to honor local gods. Other plays were performed at larger market towns, where beggars, gamblers, and fortune tellers gathered. Itinerant troupes performed different kinds of plays according to the kind of sponsor and type of audience in attendance. Lineage heads and village leaders favored plays celebrating proper Confucian virtues, while the plays designed to attract people to a temple fair were more likely to appeal to popular preferences for the supernatural, romances, or martial exploits, themes that lay beyond those actively promoted by Confucianism.

Late Ming elites, like the common people, were attracted to ideas beyond Confucianism. Disenchanted with state service, which was becoming more difficult to secure as qualified individuals increasingly outnumbered vacant positions, the gentry patronized local Buddhist monasteries and created for themselves a cultural space separate from the Confucian state. Eighteenth-century literati continued to be disenchanted with the civil service system. But instead of dissatisfaction with Confucianism leading to its further rejection, many believed that the Ming dynasty fell because intellectuals had become too interested in Buddhist-inspired metaphysics and had paid too little attention to more practical matters. Eighteenth-century literati championed a Confucian social order, in part because they were able to define career alternatives to state service. Nourished by the intellectual excitement of *kaozheng*, "evidential research," a movement to study the classics and other earlier texts with an eye to establishing authenticity, scholars avoided the pressures of bureaucratic life by becoming associated with academies that were havens

Nineteenth-century leather shadow puppet from Shanxi province. The character is a child with supernatural ability, pouring swords from a magical gourd.

outside state control. To be educated no longer necessarily meant a strong commitment to government service. Literati could gain employment teaching in local schools, writing inscriptions to commemorate major events or new buildings, and compiling records of a locale for publication as a gazetteer. These roles outside government continued to fit political definitions of acceptable cultural activity. Literati disaffection did not generate a serious critique of the state, let alone lead to a major political challenge.

Women's place in the hierarchical structure of Chinese society was reaffirmed amid the social changes of the seventeenth and eighteenth centuries. In popular stories, Chinese courtesans became heroines when they exhibited the proper virtues of loyalty to their lovers. The good courtesan ultimately married her lover, allowing her to become a good Confucian wife. Of course, most women did not live in the world of popular fiction; they were instead peasants who worked at making handicrafts and managing their households. Among the most socially vulnerable women were widows, whose chastity was promoted by officials and elites during the eighteenth century. At the same time, however, there were often great pressures on women to remarry; a dead husband's kin often wanted to repossess the widow's land,

an act more easily accomplished if the woman remarried. For peasant women generally, the economic pressures of survival dictated remarriage whenever possible, especially if the children were not yet old enough to help support her. The Qing state promoted widow chastity to demonstrate its commitment to the values stressed by Confucian elites. This commitment represented simply one feature of a much larger effort to shape popular cultural beliefs.

The state supervised China's temples, which were filled with a multitude of deities who performed a variety of functions. The state recognized a continuum between beliefs that were officially sanctioned and those that were dangerous and heterodox. So-called heterodox beliefs were prominent in the White Lotus Rebellion of 1796–1804, many of whose initial participants subscribed to a belief in a millennial age when a new social order would bring peace and prosperity to true believers. Orthodox belief, in contrast, was marked by state acceptance of deities. The state promoted a celestial bureaucracy that paralleled earthly arrangements. But officials could not force all deities into this bureaucratically inspired structure and ultimately accepted considerable diversity in local beliefs to fill in the space between the strictly orthodox and the decidedly not. Unable to patrol or even monitor local religious practices, the eighteenth-century state relied on local elites to keep popular beliefs confined within the boundaries etched out by Confucianism.

To promote actively moral indoctrination, the Qing state implemented a village lecture system modeled on earlier practices in which local elites gave moral presentations that were elaborations upon themes set out in imperial edicts. The Kangxi emperor's "Sacred Edict" offered sixteen maxims, which counseled the people in such matters as diligence, frugality, and proper treatment of relatives and friends. The Yongzheng emperor penned a set of amplified instructions that went beyond the terse classical language used by his father. Though never uniformly implemented across all of China, the lectures represented the state's interest in molding popular beliefs. The overlap of elite and official visions of acceptable cultural practices and beliefs added stability and harmony that might otherwise have been difficult to sustain. Educated elites responded to state expectations that local leaders had the power and responsibility to create and sustain social order. The more local leaders succeeded in this effort, the less the state intervened in local affairs. The bond joining state and elites was a common commitment to Confucian beliefs.

The state exercised considerable influence over the world of cultural expression. If a new vision of society was to emerge anywhere during the seventeenth and eighteenth centuries to challenge the prevailing Confucian cultural orthodoxy, it would be in the cities. But cities, which in Europe were the settings within which new attitudes were expressed about commerce, politics, and social order, remained in China under central government control and closely tied to the countryside. Shared cultural perspectives—of urban and rural sectors as well as among different classes—enabled the state to shape significantly the overall content of beliefs and preferences. Not only was the state alert to potential heterodox beliefs at the popular level, but it was vigilant about elite expression as well. During the mid-eighteenth century it launched an inquisition that led to the burning of thousands of books in Beijing, an event similar to ones that also took place in eighteenth-century Europe.

The Chinese state's success at ruling an agrarian empire depended upon its abilities to control the emergence of groups and ideas that might challenge its capacities and authority to rule. Amid commercialization, demographic growth, and a doubling of the empire's territory, the Qing state joined Chinese and Manchu elements to create a stable agrarian empire that was the widely acknowledged political center of East Asia. No stagnant society, no homogeneous country, no ineffectual and irrelevant imperial government, China was a dynamic economy and a diverse society led by a strong government that could oppress as well as promote.

The Chinese World Order

As heirs to an imperial tradition of rule, the Ming and Qing emperors conceived a world order with the emperor at the political center. All local authorities, wherever they might be, were subordinated to the emperor and expressed their understanding of this relationship through the presentation of tribute. Beyond the sphere of China's domestic government were peoples toward whom Ming and Qing rulers adopted various strategies to persuade, bribe, or coerce them to accept their places in a Chinese view of the world. Non-Chinese agreed not to challenge the empire even if they did not always agree with the Chinese view.

For China's world order, tribute relations were a key component helping to structure China's relations with peoples within and beyond its cultural orbit. The tribute system was both a political system and an economic system. The presentation of tribute by peoples from afar affirmed to the Chinese Court the centrality of their own position in the world. Through elaborate rituals of investiture, the Chinese symbolically recognized the authority of other leaders. To show their gracious recognition of tribute presentations, the Chinese offered gifts in return. Tribute presentations themselves were a kind of gift trade. Other trade often followed the presentation of tribute. In some cases—for example, Russia—the Chinese permitted trade in Beijing without tribute presentations. They also allowed this practice at some officially recognized frontier markets. These forms of administered trade were far more common than any sort of free-market trade that characterized domestic transactions. Strictly economic considerations, important though they could be, were usually secondary to the political.

Inner Asia and China: Formation of the Qing Union

For centuries the Chinese empire had a complex relationship with peoples to the north of the Great Wall. But before the Qing, no dynasty brought much territory beyond the Great Wall under formal imperial rule. It comes as no surprise that the Manchus included their own northeastern homeland in the empire, but they also subjugated other groups in Inner Asia. From what became Manchuria in the northeast through Mongolia, Xinjiang, and Tibet to the west, the Qing virtually doubled the territory of the Chinese empire and made the eighteenth-century Chinese state an impressive land-based empire flexing its military muscles in regions of interest to the Russians and British as well as the Chinese. To handle its affairs with the peoples of Inner Asia, the Qing established a specific institution, the Lifan Yuan, or Office of Border Affairs.

The Manchus divided their ancestral homeland into three provinces administered by a set of bureaucratic offices paralleling those used to rule China proper. Formally closed off to general Han immigration in order to protect the area from Chinese influence and thus protect Manchu identity, the area's fertile lands were nevertheless opened up by Han immigration. As the Qing state grew increasingly focused on China proper, the maintenance of a homeland untainted by Han influence

Pastoral Mongols live in felt-covered houses called yurts. The economy of these nomads is based on herds of cattle, horses, sheep, and goats. Their animals supply them with milk, meat, hair, and wool.

became less necessary, especially when Russian interest in territory around the Amur River, beginning in the eighteenth century, could be countered by Han settlement.

Well before the Manchus entered China proper, they had adopted the Tibetan Buddhism of the Mongols. Several eastern Mongolian tribes became attached to the Manchus; they could accept their position in an East Asian empire in which China was at the center but over which their allies the Manchus ruled. While the eastern Mongols became allied with the Manchus, others to the west remained their enemies, and the Qing had to subjugate them. The Kangxi emperor personally led the campaign against the western Mongol leader Galdan in order to destroy any lingering challenge the Mongols posed to Qing power.

In China's northwest, three distinct civilizations joined the Chinese to form the most culturally complex corner of the empire. Tibetan civilization was distinct in its origins from the Mongols, who owed their roots to Turks who dominated the steppe in the sixth century C.E. Tibetans live not only in what became Tibet under the Qing but also in western Sichuan, Yunnan, Gansu, and Xinjiang. Economically the region depended on a combination of high plateau agriculture, pastoralism, and trade. The central social institution was monasticism, which organized a large portion of the population. A Tibetanized form of Buddhism dominated their cultural life.

Along with Han Chinese, Turco-Mongolian, and Tibetan civilizations, Islam was the fourth important culture to meet in China's northwestern frontier in the eighteenth century. China contained two major groups of Islamic believers. Chinese-speaking Muslims, known as Hui, were mainly descended from Han who converted to Islam beginning in the sixteenth century. Turkic-speaking Uighurs, who generally had uneasy relations with the Hui, formed the second major group. Together with smaller groups of Muslim believers, these two groups accounted for several million people in eighteenth-century China.

The incorporation of an Inner Asian frontier into China was a Qing achievement. The administrative format adopted in different parts of Inner Asia varied considerably, but all were tied in one way or another to the Chinese imperial system, the same system whose tribute framework embraced the diverse peoples of Southeast Asia.

THE KANGXI EMPEROR'S MILITARY STRATEGY

■ *The Kangxi emperor (1662–1722) understood the solemn importance of ritual displays and the bureaucratic implications of his pronouncements to officials. Under his rule, China's agrarian economy recovered from the disruptions of the Ming-Qing transition, and state control was secured across China proper. But the Kangxi emperor was also a Manchu warrior, adept at martial skills and fond of the challenges that pursuit of a mounted enemy offered, so very different from the difficulties of creating and maintaining civilian bureaucratic rule of the agrarian empire. In this excerpt from his own writings, Kangxi recounts some of the preparations taken as he moved against the western Mongol chieftain Galdan, who represented one of the last major threats to Qing security in Inner Asia.*

Twenty years before, General Chang Yung had made secret inquiries about Galdan, and assessed his impetuous yet indecisive character, his age and family situation, his problems with the Moslems, and his love of wine and women. Since then I had observed Galdan's cunning and delight in feinting, his overconfidence, his gullibility and inability to think far ahead. After we sent the envoys, our scouts watched for the smoke of his campfires and assessed his army's movements on the evidence of hoofprints and horse dung. And as Galdan began to flee we moved into pursuit, first strengthening a base camp in which to leave the sick horses and the servants who had been marching on foot, then leaving behind the slower Green Standard Infantry, then abandoning the cannon, and finally sending Maska on ahead as commander of a flying column.

Before we moved against Galdan in 1696 I told the senior officers—Manchu, Mongol, and Chinese—to meet together by Banner and discuss how we might anticipate Galdan's movements and how we should deploy our own troops. . . . After the basic strategy of a western strike from Ninghsia and a central strike from Peking across the Gobi was agreed upon, the Council of Princes and High Officials worked out the details of rations for soldiers and servants, fodder for camels, the number of carts, and so on, basing their figures on an estimated 10,790 troops in the western army, and 8,130 in the center . . .

Again Galdan eluded us, and the following spring I pursued him for a third time, marching west to Ninghsia. The Shansi censor Chou Shih-huang tried to dissuade me, saying, "The despicable wretch is in desperate straits, and will be dead in a few days," . . . But I said that Galdan had to be finished off like Wu San-kuei . . . Then General Wang Hua-hsing also tried to divert me, suggesting that we all ride up to the Lake Hua-ma hunting grounds, and I told him: "Galdan is not yet destroyed, and the question of horses is a crucial one . . .

For in war it's experience of action that matters. The so-called *Seven Military Classics* are full of nonsense about water and fire, lucky omens and advice on the weather, all at random and contradicting each other. I told my officials once that if you followed these books, you'd never win a battle. Li Kuang-ti said that in that case, at least, you should study classical texts like the *Tso-chuan*, but I told him no, that too is high-flown but empty. All one needs is an inflexible will and careful planning. And so it was that, in the far northwest on the bend of the Yellow River in the early summer of 1697, I heard the news that Galdan, abandoned by nearly all his followers, had committed suicide.

Southeast Asia: World Religions in the Chinese World Order

The same Chinese tribute-system framework that defined the proper display of ritual relationships between the Middle Kingdom and the various peoples of Inner Asia also defined the relations between China and the polities of Southeast Asia. The Vietnamese, Thai, and Burmese all made tribute missions to the Chinese in the eighteenth and early nineteenth centuries. Relations with these countries were handled by the Ministry of

Rites, the organization also responsible for all ritual matters within the empire, such as Court ceremonials and festivals. The placement of tribute relations within the larger realm of ritual underscored the importance to the Chinese state of symbolic affirmations of the Chinese world order within and beyond China's borders.

The peoples of Southeast Asia were mostly peasants who lived in village settlements and for whom the politics linking their rulers to China were of little, if any, consequence. In Vietnam and some parts of the Philippines, family ties and broader kinship relations organized village life. For lowland peasants in Cambodia and in the Thai and Burman areas of control, the Buddhist temple was the focus of communal life. In the delta areas of the main rivers—the Red River, the Mekong, the Chao Phraya, the Salween, and the Irrawaddy—paddy rice agriculture produced the major staple. In most areas the mountains and plateaus were too dry to allow anything more than slash-and-burn agriculture. Other parts of the region were dense forest. Southeast

Asia was sparsely settled in the seventeenth and eighteenth centuries, with roughly 20 million people clustered in those places supporting either rice agriculture or maritime trading ports.

In those locales permitting permanent settlement, people formed peasant villages more similar to society in China than to the pastoralism of the steppe. Most houses were built on wooden poles to protect against flooding in the monsoon season. With thatched roofs, walls made of matting, and split bamboo flooring, houses lasted roughly ten years before being replaced. Meat and vegetable consumption was modest, but abundant fruits compensated for the limited vegetables. People suffered few famines, except those caused by war.

The mainland peninsula is divided into a series of isolated river valleys, and the archipelago is a string of islands, often with their own distinctive local variations. Spanning these diverse areas were the world's great religions—Buddhism, Islam, and Christianity.

Buddhism has two major traditions. The northern school, known as Mahayana Buddhism, spread

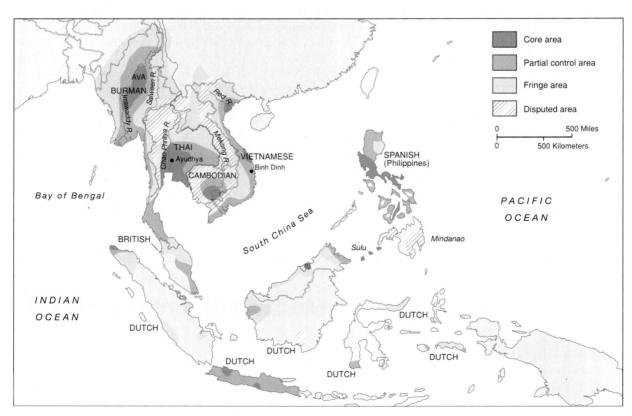

Southeast Asia, ca. 1800

The Potala, a palatial monastery at Lhasa, Tibet, was the home of the Dalai Lama.

historically from India to Nepal, Tibet, Mongolia, China, Japan, Korea, and northern Vietnam. In each area Buddhism underwent a distinctive transformation. Sometimes it gradually dominated local religious culture, as in Tibet and Mongolia. In other places, such as China, Japan, and Korea, it became one of several important religious influences. For most of Southeast Asia, Theravada Buddhism, the so-called southern school, held great influence after the thirteenth century. Every village had a monastery for its monks, and the monastery's core was a group of celibate monks clad in saffron robes who took vows of poverty and devotion to religious study. The monastery offered all village males a time and space to receive religious training and hence rudimentary literacy. The abbots and monks of each village monastery were part of an ecclesiastical hierarchy.

In contrast to Buddhism's land-centered agrarian social base, the religion of Islam followed the maritime routes weaving through the archipelago, to establish itself along the coast, a geographical and cultural area known as the *pasisir* in Indonesian. *Pasisir* Islam was rather narrowly defined and had no hierarchical religious structure. Religious life was focused at the village level, and religious sentiment was rarely mobilized to buttress or challenge secular government. Small Islamic states and societies existed all along the archipelago. Across tropical terrains inhospitable to human settlement, river-mouth cities were established as trading ports and political centers. These cities formed a political system of their own, into which the Portuguese entered in the

sixteenth century, the Dutch in the seventeenth, and the English in the eighteenth. Over time, the European presence began to grow and to weaken the powers of the Islamic port polities. During the fifteenth and sixteenth centuries the pasisir looked outward rather than toward the agrarian interior. But in the early seventeenth century a new dynasty, the Mataram, conquered all Java and absorbed the pasisir. With a hereditary king and local lords, the Javanese political system lay lightly over a myriad of local economies, some of which became tied to international trade through the Dutch East India Company. Java and the Malay sultanates, like the Spanish Philippines, lay beyond the furthest reaches of the Chinese empire. With the exception of Sulu in the Philippines, they lacked formal tributary relations with the Chinese. They did not exist in the formal political world order of the Chinese state, but they became the bases for the many migrating Chinese who engaged in trade throughout Southeast Asia.

In the Philippine Islands the competing interests of a secular government led by the Spanish and the two major religious forces of Christianity and Islam made for an unstable political situation. Christianity was actively promoted by the Spanish, whose religious zeal led them to combine the duties of priests and bureaucrats in complex ways. Priests became salaried officials, but the crown could intervene in ecclesiastical business when its interests were at stake. The governor of the Philippines was the king's personal representative and vice-patron of the Roman Catholic church. He sat atop an unresponsive bureaucracy, whose provincial governors ignored him and established virtually autonomous control over their territories. The only potentially effective link the governor had with the peasants was through the native priests recruited to serve in the villages, but tensions developed when these priests demanded more power. The Spanish governor's authority was also repeatedly tested through warfare with Muslim sultanates in Mindanao and Sulu during the eighteenth century. Making peace with the sultans could bring the governor into conflict with the Catholic church.

Closer to the Chinese political world order were the mainland polities, many of which were Theravada Buddhist monarchies. The two most prominent Buddhist monarchies of the seventeenth and eighteenth centuries were the Burmese monarchy of Ava and the Thai kingdom of Ayudhya. The Ava kings tried to control some important non-Burman peoples, such as the Mons in the south, linguistically related to the Cambodians, and the Thai-speaking people known to them as the Shan (a corruption of the word *Siam*) in the northeast; a shared Buddhism made this possible. The Thai and Burman courts became major competitors, each claiming vassal states. Their vassals reached from the Lao and Shan in the north to the peoples of the Malay Peninsula in the south. For Cambodia, the seventeenth and eighteenth centuries was a period of domination by outsiders, when monarchs sponsored by Vietnamese or Thai were often installed. When the Ayudhya state was defeated by the Burmese in 1767, a new Thai government under Rama I (1782–1809) rose to replace it.

Thai leaders, like many other leaders in Southeast Asia, could accept their minor roles in China's world order because China was not very important to them. The spread of Chinese influence in Southeast Asia had been halted by Vietnam. Vietnamese struggles to maintain independence from China meant that Chinese could not reach other parts of Southeast Asia by land and with military forces, but only by sea as peaceful traders.

Vietnam: Chinese Institutions Beyond China's Borders

Today Vietnam is a long, thin country dominated by two major river valleys, the Red River valley in the north and the Mekong Delta in the south. It was created by southern frontier expansion beginning in the fifteenth century, when the Vietnamese moved south from the Red River valley to defeat the Cham, a seafaring people influenced by Indian and Islamic cultures. In the seventeenth century Vietnamese settlers moved into the

Mekong Delta, where Cambodia had previously claimed authority. With status as a Chinese tributary state, the Vietnamese used Confucian principles to strengthen their bureaucracy and systematize their legal code as they developed their political institutions. But unity was difficult to achieve. Real power rested in the hands of two families, the Trinh in the north and the Nguyen in the south. Each formed a government with Chinese-style bureaucracies. Between 1620 and 1673 they fought with each other, and the Nguyen won recognition from the Trinh as independent rulers. The Trinh held effective power in the north and the Nguyen continued a gradual expansion in the south. For the next century there was sporadic conflict but no major wars or rebellions. This peace was broken in 1771 by a peasant rebellion in Binh Dinh province. The three Tay-son brothers sought to control central Vietnam. By 1778 Vietnam was no longer divided into two regions; now there were three. In 1786–87 Tay-son armies attacked the north, and the Trinh called upon the Qing for assistance. When Qing armies responded by invading Vietnam in order to increase their power in the region, the Tay-son declared the most gifted brother, Quang-trung, as emperor in 1788. Quang-trung initiated a program of change that was cut short by his death in 1792. His young son proved ineffective, and the exiled Nguyen leader, Phuc Anh, returned to defeat Tay-son generals between 1799 and 1801. Anh then recovered north Vietnam and proclaimed himself emperor of a united Vietnam.

The Vietnamese political and social order was centered on the three relationships borrowed from China: subject-ruler, son-father, and wife-husband. The Vietnamese subscribed to a Chinese ideology and created Chinese institutions to implement this political vision. They held Chinese-style examinations to test knowledge of the Confucian Four Books and Five Classics. In art, architecture, and literature the Vietnamese adopted Chinese models and forms with certain distinctive differences. Compared to China, Buddhism in Vietnam achieved a more prominent position, Vietnamese women's social status was a bit higher, and Vietnamese literati were more conservative in their Confucian views. The content of great literary works spoke of Vietnamese experiences, even when borrowing themes from Chinese literature, much as Shakespeare addressed his own English society in plays taken from foreign stories like the Italian *Romeo and Juliet*. During the seventeenth and eighteenth centuries, Chinese characters were adapted for the Vietnamese written language, further deepening the Chinese cultural influence. In foreign relations as well the Vietnamese modeled themselves on Chinese practices, styling themselves the "central country" to which others paid political homage and economic tribute. Envoys from Laotian and Cambodian states honored the Vietnamese just as the Vietnamese emperor recognized himself to be a tribute-bearing vassal of the Chinese.

The Chinese realized that there were peoples in Southeast Asia who lived well beyond the civilizing force of their culture, but such peoples seemed unimportant compared to the threats that peoples on the steppe could pose. With Vietnam on its southwestern border firmly within its political and cultural orbit, the Chinese empire of the seventeenth and eighteenth centuries could rest secure in the knowledge that challenges to its view of the world would not likely come from this quarter.

Europe in China's World Order

Europeans entered China's world order in two roles—as merchants and as missionaries. The Portuguese and Dutch reached China after having established trade relations in Southeast Asian ports. By the early seventeenth century the Portuguese were active in the trade between China and Japan, taking Chinese silks to Japan and returning to China with silver. The transition from the Ming dynasty to the Qing dynasty disrupted European trade relations in China and Southeast Asia. But Dutch trade relations, like those of the Portuguese, survived the dynastic change. Sino-Dutch trade declined by the late seventeenth century as the English began to assert themselves. This shift took place as the Qing government in 1685 began to regulate some foreign trade for fiscal purposes rather than as a part of the tribute system.

The so-called Canton trade system regulated China's European trade between 1760 and 1834. This system subordinated foreign traders to licensed Chinese monopolists known as the Cohong; in turn the Cohong were subordinated to the imperially appointed superintendent of maritime customs at Canton (now Guangzhou), called by the Europeans the Hoppo. The Cohong made profits by selling tea and textiles to monopoly trading firms like the British East India Company. Located at the periphery of the empire, European merchants were part of a maritime world that the Chinese state considered of little importance economically or politically. More important to the seventeenth- and eighteenth-century rulers were the Catholic missionaries.

Matteo Ricci and Ly Paulus, one of his Chinese converts. Though Ricci was held in great respect by the Chinese, he failed to make many converts to Christianity.

The most famous Jesuit pioneer, Matteo Ricci (1552–1610) reached China in 1582, where he and his colleagues tailored their Christian message to be understood in Chinese terms. To facilitate their credibility and acceptance, they adopted the Chinese scholar's gown. They captured the attention of officials and the Court by giving demonstrations of practical objects like clocks and presenting knowledge about astronomy and geography. Ricci and his seventeenth-century successors proved their worth to the Ming and Qing courts, serving as astronomers, cartographers, interpreters, architects, engineers, painters, and engravers. Their success was ended not by Chinese reactions to them so much as by criticism leveled at them by other Christian missionaries, who believed the Jesuits had gone too far in accommodating Chinese practices. The Jesuits had clearly outdistanced their Christian rivals in winning the trust and friendship of Chinese leaders.

At issue was how the Church should view several Chinese practices. Was ancestor worship simply a "civil rite" and therefore compatible with Christianity? Or was it "pagan worship" and therefore unacceptable?

What about officials praying for rain or the state's veneration of Confucius? These questions were posed to the pope by Dominicans and Franciscans who reached southeast China fresh from their successes in the Philippines, where no state power had stopped them from reaching the common people. They hoped, vainly as it turned out, to employ the same methods in China. For a century (1640–1742) the disagreements continued. In 1700 the Kangxi emperor wrote in support of the Jesuit view of Chinese rites—an outrage to the Church, which could hardly consider the Kangxi emperor an appropriate authority on matters of Christian doctrine. When the Yongzheng emperor came to power, he turned against the missionaries, who had been drawn into palace politics. In 1724 he declared Christianity a heterodox sect.

In 1742 the Catholic church closed the controversy with a papal bull forbidding all Catholics to practice the "rites and ceremonies of China." After promising beginnings, the missionaries became as unimportant as foreign merchants in eighteenth-century China. Nineteenth-century events would dramatically change this eclipse of the missionaries and the modest role of merchants. But in the seventeenth and eighteenth centuries, Europeans were but a marginal presence in the Chinese world order.

Korea and the Ryukyu Islands: Competition in China's World Order

More troubling to the Chinese government's sense of its power and authority than the European presence were events in Korea and the Ryukyu Islands, where Japanese advances challenged the centrality of the Son of Heaven. Like Vietnam, Korea experienced a period of direct Chinese control, after which a tributary relationship became the historical norm. Korea, again like Vietnam, modeled its political system on Chinese practices. From the perspective of administrative structure, political ideology, and its relationship to China, Korea appeared to be well within the Chinese world order. But Korea was also quite different from China in social and economic terms.

Korea's social system was based on a hereditary class structure. The upper class was composed of families allowed to own land, who served as either civil or military officials. They had a virtual monopoly on the right to take the civil service examinations. Below the upper class was a small group who served as petty government functionaries. Far more numerous were the commoners, who comprised the economic base of the state, working government lands and paying taxes and labor service. A final group, perhaps accounting for as much as a quarter of the population in 1600, was the lowest class of base people, who were slaves, actors, female entertainers, and other people with despised occupations.

As the year 1600 approached, Korea found itself in a difficult political situation. In 1592 the Japanese invaded Korea on their way to attack China. The Chinese met the Japanese invasion on Korean soil and achieved a military stalemate. Another major Japanese campaign of 1597 was ended in 1598 by the death of Hideyoshi, the Japanese leader responsible for the ill-fated military campaigns. In 1600, the Tokugawa family came to power in Japan; in 1609 they established friendly relations with Korea, which lasted until the second half of the nineteenth century. But before the Koreans could fully recover from the Japanese invasions, the Manchus began attacks to secure their flanks in upcoming struggles with the Ming dynasty. A 1627 incursion was followed by an invasion of 100,000 soldiers in 1637, which forced the Korean Yi dynasty to switch allegiance from the Ming to the Qing in advance of the Manchu conquest of China.

Once political relations became settled again, Korea's economy and society underwent major changes in the seventeenth and eighteenth centuries. New lands were opened and commerce expanded. The extension of irrigation facilitated double cropping rice in the south, while cotton and the potato were introduced in different parts of the country. Government land-tax collection in money rather than in kind helped to stimulate commercial activities, which broke out of the framework of licensed government monopolies. Socially, the relaxation of government regulations on slave status generally permitted more people to achieve commoner status; the manumission of all slaves in government service came in 1801. These domestic developments were joined by the spread of Christianity, about which Koreans learned from their contacts with Jesuits in Beijing. The Korean government became sufficiently anxious about the inroads made by this alien religion that it banned Christianity in 1785. While Christian influence was thereby limited, elements of Western scientific knowledge—also acquired by the Koreans from Jesuits in Beijing and from Chinese books—was not as controversial.

Chinese models clearly shaped the development of Korean statecraft in the seventeenth and eighteenth centuries. But it would be misguided to expect the simple replication of Chinese ideas and institutions on

China and the Chinese World Order, 1600–1800

1350–1767	Ayudhya begins as small Thai principality, becomes leader of Thai kingdom
1565	First permanent Spanish settlement in the Philippines
1598–1610	Jesuit missionary Matteo Ricci serves the Ming imperial court
1559–1626	Manchu state established
1604–26	Donglin Academy scholars oppose corruption in Chinese government
1630–47	Rebellions widespread across China
1644	Li Zicheng invades Beijing, overthrows Ming dynasty, Manchus invade and defeat Li Zicheng, establish Qing dynasty
1644–80	Ming loyalists resist Manchu rule
1662–1722	Reign of Kangxi emperor
1670–1750	Manchus conquer Xinjiang and Tibet
1673–81	Revolt of the Three Feudatories led by Wu Sangui
1683	Taiwan falls to the Manchus
1722–35	Reign of the Yongzheng emperor; period of autocratic control and bureaucratic reform
1736–95	Reign of the Qianlong emperor
1760–1834	Canton trade system in place to regulate China's European trade
1771	Vietnamese peasant rebellion leading to Tay-son regime
1796–1804	White Lotus Rebellion

Korea's position between China and Japan was paralleled on a far smaller scale by the uncertain status of the Ryukyu Islands to the south of Japan. The Ryukyus were once an independent kingdom, but the arrival of Chinese, Japanese, and Portuguese traders in the sixteenth century transformed the islands into an intermediary between China and Japan. While already in tributary relations with the Ming state, the Ryukyu Islands were invaded in 1603 by the feudal Japanese lord of Satsuma. With the approval of the central Japanese government, Satsuma leaders divided the Ryukyu Islands into a northern group under their direct administration and a southern group under a country administrator. But throughout the Qing dynasty, the Ryukyu kings continued to petition the Chinese emperor for investiture according to the Chinese tributary system. The ability of the Ryukyu islanders to play the Chinese and Japanese off against each other by recognizing their loyalty to each underscores the definite limits to China's world order.

As the largest state, boasting the most people, greatest territory, and most advanced economy, China in the seventeenth and eighteenth centuries, not surprisingly, had a clear vision of itself at the center of the political universe. For the Ming state there were basically two kinds of foreign governments—those modeled on Chinese principles, like the Korean or the Vietnamese, and those that had some other method of rule. The Qing dynasty recognized a third group composed of Inner Asian peoples whose ways were closer to their own than those of Southeast Asian countries, where political practices were shaped by Buddhist, Islamic, and Christian influences. European trading groups and missionaries occupied minor roles in the Chinese world order, representing peoples even more removed from the center of China's world than the most distant Southeast Asian kingdom. The Chinese could hardly be expected to be anxious about this minor presence. Japan's unification under the Tokugawa and its refusal to affirm its earlier tributary status was a more immediate potential problem to China's vision of itself and the world.

Tokugawa Japan, 1600–1800

The Tokugawa consolidation of national rule in 1600 created a new political system for a country that had been torn by a century of fighting. The leaders

Korean soil. Korean social values, for instance, clashed with Confucian norms for family organization. Even though the Korean state was modeled upon the Chinese, its actual functioning was significantly different because the monarchy was very weak. As a result the bureaucracy enjoyed more power. Government battles raged among bureaucratic factions, which became hereditary groups, each with its own academies to train scholar-officials.

succeeded in constructing new institutions to govern society and a new ideology to explain their purposes and their power. Blending ideas from native Shinto with elements from both Buddhism and Confucianism, political and social leaders created a new vision of their country. For peasants, the first two centuries of Tokugawa rule brought major changes to village life. The warriors, known as samurai, who had fought in the preceding decades of civil strife, were sent to castle towns by the government. Villages of peasants became more tightly organized as communities, in which households gradually shifted from subsistence production to crop and craft production for the market. In the cities, samurai became civil administrators served by merchants who forged new trading networks. Commercial wealth funded the development of an urban popular culture animated by new kinds of theater, fiction, and painting. Whether viewed in political, cultural, or economic terms, Tokugawa Japan was a dynamic society.

Tokugawa State Making

By the year 1600 Japan was emerging from a century of civil war. For the preceding forty years the country had been subject to unification efforts by two talented leaders, Oda Nobunaga (1534–82) and Toyotomi Hideyoshi (1536–98). The ultimate beneficiary of this process was Tokugawa Ieyasu (1542–1616), who came to power in 1600, decisively defeating his rivals at the battle of Sekigahara.

Under the Tokugawa structure, the shogun, who was the leader of the Tokugawa ruling family, directly controlled roughly one-fifth of the arable land in Japan. His administration was called the *bakufu*. The balance of the land was divided among some 245 to 295 lords with their own smaller collections of land. Their number fluctuated as new domains, or *daimyo*, were awarded to families who had aided the Tokugawa in their rise to power and older ones lacking heirs were dissolved. There were three kinds of daimyo. First were those in the hands of the ruler's collateral family. A second group included so-called house daimyo belonging to those families who had been rewarded by the Tokugawa for their service; and a third group was composed of established lords known as outside daimyo.

The bakufu and daimyo both found advantages in the political system developed in the seventeenth century. The bakufu first made several moves to strengthen itself. In the sixteenth century Japan's landscape had

been dotted with imposing castles constructed by warriors seeking to fortify their territories. The Tokugawa shogun demanded that the lords give up all castles but the ones in which they lived, and he made his own castle in the city of Edo the most spectacular and intimidating. To assert his power over the daimyo, the Tokugawa shogun also demanded that the lords personally live half their time in Edo and maintain their capital residences with other family members and staff at all times. First applied to outside daimyo, the policy was later extended to include house daimyo. During the eighteenth century, the daimyo maintained about 1,000 residences in Edo with a total of some 250,000 to 300,000 people, of whom one-half to two-thirds lived in the capital permanently, most as staff to relatives of the lord.

In many ways the bakufu was as dependent on the daimyo as the many daimyo were on the bakufu. While the bakufu set limits on daimyo authority, it was the daimyo governments that actually reached down to the village level to monitor local life across most of the country. The daimyo government collected taxes, prevented people from leaving their villages, and enforced the regulations on clothing and food that differentiated peasants, samurai, priests, and merchants. Perhaps the

Himeji Castle in Japan. During the age of the Japanese warlords such formidable fortresses dominated the countryside.

most important service the bakufu rendered the daimyo was the knowledge that they did not have to worry about violent competition among themselves because all were parts of a system stabilized by the bakufu. In the absence of military conflicts the daimyo did compete economically. By tapping the land reclamation projects for new revenues, some daimyo expanded their fiscal bases as the bakufu's income remained roughly constant.

A key component of Tokugawa state making was the transformation of the samurai from warriors into administrators. (See Special Feature, "Samurai: Warrior, Administrator, National Hero," pp. 702–703.) Rather than displacing a military elite with a civilian one, the Japanese samurai left behind his military exploits for the new challenges of civilian administration. The warrior class supplied officials for both the bakufu and daimyo administrations. Not all samurai, however, could gain employment in government. Those without any government job relied heavily on the stipends they received in recognition of their elite status, but for many of them this income was inadequate. Others were not well suited for civilian government. Nonetheless they remained the country's status elite even as their role in society was transformed and their economic security was undermined.

The bakufu closely controlled relations with other countries. The nineteenth-century Japanese view of these policies, subsequently adopted by most twentieth-century accounts, viewed the Tokugawa as isolationist. However, the concept of isolation is not one the Tokugawa leaders themselves would have understood. Instead, they first pursued a diplomacy for normalizing relations in northeast Asia after Hideyoshi's failed Korean invasions. Reestablishing peaceful relations with Korea was a means of presenting themselves as the center of their own world order, which was quite distinct from that constructed by the Chinese.

The Japanese assertion of their divine descent—making Japan a land of the gods—was made first in a diplomatic context. These beliefs allowed the Japanese to claim, at least implicitly, a kind of parity with the Chinese. As already noted in the previous section on the Chinese world order, the Ryukyu kingdom found it wise to play its part in both the Chinese and Japanese systems of foreign relations. In fact, in 1715 the Japanese persuaded Chinese merchants to acknowledge Japanese superiority, the same kind of acceptance typically demanded by the Chinese of Japanese merchants three hundred years before. The ability of the bakufu to limit

and control foreign relations was a way to distinguish its broader range of powers and authority from those of the daimyo. Foreign relations thus served to strengthen the central government's hand with respect to local governments.

The Tokugawa had been able to initiate several centralizing efforts in the seventeenth century and maintain most of them in the eighteenth. First, by 1640, the Buddhist church was subordinated to the state and Christianity eradicated; the potential for a religious threat to the Tokugawa was thereby removed. Second, the Tokugawa regulated commerce and the economy to promote economic expansion and its own security. Third, they kept the daimyo lords from becoming a challenge through effective regulation. Fourth, they sustained revenues on a routine basis even if these funds were at times insufficient and the power to levy taxes was shared with the daimyo. These successes have tempted scholars to compare the Tokugawa state with absolutist states in Europe. But there were significant differences between Japan and Europe. Japan had no political equivalent to France's Third Estate. In Japan the samurai were the ruling class; the bonds of obligation they shared with their superiors were based on a feeling of loyalty, not on a notion of contractual obligation. Beyond the state there were other major differences. Japan lacked free cities with politically independent and powerful merchants; the society was closed off economically to much of the outside world, making foreign trade a negligible factor in economic change. Nevertheless, many political and social changes in early modern Japan resonate more closely with Europe's developments than they do with conditions in China.

Political and Social Thought

When the Tokugawa established their regime, they invented a vision of their state and its relationship to society that would gain the agreement of the daimyo lords and the common people. Their goal was to transform warlord power into a form of authority that would not be challenged. The strategy adopted by Tokugawa Ieyasu and followed by later shoguns was to elevate themselves as leaders in religious terms, to seek self-deification through the Shinto religion. Using this policy, the Tokugawa could not only elevate themselves with respect to the common people and daimyo leaders but also displace the emperor from his position as the ritual center of the society. They diverted to

Japanese actors Toshiro Mifune (left) and Tatsuya Nakadai portrayed samurai in the film Joiuchi (Rebellion). *The film is an attack on the abuse of individuals under the feudal code.*

Samurai: Warrior, Administrator, National Hero

Over the common Japanese kimono, a loose-fitting robe with wide sleeves, the samurai put on a matching jacket and trousers of dark blue, dull brown, or sedate gray. Tucked into a sash beneath his jacket on his left side rested his two swords. The samurai of the Tokugawa period was easily recognized by these two swords, for only members of his hereditary class were permitted to carry both the long and the short swords. Swords had been used by many people during the war-torn sixteenth century. But by the beginning of the seventeenth century, the Tokugawa pacification had dis-

armed the peasants; swords became more important as a symbol of the samurai's status rather than as a practical weapon. Samurai made the transition from violence to peace, many of them becoming civilian administrators who served the shogun and daimyo in positions of power and authority. Others, however, who did not hold any official position, depended on modest stipends and faced economic hardships.

Whether rich or poor, samurai lived in towns and cities where the development of an urban merchant culture created luxuries and temptations that the former warriors

theoretically were not allowed to indulge in. Many of them nevertheless were attracted to the pleasure quarters, where some took on multiple mistresses and others became mired in family feuds. Not all of them could live according to the ideal code of the samurai, which combined a stress on Confucian virtues of loyalty and frugality with a Zen Buddhist approach of giving up desires and attachment to material things in order to face death easily.

Confucian loyalty and Buddhist resignation figure at the center of "Chushingura," the famous tale of forty-seven faithful samurai. When their daimyo lord is humiliated by a shogunate official in the Edo castle, he draws his sword—an offense so serious that he is ordered to commit suicide, after which his domain is confiscated. This foul act turned his many samurai retainers into *ronin*, or masterless samurai. Forty-seven of them chose to avenge his death. The shogunate, fearing that the ronin would avenge their deceased lord, monitored their leaders closely. To diminish official anxieties, the ronin leaders cleverly adopted a wild lifestyle as if wishing to escape the pain of losing their lord by losing themselves in drunken pleasures. For two years they did nothing to cause suspicion. Once the court had relaxed a bit, they planned their attack and fulfilled their bond of loyalty to their lord by assassinating the official responsible for his death.

The public was thrilled by this display of righteous loyalty and revenge. Even the government valued the virtue of loyalty the ronin's actions expressed. But the government could not allow the violation of social order that the assassination of the official represented without undermining their own authority. The government therefore forced the forty-seven ronin to commit suicide. By this action, the government transformed the forty-seven into heroic figures who have lived on in the popular imagination.

In the twentieth century few stories are as well-known. Between 1907 and 1962 the "Chushingura" story was made into a movie more than eighty times. The feudal virtues of loyalty and sacrifice have been adapted to other, more modern sensibilities in more recent films, as the forty-seven are celebrated for their sincerity, integrity, or bravery. Like the American cowboy, the samurai has become a cultural symbol with many dimensions of meaning. Outstanding examples of samurai swords are still made today according to techniques used in the Tokugawa period. The best craftsmen are honored by the government as "national living treasures" and pursue their craft subsidized by the government. More than a century after the samurai were dismantled as a class, Japanese society continues to be inspired by their heroics, and the state honors those who can still supply the finely crafted swords that these dead warriors can no longer use.

themselves the religious attention previously given the emperor.

A crucial part of the Tokugawa political vision was based on adapting Confucian thought to create a stable social order. The state promoted a four-class ideal, with samurai as the elite, followed in Confucian perspective by peasants, artisans, and merchants. Based on the Chinese idealized hierarchy, the Japanese gentleman had much more martial spirit than his Chinese counterpart. The state articulated codes for different social groups to define rules of proper behavior. The state also promoted a spatial separation of the status groups, with the samurai, merchants, and artisans living in different quarters of the cities and the peasants in the villages. Social stratification was reinforced by making samurai status hereditary. Creating a predictable and stable social order was a basic component of the Tokugawa's political logic for securing their rule. Thus, Chinese Confucian concepts were adapted to a different social situation in Japan, as they had been in Korea.

Confucianism entered Japan from China as an outside force in a culture already possessing well-developed Shinto and Buddhist traditions. In fact Confucianism was spread by Zen priests who studied Confucianism as part of acquiring a general familiarity with Chinese culture. Buddhism and Shinto had long enjoyed a division of religious labor. Shinto with its many deities and spirits was a religion for this world. Buddhism prepared one for the next, and in the Japanese context became fused with ancestor worship. The social thought of Tokugawa culture was thus composed of interwoven strands of Buddhism and Shinto, with a new prominence given to Confucianism. The state's appeal to the Confucian categories of benevolent rule and the loyalty of subjects offered a philosophy separate from the ideology associated with the emperor or the samurai warriors of the previous century.

It is easy to oversimplify the role of Confucianism in Tokugawa thought and to imagine that its influence was limited to the politics of a Tokugawa state at work crafting a new vision of political and social order. But an interest in Confucian ideas developed as well among intellectuals who lived on the margins of the ideal four-class system. Confucian ideas were also studied by merchants. In their own academies of scholarship, merchants used the Confucian category of virtue to valorize their own behavior. For them, seeking profit was the businessman's form of righteous behavior. Japanese merchants explained economics in Confucian terms. They believed that it was the duty of officials to help

nourish the people, to promote their livelihoods, and reduce the inequalities among them. Unfortunately, in many merchant eyes, the government was not strong enough to undertake many of the policies needed to reach these ends. Instead, the government often meddled in the market to squeeze resources from merchants to support the poor samurai. This kind of intervention was harmful because government attempts to regulate prices artificially in order to benefit one group undermined the economy's natural operations.

In the late seventeenth and eighteenth centuries the synthesis of Confucianism with Shinto and Buddhism was challenged by a nativist reaction to imported systems of thought. Nativist thinkers began by promoting Japanese literature as a major source from which to gain knowledge. They then broadened their efforts to include Japanese historical chronicles. Intellectuals and political leaders surveying the government's weaknesses after a century of Tokugawa rule—modest control over the domain governments, worrisome limitations to fiscal resources, difficulties in keeping stable a social order based on rigid distinctions and separations among the classes—associated the country's problems with the importance of foreign concepts in governmental practice. They urged a return to native ideas, which they distinguished from Chinese principles and practices whenever possible. Reverence for the emperor, who was believed to be part of an unbroken line of rulers descended from the gods, contrasted with the scorn nativists heaped upon the Chinese practice of ruling houses rising and falling in dynastic cycles. The Japanese emperor united political, religious, and familialistic ideas about a "national body" that nativists considered uniquely Japanese.

The stress on native elements in Japanese culture made its mark in politics in the eighteenth century, but did not by any means eradicate the deep influences of Buddhism and Confucianism in society more generally. Intellectuals synthesized imported ideas with native sensibilities to create cultural norms meaningful to peasants in the countryside and samurai, merchants, and artisans in the city.

Rural Life

Few farmhouses of the style common in the Tokugawa period remain in rural Japan today. Unlike China, where the vast majority of the population still lives in the countryside, most of Japan's population has now become urban. In Tokugawa times, peasant houses had wooden supports with walls made of loosely woven mats covered with mud and straw. Roofs were made of thatch or of wooden shingles held down by rocks. The floors were made of a straw matting known as *tatami*, still used in traditional homes today.

The management of day-to-day activities in the peasant household was usually the wife's responsibility, much as it was in China. Before reaching her position of authority, she was first a daughter-in-law to her husband's mother and before that a daughter in her own family's household. While waiting a considerable length of time before having major responsibilities and authority of their own, Japanese peasant women in the seventeenth and eighteenth centuries came to enjoy positions of importance within the family economy that would later become eroded by the development of urban industrial society and the creation of more-limited domestic roles for women as wives and mothers.

Within the Tokugawa village, landholdings varied. The rich served as village headmen to deal with higher authorities. The village itself formed a corporate unit tied politically to the outside through agricultural taxes that were levied on the village as a unit. Though this tax system placed a premium on rice production, cash crops did spread and farmers who did not grow rice bought it on the market to pay their taxes. Tokugawa Japan's household-level, labor-intensive agriculture using family labor was in many ways similar to Chinese agrarian organization. By the eighteenth century, the mix of cash crops in Japan also resembled that in China—cotton, tea, hemp, mulberry, indigo, vegetables, and tobacco made their way to markets, with a regional spread of production in major cash crops.

Sekiya-no-sato on the Sumida River, *one of the "Thirty-six Views of Mount Fuji," by the nineteenth-century artist Hokusai. Three samurai ride to Edo along a winding path between rice paddies, with Mount Fuji towering in the background. Today, this area is a bustling district of Tokyo.*

In eighteenth-century Japan, handicraft industries developed in the countryside, much as they had begun to two centuries earlier in China. The earlier expansion of trade in seventeenth-century Japan had been controlled by larger merchants serving the bakufu and daimyo governments. By the second half of the eighteenth century this pattern of production and trade was challenged by the expansion of rural industries. Rural producers of silk and cotton cloth, soy sauce, and cooking oil competed with the older, established shops in Kyoto and Osaka. Handicraft production gave rural people a new source of income, one that escaped the taxation levied on the rice fields. Peasants also increased agricultural yields through heavily fertilizing their land with mulch and livestock manure. A new rural elite emerged as commerce penetrated rural society. Evidence of agricultural improvements without any major population increases suggests that living standards improved. But even if the average standard of living moved upward, growing disparities between rich and poor meant that many peasants continued to confront the chronic threats of poor harvests and increased taxation.

Peasants expected the daimyo to provide emergency relief and to assess moderate taxes. During the seventeenth century, before commercialization created economic linkages between peasants and the cities, most villages were largely subsistence-oriented. Families consumed locally whatever they did not forward to the daimyo as tax. Because taxes were levied on the village as a community, peasants shared a common interest in protesting what they saw as too heavy a burden. Even after commercialization created opportunities for peasants as individual families, they retained a collective interest in opposing new taxes and petitioning for aid in times of natural disasters. In the seventeenth century, villages usually communicated their dissatisfactions through their headmen, who supervised as many as ten or twenty villages and were expected by the government to manage dissent within the villages and keep the number of petitions expressing grievances to a minimum. To persuade rural elites to fill these roles, the daimyo granted them partial tax exemptions, small stipends, and ceremonial swords. By the eighteenth century more nonelite peasants entered as major actors; at times they revolted against the village headman, who was often the largest landlord and moneylender and therefore became an easy target for dissatisfaction.

Conflicts became particularly widespread during the 1780s in response to a series of poor harvests and difficult conditions. Inspired by religious visions of world renewal, peasants actively challenged authorities they believed had failed to meet obligations to the communities. Peasants also moved beyond mere appeals for relief and aid to make proposals for reform that would help them in the marketplace with merchants as well as with the government. When their petitions and requests for aid were unmet, violence often occurred. Protests became visible moments of disturbance that were part of a larger structure of dialogue in which the government often compromised with peasant points of view. Peasant protest wasn't driven simply by the anger and fear of starvation amidst poverty. It developed as a form of action to express in forceful ways popular demands and expectations of elites and government.

Peasant protests became part of the popular culture in the form of oral and written accounts. Through protests, peasants engaged elites in a dialogue about how society should be run. In each community's oral tradition were stories associated with local temples and shrines that formed important public spaces in the seventeenth and eighteenth centuries. Stories of strange events and brave people were told over the decades and the centuries to create rich local traditions. Within this rural world the community complemented the family-centered vision of social order that the state sought to achieve. With the residential segregation practiced by the government, these villages were very distant from the cities of Tokugawa Japan.

Urban Society and Economy

Japanese towns and cities of the Tokugawa period had come into existence for one of three reasons. First were the towns centered on the castle of a daimyo, with separate areas for warriors and townspeople; these numbered some two hundred in the Tokugawa period. Second were the temple towns centered on a cluster of major Buddhist temples and monasteries; before the Tokugawa unification and subordination of these towns, they had often been largely self-governing. Third and finally were the trading cities, which grew up to handle the expanding trade of the Tokugawa period. Tokugawa Japan's three great cities, Osaka, Kyoto, and Edo (now Tokyo) each represented one of these urban types. Osaka became the great commercial center, Kyoto the temple city, and Edo the city of samurai.

Osaka was Tokugawa Japan's commercial and financial center. Here was the center of Japan's largest rice market, forged during the seventeenth and eighteenth

How the Four Orders of People in Mimasaka Ran Riot

■ *In 1727, thousands of peasants in the Tsuyama domain of Mimasaka province of western Japan rose to protest changes in domanial taxation policies. Within months an account, "A Record of How the Four Orders of People in Mimasaka Ran Riot," from which the following excerpt is taken, was penned by an unknown writer whose text shows him to be knowledgeable about the Japanese historical tradition and even educated enough to quote, sometimes inaccurately, the Chinese classics. Perhaps a masterless samurai, a doctor or itinerant priest, the author locates the reasons for the peasants' unjust suffering in the evil manipulations of one Kubo Chikahira, who takes people's money by levying special taxes, which he then advances to higher retainers in Mimasaka. In the following passage peasants have assembled to air their grievances with officials who only appear to be sympathetic. Later on in the narrative the peasants are defeated, their protest is crushed, and their leaders executed. The "four orders" in the story's title is a reference to Confucian categories of officials, peasants, craftsmen, and merchants. The author's Confucian outrage at evil and demands for justice from those in power are tempered by his Buddhist resignation to the fate of these failed peasant rebels who were not meant to succeed.*

"First, we do not understand why you tacked a supplementary notice onto this year's tax bill, raising taxes 4 percent, or why we have to pay our taxes in full by the end of the year. When the previous ruler was still alive, his benevolence was so widely known in other provinces that even people from the shogun's domains aspired to live in Tsuyama. Nevertheless, after Kubo got himself put in charge, he did much wrong. It is because of Chikahira and his allies among the country samurai that the first sowing of wheat in autumn was suspended and seals were attached to ox and horse plows.

"It is unlikely that the central administration ordered us to pay the land tax as soon as possible. Rather it was the district and deputy district headmen who issued these instructions. They threatened those who paid late with manacles, and the way they have made the peasants suffer through their ordeals is indescribable . . .

"Are the authorities really unaware of how the district headmen show their contempt for the peasants by subtracting the loans owed them from the tax rice, then deceiving the authorities by pretending the peasants have not paid their taxes? Herein lies the source of peasants' accumulated frustrations," they argued as shrewdly as they could.

The two magistrates listened to them. "You're absolutely right. As you have requested, we will retract the supplementary notice raising taxes, and we will allow you to pay 86 percent of the regular taxes demanded in this year's tax bill. We will abolish the district and deputy district headmen, replace the village headmen, and leave it up to you to choose whomever you please for messenger service. Debtors and creditors will negotiate their terms face to face. We will cancel your obligation to repay the rice you borrowed from the domanial authorities. Right now we will distribute to every peasant present a day's ration of rice. The former village headmen are to let us know how many there are." Since they were talking about over thirteen thousand peasants who would each receive five *go*, they realized that even 120 bales of rice would not be enough.

The poor peasants each returned to his own district, leaving behind those ordinary peasants who had become the new messengers and those who had taken the lead in being the spokesmen. The spokesmen and the magistrates then exchanged written promises, but this was all a plot on the part of the magistrates to learn the names of the leaders for the future.

centuries. The country's major rice wine, or sake, makers as well as soy sauce producers were in the area. Between 1620 and 1660 two major lines began maritime transport linking Osaka and Edo. Though goods shifted to sea transport, the roadway linking Edo and Osaka continued to bear increased traffic. Daimyo in procession to take up residence in Edo or on their return journeys offered a vivid sight, while messengers for merchants and samurai made their way with vital information for both. Merchant houses might owe their

A traditional Kabuki performance at Edo's Nakamura-za theater in 1745. The hand-colored woodblock print is by Okumura Masanobu.

origins to some smaller town, but to become successful in a major way they developed bases of operation in either Osaka or at least one of the other two major cities of Kyoto and Edo.

Kyoto was the center of learning and high culture. It was home to the country's most famous Buddhist temples and Shinto shrines, and scenes of Kyoto were celebrated in painted screens that made the city's pleasures more generally known through the country. So numerous were the visitors to Japan's capital city that by the seventeenth century guidebooks were available that detailed the shrines and temples, the palace, and other famous sights. City maps helped visitors navigate during their stays and became souvenirs when they returned home. Kyoto's aesthetic atmosphere was heavily infused with the presence of the emperor and his court. Those who served the emperor pursued pastimes like viewing flowers, reciting poetry, and appreciating the distinct odors of different incense woods. Kyoto's great Buddhist temples housed large religious communities. Shinto shrines were the sites for major festivals like the Gion festival, which climaxed two weeks of summertime celebration with a parade of colorful floats.

Edo was where the Tokugawa established their base of power. In the late eighteenth century it was probably the largest city in the world, with a population well over one million. The largest European city, London, had yet to reach a million. Commercial and artisan classes were drawn to Edo to serve the bureaucracy, which was very large because it included not only the shogun's staff but also the Edo residences of the provincial lords. The merchants and artisans accounted for roughly half a million, with the samurai warriors and provincial lords making up most of the rest. Buddhist and Shinto priests with their families numbered as many as 100,000. Finally, there were the lowlifes—indigents, transients, and entertainers. Despite their low social status, actors were a vital component of Edo society, for the merchants spent lavishly on their leisure and amusements.

Popular Culture

The theater world of Edo, as well as that found in Kyoto and Osaka, grew up near rivers, where popular entertainers of an earlier period lived. Known as "riverbank folk," entertainers were located in marginal urban spaces that reflected their marginal social status.

Stages were set up to show kabuki performances as well as puppet shows. There were also places for sumo wrestling and sideshows with dance, music, storytellers, jugglers, acrobats, tightrope walkers, and fortune-tellers.

The word *kabuki* originally meant "inclined," to suggest off-center or wild behavior. The term then became associated with the dance performances of female troupes whose skits included music and suggestive dancing. Excitement and competition over kabuki women incited brawls and duels. To avoid such incidents, the government banned women from the stage in 1629. Techniques were developed through which men could play women's roles; key aspects of a woman's gestures and speech were given exaggerated emphasis to create a formalized elegance. The themes of kabuki transformed the vision of woman in Tokugawa society—men playing women's roles portrayed the Confucian virtues of fidelity and modesty.

Puppet theater grew out of literary narratives more than plays. The performances were initially a kind of accompaniment to the recitation of texts. These texts began to utilize more dialogue and take advantage of theatrical recitation. Puppet plays mainly took as their themes heroes of earlier times, drawn from military epics, theater texts, and folktales. The gifted writer Chikamatsu developed a three-act genre that was added to a five-act period piece to form an all-day performance. These three-act plays took as their protagonists common people—shopkeepers, farmers, and courtesans. The theme that captures one central element in popular urban culture of the seventeenth and eighteenth centuries focuses on the hopeless love between a courtesan and her lover, who is a merchant or tradesman unable to purchase her freedom. The difficulties of the young man meeting his business responsibilities and of the couple creating a life together lead them to the fatal belief that they can kill themselves and be reborn together in the Amida Buddha's Western Paradise. The tension of the story centers on the conflict between duty, or *giri*, and personal feelings, or *ninjō*. The young man has duties to his family and business, but he has feelings of love for his courtesan. The impossibility of creating a relationship that supports both social obligation and private passion leads to the tragedy of double suicide.

The new popular culture was also the subject of *ukiyo-e* prints, pictures of the floating world, a new style of painting that took as its subject matter both intimate moments and public scenes of city life. "Floating world" was a Buddhist expression in medieval Japan. It referred to the pain and suffering of this world, from which followed the idea of this as a transient and uncertain world. But by the late sixteenth century the term came to refer to the culture of townsmen, whose efforts to satisfy earthly desires gave a different meaning to fleeting moments. The preface to the novel *Ukiyo monogatari* (*Tales of the floating world*), which appeared around 1665, suggests, "In this world everything is a source of interest. And yet just one step ahead lies darkness. So we should cast off all gloomy thought about our earthly lot and enjoy the pleasures of snow, moon, flowers, and autumn leaves, singing songs and drinking wine; living our lives like a gourd bobbing buoyantly downstream. This is the floating world."

Ukiyo-e depicted the world of courtesans, at rest, at play, in the company of other courtesans, or with their lovers; whether the subjects were stepping into a bath, admiring bonsai (dwarf trees) in the snow, boating across a lake, or admiring cherry blossoms, these ukiyo-e evoked images of Japanese beauty. Kabuki actors in colorful costumes with brightly painted faces were another common theme; sometimes with the actors posed in dramatic scenes, in other cases with just their faces framed, kabuki was vividly evoked by ukiyo-e prints. Landscapes were another major theme; various views of Mt. Fuji at different times of day and in different seasons were made famous by the artist Hokusai. Other landscapes depicted winter snows or summer rains,

Japan, 1600–1800

1600	Tokugawa established power following victory at Sekigahara
1637	Beginning of promotion of Neo-Confucianism
1639–40	Portuguese expelled from Japan; persecution of Christians continues
1688–1703	Growth of Kabuki and puppet theater; *ukiyo-e*; growth of Edo, Osaka, and castle towns
1701–02	The affair of the forty-seven *ronin*
1730–1800	National learning movement
1781–88	Temmei famine; great hardship in villages; peasant uprisings and urban riots

The seated courtesan by Baiooken Eishun, ca. 1725, is an example of an ukiyo-e, *or "floating world," print.*

ethic. Schooled in loyalty and frugality with a strong sense of propriety and sober reason, the samurai was expected to distance himself from the merchant's many amusements. In fact, many samurai could not resist the pleasure quarters, where they attended the theater and visited courtesans. Samurai and merchant views of the world were also linked by a common interest in Confucianism. Just as rulers could govern with Confucian benevolence and virtue, merchants could engage in trade at fair prices and seek their virtue through honest effort. Unlike China, where merchants adapted to the Confucian culture defined by scholars and gentry, in Japan merchants were able to create their own kind of Confucian purpose and social meaning.

The first two centuries of Tokugawa rule were filled with successes. The government first turned samurai warriors into virtuous rulers acceptable in Confucian terms. It then divided society into four orders, again modeled on Confucian categories, and assigned them to separate places in the social order. Within this structure there were dramatic differences. The loud and gaudy urban pleasures of the Tokugawa period contrast sharply with the peaceful and simple elegance of Zen gardens. Japanese society of the seventeenth and eighteenth centuries embraced a diversity of lifestyles and worldviews, each associated with a particular class. Social order was created and reinforced through state supervision of both the economy and popular culture. A balance of different forces, Confucian and nativist ideas, bakufu and daimyo administrations, samurai status and merchant wealth, created Tokugawa Japan's political, cultural, and social stability. This equilibrium proved fragile but sustainable through the eighteenth century. This achievement through two centuries of political, social, and economic change would become threatened by events of the first half of the nineteenth century.

SUGGESTIONS FOR FURTHER READING

LATE IMPERIAL CHINA

* Pierre-Etienne Will and R. Bin Wong, *Nourish the People: The State Civilian Granary System in China, 1650–1850* (Ann Arbor, MI: University of Michigan Center for Chinese Studies, 1991). A temporal, spatial, structural, and comparative analysis of a major Qing institution affecting the lives of peasants gives a concrete sense of the capacities and commitments of the state.

moonlit bridges, or birds perched on delicate tree branches. Ukiyo-e originated in the Kyoto-Osaka area, but during the eighteenth century the center of urban cultural life passed to Edo and ukiyo-e was considered a special product of Edo. Townspeople bought prints and rented books with ukiyo-e from shops for a small fee.

The popular urban culture of Tokugawa Japan stands at a great distance from the ruling samurai class's ideal

Frederic Wakeman, Jr. *The Great Enterprise: The Manchu Reconstruction of Imperial Order in Seventeenth-Century China* (Berkeley, CA: University of California Press, 1985). A grand narrative of the Manchu conquest, through which much of the foundation for modern China was laid.

Philip Kuhn, *Soulstealers: The Chinese Sorcery Scare of 1768* (Cambridge, MA: Harvard University Press, 1990). An engrossing story about sorcery that reveals much about popular culture and official views of the society they ruled.

* Jonathan Spence and John Wills, eds., *From Ming to Ch'ing: Conquest, Region and Continuity in Seventeenth-Century China* (New Haven, CT: Yale University Press, 1979). A fine collection of essays on different aspects of late Ming and early Qing China.

The Chinese World Order

* John Fairbank, ed., *The Chinese World Order: Traditional China's Foreign Relations* (Cambridge, MA: Harvard University Press, 1968). An excellent survey of China's relations with its neighbors, especially in the late imperial period.

Joseph Fletcher, "Ch'ing Inner Asia c. 1800," in John Fairbank, ed., *Cambridge History of China*, Vol. 10 (Cambridge: Cambridge University Press, 1978). The finest essay on Qing Inner Asia.

Morris Rossabi, *China and Inner Asia: From 1368 to the Present Day* (London: Thames and Hudson, 1975). Part One gives a good overview of Ming dynasty Inner Asia relations.

* David Joel Steinberg, ed., *In Search of Southeast Asia: A Modern History*, rev. ed. (Honolulu: University of Hawaii Press, 1986). Parts I and II give excellent thematic and country-specific accounts of Southeast Asia in the eighteenth century.

Tokugawa Japan

* Herman Ooms, *Tokugawa Ideology: Early Constructs, 1570–1680* (Princeton, NJ: Princeton University Press, 1985). A subtle study of how different kinds of Shinto and Neo-Confucian ideas were combined by different thinkers to create an ideology of rule for the early Tokugawa state.

* Stephen Vlastos, *Peasant Protests and Uprisings in Tokugawa Japan* (Berkeley, CA: University of California Press, 1986). A clear analysis of the social contexts and logic responsible for peasant conflicts.

* Tetsuo Najita, *Visions of Virtue in Tokugawa Japan: The Kaitokudō Merchant Academy of Osaka* (Chicago: University of Chicago Press, 1987). An important demonstration of the capacity of Japanese merchants to develop a positive place for themselves within a Confucian view of the world.

* Chie Nakane and Shinzaburoo Ooishi, eds., *Tokugawa Japan: The Social and Economic Antecedents of Modern Japan* (Tokyo: University of Tokyo Press, 1990). A useful set of essays by Japanese scholars on different aspects of Tokugawa Japan, including political institutions and popular culture as well as social and economic phenomena.

* Indicates paperback edition available.

CREDITS

Excerpts from "Japan's Declaration of War" from World War II: Policy and Strategy by Hans Adolf Jacobsen and Arthur J. Smith, Jr. Reprinted by permission.

Excerpts from "Roosevelt's Request for Declaration of War on Japan" from World War II: Policy and Strategy by Hans Adolf Jacobsen and Arthur J. Smith, Jr. Reprinted by permission.

"Glittering Fragments" by Hara Tamiki (p. 221) from The Penguin Book of Japanese Verse translated by Geoffrey Bownas and Anthony Thwaite (Penguin Books, 1964) translation copyright © Geoffrey Bownas and Anthony Thwaite, 1964. Reprinted by permission of Penguin Books Ltd., Letters translated by Corinner Antezana-Pernet from La Seconda Guerra Mondiale, 6th Edition by Roberto Battaglia. Reprinted by permission.

Chapter 33

"I Am the Train of Sadness" by Qabbani Nizar from New Writing From the Middle East, edited by L. Hamilian and J.D. Yohannan. Copyright © 1969 by Qabbani Nizar, translation copyright © 1974 by Abdullah al-Udhari. Reprinted by permission of The Crossroad Publishing Company.

Excerpt from Harem Years: The Memoirs of an Egyptian Feminist by Huda Shaarawi. Translation copyright © 1986 by Margot Badran from the book Harem Years: The Memoirs of an Egyptian Feminist by Huda Shaarawi. Translated and introduced by Margot Badran. Published by The Feminist Press at The City University of New York. All rights reserved.

Chapter 34

"Winston Churchill, The Iron Curtain (1946)." Excerpt from "The Sinews of Peace" by Winston Churchill from Robert Rhodes James, Winston S. Churchill: His Complete Speeches 1897–1963 Volume VII 1943–1949. Copyright © 1983 by Chelsea House Publishers. Reprinted by permission of Chelsea House Publishers.

"Subterranean Homesick Blues" by Bob Dylan. Copyright © 1965 by Warner Bros. Music, copyright renewed 1993 by Special Rider Music. All rights reserved. International copyright secured. Reprinted by permission.

Excerpts from "Report to the Twentieth Party Congress" by Nikita S. Khrushchev reprinted from Current Soviet Policies II. The Documentary Record of the Twentieth Party Congress and Its Aftermath published by The Current Digest of the Soviet Press, Columbus, Ohio. Used by permission.

Excerpts from The Second Sex by Simone De Beauvoir, translated by H.M. Parshley. Copyright 1952 and renewed 1980 by Alfred A. Knopf, Inc. Reprinted by permission of the publisher.

Chapter 35

Ian Buruma, A Japanese Mirror: *Heroes and Villains of Japanese Culture.* London: Jonathon Cape, Ltd., 1984, p. 147.

Excerpt from "A Definition of the Japanese Film" from A Lateral View: Essays on Culture and Style in Contemporary Japan by Donald Richie (Stone Bridge Press, 1992). Reprinted by permission.

Excerpt from "One Page of a Diary" from One Day in China: May 21, 1936 translated, edited and introduced by Sherman Cochran and Andrew C.K. Hsieh with Janis Cochran. Copyright © 1983 by Yale University. Reprinted by permission of Yale University Press.

PHOTO CREDITS

Positions of the photographs are indicated in the abbreviated form as follows: top (t), bottom (b), center (c), left (l), right (r).

Unless otherwise acknowledged, all photographs are the property of ScottForesman.

Chapter 1

xxxiv Satellite image of the Earth. © Tom Van Sant, Science Source/Photo Researchers

xviii (Volume I) Satellite image of the Earth. © Tom Van Sant, Science Source/Photo Researchers

xxiv (Volume II) Satellite image of the Earth. © Tom Van Sant, Science Source/Photo Researchers

xviii (Volume A) Satellite image of the Earth. © Tom Van Sant, Science Source/Photo Researchers

xxx (Volume B) Satellite image of the Earth. © Tom Van Sant, Science Source/Photo Researchers

xxvi (Volume C) Satellite image of the Earth. © Tom Van Sant, Science Source/Photo Researchers

3 Kathleen M. Kenyon/Jericho Excavations

5 © Kazuyoshi Nomachi/Pacific Press Service

6 Courtesy Federal Department of Antiquities, Nigeria

13 Hirmer Fotoarchiv, Munich

15 Hirmer Fotoarchiv, Munich

18 Hirmer Fotoarchiv, Munich

19 The Metropolitan Museum of Art, Rogers Fund, 1931 (31.3.157)

23 Erich Lessing/Art Resource, NY

27 National Museum of India, New Delhi

28 Government of India Information Services

32 From *Sources of Shang History: The Oracle-Bone Inscriptions of Bronze Age China* by David N. Keightley. University of California Press, 1978. Copyright © 1978 by The Regents of the University of California

34 Courtesy of The Cultural Relics Bureau, Beijing and The Metropolitan Museum of Art

36 Emil Muench

41 Doug Bryant/D. Donne Bryant Stock

42 Peabody Museum, Harvard University

Chapter 2

44 Black-figure Hydria. *Achilles Dragging the Body of Hector around the Walls of Troy*, ca. 520 B.C. William Francis Warden Fund. Courtesy, Museum of Fine Arts, Boston

46 The Metropolitan Museum of Art, Rogers Fund, 1947 (47.100.1)

48 Copyright British Museum

50 Copyright British Museum

52 Copyright British Museum

54 Bibliothèque Nationale, Paris

55 Staatliche Museen Preussischer Kulturbesitz, Antikenmuseum, Berlin

56 Alexander Tsiaras/Stock, Boston

59 Scala/Art Resource, NY

61 The Metropolitan Museum of Art, Fletcher Fund, 1932 (32.11.1)

62 Hirmer Fotoarchiv, Munich

63 Wadsworth Atheneum, Hartford, J. Pierpont Morgan Collection

66 Lee Boltin

Chapter 3

70 *Battle of Issus* and a detail showing Alexander the Great. Mosaic copy of a Hellenistic painting. (both) Alinari/Art Resource, NY

73 American School of Classical Studies at Athens: Agora Excavations

74 Staatliche Museen Preussischer Kulturbesitz, Antikenmuseum, Berlin

75 The Metropolitan Museum of Art, Fletcher Fund, 1931 (31.11.0)

78 Hirmer Fotoarchiv, Munich

80 Copyright British Museum

81 Martin-von-Wagner Museum, University of Würzburg

83 The Metropolitan Museum of Art, Rogers Fund, 1952 (52.11.4)

85 Hirmer Fotoarchiv, Munich

87 Copyright British Museum

90 Alinari/Art Resource, NY

93 Hirmer Fotoarchiv, Munich

95 The Metropolitan Museum of Art, Rogers Fund, 1911 (11.90)

Chapter 4

100 Halebid, Hoysaleśvara Temple: Draupadī about to wash her hair with the blood of Duḥśāsana, offered to her by Bhīma. Photo by Helen Hiltebeitel, Courtesy of Alf Hiltebeitel

104 Seth Joel/Courtesy The Metropolitan Museum of Art

105 Shanghai Museum

106 From Lo Chen-yu, *Yin-hsu Shu-ch'i Ching-hua*, 1914

108 Field Museum of Natural History, Chicago

111 Worcester Art Museum

112 Seth Joel/Courtesy The Metropolitan Museum of Art

115 Shensi Provincial Museum

116 Courtesy of the Freer Gallery of Art, Smithsonian Institution, Washington, D.C.

117 Originally published by the University of California Press; Reprinted by permission of The Regents of the University of California

123 National Museum of India, New Delhi

124 The Seattle Art Museum, Eugene Fuller Memorial Collection

126 Copyright British Museum

128 Archaeological Survey of India

129 Government of India Information Services

Chapter 5

132 The Roman Forum. Istituto Geografico de Agostini, Milan. Photo: A. De Gregorio

137 Hirmer Fotoarchiv, Munich

139 Bibliothèque Nationale, Paris

142 Museo Nazionale, Naples

145 Alinari/Art Resource, NY

149 Giraudon/Art Resource, NY

150 Carbone & Danno, Naples

151 Alinari/Art Resource, NY

153 Römische-Germanisches Zentralmuseum, Mainz

155 Alinari/Art Resource, NY

158 Roger-Viollet

Chapter 6

Barbarian medallion (front and back) of Valentinian I and Valens. (both) Hirmer Fotoarchiv, Munich

165 Scala/Art Resource, NY

169 Alinari/Art Resource, NY

170 Alinari/Art Resource, NY; (inset) Staatliche Skulpturen-sammlung, Dresden
174 Alinari/Art Resource, NY
176 Bibliothèque Nationale, Paris
177 Rheinisches Landesmuseum, Trier
178 Alinari/Art Resource, NY
179 Hirmer Fotoarchiv, Munich
182 (l) Hirmer Fotoarchiv, Munich; (r) André Held
184 (l) Hirmer Fotoarchiv, Munich; (r) Copyright British Museum
186 Vatican Museums
189 © Photo RMN

Chapter 7
192 (t) The main mosque at Timbuktu. Werner Forman/Art Resource, NY; (b) Courtyard of the Great Mosque, Damascus. Hubertus Kanus/SuperStock
196 Hirmer Fotoarchiv, Munich
198 Bibliothèque Nationale, Paris
202 Courtesy of the Freer Gallery of Art, Smithsonian Institution, Washington, D.C. 30.60
204 Bibliothèque Nationale, Paris
205 Arxiu Mas, Barcelona
207 The Metropolitan Museum of Art, Bequest of Edward C. Moore, 1891 (91.1.535)
210 Bibliothèque Nationale, Paris
213 (t) The British Library
216 Authenticated News International; (inset) Zimbabwe Ministry of Information

Chapter 8
220 Frontispiece to the *Diamond Sutra* (detail). The British Library
224 The Nelson-Atkins Museum of Art, Kansas City, Missouri (Nelson Fund) 34-10
226 Courtesy of the Arthur M. Sackler Gallery, Smithsonian Institution, Washington, D.C. 44.46
230 The Nelson-Atkins Museum of Art, Kansas City, Missouri (Acquired through the generosity of Mrs. Katherine Harvey) 48-31/1-4
231 From *Murals from the Han to the Tang Dynasty*. Foreign Language Press, Beijing, 1974
232 National Palace Museum, Taipei, Taiwan, Republic of China
234 Copyright British Museum
236 Indian Museum, Calcutta
239 The Cleveland Museum of Art, Purchase from the J. H. Wade Fund 30.331
240 Werner Forman/Art Resource, NY
246 The Seattle Art Museum, Eugene Fuller Memorial Collection
251 Tokugawa Reimeikai Foundation

Chapter 9
254 Interior of the Palatine Chapel, Aachen. Domkapitel Aachen. Photo: Ann Münchow
258 Bodleian Library, Oxford MS. OPP. 154, fol. 39v
262 The British Library
264 Austrian National Library, Vienna, Picture Archives
265 Copyright British Museum

268 Bibliothek der Rijksuniversiteit, Utrecht, The Netherlands
272 Bridgeman/Art Resource, NY
274 The British Library
277 Bodleian Library, Oxford MS. Bodl. 264, fol. 218r
280 The British Library
282 The Saint Louis Art Museum, Purchase

Chapter 10
284 Details of the Bayeux Tapestry, c. 1073–83. (all) Giraudon/Art Resource, NY
288 Larousse
292 Giraudon/Art Resource, NY
296 Windsor Castle, Royal Library. © 1994 Her Majesty Queen Elizabeth II
297 Lambeth Palace Library
299 Giraudon/Art Resource, NY
302 Bibliothèque Nationale, Paris
305 The Metropolitan Museum of Art, The Cloisters Collection, 1969 (69.86)
306 Bibliothèque Nationale, Paris
312 State Library of the Czechoslovak Socialist Republic, Prague: University Library
313 The British Library

Chapter 11
316 (t) Chinese scroll painting, *Rice Farming, Irrigating*, 13th century. Courtesy of the Freer Gallery of Art, Smithsonian Institution, Washington, D.C. 54.21-14; (b) *Ladies Classic of Filial Piety* (section 5) by Ma Ho-chih and Emperor Sung Kao-tsung. National Palace Museum, Taipei, Taiwan, Republic of China
320 From *The Chinese Spirit Road: The Classical Tradition of Stone Tomb Statuary* by Ann Paludan. Yale University Press, 1991. Copyright © 1991 by Yale University. All rights reserved.
321 National Palace Museum, Taipei, Taiwan, Republic of China
323 Courtesy of the Freer Gallery of Art, Smithsonian Institution, Washington, D.C. 35.8
325 Photograph by permission of the Kyoto temple, Konkoji and courtesy of the Tokyo National Research Institute of Cultural Properties
328 Kodansha Ltd., Tokyo
332 The Nelson-Atkins Museum of Art, Kansas City, Missouri (Purchase: Nelson Trust) 45-51/2
334 Tokyo National Museum
335 Imperial Household Agency, Kyoto
340 Tokyo National Museum
342 (t) from *Nikyoku Santai no Ezu* by Zeami; (b) Kodansha Ltd., Tokyo
345 Courtesy of The Art Institute of Chicago

Chapter 12
348 *The Procession of the Relic of the Holy Cross* (detail) by Gentile Bellini, 1496. Alinari/Art Resource, NY
351 Rijksmuseum, Amsterdam
353 Alinari/Art Resource, NY
355 (l) Giraudon/Art Resource, NY; (r) *Ginevra de' Benci (obverse)* by Leonardo da Vinci, c. 1474. National Gallery of Art, Washington, Ailsa Mellon Bruce Fund

786 National Archives
788 National Army Museum, London/Weidenfeld & Nicolson Archives
791 Museum of London
796 Staatsbibliothek, Berlin
799 Bibliothèque Nationale, Paris

Chapter 27
802 Map of the British Empire in 1886. Mansell Collection
807 Altonaer Museum, Hamburg
813 Mansell Collection
814 Staatsbibliothek, Berlin
815 Courtesy Department of Library Services, American Museum of Natural History, 322202
816 National Archives of Zimbabwe
819 R. B. Fleming
825 The Bettmann Archive
826 The Hulton Deutsch Collection
829 Hawaii State Archives
830 The Hulton Deutsch Collection

Chapter 28
834 Santa Anna, daguerrotype by F. W. Seiders, ca. 1850. The San Jacinto Museum of History, Houston, Texas
840 Library of Congress
843 Courtesy of the Board of Trustees of the Victoria & Albert Museum
844 Museo Nacional de Historia, Castillo de Chapultepec, Mexico City
847 California Historical Society
849 Courtesy of The Newberry Library, Chicago
855 Church Missionary Society, London
857 Copyright British Museum
859 From *Zanzibar: Tradition and Revolution* by Esmond Bradley Martin. Hamish Hamilton Ltd., London, 1978. Copyright © 1978 by Esmond Bradley Martin
864 National Archives of Malawi

Chapter 29
868 (t) *Deutsche Frauen Arbeitet im Heimat-Heer! Kriegsamtstelle Magdeburg (German Women Work in the Home-Army! Magdeburg War Office)* by Georg Kirchbach, Germany, 1914–18; (b) *Take Up the Sword of Justice* by Sir Bernard J. Partridge, England, 1915. (both) From copy in Bowman Gray Collection, Rare Book Collection, UNC Library, Chapel Hill, North Carolina
871 Copyright British Museum
873 UPI/Bettmann
877 Trustees of the Imperial War Museum, London
878 Trustees of the Imperial War Museum, London
882 Trustees of the Imperial War Museum, London
883 UPI/Bettmann
885 Trustees of the Imperial War Museum, London
888 UPI/Bettmann
890 Sovfoto
893 Novosti
896 Novosti/Sovfoto
897 Staatliche Museen Preussischer Kulturbesitz, Nationalgalerie, Berlin

Chapter 30
902 *Guernica* by Pablo Picasso, 1937. Museo del Prado,

Madrid. © 1994 ARS, New York/SPADEM, Paris
906 *Project for a Glass Skyscraper* by Ludwig Mies van der Rohe, 1921, model—no longer extant. Photograph courtesy The Museum of Modern Art, New York
911 William A. Ireland, *The Columbus Dispatch*
912 AP/Wide World
914 Historical Pictures/Stock Montage
917 The Hulton Deutsch Collection
920 Novosti
921 Novosti
924 Margaret Bourke-White, *Life* Magazine © Time Warner Inc.
927 UPI/Bettmann
929 Landesbildstelle Berlin
932 Weidenfeld & Nicolson Archives
933 Copyright: Wiener Library, London
936 The Hulton Deutsch Collection

Chapter 31
938 Cherry-blossom time at Ueno Park, with the statue of Saigō Takamori, leader of the Satsuma Rebellion of 1877. From a lithograph dated 1915. From *Low City, High City: Tokyo from Edo to the Earthquake* by Edward Seidensticker. Alfred A. Knopf, 1983. Copyright © 1983 by Edward Seidensticker
942 Courtesy, Peabody & Essex Museum, Salem, Mass./ Peabody Museum Collection
943 Courtesy, Peabody & Essex Museum, Salem, Mass./ Peabody Museum Collection
945 Courtesy, Peabody & Essex Museum, Salem, Mass./ Peabody Museum Collection
946 Library of Congress
948 Culver Pictures
950 Bettmann/Hulton
953 Bettmann/Hulton
955 Library of Congress
957 YMCA of the USA Archives, University of Minnesota Libraries
960 From *North China Villages: Social, Political, and Economic Activities before 1933* by Sidney D. Gamble, University of California Press, 1963
961 Laurie Platt Winfrey
964 Royal Tropical Institute, Amsterdam APA Photo Agency
966 National Archives

Chapter 32
972 The shell of the first atomic bomb being lifted into the detonating tower at the Trinity bomb test site near Alamagordo, New Mexico. Ap/Wide World
977 Austrian National Library, Vienna, Picture Archives
979 UPI/Bettmann
981 British Information Services
985 Roger-Viollet
988 Courtesy of Friends of Le Chambon
990 Johnny Florea, *Life* Magazine © Time Warner Inc.
992 UPI/Bettmann
993 Tass/Sovfoto
995 AP/Wide World
999 U.S. Coast Guard
1000 (both) from *Unforgettable Fire: Pictures Drawn by Atomic*

Bomb Survivors edited by The Japan Broadcasting Association. Copyright © 1977 by NHK. Reprinted by permission by Pantheon Books, a division of Random House, Inc.
1002 U. S. Navy
1004 Franklin D. Roosevelt Library, National Archives and Records Service

Chapter 33
1006 Mourners surrounding the flag-draped coffin of UAR President Gamal Abdel Nasser during his funeral procession. UPI/Bettmann
1012 UPI/Bettmann
1014 AP/Wide World
1016 N.R. Farbman, *Life* Magazine © Time Warner Inc.
1020 UPI/Bettmann
1023 East African Standard Newspapers Ltd.
1024 AP/Wide World
1026 Betty Press/Woodfin Camp & Associates
1029 Trustees of the Imperial War Museum, London
1033 Courtesy of United Jewish Appeal
1039 Ralph Crane, *Life* Magazine © Time Warner Inc.
1040 Reuters/Bettmann

Chapter 34
1044 *The Poster Scene*, 1967. Topham/Image Works
1048 UPI/Bettmann
1050 European Community Information Service
1054 UPI/Bettmann
1057 Erich Lessing/Magnum
1062 UPI/Bettmann
1065 Bruno Barbey/Magnum
1067 Peter Marlow/Magnum
1068 Vlastimir Shone/Gamma-Liaison
1069 DeKeerle/Grochowiak/Sygma
1070 AP/Wide World
1073 Leh/Saukkomaa/Woodfin Camp & Associates
1075 AP/Wide World
1076 AP/Wide World
1079 Reuters/Bettmann

Chapter 35
1082 Shanghai Sampan. Hiroji Kubota/Magnum
1086 UPI/Bettmann
1089 AP/Wide World
1093 UPI/Bettmann
1095 AP/Wide World
1098 UPI/Bettmann
1099 AP/Wide World
1101 AP/Wide World
1104 (l) AP/Wide World; (r) Reuters/Bettmann
1106 Courtesy of *Baseball Magazine Sha*
1109 T. Matsumoto/Sygma
1111 Andy Hernandez/Sygma

Color Essay 1 following page 126
1 Erich Lessing/Art Resource, NY
2 B. Norman/Ancient Art & Architecture Collection
3 TAP Service/National Museum, Athens
4 Hirmer Fotoarchiv, Munich

Color Essay 2 following page 222
1 Scala/Art Resource, NY
2 The Metropolitan Museum of Art, Purchase, Lita Annenberg Hazen Charitable Trust Gift, in honor of Cynthia Hazen and Leon Bernard Polsky, 1982 (1982.220.8)
3 The Board of Trinity College Dublin
4 Scala/Art Resource, NY

Color Essay 3 following page 318
1 Erich Lessing/Art Resource, NY
2 Scala/Art Resource, NY
3 Reproduced by courtesy of the Trustees, The National Gallery, London
4 Reproduced by courtesy of the Trustees, The National Gallery, London

Color Essay 4 following page 414
1 The Granger Collection, New York
2 Scala/Art Resource, NY
3 Derby Museums and Art Gallery
4 Werner Forman/Art Resource, NY

Color Essay 5 following page 590
1 Giraudon/Art Resource, NY
2 Courtesy of The Arthur M. Sackler Museum, Harvard University Art Museums, Private Collection
3 Colorphoto Hans Hinz
4 Reproduced by permission of the Trustees of the Wallace Collection

Color Essay 6 following page 718
1 Bridgeman/Art Resource, NY
2 Royal Academy of Arts, London
3 Erich Lessing/Art Resource, NY
4 Erich Lessing/Art Resource, NY

Color Essay 7 following page 814
1 Pablo Picasso. *Les Desmoiselles d'Avignon.* Paris (June–July 1907). Oil on canvas, 8′ × 7′ 8″. The Museum of Modern Art, New York. Acquired through the Lillie P. Bliss Bequest
2 M. Felix Collection, Brussels. Photo: Dick Beaulieux
3 Private Collection. Photo: Jeffrey Ploskonka
4 Frida Kahlo. *Self Portrait with Cropped Hair.* 1940. Oil on canvas, 15¾ × 11″. The Museum of Modern Art, New York. Gift of Edgar Kaufmann, Jr.

Color Essay 8 following page 1102
1 Kitagawa Utamaro, Japanese, 1753–1806, *Joshoku Kaiko Tewaza Gusa (Women's Work in Silk Culture)*, woodblock print, c. 1802, 38.1 × 25.4 cm, Departmental Funds, 1925.3257, photograph © 1993, The Art Institute of Chicago. All Rights Reserved
2 Tate Gallery, London/Art Resource, NY
3 Library of Congress
4 From *Prop Art: Over 1000 Contemporary Political Posters* by Gary Yanker. Darien House, New York, distributed by New York Graphic Society, 1972. Copyright © 1972 by Gary Yanker

INDEX